D1587988

# THE LATER PREHISTORY OF NORTH-WEST EUROPE

# MATHEMATICS EMERGING

A SOURCEBOOK 1540–1900

Jacqueline Stedall

OXFORD

UNIVERSITY PRESS

# OXFORD
UNIVERSITY PRESS

Great Clarendon Street, Oxford OX2 6DP

Oxford University Press is a department of the University of Oxford.
It furthers the University's objective of excellence in research, scholarship,
and education by publishing worldwide in

Oxford  New York

Auckland  Cape Town  Dar es Salaam  Hong Kong  Karachi
Kuala Lumpur  Madrid  Melbourne  Mexico City  Nairobi
New Delhi  Shanghai  Taipei  Toronto

With offices in

Argentina  Austria  Brazil  Chile  Czech Republic  France  Greece
Guatemala  Hungary  Italy  Japan  Poland  Portugal  Singapore
South Korea  Switzerland  Thailand  Turkey  Ukraine  Vietnam

Oxford is a registered trade mark of Oxford University Press
in the UK and in certain other countries

Published in the United States
by Oxford University Press Inc., New York

© Oxford University Press 2008

The moral rights of the authors have been asserted
Database right Oxford University Press (maker)

First published 2008

British Library Cataloguing in Publication Data
Data available

Library of Congress Cataloging in Publication Data
Data available

Typeset by Newgen Imaging Systems (P) Ltd., Chennai, India
Printed in Great Britain
on acid-free paper by
CPI Antony Rowe, Chippenham, Wiltshire

ISBN  978–019–922690–0

10 9 8 7 6 5 4 3 2 1

*For Tom, who loves mathematics,*

*and*

*for Ellie, who loves old books.*

# CONTENTS

# ACKNOWLEDGEMENTS

This book is based on a course designed by Raymond Flood, Peter Neumann, Robin Wilson, and me for mathematics undergraduates at the University of Oxford, and taught by us since 2003 . Any expression of gratitude to my three colleagues falls very far short of what I owe them for all they have done directly or indirectly to make this book possible, and for their unfailing commitment, generosity, friendship, and good humour. Peter Neumann read and commented on the entire text in draft; I learned enormously, and I believe even he learned a little, from our efforts to tease out some of the finer points of mathematics, language, and history.

Apart from the exceptions mentioned below, I have provided fresh translations for all the extracts in this book. Those from Latin or French are my own, those from German were done with invaluable help from Annette Imhausen and further assistance from Peter Neumann. The translation of the cuneiform tablet in 12.1.1 was provided by Eleanor Robson, who also kindly read and checked Chapter 1. For extracts from Bolzano I have used the translations made by Steve Russ in *The mathematical works of Bernard Bolzano*, which were so carefully done that I cannot possibly improve on them. To everyone mentioned here I extend my warmest thanks.

Best efforts have been made to trace copyright holders wherever necessary. The following people and institutions are gratefully acknowledged. British Library for 2.3.1 (C.74.e), 2.4.1 (530.i.25), 3.2.3 (8532.b.41), 7.1.2 (529.f.17), 8.2.1 (51.e.5), 17.1.1 (530.a.16); Bodleian Library, University of Oxford, for 2.1.2 (1801 d.1, p. 4), 3.2.4 (Savile G.26, pp. 28–29), 5.1.1–5.1.6 (Savile G.7, pp. 12–13, 26–27, 30, 35–38, 41–42, 53–55), 12.1.1 (Savile N.15, ff. 16, 30); Cambridge University Library for 8.1.1 (CUL Add. 3958.3:72r); Eighteenth Century Collections On-line, Gale Digital Collection for 4.1.2 (CW3306752059–60, CW3306752062–64, CW3306752082–84), 4.1.3 (CW3309835158, CW3309835160, CW3309835163–64), 7.1.3 (CW3308607677–78), 10.2.1 (CW3319154613–14), 14.1.1 (CW3309363369–72); the Euler Archive, http://www.math.dartmouth.edu/~euler/ for 8.2.3, 9.1.2–9.2.3; Il Giardino di Archimede for 8.3.2, 11.2.3, 14.1.2; Koninklijke Nederlandse Akademie van Wetenschappen for 2.1.1; Lawrence Schoenberg for 1.1.2; University of Chicago Press, who retain the copyright, for 1.1.1. Other material comes from the Fauvel Collection at the Open University, the Gerrans Collection at the Mathematical Insititute, Oxford, and the library of The Queen's College, Oxford. I am particularly grateful to the librarians, Provost, and Governing Body of The Queen's College, Oxford, without whose generous support this book would never have been possible.

# INTRODUCTION

Mathematics has the longest and richest history of any subject in the academic curriculum. It has been practised in every society and culture, with written records reaching back in some cases as far as four thousand years, so that those who learn mathematics in schools and universities today are studying a subject whose origins lie in civilizations and historical periods often very remote from our own. This book will focus on just a small part of the story, in a sense the most recent chapter of it: the mathematics of western Europe from the sixteenth to the nineteenth centuries. This is because this book evolved from a course designed to provide mathematics undergraduates with some historical background to the material that is now taught universally to students in their final years at school and the first years at college or university: the core subjects of calculus, analysis, and abstract algebra, along with others such as mechanics, probability, and number theory. All of these evolved into their present form in a relatively limited area of western Europe from the mid sixteenth century onwards, and it is there that we find the major writings that relate in a recognizable way to contemporary mathematics. Hence the relatively narrow focus of this book.

There are many different ways of approaching the history of mathematics. The most common are by topic or by period, and in this book you will find both. The first six chapters deal mainly with the seventeenth century, the next six with the eighteenth, and the final six with the nineteenth, but the divisions are very far from rigid, and several chapters deliberately overstep these boundaries. Within that broad framework each chapter focuses on a particular topic and outlines its history, as far as possible through extracts from primary sources. The aim of this book is not to present a conventional account or a predigested version of history, but to encourage you, the reader, to develop critical historical thinking for yourself. It therefore offers mathematics as it was originally written, and invites you to read it for yourselves, to ask your own questions, and make your own judgements.

It can be argued, of course, that the selection of sources and the surrounding commentary already lend support to one interpretation rather than another. That is true but unavoidable, and I very much hope that readers will counter it by feeling free to discuss and argue about anything and everything that is written in these pages. It may also be objected that brief extracts from otherwise lengthy books and articles can never give more than a partial picture. That is also true, but for beginners a complete picture would be overwhelming. Selected themes and examples, on the other hand, can serve as a helpful introduction to what is available, and those who enjoy what is offered in this book will have no difficulty pursuing particular authors or topics much further if they wish to do so. More and more source material is becoming available electronically, but the sheer amount of it can be bewildering and I believe there is still a place for a book like this that can serve as a guide to some of the key mathematical literature of the past.

Sourcebooks in mathematics over the last eighty years have always tended to reflect current trends in the history of mathematics, and this one is no exception. One of the earliest such books was David Eugene Smith's *A source book in mathematics* (1929), a collection of translations grouped under the general headings of number, algebra, geometry, probability, and (lumped together) calculus, functions, and quaternions. Within each section the extracts appear in random order, so that, for instance, Chebyshev on the totality of primes (1851) is immediately followed by Napier on the invention of logarithms (1614). The book therefore presents the reader with a collection of raw material but obscures any sense of historical development. Later popular source books, for example Struik's *A source book in mathematics, 1200–1800* (1969) or Calinger's *Classics of mathematics* (1982) are better arranged, and the latter in particular has useful introductions to each chapter, and extensive suggestions for further reading, but remains primarily an anthology, a collection of diverse and unrelated texts. Such books are based on the premise that the selected extracts will somehow speak for themselves, but unfortunately they do not. The originals were written in particular historical, personal, and mathematical circumstances that influenced both their style and their content, and without some knowledge of that context the reader is likely at best to lack understanding and at worst to be misled. Further, and crucially, mathematics is not a subject carried on by mathematicians working in isolation, in which every few years or centuries some new discovery emerges for us to wonder at; on the contrary, all mathematicians rely on the work of their predecessors and all owe an enormous debt to the past. How mathematics is communicated from one generation or culture to another is not a side issue, but an integral part of mathematics as a human activity.

By far the most widely used source book in recent years has been Fauvel and Gray's *The history of mathematics: a reader*, which has done much to overcome the shortcomings of the earlier books. The sources have been imaginatively and astutely chosen to illustrate periods or themes, and there are helpful introductory notes to each chapter and section. The *Reader* was not designed to stand alone, however, but to be read alongside comprehensive study material produced by the Open University, so that to use it in an effective way the reader must refer to that or other supporting material. Jeremy Gray, one of the original editors, is currently compiling the material from the Open University course units into a companion volume to the *Reader*, so that the two books together will provide an excellent introduction to the general history of mathematics.

Nevertheless, I believe there is also room for this present book, not as an alternative to the *Reader* but to complement it. The *Reader* reflects (as all source books are bound to do) the predilections of its editors, but also it was designed for students who could not be assumed to have any mathematical background. It addresses that audience very successfully, but necessarily its emphasis is either on earlier periods of history (up to the seventeenth century), or on topics where technical detail can be presented in a way that is not too daunting. The expected readership of the present book is quite different: students, teachers, or others, who do have some mathematical training, and would like to learn more about what lies behind the mathematics they know. This book therefore offers extracts in which the mathematics stands exactly as it was originally written, in the hope that readers will engage with it for themselves. Just as new mathematics can hardly ever be learned without taking pencil and paper in hand, so there is no better way of entering into the mind of a mathematician than by trying to think as he did (I am afraid there is no 'she' in this book). Some of the mathematics is easy, some is more difficult, but that is the nature of the subject, and it would present an unrealistically anodyne picture if the hard bits were all edited out. It is not necessary to follow every single step of every argument, but it is already a useful historical exercise to observe just where the difficulties arise, and whether or how they were overcome.

The feature of this book that otherwise distinguishes it most sharply from its predecessors is that almost every source is given in its original form, not just in the language in which it was first written, but as far as practicable in the layout and typeface in which it was read by contemporaries. Every researcher knows the thrill of handling old books and journals, and while it is impossible in any modern book to convey a sense of dustiness, or crinkled pages, or battered bindings, or the unmistakable smell of an old library, I hope the extracts will offer some sense of what it is like to see and handle the originals. Modern typeface is clean, clear, and regular, but this was not so in the seventeenth or eighteenth centuries when everything had to be painstakingly set by hand by printers who probably understood little or nothing of the mathematics they were dealing with. Paper was of variable quality, ink was spread unevenly, so that sometimes it bled through the page but at other times failed to make a mark at all, and page edges were often rough and irregular; beyond that, time and age have added further blemishes, some of which are visible in these extracts. The printed page of two or three hundred years ago had a much more homespun look than a modern page, sometimes rough and awkward, but at other times quite beautiful, and difficult to copy or surpass even with all the possibilities of modern technology. The reasons for reproducing the pages in their original form, however, are more than aesthetic. It is only by studying the originals that one sees exactly how notation was invented and used, how equations were laid out, where and how the diagrams were set, and so on. Later editors and translators take liberties with all these things, perhaps producing clearer text, but at the same time distancing us from the original. In this book, sources originally written in English have not been transcribed except where the original presents problems of legibility, and diagrams throughout have been left in their original form and context.

Unfortunately for many of the readers to whom this book is addressed, most of the sources are not in English, which became an international language of intellectual discourse only in the twentieth century. In the earlier chapters, the predominant language is Latin, later giving way to French and then to German. Because it is too much to expect modern readers to know all or even one of these, translations are provided for all the extracts, but it is my hope that anyone with even a rudimentary knowledge of the other languages will try their hand at the originals, with or without the offered translation alongside. Translation is at the best of times a subtle and difficult task for which there is no single correct outcome, and just as in the choice and arrangement of sources, new ways of thinking about the history of mathematics are reflected in changing attitudes to translation. Many older translations reveal the content of a text and can be a useful starting point, but the translators were sometimes very free in their interpretations of the original, and unfortunately have all too often been copied without question in later volumes: Calinger, for instance, and even Fauvel and Gray, draw quite heavily on translations to be found in Smith or Struik. The translations in the present book, apart from two exceptions noted in the Acknowledgements below, have been made entirely afresh, with the following precepts in mind: (i) that vocabulary and sentence structure should remain as true as possible to the original; (ii) that mathematical notation should not be changed unless it cannot be reproduced, or is actually misleading; in this last case any changes have been clearly noted. These rules may sound straightforward but in practice they are not.

Retaining the thought forms of another language is never easy, especially (in this book) translating from Latin or German where word order is markedly different from English. Even from French, which is much closer to English in its modes of expression, the problems are subtle. Lacroix, for instance, in his account of the development of the calculus in the introduction to his *Traité du calcul* wrote (of Newton): 'il appela fluxions les vîtesses qui régulaient ces mouvemens'.[1] Translating literally we have: 'he called fluxions the speeds which regulate these movements', but since the sentence is offering a definition of fluxions it is much more natural to say in English: 'he called the speeds which regulate these movements fluxions'. In other words, English witholds the emphasis on the new concept to the end of the sentence, where French has it up front. Do such fine distinctions matter? They do, because by changing word order it is all too easy to alter the balance of a sentence, and therefore of a thought, in ways that the author did not intend. Strictly literal translations, on the other hand, can be awkward to the point of being unreadable and, as in the example above from Lacroix, can even get the meaning wrong. In the end, every translator has to take a little licence with the original for the sake of fluency. Seventeenth- and eighteenth-century Latin, for example, is often riddled with 'moreovers' and 'therefores', and I confess to having silently eliminated quite a few of them. Nevertheless I have kept these and other stylistic

---

1. Lacroix 1810, xv.

changes to a minimum and have tried to avoid the temptation to modernize or 'improve' other people's writing. Not the least of my reasons for doing so is to enable the reader to compare originals and translations as directly as possible.

The problems outlined above are common to all translation, but the translation of historical mathematical texts poses yet further levels of difficulty, in the handling of technical words and mathematical notation. Most readers of this book will almost certainly want to re-write some of its mathematics in modern symbolism to understand it more easily; this is a natural and reassuring thing to do, and indeed we have all learned mathematics by precisely this technique of writing it 'in our own words'. A modern translation should not be confused, however, with what the author himself had in mind. When, for instance, we change Cardano's equation

$$1 \; cubum \;\; p : 8 \; rebus, \; aequalem \;\; 64$$

into

$$x^3 + 8x = 64$$

we are translating an obscure form of words into something we can immediately recognize. But it also takes us a long way from the original, turning Cardano's 'rebus', or 'things', which had its own history and meaning, into our '$x$', which has its own quite different history and meaning. To understand Cardano's thought we need to return to his text armed with modern formulas only as a guide. The symbolic version can certainly give us some hints and clues as to the richness of the original, but should never be mistaken for it.

Similar problems arise with words and phrases that were once in common currency but which have now lost their meaning. Sixteenth- and seventeenth-century mathematicians, for instance, frequently used the Latin word '*in*' in phrases like '*A in B*'. Literally, this refers to the construction of a line segment $A$ on ('*in*'), and perpendicular to, a line segment $B$; together the lines define or 'produce' a rectangular space. The phrase is usually most easily translated as '$A$ multiplied by $B$' or '$A$ times $B$', but the words 'multiplied by' or 'times' strictly apply to numbers, not lengths, and in themselves carry no geometric overtones. Similarly, the geometric '*applicare ad*' (to lay against) is generally translated as 'to divide by', but again the geometric connotation is lost. Does it matter? Yes, because we cannot really understand meaning if we ignore historical roots, and yet it is almost impossible to preserve or convey those roots in the very different language of today.

In other cases there are words that have remained outwardly the same while their meaning has changed many times over: 'algebraic' and 'analytic', for instance, which can only ever be understood in relation to a particular time and context. There are also words or phrases that simply have no exact counterparts in English. Euler, for example, used the expression *functio integra* (literally a whole or complete function) for a function that can be expressed as a finite sum of positive powers. The same phrase appears in French as *fonction entière* or in German as *ganze Function*, but there is no English equivalent. Cayley tried 'integral function' but that simply confuses matters with the calculus. A technically correct translation is 'polynomial function', but that is unsatisfactory because 'polynomial' means literally 'having many terms', something almost the opposite of the sense Euler was trying to convey of being complete, finished, rounded off.

Finally, in translating mathematics it is often all too tempting to introduce words that now have a precise technical meaning, as though that was what an author in the past would have used if he could. Thus, for example, a recent translation of Cantor's proof of the countability of algebraic numbers, uses the terms 'set' and 'one-to-one', both of them thoroughly familiar to modern mathematicians, but nowhere to be seen in Cantor in 1874; on the contrary, Cantor had to explain his new meaning as best he could *without* the help of such words and in everyday vocabulary.[2] To read the present into the language of the past is to imagine that modern mathematics was somehow always in existence, just waiting for someone to notice it. This attitude is not only ahistorical but it belittles the struggles and insights of those who had to grapple for the first time with strange and difficult ideas, and express them in whatever words they could muster.

The process of change in style and language continues even now, and with increasing rapidity. Those who were educated in the 1960s or 1970s will still be intimately familiar with some of the terms and concepts to be found in the extracts in this book, in a way that those educated even twenty or thirty years later will not. As a reader of this book you need to be constantly aware of the problems of language and translation, and if you have any knowledge at all of the source languages, look at the originals and decide for yourself how to interpret them. Discuss the problems with others, and make whatever changes or improvements you see fit to the translations offered.

The same direction to discuss and improve applies to every other feature of this book. Everyone who reads it with any seriousness is likely sooner or later to complain that this or that source should have been included but is not: in that case, follow it up and make the missing source the starting point of an alternative or more complete story. Around every extract in the book there is some commentary to explain how it fits into a broader picture, or to elucidate those parts where the mathematics may seem to modern eyes (and perhaps to contemporary eyes also) particularly difficult or obscure, but these relatively brief remarks should by no means be taken as all there is to say. Compare them with interpretations made by other historians; weigh up the points of agreement or disagreement; make your own judgements based on the source material available to you here and elsewhere; become not just a reader but a historian.

Part of this process will be to understand that mathematics does not separate itself into sections as neatly as might appear from the eighteen chapter divisions of this

---

2. Ewald 1996, II, 840.

book. There are already many cross-references from one chapter to another, as there are bound to be in a subject where apparently unrelated topics have a way of turning out to belong to the same larger picture. I hope you will find other connections, both within this book and to material outside it. I also hope that you will look for relationships and influences not just between one piece of mathematics and another, but between mathematicians themselves. Mathematics, perhaps more than any other academic subject, develops out of insights and understanding accumulated over time and passed from person to person, sometimes through books and printed papers, but also through letters, lectures, and conversations. The significance of personal meetings and friendships between mathematicians is often overlooked, but they are very much part of the intricate social history of mathematics.[3] The brief biographical notes at the end of the book are intended to help illustrate this.

Mathematics is a thoroughly human endeavour in yet another sense, and this time with the emphasis on endeavour. Mathematics, for obvious reasons, is generally taught as a set of tried and tested theorems, carefully built up in a sensible and convincing way from accepted starting points, but it will not take you long as you peruse the extracts in this book to see that mathematics was not discovered or invented that way at all. Here you will find mathematicians groping in the dark, experimenting with new ideas, making hypotheses and guesses, proving correct theorems wrongly, and even on occasion proving incorrect theorems wrongly too. Mathematics is for everyone, beginner or expert, a process of discovery that is prone to error, false starts, and dead ends. Some past mistakes have been included in this book quite deliberately to demonstrate that not even for an Euler, a Lagrange, or a Cauchy was it all plain sailing.

My hope is that through the pages of this book you will see the emergence of mathematics that is universally taught today, as it took shape in the minds of those who created it. Often, especially in the earlier years of the seventeenth century, it was developed in contexts that now appear strange and perhaps unwelcoming, and expressed in language that can seem difficult and obscure. Yet gradually it becomes more recognizable and familiar, until by the early nineteenth century we are in touch with those who directly formed much of our present day curriculum. If this book helps you to a better understanding of some of the mathematics you know, it will have served one good purpose; if it leads to you to read historical texts with perception and judgement it will have served another, no less valuable.

---

3. For a remarkable example of a mathematician working alone see Simon Singh's account of Andrew Wiles in *Fermat's last theorem* (2002); for an equally remarkable example of mathematicians working in collaboration see Mark Ronan's *Symmetry and the Monster* (2006).

# CHAPTER 1

# BEGINNINGS

New mathematics rarely emerges out of the blue. Mathematicians always work within a framework of existing ideas, their own or other people's, sometimes worked out a few days or a few years earlier, sometimes inherited from the far distant past. To understand the development of mathematics at any period of history we need to know what was already alive and stirring in the contemporary mathematical culture, and in European mathematics this becomes particularly important for the crucial time around the later sixteenth and early seventeenth century. From the Renaissance onwards mathematics, like every other aspect of intellectual life in western Europe, had been invigorated by the rediscovery and translation of Greek texts, by ideas stemming from Islamic sources, and by new technical challenges. To set the scene for all that follows, this first chapter is devoted to extracts from some of the texts that provided the foundations upon which European mathematics was developed from the late sixteenth century onwards.

The first example in this book is a Babylonian clay tablet dating from about 1800 BC. No sixteenth- or seventeenth-century European mathematician ever saw or read such a tablet, but if they had they would certainly have recognized the mathematics, including the lengthy calculations in base 60, which at that time were still commonplace. Other features of the tablet remain in use to this day: even the most modern mathematics bears traces of some very ancient ideas.

The next historical era that concerns us is that of the Greek and Hellenistic civilizations that together stretched from approximately 600 BC to 500 AD. The mathematics of this period has been intensively studied, but the evidence is often fragmentary. Almost always we are dependent on copies, translations, or commentaries, made long after the originals themselves were composed. After the collapse of the Roman Empire in the west in the fifth century AD, Greek as a language, and with it almost all traces of Greek mathematics, virtually disappeared from most of Europe.

Fortunately, mathematical and scientific texts were preserved and studied in the Islamic culture that spread rapidly around the shores of the Mediterranean after the sixth century AD, and were incorporated into a new and vigorous period of Islamic learning. By the ninth century Baghdad, close to the site of ancient Babylon, was again a vital intellectual centre, where mathematics and astronomy flourished, and through which ideas could spread from as far east as India to as far west as Spain. By the twelfth century scholars from more northern parts of Europe had discovered the existence of important mathematical, scientific, and philosophical texts in Spain and Sicily, and began the long process of translation into Latin, first from Arabic, later directly from Greek.

Over the next four centuries, ancient and eastern learning spread gradually into north western Europe, disseminated through schools and monasteries and the fledgling universities of Oxford, Cambridge, and Paris, but mathematical knowledge at any level would have been available only to the very few who had access to laboriously copied manuscripts or to personal tuition. From the late fifteenth century onwards, however, mathematics began to appear in print in many different ways, from basic textbooks of geometry, arithmetic, and algebra, to lavish printed editions of Euclid, Archimedes, Apollonius, Ptolemy, and Diophantus, whose works now began to inspire a new generation of scholars.

The aim of this chapter is to introduce some of the authors and concepts that would have been familiar by around 1600 to any serious student of the mathematical sciences, in other words to offer an overview of the mathematical 'common knowledge' of western Europe in the late Renaissance.

## 1.1 BEGINNINGS OF ARITHMETIC

### 1.1.1 Large number calculations, *c.* 1800 BC

All societies have developed systems of recording and manipulating numbers, from the simple use of counters or tally marks to sophisticated methods of calculation. The clay tablet shown below is from Mesopotamia (roughly the same region as modern Iraq) from around 1800 BC (the Old Babylonian period), and bears witness to a highly developed ability to work with large numbers.

Apart from a single repeated instruction down the left hand side, the tablet is entirely numerical. Each upright stroke represents a unit, or 1, and each slanted stroke represents 10, so the repeated number down the right hand side of the first column is 1 40. Since the base of this arithmetic is 60, this number may be read as $1 + \frac{40}{60} = 1\frac{2}{3}$, or $1 \times 60 + 40 \times 1 = 100$, or $1 \times 60^2 + 40 \times 60 = 6000$, or .... There is no clue to the correct reading in the text itself, but other similar tables suggest that in this case we should read 1 40 as $1 \times 60 + 40$, or 100. The numbers in the right hand column are then respective powers, $100^2, 100^3, 100^4, \ldots, 100^{10}$.

There was no symbol for zero, and in the fifth line there is nothing to mark the empty place between the second number ($=26$) and the third ($=29$). It is hardly surprising that by the next line the scribe has lost sight of the space, so that all his subsequent calculations are wrong. Though frustrating to the mathematician, mistakes like this can be very helpful to the historian: first, because they provide an insight into the process that the writer was following (for another example of this see 8.1.4); second, because they can sometimes enable us to identify 'family trees' of borrowers or copyists.

On the reverse of the tablet is a similar table of powers of 5, up to $5^{10}$, and a small number of other tablets survive with powers of 9, 16, and 225, but we have no idea what, if anything, such tables were for.

The practice of raising numbers to powers, the concept of place value, and even the use of 60 as a base (in the measurement of time and angle), are all still part of today's mathematics.

## A table of powers

from an unkown scribe, *c.* 1800 BC, British Museum 22706, reproduced from Nissen *et al* 1993, 151

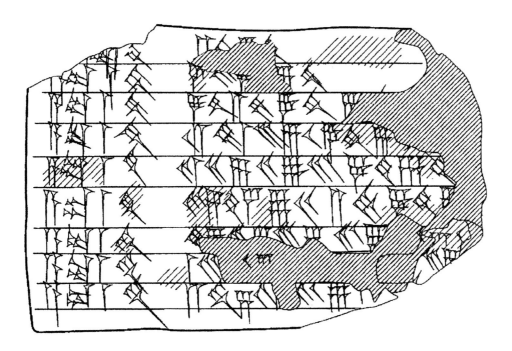

*Notation*
Square brackets indicate restorations of broken text.

TRANSCRIPT

| | | |
|---|---|---|
| [1 40 a]ra | 1 40 | 2 46 40 |
| ara | 1 40 | 4 37 46 40 |
| ara | 1 40 | 7 42 57 46 [40] |
| ara | 1 40 | 12 51 36 17 46 [40] |
| ara | 1 40 | 21 26 {0} 29 37 46 40 |
| ara | 1 40 | 35 44 9 22 57 46 40 |
| ara | 1 40 | 59 33 35 38 [16 17 46 40] |
| ara | 1 40 | 1 3[9] 15 [59 40 27 8] 37 [46 40] |
| ara | 1 40 | 2 45 2[6] 39 [28 25 14 22 57 46 40] |

The last four lines should actually read:

35 43 20 49 22 57 46 40
59 32 14 43 18 16 17 46 40
1 39 13 44 32 10 27 9 37 46 40
2 38 42 54 13 57 25 16 3 3 46 40

TRANSLATION

| | |
|---|---|
| 100 steps of 100 | 10000 |
| steps of 100 | 1000000 |
| steps of 100 | 100000000 |
| steps of 100 | 10000000000 |
| steps of 100 | 1000000000000 |
| steps of 100 | 100000000000000 |
| steps of 100 | 10000000000000000 |
| steps of 100 | 1000000000000000000 |
| steps of 100 | 100000000000000000000 |

## 1.1.2 Sacrobosco's *Algorismus*, *c.* 1230 AD

A system of writing numbers using place value, and nine symbols together with zero, emerged in central India during the late sixth and early seventh centuries AD, and gradually spread into all neighbouring cultures. By the end of the eighth century it had reached Baghdad where, around 825 AD, Muhammad ibn Mūsa al-Khwārizmī wrote a treatise explaining Indian numerals and the associated methods of addition and subtraction, multiplication and division, and easy extraction of roots. Unfortunately, the original treatise is now lost, but knowledge of its contents spread throughout the Islamic world, including Spain.

The Hindu-Arabic numerals, as they came to be called, are known to have made a fleeting appearance in north-west Europe in the tenth century as markers on the abacus counters of the French monk and scholar Gerbert (later Pope Sylvester II) who had studied in Spain, but there is no evidence of their use for calculation. In the eleventh century they would almost certainly have became known to the crusaders. During the twelfth century, they came into France and England through two kinds of mathematical text: (i) astronomical tables, for example, the Toledan tables from Spain which were translated from Arabic into Latin and adjusted for the cities of Marseilles (1140) and London (1150); (ii) Latin texts based on al-Khwārizmī's treatise of 825 AD, which explicitly taught the use of the new numerals, and which came to be known as 'algorisms' from the opening words 'Dixit Algorismi ...', ('al-Khwārizmī said ...').[1]

From the beginning of the thirteenth century the numerals gradually became better understood, in Italy through the *Liber abaci* (1202) of Leonardo Pisano (later known as Fibonacci), who had travelled extensively through north Africa and the eastern Mediterranean. Further north the *Liber abaci* was unknown and the crucial texts were the algorisms, such as those of Alexander de Ville Dieu (*c.* 1200) and Sacrobosco (*c.* 1230). The algorism of Sacrobosco was particularly influential and often copied, and remained in use as a university text until the fifteenth century.

Shown below is the opening of Sacrobosco's algorism, from a copy made on vellum in Florence in 1399. To save time and materials, manuscript copyists used many abbreviations, which here appear as squiggles and dashes throughout the text and render it illegible to the untrained reader, but there is no difficulty in spotting the subject of the piece, the numerals 0, 9, 8, 7, 6, 5, 4, 3, 2, 1, (Arabic ordering) in the fourth line of the second page. Note that while the text is known as an 'algorism', the historical figure of al-Khwārizmī has been replaced by the mythical philosopher Algus.

---

1. Three such texts survive from the twelfth century; for details see Folkerts 2001.

# Sacrobosco and Hindu-Arabic numerals
from a fourteenth-century copy of Sacrobosco's 'Algorismus'

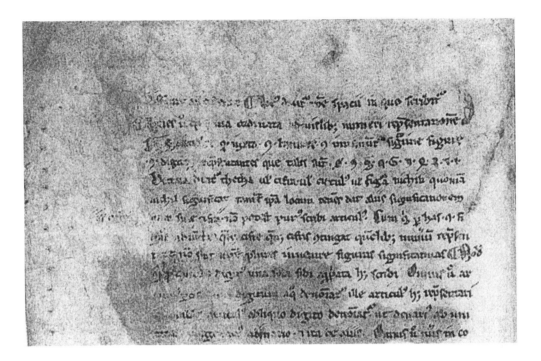

Note:
In the translation that follows the Latin *differentia* has been translated as 'scale', because its meaning in this context is the change in magnitude between consecutive figures (from ones to tens, tens to hundreds, and so on). Another difficult word is *limes*, literally a boundary, but here the 'range of values' that a particular figure can take: 2, for instance, can take the values 2, 20, 200, ... according to position. The word *digitus* gives rise to the modern 'digit', but I have kept the literal translations 'finger' and 'knuckle' for *digitus* and *articulus* as a reminder of the practical counting methods on which these terms were based.

## TRANSLATION

All that has proceeded from the first beginning of things has been formed by reason of number, and how is to be known thus: that in the entire understanding of things, the art of numbering is at work. Therefore a philosopher by the name of Algus wrote this brief knowledge of number, whence it is called *algorismus*, or the art of numbering. A number is known in two ways: in form a number is a multitude gathered from units; materially a number is units collected. A unit, moreover, is that by which any one thing is said to be one. Among numbers there are fingers, knuckles, and composite numbers. Every number smaller than ten is said to be a finger [*digitus*]; but a knuckle [*articulus*] is any number that may be divided into ten equal parts, in such a way that nothing is left over. A composite or mixed number is one consisting of finger and knuckle. And it is to be understood that every number between two neighbouring knuckles is a composite number. Moreover there are nine classes of this art: namely, denomination, addition, subtraction, halving, doubling, multiplication, division, progression, and extraction of roots, and the latter is twofold, for square numbers and cube numbers; amongst which we speak first of numeration and afterwards of the others in turn.

The denomination of any number by suitable figures is a skilled representation. Indeed figure, scale, place, and range of value assume the same [method], but are put here for different reasons. What is traced by a line is said to be a figure. The scale is shown by how much a subsequent figure differs from a preceding one. A place is so called by reason of the space within which [a number] is written. Range of value is the method devised for representing any number whatever. Therefore for the nine ranges of value, there are found to be nine figures, representing nine fingers; which are these, 9.8.7.6.5.4.3.2.1. The tenth figure is called theta, or circle, or cipher, or the figure nothing because it signifies nothing, but holding a place it gives significance to the others: for without a cipher or ciphers a correct number cannot be formed. Therefore with these nine signifying figures together with a cipher or ciphers it is possible to represent any number whatever, and it is not necessary to find more signifying figures. Thus it is to be noted that any finger can be written with one single figure appropriate to it. But every knuckle by a cipher placed first, and by the figure of the finger by which it is denominated, that knuckle may be represented or denominated. Any knuckle can be represented by some finger, as ten by one, twenty by two, and so on for others.

---

## 1.2 BEGINNINGS OF GEOMETRY

In medieval Europe it was believed that the yearly flooding of the Nile gave rise to geometry ('earth measurement') and that Pythagoras learned geometry from the Egyptians. There is no evidence on either count. Pythagoras is thought to have lived on the island of Samos in the sixth century BC but he became a legendary figure who survived at the interface between fact and fiction, and almost nothing is known about him with any certainty. As far as we can tell, geometry in the form that it has been studied and taught in Europe for over two thousand years began in the Greek speaking world itself after about 500 BC.

The most comprehensive surviving treatise on Greek geometry is Euclid's *Elements*, which modern scholars suppose to have been written around 250 BC. There are no contemporary references to the *Elements*, however, and this date is based on the estimated date of other works by Euclid. No more is known about Euclid himself than about Pythagoras, but the *Elements* has been one of the most influential mathematical texts ever written. It consists of thirteen Books, nine of which (I–VI and XI–XIII) are concerned with plane and solid geometry, culminating in a study of the five Platonic solids. The four middle Books (VII to X) deal with number (in Greek, *arithmos*; see 1.3.1 and 1.3.2).

The *Elements* appears to have been a systematic compilation of known theorems of plane and solid geometry, and of elementary number theory. Euclid's achievement was to bring all this material together in a logical arrangement, beginning with definitions and axioms, and proceeding to theorems and corollaries in a series of careful deductive arguments. The *Elements* became the longest running textbook ever, and generations of students until well into the twentieth century continued to learn basic geometry from Euclidean principles. Even more importantly, it set standards of mathematical proof and rigour that later mathematicians continually aspired to. That is not to say, however, that every statement in the *Elements* was indisputable, and attempts to understand or improve on Euclid have over the years led to much new and profound mathematics.

The textual history of the *Elements* is long and complex. No ancient Greek copy has survived, and the text has come down to us only through multiple translations and renditions, with no single definitive version. Some of the more elementary material made its way into the work of early Latin writers like Boethius, and as Islam spread into the old Hellenistic empire translations were made from Greek to Arabic. Full Latin translations were made in the twelfth century, first from Arabic, and later from rediscovered Greek manuscripts. From the fifteenth century onward there have been hundreds of printed editions in numerous languages, ranging from large and lavish library editions to pocket-sized versions for students. And like any great text, the *Elements* has accrued many layers of commentary and explanation.

The edition chosen for this book is the English translation published in 1660 by Isaac Barrow, Lucasian Professor of Mathematics at Cambridge. One reason for selecting Barrow's edition from among the many on offer is that it is in English; another is that it was aimed at precisely the same kind of audience as the present book, namely, undergraduates learning mathematics. Students at the two English universities, Cambridge and Oxford, began their studies at the age of about sixteen or seventeen, and although there was as yet no such thing as a degree in mathematics anyone who wanted to study the subject would certainly have begun with Euclid. To the modern reader Barrow's vocabulary, spelling, and punctuation may seem archaic: 'longitude' for 'length', 'latitude' for 'width', 'right' for 'straight', 'superficies' for 'surface', and 'contained under' for 'enclosed by' are all closer to their Latin equivalents than to modern English, while 'it's' was a common seventeenth-century form of 'its' which should not be imitated now. Nevertheless, compared with the only other English translation then available, Billingsley's large and expensive edition of 1572, Barrow's version is homely and readable. All remarks in *italic* are Barrow's own comments on the text.

### 1.2.1 Euclid's definitions, *c.* 250 BC

Euclid's definitions of point, line, surface, angle, and circle, of various kinds of triangle and quadrilateral, and of parallel lines, are gathered together at the beginning of Book I.

## Euclid's geometric definitions
from *Euclide's Elements*, edited by Barrow, 1660, Definitions 1–21

---

**1**

# THE FIRST BOOK
## OF
# EUCLIDE'S
# ELEMENTS.

---

### *Definitions.*

I.   A Point is that which hath no part.

II. A Line is a longitude without latitude.

III. The ends, or limits, of a line are points.

IV. A right line is that which lyes equally betwixt it's points.

V. A Superficies is that which hath only longitude and latitude.

VI. The extremes, or limits, of a superficies are lines.

VII. A plaine superficies is that which lyes equally betwixt it's lines.

VIII. A plaine Angle is the inclination of two lines the one to the other, the one touching the other in the same plain, yet not lying in the same strait line.

IX. And if the lines which contein the angle be right lines, it is called a right-lined angle.

A                              X. When

*The firſt Book of*

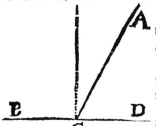

X. When a right line **C G** ſtanding upon a right line A **B**, makes the angles on either ſide thereof, C G A, **C G B**, equall one to the other, then both thoſe equall angles are right angles ; and the right line **C** G, which ſtandeth on the other, is termed a **P**erpendicular to that ( A B ) whereon it ſtandeth.

Note. *When ſeverall angles meet at the ſame point ( as at* G) *each particular angle is deſcribed by three letters ; whereof the middle letter ſheweth the angular point, and the two other letters the lines that make that angle :  As the angle which the right lines* C G, A G *make at* G, *is called* C G A, *or* A G C.

X I. An obtuſe angle is that which is greater then a right angle; as A C B.

X I I. An acute angle is that which is leſſe then a right angle; as A C D.

XIII. A Limit, or Term, is the end of any thing.

X I V. A Figure is that which is conteined under one or more terms.

X V. A Circle is a plain figure conteined under one line , which is called a Circumference ; unto which all lines drawn from one point within the figure , and falling upon the circumference thereof, are equall the one to the other.

X V I. And that point is called the Centre of the circle.

X V I I. A Diameter of a circle is a right line drawn through the centre thereof, and ending at the circumference on either ther

**EUCLIDE'S** *Elements.*                                    **3**

ther fide, dividing the circle into two equall parts.

XVIII. A Semicircle is a figure which is conteined under the diameter and under that part of
the circumference which is cut off by the diameter.

*In the circle* E A B C D, E *is the centre,* A C *the
diameter,* A B C *the femicircle.*

XIX. Right-lined figures are fuch as are conteined under right lines.

XX. Three-fided or Trilateral figures are fuch as
are conteined under three right lines.

XXI. Four-fided or Quadrilateral figures are
fuch as are conteined under four right lines.

### 1.2.2  Euclid's construction of proportionals, *c.* 250 BC

In Book V of the *Elements*, Euclid defined the concept of a *ratio* between two magnitudes such as lines or surfaces, and after that the geometry of the *Elements* is
everywhere permeated with the language of ratio and proportion. (In Book VII he
attempted corresponding definitions for numbers, hence the later idea of 'rational'
numbers, those that can be expressed as ratios of whole numbers.) These concepts
are important because they determined the language and style of geometric discourse
for centuries: Euclidean ratio arguments are still clearly visible in the work of Fermat
and Newton in the seventeenth century, for example (see 3.2.1 and 5.1.5). The extract
below describes two constructions that were well known and frequently used by later
mathematicians.

## The construction of proportionals

from *Euclide's Elements*, edited by Barrow, 1660, Propositions VI.12, VI.13

*Notation*

A *mean proportional* is what is now known as a geometric mean. Given three consecutive terms in a geometric progression, a *fourth proportional* is the next term in the sequence. Barrow used ratio notation invented by William Oughtred in his *Clavis mathematicae* of 1631, namely, *A.B :: C.D* for what we would now write as $A : B = C : D$. Barrow's margin notes refer to earlier propositions in Euclid, thus 2.6 means Book VI, Proposition 2.

### P R O P.  XII.

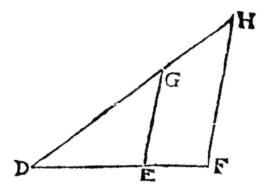

*Three right lines being given* DE, EF, DG, *to find out a fourth proportionall* GH.

Join EG, and thorough F draw FH parallel to EG; with which let DG produced to H meet. Then it is evident that DE. EF *a* :: DG. GH. *W. W. to be Done.*    **a** *2. 6.*

### P R O P.  XIII.

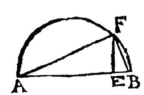

*Two right lines being given* AE, EB, *to find out a mean proportionall* E-F.

Upon the whole line A B as a diameter describe a semicircle AFB, & from E erect a perpendicular EF meeting with the periphery in F. then AE.EF :: EF. EB. For let AF & FB be drawn; *a* then from the right angle of the right-angled triangle AFB is drawn a right line FE perpendicular to the base. *b* Therefore AE.FE :: FE.EB. *W.W. to be Done.*    **a** *31. 3.*   **b** *cor. 8. 6.*

### 1.2.3 Archimedes on circle measurement, *c.* 250 BC

Archimedes (287–212 BC) spent part of his life in Egypt and is thought to have studied at Alexandria. He is renowned both for his mechanical inventions, and for a number of sophisticated mathematical treatises, the best known of which are *On the sphere and cylinder, Measurement of a circle, On spirals,* and *The sand-reckoner,* the last being his attempt to calculate the number of grains of sand needed to fill the universe.

Archimedes used two mathematical techniques which came to epitomize standards of classical rigour: the method of exhaustion, and proof by contradiction. The method of exhaustion can be used, for instance, to estimate the space inside a circle by inscribing or circumscribing polygons, and increasing the number of sides as far as necessary so that the space between circle and polygon is steadily 'exhausted'. The method relies essentially on a proposition to be found in Euclid X.1 which states that if a quantity (in this case the excess space) is continually reduced by more than half of itself, it can be made less than any preassigned quantity. Circle and polygon are never supposed actually equal, however, and it is important to note that there is no limiting process involved here or anywhere else in Greek mathematics.

Proof by contradiction, or *reductio ad absurdum,* was known before the time of Archimedes (it had been used, for instance, in the simple and beautiful proof that the diagonal and side of a square are incommensurable), but he made particularly effective use of the method. It cannot be faulted on grounds of rigour, but later mathematicians complained bitterly that such proofs gave no insight into how theorems were conceived in the first place, and that Archimedes and others had deliberately hidden their working. (Only in the twentieth century with the discovery of the Archimedes palimpsest do we have some clues as to how Archimedes found some of his results on areas and volumes, and his method appears to anticipate the 'cutting into strips' that was later used in the development of the calculus.)

In the first proposition of *Measurement of a circle* Archimedes used the methods of exhaustion and double *reductio* to prove that the area of a circle is equal to that of a right-angled triangle in which the perpendicular sides are the length of the radius and the circumference respectively. In the third and last proposition (not given here) he showed in a remarkable feat of calculation that the ratio of the perimeter to the diameter lies between $3\frac{1}{7}$ and $3\frac{10}{71}$.

## Archimedes' theorem
from *Archimedis opera*, edited by Commandino, 1558, Proposition 1

I

# ARCHIMEDIS

### CIRCVLI DIMENSIO.

### PROPOSITIO I.

VILIBET circulus æqualis eſt
triangulo rectangulo : cuius quidem ſemidiameter uni laterum,
quæ circa rectũ angulũ ſunt, ambitus uero baſi eius eſt æqualis .

Sɪт a b c d circulus, ut ponitur .
Dico eum æqualem eſſe triangulo e . ſi
enim fieri poteſt , ſit primum maior circulus : & ipſi inſcribatur
quadratum a c : ſecenturǫ circumferentiæ bifariam : & ſint portiones iam minores exceſſu, quo circulus ipſum triangulum excedit . erit figura rectilinea adhuc triangulo maior. Sumatur cen
trum n ; & perpendicularis n x . minor eſt igitur n x trianguli latere . eſt autem & ambitus rectilineæ figuræ reliquo latere minor ;
quoniam & minor eſt circuli ambitu . quare figura rectilinea mi
nor eſt triangulo e : quod eſt abſurdum .

Sit deinde , ſi fieri poteſt , circulus minor triangulo e : & cir-
cumſcribatur quadratum : circũferentiisǫ bifariam ſectis , per
ea puncta contingentes lineæ ducãtur. erit angulus o ɑ r rectus.
& idcirco linea o r maior, quàm ɑ m ; quòd r m ipſi r a ſit æqualis.
triangulum igitur r o p maius eſt , quàm dimidium figuræ o f a m .
itaque ſumantur portiones, ipſi p f a ſimiles ; quæ quidem mino
res ſint eo , quo triangulum e excedit circulum a b c d . erit figura circumſcripta adhuc triangulo e minor : quod item eſt abſurdum , cum ſit maior : nam ipſa quidem n a æqualis eſt trianguli
catheto : ambitus uero maior eſt baſi eiuſdem . ex quibus ſequitur circulum triangulo e æqualem eſſe .

### PROPOSITIO II.

Circulus
ad quadratũ
diametri eam
proportionẽ
habet, quam
XI ad XIIII.

Sɪт circulus,
cuius diameter a
b : & circumſcri-
batur quadratũ c
g : & ipſius c d du
pla ſit d e : ſit au-
tem e f, ſeptimɑ
eiuſdẽ c d. Quo-

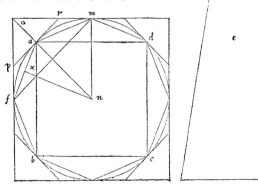

TRANSLATION

ARCHIMEDES'
MEASUREMENT OF A CIRCLE

PROPOSITION I.

ANY circle is equal to a right-angled triangle, in which the semidiameter is one of the sides next to the right angle, while the perimeter is equal to its base.

LET the circle *abcd* be as shown. I say that it is equal to triangle *e*. For, if it is possible, first suppose the circle is greater; and let the square *ac* be inscribed in it; and the arcs be cut in two; and let the portions now become less than the excess by which the circle exceeds the triangle. The straight-edged figure this far will be greater than the triangle. There is taken a centre *n*, and a perpendicular *nx*. Therefore *nx* is less than the side of the triangle. And the perimeter of the straight-edged figure is also less than the remaining side; since it is also less than the perimeter of the circle. Whence the straight-edged figure is less than the triangle *e*; which is absurd.

Then, if it is possible, suppose the circle is less than triangle *e*; and let a square be circumscribed around it; and the arcs being cut in two, through the points there are taken tangents. Therefore angle *oar* will be a right angle, and therefore the line *or* is greater than *rm*, because *rm* is equal to *ra*. Therefore triangle *rop* is more than half the figure *ofam*. And therefore there may be taken portions similar to *pfa*, which are indeed less than that amount by which the triangle *e* exceeds the circle *abcd*. The straight-edged figure circumscribed this far is less than the triangle *e*; which is likewise absurd, for it is greater; for indeed *na* is equal to the upright of the triangle; but the perimeter is greater than the base of it. From which it follows that the circle is equal to the triangle *e*.

## 1.2.4 Apollonius' *Conics, c.* 185 BC

Apollonius is thought to have been active around 185 BC and, like Archimedes, he studied at Alexandria. He is now best known for his *Conics*, a comprehensive study of conic sections: circle, ellipse, parabola, and hyperbola. The *Conics* was written in eight books, of which the first seven are known from Arabic translations, but only the first four have survived in Greek. The eighth book is completely lost, though some of its contents can be reconstructed from the description of it given by Pappus in his *Synagoge* (*Collection*) in the early fourth century AD.

At the beginning of Book I Apollonius gave his basic definitions (of cone, diameter, ordinates, and so on). In Proposition 11 (given below) he described the curve obtained by making a cut parallel to one of the sides of the cone. He demonstrated that such a curve must have certain geometric properties, and called it a *parabola*. The crucial line *fh* is now known as the *latus rectum*, and its length is that of the ordinate taken through the focus (so for a parabola with equation $y^2 = 4ax$ its length is $2a$).

Apollonius' proof uses several propositions that are to be found in Euclid's *Elements*, and margin references to these and to earlier propositions in the *Conics* were inserted by later editors. Though written in language that is now unfamiliar, the argument is well worth pursuing: there are few better introductions to the style and sophistication of classical Greek mathematics.

---

### Apollonius' definition of a parabola

from *Apollonii Pergaei conicorum*, edited by Commandino, 1566, Proposition I.11

---

#### THEOREMA XI. PROPOSITIO XI.

S I conus plano per axem fecetur: fecetur autem & altero plano fe-cante bafim coni fecundum rectam lineam, quæ ad bafim trianguli per axem fit perpendicularis: & fit diameter fectionis uni laterum triangu-li per axem æquidiftans: recta linea, quæ à fectione coni ducitur æqui-diftans communi fectioni plani fecantis, & bafis coni, ufque ad fectionis diametrum; poterit fpatium æquale contento linea, quæ ex diametro abfciffa inter ipfam & uerticē fectionis interiicitur, & alia quadam, quæ ad lineam inter coniangulum, & uerticem fectionis interiectam, eam proportionem habeat, quàm quadratum bafis trianguli per axem, ad id quod reliquis duobus trianguli lateribus continetur. dicatur autem hu-iufmodi fectio parabolē.

SIT conus, cuius uertex punctum a; bafis b c circulus: fecetur ́q; plano per axem, quód fectionem faciat triangulum a b c: & fecetur altero plano fecante bafim coni fe cundum rectam lineam d e, quæ ad b c fit perpendicularis; & faciat fectionem in fu-perficie coni d f e lineam: diameter autem fectionis f g æquidiftans fit uni laterum trianguli per axem, uidelicet ipfi a c; atque à puncto f lineæ f g ad rectos angulos du
**A**   catur f h: & fiat ut quadratum b c ad rectangulum b a c, ita linea h f ad f a. fumatur præterea in fectione quodlibet punctum k: & per k ducatur k l ipfi d e æquidiftans. Dico quadratum k l rectangulo h f l æquale effe. Ducatur enim per l ipfi b c æquidi-
15.unde-   ftaus m n: & eft k l æquidiftans ipfi d e. ergo planum, quod tranfit per k l m n plano per
cimi   b c d e, hóc eft ipfi bafi coni æquidiftat. ideóq; planum per k l m n circulus eft, cuius
4.huius   diametér m n. eft autem k l ad m n perpendicularis, quòd & d e ad b c. rectangulum
10.unde.   igitur m l n æquale eft k l quadrato. itaque quoniam linea h f ad f a eft ut quadratum
b c ad rectangulum b a c: quadratum autem b c ad b a c rectangulum compofitam
proportionem habet ex proportione, quàm b c ad c a, & ex ea, quàm c b habet ad b a.
quare proportio h f ad f a componitur ex proportione b c ad c a, & c b ad b a. Vt autem

## CONICORVM LIB. I.

tem b c ad c a,ita m n ad n a,hoc eſt m l ad l f: & ut c b ad b a,ita n m ad m à,hoc eſt l m ad m f, & reliqua n l ad f a. proportio igitur h f ad f a componitur ex proportione m l ad l f,& n l ad f a. ſed proportio compoſita ex proportione m l ad l f, & n l ad f a eſt ea,quam habet m l n rectangu lum ad rectangulum l fa.ergo ut h f ad f a; ita re‒ ctangulum m l n ad l f a rectangulum.ut autem h f ad f a,ſumpta f l communi altitudine,ita h f l re‒ ctangulum ad rectangulum l f a. Vt igitur rectan‒ gulum m l n ad ipſum l fa,ita rectangulum h f l ad l fa:& idcirco æquale eſt rectangulum m l n rectan gulo h f l. ſed rectangulum m l n æquale eſt qua‒ drato k l. ergo quadratum k l rectangulo h f l æ‒ quale erit. Vocetur autem huiuſmodi ſectio pa‒ rabole;& linea h f,iuxta quam poſſunt, quæ ad f g diametrum ordinatim applicantur: quæ quidem etiam recta appellabitur.

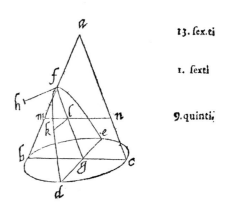

19.quinti

13.ſex.ti

1. ſexti

9.quinti

### TRANSLATION

## THEOREM XI. PROPOSITION XI.

SUPPOSE a cone is cut by a plane along its axis; and moreover that it is cut also by another plane cutting the base of the cone in a straight line, which is perpendicular to the base of the triangle through the axis; and let the diameter of the section be parallel to one side of the triangle through the axis; and let there be a straight line, which is drawn from the section of the cone, parallel to the intersection of the cutting plane and the base of the cone, as far as the diameter of the section. The line with itself will form a space equal in content to that formed from the diameter cut off between that and the vertex of the section, and another, which has the same ratio to the line between the angle of the cone and the vertex of the section, as the square on the base of the triangle through the axis to that formed by the remaining two sides of the triangle. Moreover, a section of this kind is said to be a parabola.

LET there be a cone, whose vertex is the point *a* and whose base is the circle *bc*. Let it be cut by a plane through the axis, which section makes a triangle *abc*; and let it be cut by another plane cutting the base of the cone in a straight line *de*, which is perpendicular to *bc*; and let it make a line *dfe* on the surface of the cone; moreover, the diameter *fg* of the section is parallel to one side of the triangle through the axis, suppose to *ac*; and from the point *f* there is taken *fh* at right angles to the line *fg*; done so that *hf* to *fa* is as the square on *bc* to the rectangle *bac*. Further, there is taken in the section any point *k*; and through *k* there is drawn *kl* parallel to *de*. I say that the square on *kl* is equal to the rectangle *hfl*. For there is taken *mn* through *l* parallel to *bc*; and *kl* is parallel to *de*. Therefore the plane which passes through *klmn* is parallel to the plane through *bcde*, that is, the base of the cone. And therefore, the plane through *klmn* is a circle, whose diameter is *mn*. Moreover *kl* is perpendicular to *mn*; because so is *de* to *bc*. Therefore the rectangle *lmn* is equal to the square *kl*. Since the line *hf* to *fa* is as the square on *bc* to the rectangle *bac* and, moreover, the square on *bc* has a ratio to the rectangle *bac* which is composed from the ratio of *bc* to *ca* and that of *cb* to *ba*, therefore the ratio of *hf* to *fa* is composed from the ratio of *bc* to *ca* and that of *cb* to *ba*. Moreover, as [14] *bc* is to *ca*, so is *mn* to *na*, that is, as *ml* to *lf*; and as *cb* is to *ba*, so is *nm* to *ma*, that is, as *lm* to *mf*, and the difference *nl* to *fa*. Therefore the ratio of *hf* to *fa* is composed from the ratio of *ml* to *lf* and that of *nl* to *fa*. But the ratio composed from the ratio of *ml* to *lf* and that of *nl* to *fa* is that of rectangle *mln* to rectangle *lfa*. Therefore as *hf* is to *fa* so is rectangle *mln* to rectangle *lfa*. Moreover, as *hf* is to *fa* so is rectangle *hfl* to rectangle *lfa*, taking a common altitude *fl*. Therefore as rectangle *mln* is to *lfa* so is rectangle *hfl* to *lfa*, and therefore rectangle *mln* is equal to rectangle *hfl*. But rectangle *mln* is equal to the square on *kl*. Therefore the square on *kl* is equal to rectangle *hfl*. Moreover, a section of this kind is called a parabola; and the line *hf*, placed where it fits alongside those laid against the diameter *fg* as ordinates, is also called the *latus rectum*.

15. eleventh
4. of this
10. eleventh

19. fifth

13. sixth
1. sixth

9. fifth

———————

## 1.3 BEGINNINGS OF A THEORY OF NUMBERS

### 1.3.1 Euclid's definitions of number, *c.* 250 BC

Nowadays we tend to think of arithmetic as elementary calculation. Historically this has been known as common or vulgar arithmetic, or in Latin *logistica*. For the Greeks, *arithmetica* (from *arithmos*, a collection of units) was concerned with properties of *whole* numbers: whether they were odd or even, prime, square, triangular, perfect, and so on, and so had qualitative as well as quantitative aspects. Four books of Euclid's *Elements* (VII–X) deal with arithmetic in this second and more abstract sense: no-one expected to read the *Elements* to learn how to add or subtract.

Even when Euclid was writing about numbers his approach remained primarily geometric. A unit was a line segment of fixed length, and any whole number was regarded as some appropriate multiple of it. Thus Euclid's descriptions of numbers and what one can do with them abound in geometric references: one number divides another exactly, for example, if the line representing the first can be used to 'measure' the line representing the second. Many editions of Euclid illustrate propositions about numbers with lines of appropriate lengths, but we have no idea at all what diagrams, if any, were drawn in the original text. Barrow, writing in 1660, used (dotted) lines to suggest numbers of different sizes, but also went some way beyond of his predecessors in introducing some elementary algebraic notation.

---

## Euclid's definitions of number

from *Euclide's Elements*, edited by Barrow, 1660, VII, Propositions 1–22

---

# THE SEVENTH BOOK
# O F
# EUCLIDE'S ELEMENTS.

---

## *Definitions.*

I. UNity is that, by which every thing that is, is called One.

II. Number is a multitude composed of unities.

III. One number is a Part of another, the lesser of the greater, when the lesser measureth the greater.

*Every part is denominated from that number, by which it measures the number whereof it is a part; as 4 is called the third part of 12, because it measures 12 by 3.*

IV. But the lesser number is termed Parts, when it measureth not the greater.

*All parts whatsoever are denominated from those two numbers, by which the greatest common measure of the two numbers measures each of them; as 10 is said to be ⅔ of the number 15; because the greatest common measure, which is 5, measures 10 by 2, and 15 by 3.*

V. A number is Multiplex (or Manifold) a greater in comparison of a lesser, when the lesser measureth the greater.

VI. An Even number is that which may be divided into two equall parts.

VII. But an Odde number is that which cannot be divided into two equall parts; or, that which differeth from an even number by an unitie.

VIII. A number Evenly Even is that which an even number measureth by an even number.

IX. But a number Evenly Odde is that which an even number measureth by an odde number.

X. A

*The seventh Book of*

**X.** A number Oddly Odd is that which an odd number measureth by an odd number.

**X I.** A Prime (or first) number is that , which measured only by an unitie.

**X I I.** Numbers Prime the one to the other , is such as onely an unitie doth measure, being their common measure.

**X I I I.** A Composed number is that which some certain number measureth.

**X I V.** Numbers Composed the one to the other, are they, which some number, being a common measure to them both, doth measure.

*In this, and the preceding  definition , unitie is not a number.*

**X V.** One number is said to Multiply another, when the number multiplied is so often added to it self, as there are unities in the number multiplying, and another number is produced.

*Hence in every multiplication  a  unitie is to the multiplier, as the multiplied is to the product.*

*Obs. That many times , when any numbers are to be multiplied (as A into B) the conjunction of the letters denotes the Product: So AB = A x B, and CDE = C x D x E.*

**X V I.** When two numbers multiplying themselves produce another, the number produced is called a Plane number; and the numbers which multiplied one another, are called the Sides of that number: So 2 (C) x 3 (D) = 6 = CD *is a plane number.*

**XVII.** But when three numbers multiplying one another produce any number, the number produced is termed a Solid number ; and the numbers multiplying one another, are the sides thereof: So 2 (C) x 3 (D) x 5 (E) = 30 = CDE *is a solid number.*

**XVIII.** A Square number is that which is equally equall ; or, which is conteined under two equall numbers. *Let A be the side of a square; the square is that noted,* A A, *or* Aq.

**XIX.** A Cube is that number which is equally equall

# EUCLIDE'S *Elements.*                    143

quall equally; or, which is conteined under three e-
quall numbers. *Let* **A** *be the fide of a Cube; the Cube is
thus noted,* **AAA**, *or* Ac.

*In this definition, and the three foregoing , unitie is a
number.*

XX. Numbers are proportionall, when the firft is as
multiplex of the fecond as the third is of the fourth;
or, the fame part; or, when a part of the firft number
meafures the fecond , and the fame part of the third
meafures the fourth, equally : and on the contrary.
*So* A. B :: C. D. *that is*, 3. 9 :: 5. 15.

XXI. Like Plane , and folid numbers are they ,
which have their fides proportionall : *Namely, not all
the fides, but fome.*

XXII. A Perfect number is that which is equall to
its own parts.

*As* 6. & 28. *But a number that is leffe then it's parts
is called an* Abounding *number; and a greater a* Diminutive : *fo* 12 *is an abounding*, 15 *a diminutive number.*

### 1.3.2 Euclid's proof of the infinity of primes, *c.* 250 BC

In Book IX of the *Elements*, Euclid stated a number of properties of the natural numbers, one of the best known of which is the existence of infinitely many primes, together with his beautifully concise proof. The proposition that follows it is, by contrast, somewhat mundane.

---

### The infinity of primes
from *Euclide's Elements*, edited by Barrow, 1660, IX, Propositions 20, 21

---

#### P R O P.  XX.

A,2. B,3. C,5.    *More prime numbers may be given*
D, 30. G - - - -  *then any multitude whatsoever of*
                  *prime numbers* A,B,**C**,*propounded.*

*a* 38. 7.      *a* Let D be the leaſt which A,B,**C**, meaſure ; Iſ D
*b* 33.7.      ─┼ 1 be a prime, the caſe is plain; if compoſed,*b* then
               ſome prime number, conceive G , meaſures D ─┼ 1;
                                                                which

#### E U C L I D E' S  *Elements.*          1**8**7

which is none of the three **A,**B,**C;** For if it be, ſeeing
it *c* meaſures the whole D ─┼ 1, *d* and the part taken    *c ſuppoſ.*
away D, *e* it ſhall alſo meaſure the remaining unite.   *d conſtr.*
*which is Abſ.* Therefore the propounded number of        *e* 13.0x.7.
prime numbers is increaſed by D ─┼ 1, or at leaſt
by **G.**

#### P R O P.  XXI.

         ſ     ſ   3   3   2   2
    A .....E .....B ...F...C ..G..D 20.

*If even numbers, how many ſoever,* AB, BC, CD, *be*
*added together, the whole* AD *ſhall be even.*
*a* Take EB ═ ½ AB, and FC ═ ½ BC,  and GD    *a* 6.*def.*7.
═ ½ CD. *b* it is plain that EB ─┼ FC ─┼ GD ═ ½     *b* 12. 7.
AD. *c* therefore AD is an even number. *Which was to*    *c,*6 *def.*7.
*be Dem.*

### 1.3.3 The *Arithmetica* of Diophantus, (after 150 AD)

Only one Greek text departs from the otherwise overwhelmingly geometric discourse of surviving Greek mathematics: the *Arithmetica* of Diophantus. All we can say with certainty about Diophantus himself is that he wrote after 150 AD (because he referred to an earlier writer, Hypsicles). The *Arithmetica* was originally written in thirteen books, of which only the first six survive in Greek, but an Arabic manuscript of Books IV to VII was discovered in the twentieth century. All the problems in the *Arithmetica* are concerned with finding numbers that satisfy certain conditions, and with the implicit requirement that the solutions should be integers or fractions.

The surviving books made a profound impression on European mathematicians when they were eventually rediscovered and published in the sixteenth century. Rafael Bombelli re-wrote a large part of his *Algebra* (published in 1572) in order to incorporate problems from a manuscript of the *Arithmetica* that he read in the Vatican Library, and François Viète also used problems from Diophantus in his *Zetetica* of 1593. In the late 1620s the young Pierre de Fermat read Claude Gaspar Bachet's new edition of the *Arithmetica* (1621) and made a number of notes in the margin: one of them was his statement of what came to be known as 'Fermat's last theorem' (see 6.3).

The problem that gave rise to Fermat's theorem is given below, from the 1621 edition of the *Arithmetica* that Fermat himself read. The problem is to partition any square number into two (integer or fractional) squares. Diophantus illustrated the method for 16, but his method is clearly applicable to any other square number. In modern notation, his solution is as follows. If 16 is the sum of two squares, say $x^2 + y^2$, then $16 - x^2$ is a square. Now suppose, as a particular and convenient case, that it is $(2x - 4)^2$. We then have the equation

$$16 - x^2 = 4x^2 - 16x + 16$$

in which the numerical terms cancel each other out. We are left with $5x^2 = 16x$, with solutions $x = \frac{16}{5}, y = \frac{12}{5}$. In fact there are infinitely many other solutions, but Diophantus required only one of them, and so his problem was solved.

## A square as a sum of two squares
from *Diophanti Alexandrini arithmeticorum libri sex*, edited by Bachet, 1621,
Proposition II.8

# Arithmeticorum Lib. II.    85

teruallo quadratorum , & Canones iidem hic etiam locum habebunt , vt manifeftum eſt.

### QVÆSTIO VIII.

Propositvm quadratum
diuidere in duos quadratos.
Imperatum fit vt 16. diuidatur
in duos quadratos. Ponatur
primus 1 Q. Oportet igitur 16
– 1 Q. æquales eſſe quadrato.
Fingo quadratum à numeris
quotquot libuerit , cum defe-
ctu tot vnitatum quot continet latus ipſius 16. eſto à 2 N.
– 4. ipſe igitur quadratus erit
4 Q. –+ 16. – 16 N. hæc æqua-
buntur vnitatibus 16 – 1 Q.
Communis adiiciatur vtrimque
defectus , & à ſimilibus aufe-
rantur ſimilia, fient 5 Q. æquales 16 N. & fit 1 N. ⅘ Erit igi-
tnr alter quadratorum ⁚⁚ . alter
verò ⁚⁚ . & vtriuſque ſumma eſt
⁚⁚ ſeu 16. & vterque quadratus
eſt.

ΤΟΝ ἐπιταχθέντα τετράγωνον
διελεῖν εἰς δύο τετραγώνους. ἐ-
πιτετάχθω δὴ τ̄ 15 διελεῖν εἰς δύο τετραγώνους. καὶ τετάχθω ὁ πρῶτος
δυνάμεως μιᾶς. δεήσει ἄρα μονάδας 15 λείψ δυνάμεως μιᾶς ἴσας
εἶ τετραγώνῳ. πλάσσω τ̄ τετράγωνον ἀπὸ ϛϛ. ὅσων δήποτε λείψ το-
σούτων μ̄ ὅσων ἐστὶν ἡ τ̄ 15 μ̄ πλά-
εϛ. ἔστω ϛϛ β̄ λείψ μ̄ δ. αὐτὸς
ἄρα ὁ τετράγωνός ἐσται δυνάμεων
δ̄ μ̄ 15 [ λείψ ϛϛ 15 ] ταῦτα ἴσα
μονάσι 15 λείψ δυνάμεως μιᾶς.
κοινὴ προσκείσθω ἡ λεῖψις, κὴ ἀπὸ
ὁμοίων ὅμοια. δυνάμεις ἄρα ε ἴσαι
ἀριθμοῖς 15. κὴ γίνεται ὁ ἀριθμὸς
15 πέμπτων. ἔσται ὁ μὴ ὅνϛ εἰκοσο-

πέμπλων. ὁ δὲ ρμδ̄ εἰκοσοπέμπλων, ἐ ⅔ δύο συντεθέντες ποιοῦσι ῡ
εἰκοστόπεμπλα, ἤτοι μονάδας 15 . καὶ ἔστιν ἑκάτερος τετράγων⊕ .

## QUESTION VIII

It is proposed to divide a square into two squares. As though it is required to divide 16
into two squares. The first is put as one square. Therefore 16 minus that square must
be equal to a square. I form a square from any number you please, so that the defect
has as many units as are contained in the side of 16. Let this be twice the root [of the

supposed square] minus 4, of which the square will therefore be 4 times the square +16 − 16 times the root, this being equal to the units of 16 minus the square. Adding the same defect to both sides, and taking like from like, it comes out that 5 times the square equals 16 times the root, and so the root is $\frac{16}{5}$. Therefore one square will be $\frac{256}{25}$ and the other $\frac{144}{25}$, and the sum of both is $\frac{400}{16}$ or 16, and both are squares.

---

## 1.4 BEGINNINGS OF ALGEBRA

Algebra has been left until last in this chapter because while it is relatively easy to understand what is meant by 'arithmetic' or 'geometry' it is much more difficult to define 'algebra'. The popular understanding is that it is a kind of calculation with 'letters for numbers' and this is indeed one aspect of it, but those who have studied mathematics far enough know that the word 'algebra' is also used in a quite different sense for the study of abstract structures such as groups or vector spaces; indeed there are now entire systems that are themselves called 'algebras'. The different meanings are not unrelated, and in Chapters 12 and 13 we shall try to untangle some of the threads that are woven into modern algebra, but here we look only at the earliest precursors of the subject. The Arabic word *al-jabr* first entered mathematics in connection with equation-solving, and so that is where we shall begin.

### 1.4.1  Completing the square, *c.* 1800 BC

Problems involving unknown numbers that must satisfy certain conditions have been posed in many cultures; we have already seen some in the *Arithmetica* of Diophantus, and many others are to be found in Indian texts from about 500 AD onwards. Of particular interest with regard to the later development of algebra, however, are some much earlier examples, from Babylonian tablets of around 1800 BC, in which it was required to find two numbers whose sum (or difference) and product were known. Transcribed into modern notation, such questions lead to quadratic equations, but in 1800 BC they were solved by a kind of cut-and-paste geometry. In the problem below, for example, one is asked to find two numbers that are reciprocal with respect to 60 (that is, whose product is 60) and whose difference is 7. This can be solved by representing the two unknowns as sides of a rectangle of area 60, with one side 7 units longer than the other, and by then supplementing and rearranging the pieces to form a square whose side can be calculated.

With practice, the geometric manoeuvres can be replaced by a set of instructions that can be carried out without drawing figures, but in the example below many traces of practical activity linger on in the language, and the process as a whole is still described as 'completing the square'.[2]

---

2. For further details see Robson 2002, 114–116.

## Completing the square

from an unkown scribe, *c.* 1800 BC, Yale Babylonian Collection 6967, reproduced from
Neugebauer and Sachs, 1945, as translated by Eleanor Robson, 2002

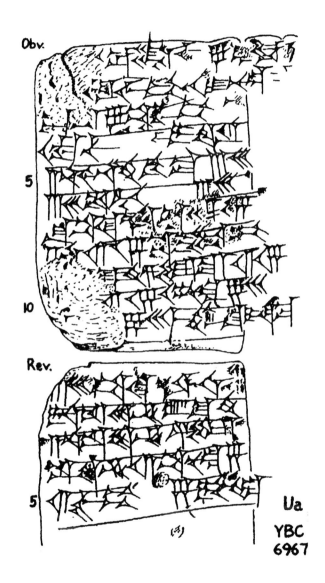

*Notation*
Square brackets show restorations of missing text.

## TRANSLATION

[A reciprocal] exceeds its reciprocal by 7. What are [the reciprocal] and its reciprocal?

You: break in half the 7 by which the reciprocal exceeds its reciprocal, and 3; 30 (will come up). Multiply 3; 30 by 3; 30 and 12; 15 (will come up).

Append [1 00, the area,] to the 12; 15 which came up for you and 1 12; 15 (will come up). What is [the square-side of 1] 12; 15? 8; 30.

Put down [8; 30 and] 8; 30, its equivalent, and subtract 3; 30, the takiltum-square, from one (of them); append (3; 30) to one (of them). One is 12, the other is 5. The reciprocal is 12, its reciprocal 5.

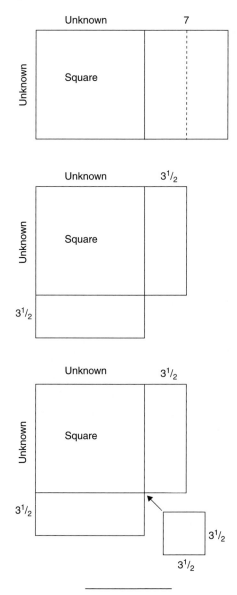

## 1.4.2 Al-Khwārizmī's *Al-jabr*, *c.* 825 AD

Babylonian two-number problems recur (though with long gaps in the record) until about 200 BC, but then disappear. One thousand years later, however, a seminal treatise on equation-solving, the inspiration for all subsequent work on the subject, came from the same part of the world: al-Khwārizmī's *Al-kitāb almukhtasar fi hisāb al-jabr w'al-muqābala* (*The book on restoration and balancing*), written in Baghdad around 825 AD. *Al-jabr* means 'restoration', especially of broken bones,[3] and presumably referred originally to the geometric process of putting together a square. Later it came to have the more abstract but equivalent meaning of supplying a term in an equation, in particular a positive term to counteract a negative. Of course, such a quantity must be added to *both* sides of an equation, and hence the concept of *al-muqābala*, or balancing, another practical word that came to acquire a more abstract meaning.

Al-Khwārizmī dealt entirely with equations between 'squares', 'roots', and 'numbers' and classified them into six types, for each of which he gave rules for solution. These were:

squares equal to roots
squares equal to numbers
roots equal to numbers
squares and roots equal to numbers
squares and numbers equal to roots
roots and numbers equal to squares

Although they are separated by over 2500 years, there are striking resemblances between al-Khwārizmī's text and the Mesopotamian example given earlier: the 'recipes' for solution are essentially the same, and so is the way the instructions are addressed directly to the reader. Although the concrete instructions of the Mesopotamian text ('break in half', 'append', 'put down') have been replaced by arithmetic operations such as 'divide into two', 'add', or 'subtract', traces of older geometric thinking are still discernible. Indeed, al-Khwārizmī provided geometric demonstrations for several of his examples by drawing and completing squares. The list of instructions could be applied by rote, but geometry was still regarded as the justification and foundation of the method. At the same time, as one might expect, the later text shows an increased sophistication of understanding. It states more explicitly that we are dealing with entire classes of equations and that the rules will apply to all others of the same type. It is understood that the type 'squares plus numbers equal roots' gives rise to two (positive) solutions, and the text also points out some possible pitfalls: cases where the method either breaks down or becomes trivial.

---

3. In the Spanish of Cervantes' *Don Quixote*, for example, an *algebrista* is a bone-setter.

Al-Khwārizmī's treatise ends with a lengthy collection of problems arising, for example, from Islamic inheritance laws, but with no further application to quadratic equations.

The rules for solving equations were taken up by other Islamic writers, particularly abū-Kāmil (*c.* 850–930) and al-Karajī (*c.* 1010), but it was not until the twelfth century that they reached western Europe, initially through Latin translations of al-Khwārizmī's *Al-jabr* by Robert of Chester (1145) and Gerard of Cremona (*c.* 1175).

Given below is Chapter V of al-Khwārizmī's treatise, here translated into English from the twelfth-century Latin version made by Robert of Chester. Observe that the idea of a square as a geometric shape still persists in the phrase '49 [units] fill (*adimplent*) the square'.

---

### Al-Khwārizmī's treatment of a quadratic equation

Al-Khwārizmī, *Al-jabr wa'l-muqābala*, Chapter V, translated into English from the Latin version given in Karpinski, 1915, 74 and 76

---

TRANSLATION

*On squares and numbers equalling roots* Chapter V.

The proposition is of this kind, as you say:

A square and 21 units are equal to 10 roots.

For this investigation a rule of this kind is given, as you say: What is the square, to which if you adjoin 21 units the whole sum at the same time is worth 10 roots of the same square. The solution to questions of this kind is conceived in this way, that first you divide the [number of] roots into two, and they come in this case to 5, this multiplied with itself produces 25. From this subtract the 21 units, which a little earlier we mentioned together with the square, and there remain 4, of which you take the square root, which is 2, which you subtract from half the roots, 5, and there is left 3, constituting one root of this square, and clearly the number nine gives the square. If you so wish, you may of course add this 2, which you have already subtracted from half the roots, to half the roots, 5, and there comes 7; which gives one root of the square, and 49 [units] fill the square. Therefore when any problem of this kind is proposed to you, investigate it by this method of addition, as we have said, but when you cannot find it by addition, without doubt you will find it by subtraction. For this kind alone requires both addition and subtraction which in other previous kinds you do not find at all.

It must also be understood, when according to this case you take half the roots, and then you multiply the half with itself, if what arises from the multiplication turns out to be less than the number of units announced with the square: the question proposed to you is void. But if it is equal to the units, or if the root of the square turns out to be the same as half the roots that are with the square, it is solved, without either addition or subtraction.

---

Robert of Chester's translation does not appear to have become widely known, but in 1202 Leonardo Pisano, towards the end of his *Liber abaci*, gave rules for al-Khwārizmī's six types of equation, drawing extensively on problems from abū-Kāmil. Through the *Liber abaci* and later texts derived from it, the technique of *al-jabr*, or algebra, gradually spread during the thirteenth to fifteenth centuries into France and Germany, and became known as the 'cossick art', from the Italian *cosa* (thing) for an unknown quantity. By the sixteenth century al-Khwārizmī's rules, by now attributed in a vague way to someone called Mohammed, or sometimes to an astronomer named al-Geber, were available in printed textbooks in Spain, France, Germany, and England.

# CHAPTER 2

# FRESH IDEAS

I n Chapter 1 we looked at some of the key ideas from the Middle East, India, and the countries around the Mediterranean, that were eventually absorbed into the mathematics of western Europe: in arithmetic, a ten-digit number system with place value and efficient algorithms for calculation, and some rudimentary number theory; in geometry, a rich but fragmentary legacy of theorems about plane and solid figures, together with a formal and deductive method of working from definitions and axioms; in algebra, techniques for solving quadratic equations. Astronomy, no longer part of the mathematics curriculum and therefore not treated in this book, was also a major branch of the subject up to the Renaissance and beyond, requiring detailed measurement and calculation of lengths and angles.

Most of this knowledge found its way into north-western Europe only gradually from the twelfth century onwards, but by the sixteenth century was becoming more easily available and better understood. Scholars in Italy, France, England, and the Netherlands, stimulated and inspired by the texts they had inherited, began to make new and significant advances in their own right, and the most important of their innovations and insights are outlined in this chapter. Some were practical: more powerful methods of calculation, and the development of concise symbolic notation. Others were conceptual: a gradual recognition of the power of algebra in mathematical problem-solving, and new and bold ideas about infinitely small quantities. All were to become a vital part of later mathematical thinking.

## 2.1 IMPROVEMENTS IN CALCULATION

It is always illuminating to discover what mathematicians themselves have regarded as important advances, and there will be several examples in this book of mathematicians writing about the history of their subject (see, for example, 9.3, 10.2.4, 12.3.1). One of the first to do so extensively was John Wallis, Savilian Professor of Geometry at Oxford from 1649 to 1703. Wallis's *Treatise of algebra, historical and practical* (1685) was written to promote his own views (what history is not?) but it nevertheless provides some fascinating insights into contemporary mathematics. Wallis noted two developments that had greatly eased the labour of calculation,[1] both of which had come about less than one hundred years before he wrote. The first was the introduction of decimal fractions by Simon Stevin in 1585; the second was the invention of logarithms by John Napier in 1614.

### 2.1.1 Stevin's decimal fractions, 1585

The Old Babylonians used place value for fractions as well as whole numbers in the second millennium BC (giving us minutes, seconds, thirds, and so on, in the measurement of angles and time), but it was not until the end of the sixteenth century that the same idea was routinely extended to the decimal system. Before that, writers had either handled fractions as 'parts' (see 1.3.1), or had avoided them by using large whole numbers (taking the sine of 90°, for example, to be 10 000 000).

Wallis in 1685 explained to his readers the 'great advantage' of decimal fractions:[2]

Thus instead of $3\frac{1}{8}$, or $3°7'30''$, we say 3.125; that is $3\frac{125}{1000}$ or, 3 Integers and 125 Millesins.

The great advantage of these Decimal Parts or Fractions, now introduced beyond the Sexagesimal formerly in use, consists mainly in this; That by this means, Fractions are now managed in the same way, and with like ease, as Integer Numbers.

The first European writer to introduce decimal fractions (as Wallis also explained) was Simon Stevin, in a short treatise in Dutch entitled *De thiende* (literally *Of tenths*), published in Leiden in 1585. Stevin also translated it into French as *La disme* and appended it to his *L'arithmetique . . . aussi l'algebre*, which was also published in 1585. An engineer himself, he offered *De thiende* to such practical men as astronomers, surveyors, and merchants, and promised to teach all computations using only 'whole numbers without fractions' ('heele ghetalen sonder ghebrokenen').

---

1. Wallis 1685, 22–35 and 55–61.     2. Wallis 1685, 22.

## Stevin's decimal fractions
from Stevin, *De thiende*, 1585, 10–12

10      S. STEVINS

# HET EERSTE DEEL
### DER THIENDE VANDE
#### BEPALINGHEN.

### I. BEPALINGHE.

THIENDE *is eē specie der Telconsten,
door de vvelcke men alle rekeninghen onder
den Menschē noodich vallende, afveerdicht
door heele ghetalen, sonder ghebrokenen,
ghevonden uyt de thiende voortganck, be-
staende inde cijfferletteren daer eenich ghetal door beschreven vvort.*

#### VERCLARINGHE.

HET sy een ghetal van Duyst een hondert
ende elf, beschreven met cijfferletteren aldus
1111, inde welcke blijct, dat elcke 1, het thiende
deel is van sijn naest voorgaende. Alsoo oock in
1378 elcke een vande 8, is het thiende deel van
elcke een der 7, ende alsoo in allen anderen: Maer
want het voughelick is, dat de saecken daermen af
spreecken wil, namen hebben, ende dat dese maniere van rekeninghe ghevonden is uyt d'anmerc-
kinghe van alsulcken thienden voortganck, ja
wesentlick in thiende voortganck bestaet, als int
volghende claerlick blijcken sal , soo noemen wy
den

den handel van dien eyghentlick ende bequame-
lick, de THIENDE. Door de selve worden alle
rekeninghen ons ontmoetende volbrocht met be-
sondere lichticheyt door heele ghetalen sonder ge-
brokenen als hier naer opentlick bewesen sal
worden.

## II. BEPALINGHE.

*Alle voorgestelde heel ghetal, noemen vvy*
*BEGHIN, sijn teecken is soodanich ⓪.*

### VERCLARINGHE.

ALs by ghelijckenis eenich heel ghegheven
ghetal van driehondert vierentsestich, wy
noement driehondert vierentsestich BEGHIN-
SELEN, die aldus beschrijvende 364⓪. Ende
alsoo met allen anderen dier ghelijcken.

## III. BEPALINGHE.

*Ende elck thiendedeel vande eenheyt des*
*BEGHINS, noemen vvy EERSTE,*
*sijn teecken is ①; Ende elck thiendedeel van-*
*de eenheyt der Eerste, noemē vvy TWEE-*
*DE, sijn teecken is ②; Ende soo voort elck*
*thiendedeel der eenheyt van sijn voorgaen-*
*de, altijt in d'oirden een meer.*

VER-

12                S. STEVINS

VERCLARINGHE.

ALS 3 ① 7 ② 5 ③ 9 ④, dat is te segghen 3 Eerſten, 7 Tweeden, 5 Derden, 9 Vierden, ende
ſoo mochtmen oneyndelick voortgaen. Maer om
van hare weerde te ſegghen, ſoo is kennelick dat
naer luyt deſer Bepalinge, de voornoemde ghetalen doen $\frac{3}{10}$, $\frac{7}{100}$, $\frac{5}{1000}$, $\frac{9}{10000}$, tſamen $\frac{3759}{10000}$.
Alſoo oock 8 ⓪ 9 ① 3 ② 7 ③, ſijn weert 8 $\frac{9}{10}$, $\frac{3}{100}$,
$\frac{7}{1000}$, dat is tſamen 8 $\frac{937}{1000}$ ende ſoo met allen
anderen dier ghelijcke. Het is oock te anmercken,
dat wy inde THIENDE nerghens ghebroken getalen en ghebruycken: Oock dat het ghetal vande
menichvuldicheyt der Teeckenen, uytghenomen
⓪, nummermeer boven de 9 en comt. By exempel, wy en ſchrijven niet 7 ① 12 ② maer in diens
plaetſe 8 ① 2 ②, want ſy ſoo veel weert ſijn.

## IIII.   BEPALINGHE.

*De ghetalen der voorgaender tvveeder
ende derder bepalinghe, noemen vvy int ge-
meen* THIENDETALEN.

EYNDE DER BEPALINGHEN.

TRANSLATION

# THE FIRST PART OF DECIMALS
## ON THE DEFINITIONS

### I DEFINITION

DECIMAL *is a kind of arithmetic, by which one can do all the calculations mankind has
need of, with whole numbers, without fractions, making use of a progression of tenths, and
setting a symbol by each whole number to denote its value.*

EXPLANATION

LET there be a whole number, for example, one hundred and eleven, written with symbols thus 111, in which it appears that each 1 is one tenth part of that next before it. So also in 2378 each unit of 8 is a tenth part of each unit of 7, and so in all the others. But because it is convenient that the things of which we will speak have names, and because this manner of calculation is based on marking progressions of tenths, indeed rests wholly on progression of tenths, as we shall afterwards clearly see, so we name [11] this treatise by the appropriate title, DECIMALS. By the teachings of which all calculations we meet with may be done in a special way with whole numbers without fractions as here shall be clearly established.

II DEFINITION

*Any proposed whole number we call a* BEGINNING, *and its sign is* ⓪.

EXPLANATION

So for example given a whole number three hundred and sixty-four, we call three hundred and sixty-four the BEGINNING, written thus, 364 ⓪. And so with all others like this.

III DEFINITION

*And each tenth part of the unit of the* BEGINNING, *we call the* FIRST, *whose sign is* ①; *and each tenth part of the unit of the First, we call the* SECOND, *whose sign is* ②; *and so for each tenth part of the unit of the foregoing sign, always in order one more.*

EXPLANATION

[12] Thus 3 ① 7 ② 5 ③ 9 ④, that is to say 3 *Firsts*, 7 *Seconds*, 5 *Thirds*, 9 *Fourths*, and so on without end. But to speak of their value, it is known that according to these definitions, the said numbers are $\frac{3}{10}$, $\frac{7}{100}$, $\frac{5}{1000}$, $\frac{9}{10000}$, together $\frac{3759}{10000}$. Likewise 8 ⓪ 9 ① 3 ② 7 ③ are worth $8\frac{9}{10}$, $\frac{3}{100}$, $\frac{7}{1000}$, that is together $8\frac{937}{1000}$, and so for all others like this. This is also to be understood, that in DECIMALS we never make use of fractions. Also that the number collected by a symbol, excluding ⓪, never goes over 9 in count. For example, we do not write 7 ① 12 ② but in their place 8 ① 2 ②, for they are worth the same.

IIII DEFINITION

*The numbers of the foregoing second and third definitions, we generally call* DECIMAL NUMBERS.

END OF THE DEFINITIONS

### 2.1.2 Napier's logarithms, 1614

The second improvement in calculation mentioned by Wallis in 1685 was the invention of logarithms. Those who have grown up with pocket calculators arrive at logarithms only relatively late in their mathematical education, probably in the context of inverting the exponential function, and it is easy to forget that they were devised first and foremost as an aid to calculation. John Napier (also remembered for the calculating device known as 'Napier's bones') published his *Mirifici logarithmorum canonis descriptio* in 1614. Two years later it was translated into English by Edward Wright as *A description of the admirable table of logarithms*, and in the preface to that translation Napier wrote:[3]

Seeing there is nothing (right well beloved Students in the Mathematickes) that is so troublesome to Mathematicall practice, nor that doth molest and hinder Calculators, then the Multiplications, Divisions, square and cubical Extractions of great Numbers, which besides the tedious expence of time, are for the most part subject to many slippery errors. I began therefore to consider in my minde, by what certaine and ready Art I might remove those Hindrances.

The calculations that Napier had in mind came in particular from astronomy and trigonometry, leading him to define logarithms initially for sines rather than for ordinary numbers. For Napier, the sine corresponding to a given arc was the length of half the chord subtended by the arc. Napier chose his radius to be 10 000 000 so that sines (and tangents) could be represented as whole numbers (whereas the modern convention is to take the radius to be 1).

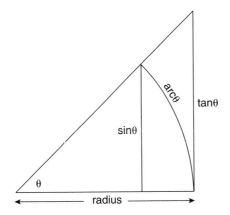

In Napier's diagrams the radius (which is also the sine of 90°, or the 'whole sine') is represented by the line $\alpha\omega$. Sines of smaller angles are thus represented by $\gamma\omega$, $\delta\omega$, and so on. Napier then imagined a point $B$ that moves at a steady speed along the

---

3. Napier 1616, Preface.

line $AC$. At the same time a second point $\beta$ starts with the same speed, but moves along $\alpha\omega$ in such a way that the segments $\alpha\gamma$, $\alpha\delta$, $\alpha\varepsilon$, ... decrease in geometric proportion. $AC$ is then defined to be the logarithm of $\gamma\omega$; $AD$ is the logarithm of $\delta\omega$; and so on.

In this system the logarithm of the 'whole sine' $\alpha\omega$ is 0, and logarithms increase as sines decrease (so that $\log 0 = \infty$). These are not the modern conventions, but Naperian logarithms nevertheless have the crucial property that multiplication and division of lengths on the line $\alpha\omega$ are related to addition and subtraction of the corresponding lengths on the line $AO$ (the precise relationship is Naperian $\log X +$ Naperian $\log Y =$ Naperian $\log \frac{XY}{10^7}$).

Napier's ideas met with immediate acclaim. Henry Briggs, then Savilian Professor of Geometry at Oxford, journeyed to Scotland to meet and work with Napier, and together they modified the original definition, setting $\log 1 = 0$ and $\log 10000000 = 1$. Napier died in 1619, but Briggs went on to calculate and publish tables of logarithms to 14 decimal places, for numbers from 1 to 20000 and from 90000 to 100000, in his *Arithmetica logarithmica* of 1624. The missing central portion was completed (though only to 10 decimal places) by Adrian Vlacq in 1628. Tables of logarithms essentially identical to those calculated by Briggs and Vlacq remained in everyday use until the 1980s when pocket calculators finally rendered them redundant.

## Napier's definition of logarithms

from Napier, *Mirifici logarithmorum canonis descriptio*, 1614, 3–4

6.def.  *Logarithmus ergò cujusque sinus, est numerus quàm proximè defi-*
*niens lineam, quæ æqualiter crevit interea dum sinus totius linea pro-*
*portionaliter in sinum illum decrevit, existente utroque motu synchrono,*
*atque initio æquiveloce.*

B 2                                     Exem-

### LIBER I. CAP. I.

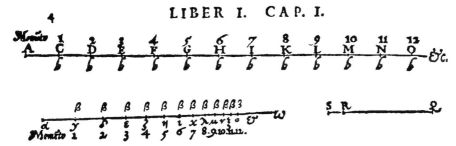

Exempli gratia  Repetantur ambo superiora schemata
& moveatur B. semper & ubique eadem seu æquali velocitate qua cœpit moveri C initio quum est in α. deinde primo momento procedat B. ab A in C, & eodem momento
procedat C ab α in γ. proportionaliter : erit numerus definiens A C logarithmus lineæ, seu sinus γ ω. Tum secun-
do mométo promoveatur B à C in D, & eodem momento promoveatur proportionaliter C à γ in ε, erit numerus
definiens A D logarithmus sinus ε ω. Sic tertio momento
procedat æqualiter B à D in E, & eodem momento promoveatur proportionaliter C à ε in ι. erit numerus definiens A E logarithmus ipsius sinus ι ω. Item quarto momento procedat B in F, & β in ζ. erit numerus A F Logarithmus sinus ζ ω. Atque eodem continuò servato ordine
erit ( ex difinitione superius tradita ) numerus A G logarithmus sinus η ω. A H logarithmus sinus θ ω. A I log. sinus
K ω. A K log. sinus λ ω. & ita in infinitum.

Cor.    *Unde sinus totius 10000000. nullum seu o est logarithmus : & per*
*consequens, numerorum majorum sinu toto logarithmi sunt nihilo mi-*
*nores.*

Quum enim ex definitione pateat.quod à sinu toto decrescentibus sinibus, à nihilo accrescant logarithmi, ideò
contrà crescentibus numeris (quos adhuc sinus vocamus)
in sinum totum, scilicet in 10000000. decrescant, in o, seu
nihilum logarithmi est necesse. Et per consequens numerorum crescentium ultra sinum totum 10000000. ( quos
secantes aut tangentes, & non amplius sinus vocamus) logarithmi erunt minores nihilo.

*Itaque*

Definition 6. *Therefore the logarithm of any sine is the number denoting as closely as possible a line, which has increased evenly while the line of the whole sine has decreased proportionally to that sine, both motions taking place at the same time, and from the same initial velocity.*

For example. Repeat both the above diagrams, and let $B$ move always and everywhere with the same or equal velocity as that with which $\beta$ began to move initially when it was at $\alpha$; then in the first moment let $B$ proceed from $A$ to $C$, and in the same moment let $\beta$ proceed from $\alpha$ to $\gamma$ proportionally. The number denoting $AC$ will be the logarithm of the line, or sine, $\gamma\omega$. Then in the second moment let $B$ be moved on from $C$ to $D$, and in the same moment let $\beta$ be moved on proportionally from $\gamma$ to $\delta$; the number denoting $AD$ will be the logarithm of the sine $\delta\omega$. Thus in the third moment let $B$ proceed evenly from $D$ to $E$, and in the same moment let $\beta$ be moved on proportionally from $\delta$ to $\varepsilon$; the number denoting $AE$ will be the logarithm of the sine $\varepsilon\omega$. Likewise in the fourth moment let $B$ proceed to $F$, and $\beta$ to $\zeta$, and the number $AF$ will be the logarithm of the sine $\zeta\omega$. And continually using the same scheme, the number $AG$ (by the definition taught above) will be the logarithm of sine $\eta\omega$; $AH$ the logarithm of $\iota\omega$; $AI$ log sine $\kappa\omega$; $AK$ log sine $\lambda\omega$; and thus indefinitely.

Corollary *Whence the logarithm of the whole sine, 10000000, is nothing, or 0. And consequently, the logarithms of numbers greater than the whole sine are less than nothing.*

For since from the definition it is clear that for sines decreasing from the whole sine, the logarithms increase from nothing, therefore conversely, for numbers (which up to here we have called sines) increasing to the whole sine, namely to 10000000, it must be that the logarithms decrease to 0 or nothing. And consequently the logarithms of numbers increasing beyond the whole sine 10000000 (which we call secants or tangents, and no longer sines) will be less than nothing.

---

Decimal fractions and logarithms have both been described in this section as aids to practical calculation, which is exactly what they were in the minds of their inventors. In the rest of this book we shall not be much concerned with numerical calculations, but we shall be drawn back repeatedly to the deeper significance of Stevin's and Napier's ideas. One of the most important aspects of their work was that both opened up the possibility of operating with a continuous range of numbers, not just the integers, fractions, or surds of Euclidean arithmetic. Stevin's decimal fractions allowed any number at all to be expressed to as fine a degree of accuracy as one chose; while Napier assumed that every point on a continuous line can be designated by a number and *vice versa*. Both of them thus conceived of numbers as a *continuum*, an idea that was not yet explicit, but which was eventually to become extremely important (see in particular 11.2.6 and 16.3).

## 2.2 IMPROVEMENTS IN NOTATION

Good mathematical notation serves more than one purpose. First, it displays mathematics in a clear and concise form, often encapsulating in a few symbols ideas that cannot be at all easily or briefly expressed in words; once one know the rules, mathematics written symbolically is more easily visualized, communicated, and understood. This in turn helps to generate new ideas, sometimes because the symbols themselves can be manipulated to show new connections, but at a deeper level because clear exposition almost invariably opens the way to further and faster progress in the mind of both reader and writer.

New symbols usually lag some way behind the concepts they are required to express, and can take some time to settle into a standard form. Mathematical notation continues to evolve today, but widespread publication and rapid communication have made the process very much faster than it was four hundred years ago. Modern notation did not begin to appear until the late fifteenth century, when + and − were first used in Germany. They were followed some time later by the = sign, which first appeared in Robert Recorde's *Whetstone of witte* in 1557 (and was described by Recorde as 'a paire of paralleles, or Gemowe [twin] lines of one lengthe, thus: ====== bicause noe .2. thynges, can be moare equalle'). It was many years, however, before these signs or any others became standard; many sixteenth-century writers continued to use *p.* for plus and *m.* for minus (or other inventions of their own), and continental writers followed René Descartes in using a version of $\infty$ as an equality sign well into the seventeenth century.

Girolamo Cardano's great book, the *Ars magna*, of 1545 (see 12.1.1), was written entirely verbally, with some useful abbreviations but no genuine symbolic notation. Rafael Bombelli, trying to present Cardano's work more clearly, devised the notation $\smile\kern-0.5em{\scriptstyle 2}$, $\smile\kern-0.5em{\scriptstyle 3}$, and so on, for squares, cubes, and higher powers, an idea that was taken up with slight modification by Stevin, who greatly admired Bombelli. François Viète, writing in the 1590s, retained the verbal forms *quadratus* and *cubus* for 'squared' and 'cubed', but contributed the idea of using vowels $A, E, I, \ldots$ for unknowns, and consonants $B, C, D, \ldots$ for known or given quantities, which meant that equations could be expressed entirely in letters or, as he called them, 'species'. Viète still used words, however, for the linking operations ('multiplied by', 'equals', and so on), so that his text remained primarily verbal rather than symbolic.

### 2.2.1  Harriot's notation, *c.* 1600

The earliest mathematical notation that appears to a modern reader both familiar and easy to read is that of Thomas Harriot, whose gift for devising lucid symbolism is apparent in all aspects of his mathematical and scientific work from the early 1590s onwards. Harriot's mathematical notation was based on Viète's insofar as it used vowels $a$, $e$, ... for unknown quantities, and consonants $b$, $c$, $d$, ... for known quantities or coefficients, but now in lower case rather than as capitals. He also introduced the convention of writing $ab$ for $a \times b$, with $aa$, $aaa$, and so on, for squares, cubes, and higher powers. His equals sign incorporated two short cross strokes to distinguish it from Recorde's simple parallels (since the latter were sometimes used by Viète to indicate subtraction) but these were abandoned in the printed versions. He also invented the now standard inequality signs $<$ and $>$; in manuscript they, like his equals sign, included two vertical cross strokes, but these too were dropped as soon as the signs went into print. Also to be found in Harriot's manuscripts is the three-dot 'therefore' sign, designed to suggest that two propositions imply a third.

Below is a single page from Harriot's posthumously published *Artis analyticae praxis* (*The practice of the analytic art*) of 1631, one of the few extracts in this present book that needs almost no translation.

## Harriot's notation

from Harriot, *Artis analyticae praxis*, 1631, 10

10    SECTIO PRIMA.

*Comparationis signa in sequentibus vsurpanda.*

AEqualitatis ——— vt a ——— b. significet a æqualem ipsi b.

Maioritatis —▷— vt a —▷— b. significet a maiorem quam b.

Minoritatis —◁— vt a —◁— b significet a minorem quam b.

*Fractiones reducibiles reductitijs suis æquat.c.*

Æquatio

### TRANSLATION

*Signs of comparison used in what follows.*

*Equality = as a = b signifies a is equal to b.*
*Greater > as a > b signifies a is greater than b.*
*Less < as a < b signifies a is less than b.*

*Reducible fractions reduced to their equivalents*
[...]

### 2.2.2 Descartes' notation, 1637

Because of its enormous influence, Descartes' *La géométrie* (1637) was the book that did more than any other to standardize modern algebraic notation. Like Harriot, Descartes used lower case letters, and he began by using $a$, $b$, $\dots$, from the beginning of the alphabet, but later adopted the convention of using $x$, $y$, and $z$ as unknown quantities. Also like Harriot, he wrote $xy$ for $x$ times $y$, and $xx$ for $x$ times $x$, but introduced superscript notation $x^3$, $x^4$, $\dots$ for higher powers (though for some reason the convention of writing $xx$ for $x$-squared lingered on well into the eighteenth century).

Continental mathematicians took up Descartes' notation wholeheartedly. In England, Harriot's $a$ rather than Descartes' $x$ survived until at least the end of the seventeenth century, but then fell out of use. On the other hand, Descartes' $\infty$ for equality was eventually ousted by Recorde's $=$, and Descartes' $\sqrt{C}$. by the more adaptable $\sqrt[3]{}$.

The extract below is a very short section from Descartes' *La géométrie*, illustrating not only his notation but also some of the difficulties of contemporary typesetting.

---

### Descartes' notation
from Descartes, *La géométrie*, 1637, 326

---

Mais suppofons la icy eftre poffible, & pour en abreger les termes, au lieu des quantités $\dfrac{cfglz - de\ell zz}{}$ efcriuons $2m$, & au lieu de $\dfrac{dezz + cfgz - bcg z}{ez - cgzz}$ efcriuons $\dfrac{2n}{z}$; & ainfi nous aurons

$$yy \infty 2my - \frac{2n}{z}\, xy\; \frac{+\,bcfglx - bcfgxx}{ez - cgzz},\ \text{dont la raci-}$$

ne eft

$$y \infty m - \frac{nx}{z} + \sqrt{\, mm' - \frac{2mnx}{z} + \frac{nnxx + bcfglx - bcfgxx}{z z \cdot ez - cgzz}}.$$

& derechef pour abreger, au lieu de $-\dfrac{2mn}{z} + \dfrac{bcfgl}{ez - cgzz}$ efcriuons $o$, & au lieu de $\dfrac{nn}{zz} - \dfrac{bcfg}{e - cgzz}$ efcriuons $\dfrac{p}{m}$. car ces quantités eftant toutes données, nous les pouuons nommer comme il nous plaift. & ainfi nous auons

$$y \infty m - \frac{n}{z}x + \sqrt{\, mm + ox - \frac{p}{m}xx},\ \text{qui doit eftre la}$$

longeur de la ligne B C, en laiffaut A B, ou $x$ indeterminée.

But let us suppose here that it is possible, and to shorten the terms, in place of the quantities $\dfrac{cflgz - dekzz}{ez^3 - egzz}$ let us write $2m$, and in place of $\dfrac{dezz + cfgz - bcgz}{ez^3 - cgzz}$ let us write $\dfrac{2n}{z}$; and thus we will have $yy = 2my - \dfrac{2n}{z}xy + \dfrac{bcfglx - bcfgxx}{ez^3 - cgzz}$ of which the root is

$$y = m - \frac{nx}{z} + \sqrt{mm - \frac{2mnx}{z} + \frac{nnxx}{zz} + \frac{bcfglx - bcfgxx}{ez^3 - egzz}}.$$

And again to shorten it, in place of $-\dfrac{2mn}{z} + \dfrac{bcfgl}{ez^3 - egzz}$ let us write $o$, and in place

of $\dfrac{nn}{zz}[+]\dfrac{-bcfg}{ez^3 - cgzz}$ let us write $\dfrac{p}{m}$. For these quantities all being given, we can name

them as we please, and thus we have $y = m - \dfrac{n}{z}x + \sqrt{mm + ox - \dfrac{p}{m}xx}$, which must

be the length of the line $BC$, leaving $AB$, or $x$ undetermined.

---

## 2.3 ANALYTIC GEOMETRY

The invention of analytic geometry is usually attributed to Descartes and Fermat, but the foundations were laid before either was born, by the French lawyer and mathematician François Viète in the early 1590s. In this section we look at some of the difficult but important ideas put forward by Viète, and how they were used, adapted, and eventually superseded by Fermat and Descartes.

### 2.3.1 Viète's introduction to the analytic art, 1591

Viète's most important contribution to mathematics was his recognition that geometric relationships could be expressed and explored through algebraic equations, leading to a powerful fusion of two previously distinct legacies: classical Greek geometry and Islamic algebra. The central technique of algebra, taught in many sixteenth-century texts as the 'Rule of Algebra', was that one should assign a symbol or letter to an unknown quantity and then, bearing in mind the requirements of the problem, manipulate it alongside known quantities to produce an equation. For Viète, never content with a simple idea unless he could clothe it in a Greek term, this was the classical method of 'analysis' in which, he claimed, one assumes that what one is seeking is somehow known and then sets up the relationships or equations it must satisfy. Thus Viète saw the application of algebra to geometric quantities as the restored art of analysis.

From this there followed some important consequences. One was that, in solving a problem or proving a theorem, all the relevant geometric magnitudes, given or sought, had to be represented by letters or 'species'. Viète set up a scale of dimensions: length, square, cube, square-square, square-cube, and so on, and frequently introduced artificially contrived 'species' such as $A_{planum}$ or $Z_{solidum}$ to keep his equations homogeneous. This made his notation almost impossible to generalize beyond three or four dimensions, but it led for the first time to equations in which all the quantities, known or unknown, were represented by letters rather than numbers.

A second consequence of Viète's method was that the art of creating equations (which he called *zetetics*) and solving them (which he called *exegetics*) came to be seen as essential tools for analysing and solving geometric problems, and Viète wrote separate treatises on each. In particular he introduced a numerical method for solving equations that could not be handled algebraically, the first European mathematician to do so.[4] Viète believed that his methods of analysis and equation-solving could not only help to restore the lost or incomplete work of the Greek geometers, but could also enable mathematicians to handle previously intractable problems, in particular the classical problems of doubling the cube and trisecting an angle. So inspired was he by these new possibilities that he ended his first treatise, *Ad artem analyticem isagoge* (*Introduction to the analytic art*) of 1591, with his hopes for the future written in capital letters: Nullum non problema solvere (To leave no problem unsolved).

Viète's idiosyncratic blend of Greek terminology and awkward notation make him a difficult author to read. Understanding of his ideas grows only with time and repeated reading of his various tracts, both singly and in relation to each other. Nevertheless, the opening chapter of the *Isagoge* is given below because it contains the seeds of some vitally important ideas. It was here, for example, that the word 'analysis' first entered modern European mathematics; it has since evolved through several changes of meaning but has never disappeared from the mathematical lexicon. It was here too that Viète first claimed that geometric magnitudes could be discovered through setting up and solving equations, and argued that all of this could be done in symbols. These were profound ideas that were to lead eventually to the development of powerful general techniques.

---

4. The relevant treatises are *Zeteticorum libri quinque* (1593), *De numerosa potestatum ad exegesin resolutione* (1600), and *De recognitione aequationum* (1615).

## Viète's vision of the 'analytic art'

from Viète, *Isagoge*, 1591, 4

# IN ARTEM ANALYTICEM
## ISAGOGE.

*De definitione & partiĉione Analyſeos , & de ijs quæ iuuant*
*Zeteticem.*    CAPVT I.

EST veritatis inquirendæ via quædam in Mathematicis,quam Plato primus inueniſſe dicitur, à Theone nominata Analyſis,& ab eodem definita,Adſumptio quæſiti tanquam conceſſi per conſequentia ad verum conceſſum. Vt contra Syntheſis,Adſumptio conceſſi per conſequentia ad quæſiti finem & comprehenſionem.   Et quanquam veteres duplicem tantùm propoſuerunt Analyſim ζητητικὼ ἢ πορισκὼ,ad quas definitio Theonis maximè pertinet,conſtitui tamen etiam tertiam ſpeciem,quæ dicatur ῥητικὴ ἢ ἐξηγητικὴ , conſentaneum eſt , vt ſit Zetetice quâ inuenitur æqualitas proportioue magniiudinis de quâ quæritur cum ijs quæ data ſunt. Poriſtice, quâ de æqualitate vel proportione ordinati Theorematis veritas examinatur. Exegetice, quâ ex ordinata æqualitate vel proportione ipſa de qua quæritur exibetur magnitudo. Atque adeò tota ars Analytice triplex illud ſibi vendicans officium definiatur,doĉtrina bene inueniendi in Mathematicis. Ac quod ad Zeteticem quidem attinet, inſtituitur arte logicâ per ſyllogiſmos & enthymemata,quorum firmaméta ſunt ea ipſa quibus æqualitates & proportiones concluduntur ſymbola , tam ex communibus deriuanda notionibus,quàm ordinandis vi ipſius Analyſeos theorematis.Forma autè Zeteſim ineundi ex arte propriâ eſt,non iam in numeris ſuam-logicam exercente, quæ fuit oſcitantia veterum Analyſtarum,ſed per logiſticem ſub ſpecie nouiter inducendam, feliciorem multò & potiorem numeroſâ ad comparandum inter ſe magnitudines,propoſitâ primùm homo-geneorum lege,& inde conſtitutâ,vt ſit, ſolemni magnitudinum ex genere ad genus vi ſuâ proportionaliter adſcendentium vel deſcendentium ſerie ſeu ſcalâ, quâ gradus earundem & genera in comparationibus deſignentur ac diſtinguantur.

*De Symbolis æqualitatum & proportionum.*    CAPVT II.

SYmbola æqualitatum & proportionum notiora quæ habentur in Elementis adſumit Analytice vt demonſtrata,qualia ſunt ferè, .

1    Totum ſuis partibus æquaii.
2    Quæ eidem æquantur,inter ſe eſſe æqualia.
3    Si æqualia æqualibus addantur,tota eſſe æqualia.

A iiij

## INTRODUCTION
## TO THE ANALYTIC ART

*On the definition and parts of Analysis, and thence what is useful to*
*Zetetics.*  CHAPTER I.

There is a certain way of seeking the truth in mathematics, which Plato is said to have
first discovered, called Analysis by Theon, and defined by him as: assuming what is
sought as though given, from the consequences the truth is given. As opposed to Synthesis: assuming what is given, from the consequences one arrives at and understands
what is sought. And although the ancients proposed only two kinds of analysis, zetetics
and poristics, to which the definition of Theon wholly applies, I have nevertheless also
added a third kind, which is called rhetics or exegetics, agreeing that it is zetetic by
which are found equalities in the ratios of magnitudes, between that which is sought
and those that are given. Poristic is that by which the truth of a stated theorem is examined from the equality or ratio. Exegetic is that by which the magnitude one seeks
is discovered from that stated equality or ratio. And therefore the whole analytic art
taking these three tasks to itself, may be defined as the doctrine of proper discovery
in mathematics. And what particularly pertains to zetetics is founded on the art of
reasoning with syllogisms and enthymemes, of which the main features are those laws
from which equalities and ratios may be deduced, to be derived as much from common
notions as from the theorems stated on the strength of Analysis itself. Moreover the
way of discovery by zetetics is by its own art, exercising its reasoning not now in numbers, which was the shortcoming of the ancient analysts; but by a newly introduced
reasoning with symbols, much more fruitful and powerful than the numerical kind for
comparing magnitudes, first by the proposed law of homogeneity, and then by setting
up, as it were, of an ordered series or scale of magnitudes, ascending or descending
proportionally from one kind to another by power, from which the degree of each and
comparisons between them are denoted and distinguished.

### 2.3.2 Fermat and analytic geometry, 1636

Pierre de Fermat was introduced to the mathematics of Viète by his friend Etienne
d'Espagnet while he was studying law in Bordeaux between 1626 and 1630; d'Espagnet's
father had known Viète personally and owned copies of his books, which were otherwise
not easy to obtain. Fermat was profoundly influenced by what he read, and Viète's style
of thinking and writing are clearly discernible in Fermat's early work.

Viète had firmly established the connection between algebra and geometry, but his
constructions remained essentially fixed and static, whereas Fermat began to investigate
the *locus*, or range of possible positions, of a point constrained by certain conditions.
In 1636 he attempted a restoration of two lost books of Apollonius on plane loci, and
shortly afterwards wrote a short treatise entitled 'Ad locos planos et solidos isagoge'

('An introduction to plane and solid loci'), where he showed that all second degree equations correspond to one or other of the conic sections. (Fermat referred to general second-degree equations as 'affected equations', that is to say, the square term is 'affected' by the addition or subtraction of terms of lower degree.)

Fermat's treatment was based directly on that of Apollonius, where each conic section is distinguished by a particular relationship between the ordinates and the diameter (see 1.2.4 for the parabola). That is to say, each section has a natural co-ordinate representation in which the diameter is taken as one axis and any line parallel to the ordinates as the other. The axes are not external, but embedded into the curve itself, and need not be at right angles, and Fermat was able to demonstrate that simple variations in the equation correspond only to changes in the choice of axes.

Fermat sent 'Ad locos' to Marin Mersenne in Paris in 1637, but by the end of the year it was overtaken by the publication of Descartes' *La géométrie*, and remained unpublished in Fermat's lifetime. After his death, his son Samuel published some of his papers and letters in a compilation entitled *Varia opera mathematica* (1679), and the extract below is taken from that edition. While editors of mathematical texts generally try to remain true to the words of an original, they sometimes have less compunction about 'improving' the notation or diagrams, and Samuel was no exception. Fermat had used Viète's notation *A quadratus* or *Aq*, but Samuel upgraded this to the more modern $A^2$. It is likely that Fermat's diagrams were also redrawn for the printed edition, and we do not know how close they are to the originals. Later editions and translations have introduced yet further changes to notation and diagrams (compare, for example, the various extracts from Fermat in this book with those in Fauvel and Gray or other source books).

## Fermat's co-ordinate description of the parabola

from Fermat, *Varia opera*, 1679, 4–5

A² ∞ D E.        Si A² æq. D in E, punctum I, est ad Parabolem.

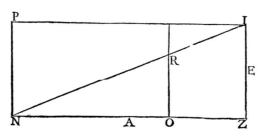

constituantur N Z, & Z I, ad quemcumque angulum Z.

Fiat N P, Parallela Z I, & circa diametrum N P describatur parabole, cujus rectum latus recta D, datæ, & applicatæ sint parallellæ N Z. punctum I. erit ad parabolem hanc positione datam. Ex constructione rectangulum sub D, in N P, æquabitur quadrato P I, hoc est, si P I, intelligatur esse A, & N P, intelligatur esse E, D, in E, æquabitur A².

Ad hanc æquationem facillimè reducentur omnes in quibus A,² miscetur homogeneis sub datis in E, aut E,² homogeneis sub datis in A, idemque continget, licèt homogenea omnino data æquationibus misceantur.

Sit E,² æquale D in A.

E² ∞ D A.    In præcedenti figura vertice N, circa diametrum N Z, describatur parabole, cujus rectum latus sit D, & applicatæ rectæ N P, parallela, præstabit propositum, ut patet,

B²—A² ∞    Ponatur B² —A² æqu. D in E. Ergo B² — D in E æquabitur A².
D E B²—
D E ∞ A².

Applicetur B² ad D, & sit æquale D. in R.

Ergo D in R — D in E, æquabitur A² Ideoque D in R — E æquabitur A².

Ideoque hæc æquatio reducetur ad præcedentem. Recta quippe R — E, succedet ipsi E.

Fiat quippe N M, parallela Z I, & æqualis R, & per punctum M ducatur M O, parallela N Z, datur punctum M, & recta M O, positione, in hac constructione O I, æquatur R — E. ergo D. in O I, æquabitur N E quad. sive M O quad. vertice M. circa diametrum M N, descripta parabole, cujus dextrum latus D, & applicatæ ipsi

# Mathematica.

N Z, parallelæ, præstabit propositum, ut patet ex constructione.

Si B² — A² æqu. D in E.

D in E — B² æquabitur A² &c. vt supr. similiter omnes æquationes affectæ construentur.

*Notation*
The expression 'A *in* B' arises from the geometric construction of a line A on (*in*) and perpendicular to a line B, thus producing a rectangle, or 'product'. There is no simple modern English equivalent for *in* except perhaps 'by' as in '3 by 4', which is used in carpentry but not in theoretical mathematics. I have therefore fallen back, though reluctantly, on 'times'.

TRANSLATION
_____

If $A^2$ is equal to $D$ times $E$, the point $I$ is on a parabola.

Let there be constructed $NZ$ and $ZI$ at any angle $Z$.

Let $NP$ be parallel to $ZI$, and around the diameter $NP$ let there be described a parabola, whose *latus rectum* is $D$, and also let there be given ordinates parallel to $NZ$. The point $I$ will be on the parabola given in this position. From the construction, the product of $D$ and $NP$ will be equal to the square of $PI$, that is, if $PI$ is understood to be $A$, and $NP$ is understood to be $E$, then $D$ times $E$ equals $A^2$.

To this equation are easily reduced all those in which $A^2$ is mixed with terms formed from given quantities times $E$, or $E^2$ with terms formed from given quantities times $A$, and the same holds if we allow terms that are entirely given to be mixed in the equation.

Let $E^2$ equal $D$ times $A$.

In the preceding figure with vertex $N$, around the diameter $NZ$, let there be described a parabola, whose *latus rectum* is $D$, and with ordinates parallel to $NP$; this will demonstrate the proposed equation, as is clear.

Suppose $B^2 - A^2$ equals $D$ times $E$. Therefore $B^2 - D$ times $E$ will be equal to $A^2$.

Divide $B^2$ by $D$ and let it $[B^2]$ be equal to $D$ times $R$.

Therefore $D$ times $R - D$ times $E$ will be equal to $A^2$. And therefore $D$ times $R - E$ will be equal to $A^2$.

And therefore this equation is reduced to the preceding one. Indeed the line $R - E$ replaces $E$ there.

Indeed let $NM$ be parallel to $ZI$ and equal to $R$, and through the point $M$ let there be taken $MO$ parallel to $NZ$; given the point $M$ and line $MO$ in position, in this construction $OI$ is equal to $R - E$. Therefore $D$ times $OI$ will be equal to $N[Z]$ squared, or $MO$ squared. With vertex $M$ and around diameter $MN$ there is described a parabola with *latus rectum* $D$ and ordinates [5] parallel to $NZ$, which demonstrates the proposed equation, as is clear from the construction.

Let $B^2 + A^2$ equal $D$ times $E$

$D$ times $E - B^2$ will equal $A^2$ etc. as above. All affected equations can be constructed similarly.

_____

Margin notes:

$A^2 = DE$

$E^2 = DA$

$B^2 - A^2 = DE$
$B^2 - DE = A^2$

### 2.3.3 Descartes and analytic geometry, 1637

The influence of Viète on Fermat is clear, but for Descartes the story is not so straight-forward. After he published *La géométrie* in 1637, Descartes denied that he had ever read Viète, which may have been true, but he was never generous about acknowledging the achievements of others, and his claims to complete originality must be regarded with some circumspection. He was part of the scientific community in Paris during the 1620s, continued to correspond with Mersenne after he went to live in the Netherlands in 1628, and quarrelled by letter with Fermat in the mid 1630s, so cannot have been entirely unaware of mathematical ideas that had by then been alive in France for some thirty years or more.

*La géométrie*, was published as an appendix to Descartes' *Discours sur la méthode* and was intended primarily as a demonstration of his philosophical method. It rapidly came to be seen as a seminal book in its own right and had a profound influence on the development of mathematics in the mid-seventeenth century. Originally in French, it was written in three short Books, leaving much of the detail as an exercise for the reader. It was reprinted in Latin with a commentary by Francis van Schooten in 1649, and a second Latin edition followed in 1659–61, by now in two volumes to accommodate the wealth of research and commentary that had already accumulated around it.

The title was brief and explicit: Descartes wrote about geometric problems and geometric solutions. Like Viète he recognized algebra as an invaluable tool for analysis and simplification, but a geometric problem could only be fully solved by a geometric construction. This thinking is already evident in Descartes' description of Book I: 'Des problèmes qu'on peut construire sans y employer que des cercles & des lignes droites' ('On problems one may construct using only circles and straight lines'). With this end in view, Book I begins with ruler and compass constructions corresponding to the algebraic processes of multiplication, division, and taking square roots (see also 1.2.2).

Geometric constructions for algebraic operations
from Descartes, *La géométrie*, 1637, 297–299

297

# LA
# GEOMETRIE.
## LIVRE PREMIER.

*Des problefmes qu'on peut conftruire fans*
*y employer que des cercles & des*
*lignes droites.*

Ous les Problefmes de Geometrie fe peuuent facilement reduire a tels termes, qu'il n'eft befoin par aprés que de connoi-ftre la longeur de quelques lignes droites, pour les conftruire.

Et comme toute l'Arithmetique n'eft compofée, que de quatre ou cinq operations, qui font l'Addition, la Souftraction, la Multiplication, la Diuifion, & l'Extra-ction des racines, qu'on peut prendre pour vne efpece de Diuifion : Ainfi n'at'on autre chofe a faire en Geo-metrie touchant les lignes qu'on cherche, pour les pre-parer a eftre connuës, que leur en adioufter d'autres, ou en ofter, Oubien en ayant vne, que ie nommeray l'vnité pour la rapporter d'autant mieux aux nombres , & qui peut ordinairement eftre prife a difcretion, puis en ayant encore deux autres, en trouuer vne quatriefme, qui foit à l'vne de ces deux, comme l'autre eft a l'vnité, ce qui eft le mefme que la Multiplication ; oubien en trouuer vne quatriefme, qui foit a l'vne de ces deux, comme l'vnité

*Commēt le calcul d'Ari-thmeti-que fe rapporte aux ope-rations de Geome-trie.*

P p                                eft

298        LA GEOMETRIE.

eſt a l'autre, ce qui eſt le meſme que la Diuiſion; ou enfin trouuer vne, ou deux, ou pluſieurs moyennes proportionnelles entre l'vnité, & quelque autre ligne; ce qui eſt le meſme que tirer la racine quarrée, on cubique, &c. Et ie ne craindray pas d'introduire ces termes d'Arithmetique en la Geometrie, affin de me rendre plus intelligibile.

La Multiplication.

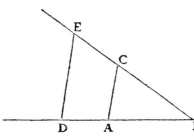

Soit par exemple A B l'vnité, & qu'il faille multiplier B D par B C, ie n'ay qu'a ioindre les poins A & C, puis tirer D E parallele a C A, & B E eſt le produit de cete Multiplication.

La Diviſion.    Oubien s'il faut diuiſer B E par B D, ayant ioint les poins E & D, ie tire A C parallele a D E, & B C eſt le produit de cete diuiſion.

l'Extraction de la racine quarrée.

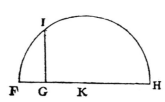

Ou s'il faut tirer la racine quarrée de G H, ie luy adiouſte en ligne droite F G, qui eſt l'vnité, & diuiſant F H en deux parties eſgales au point K, du centre K ie tire le cercle F I H, puis eſleuant du point G vne ligne droite iuſques à I, à angles droits ſur F H, c'eſt G I la racine cherchée. Ie ne dis rien icy de la racine cubique, ny des autres, à cauſe que i'en parleray plus commodement cy aprés.

Commēt on peut    Mais ſouuent on n'a pas beſoin de tracer ainſi ces ligne

gne

LIVRE PREMIER.                299

gnes fur le papier, & il fuffift de les defigner par quelques $_{vfer de}$
lettres, chafcune par vne feule.   Comme pour adioufter $^{chiffres en}$
la ligne B D a G H, ie nomme l'vne $a$ & l'autre $b$, & efcris $_{trie.}^{Geome-}$
$a + b$; Et $a -- b$, pour fouftraire $b$ d'$a$; Et $a\,b$, pour les multiplier l'vne par l'autre; Et $\frac{a}{b}$, pour diuifer $a$ par $b$; Et $a\,a$,
ou $a^2$, pour multiplier $a$ par foy mefme; Et $a^3$, pour le
multiplier encore vne fois par $a$ , & ainfi a l'infini; Et
$\sqrt{a^2 + b^2}$, pour tirer la racine quarrée d' $a^2 + b^2$; Et
$\sqrt{C. a^3 -- b^3 + a\,b\,b}$, pour tirer la racine cubique d' $a^3 -- b^3$
$+ a\,b\,b$, & ainfi des autres.

Où il eft a remarquer que par $a^2$ ou $b^3$ ou femblables,
ie ne conçoy ordinairement que des lignes toutes fimples, encore que pour me feruir des noms vfités en l'Algebre, ie les nomme des quarrés ou des cubes, &c.

---

TRANSLATION

# GEOMETRY
## FIRST BOOK
*Problems that one may construct*
*using only circles and straight lines.*

All problems in geometry may be easily reduced to such terms, that there is no need until afterwards to know the length of certain straight lines, in order to construct [the problems].

And since all of arithmetic is composed of only four or five operations, which are addition, subtraction, multiplication, division, and extraction of roots, which one may take for a kind of division, thus one has nothing else to do in Geometry concerning the lines that one seeks, in order to prepare them to be known, than to join them to others, or to show them. Or rather, on having one, which I will call the unit in order to relate it better to numbers, and which can normally be taken at discretion, then on having two others, to find a fourth, which will be to one of these two as the other is to the unit, which is the same as multiplication; or rather, to find a fourth, which will be to one of these two as the unit [298] is to the other, which is the same as division; or finally to find one, or two, or more mean proportionals between the unit and any other line, which is the same as taking the square root, or cube root, etc. And I shall not

How the operations of arithmetic relate to constructions in geometry

Multiplication.

hesitate to introduce these terms of arithmetic into geometry in order to make myself better understood.

Suppose, for example, $AB$ is the unit, and that it is required to multiply $BD$ by $BC$; I have only to join the points $A$ and $C$, then draw $DE$ parallel to $CA$, and $BE$ is the product of this multiplication.

Division.

Or instead if one must divide $BE$ by $BD$, having joined the points $E$ and $D$, I draw $AC$ parallel to $DE$, and $BC$ is the outcome of this division.

Extraction of
square roots.

Or if one must draw the square root of $GH$, I adjoin to it the straight line $FG$, which is the unit, and dividing $FH$ into two equal parts at the point $K$, from the centre $K$, I draw the circle $FIH$, then erecting from the point $G$ a straight line as far as $I$, at right angles to $FH$, the root sought is $GI$. I say nothing here of the cube root, nor of others, because I will speak more conveniently of them after this.

How one may
use symbols
in geometry.

But often one has no need thus to trace lines [299] on paper, and it suffices to denote them by certain letters, each by just one. Thus to adjoin the line $BD$ to $GH$, I name one $a$ and the other $b$, and write $a + b$; and $a - b$ to subtract $b$ from $a$; and $ab$ to multiply one by the other; and $\frac{a}{b}$ to divide $a$ by $b$; and $aa$ or $a^2$ to multiply $a$ by itself; and $a^3$ to multiply it once again by $a$; and so on indefinitely; and $\sqrt{a^2 + b^2}$ to take the square root of $a^2 + b^2$; and $\sqrt{C.a^3 - b^3 + abb}$ to take the cube root of $a^3 - b^3 + abb$, and so on for others.

Where it must be remarked that by $a^2$ or $b^3$ or similar, I normally conceive only completely simple lines, although to avail myself of the names used in algebra, I call them squares or cubes, etc.

---

Having established the precise connection between the operations of arithmetic and algebra on the one hand, and geometric constructions on the other, Descartes went on to explain his 'method'. It was based on the principle that Viète had called 'analysis', in which what is sought is assumed known. Thus, first suppose that the problem has been solved, that is, that the necessary construction has been carried out. Then assign a letter to each line; strictly speaking the letters represent lengths, but Descartes called them simply *des noms*, or names. In this way even unknown quantities are named and handled as if they are known. Now use geometric relationships to construct equations and reduce these to a single equation in one unknown. Finally, by solving the equation, it should be possible to provide a construction for the solution based only on given quantities: this is the geometric *synthesis* derived from the *analysis*.

(In general Descartes left his readers to work out the details for themselves, but one of his few worked examples of the method, for finding the tangent to an ellipse, is given in 3.1.2.)

## The analytic method
from Descartes, *La géométrie*, 1637, 300–302

Commēt
il faut ve-
nir aux
Equatiōs
qui fer-
uent a re-
foudre les
problef-
mes.

Ainfi voulant refoudre quelque problefme, on doit d'a-
bord le confiderer comme defia fait, & donner des noms
a toutes les lignes, qui femblent neceffaires pour le conftruire, auffy bien a celles qui font inconnuës, qu'aux
autres. Puis fans confiderer aucune difference entre ces
lignes connuës, & inconnuës, on doit parcourir la difficulté, felon l'ordre qui monftre le plus naturellement
de tous en qu'elle forte elles dependent mutuellement.
les vnes des autres, iufques a ce qu'on ait trouué moyen
d'exprimer vne mefme quantité en deux façons: ce qui
fe nomme vne Equation; car les termes de l'vne de ces
deux façons font efgaux a ceux de l'autre. Et on doit
trouuer autant de telles Equations, qu'on a fuppofé de lignes, qui eftoient inconnuës. Oubien s'il ne s'en trouue
pas tant, & que nonobftant on n'omette rien de ce qui eft
defiré en la queftion, cela tefmoigne qu'elle n'eft pas en-
tierement determinée. Et lors on peut prendre a difcretion des lignes connuës, pour toutes les inconnuës auf-
qu'elles ne correfpond aucune Equation. Aprés cela s'il
en refte encore plufieurs, il fe faut feruir par ordre de
chafcune des Equations qui reftent auffy, foit en la con-
fiderant toute feule, foit en la comparant auec les autres,
pour expliquer chafcune de ces lignes inconnuës; & faire

ainfi

ainſi en les demeſlant, qu'il n'en demeure qu'vne ſeule, eſgale a quelque autre, qui ſoit connuë, oubien dont le quarré, ou le cube, ou le quarré de quarré, ou le ſurſolide, ou le quarré de cube, &c. ſoit eſgal a ce, qui ſe produiſt par l'addition, ou ſouſtraction de deux ou pluſieurs autres quantités, dont l'vne ſoit connuë, & les autres ſoient compoſées de quelques moyennes proportionnelles entre l'vnité, & ce quarré, ou cube, ou quarré de quarré, &c. multipliées par d'autres connuës. Ce que i'eſcris en cete ſorte.

$$z \infty\ b.\ \text{ou}$$
$$z^2 \infty -a\ z + bb.\ \text{ou}$$
$$z^3 \infty +a\ z^2 + bbz - c^3.\ \text{ou}$$
$$z^4 \infty\ a\ z^3\ - c^3z + d^4.\ \&c.$$

C'eſt a dire, z, que ie prens pour la quantité inconnuë, eſt eſgalé a b, ou le quarré de z eſt eſgal au quarré de b moins a multiplié par z. ou le cube de z eſt eſgal à a multiplié par le quarre de z plus le quarré de b multiplié par z moins le cube de c. & ainſi des autres.

Et on peut touſiours reduire ainſi toutes les quantités inconnuës à vne ſeule, lorſque le Probleſme ſe peut conſtruire par des cercles & des lignes droites, ou auſſy par des ſections coniques, ou meſme par quelque autre ligne qui ne ſoit que d'vn ou deux degrés plus compoſée. Mais ie ne m'areſte point a expliquer cecy plus en detail, a cauſe que ie vous oſterois le plaiſir de l'apprendre de vous meſme, & l'vtilité de cultiuer voſtre eſprit en vous y exerceant, qui eſt a mon auis la principale, qu'on puiſſe

tirer

Thus in wishing to resolve any problem, one must first consider it as already done, and give names to all the lines that seem necessary to construct it, as much to those that are unknown as to others. Then without making any distinction at all between these known and unknown lines, one must run through the problem, in the order that shows most naturally how they mutually depend on one another, until one has found a means of expressing a single quantity in two ways: this is called an equation; for the terms from one of the two ways are equal to those of the other. And one must find as many such equations as one supposes there are lines that are unknown. Or rather, if one cannot find so many, and notwithstanding one has omitted nothing that is desired in the question, that suggests that it is not completely determined. And then one may take at one's discretion known lines, for every unknown to which there corresponds no equation. After that if there still remain several [unknowns] one must make use in turn of each of the equations that remain, either considering it all alone, or in comparison with the others, to display each of the unknown lines; [301] and so to combine them that there remains only a single one, equal to some other which is known, or rather, of which the square, or the cube, or the square of the square, or the sursolid [fifth power], or the square of the cube, etc. is equal to something which is produced by addition, or subtraction of two or more other quantities, of which one is known, and the others are composed of certain mean proportionals between the unit and this square, or cube, or square of square, etc. multiplied by other known quantities. Which I write in this way.

*How one arrives at equations that can be used to solve problems.*

$$z = b, \quad \text{or}$$

$$z^2 = -az + bb, \quad \text{or}$$

$$z^3 = az^2 + bbz - c^3, \quad \text{or}$$

$$z^4 = az^3 - c^3z + d^4, \quad \text{etc.}$$

That is to say, $z$, which I take for the unknown quantity, is equal to $b$, or the square of $z$ is equal to the square of $b$ less $a$ multiplied by $z$, or the cube of $z$ is equal to $a$ multiplied by the square of $z$ plus the square of $b$ multiplied by $z$ less the cube of $c$, and so on for others.

And in this way one can always reduce all unknown quantities to a single one, as long as the problem can be constructed by circles and straight lines, or also by conic sections, or even by some other [curved] line which may be only one or two degrees higher. But I will not stop at all to explain this in more detail, since I would deprive you of the pleasure of learning it yourself, and of the usefulness of cultivating your mind by exercising yourself in it, which in my opinion is the main thing one can [302] draw from this study.

## 2.4 INDIVISIBLES

### 2.4.1 Cavalieri's theory of indivisibles, 1635

For ancient Greek philosophers, an indivisible quantity was something so small that it could not conceivably be divided any further: in the physical world an atom, in geometry a point. During the 1620s similar ideas were once again taken up, this time by geometers, and now indivisibles might be not only Euclidean points, but also, perhaps, the lines in a plane surface, or the planes in a solid. Ideas of this kind were explored by the Jesuit Grégoire de Saint Vincent in the low countries around 1623, by Gilles Personne de Roberval in Paris from about 1628 to 1634, and by Bonaventura Cavalieri in Bologna from about 1629. All three achieved some remarkable results. Saint Vincent's massive *Opus geometricum*, however, was not published until 1647. Roberval's 'Traité des indivisibles' did not appear in print until almost fifty years after that, in 1693, by which time its value was mainly historical. Only Cavalieri published a contemporary account of his work, and thus became the most influential figure of the three.

Cavalieri was a monk of the Jesuati order in Pisa, and a pupil and correspondent of Galileo. On Galileo's recommendation, he was made professor of mathematics at Bologna in 1629, and it was at about this time that he began to devise his theory of indivisibles. He published it a few years later in his *Geometria indivisibilibus continuorum nova quadam ratione promota* in 1635, with a second edition in 1653. Cavalieri's key definition of 'all the lines' ('omnes lineae') of a plane figure appears at the beginning of Book II:[5]

If through opposite tangents to any given plane figure there are drawn two planes parallel to each other, either at right angles or inclined to the plane of the given figure, and produced indefinitely, one of which is moved towards the other, always remaining parallel until it coincides with it, then the single lines, which in the motion as a whole are the intersections of the moving plane and the given figure, collected together are called: All the lines of the figure, taken from one of them as *regula*;

Cavalieri's basic theorem, stated a few pages later, was that two figures could be said to be in the same ratio as 'all their lines':[6]

Plane figures have the same ratio to each other, as that of all their lines taken from whatever *regula*;

---

5. 'Si per oppositas tangentes cuiuscunque datae planae figurae ducantur duo plana invicem parallela, recta, sive inclinata ad planum datae figurae, hinc inde indefinite producta; quorum alterum moveatur versus reliquem eidem semper aequidistans donec illi congruerit: singula rectae lineae, quae in toto motu fiunt communes sectiones plani moti, et datae figurae, simul collectae vocentur: Omnes lineae talis figurae, sumptae regula une earundem;' Cavalieri 1635, Book II, Definition I.

6. 'Figurae planae habent inter se eandem rationem, quam eorum omnes lineae iuxta quamvis regulam assumptae;' Cavalieri 1635, Book II, Theorem III.

As an example of the way Cavalieri used his theory of indivisibles to compare areas, we reproduce his Theorem IV from Book II.

---

### Cavalieri's comparison of areas

from Cavalieri, *Geometria indivisibilibus*, 1635, Book II, Theorem 4, here from the second edition, 1653, 115–116

---

## THEOREMA IV. PROPOS. IV.

SI duæ figuræ planæ, vel folidæ, in eadem altitudine fue-rint conftitutæ, ductis autem in planis rectis lineis, & in figuris folidis ductis planis vtcumque inter fe parallelis, quorum refpectu prædicta fumpta fit altitudo, repertum fue-rit ductarum linearum portiones figuris planis interceptas, feu ductorum planorum portiones figuris folidis interceptas, effe magnitudines proportionales, homologis in eadem figu-ra femper exiftentibus, dictæ figuræ erunt inter fe, vt vnum quodlibet eorum antecedentium, ad fuum confequens in a-lia figura eidem correfpondens.

Sint primò duæ figurę planæ in eadem altitudine conftitutæ, C A M, C M E, in quibus duæ vtcunque rectæ lineæ inuicem parallelæ ductæ intelligantur, A E, B D, refpectu quarum communis altitu-do affumpta intelligatur, fint au-tem portiones figuris interceptæ ipfæ, A M, B R, in fig. C A M, &, M E, R D, in fig. C M E, reperiatur autem, vt, A M, ad, M E, ita effe, B R, ad, R D. Dico figuram, C A M, ad figu-ram, C M E, effe vt, A M, ad, M E, vel, B R, ad, R D, quoniam enim, B D, A E, vtcumq; du-ctæ funt inter fe æquidiftantes, patet, quod quęlibet earum, quę di-cuntur omnes lineæ figuræ, C A M, fumpta regula altera ipfarum,

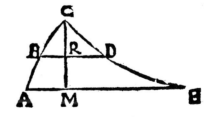

P   2                    A M,

**116**           # GEOMETRIÆ

A M , B R , ad eam , quæ illi indirectum iacet in figura , C M E , erit
vt , B R , ad , R D , vel vt , A M , ad , M E , vt igitur , A M , ad , M
E , vnum .f. antecedentium ad vnum confequentium , ita erunt omnia antecedentia , nempè omnes lineę figurę , C A M , regula , A M
ad omnia confequentia , fcilicet
ad omnes lineas figuræ , C M E,
regula , M E ; indefinitus .n. numerus omnium antecedentium ,
& confequentium , qui pro vtrif-
que hic idem eft , quicunque fit
( & hoc nam figuræ funt in eadem altitudine , & cuilibet ante-
cedenti in figura , C A M , affumpto refpondet fuum confequens illi
in directum in alia figura conftitutum ) non obftat quin omnes lineę
1. huius . figurę , C A M ; fint comparabiles omnibus lineis figurę , C M E , cum
ad illas rationem habeant , vt probatum eft , & ideò omnes lineæ figuræ , C A M , regula , A M , ad omnes lineas figurę , C M E , regula , M E , erunt vt , A M , ad , M E , verum , vt omnes lineæ figuræ,
5. huius . C A M , ad omnes lineas figurę , C M E , ita fig. C A M , eft ad figuram , C M E , ergo figura , C A M , ad figuram , C M E , erit vt , B
R , ad , R D , vel , A M , ad , M E , quod in figuris planis oftendere
opus erat .

Si verò fupponamus , C A M , C M E , effe figuras folidas , & vice
rectarum , A M , B R , M E , R D , plana intelligamus figuris , C A
M , C M E , intercepta inuicem parallela , & ita conftituta, vt plana,
A M , M E , iaceant in eodem plano , veluti fe habeant etiam plana,
B R , R D , refpectu quorum præfata altitudo affumpta quoq; intelligatur , eadem methodo procedentes oftendemus omnia plana figuræ , C A M , ad omnia plana figuræ , C M E , ideft figuram folidam,
3. huius . C A M , ad figuram folidam , C M E , effe vt planum , B R , ad planum , R D , vel vt planum , A M , ad planum , M E , quod & in folidis oftendere opus erat .

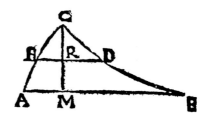

*Notation*

Cavalieri marked all geometric quantities with commas, as , *AB*, or ,*CAM*. Because we now use
commas to indicate pauses or separations, they render the passage almost unreadable, and so
have been silently dropped in the translation.

TRANSLATION

THEOREM IV. PROPOSITION IV.

Suppose two plane figures, or solids, are constructed to the same altitude; moreover having taken straight lines in the planes, or planes in the solids, parallel to each other in whatever way, with respect to which the aforesaid altitude is taken, if it is found that segments of the taken lines intercepted in the plane figures, or portions of the taken planes intercepted in the solids, are proportional quantities, always in the same way in each figure, then the said figures will be to each other as any one of the former to the latter corresponding to it in the other figure.

First suppose the two plane figures constructed to the same altitude are *CAM*, *CME*, in which there are understood to be taken any two straight lines parallel to each other, *AE*, *BD*, with respect to which the common altitude is understood to be taken; moreover let there be intercepted segments *AM*, *BR*, inside figure *CAM*, and *ME*, *RD*, inside figure *CME*; and suppose it is found that *AM* to *ME* is as *BR* to *RD*. I say that figure *CAM* to figure *CME*, will be as *AM* to *ME*, or *BR* to *RD*, for since *BD*, *AE*, however taken, are parallel to each other, it is clear that any one of those which are said to be all the lines of figure *CAM*, taken from either *AM*, *BR*, as *regula* [116] to that which lies opposite to it in figure *CME*, will be as *BR* to *RD*, or as *AM* to *ME*; therefore as *AM* to *ME*, that is, as one of the former to one of the latter so will be all of the former, namely all the lines of figure *CAM*, from *regula AM*, to all the latter, that is, to all the lines of the figure *CME*, from *regula ME*. The indefinite number .n. of all the former, or latter, is here the same for both, whatever it is (for here the figures are to the same altitude, and to any supposed former line in the figure *CAM* there corresponds a latter constructed opposite to it in the other figure) so it cannot be but that all the lines of figure *CAM* are comparable to all the lines of figure *CME*, since they have a ratio to them, as has been shown. And therefore all the lines of figure *CAM*, from *regula AM*, to all the lines of figure *CME*, from *regula ME*, will be as *AM* to *ME*; but as all the lines of figure *CAM* to all the lines of figure *CME*, so is figure *CAM* to figure *CME*; therefore figure *CAM* to figure *CME* will be as *BR* to *RD*, or *AM* to *ME*, which it was required to show for plane figures.

But if we assume *CAM*, *CME*, to be solid figures, and instead of the lines *AM*, *BR*, *ME*, *RD*, we understand intercepted planes parallel to each other inside the figures *CAM*, *CME*, and so constructed that planes *AM*, *ME*, lie in the same plane, just as do the planes *BR*, *RD*, with respect to which the aforesaid altitude is again understood to be taken, then proceeding by the same method we show that all the planes of figure *CAM* to all the planes of figure *CME*, that is the solid figure *CAM* to the solid figure *CME*, are as the plane *BR* to the plane *RD*, or as the plane *AM* to the plane *ME*, which it was required to show also for solid figures.

1. of this.

3. of this.

3. of this.

## 2.4.2 Wallis and Hobbes on indivisibles, 1656

Cavalieri was well aware of the paradoxes that can arise from handling the infinitely large and the infinitely small, and tried to avoid them by making precise stipulations about the movement of the intersecting plane, or (in a later addition to his book) by comparing individual lines rather than collections of 'all the lines'.

Evangelista Torricelli had no such scruples when he took up Cavalieri's work in the 1640s. He regarded planes simply as 'sums' of lines, and volumes as 'sums' of planes, and in his *Opera geometrica* of 1644 successfully used this simplified version of the theory to solve two problems: the quadrature (area) of the parabola and the cubature (volume) of a hyperbolic solid. It was from Torricelli's *Opera geometrica* that John Wallis also learned the theory of indivisibles, in the early 1650s.[7] Wallis was no more concerned than Torricelli had been with painstaking discussion of the nature of indivisibles, but took them to be either 'lines' or 'parallelograms' as required, and introduced the symbol $\infty$ to denote the number of them.

Wallis pursued the method much further than any previous writer (see 3.2.3) but not everyone was convinced by his manipulations, and the philosopher Thomas Hobbes raised the first doubts, to be echoed by many others later, on the use of infinitely small or indivisible quantities (see below and 10.2). Wallis was undaunted; for him the method was more than justified by a flood of new and useful results, some of which we will see in Chapter 3.

---

7. Wallis read the copy of Torricelli's *Opera geometrica* in the Savilian Professors' library (modern shelfmark Savile Y.1), and his annotations of the relevant passages show just how interested he was in the new theory of indivisbles.

## Wallis's description of indivisibles
from Wallis, *De sectionibus conicis*, 1656, Proposition 1

**4**    *De Sectionibus Conicis.*    **PROP. 1.**

# PARS PRIMA.

### PROP. I.
*De Figuris planis juxta Indivisibilium
methodum considerandis.*

 Uppono in limine (juxtâ Bonaventuræ
Cavallerii *Geometriam Indivisibilium*)
Planum quodlibet quasi ex infinitis lineis
parallelis conflari: Vel potiùs (quod e-
go mallem) ex infinitis Prall-logram-
mis æquè altis; quorum quidem singulo-
rum altitudo sit totius altitudinis $\frac{1}{\infty}$, sive aliquota pars
infinite parva; (esto enim $\infty$ nota numeri infini-
ti;) adeóq; omnium simul altitudo æqualis altitudi-
ni figuræ.

Utrovis autem modo res explicetur (sive per infinitas lineas parallelas, sive per infinita parallelogramma æquè al-
ta infinitis illis lineis interjecta) eodem res redibit. Nam Parallelogrammum cuius altitudo supponitur infinite parva, hoc
est, nulla, (nam quantitas infinite parva perinde est atq; non-
quanta,) vix aliud est quàm linea (In hoc saltem differunt,
quòd linea hæc supponitur dilatabilis esse, sive tantillàm saltem spissitudinem habere ut infinitâ multiplicatione certam tandem altitudinem sive latitudinem possit acquirere, tantam
nempe quanta est figuræ altitudo.) Nos igitur deinceps ( partim quod ille mos loquendi in Cavallerii methodo de *Indivisibilibus* videatur obtinuisse, partim etiam ut brevitati consula-
mus) Linearum potiùs quàm Parallelogrammorum nomine
partes illas figurarum infinite exiguas ( sive altitudinis infinite
exiguæ) nonnunquam appellabimus, quando saltem determi-

**PROP.** 2.     *De Sectionibus Conicis.*

**nata altitudinis** confideratio non habetur; Ubi autem deter⁻

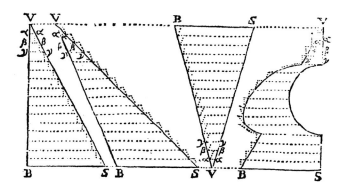

m'natæ altitudinis inftituetur confideratio (quod aliquando fiet) exiguæ illius altitudinis eoulq; ratio habenda erit, ut ea infinities multiplicata totam figuræ altitudinem fupponatur ad · quare.

TRANSLATION

---

## FIRST PART

### PROPOSITION I.

*Plane figures considered according to the method of indivisibles*

I suppose at the start (according to the *Geometria indivisibilium* of Bonaventura Cavalieri) that any plane whatever consists, as it were, of an infinite number of parallel lines. Or rather (which I prefer) of an infinite number of parallelograms of equal altitude; of which indeed the altitude of a single one is $\frac{1}{\infty}$ of the whole altitude, or an infinitely small divisor; (for let $\infty$ denote an infinite number); and therefore the altitude of all of them at once is equal to the altitude of the figure.

Moreover, in whichever way the thing is explained (whether by infinitely many parallel lines, or by infinitely many parallelograms of equal altitude interposed between those infinitely many lines) it comes down to the same thing. For a parallelogram whose altitude is supposed infinitely small, that is, nothing (for an infinitely small quantity is just the same as no quantity) is scarcely other than a line. (In this at least they differ, that a line is here supposed to be dilatable, or at least to have a certain such thickness that by infinite multiplication it can acquire a definite altitude or latitude, namely as much as the altitude of the figure.) Therefore from now on (partly because strictly speaking this seems to have been the case in Cavalieri's method of *indivisibles*, partly also so that we may deliberate with brevity) we sometimes call those infinitely tiny parts of figures (or, of infinitely tiny altitude) by the name of LINES rather than PARALLELOGRAMS, at least when [5] we do not have to consider the determination of the altitude. Moreover when we do have to take into consideration the determination of the altitude (as sometimes happens) those tiny altitudes must have a ratio, so that infinitely multiplied they are assumed to become equal to the whole altitude of the figure.

---

# Hobbes' response to Wallis

from Hobbes, *Six lessons to the Professors of Mathematicks*, 1656, 46

---

### TRANSCRIPT

Therefore though your *Lemma* be true, and by me (Chap.13. Art.5.) demonstrated; yet you did not know why it is true; which also appears most evidently in the first Proposition of your *Conique-sections*. Where first you have this, *That a Parallelogram whose Altitude is* infinitely little, *that is to say*, none, is scarce *anything else but a Line*. Is this the Language of Geometry? How do you determine this word *scarce*? The least Altitude, is Somewhat or Nothing. If Somewhat, then the first character of your Arithmeticall Progression must not be zero; and consequently the first eighteen Propositions of this your *Arithmetica Infinitorum* are all naught. If Nothing, then your whole figure is without Altitude, and consequently your Understanding naught. Again, in the same Proposition, you say thus, *We will sometimes call those Parallelograms rather by the name of Lines then of Parallelograms, at least, when there is no* consideration *of a determinate Altitude; But where there is a* consideration *of a determinate Altitude (which will happen sometimes) there that little Altitude shall be so far* considered, *as that being infinitely multiplyed it may be equall to the* Altitude *of the whole Figure.* See here in what a confusion you are when you resist the truth. When you *consider* no determinate Altitude (that is, *no Quantity* of Altitude) then you say your Parallelogram shall be called a *Line*. But when the Altitude is determined (that is, when it is *Quantity*) then you will call it a Parallelogram. Is not this the very same doctrine which you so much wonder at and reprehend in me, in your objections to my eighth Chapter, and your word *considered* used as I used it? 'Tis very ugly in one that so bitterly reprehendeth a doctrine in another, to be driven upon the same himself by the force of truth when he thinks not on't. Again, seeing you admit in any case, those *infinitely little* altitudes to be quantity, what need you this limitation of yours, *so far forth as that by multiplication they may be made equall to the Altitude of the whole figure*? May not the half, the third, the fourth, or the fifth part, etc. be made equall to the whole by multiplication? Why could you not have said plainly, *so far forth as that every one of* those infinitely little *Altitudes be not only* something *but an* aliquot part [divisor] *of the whole*? So you will have an *infinitely little* Altitude, that is to say *a Point, to be both nothing and something and an aliquot part.* And all this proceeds from not understanding the ground of your Profession.

---

CHAPTER 3

# FORESHADOWINGS
# OF CALCULUS

The emergence of the differential and integral calculus in the seventeenth century increased the scope and power of mathematics dramatically. We will be concerned with the calculus in one way or another for much of the rest of this book but first, in this chapter, we examine some of the ideas that lay behind it. As with any major breakthrough, these can be traced back for some time and to a variety of sources. Early hints of later methods are (with the benefit of hindsight) already discernible in the 1620s in the work of de Saint Vincent in the low countries, Fermat in France, and Cavalieri in Italy. Over the next fifty years, many others added to the gradual development and cohesion of ideas: Roberval and Pascal in France, Descartes in the Netherlands, Torricelli in Italy, and Wallis in England. We can do no more than touch upon the full richness and complexity of the story, but in this chapter we look at some of the key problems that were explored from the 1620s onwards. Very often these arose from the effort to understand or improve upon the legacy of Greek geometry. Given some curve, perhaps a spiral or a parabola or a cycloid, can one find its tangent at particular point? Is it possible to find the exact length of a portion of the curve? And how can one determine areas bounded by it?

## 3.1 METHODS FOR TANGENTS

### 3.1.1  Fermat's tangent method, 1629

Near the beginning of his mathematical studies, in 1629, Fermat described an innovative method for finding tangents in a piece entitled 'Methodus ad disquirendam maximam et minimam et de tangentibus linearum curvarum' ('Method of discovering maxima and minima, and on tangents to curved lines'). His interest in maximization problems was inspired by his reading of Pappus, Book VII, which poses a set of problems about the unique least ratio of two rectangles (propositions 59 to 64). His motivation therefore, as so often for Fermat, came directly from classical mathematics, but his methods were very far from traditional. In the 'Methodus' Fermat showed first how to maximize the product of two line segments, and then applied the method to finding tangents. His argument involved a quantity $E$ (Viète's notation) that was eventually neglected, but not before he had divided by it throughout his key equation. It was a clever idea that led rapidly and easily to a result, but already it presented a fundamental difficulty that was to plague the calculus later: how could one divide by something that was then assumed to be nothing? Yet Fermat, or anyone else who had studied Apollonius, knew that the answer he arrived at was correct.

Fermat's original manuscript is now lost, but copies of it were sent by his friend d'Espagnet to Roberval in 1636 and to Mersenne by the end of 1637, and by Mersenne to Descartes in 1638. Mersenne also took it to Italy in 1644. At some stage Francis van Schooten made his own copy, and by 1650 further copies were owned by Sir Charles Cavendish and John Pell, both of whom lived in continental Europe during the later part of the 1640s. Thus Fermat's method circulated widely and was well known in the mathematical circles of the day.

The text was first printed in Fermat's posthumous *Varia opera* of 1679, edited by his son Samuel, probably from the original manuscript although the notation has been updated and several errors have crept in. At one point, for example, the copyist has written '$D$, aut $D - E$', where the context clearly requires '$D$ ad $D - E$'. Corrections are shown in square brackets in the translation below.

## Fermat's tangent method
from Fermat, *Varia opera*, 1679, 64

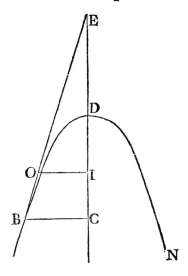

64            Varia Opera

Sit data, verbi gratià, Parabole B D N, cujus vertex D, diameter D C, & punctum in
ea datum B, ad quod ducenda est recta B E, tangens parabolen, & in puncto E, cum
diametro concurrens, ergo sumendo quodlibet punctum O I, in recta B E, & ab eo
ducendo ordinatam O I, à puncto autem B, ordinatam B C major erit proportio
C D, ad D I, quàm quadrati B C, ad quadratum O I, quia punctum O, est extra
parabolen, sed propter similitudinem triangulorum, ut B C, quad. ad O I, quad. ita
C E, quad. ad I E, quad. Major igitur erit proportio C D  ad D I, quàm quadrati
C E ad quad. I E, Cum autem punctum B detur, datur applicata B C, ergo punctum
C datur etiam  C D, Sit igitur C D, æqualis D, datæ. Ponatur C E, esse A, ponatur
C I esse E, ergo D, aut D —E habebit majorem rationem, quàm A² ad A² + E² -- A,
in E. Et ducendo inter se medias & extremas D in A² + D in E² — D in A in E,
majus erit quàm D, in A² — A² in E, Adæquentur igitur juxta superiorem methodum, demptis itaque communibus D, in E² — D, in A in E adæquabitur— A² in
E, aut quod idem est, D in E², + A² in E, adæquabitur D in A in E, Omnia
dividantur per E, ergo D in E + A² adæquabitur D in A, elidatur D in E,
ergo A² æquabitur D in A², ideoque A æquabitur D, ergo C E, probavimus du-
plam ipsius C D, quod quidem ita se habet.

Nec unquam fallit methodus, imò ad plerasque quæstiones pulcherrimas potest ex-
tendi, ejus enim beneficio centra gravitatis in figuris lineis curvis & rectis comprehen-
sis, & in solidis invenimus, & multa alia, de quibus fortasse aliàs, si otium suppetat.
De quadraturis spatiorum sub lineis curvis & rectis contentorum, imò & de proportione solidorum ab eis ortorum ad conos ejusdem basis & altitudinis, fusè cum Domi-
no de Roberval egimus.

Suppose there is given, for example, a parabola $BDN$, with vertex $D$, and diameter $DC$, and a given point on it $B$, at which there must be drawn the straight line $BE$ touching the parabola, through the point $E$ where it meets the diameter; therefore take any point $O$ [the printed text has $OI$] on the line $BE$, and from that draw the ordinate $OI$, and from the point $B$, the ordinate $BC$. The ratio of $CD$ to $DI$ will be greater than that of the square of $BC$ to the square of $OI$, because the point $O$ is outside the parabola; but because of similarity of triangles, $BC$ squared to $OI$ squared, is as $CE$ squared to $IE$ squared. Therefore the ratio $CD$ to $DI$ will be greater than that of the square of $CE$ to the square of $IE$. Moreover, since the point $B$ is given, the ordinate $BC$ is given, so the point $C$ is given and also $CD$. Therefore let $CD$ be equal to a given quantity $D$. Put $CE$ equal to $A$, and $CI$ equal to $E$, therefore $D$ [to] $D - E$ will have a ratio greater than $A^2$ to $A^2 + E^2 - [2]A$ times $E$. And taking from these the means and extremes, $D$ times $A^2 + D$ times $E^2 - [2]D$ times $A$ times $E$ will be greater than $D$ times $A^2 - A^2$ times $E$. Therefore adequating according to the method above, and removing common terms, $D$ times $E^2 - [2]D$ times $A$ times $E$ will adequate to $-A^2$ times $E$, or, which is the same thing, $D$ times $E^2 + A^2$ times $E$ will adequate to $[2]D$ times $A$ times $E$. Dividing everything by $E$, therefore, $D$ times $E + A^2$ will adequate to $[2]D$ times $A$; eliminating $D$ times $E$ , therefore, $A^2$ will equal $[2]D$ times $A$, and therefore $A$ will equal $[2]D$. Therefore we have proved that $CE$ is twice $CD$, which indeed is the case.

This method never fails, and can be extended immediately to several beautiful problems, for with its help I have found centres of gravity in figures bounded by curves and straight lines, and in solids, and much else, of which perhaps elsewhere if leisure permits.

---

### 3.1.2  Descartes' tangent method, 1637

When Descartes read Fermat's 'Methodus' in 1638, he was sceptical, complaining that the method of tangents was not properly derived from the method of maxima and minima, and that it applied only to the particular example Fermat had used, the parabola. Both criticisms were misunderstandings arising from Fermat's usual brevity of explanation. A further reason for Descartes' negative response, however, was that he had offered his own tangent method in his recently published *La géométrie*, and was as proud of it as Fermat was of his, describing it as 'the most useful problem, and the most general, not only that I know but even that I have ever desired to know in geometry'.[1]

Descartes' method was based on finding a circle that touches the curve at the point in question, so that the tangent to the circle at that point is also a tangent to the curve. The correct circle is to be found algebraically, by searching for double roots of the equation

---

1. 'Et i'ose dire que c'est cecy le problesme le plus vtile, & le plus general non seulement que ie sçache, mais mesme que i'aye iamais desiré sçavoir en Geometrie.' Descartes, *La Géométrie*, 1637, 342.

of intersection. In principle the method can be applied to any curve, but it is laborious, and Descartes gave only two fully worked examples (ellipse and parabola).

Each curve was described in relation to $x$- and $y$-axes but, like Fermat's axes in 'Ad locos' (see 2.3.2), they were intrinsic to the curve and not necessarily at right angles. 'Cartesian' co-ordinates in the modern form, with fixed orthogonal axes, were not to become standard until the eighteenth century.

---

### Descartes' tangent method
from Descartes, *La géométrie*, 1637, 342–343, 347–348

---

Façon
generale
pour
trouuer
des lignes
droites,
qui coup-
pent les
courbes
données,
ou leurs
contin-
gentes, a
angles
droits.

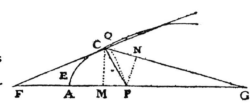

Soit C E
la ligne courbe,
& qu'il faille ti-
rer vne ligne
droite par le
point C, qui fa-

ce auec elle des angles droits. Ie fuppofe la chofe defia faite, & que la ligne cherchée eft C P, laquelle ie pro-longe iufques au point P, ou elle rencontre la ligne droi-te G A, que ie fuppofe eftre celle aux poins de laquelle on rapporte tous ceux de la ligne C E : en forte que fai-fant M A ou C B ∞ *y*, & C M, ou B A ∞ *x*, iay quelque equation, qui explique le rapport, qui eft entre *x* & *y*. Puis ie fais P C ∞ *s*, & P A ∞ *v*, ou P M ∞ *v* -- *y*, & a caufe du triangle rectangle P M C iay *ss*, qui eft le quar-ré de la baze efgal à $xx + vv - 2vy + yy$, qui font les quarrés des deux coftés. c'eft a dire iay *x* ∞

$\sqrt{ss - vv + 2vy - yy}$, oubien $y ∞ v + \sqrt{ss - xx}$, & par le moyen de cete equation, i'ofte de l'autre equa-tion qui m'explique le rapport qu'ont tous les poins de la courbe C E a ceux de la droite G A, l'vne des deux quan-tités indeterminées *x* ou *y*. ce qui eft ayfé a faire en mettant partout $\sqrt{ss - vv + 2vy - yy}$ au lieu d'*x*, & le quarré de cete fomme au lieu d'*xx*, & fon cube au lieu d'*x*³, & ainfi des autres, fi c'eft *x* que ie veuille ofter; oubien

bien fi c'eft $y$, en mettant en fon lieu $x + \overline{\sqrt{ss - xx}}$, &
le quarré, ou le cube, &c. de cete fomme, au lieu d'$yy$, ou
$y$ &c. De façon qu'il refte toufiours aprés cela vne equation, en laquelle il ny a plus qu'vne feule quantité indeterminée, $x$, ou $y$.

Comme fi C E eft vne Ellipfe , & que M A foit le
fegment de fon diametre, auquel C M foit appliquée par
ordre, & qui ait $r$ pour fon cofté droit , & $q$ pour le tra-
uerfant, on à par le 13 th.

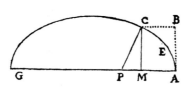

du 1 liu. d'Apollonius.

$xx \infty ry - \frac{r}{q}yy$ , d'on
oftant $xx$, il refte $ss -$
$- vv + 2vy - yy \infty ry - \frac{r}{q}yy$.
oubien,

$$yy \frac{\pm qry - 2qvy \pm qvv - qss}{q - r}$$ efgal a rien. car il eft mieux en
cet endroit de confiderer ainfi enfemble toute la fom-
me , que d'en faire vne partie efgale a l'autre.

[...]

Comme par exemple ie dis que la premiere equation trouuée cy deſſus, a ſçauoir

$$yy \frac{\pm qry - 2qvy \pm qvv - qss}{q-r}$$ doit auoir la meſme forme que celle qui ſe produiſt en faiſant $e$ eſgal a $y$, & multipliant $y - e$ par ſoy meſme, d'où il vient $yy - 2ey + ee$, en ſorte qu'on peut comparer ſeparement chaſcun de leurs termes, & dire que puiſque le premier qui eſt $yy$ eſt tout le meſme en l'vne qu'en l'autre, le ſecond qui eſt en l'vne

$$\frac{qry - 2qvy,}{q-r}$$ eſt eſgal au ſecõd de l'autre qui eſt $-2ey$, d'où cherchant la quantité $v$ qui eſt la ligne P A, on a

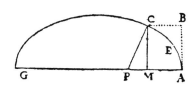

$v \infty e -\frac{r}{q}e + \frac{1}{2}r$, oubiẽ a cauſe que nous auons ſuppoſé $e$ eſgal a $y$, on a

$v \infty y -\frac{r}{q}y + \frac{1}{2}r$. Et

X x 2                    ainſi

348              LA GEOMETRIE.

ainſi on pourroit trouuer $s$ par le troiſieſme terme

$ee \infty \frac{qvv - qss,}{q - r}$ mais pourceque la quantité $v$ determine aſſés le point P, qui eſt le ſeul que nous cherchions, on n'a pas beſoin de paſſer outre.

---

TRANSLATION

Suppose $CE$ is the curve, and that one must draw a straight line through the point $C$, which makes right angles with it. I suppose the thing already done, and that the sought line is $CP$, which I lengthen to the point $P$, where it meets the straight line $GA$, which I suppose to be the one to whose points one may relate all those of the curve $CE$; so that making $MA$ or $CB$ equal to $y$, and $CM$ or $BA$ equal to $x$, I have some equation that explains the relationship between $x$ and $y$. Then I make $PC = s$, and $PA = v$, or $PM = v - y$, and because of the right angled triangle $PMC$, I have $ss$, which is the square of the base, equal to $xx + vv - 2vy + yy$, which are the squares of the two sides. That is to say I have $x = \sqrt{ss - vv + 2vy - yy}$, or rather $y = v + \sqrt{ss - xx}$, and by means of this equation, I eliminate from the other equation, which explains the relationship of the points of the curve $CE$ to those of the straight line $GA$, one of the two unknown quantities $x$ or $y$. This is easy to do putting everywhere $\sqrt{ss - vv + 2vy - yy}$ instead

General method for finding straight lines that cut given curves, or their tangents, at right angles.

of $x$, and the square of this sum instead of $xx$, and its cube instead of $x^3$, and so on for others, if it is $x$ that I want to eliminate; or [343] instead, if it is $y$, by putting in its place $v + \sqrt{ss - xx}$, and the square, cube, etc. of this sum in place of $yy$, or $y^3$ etc. In such a way that there always remains after this an equation in which there is no more than a single unknown quantity $x$ or $y$.

If $CE$ is an ellipse, and $MA$ is the segment of its diameter to which $CM$ is applied as an ordinate, and which has $r$ for its *latus rectum*, and $q$ for the transverse diameter, one has by Proposition 13 of Book I of Apollonius $xx = ry - \frac{r}{q}yy$, where eliminating $xx$ there remains $ss - vv + 2vy - yy = ry - \frac{r}{q}yy$. Or rather, $yy\frac{+qry - 2qvy + qvv - qss}{q - r}$ is equal to nothing. For it is better in this case to consider the whole sum together in this way, than to make one part equal to another.

$$[\ldots]$$

Descartes went on to explain that the equation thus found is to be used to discover $v$ or $s$. Further, he argued, if $P$ is the point required, then the circle through $C$ with $P$ as the centre will touch the curve without cutting it, and so the equation between $y$, $v$, and $s$ will have two equal roots.

[347] As if, for example, I say that the first equation found above, namely $yy\frac{+qry - 2qvy + qvv - qss}{q - r}$ must take the same form as that produced by making $e$ equal to $y$ and multiplying $y - e$ by itself, from which there comes $yy - 2ey + ee$, so that one may compare each of their terms separately, and say that because the first, which is $yy$ is just the same in one as in the other, the second which is in one $\frac{qry - 2qvy}{q - r}$, is equal to the second of the other, which is $-2ey$, from which, seeking the quantity $v$, which is the line $PA$, we have $v = e - \frac{r}{q}e + \frac{1}{2}r$, or rather, because we have supposed $e$ equal to $y$, we have $v = y - \frac{r}{q}y + \frac{1}{2}r$. And [348] thus one may find $s$ from the third term $ee = \frac{qvv - qss}{q - r}$ but because the quantity $v$ sufficiently determines the point $P$, which is the only one we were seeking, one has no need to go further.

## 3.2 METHODS OF QUADRATURE

### 3.2.1 Fermat's quadrature of higher hyperbolas, early 1640s

A problem of much wider concern than finding tangents was that of quadrature: literally, finding a square equal to a given space or, in modern terms, finding an area. Attempts at quadrature were many and varied, giving rise to numerous special methods for special cases. Here we can present only a few examples, chosen to illustrate some of the more important ideas that were beginning to emerge during the seventeenth century. For ease of reading in what follows we will borrow modern notation for summations and for equations of curves.

By 1636, both Roberval and Fermat knew that the value of $\sum_{x=0}^{X} x^n$ is approximately $\frac{X^n}{n+1}$ when $n$ is a positive integer and $x$ is taken at sufficiently small intervals between 0 and $X$. Both used this relationship to find the quadrature of curves of the form $y = x^n$. Fermat continued to explore such questions privately during the early 1640s, and appears to have found methods of quadrature also for curves of the form $y^m = x^n$ (higher parabolas) and $y^m = x^{-n}$ (higher hyperbolas), but unfortunately it is impossible to date his work precisely. We know that he corresponded with Torricelli on the subject in 1644, but the letters themselves are now lost.

Only in 1658–59 did Fermat bring his results together in a treatise headed 'De aequationum localium transmutatione …cui annectitur proportionis geometricae in quadrandis infinitis parabolis et hyperbolis usus' ('On the transformation of equations of place …to which is adjoined the use of geometric progressions for squaring infinite parabolas and hyperbolas'). This was almost certainly written in response to Wallis's *Arithmetica infinitorum* of 1656, which treated similar problems in a rather different way. By the late 1650s, however, Fermat's results were no longer new, and the treatise remained unpublished until 1679, long after his death.

The procedure below is from the opening of 'De aequationum localium'. It can be applied to any curve of the form $y = x^{-n}$ except when $n = 1$, the case Fermat described as the hyperbola of Apollonius. The method is based on dividing the required area into strips whose bases increase in geometric progression. Because of the rapid fall of the curve the areas of the corresponding rectangles decrease, also in geometric progression. Fermat knew (from Euclid IX.35) how to sum a finite geometric progression and, like Viète before him, extended the result to an infinite progression by taking the 'last' term to be zero.

In many respects Fermat's proof remains strongly reminiscent of the Greek mathematics to which he made such frequent reference: it is entirely geometric, and couched throughout in the Euclidean language of ratio. In other ways, however, he went far beyond the classical methods of exhaustion and contradiction. In August 1657 he had complained that Wallis could just as well have handled quadratures in the traditional Archimedean way,[2] yet in his own treatment he discussed the Archimedean method only to dismiss it and move on. His summation of a geometric progression with an infinite number of terms was an idea learned from Viète, not from Euclid. And just as in his tangent method he had introduced quantities that were allowed to vanish once they had served their purpose, here too he used a similar procedure: the parallelogram *EGH* plays a crucial role in his argument, but when no longer needed it simply 'goes to nothing' ('abit in nihilum').

---

2. Wallis 1658, letter 12.

**Fermat's quadrature of a hyperbola**

from Fermat, *Varia opera*, 1679, 44–46

44   ## Varia Opera

# DE ÆQUATIONUM LOCALIUM TRANS

mutatione, & emendatione, ad multimodam curvilineorum inter fe, vel cum rectilineis comparationem.

## CVI ANNECTITVR

*PROPORTIONIS GEOMETRICÆ in quadrandis infinitis parabolis & hyperbolis ufus.*

N unica paraboles quadraturâ proportionem geometricam ufurpavit Archimedes. In reliquis quantitatum heterogenearum comparationibus, arithmeticæ dumtaxat proportioni fefe adftrinxit. An ideo quia proportionem geometricam minùs π/ραγωνίζωσαν eft expertus? An verò quia peculiare ab illa proportione petitum artificium ad quadrandam primariam parabolam, ad ulteriores derivari vix poteft? Nos certè hujufmodi proportionem quadrationum feraciffimam & agnofcimus, & experti fumus, & inventionem noftram quæ eadem omnino methodo & parabolas & hyperbolas quadrat, recentioribus geometris haud illibenter impertimur.

Unico quod notiffimum eft proportionis geometricæ attributo, tota hæc methodus innititur.

Theorema hoc eft : Datâ quavis proportione geometricâ cujus termini decrefcant in infinitum, eft ut differentia terminorum progreffionem conftituentium, ad minorem terminum, ita maximus progreffionis terminus ad reliquos omnes in infinitum fumptos.

Hoc pofito, proponantur primo hyperbolæ quadrandæ. Hyperbolas autem definimus infinitas diverfæ fpeciei curvas, ut D S E F, quarum hæc eft proprietas, ut pofitis in quolibet angulo dato R A C, ipfarum afymptotis rectis A R, A C, in infinitum, fi placet, non fecùs ac ipfa curva extendendis, & ductis uni afymptotωn parallelis rectis quibuflibet G E, H I, O N, M P, R S, &c. fit ut poteftas quædam rectæ A H, ad poteftatem fimilem rectæ A G, ita poteftas rectæ G E, vel fimilis vel diverfa à præcedente, ad poteftatem ipfi homogeneam rectæ H I, poteftates autem intelligimus, non fo-

# Mathematica.                    45

lùm quadrata, cubos, quadratoquadrata, &c. quarum exponentes funt. 2. 3. & 4. &c. fed etiam latera fimplicia, quorum exponens eft unitas. Aio itaque omnes in infinitum hujufmodi hyperbolas, unicâ demptâ, quæ Apolloniana eft, five primaria, beneficio proportionis geometricæ uniformi & perpetua methodo quadrari poffe.

Exponatur, fi placet, hyperbola, cujus ea fit proprietas, ut fit femper ut quadratum rectæ H A, ad quadratum rectæ A G, ita recta G E, ad rectam H I, & ut quadratum

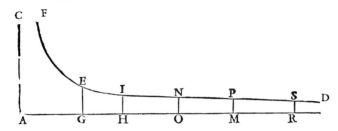

O A, ad quadratum A H, ita recta H I, ad rectam O N, &c. Aio fpatium infinitum, cujus bafis G E, & curva E S, ex uno latere, ex alio vero afymptotos infinita G O R, æquari fpatio rectilineo dato. Fingantur termini progreffionis geometricæ in infinitum extendendi, quorum primus fit A G, fecundus A H, tertius A O, &c. in infinitum, & ad-fe fe per approximationem tantum accedant quantum fatis fit ut juxta Methodum Archimedæam, parallelogrammum rectilineum fub GE, in G H, quadrilineo mixto G H E, adæquetur, ut loquitur Diophantus, aut ferè æquetur.

GE, in G H.

Item ut priora ex intervallis rectis proportionalium G H, H O, O M, & fimilia funt ferè inter fe æqualia, ut commodè per ἀπαγωγὴν εἰς ἀδύνατον, per circumfcriptiones & infcriptiones Archimedæa demonftrandi ratio inftitui poffit, quod femel monuiffe fufficiat, ne artificium quibuflibet geometris jam fatis notum inculcare fæpius & iterare cogamur.

His pofitis, cum fit ut A G, ad A H, ita A H, A O, & ita A O ad A M, erit pariter ut A G, ad A H: ita intervallum G H, ad H O, & ita intervallum H O, ad O M, &c. Parallelogrammum autem fub E G, in G H, erit ad parallelogrammum fub H I, in H O, ut parallelogrammum fub H I, in H O, ad parallelogrammum fub N O, in O M, cùm enim ratio parallelogralemi fub G E, in G H, ad parallelogrammum fub H I, in H O, componatur ex ratione rectæ G E, ad rectam H I, & ex ratione rectæ G H, ad rectam H O : fit autem ut G H, ad H O, ita A G, ad A H, ut præmonuimus. Ergo ratio parallelogrammi fub E G, & G H, ad parallelogrammum fub H I, in H O, componitur ex ratione G E, ad H I, & ex ratione A G, ad A H, fed ut G E, ad H I, ita ex conftructione H A, quadratum, ad quadratum G A, five propter proportionales : ita recta A O, ad rectam G A. Ergo ratio parallelogrammi fub E G, in G H, ad parallelogrammum fub H I, in H O, componitur ex ratione A O, ad A G, & A G, ad A H, fed ratio A O ad A H, componitur ex illis duabus. Ergo parallelogrammum fub G E, in G H, eft ad parallelogrammum fub H I, in H O, ut O A, ad H A; five ut H A, ad A G.

Similiter probabitur parallelogrammum fub H I, in H O, effe ad parallelogrammum fub O N, in O M, ut A O, ad H A, fed tres rectæ quæ conftituunt rationes parallelogrammorum, rectæ nempe A O, H A. G A, funt proportionales ex conftructione.

F 3

## 46    Varia Opera

Ergo parallelogramma in infinitum fumpta fub G E, in G H, fub H I, in H O, fub O N, in O M, &c. erunt femper continuè proportionalia in ratione rectæ H A, ad G A. Eſt igitur ex theoremate hujus methodi conſtitutivo ut G H, differentia terminorum rationis ad minorem terminum G A, ita primus parallelogrammorum progreſſionis terminus, hoc eſt parallelogrammum fub E G, in G H, ad reliquos in infinitum parallelogrammos, hoc eſt ex adæquatione Archimedæa ad figuram fub H I, afymptoto H R, & curvâ in I N D, in infinitum extendendâ contentam. Sed ut H G, ad G A, ita fumptâ communi latitudine rectâ G E, parallelogrammum fub G E, in G H, ad parallelogrammum fub G E in G A. Eſt igitur ut parallelogrammum fub G E, in G H, ad figuram illam infinitam, cujus bafis H I, ita idem parallelogrammum fub G E, in G H, ad parallelogrammum fub G E, in G A, ergo parallelogrammum fub G E, in G A, quod eſt ſpatium rectilineum datum, adæquatur figuræ prædictæ. Cui fi addas parallelogrammum fub G E, in G H, quod propter minutiſſimos τμαχισμὸς evanefcit & abit in nihilum, ſupereſt veriſſimum, & Archimedæâ licet prolixiore demonſtratione facillimè firmandum, parallelogrammum A E, in hac hyperbolæ fpecie, æquari figuræ fub bafe G E, afymptoto G R, & curvâ E D, in infinitum producendâ contentæ. Nec operofum ad omnes omnino hujufmodi hyperbolas, unâ, ut diximus, demptâ, inventionem extendere.

TRANSLATION

## ON THE TRANSFORMATION AND EMENDATION OF EQUATIONS OF PLACE
in order to compare curves in various ways with each other, or with straight lines

### TO WHICH IS ADJOINED

### THE USE OF GEOMETRIC PROGRESSIONS
*in the quadrature of infinite parabolas or hyperbolas*

Archimedes made use of geometric progressions only for the quadrature of one parabola. In the remaining comparisons of heterogeneous quantities he restricted himself merely to arithmetic progressions. Whether because he found geometric progressions less appropriate? Or because the required method with the particular progression used for squaring the first parabola could scarcely be extended to the others? I have certainly recognized, and proved, progressions of this kind very productive for quadratures, and my discovery, by which one may square both parabolas and hyperbolas by exactly the same method, I by no means unwillingly communicate to more modern geometers.

I attribute to geometric progressions only what is very well known, on which this whole method is based.

The theorem is this: Given any geometric progression whose terms decrease infinitely, as the difference of two [consecutive] terms constituting the progression is to the smaller of them, so is the greatest term of the progression to all the rest taken infinitely.

This established, there is proposed first the quadrature of hyperbolas. Moreover we define hyperbolas as infinite curves of various kinds, like *DSEF*, of which this is a property, that having placed at any given angle *RAC* its asymptotes, *AR*, *AC*, extended infinitely if one pleases but not cut by the curve, and taking whatever straight lines, *GE*, *HI*, *ON*, *MP*, *RS*, etc. parallel to one asymptote, we suppose that a certain power of the line *AH* to the same power of the line *AG* is as a power of the line *GE*, whether the same or different from the preceding one, to that same power of the line *HI*; moreover we understand the powers to be not [45] only squares, cubes, square-squares, etc. of which the exponents are 2, 3, 4, etc. but also simple lines, whose power is one. I say, therefore, that all hyperbolas of this kind indefinitely, with one exception, which is that of Apollonius, or the first, can be squared with the help of the same and always applicable method of geometric progressions.

Let there be, if one likes, a hyperbola of which it is the property that the square of the line *HA* to the square of the line *AG* is always as the line *GE* to the line *HI*, and that the square of *OA* to the square of *AH* is as the line *HI* to the line *ON*, etc. I say that the infinite space whose base is *GE*, and with the curve *ES* for one side, but for the other the infinite asymptote *GOR*, is equal to a given rectilinear space. It is supposed that the terms of a geometric progression can be extended infinitely, of which the first is *AG*, the second *AH*, the third *AO*, etc. infinitely, and these approach each other by approximation as closely as is needed, so that by the method of Archimedes the parallelogram made by *GE* and *GH* adequates, as Diophantus says, to the irregular four-sided shape *GHE*, or very nearly equals.

*GE* times *GH*.
_____

Likewise, the first of the straight line intervals of the progression *GH*, *HO*, *OM*, and so on, are similarly very nearly equal amongst themselves, so that we can conveniently use the method of exhaustion, and by Archimedean circumscriptions and inscriptions the ratio to be demonstrated can be established, which it is sufficient to have shown once, nor do I wish to repeat or insist more often on a method already sufficiently known to any geometer.

This said, since *AH* to *AO* is as *AG* to *AH*, so also will *AO* to *AM* be as *AG* to *AH*. So also will be the interval *GH* to *HO*, and the interval *HO* to *HM*, etc. Moreover the parallelogram made by *EG* and *GH* will be to the parallelogram made by *HI* and *HO*, as the parallelogram made by *HI* and *HO* to the parallelogram made by *NO* and *OM*, for the ratio of the parallelogram made by *GE* and *GH* to the parallelogram made by *HI* and *HO* is composed from the ratio of the line *GE* to the line *HI*, and from the ratio of the line *GH* to the line *HO*; and as *GH* is to *HO*, so is *AG* to *AH*, as we have shown. Therefore the ratio of the parallelogram made by *EG* and *GH* to the parallelogram made by *HI* and *HO* is composed from the ratio *GE* to *HI*, and from the ratio *AG* to *AH*, but as *GE* is to *HI* so by construction will be the square of *HA* to the square of *GA*, or because of proportionality, as the line *AO* to the line *GA*. Therefore the ratio of the parallelogram made by *EG* and *GH* to the parallelogram made by *HI* and *HO*, will be composed of the ratios *AO* to *AG*, and *AG* to *AH*; but the ratio *AO* to *AH* is composed of these two. Therefore the parallelogram made by *GE* and *GH* is to the parallelogram made by *HI* and *HO*, as *OA* to *HA*; or as *HA* to *AG*.

Similarly it can be proved that the parallelogram made by *HI* and *HO* is to the parallelogram made by *ON* and *OM*, as *AO* to *HA*, but the three lines that constitute the ratios of the parallelogams, namely *AO*, *HA*, *GA*, are proportionals by construction.

[46] Therefore the parallelograms made by *GE* and *GH*, by *HI* and *HO*, by *ON* and *OM*, etc. taken indefinitely, will always be continued proportionals in the ratio of the lines *HA* to *GA*. Therefore, from the theorem that is the foundation of this method, as *GH*, the difference of the terms of the progression, is to the smaller term *GA*, so will be the first term of the progression of parallelograms, that is, the parallelogram made by *EG* and *GH*, to the rest of the parallelograms taken infinitely, that is, by the adequation of Archimedes, to the space contained by *HI*, the asymptote *HR*, and the curve *IND* extended infinitely. But as *HG* is to *GA* so, taking as a common side the line *GE*, is the parallelogram made by *GE* and *GH* to the parallelogram made by *GE* and *GA*. Therefore, as the parallelogram made by *GE* and *GH* is to that infinite figure whose base is *HI*, so is the same parallelogram made by *GE* and *GH* to the parallelogram made by *GE* and *GA*; therefore the parallelogram made by *GE* and *GA*, which is the given rectilinear space, adequates to the aforesaid figure. To which if there is added the parallelogram made by *GE* and *GH*, which on account of the minute divisions vanishes and goes to nothing, there remains the truth, which may be easily confirmed by a more lengthy Archimedean demonstration, that the parallelogram *AE* in this kind of hyperbola, is equal to the space contained between the base *GE*, the asymptote *GR*, and the curve *ED*, infinitely produced. Nor is it onerous to extend this discovery to all hyperbolas of this kind, except, as I said, one.

---

### 3.2.2 Brouncker and the rectangular hyperbola, *c.* 1655

The quadrature of the Apollonian, or rectangular, hyperbola ($y = x^{-1}$) had eluded Fermat, but some partial results had been found by de Saint Vincent as early as 1625. When de Saint Vincent's work was eventually published in his massive *Opus geometricum* in 1647, his fellow Jesuit Alphonse Antonio de Sarasa noted that certain areas under the hyperbola are related to each other in the same way as logarithms, but at this stage this was no more than an empirical observation.

A numerical quadrature of the hyperbola was finally discovered by William Brouncker in the early 1650s while he was working with Wallis on the related problem of the quadrature of the circle (see 3.2.3). Brouncker's quadrature was published in 1668 in the third volume of the *Philosophical transactions of the Royal Society*, the first mathematical result to be published in a scientific journal. (Brouncker himself was the first president of the Royal Society, which had been founded in 1660.)

Though an able mathematician, Brouncker was never forthcoming about his methods, and offered only diagrams and results, without any intermediate calculations. He did however, offer the first and almost only seventeenth-century attempt at a convergence proof.

# Brouncker's quadrature of the hyperbola

from Brouncker, 'The squaring of the hyperbola by an infinite series of rational numbers',
*Philosophical transactions of the Royal Society*, 3 (1668), 645–647

*Notation*
Although Brouncker adopted Descartes' superscript notation for powers, he retained Harriot's *a*
rather than Descartes' *x*.

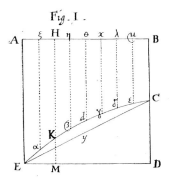

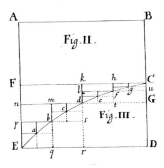

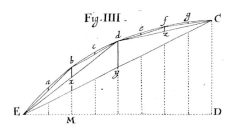

(645)    *Numb.34.*

# PHILOSOPHICAL
# TRANSACTIONS.

Monday, *April* 13. 1668

## The Contents.

*The Squaring of the* Hyperbola *by an infinite series of* Rational *Numbers, together with its Demonstration, by the Right Honourable the Lord Viscount* Brouncker. *An Extract of a Letter sent from* Danzick, *touching some Chymical, Medicinal and Anatomical particulars.* Two Letters, *written by* Dr. John Wallis *to the Publisher; One, concerning the Variety of the Annual High-Tides in respect to several places: the other, concerning some Mistakes of a Book entituled SPECIMINA MATHEMATICA* Francisci Dulaurens, *especially touching a certain Probleme, affirm'd to have been proposed by* Dr. Wallis *to the Mathematicians of all* Europe, *for a solution.* An Account of some *Observations concerning the* true Time of the Tydes, *by* Mr. Hen. Philips. *An Account of three Books : I. W.SENGWERDIUS PH.D.de* Tarantula. *II.REGNERI de GRAEF M.D.* Epistola de nonnullis circa Partes *Genitales* Inventis Novis. *III.JOHANNIS* van *HORNE M.D.* Observationum suarum circa Partes *Genitales* in utroque sexu, *PRODROMUS.*

*The Squaring of the* Hyperbola, *by an infinite series of Rational Numbers, together with its Demonstration, by that Eminent Mathematician, the Right Honourable the Lord Viscount* Brouncker.

What the Acute Dr. *John Wallis* had intimated, some years since, in the Dedication of his Answer to M. *Meibomius de proportionibus*, *vid.* That the World one day would learn from the Noble Lord *Brounker*, the *Quadrature of the Hyperbole*; the Ingenious Reader may see performed in the subjoyned operation, which its Excellent Author was now pleased to communicate, as followeth in his own words;

Z z z                    My

(646)

*My Method for Squaring the* Hyperbola *is this*:

Let AB be one *Asymptote* of the Hyperbola E d C; and let A E and B C be parallel to th'other: Let also A E be to B C as 2 to 1; and let the Parallelogram ABDE equal 1. See *Fig.* 1. And note, that the Letter x every where stands for Multiplication.

Supposing the Reader knows, that E A. $\alpha\zeta$. K H. $\beta\eta$. d $\theta$. $\gamma\kappa$. $\delta\lambda$. $\epsilon\mu$. C B.&c. are in an *Harmonic* series, or a *series reciproca primanorum seu arithmetice proportionalium* ( otherwise he is referr'd for satisfaction to the 87, 88, 89, 90, 91, 92, 93, 94, 95, prop. *Arithm. Infinitor. Wallisij*: )

I say $ ABCdEA = \dfrac{1}{1\times2} + \dfrac{1}{3\times4} + \dfrac{1}{5\times6} + \dfrac{1}{7\times8} + \dfrac{1}{9\times10}$ &c.

$ EdCDE = \dfrac{1}{2\times3} + \dfrac{1}{4\times5} + \dfrac{1}{6\times7} + \dfrac{1}{8\times9} + \dfrac{1}{10\times11}$ &c.

$ EdCyE = \dfrac{1}{2\times3\times4} + \dfrac{1}{4\times5\times6} + \dfrac{1}{6\times7\times8} + \dfrac{1}{8\times9\times10}$ &c.

} *in infinitum.*

For ( *in Fig.* 2, & 3 ) the *Parallelog*.    And ( *in Fig.* 4. ) the *Triangl*.

| | | | *Note*. |
|---|---|---|---|
| $CA = \dfrac{1}{1\times2}$ | | $EdC = \dfrac{1}{2\times3\times4} = \dfrac{\square dD - \square dF}{2}$ | $CA = dD + dF$ |
| $dD = \dfrac{1}{2\times3}$ $dF = \dfrac{1}{3\times4}$ | | $Ebd = \dfrac{1}{4\times5\times6} = \dfrac{\square br - \square bn}{2}$ | $dD = br + bn$ |
| $br = \dfrac{1}{4\times5}$ $bn = \dfrac{1}{5\times6}$ | | $dfC = \dfrac{1}{6\times7\times8} = \dfrac{\square fG - \square fk}{2}$ | $dF = fG + fk$ |
| $fG = \dfrac{1}{6\times7}$ $fk = \dfrac{1}{7\times8}$ | | $Eab = \dfrac{1}{8\times9\times10} = \dfrac{\square aq - \square ap}{2}$ | $br = aq + ap$ |
| $aq = \dfrac{1}{8\times9}$ $ap = \dfrac{1}{9\times10}$ | | $bcd = \dfrac{1}{10\times11\times12} = \dfrac{\square cs - \square cm}{2}$ | $bn = cs + cm$ |
| $cs = \dfrac{1}{10\times11}$ $cm = \dfrac{1}{11\times12}$ | | $def = \dfrac{1}{12\times13\times14} = \dfrac{\square et - \square el}{2}$ | $fG = et + el$ |
| $et = \dfrac{1}{12\times13}$ $el = \dfrac{1}{13\times14}$ | | $fgC = \dfrac{1}{14\times15\times16} = \dfrac{\square gu - \square gh}{2}$ | $fk = gu + gh$ |
| $gu = \dfrac{1}{14\times15}$ $gh = \dfrac{1}{15\times16}$ | | &c. | &c. |
| &c. &c. | | | |

And

$$( 647 )$$

And that therefore in the firſt ſeries half the firſt term is greater than the ſum of the two next, and half this ſum of the ſecond and third greater than the ſum of the four next, and half the ſum of thoſe four greater than the ſum of the next eight, &c. *in infinitum.* For $\frac{1}{2} dD = br + bn$; but $bn > fG$, therefore $\frac{1}{2} dD > br + fG$, &c. And in the *ſecond* ſeries half the firſt term is leſs then the ſum of the two next, and ſecond half this ſum leſs then the ſum of the four next, &c. *in infinitum.*

That the firſt *ſeries* are the *even* terms, *viz.* the $2^d$, $4^{th}$, $6^{th}$, $8^h$, $10^{th}$, &c. and the ſecond, the *odd,* viz. the $1^s$, $3^s$, $5^s$, $7^h$, $9^h$, &c. of the following ſeries, viz. $\frac{1}{1\times2} \cdot \frac{1}{2\times3} \cdot \frac{1}{3\times4}$ &c. *in infinitum* = 1. Whereof *a* being put for the number of terms taken at pleaſure, $\frac{1}{a+a}$ is the laſt, $\frac{a}{a+1}$ is the ſum of all thoſe terms from the beginning, and $\frac{1}{a+1}$ the ſum of the reſt to the end.

That $\frac{1}{4}$ of the firſt terme in the *third* ſeries is leſs than the ſum of the two next, and a quarter of this ſum, leſs than the ſum of the four next, and one fourth of this laſt ſum leſs than the next eight, I thus demonſtrate.

Let a = the $3^d$ or laſt number of any term of the firſt Column, *viz.* of Diviſors,

$$\frac{1}{\frac{a}{x}\frac{a-1}{x}a-2} = \frac{1}{a^3-3a^2+2a} = \frac{16a^3-48a^2+56a-24}{16a^6-96a^5+232a^4-288a^3+184a^2-48a} = A$$

$$\left. \begin{array}{c} \frac{1}{\frac{2a}{x}\frac{2a-1}{x}2a-2} = \frac{1}{8a^3-12a^2+4a} \\[2ex] \frac{1}{\frac{2a-2}{x}\frac{2a-3}{x}2a-4} = \frac{1}{8a^3-36a^2+52a-24} \end{array} \right\} = \frac{16a^3-48a^2+56a-24}{64a^6-384a^5+880a^4-960a^3+496a-96} = B$$

$$\frac{64a^6-384a^5+928a^4-1152a^3+736a^2-192a}{64a^6-384a^5+880a^4-960a^3+496a-96} \times \frac{1}{4}A \gtrless B. \qquad \qquad =$$

And $48a^4 -192a^3 +240a^2 -96a =$ *Exceſs of the Numerator above Denomin.*

But —— The affirm. $>$ the Negat.
That is , $48a^4 +240a^2 > 192a^3 +96a$ $\left.\begin{array}{c} \\ \\ \\ \end{array}\right\}$ if $a > 2$.
Becauſe $a^4 + 5a^2 > 4a^3 + 2a$
$a^3 + 5a > 4a^2 + 2$

Therefore B $> \frac{1}{4}$A.

Therefore $\frac{1}{4}$ of any number of A. or Terms, is leſs than their ſo many reſpective B. that is , than twice ſo many of the next Terms. *Quod, &c.*

Aaaa 2                                    By

### 3.2.3 Wallis's use of indivisibles, 1656

Wallis learned of the theory of indivisibles through Torricelli's *Opera geometrica* (see 2.4.2 and 3.3.1) and saw immediately how to apply the idea to a variety of plane and solid figures. Ultimately he hoped that he could use it to find the elusive and long sought quadrature of the circle.

First Wallis demonstrated that $\sum_{a=0}^{R} a^n$ becomes arbitrarily close to $R^n/(n + 1)$, when $n$ is an integer and when the powers of $a$ are taken at sufficiently small intervals between 0 and $R$. He then went on to show that the same result also holds for fractional and negative values of $n$ (except $n = -1$). These findings were not entirely new; Fermat and Descartes, and probably also Roberval, had arrived at similar conclusions by the early 1640s, at least in a number of special cases, but none had published their discoveries, and Wallis was unaware of them.[3] Further, Wallis's methods were based on numerical sums of infinite sequences rather than on geometric arguments, and he came to rely more and more on numerical interpolation, an approach that was later to prove particularly powerful in the hands of Newton (see 8.1.1). Wallis knew that his results could be demonstrated by traditional geometric methods if required, but argued that he had shown a new way of finding them, more transparent and more widely applicable than those used by 'the Ancients'.

Wallis introduced several new ideas through the pages of the *Arithmetica infinitorum*. His methods were based on 'induction', by which he meant simply that a well established pattern could be assumed to continue indefinitely. He also made the important assertion that a quantity that can be made less than any preassigned amount may be taken to be zero. This last statement was taken up by Newton (5.1.2), Leibniz (8.3), and Euler (10.2.3), and came to be increasingly significant later (see 11.1).

---

3. In the preface to 'Tractatus mechanica' in his *Cogitata physico-mathematica* of 1644, Mersenne gave the correct quadrature for the case $y^4 = x^3$, and attributed it to Descartes. For Fermat, see 3.2.1 above and Mahoney 1994, chapter 5. For Roberval see Auger 1962 and Walker 1932.

## Wallis and sums of squares

from Wallis, *Arithmetica infinitorum*, 1656, Propositions 19–23

---

PROP. XIX. *Lemma.*

SI proponatur feries Quantitatum in *duplicata* ratione Arithmeticè-proportionalium, (five juxta feriem numerorum quadraticorum,) continuè crefcentium, a puncto vel o inchoatarum, ( puta ut 0, 1, 4, 9, 16, &c. ) propofitum fit inquirere, quam habeat illa rationem ad feriem totidem maximæ æqualium?

Fiat invefligatio per modum inductionis, ( ut in prop. 1.)

eritq; $\dfrac{0+1=1}{1+1=2} = \frac{1}{6} = \frac{1}{3} + \frac{1}{6}.$   $\dfrac{0+1+4=5}{4+4+4=12} = \frac{1}{3} + \frac{1}{12}.$

$\dfrac{0+1+4+9=14}{9+9+9+9=36} = \frac{7}{18} = \frac{1}{3} + \frac{1}{18}$   $\dfrac{0+1+4+9+16=30}{16+16+16+16+16=80} = \frac{3}{8} =$

$\frac{1}{24} = \frac{1}{3} + \frac{1}{24}.$   $\dfrac{0+1+4+9+16+25=55}{25+25+25+25+25+25=150} = \frac{11}{30} = \frac{1}{3} + \frac{1}{30}.$

o+

16     *Arithmetica Infinitorum.*     Prop 20

$$\frac{0+1+4+9+16+25+36}{36+36+36+36+36+36+36} = \frac{91}{252} = \frac{13}{36} = \frac{1}{3}+\frac{1}{36}$$ Et fic deinceps.

Ratio proveniens eft ubiq; major quam fubtripla, feu $\frac{1}{3}$ Exceffus autem perpetuò decrefcit prout numerus terminorum augetur; puta $\frac{1}{6}, \frac{1}{12}, \frac{1}{18}, \frac{1}{24}, \frac{1}{30}, \frac{1}{36}$ &c², audto nimirum fractionis denominatore, five confequente rationis, in fingulis locis numero fenario, ( ut patet,) ut fit rationis provenientis exceffus fupra fubtriplum, ea quam habet unitas ad fextuplum numeri terminorum poft o, adeoq; ----

## PROP. XX.     *Theorema.*

SI proponatur feries quantitatum in duplicata ratione Arithmetice-proportionalium (five juxta feriem numerorum quadraticorum ) continue crefcentium, a puncto vel o inchoatarum; ratio quam habet illa ad feriem totidem maxime æqualium, fubtriplam fuperabit; eritq; exceffus, ea ratio quam habet unitas ad fextuplum numeri terminorum poft o; five, quam habet radix quadratica termini primi poft o, ad fextuplum radicis quadraticæ termini maximi.

Puta ( fi terminus poft o primus ponatur 1, & ultimi latus)
$$\frac{1+1}{3} \mathrm{I}^2 + \frac{1+1}{61} \quad \mathrm{I}^2. \text{ Vel(pofito numero terminorum } a, \&$$
ultimi latere $l,) \frac{a}{3}\mathrm{I}^2 + \frac{a}{6a-6}\mathrm{l}.$

Patet ex Prop. præced.

Cùm autem crefcente numero terminorum, exceffus ille fupra rationé fubtriplum ita continuo minuatur, ut tandem quælibet affignabili minor evadat, ( ut patet;) fi in infinitum procedatur, prorfus evaniturus eft. Adeoq; ----

### PROP. XXI.   *Theorema.*

SI pro ponatur feries infinita Quantitatum in duplicata ratione arithmetice-proportionaliũ, (five juxta feriem numerorum quadraticorum,) continue crefcentium, a puncto feu o inchoatarum; erit illa ad feriem totidem maximæ æqualiũm, ut 1 ad 3.

Patet ex præced.

### PROP. XXII.   *Corollarium.*

IDeoq; *Conus vel Pyramis ad Cylindrum vel Prifma (fuper eadem vel æquali bafe æquè altum) eft ut 1 ad 3.*

Conftare enim fupponimus tam Conum quam Pyramidem ex infinitis planis fimilibus & parallelis, in duplicata ratione Arithmetice-proportionalium conftitutis, quorum minimum fupponitur Punctum, maximum verò bafis; (per ea quæ diximus ad Prop 6. Con. Sect.) Cylindrus autem vel Prifma, ex totidem maximo æqualibus (ut patet:) Ratio igitur eft ut 1 ad 3. per præced.

### PROP. XXIII.   *Coroll:*

ITem *Complementum Semi-parabolæ (intellige figuram AOT quæ cum ipfa femi-parabola complet Parallelogrammum,) eft ad Parallelogrammum TD (fuper eadem vel æquali bafe æquè-altum) ut 1 ad 3. (Et confequenter, ipfa femi-parabola eft ad idem Parallelogrammum, ut 2 ad 3.)*

Efto enim Figuræ AOT vertex A, diameter AT, bafis TO, eiq; parallela quotlibet (Eafem inter & verticem) TO, TO, &c. Quoniam funt (per prop. 21 Con Sect.) recta DO, LO, &c. in fubduplicata ratione rectarum AD, AD, &c. Erunt

E e                                    è contra

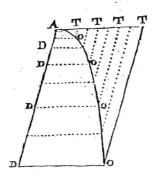

18        *Arithmetica Infinitorum.*        Prop.24.

è contra ipfæ AD, AD, &c. hoc eſt TO, TO, &c. in ratione duplicata ipfarum DO, DU, &c. hoc eſt AT, AT, &c. Tota igitur figura AOT ( conſtans ex infinitis rectis TO, TO, &c. in duplicata ratione rectarum AT, AT, &c. Arithmetice proportionalium ) erit ad Parallelogrammum æquè altum TD ( conſtans ex totidem rectis ipſi TO maximæ æqualibus) ut 1 ad 3. per prop. 21. (Quod erat oſtendendum.)Et conſequenter , ſemiparabola AOD ( parallelogrammi reliduum) ad idem Parallelogrammum ut 2 ad 3.

---

TRANSLATION

---

## PROPOSITION XIX *Lemma*

Suppose there is given a series of quantities in duplicate ratio to arithmetic proportionals (or as a series of square numbers), continually increasing, beginning from a point or 0 (thus as 0, 1, 4, 9, 16, etc.); it is proposed to enquire, what ratio does it have to a series of the same number of terms equal to the greatest?

The investigation can be carried out by means of induction (as in proposition 1), and we will have:

$$\frac{0+1=1}{1+1=2} = \frac{1}{6} = \frac{1}{3}+\frac{1}{6}. \qquad \frac{0+1+4=5}{4+4+4=12} = \frac{1}{3}+\frac{1}{12}.$$

$$\frac{0+1+4+9=14}{9+9+9+9=36} = \frac{7}{18} = \frac{1}{3}+\frac{1}{18}.$$

$$\frac{0+1+4+9+16=30}{16+16+16+16+16=80} = \frac{3}{8} = \frac{9}{24} = \frac{1}{3}+\frac{1}{24}.$$

$$\frac{0+1+4+9+16+25=55}{25+25+25+25+25+25=150} = \frac{11}{30} = \frac{1}{3}+\frac{1}{30}.$$

$$\frac{0+1+4+9+16+25+36=91}{36+36+36+36+36+36+36=252} = \frac{13}{36} = \frac{1}{3}+\frac{1}{36}.$$

And so on.

The ratio that arises is everywhere greater than one third, or $\frac{1}{3}$. Moreover, the excess decreases continually as the number of terms is increased; thus $\frac{1}{6}$, $\frac{1}{12}$, $\frac{1}{18}$, $\frac{1}{24}$, $\frac{1}{30}$, $\frac{1}{36}$, etc.; indeed the increased denominator of the fraction, or the consequent term of the ratio, is in each place a multiple of 6 (as is clear) which makes the excess above one third, of the ratio arising, one over six times the number of terms after 0, and therefore . . .

## PROPOSITION XX *Theorem*

Suppose there is given a series of quantities in duplicate ratio to arithmetic proportionals (or as a series of square numbers) continually increasing, beginning from a point or 0, its ratio to a series of the same number of terms equal to the greatest will exceed one third; and the excess will be one over six times the number of terms after 0, or the square root of the first term after 0 over six times the square root of the greatest term.

Thus (if for the first term after 0 there is put 1, and for the root of the last [$l$]), $\frac{l+1}{3}l^2 + \frac{l+1}{6l}l^2$. Or (putting $a$ for the number of terms, and $l$ for the last root) $\frac{a}{3}l^2 + \frac{a}{6a-6}l.$

This is clear from the preceding proposition.

Moreover, since the number of terms is increasing, the excess above one third will thus continually decrease, so that at length it will pass below any assignable quantity (as is clear); if one proceeds to infinity, it will eventually vanish. And therefore . . . [17]

## PROPOSITION XXI *Theorem*

Suppose there is given an infinite series of quantities in duplicate ratio to arithmetic proportionals (or as a series of square numbers), continually increasing, beginning from a point or 0; it will be to a series of the same number of terms equal to the greatest as 1 to 3.

This is clear from what has gone before.

## PROPOSITION XXII *Corollary*

*Therefore a cone or pyramid to a cylinder or prism (on the same or equal base and of equal height) is as* 1 *to* 3.

For let us suppose the cone or pyramid to consist of infinitely many similar and parallel planes, being in duplicate ratio to arithmetic proportionals, of which the smallest is supposed to be a point, but the greatest the base (by what was said in Proposition 6 of *De conicis sectionibus*); moreover the cylinder or prism is [composed] of the same number equal to the greatest (as is clear). Therefore the ratio is as 1 to 3, by what has gone before.

PROPOSITION XXIII *Corollary*

*Likewise the complement of a half-parabola (to be understood as the figure AOT which with the half-parabola itself completes the parallelogram) is to the parallelogram TD (on the same or equal base and of equal height) as 1 to 3. (And consequently the half-parabola itself is to the same parallelogram as 2 to 3.)*

For let there be the figure *AOT* with vertex *A*, diameter *AT*, base *TO*, and as many parallels as one likes (between that and the vertex) *TO, TO*, etc. Since (by Proposition 21 of *De sectionibus conicis*) the lines *DO, DO*, etc. are in subduplicate ratio to the lines *AD, AD*, etc., [18] conversely *AD, AD* etc., that is, *TO, TO*, etc. will be in duplicate ratio to *DO, DO*, etc., that is, *AT, AT*, etc. Therefore the whole figure *AOT* (consisting of infinitely many lines *TO, TO*, etc. in duplicate ratio to the lines *AT, AT*, etc., which are arithmetic proportionals) will be to the parallelogram *TD* of equal height (consisting of the same number of lines equal to the greatest *TO*) as 1 to 3 by Proposition 21 (which was to be shown). And consequently, the half-parabola *AOD* (the remainder of the parallelogram) will be to the same parallelogram as 2 to 3.

------

### 3.2.4 Mercator and the rectangular hyperbola, 1668

Mercator's method of finding the area under a hyperbola, published in his *Logarithmotechnia* of 1668, was based on the work of Wallis in the *Arithmetica infinitorum* of 1656. Wallis, like Fermat earlier, had been unable to deal with the rectangular hyperbola because his 'integration rule' (that $\sum_{a=0}^{R} a^n$ approximates to $\frac{R^n}{n+1}$) broke down for $n = -1$. Mercator got around the problem by a change of axes so that he was handling $\frac{1}{1+a}$ instead of $\frac{1}{a}$, and then carried out long division to produce a power series for $\frac{1}{1+a}$. He was then able to 'integrate' term by term using Wallis's rule.

Mercator used the known relationship between logarithms and sections of area under a rectangular hyperbola to check his procedure. The fact that the area for $1 + a = 1.21$ (namely, 0.190620361) was exactly twice that for $1 + a = 1.1$ (namely, 0.095310181) convinced him that his calculations, and therefore his method, were correct.

It was almost certainly the publication of *Logarithmotechnia* that prompted Brouncker to publish his own quadrature of the hyperbola worked out some years previously (see 3.2.4), and Newton to write an account of the discoveries he had made in 1664–65 (see 4.1.1 and 8.1.2).

---

## Mercator's quadrature of the hyperbola

from Mercator, *Logarithmotechnia*, 1668, Proposition 14

---

18   *LOGARITHMOTECHNIA.*

### Propofitio XIV.

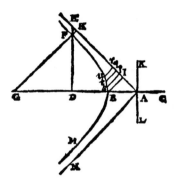

Sit Hyperbole *M B F*, cujus latus rectum *K L* æquale fit tranfver-
fo *B C*; erunt afymptoti *A N* & *A E* ad angulos rectos, & quadratum *D F* æquale rectangulo *C D B* per 21. I. Conicor. Ex *B*
& cadant perpendiculares ad afymptoton *B I* & *F H*. Dico, *A H*
effe ad *A I*, ut *B I* ad *F H*.

Demonftratio.   Sit $AB = 1 \sqsubset AC$

$BC = AB + AC = 2$

$BD = a$

$AD = AB + BD = 1 + a = DE$

$CD = BC + BD = 2 + a$

$CD \star BD = 2 + a \text{ in } a = 2a + aa = Q : DF$

$DF = \sqrt{2a + aa} = DG$

$AG = AD + DG = 1 + a + \sqrt{2a + aa}$

$\sqrt{2} \cdot 1 :: AG. AH$

$AH = \dfrac{1 + a + \sqrt{2a + aa}}{\sqrt{2}}$

$EF = DE - DF = 1 + a - \sqrt{2a + aa}$

$\sqrt{2} \cdot 1 :: EF. FH$

*FH*

*LOGARITHMOTECHNIA.*    29

$$FH = \frac{1 + a - \sqrt{2a + aa}}{\sqrt{2}}$$

Ducatur $AH$ in $FH$;

ponendo $1 + a = c$, & $\sqrt{2a + aa} = d$

erit $\quad 1 + 2a + aa = cc$ ⎫ subtrahe
& $\qquad\qquad 2a + aa = dd$ ⎭

$$\underline{\qquad 1 \qquad\qquad = cc - dd}$$

$$\frac{cc - dd}{\sqrt{2} * \sqrt{2}} = \frac{1}{2} = AH * FH \qquad \alpha$$

$$\sqrt{2} . 1 :: AB . AI$$

$$AI = \frac{1}{\sqrt{2}}$$

$$AI * BI = \frac{1}{\sqrt{2}} * \frac{1}{\sqrt{2}} = \frac{1}{2} \qquad \beta$$

Ergo per $\alpha$ & $\beta$, $AH * FH = AI * BI$

& $AH . AI :: BI FH \qquad$ q. e. d.

### Propofitio XV.

In diagrammate præcedenti, pofitâ $AI = BI = 1$, & $HI = a$; oporteat invenire $FH$.

Dic per præcedentem: ut $AH$ ad $AI$, ita $BI$ ad $FH$; hoc eſt,

$1 + a . 1 :: 1 . \frac{1}{1 + a}$; nimirum $FH$ æqualit eſt unitati divifæ per $1 + a$. Perficitur autem divifio ipfo opere fic :

$$
\begin{array}{ll}
\begin{array}{l}
b \quad c \;)\; d \\
1+a \;)\; 1 \\
\quad\; f \quad g \\
\quad\; 1+a \\
\overline{\quad\; h \quad i} \\
\quad\; o - a \\
\qquad 1 \quad m \\
\quad \overline{-a - aa} \\
\qquad\; n \quad o \\
\qquad\; o + aa \\
\qquad\qquad\quad r \\
\qquad\; q \quad 3 \\
\quad \overline{aa + a} \\
\qquad\qquad\; t \\
\qquad\; 5 \quad 3 \\
\qquad\; o - a
\end{array}
&
\begin{array}{l}
e \\
1 \\
\\
\\
k \\
- a \\
\\
\\
p \\
+ aa \\
\\
\\
u \\
3 \\
- a
\end{array}
\end{array}
$$

Ap-

30                    *LOGARITHMOTECHNIA.*

$$\overset{b}{\phantom{}}\overset{c}{\phantom{}}\quad\overset{d}{\phantom{}}\qquad\overset{e}{\phantom{}}\qquad\overset{e}{\phantom{}}\overset{b}{\phantom{}}\overset{c}{\phantom{}}\qquad\overset{f}{\phantom{}}\overset{g}{\phantom{}}$$

Applica $1+a$ ad $1$, oritur $1$; tum $1$ in $1+a$ producit $1+a$ fub-

ducendum ex $1$, & reſtat $o-a$. Rurſus $1+a$ applicetur ad $o-a$,

oritur $-a$; tum $-a$ in $o-a$ producit $-a-aa$, fubducendum ex

$o-a$, & reſtat $o+aa$. Ad hoc applica $1+a$, oritur $+aa$; quod

ductum in $1+a$ gignit $aa+a$, fubducendum ex $o+aa$, & reſtat $o-a$.

Atque ita continuatâ operatione, deprehenditur $\dfrac{1}{1+a} = 1-a+aa-a^3$

$+a^4$ (&c.) $= FH.$

*Notation*

Mercator used a mixture of contemporary notations and some inventions of his own. In this extract we see Harriot's *a*, Oughtred's :: for equality of ratios, the symbol ∗ invented by Mercator's friend John Pell, and his own $Q : DF$ for $DF^2$.

TRANSLATION

---

Proposition XIV

Suppose there is a hyperbola *MBF* whose *latus rectum KL* is equal to the transverse diameter *BC*; there will be asymptotes *AN* and *AE* at right angles, and the square of *DF* will be equal to the rectangle *CDB* by Proposition I.21 of the Conics [of Apollonius]. From *B* there also fall perpendiculars to the asymptotes, *BI* and also *FH*. I say that *AH* is to *AI* as *BI* to *FH*.

Demonstration. Let $AB = 1 = AC$.

$$BC = AB + AC = 2$$
$$BD = a$$
$$AD = AB + BD = 1 + a = DE$$
$$CD = BC + BD = 2 + a$$
$$CD * BD = 2 + a \quad \text{times} \quad a = 2a + aa = Q : DF$$
$$DF = \sqrt{2a + aa} = DG$$
$$AG = AD + DG = 1 + a + \sqrt{2a + aa}$$
$$\sqrt{2}.1 :: AG.AH$$
$$AH = \frac{1 + a + \sqrt{2a + aa}}{\sqrt{2}}$$
$$EF = DE - DF = 1 + a - \sqrt{2a + aa}$$

$$\sqrt{2}.1 :: EF.FH$$
$$FH = \frac{1 + a - \sqrt{2a + aa}}{\sqrt{2}}$$

[29]

Multiply *AH* by *FH*;

putting $1 + a = c$ and $\sqrt{2a + aa} = d$ we will have

$$1 + 2a + aa \; = \; cc$$
$$\text{and} \qquad 2a + aa \; = \; dd$$
$$\overline{\phantom{\text{and}} \qquad 1 \qquad\quad = \; cc - dd}$$

$$\frac{cc - dd}{\sqrt{2} * \sqrt{2}} = \frac{1}{2} = AH * FH \qquad\qquad \alpha$$

$$\sqrt{2}.1 :: AB.AI$$

$$AI = \frac{1}{\sqrt{2}}$$

$$AI * BI = \frac{1}{\sqrt{2}} * \frac{1}{\sqrt{2}} = \frac{1}{2} \qquad\qquad \beta$$

Therefore by $\alpha$ and $\beta$, $AH * FH = AI * BI$, and

$$AH.AI :: BI.FH$$

*which was to be proved.*

Proposition XV

In the preceding diagram, putting $AI = BI = 1$, and $HI = a$; it is required to find $FH$.

I say, by what has gone before, that as $AH$ is to $AI$, so is $BI$ to $FH$; that is, $1 + a.1 ::$ $1.\frac{1}{1+a}$; certainly $FH$ is equal to one divided by $1 + a$. Moreover the division can be carried out in this way:

$$
\begin{array}{r}
1 + a) \qquad 1 \phantom{+aaaa} \\
\underline{1 + a \phantom{aa}} \\
0 - a \phantom{aa} \\
\underline{-a \quad -aa} \\
0 \quad +aa \\
\underline{aa \quad +a} \\
0 \quad -a
\end{array}
$$

[30] Dividing $1 + a$, into 1 there arises 1, then 1 times $1 + a$ produces $1 + a$ to be subtracted from 1, and there remains $0 - a$. Again $1 + a$ is divided into $0 - a$, there arises $-a$; then $-a$ times $[1 + a]$ produces $-a - aa$, to be subtracted from $0 - a$, and there remains $0 + aa$. This is divided by $1 + a$, there arises $+aa$; which multiplied by $1 + a$ produces $aa + a^3$, to be subtracted from $0 + aa$, and there remains $0 - a^3$. And having thus continued the operation, there is to be had $\dfrac{1}{1 + aa} = 1 - a + aa - a^3 + a^4$ (etc.) $= FH$.

## 3.3 A METHOD OF CUBATURE

### 3.3.1 Torricelli's infinite solid, 1644

One of the most remarkable examples of the early use of indivisibles was Torricelli's discovery of the cubature (volume) of the solid formed by rotation of a rectangular hyperbola about one of its asymptotes. Torricelli treated the solid as a 'sum' of nested cylindrical surfaces, and concluded correctly that the solid, though unbounded, was of finite volume. The result was published in his *Opera geometrica* of 1644.

---

### The cubature of an infinite solid
from Torricelli, *Opera geometrica*, 1644, 115–116

---

### Theorema.

S Olidum acutum hyperbolicum infinitè longum, fectum plano ad axem erecto, vnà cum cylindro fuæ bafis, æquale eft cylindro cuidam recto, cuius bafis diameter fit latus verfum, fiue axis hyperbolæ, altitudo verò fit æqualis femidiametro bafis ipfius acuti folidi .

Efto hyperbola cuius afymptoti *a b*, *a c* angulum rectum contineant; fumptoq; in hyperbola quolibet puncto *d*, ducatur *d c* æquidiftans ipfi *a b*, & *d p* æquidiftans *a c*. Tù conuertatur vniuerfa figura circa axê *a b*. ità vt fiat folidum acutum byperbolicum *e b d*, vnà cum cylindro fuæ bafis *f e d c*. Poducatur *b a* in *h* . ita vt *a h*. æqualis fit integro axi, fiue lateri verfo hyperbolæ. Et circa diametrum

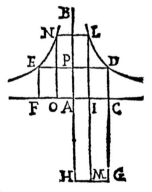

*a h* intelligatur circulus erectus ad afymptoton *a c* : & fuper bafi *a h* concipiatur cylindrus rectus *a c g h*, cuius altitudo fit *a c*, nempe femidiameter bafis acuti folidi . Dico folidum vniuerfum *f e b d c*, quanquam fine fine longum, æquale tamen effe cylindro *a c g h*.

Accipiatur in recta *a c* quodlibet punctum *i*, & per *i* intelligatur ducta fuperficies cylindrica *o n l i* in folido acuto

P  2                 com-

### 116    *De folido Hyperbolico*

compræhenfa circa axem *ab*: item circulus *im* in cylindro *acgh* æquidiftans bafi *ah*.

Erit ergo prædicta fuperficies cylindrica *onli* ad circulum *im*, vt rectangulum per axem *ol*, ad quadratum radij circuli *im*; nempe vt rectangulum *ol*, ad quadratum femiaxis hyperbolæ; & ideo æqualis ex lemmate. Et hoc femper verum erit, vbicunq; fumatur punctum *i*. Propterea omnes fimul fuperficies cylindricæ, hoc eft ipfum folidum acutum *ebd*, vna cum cylindro bafis *fedc*, æquale erit omnibus circulis fimul, hoc eft cylindro *acgh*. Quod erat &c.

---

TRANSLATION

Theorem

An infinitely long acute hyperbolic solid, cut by a vertical plane through its axis, and the same as a cylinder at its base, is equal to a straight cylinder, the diameter of whose base is the *latus versum* or axis of the hyperbola, but whose altitude is equal to the semidiameter of the base of the acute solid itself.

Let this be a hyperbola, whose asymptotes *ab*, *ac* contain a right angle; and taking any point *d* on the hyperbola, there is drawn *dc* parallel to *ab*, and *dp* parallel to *ac*. Then the whole figure is turned about the axis *ab*, so that it creates an acute hyperbolic solid *ebd*, the same as a cylinder at its base *fedc*. Produce *ba* to *h* so that *ah* is equal to the whole axis, or *latus versum* of the hyperbola. And around the diameter *ah* there is understood to be a circle standing against the asymptote *ac*; and on the base *ah* there is constructed a straight cylinder *acgh*, whose altitude is *ac*, namely the semidiameter of the base of the acute solid. I say that the whole solid *febdc*, although not of finite length, is nevertheless equal to the cylinder *acgh*.

Let there be taken on the line *ac* any point *i*, and through *i* it is understood that there is drawn a cylindrical surface *onli* contained in the acute solid [116] around the axis *ab*; likewise the circle *im* in the cylinder *acgh* parallel to the base *ah*.

Therefore the said cylindrical surface *onli* is to the circle *im*, as the rectangle *ol* through the axis is to the square of the radius of the circle *im*; namely as the rectangle *ol* to the square of the semiaxis of the hyperbola; and therefore equal by the lemma. And this will always be true wherever the point *I* is taken. Therefore all the cylindrical surfaces taken at once, that is the acute solid *ebd* together with the cylindrical base *fedc*, will be equal to all the circles at once, that is the cylinder *acgh*. Which was to be demonstrated.

---

## 3.4 A METHOD OF RECTIFICATION

### 3.4.1 Neile and the semicubical parabola, 1657

In 1637 Descartes claimed that it was not possible to compare a curve with a straight line, in other words, that finding a line equal in length to a given curve (rectification) was in general impossible.[4] Twenty year later, however, William Neile, then a student at Wadham College, Oxford, succeeded in finding the length of the curve now known as the semicubical parabola (in modern notation $y^2 = kx^3$) by means of a clever geometrical construction that compared length with area. Neile's method was almost immediately re-written algebraically by both Wallis and Brouncker, and Wallis sent all three methods in a letter to Christiaan Huygens, and published them in an appendix to his *Tractatus duo de cycloide …et de cissoide* in 1659.

Meanwhile, in the Netherlands, Hendrick van Heuraet had independently found the same result, also in 1657, giving rise to a priority dispute that rumbled on for years between Wallis and Huygens, the respective champions of Neile and van Heuraet. In 1659, Fermat, isolated in Toulouse, and unaware of either Neile's work or van Heuraet's, also wrote a treatise on rectification, entitled 'De linearum curvarum cum lineis rectis comparatione dissertatio geometrica' ('Geometric dissertation on the comparison of curved lines with straight lines').

The extract below is Wallis's description of Neile's method, taken from his 1659 letter to Huygens. Neile made no use of co-ordinate geometry, but as a first step towards understanding his method, it is perhaps helpful to consider $AD$ and $AI$ in his diagram as $x$- and $y$-axes, respectively. Neile constructed the following sequence of curves, whose equations are also given in modern notation.

| | | |
|---|---|---|
| (1) curve | $AbC$ | $y = x^{\frac{1}{2}}$ |
| (2) curve | $AfC$ | $y = \int_0^x t^{\frac{1}{2}} dt = \frac{2}{3} x^{\frac{3}{2}}$ |
| (3) straight line | $IsS$ | $y = 1$ |
| (4) curve | $IhH$ | $y = \sqrt{1+x}$ |

An ordinate of curve (2) $AfC$, is defined as the 'area-so-far' under curve (1) $AbC$. Taking a small section along the curve $AfC$, Neile treated it as the hypotenuse of a small right-angled triangle, and applied Pythagoras' theorem to find its length. In modern notation we might write $(\delta s)^2 = (\delta x)^2 + (\delta y)^2$, where $\delta x$ is a small change in the $x$ direction (*ee* in Neile's diagram). The length $\delta y$ is, by definition, the change in area under $AbC$ for the same $\delta x$. Then $\delta y = x^{\frac{1}{2}} \delta x$ and so $\delta s = \sqrt{1+x}\, \delta x$. Neile could now construct a further curve (4) $IhH$ whose 'area-so-far' represents 'length-so-far' of $AfC$. Neile recognised that $IhH$ is in fact a section of a parabola, and so its quadrature was already known and the problem was solved.

---

4. Descartes 1637, 90–91.

Neile's argument is entirely geometric; nevertheless he came very close in this particular case to what later became known as the fundamental theorem of calculus, observing that the rate of change of 'area-so-far' for the curve *AbC* reproduces the curve *AbC* itself. But his construction was for one special curve only, and he had no general algorithm for the calculation of areas or tangents. (Isaac Barrow in his *Lectiones geometricae* of 1670 likewise constructed a curve representing 'area-so-far', and made the relationship between area and tangent more explicit. For this reason Barrow is sometimes credited with having foreseen the fundamental theorem of calculus, but by then Barrow had seen some of Newton's early work, in which the fundamental theorem had been made clear.)

---

### Neile's rectification of the semicubical parabola

from Wallis, *Tractatus duo de cycloide …et de cissoide …et de curvarum*, 1659, 92

---

*Curva Pa-*
*raboloidis*
*Semicubi-*
*calis.*
**Fig. 23.**

Nelii demonſtratio,quam (ut dictum eſt) ante duos annos vulgavit, hæc erat.

*Sit* A b C D *parabola recta; cujus axis* A D *dividatur in æquales partes minimas* e e; *atque ad puncta* e *ordinatim applicentur* e f *recta, parabolis* A e b *proportionales. Et fiat* D S I *rectangulum, ad parabolam* A D C, *ut* A D *ad* D C. *Denique fit* e h *ubique æqualis potentiâ utriſque* e s, e b.

*Dico primo, eandem eſſe inter ſe proportionem figura* A D H I, *rectanguli* D I, *& parabola* A D C, *qua eſt linearum* A f C *curva, & rectarum* A D, D C.

2°. *Rectas* e h *eſſe ordinatim applicatas in Parabola.*

*Sunt enim recta* e f, *per conſtructionem, parabolis* A e b *proportionales ; & propterea rectarum differentia, commode repreſentantur per rectangula* e e b. *Rectangula* e e s *ſunt æqualia: (eorumque omnium ſumma, ad ſummam omnium* e e b, *ut* A D *ad* D C;) *repreſentant itaque rectas* e e. *Recta* f f *ſunt æquales potentiâ tum rectis* e e *tum rectarum* e f *differentiis. Et rectangula* e e h *ſunt ubique in eadem proportione ad quantitatum illarum repreſentativas. Conſtat itaque propoſitionis pars prior.*

*Quadrata rectarum* e b *ſunt arithmetice proportionalia. Quadrata rectarum* e e *ſunt æqualia. Ergo & quadrata* e h *ſunt Arithmetice proportionalia; ipſaque* E H *recta quadratorum arithmetice proportionalium latera : adeoque ſunt ut ſeries ordinatim-applicatarum in parabola.*

*Et conſequenter ;* Exhiberi poterit linea recta æqualis curvæ A F C.

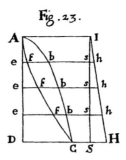

Fig. 23.

### TRANSLATION

Neile's demonstration which (as has been said) he made public two years ago, was this.

*Let* AbCD *be an erect parabola; whose axis* AD *is divided into equal small parts* ee; *and to each point* e *are applied ordinates* ef, *proportional the parabolic area* AeB. *And let the rectangle* DSI *to the parabola* ADC, *be as* AD *to* DC. *And then let the square of* eh *be everywhere equal to the squares of both* es *and* eb *together.*

*I say first that the figures* ADHI, *the rectangle* DI, *and the parabola* ADC, *have the same ratio to each other as the curved line* AfC, *and the straight lines* AD, AC.

*Second, the lines* eh *are ordinates of a parabola.*

*For the lines* ef *are, by construction, proportional to a parabolic area* Aeb; *and therefore the differences of the lines are conveniently represented by the rectangles* eeb. *The rectangles* ees *are equal (and the sum of all of them to the sum of all* eeb *is as* AD *to* DC), *and therefore represent the lines* ee. *The squares of the lines* ff *are equal to the squares of the lines* ee *together with the squares of the differences of the lines* ef. *And the rectangles* eeh *are everywhere in the same proportion to the representations of those quantities. Therefore the first part of the proposition stands.*

*The squares of the lines* eb *are arithmetic proportionals. The squares of the lines* ee *are equals. Therefore the squares of* eh *are also arithmetic proportionals; and the lines* [eh] *are the sides of these arithmetically proportional squares; and therefore as a series of ordinates of a parabola.*

*And consequently.* It is possible to exhibit a straight line equal to the curve AFC.

# CHAPTER 4

# THE CALCULUS OF NEWTON AND OF LEIBNIZ

We have seen in Chapter 3 that many of the methods and ideas that were eventually absorbed into the differential and integral calculus were already emerging from the late 1620s onwards. Only with the work of Newton in the 1660s and Leibniz in the 1670s, however, did the pieces come together in a recognizable whole. Both Newton and Leibniz, working independently and from different starting points, discovered systematic rules for finding tangents and areas, and both observed what on the face of it is quite unexpected: that the two kinds of problem are intimately related. Differentiation and integration turn out to be inverse processes. This discovery is now known as the Fundamental Theorem of the Calculus, but in the seventeenth century it was not yet a theorem. Rather, like so much of the mathematics of this innovative period it was a purely empirical discovery.

## 4.1 THE CALCULUS OF NEWTON

### 4.1.1 The chronology of Newton's calculus

Newton's development of the calculus in the mid 1660s was a complex process that brought together several different strands of thought. In the late 1960s the manuscripts associated with his discoveries were transcribed, translated, and annotated by D T Whiteside in the first of eight volumes of Newton's mathematical papers, and they are well worth exploring, though for beginners the amount and variety of material can be daunting. It is clear that Newton developed the essentials of his calculus, which he later called his method of fluxions, over one astonishingly productive year from the autumn of 1664 to the autumn of 1665, during which he passed his twenty-second birthday.

For most of this period Newton worked alone at his home in Lincolnshire, but was by no means oblivious of earlier work. From Descartes' *La géométrie*, which he read in September 1664, he gleaned ideas about the algebraic handling of curves, tangents, and curvature, while some of his most important ideas on quadrature were inspired by his reading of Wallis's *Arithmetica infinitorum* later that same autumn. To all this Newton added discoveries of his own, not least the general binomial theorem (see 8.1.1), and his intuition of lines and areas as 'fluent' quantities whose rates of change were measured by 'fluxions'. By the summer of 1665 Newton had recognized the inverse relationship between tangent and area problems, and by autumn of that year was treating both by the method of fluxions.

The diagram below is reproduced to give some sense of the richness and complexity of the ideas that went into the calculus. It also serves as a useful reminder that mathematical progress in any but the simplest problems is rarely straightforwardly linear.

## The chronology of Newton's calculus
as reconstructed by D T Whiteside in Newton 1967–1981, I, 154

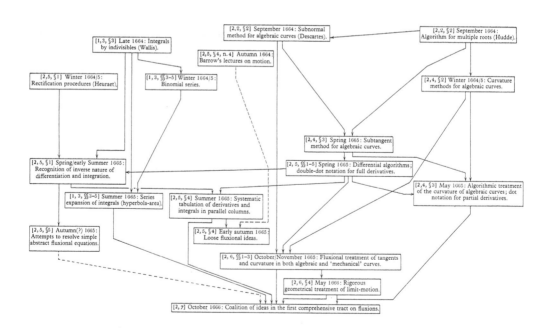

### 4.1.2 Newton's treatise on fluxions and series, 1671

As far as we know, Newton made no attempt to communicate his discoveries until prompted to do so by the publication of Mercator's *Logarithmotechnia* in 1668, from which it was clear that Mercator too had discovered the quadrature of the hyperbola as an infinite series (see 3.2.4). Newton responded with a treatise entitled 'De analysi per aequationes infinitas' ('On analysis by infinite equations'), in which he set out some of his own results on the integration of infinite series, results that were considerably more sophisticated than Mercator's. In 1669 he showed 'De analysi' to Isaac Barrow in Cambridge and to John Collins in London and the treatise probably helped persuade Barrow to resign the Lucasian chair of mathematics in Newton's favour, but for the time being it went no further. The following year, Newton began to write what he referred to as a 'larger Tract' showing how to use his methods of series and fluxions to solve a range of problems, and by late 1671 it was close to completion. He planned to have it printed alongside his Cambridge lectures on optics, but the controversy that erupted around his theory of light and colour early in 1672 put paid to that scheme. Newton withdrew not only the lectures but also the treatise on fluxions, setting back the publication of his most important mathematical discoveries for more than thirty years.

'De analysi', written in 1669, was eventually published in 1711, by William Jones. The 1671 treatise on fluxions, however, was not printed until 1736, translated into English by John Colson under the title *The method of fluxions, and infinite series*. By this time it was long out of date, but it was, and remains, a text of enormous historical interest for what it tells us about Newton's achievements in the calculus by 1671. The extract below shows how to find the relationship between fluxions ($\dot{x}$ and $\dot{y}$) from a relationship between fluents ($x$ and $y$) and, conversely, how to find fluents from fluxions.

---

### Newton's 1671 treatise on fluxions

from Newton, *The method of fluxions, and infinite series*, 1736, 21–22, 24–26, 44–46

Eighteenth Century Collection Online, Gale Digital Collection

---

*Notation*

Recall from Chapter 2 that in expressions involving ratios :: is to be read as =.

# PROB. I.

*The Relation of the Flowing Quantities to one another being given, to determine the Relation of their Fluxions.*

## SOLUTION.

1. Difpofe the Equation, by which the given Relation is exprefs'd, according to the Dimenfions of fome one of its flowing Quantities, fuppofe $x$, and multiply its Terms by any Arithmetical Progreffion, and then by $\frac{\dot{x}}{x}$. And perform this Operation feparately for every one of the flowing Quantities. Then make the Sum of all the Products equal to nothing, and you will have the Equation required.

2. EXAMPLE I. If the Relation of the flowing Quantities $x$ and $y$ be $x^3 - ax^2 + axy - y^3 = 0$; firft difpofe the Terms according to $x$, and then according to $y$, and multiply them in the following manner.

| Mult. | $x^3$ | $-ax^2$ | $+axy$ | $-y^3$ | $\bigg\vert$ | $-y^3$ | $+axy$ | $\begin{matrix}-ax^2\\+x^3\end{matrix}$ |
|---|---|---|---|---|---|---|---|---|
| by | $\frac{3\dot{x}}{x}$ . | $\frac{2\dot{x}}{x}$ . | $\frac{\dot{x}}{x}$ . | $0$ | | $\frac{3\dot{y}}{y}$ . | $\frac{\dot{y}}{y}$ . | $0$ |
| makes | $3\dot{x}x^2$ | $-2a\dot{x}x$ | $+a\dot{x}y$ | $*$ | | $-3\dot{y}y^2$ | $+a\dot{y}x$ | $*$ |

The Sum of the Products is $3\dot{x}x^2 - 2a\dot{x}x + a\dot{x}y - 3\dot{y}y^2 + a\dot{y}x = 0$, which Equation gives the Relation between the Fluxions $\dot{x}$ and $\dot{y}$. For if you take $x$ at pleafure, the Equation $x^3 - ax^2 + axy - y^3 = 0$ will give $y$. Which being determined, it will be $\dot{x} : \dot{y} :: 3y^2 - ax : 3x^2 - 2ax + ay$.

3. Ex. 2. If the Relation of the Quantities $x$, $y$, and $z$, be exprefs'd by the Equation $2y^3 + x^2y - 2cyz + 3yz^2 - z^3 = 0$,

| Mult. | $2y^3 \begin{matrix}+xx\times y\\-2cz\\+3z^2\end{matrix} -z^3$ | $\bigg\vert$ | $yx^2 \begin{matrix}+2y^3\\-2cyz\\+3yz^2\\-z^3\end{matrix}$ | $\bigg\vert$ | $-z^3 +3yz^2 -2cyz +x^2y +2y^3$ |
|---|---|---|---|---|---|
| by | $\frac{2\dot{y}}{y}$ . $0$ . $-\frac{\dot{y}}{y}$ | | $\frac{2\dot{x}}{x}$ . $0$ . | | $\frac{3\dot{z}}{z}$ . $\frac{2\dot{z}}{z}$ . $\frac{\dot{z}}{z}$ . $0$ . |
| makes | $4\dot{y}y^2$ $*$ $+\frac{\dot{y}z^3}{y}$ | | $2\dot{x}xy$ $*$ | | $-3\dot{z}z^2 +6\dot{z}zy -2c\dot{z}y$ $*$ |

Where-

Wherefore the Relation of the Celerities of Flowing, or of the Fluxions $\dot{x}$, $\dot{y}$, and $\dot{z}$, is $4\dot{y}y^2 + \frac{\dot{y}z^3}{y} + 2\dot{x}xy - 3\dot{z}z^2 + 6\dot{z}zy - 2c\dot{z}y = 0$.

4. But since there are here three flowing Quantities, $x$, $y$, and $z$, another Equation ought also to be given, by which the Relation among them, as also among their Fluxions, may be intirely determined. As if it were suppofed that $x + y - z = 0$. From whence another Relation among the Fluxions $\dot{x} + \dot{y} - \dot{z} = 0$ would be found by this Rule. Now compare these with the foregoing Equations, by expunging any one of the three Quantities, and also any one of the Fluxions, and then you will obtain an Equation which will intirely determine the Relation of the reft.

5. In the Equation propos'd, whenever there are complex Fractions, or furd Quantities, I put fo many Letters for each, and fuppofing them to reprefent flowing Quantities, I work as before. Afterwards I fupprefs and exterminate the affumed Letters, as you fee done here.

6. Ex. 3. If the Relation of the Quantities $x$ and $y$ be $yy - aa - x\sqrt{aa - xx} = 0$; for $x\sqrt{aa - xx}$ I write $z$, and thence I have the two Equations $yy - aa - z = 0$, and $a^2x^2 - x^4 - z^2 = 0$, of which the firft will give $2\dot{y}y - \dot{z} = 0$, as before, for the Relation of the Celerities $\dot{y}$ and $\dot{z}$, and the latter will give $2a^2\dot{x}x - 4\dot{x}x^3 - 2\dot{z}z = 0$, or $\frac{a^2\dot{x}x - 2\dot{x}x^3}{z} = \dot{z}$, for the Relation of the Celerities $\dot{x}$ and $\dot{z}$. Now $\dot{z}$ being expunged, it will be $2\dot{y}y \frac{-a^2\dot{x}x + 2\dot{x}x^3}{z} = 0$, and then reftoring $x\sqrt{aa - xx}$ for $z$, we fhall have $2\dot{y}y \frac{-a^2\dot{x} + 2\dot{x}x^2}{\sqrt{aa - xx}} = 0$, for the Relation between $\dot{x}$ and $\dot{y}$, as was required.

[...]

### DEMONSTRATION *of the Solution.*

13. The Moments of flowing Quantities, (that is, their indefinitely small Parts, by the accession of which, in indefinitely small portions of Time, they are continually increased,) are as the Velocities of their Flowing or Increasing.

14. Wherefore if the Moment of any one, as $x$, be represented by the Product of its Celerity $\dot{x}$ into an indefinitely small Quantity $o$ (that is, by $\dot{x}o$,) the Moments of the others $v$, $y$, $z$, will be represented by $\dot{v}o$, $\dot{y}o$, $\dot{z}o$; because $\dot{v}o$, $\dot{x}o$, $\dot{y}o$, and $\dot{z}o$, are to each other as $\dot{v}$, $\dot{x}$, $\dot{y}$, and $\dot{z}$.

15. Now since the Moments, as $\dot{x}o$ and $\dot{y}o$, are the indefinitely little accessions of the flowing Quantities $x$ and $y$, by which those Quantities are increased through the several indefinitely little intervals of Time; it follows, that those Quantities $x$ and $y$, after any indefinitely small interval of Time, become $x + \dot{x}o$ and $y + \dot{y}o$. And therefore the Equation, which at all times indifferently expresses the Relation of the flowing Quantities, will as well express the Relation between $x + \dot{x}o$ and $y + \dot{y}o$, as between $x$ and $y$: So that $x + \dot{x}o$ and $y + \dot{y}o$ may be substituted in the same Equation for those Quantities, instead of $x$ and $y$.

16. Therefore let any Equation $x^3 - ax^2 + axy - y^3 = o$ be given, and substitute $x + \dot{x}o$ for $x$, and $y + \dot{y}o$ for $y$, and there will arise

$$\left. \begin{array}{l} x^3 + 3\dot{x}ox^2 + 3\dot{x}^2oox + \dot{x}^3o^3 \\ - ax^2 - 2a\dot{x}ox - a\dot{x}^2oo \\ + axy + a\dot{x}oy + a\dot{y}ox + a\dot{x}\dot{y}oo \\ - y^3 - 3\dot{y}oy^2 - 3\dot{y}^2ooy - \dot{y}^3o^3 \end{array} \right\} = o.$$

17.

*and* INFINITE SERIES.                              25

17. Now by Suppofition $x^3 - ax^2 + axy - y^3 = 0$, which therefore being expunged, and the remaining Terms being divided by $o$, there will remain $3\dot{x}x^2 + 3\dot{x}^2 ox + \dot{x}^3 oo - 2a\dot{x}x - a\dot{x}^2 o + a\dot{x}y + a\dot{y}x + a\dot{x}yo - 3\dot{y}y^2 - 3\dot{y}^2 oy - \dot{y}^3 oo = 0$. But whereas $o$ is fuppofed to be infinitely little, that it may reprefent the Moments of Quantities; the Terms that are multiply'd by it will be nothing in refpect of the reft. Therefore I reject them, and there remains $3\dot{x}x^2 - 2a\dot{x}x + a\dot{x}y + a\dot{y}x - 3\dot{y}y^2 = 0$, as above in Examp. 1.

18. Here we may obferve, that the Terms that are not multiply'd by $o$ will always vanifh, as alfo thofe Terms that are multiply'd by $o$ of more than one Dimenfion. And that the reft of the Terms being divided by $o$, will always acquire the form that they ought to have by the foregoing Rule: Which was the thing to be proved.

19. And this being now fhewn, the other things included in the Rule will eafily follow. As that in the propos'd Equation feveral flowing Quantities may be involved ; and that the Terms may be multiply'd, not only by the Number of the Dimenfions of the flowing Quantities, but alfo by any other Arithmetical Progreffions ; fo that in the Operation there may be the fame difference of the Terms according to any of the flowing Quantities, and the Progreffion be difpos'd according to the fame order of the Dimenfions of each of them. And thefe things being allow'd, what is taught befides in Examp. 3, 4, and 5, will be plain enough of itfelf.

# P R O B.  II.

*An Equation being propofed, including the Fluxions of Quantities, to find the Relations of thofe Quantities to one another.*

### A PARTICULAR SOLUTION.

1. As this Problem is the Converfe of the foregoing, it muft be folved by proceeding in a contrary manner. That is, the Terms multiply'd by $\dot{x}$ being difpofed according to the Dimenfions of $x$ ; they muft be divided by $\frac{\dot{x}}{x}$, and then by the number of their Dimenfions, or perhaps by fome other Arithmetical Progreffion. Then the fame work muft be repeated with the Terms multiply'd by $\dot{v}$, $\dot{y}$,

E                                                    or

26          *The Method of* FLUXIONS,

or $\ddot{z}$, and the Sum refulting muſt be made equal to nothing, re-
jecting the Terms that are redundant.

2. EXAMPLE. Let the Equation propoſed be $3\dot{x}x^2 - 2a\dot{x}x + a\dot{x}y$
$- 3\dot{y}y^2 + a\dot{y}x = 0$. The Operation will be after this manner :

Divide     $3\dot{x}x^2 - 2a\dot{x}x + a\dot{x}y$ | Divide     $- 3\dot{y}y^2 \ast + a\dot{y}x$
by $\frac{\dot{x}}{x}$. Quot. $3x^3 - 2ax^2 + ayx$ | by $\frac{\dot{y}}{y}$. Quot. $- 3y^3 \ast + axy$
Divide by   3 . 2 . 1.          | Divide by   3 . 2 . 1.
Quote       $x^3 - ax^2 + ayx$  | Quote       $- y^3 \ast + axy$

Therefore the Sum $x^3 - ax^2 + axy - y^3 = 0$, will be the required
Relation of the Quantities $x$ and $y$. Where it is to be obſerved,
that tho' the Term $axy$ occurs twice, yet I do not put it twice in
the Sum $x^3 - ax^2 + axy - y^3 = 0$, but I reject the redundant
Term. And ſo whenever any Term recurs twice, (or oftener when
there are ſeveral flowing Quantities concern'd,) it muſt be wrote
only once in the Sum of the Terms.

3. There are other Circumſtances to be obſerved, which I ſhall
leave to the Sagacity of the Artiſt ; for it would be needleſs to dwell
too long upon this matter, becauſe the Problem cannot always be
ſolved by this Artifice. I ſhall add however, that after the Relation of the Fluents is obtain'd by this Method, if we can return,
by Prob. 1. to the propoſed Equation involving the Fluxions, then
the work is right, otherwiſe not.

[...]

## PROB. III.

*To determine the* Maxima *and* Minima *of* Quantities:

1. When a Quantity is the greateſt or the leaſt that it can be,
at that moment it neither flows backwards or forwards. For if it
flows forwards, or increaſes, that proves it was leſs, and will pre-
ſently be greater than it is. And the contrary if it flows backwards,
or decreaſes. Wherefore find its Fluxion, by Prob. 1. and ſuppoſe
it to be nothing.

2. EXAMP. 1. If in the Equation $x^3 - ax^2 + axy - y^3 = 0$ the
greateſt Value of $x$ be required; find the Relation of the Fluxions
of $x$ and $y$, and you will have $3\dot{x}x^2 - 2a\dot{x}x + a\dot{x}y - 3\dot{y}y^2 + a\dot{y}x$
$= 0$. Then making $\dot{x} = 0$, there will remain $- 3\dot{y}y^2 + a\dot{y}x = 0$,
or $3y^2 = ax$. By the help of this you may exterminate either $x$
or $y$ out of the primary Equation, and by the reſulting Equation you
may determine the other, and then both of them by $- 3y^2 +$
$ax = 0$.

3. This Operation is the ſame, as if you had multiply'd the
Terms of the propoſed Equation by the number of the Dimenſions
of the other flowing Quantity $y$. From whence we may derive the

famous Rule of *Huddenius*, that, in order to obtain the greateſt or leaſt Relate Quantity, the Equation muſt be diſpoſed according to the Dimenſions of the Correlate Quantity, and then the Terms are to be multiply'd by any Arithmetical Progreſſion.   But ſince neither this Rule, nor any other that I know yet publiſhed, extends to Equa-tions affected with ſurd Quantities, without a previous Reduction; I ſhall give the following Example for that purpoſe.

4. EXAMP. 2. If the greateſt Quantity $y$ in the Equation $x^3 -$ $ay^2 + \frac{b y^3}{a+y} - xx\sqrt{ay+xx} = 0$ be to be determin'd, ſeek the Fluxions of $x$ and $y$, and there will ariſe the Equation $3\dot{x}x^2 - 2a\dot{y}y +$ $\frac{3ab\dot{y}y^2 + 2b\dot{y}y^3}{a^2 + 2ay + y^2} - \frac{4a\dot{x}xy + 6\dot{x}x^3 + a\dot{y}x^2}{2\sqrt{ay+xx}} = 0.$   And ſince by ſuppoſition $\dot{y} = 0$, omit the Terms multiply'd by $\dot{y}$, (which, to ſhorten the labour, might have been done before, in the Operation,) and divide the reſt by $\dot{x}x$, and there will remain $3x - \frac{2ay + 3xx}{\sqrt{ay+xx}} = 0.$   When the Re-duction is made, there will ariſe $4ay + 3xx = 0$, by help of which you may exterminate either of the quantities $x$ or $y$ out of the pro-poſ'd Equation, and then from the reſulting Equation, which will be Cubical, you may extract the Value of the other.

5. From this Problem may be had the Solution of theſe fol-lowing.

I. *In a given Triangle, or in a Segment of any given Curve, to inſcribe the greateſt Rectangle.*

II. *To draw the greateſt or the leaſt right Line, which can lie between a given Point, and a Curve given in poſition.   Or, to draw a Perpendicular to a Curve from a given Point.*

III. *To draw the greateſt or the leaſt right Lines, which paſſing through a given Point, can lie between two others, either right Lines or Curves.*

IV. *From a given Point within a Parabola, to draw a right Line, which ſhall cut the Parabola more obliquely than any other. And to do the ſame in other Curves.*

V. *To determine the Vertices of Curves, their greateſt or leaſt Breadths, the Points in which revolving parts cut each other, &c.*

VI. *To find the Points in Curves, where they have the greateſt or leaſt Curvature.*

VII. *To find the leaſt Angle in a given Ellipſis, in which the Ordinates can cut their Diameters.*

VIII.

46 *The Method of* FLUXIONS,

VIII. *Of Ellipses that pass through four given Points, to determine the greatest, or that which approaches nearest to a Circle.*

IX. *To determine such a part of a Spherical Superficies, which can be illuminated, in its farther part, by Light coming from a great distance, and which is refracted by the nearer Hemisphere.*

And many other Problems of a like nature may more easily be proposed than resolved, because of the labour of Computation.

## PROB. IV.

### *To draw Tangents to Curves.*

#### *First Manner.*

1. Tangents may be variously drawn, according to the various Relations of Curves to right Lines. And first let BD be a right Line, or Ordinate, in a given Angle to another right Line AB, as a Base or Abscis, and terminated at the Curve ED. Let this Ordinate move through an indefinitely small Space to the place *bd*, so that it may be increased by the Moment *cd*, while AB is increased by the Moment B*b*, to which D*c* is equal and parallel. 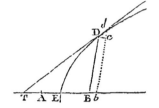 Let D*d* be produced till it meets with AB in T, and this Line will touch the Curve in D or *d*; and the Triangles *dc*D, DBT will be similar. So that it is TB : BD :: D*c* (or B*b*) : *cd*.

2. Since therefore the Relation of BD to AB is exhibited by the Equation, by which the nature of the Curve is determined; seek for the Relation of the Fluxions, by Prob. 1. Then take TB to BD in the Ratio of the Fluxion of AB to the Fluxion of BD, and TD will touch the Curve in the Point D.

3. Ex. 1. Calling AB $= x$, and BD $= y$, let their Relation be $x^3 - ax^2 + axy - y^3 = 0$. And the Relation of the Fluxions will be $3\dot{x}x^2 - 2a\dot{x}x + a\dot{x}y - 3\dot{y}y^2 + a\dot{y}x = 0$. So that $\dot{y} : \dot{x} :: 3xx - 2ax + ay : 3y^2 - ax ::$ BD $(y)$ : BT. Therefore BT $= \frac{3y^3 - axy}{3x^2 - 2ax + ay}$. Therefore the Point D being given, and thence DB and AB, or *y* and *x*, the length BT will be given, by which the Tangent TD is determined.

4.

## 4.1.3 Newton's first publication of his calculus, 1704

Only in 1704 after the death of his chief adversary Robert Hooke, did Newton finally publish his *Opticks*. Just as he had planned thirty years earlier, his discoveries in calculus appeared as an appendix. This was not now the 1671 treatise of fluxions, however, but a newer treatise, the *Tractatus de quadrature curvarum* (*A treatise on the quadrature of curves*), composed during the 1690s.

Observe that in 1671 Newton had found fluents from fluxions by simply reversing the rules for finding fluxions from fluents (4.1.2, Problems II and III). In 1704 he presented instead a geometric picture, relating fluxions and fluents to the equations defining curves and their areas, respectively.

---

### Newton's first publication of his calculus

from Newton, *Tractatus de quadratura curvarum*, 1704, 170, 172, 175–176
Eighteenth Century Collection Online, Gale Digital Collection

---

[ 170 ]

# T R A C T A T U S

## D E

# Quadratura Curvarum.

QUantitates indeterminatas ut motu perpetuo crefcentes vel decrefcentes, id eft ut fluentes vel defluentes in fequentibus confidero, defignoq; literis z, y, x, v, & earum fluxiones feu celeritates crefcendi noto iifdem literis punctatis $\dot{z}$, $\dot{y}$, $\dot{x}$, $\dot{v}$. Sunt & harum fluxionum fluxiones feu mutationes magis aut minus celeres quas ipfarum z, y, x, v fluxiones fecundas nominare licet & fic dignare $\ddot{z}$, $\ddot{y}$, $\ddot{x}$, $\ddot{v}$, & harum fluxiones primas feu ipfarum z, y, x, v fluxiones tertias fic $\dddot{z}$, $\dddot{y}$, $\dddot{x}$, $\dddot{v}$, & quartas fic $\ddddot{z}$, $\ddddot{y}$, $\ddddot{x}$, $\ddddot{v}$. Et quemadmodum $\ddot{z}$, $\ddot{y}$, $\ddot{x}$, $\ddot{v}$ funt fluxiones quantitatum $\dot{z}$, $\dot{y}$, $\dot{x}$, $\dot{v}$, & hæ funt fluxiones quantitatum z, y, x, v & hæ funt fluxiones quantitatum primarum z, y, x, v : fic hæ quantitates confiderari poffunt ut fluxiones aliarum quas fic defignabo,

$\dot{z}$,

[...]

# [ 172 ]

## PROP. I. PROB. I.

*Data æquatione quotcunq; fluentes quantitates invol-*
*vente, invenire fluxiones.*

### Solutio.

Multiplicetur omnis æquationis terminus per in-
dicem dignitatis quantitatis cujufq; fluentis quam
involvit, & in fingulis multiplicationibus mutetur
dignitatis latus in fluxionem fuam, & aggregatum factorum omnium fub propriis fignis erit
æquatio nova.

### Explicatio.

Sunto a, b, c, d &c. quantitates determinatæ &
immutabiles, & proponatur æquatio quævis quantitates fluentes z, y, x &c. involvens, uti $x^3 - xyy$
$+ aaz - b^3 = 0$. Multiplicentur termini primo per
indices dignitatum x, & in fingulis multiplicationibus pro dignitatis latere, feu x unius dimenfionis,
fcribatur $\dot{x}$, & fumma factorum erit $3\dot{x}x^2 - \dot{x}yy$. Idem
fiat in y & prodibit $-2\dot{x}yy$.   Idem fiat in z & prodibit $aa\dot{z}$.   Ponatur fumma factorum æqualis nihilo, & habebitur æquatio $3\dot{x}x^2 - \dot{x}yy - 2\dot{x}y\dot{y}$
$+ aa\dot{z} = 0$.   Dico quod hac æquatione definitur relatio fluxionum.

[...]

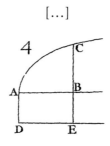

## PROP. II.   PROB. II.

*Invenire Curvas quæ quadrari poſſunt.*

Sit ABC figura invenienda, BC Ordinatim ap-*Fig.* 4
plicata rectangula, & AB abſciſſa.   Producatur
CB ad E ut ſit BE= 1, & compleatur parallelogrammum ABED : & arearum ABC, ABED
fluxiones erunt ut BC & BE.   Aſſumatur igitur
æquatio quævis qua relatio arearum definiatur, &
inde dabitur relatio ordinatarum BC & BE per
Prop. I.   Q. E. I.

Hujus rei exempla habentur in Propoſitionibus
duabus ſequentibus.

[ **176** ]

## PROP. III.   THEOR. I.

Si pro abſciſſa AB & area AE ſeu AB×1 pro-
miſcue ſcribatur z, & ſi pro e $+$ fz$^n$ $+$ gz$^{2n}$ $+$ hz$^{3n}$ $+$ &c.
ſcribatur R : ſit autem area Curvæ z$^\theta$R$^\lambda$ erit.
ordinatim applicata BC=

$$\theta e \genfrac{}{}{0pt}{}{+}{+} \genfrac{}{}{0pt}{}{\theta}{\lambda n} fz^n \genfrac{}{}{0pt}{}{+}{+} \genfrac{}{}{0pt}{}{\theta}{2\lambda n} gz^{2n} \genfrac{}{}{0pt}{}{+}{+} \genfrac{}{}{0pt}{}{\theta}{3\lambda n} hz^{3n} + \&c. \text{ in } z^{\theta-1} R^{\lambda-1}.$$

### *Demonſtratio.*

Nam ſi ſit z$^\theta$R$^\lambda$=v, erit per Prop. 1, $\theta \dot{z}z^{\theta-1}$R$^\lambda$
$+\lambda z^\theta \dot{R}$R$^{\lambda-1}$=$\dot{v}$.   Pro R$^\lambda$ in primo æquationis termino & z$^\theta$ in ſecundo ſcribe RR$^{\lambda-1}$ & zz$^{\theta-1}$, & ſiet
$\theta \dot{z}R+\lambda z\dot{R}$ in z$^{\theta-1}$R$^\lambda_{-1}$=$\dot{v}$.   Erat autem R=e $+$ fz$^n$
$+$gz$^{2n}+$hz$^{3n}$ &c. & inde per Prop. 1. ſit $\dot{R}$ =
$n$fżz$^{n-1}+2n$gżz$^{2n-1}+3n$hżz$^{3n-1}+$ &c. quibus ſubſtitu-
tis & ſcripta BE ſeu 1 pro z, ſiet
$\theta e+\genfrac{}{}{0pt}{}{\theta}{\lambda n}+$fz$^n+\genfrac{}{}{0pt}{}{\theta}{2\lambda n}$gz$^{2n}+\genfrac{}{}{0pt}{}{\theta}{3\lambda n}$hz$^{3n}+$ &c. in z$^{\theta-1}$ R$^{\lambda-1}$=v= BC.
Q. E. D.

*Notation*

For the sake of clarity in Proposition III, modern brackets have been introduced around the coefficients in each equation.

TRANSLATION

# TREATISE
## on the quadrature of curves

In what follows I consider unknown quantities in perpetual motion, increasing or decreasing, that is as flowing or receding, and I designate them by the letters $z, y, x, v$, and their fluxions or increasing speeds I denote by these pointed letters $\dot{z}, \dot{y}, \dot{x}, \dot{v}$. There are also changes or fluxions of these fluxions, more or less than the speeds of $z, y, x, v$; one may call these second fluxions and denote them thus $\ddot{z}, \ddot{y}, \ddot{x}, \ddot{v}$, and the first fluxions of these, or third fluxions of $z, y, x, v$, by $\dddot{z}, \dddot{y}, \dddot{x}, \dddot{v}$, and the fourth thus $\ddddot{z}, \ddddot{y}, \ddddot{x}, \ddddot{v}$. And in whatever way, $\dddot{z}, \dddot{y}, \dddot{x}, \dddot{v}$, are fluxions of the quantities $\ddot{z}, \ddot{y}, \ddot{x}, \ddot{v}$, and these are fluxions of the quantities $\dot{z}, \dot{y}, \dot{x}, \dot{v}$, and these are fluxions of the original quantities $z, y, x, v$;

[...]

[172]

## PROPOSITION I, PROBLEM I
*Given any equation involving fluent quantities, to find the fluxions*

*Solution*

Let every term of the equation be multiplied by the index of the power of that fluent quantity it contains, and in each multiplication let a root of the power be changed into its fluxion, and the sum of all the terms under the proper sign will be a new equation.

*Explanation*

Let $a, b, c, d$, etc. be known and unchangeable quantities, and let there be proposed any equation involving fluent quantities $z, y, x$, etc., such as $x^3 - xyy + aaz - b^3 = 0$. Let the terms be multiplied first by the indices of the powers of $x$, and in each multiplication, for the root of the power, or one dimension of $x$, there is written $\dot{x}$, and the sum of the terms will be $3\dot{x}x^2 - \dot{x}yy$. Do the same for $y$ and it will produce $2xy\dot{y}$. Do the same for $z$ and it will produce $aa\dot{z}$. The sum of the terms is put equal to nothing, and there will be had the equation $3\dot{x}x^2 - \dot{x}yy - 2xy\dot{y} + aa\dot{z} = 0$. I say that the relationship between the fluxions is defined by this equation.

[...]

[175]

## PROPOSITION II, PROBLEM II
*To find curves when the quadrature can be done*

*Figure 4*

Suppose $ABC$ is the figure to be found, $BC$ a perpendicular ordinate, and $AB$ the abscissa. Produce $CB$ to $E$ so that $BE = 1$, and complete the parallelogram $ABED$; then the fluxions of the areas $ABC$, $ABED$, will be as $BC$ and $BE$. Therefore taking any equation by which the relationship of the areas is defined, thence also will be given the relationship of the ordinates $BC$ and $BE$ by Proposition I. Which was to be found.

There are examples of this in the two following propositions.

### PROPOSITION III, THEOREM I

[176] For the abscissa $AB$ and the area $AE$ or $AB \times 1$ let there be everywhere written $z$, and for $e + fz^n + gz^{2n} + hz^{3n}+$ etc. let there be written $R$; if, moreover, suppose the area of the curve is $z^\theta R^\lambda$. Then the ordinate $BC$ will be $\theta e + (\theta + \lambda n)fz^n + (\theta + 2\lambda n)gz^{2n} + (\theta + 3\lambda n)hz^{3n}+$ etc. times $z^{\theta-1}R^{\lambda-1}$.

#### *Demonstration*

If $z^\theta R^\lambda = v$, then by Proposition I, $\theta \dot{z} z^{\theta-1} R^\lambda + \lambda z^\theta \dot{R} R^{\lambda-1} = \dot{v}$. Instead of $R^\lambda$ in the first term of the equation and $z^\theta$ in the second write $RR^{\lambda-1}$ and $zz^{\theta-1}$, and then $\theta \dot{z} R + \lambda z \dot{R}$ times $z^{\theta-1}R^{\lambda-1} = \dot{v}$. Moreover, $R = e + fz^n + gz^{2n} + hz^{3n}$ etc. and thence by Proposition I, $\dot{R} = nf\dot{z}z^{n-1} + 2ng\dot{z}z^{2n-1} + 3nh\dot{z}z^{3n-1}+$ etc. Substituting this and writing $BE$ or 1 for $\dot{z}$, gives $\theta e + (\theta + \lambda n)fz^n + (\theta + 2\lambda n)gz^{2n} + (\theta + 3\lambda n)hz^{3n}+$ etc. times $z^{\theta-1}R^{\lambda-1} = v = BC$.

Which was to be demonstrated.

---

## 4.2 THE CALCULUS OF LEIBNIZ

In 1672, at the age of twenty-six, Leibniz accompanied a diplomatic mission from the Rhineland to Paris, where he continued to live until 1676. Between January and March 1673 he visited London and made contact with several prominent members of the Royal Society, to which he was admitted on the strength of his promised work on a calculating machine. As a mathematician, however, he was still very much a novice, and was embarrassed to discover that he was rather less well informed on the subject than some of the Fellows of the Royal Society. On his return to Paris he began to study mathematics seriously under the guidance of Christiaan Huygens, and thereafter rapidly mastered the contemporary literature. Among the books he studied intensively at this time were Cavalieri's *Geometria indivisibilibus* (1635), Descartes' *La géométrie* (1637), de Saint Vincent's *Opus geometricum* (1647), Pascal's *Lettres de A Dettonville* (1659), and Barrow's *Lectiones geometricae* (1670).

During 1673 Leibniz already came to see the importance of the 'characteristic triangle', a right-angled triangle with a tiny length of a curve as its hypotenuse. He saw that useful results could be obtained by regarding this as similar to a triangle of finite size, and then neglecting small parts as required. He also recognized that finding a curve from its tangent was essentially a process of summation of small differences, and therefore equivalent to finding a quadrature.

By 1674 he was beginning to develop his transmutation theorem for quadrature. In principle it was simple: instead of seeing an area under a curve as a sum of strips parallel to the ordinates, Leibiniz regarded it as a sum of triangles with a common vertex at the origin. The 'transmutation' from strips to triangles requires only addition or subtraction of constants, and is essentially a special case of what later came to be called integration by parts. An important feature of the method, apart from its practical usefulness, is that the transformed integral involves the slope of the tangent, showing again how intimately area and slope are connected.

One of Leibniz's early successes with the method was the quadrature of the circle,[1] which he was able to reduce to what we may write in modern notation as $1 - \int_0^1 \dfrac{z^2}{1+z^2}\,dz$. He then used long division (as Mercator had done, see 3.2.4) to write $\dfrac{1}{1+z^2}$ as $1 - z^2 + z^4 - z^6 + \ldots$, and integrated term by term to obtain

$$\frac{\pi}{4} = 1 - \frac{1}{3} + \frac{1}{5} - \frac{1}{7} + \ldots.$$

By October 1675 Leibniz began, hesitatingly at first, to devise his own notation.[2] He introduced $\int$ (an elongated $S$) to replace the abbreviation *omn.* (for *omnes*, all); and at first $\dfrac{x}{d}$ but later $dx$ for small changes in $x$.

### 4.2.1 Leibniz's first publication of his calculus, 1684

The *Acta eruditorum* was founded in 1682, and Leibniz published his first paper on the calculus in it two years later. Translations of this important article have appeared in many source books, but modern translations do not usually retain Leibniz's ratio notation, nor reveal the contemporary difficulties of typesetting even such a simple fraction as $\dfrac{v}{y}$, and so the article is given here in full except for the final example.

---

1. Child 1920, 42–45.    2. Child 1920, 72–83.

## Leibniz's first paper on the calculus

from Leibniz, 'Nova methodus pro maximis et minimis, itemque tangentibus, ... per
G.G.L.', *Acta eruditorum*, (1684), 467–472

---

# MENSIS OCTOBRIS A. M DCLXXXIV.   467

## NOVA METHODVS PRO MAXIMIS ET MI.
*nimis, itemque tangentibus, quæ nec fractas, nec irrati-*
*onales quantitates moratur, & singulare pro*
*illis calculi genus, per G.G.L.*

SIt axis AX, & curvæ plures, ut VV, WW, YY, ZZ, quarum ordi- **TAB. XII.**
natæ, ad axem normales, VX, WX, YX, ZX, quæ vocentur respective, *v, vv, y, z*; & ipsa AX abscissa ab axe, vocetur x. Tangentes sint
VB, WC, YD, ZE axi occurrentes respective in punctis B, C, D, E.
Jam recta aliqua pro arbitrio assumta vocetur dx, & recta quæ sit ad
dx, ut *v* (vel vv, vel y, vel z) est ad VB (vel WC, vel YD, vel ZE) vocetur d*v* (vel d vv, vel dy vel dz) sive differentia ipsarum *v* (vel ipsarum vv, aut y, aut z) His positis calculi regulæ erunt tales:

Sit a quantitas data constans, erit da æqualis o, & d $\overline{ax}$ erit æqu-
a dx: si sit y æqu *v* (seu ordinata quævis curvæ YY, æqualis cuivis ordinatæ respondenti curvæ VV) erit dy æqu. d*v*. Jam *Additio & Sub-*
*tractio*: si sit z -y † vv † x æqu. *v*, erit $\overline{dz -y † vv † x}$ seu d*v*, æqu.
dz -dy † dvv † dx. *Multiplicatio*, $\overline{d x v}$ æqu. x d*v* † *v* dx, seu posito
y æqu. x*v*, fiet dy æqu. x d*v* † *v* dx. In arbitrio enim est vel formulam,
ut x*v*, vel compendio pro ea literam, ut y, adhibere.   Notandum & x
& dx eodem modo in hoc calculo tractari, ut y & dy, vel aliam literam
indeterminatam cum sua differentiali.   Notandum etiam non dari
semper regressum a differentiali Æquatione, nisi cum quadam cautio-

ne, de quo alibi.   Porro *Divisio*, d$\frac{v}{---}$vel (posito z æqu. $\frac{v}{---}$) dz æqu.

$\frac{\text{† } v \text{ dy † y d} v}{\overline{\phantom{xx}}}$        y        y

yy

Quoad *Signa* hoc probe notandum, cum in calculo pro litera
substituitur simpliciter ejus differentialis, servari quidem eadem signa,
& pro † z scribi † dz; pro -z scribi -- dz, ut ex additione & subtra-
ctione paulo ante posita apparet; sed quando ad exegesin valorum
venitur, seu cum consideratur ipsius z relatio ad x, tunc apparere, an
valor ipsius dz sit quantitas affirmativa, an nihilo minor seu negativa:
quod posterius cum fit, tunc tangens ZE ducitur a puncto Z non versus A, sed in partes contrarias seu infra X, id est tunc cum ipsæ ordinatæ

z decre-

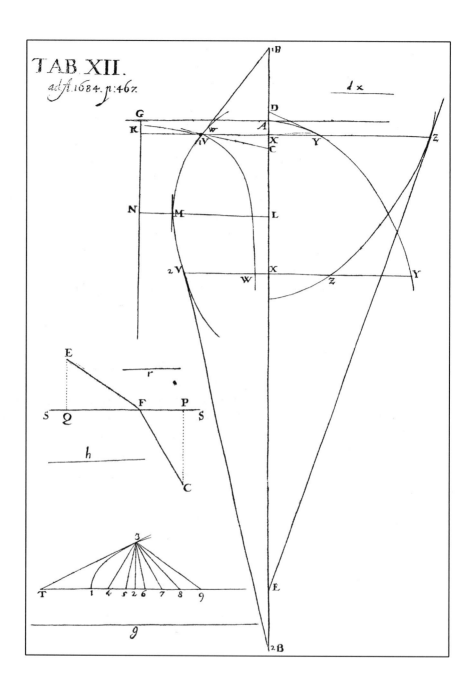

### 468    ACTA ERUDITORUM

z decrescunt crescentibus x.   Et quia ipsæ ordinatæ $v$ modo crescunt, modo decrescunt, erit d $v$ modo affirmativa modo negativa quantitas, & priore casu 1 V 1 B tangens ducitur versus A; posteriore 2 V 2B in partes aversas: neutrum autem fit in medio circa M, quo momento ipsæ $v$ neque crescunt neque decrescunt, sed in statu sunt, adeoque fit d $v$ æqu. o, ubi nihil refert quantitas sit ne affirmativa an negativa, nam +o æqu.—o: eoque in loco ipsa $v$, nempe ordinata L M, est *maxima* (vel si convexitatem Axi obverteret, *Minima*) & tangens curvæ in M neque supra X ducitur ad partes A ibique axi propinquat, neque infra X ad partes contrarias, sed est axi parallela. Si d$v$ sit infinita respectu ipsius d x, tunc tangens est ad axem recta, seu est ipsa ordinata.   Si d$v$ & d x æquales, tangens facit angulum semirectum ad axem.   Si crescentibus ordinatis $v$, crescunt etiam ipsa earum incrementa vel differentiæ, d$v$; (seu si positis d $v$ affirmativis etiam d d$v$ differentiæ differentiarum sunt affirmativæ, vel negativis negativæ) curva axi obvertit *concavitatem*; alias *convexitatem*: ubi vero est maximum vel minimum incrementum, vel ubi incrementa ex decrescentibus fiunt crescentia aut contra, ibi est *punctum flexus contrarii*, & concavitas atque convexitas inter se permutantur, modo non & ordinatæ ibi ex crescentibus fiant decrescentes, vel contra, tunc enim concavitas aut convexitas maneret: ut autem crementa continuent crescere aut decrescere, ordinatæ vero ex crescentibus fiant decrescentes vel contra, fieri non potest. Itaque punctum flexus contrarii locum habet, quando neque $v$ neque d $v$ existente o, tamen dd$v$ est o.   Unde etiam problema flexus contrarii non duas ut problema maximæ, sed tres habet radices æquales. Atque hæc omnia quidem pendent a recto usu signorum.

Interdum autem adhibenda sunt *Signa Ambigua*, ut nuper in *divisione*, antequam scilicet constet quomodo explicari debeant.   Et quidem si crescentibus x, crescunt $\left(\text{decrescunt}\right) - \dfrac{v}{y},$ debent signa ambigua in d $\dfrac{v}{y}$ seu $\mathrm{in} \dfrac{+vdy + ydv}{yy}$ ita explicari, ut hæc fractio fiat quantitas affirmativa (negativa.)   Significat autem † contrarium ipsius †, ut si hoc sit + illud sit —, vel contra. Possunt & in eodem calculo occurrere plures ambiguitates, quas distinguo parenthesibus, exempli

pli caufa fi effet $\dfrac{v}{y} \dfrac{\mp y}{z} \dfrac{x}{v} = w$ foret $\dfrac{\pm vdy \mp ydv}{yy}$

$\dashuparrow \dfrac{(\mp)\, y\, dz\, (\mp)\, zdy}{zz} \mp \dfrac{((\mp))\, x\, dv\, ((\mp))\, v\, dx}{vv} = dw \,;\text{alioqui}$

ambiguitates ex diverfis capitibus ortæ confunderentur.   Ubi notandum fignum ambiguum in fe ipfum ductum dare †, in fuum contrarium dare —, in aliud ambiguum formare novam ambiguitatem ex ambabus dependentem

*Potentiæ* d $X^a$, $= a. X^{a-1}\, dx$, exempli gratia d, $X^3 = 3X^2\, dx$

d $\dfrac{1}{X^a} = \dfrac{a\, dx}{X^{a+1}}$ ex. gr. fi w fit $= \dfrac{1}{X^3}$ fiet d w $= -\dfrac{3\, dx}{X^4}$.

*Radices:* d $\sqrt[b]{X^a} = \dfrac{a}{b}\, dx \sqrt[b]{X^{a-b}}$ (Hinc d $\sqrt[2]{y} \doteq \dfrac{dy,}{2 \sqrt[2]{y}}$

nã eo cafu a eft 1, & b 2; ergo $\dfrac{a}{b} dx \sqrt[b]{X^{a-b}}$ eft $\dfrac{1}{2} \sqrt[2]{Y^{-1}}$ jam $Y^{-1}$ idem

eft quod $\dfrac{1}{y}$ ex natura exponentium progreffionis Geometricæ, &

$\sqrt[2]{Y^1}$ eft $\dfrac{1}{\sqrt[2]{y}}$ $\dfrac{1}{\sqrt[2]{Y}}$ ) d $\dfrac{1}{\sqrt[b]{X^a}} = \dfrac{-bdx}{a \sqrt[b]{X^{b-a}}}$ Suffeciffet autem regula po-

tentiæ integræ tam ad fractas quam ad radices determinandas, potentia enim fit fracta cum exponens eft negativus, & mutatur in radicem cum exponens eft fractus: fed malui confequentias iftas ipfe deducere, quam aliis deducendas relinquere, cum fint admodum generales, & crebro occurrentes, & in re per fe implicita præftet facilitati confulere.

Ex cognito hoc velut *Algorithmo*, ut ita dicam, calculi hujus, quem voco *differentialem*, omnes aliæ æquationes differentiales inveniri poffunt per calculum communem, maximæque & minimæ, itemque tangentes haberi, ita ut opus non fit tolli fractas aut irrationales, aut alia vincula, quod tamen faciendum fuit fecundum Methodos hactenus editas. Demonftratio omnium facilis erit in his rebus verfato, & hoc unum hactenus non fatis expenfum confideranti, ipfas dx, dy, dv, dw, dz, ut ipfarum x, y, v, vv, z, (cujusque in fua ferie) differentiis five incrementis vel decrementis momentaneis proportionales haberi poffe. Unde fit ut propofita quacunq; æquatione fcribi poffit ejus æquatio differenti-

**470** ## ACTA ERUDITORVM

alis, quod fit pro quolibet *membro* (id eſt parte, quæ ſola additione vel
ſubtractione ad æquationem conſtituendam concurrit) ſubſtituendo
ſimpliciter quantitatem membri differentialem, pro alia vero quantitate, (quæ non ipſa eſt membrum, ſed ad membrum formandum concurrit) ejus quantitatem differentialem ad formandam quantitatem
differentialem ipſius membri adhibendo, non quidem ſimpliciter, ſed
ſecundum Algorithmum hactenus præſcriptum. Editæ vero hactenus Methodi talem tranſitum non habent, adhibent enim plerumque
rectam ut DX, vel aliam hujusmodi, non vero rectam dy quæ ipſis
DX, XY, dx eſt quarta proportionalis, quod omnia turbat; hinc
præcipiunt ut fractæ & irrationales (quas indeterminatæ ingrediun-
tur) prius tollantur, patet etiam methodum noſtram porrigi ad lineas tranſcendentes, quæ ad calculum Algebraicum revocari non poſſunt, ſeu quæ nullius ſunt certi gradus, idque univerſaliſſimo modo,
ſine ullis ſuppoſitionibus particularibus non ſemper ſuccedentibus,
modo teneatur in genere, *tangentem* invenire, eſſe rectam ducere, quæ
duo curvæ puncta diſtantiam infinite parvam habentia, jungat, ſeu
latus productum polygoni infinitanguli, quod nobis *curvæ* æquivalet.
Diſtantia autem illa infinite parva ſemper per aliquam differentialem
notam, ut d*v*, vel per relationem ad ipſam exprimi poteſt, hoc eſt per
notam quandam tangentem. Speciatim, ſi eſſet y, quantitas tran-
ſcendens exempli cauſa ordinata cycloeidis, eaque calculum ingrede-
retur, cujus ope ipſa Z ordinata alterius curvæ eſſet determinata, &
quæreretur dz ſeu per eam tangens hujus curvæ poſterioris, utique de-
terminanda eſſet dz per dy, haberetur autem dy, quia habetur tangens
cycloeidis. Ipſa autem tangens cycloeidis, ſi nondum haberi fingere-
tur, ſimiliter calculo inveniri poſſet ex data proprietate tangentium
circuli.

Placet autem exemplum calculi proponere, ubi notetur me di-
viſionem hic deſignare hoc modo, x: y quod idem eſt ac x diviſ. per y

ſeu $\frac{x}{y}$. Sit æquatio *prima* ſeu data, x: y † a † b x c-xx: quadrat.

$$\overline{ex † f xx † a x} \; \vee \; gg † y y † y y: \; \vee \; h h † l x † m x x \; æqu. \; o.$$

exprimens relationem inter x & y ſeu inter AX & XY, poſito ipſas a,b,c,
e,f,g,h,l, m eſſe datas; quæritur modus ex dato puncto Y educendi
YD

## MENSIS OCTOBRIS A. M DC LXXXIV.   471

YD quæ curvam tangat, feu quæritur ratio rectæ DX ad rectam datam
XY. Compendii caufa pro a ✛ b x fcribamus n; pro c-xx, p; pro
ex ✛ fxx, q; pro gg✛yy, r; pro hh ✛l x✛m x x, s. fiet x : y ✛n p :
qq ✛ax ᴠ r ✛y y : ᴠ s æqu. o. Quæ fit Æquatio *Secunda.* Jam ex
calculo noftro conftat d, x : y effe ✛x d y ✛ y d x, :yy; & fimiliter d,
np : qq effe (†) 2 n p d q (†̄) q n d̄p̄ † p d̄n̄, : q³ & d, ax ᴠ r
effe --ax d r : 2 r y†ad x √ r; & d, y y : √ s effe ((†)) y y d s ((†̄))
4 y s d y, : 25 ᴠ s, quæ omnes quantitates differentiales inde ab ipfo d,
x : y ufq; ad d, y y : ᴠ s in unum additæ, facient o, & dabunt hoc modo
Æquationem *tertiam,* ita enim pro membris fecundæ æquationis fub-
ftituuntur quantitates eorum differentiales. Jam d n eft b d x, & d p eft
--2x d x, & d q eft e d x ✛ 2 fx d x, & d r eft 2 y d y, & d s eft l dx ✛2 mx d x.
Quibus valoribus in Æquatione tertia fubftitutis habebitur æquatio
*quarta,* ubi quantitates differentiales quæ folæ fuperfunt, nempe dx, dy,
femper reperiuntur extra nominatores & vincula, & unum quodque
membrum afficitur vel per dx vel per dy, fervata femper lege homo-
geneorum quoad has duas quantitates, quomodocunque implicatus
fit calculus; unde femper haberi poteft valor ipfius dx : d y feu rationis
dx ad d y hoc eft DX quæfitæ ad XY datam, quæ ratio in hoc noftro
calculo (mutando æquationem quartam in Analogiam) erit ut ✛x : y
✛ax y : ᴠ r ((✛)) 2 y : ᴠ s eft ad ✛̄ l : y (✛) 2 n p e ✛2 fx : q³
(✛)-- 2 nx ✛ p b : qq ✛a ᴠ r (( ✛ )) y y l ✛2 m x : 2 s √ s. Dantur autem x & y ex dato puncto Y Dantur & valores fupra fcripti literarum n, p, q, r, s, per x & y. Habetur ergo quæfitum. Atque hoc exemplum fatis implicatum ideo tantum afcripfimus, ut modus fuperiori-
bus regulis in calculo etiam difficiliore utendi appareret. Nunc præftat
ufum in exemplis intellectui magis obviis oftendere.

Data fint duo puncta C & E, & recta SS in eodem cum ipfis plano, quæritur punctum F in recta SS ita fumendum, ut junctis CF, FE,
fit aggregatum rectangulorum, CF in datam h, & FE in datam r, omnium poffibilium minimum, hoc eft fi SS fit mediorum feparatrix, &
h repræfentet denfitatem medii, ut aquæ, a parte C & r denfitatem medii ut aeris, a parte E, quæritur punctum F tale, ut via a C ad E per F fit
omnium poffibilium facillima. Ponamus omnia ifta rectangulorum
aggregata poffibilia, vel omnes viarum poffibilium difficultates, re-

O o o                                    præ-

**472**     ## ACTA ERVDITORVM

præfentari per ipfas K V, curvæ VV ordinatas ad rectam G K normales, quas vocabimus ω, quærique minimam earum, NM. Quia dantur
puncta C & E, dabuntur & perpendiculares ad SS, nempe C P (quam
vocabimus c) & E Q (quam e) & præterea P Q ( quam p ) ipfam autem Q F quæ fit æqualis ipfi G N (vel AX) vocabimus x, & CF, f; &
E F, g; fiet FP, p -- x ; f æqu. $\curlyvee$ c c $+$ p p -- 2 p x $+$ xx, feu compendio $\curlyvee$ l, & g æq. $\sqrt{}$ e e $+$ x x feu compendio $\curlyvee$ m. Habemus ergo
ω æqu. h $\curlyvee$ l $+$ r $\curlyvee$ m, cujus æquationis æquatio differentialis (pofito d ω efle o, in cafu minimæ) eft o æqu -- h d l : 2 $\sqrt{}$ l -- r d m : 2 $\curlyvee$ m
per regulas calculi noftri traditas ; jam d l eft -- 2 d x -- $\overline{p + x}$, & d m
eft 2 x d x, ergo fit : h p -- x : f æqu. r x : g.     quod fi jam hæc accom-
modentur ad dioptricam, & ponantur f & g, feu C F & E F æquales,
quia eadem manet refractio in puncto F quantacunque ponatur longitudo rectæ C F, fiet h p -- x æqu. r x, feu h : r : : x : p -- x, feu h ad r ut
Q F ad FP, hoc eft finus angulorum incidentiæ & refractionis FP & QF
erunt reciproce ut r & h, denfitates mediorum in quibus fit incidentia
& refractio. Quæ denfitas tamen non refpectu noftri, fed refpectu ref-
ftentiæ, quam radiis lucis faciunt, intelligenda eft.     Et habetur ita demonftratio calculi, alibi a nobis in his ipfis Actis exhibiti, quando generale Opticæ, Catoptricæ & Dioptricæ fundamentum exponeba-
mus. Cum alii doctiffimi Viri multis ambagibus venati fint, quæ hujus
calculi peritus tribus lineis impofterum præftabit.

*Notation*
Leibniz's overlines are the equivalents of modern brackets, but were not always accurately placed
in the original, and have been silently corrected in the translation. Other corrections are shown
in square brackets.

### TRANSLATION

## A NEW METHOD FOR MAXIMA AND MINIMA
### and the same for tangents, unhindered by either fractional or irrational powers, and a unique kind of calculus for that, by G. G. L.

Tab. XII.

Let there be an axis *AX* and several curves, such as *VV*, *WW*, *YY*, *ZZ*, of which the
ordinates, normal to the axis, are *VX*, *WX*, *YX*, *ZX*, which may be called respectively *v*,
*w*, *y*, *z*; and *AX*, the length along the axis may be called *x*. Let the tangents be *VB*, *WC*,
*YD*, *ZE*, meeting the axis respectively in the points *B*, *C*, *D*, *E*. Now any other straight
line taken arbitrarily may be called *dx*, and the line which is to *dx* as *v* (or *w*, or *y*, or *z*)

is to $VB$ (or $WC$, or $YD$, or $ZE$) may be called $dv$ (or $dw$, or $dy$, or $dz$), or the differences of $v$ (or $w$, or $y$, or $z$). This said, the rules of the calculus will be these:

Let $a$ be a given constant quantity, then will $da$ equal 0, and $d\,\overline{ax}$ will equal $a\,dx$; if $y$ equals $v$ (or the ordinate of any curve $YY$ is equal to the corresponding ordinate of the curve $VV$) then will $dy$ equal $dv$. Now *addition* and *subtraction*: if $z - y + w + x$ equals $v$, then will $d\,\overline{z - y + w + x}$ or $dv$ equal $dz - dy - dw + dx$. *Multiplication*: $d\,\overline{xv}$ equals $xdv + vdx$, or putting $y$ equal to $xv$, then $dy$ equals $xdv + vdx$. For it is arbitrary whether one uses the formula $xv$, or a letter short for them, like $y$. It is to be noted also that $x$ and $dx$ are treated in the same way in this calculus, as $y$ and $dy$, or other unknown letters and their differentials. It is also to be noted that one can not always come back from an equation of the differentials, unless with a certain care, of which elsewhere. Then *division*, $d\dfrac{v}{y}$ or (putting $z$ equal to $\dfrac{v}{y}$) $dz$ equals $\dfrac{\pm vdy \mp ydv}{yy}$.

As to the *sign* it is here rightly noted that, when in this calculus there are simply substituted for letters their differentials, the same signs are used, and instead of $+z$ there is written $+dz$, and instead of $-z$ there is written $-dz$, as is clear from the addition and subtraction given a short time ago; but when one comes to working out the value, or when considering the relationship of $z$ to $x$, then it will appear whether the value of $dz$ is a positive quantity, or less than nothing, or negative. If the latter happens, then the tangent $ZE$ drawn from the point $Z$ is not behind $A$ but in the opposite direction or below $X$, and then the ordinates $z$ [468] are decreasing with increasing $x$. And as the ordinates $v$ either increase or decrease, $dv$ will be either a positive or a negative quantity, and in the former case the tangent $V_1B_1$ will be drawn behind $A$; in the latter, $V_2B_2$ in the other direction. Moreover it becomes neutral in the the the middle around $M$, at which moment the [ordinates] $v$ neither increase nor decrease, but stay still, and therefore $dv$ becomes 0, where nothing means a quantity that is neither positive or negative, for $+0$ equals $-0$; and at that point $v$, namely the ordinate $LM$, is a *maximum* (or if turning convexly to the axis a *minimum*), and the tangent to the curve at $M$ is drawn neither above $X$ approaching the axis in the direction of $A$, nor below $X$ in the opposite direction, but is parallel to the axis. If $dv$ is infinite with respect to $dx$, then the tangent is at right angles to the axis, or itself an ordinate. If $dv$ and $dx$ are equal, the tangent makes half a right angle with the axis. If as the ordinates $v$ increase, their increments or differences, $dv$, also increase (or, if having assumed $dv$ positive, the differences $ddv$ of the differences are also positive, or if negative then negative), the curve turns towards the axis *concavely*; otherwise *convexly*; but where there is a maximum or minimum increment, or where the increments from decreasing become increasing, or conversely, there is a *point of contrary flexion*, and concavity and convexity are interchanged, provided only that there also the ordinates do not become decreasing from increasing, or conversely, for then concavity or convexity would remain; moreover, as the increments continue to increase or decrease, indeed it is not possible for the ordinates to go from increasing to decreasing, or conversely. Therefore the point of contrary flexion occurs when, neither $v$ nor $dv$ being 0, nevertheless $ddv$ is 0. Whence also the problem of contrary flexion does not have two equal roots as in the problem of maxima, but three. And all this depends on the correct use of signs.

Meanwhile there must be used *ambiguous signs*, as above for *division*, before it is known for certain in what way they must be explained. And indeed if for $x$ increasing,

$\frac{v}{y}$ increases (or decreases) the ambiguous signs in $d\frac{v}{y}$ or in $\frac{\pm vdy \mp ydv}{yy}$ must be explained in such a way that this fraction becomes a positive (or negative) quantity. Moreover the sign $\mp$ signifies the opposite of $[\pm]$, so that if the latter is $+$, the former is $-$, or conversely. There may also occur in this calculus several ambiguities, which I distinguish by parentheses, [469] for example if $\frac{v}{y} + \frac{y}{z} + \frac{x}{y} = w$ we would write

$$\frac{\pm vdy \mp ydv}{yy} + \frac{(\pm)ydz(\mp)zdy}{zz} + \frac{((\pm))xdv((\mp))vdx}{vv} = dw;$$ otherwise the ambiguities

arising from different terms would be confused. It is to be noted that an ambiguous sign multiplied by itself gives $+$, by its opposite it gives $-$, by another ambiguity it will form a new ambiguity depending on the others.

*Powers* $dX^a, = aX^{a-1}dx$, for example, $dX^3 = 3X^2dx$. $d\frac{1}{X^a} = \frac{adx}{X^{a+1}}$, for example,

if $w = \frac{1}{X^3}$, it will give $dw = -\frac{3dx}{X^4}$.

*Roots* $d\sqrt[b]{X^a} = \frac{a}{b}dx\sqrt[b]{X^{a-b}}$. (Hence $d\sqrt[2]{y} = \frac{dy}{2\sqrt[2]{y}}$ because $a$ is 1 and $b$ is 2; therefore

$\frac{a}{b}dx\sqrt[b]{X^{a-b}}$ is $\frac{1}{2}\sqrt[2]{Y^{-1}}$; now $Y^{-1}$ is the same as $\frac{1}{Y}$ from the nature of geometric

progressions, and $\sqrt[2]{\frac{1}{Y}}$ is $\frac{1}{\sqrt[2]{Y}}$. Also $d\frac{1}{\sqrt[b]{X^a}} = \frac{-bdx}{a\sqrt[b]{X^{b-a}}}$. Moreover the rules for whole

powers would suffice for determining both fractions and roots, for the power is a fraction when the exponent is negative, and is changed into a root when the exponent is a fraction; but I have preferred to deduce the consequences this way, than to leave the deductions to others, and to take steps to facilitate what appears complicated, since they are quite general and occur often.

From knowledge of this *Algorithm*, as I call it, of this calculus, which I call *differential*, all other differential equations can be found by a similar calculation; also maxima and minima, and likewise tangents, can be found with no need to remove fractions or irrationals or other roots, which, however, had to be done according to methods previously published. The demonstration of all this will be easy to one versed in these things, and who bears in mind one thing, not satisfactorily explored until now, that $dx$, $dy$, $dw$, $dz$, can be proportional to instantaneous differences, whether increasing or decreasing, of $x$, $y$, $w$, $z$, (of each in turn). Whence it comes about that for any proposed equation, its differential equation can be written, [470] which may be done by substituting for each *term* (that is a part which occurs in the given equation only by addition or subtraction) the simple differential of the term, but for any other quantity (which is not itself a term, but occurs in the formation of a term) using its differential quantity in the formation of the differential quantity of the term, not indeed simply, but according to the algorithm already prescribed. But the methods published so far do not have this transformation, for they use several lines such as $DX$, or others of this kind, but not the line $dy$ which is the fourth proportional to $DX$, $XY$, $dx$, which confuses everything; hence they advise that fractions and irrationals (which enter into the unknown quantities) should first be removed; also it is clear that my method can be extended to transcendent curves, which cannot be reduced to algebraic calculations, or which are not of certain degree, and therefore by a most general method, without any particular suppositions which are not always satisfied, we only need recall that in general to find a *tangent* is to draw a line which joins two points of the curve an infinitely small distance apart, or the extended side of an infinite-angled polygon, which to us is equivalent to the *curve*. Moreover that infinitely small distance can always be expressed as some known differential, such as $dv$, or in relation to it, that is by means of some known tangent. In particular, if $y$ is a transcendent quantity, for example, the ordinate of a cycloid, and if it enters into the calculation, by means of which $Z$, the ordinate of another curve, is determined, and also there is sought $dz$ or by means of it the tangent to this latter curve, there must everywhere be determined $dz$ by means of $dy$; moreover $dy$ will be known, because we have the tangent to the cycloid. Moreover, the tangent to the cycloid, if we suppose that we do not yet have it, can be found by a similar calculation from the given properties of tangents to a circle.

Further, I wish to give an example of this calculus, in which I indicate division by denoting it in this way $x : y$ which is the same as $x$ divided by $y$, or $\frac{x}{y}$. Let the *first* or given equation be $x : y + \overline{a + bx} \times \overline{c - xx} : \overline{ex + fxx}$ squared $+ax\sqrt{gg + yy} + yy : \sqrt{hh + lx + mxx}$ equals 0, expressing the relationship between $x$ and $y$ or between $AX$ and $XY$, supposing $a, b, c, e, f, g, h, l, m$, to be given. It is sought how to draw from a given point $Y$ [471] the line $YD$ that touches the curve, or the ratio of the line $DX$ to the given line $XY$. If for brevity we write $n$ for $a + bx$; $p$ for $c - xx$; $q$ for $ex + fxx$; $r$ for $gg + yy$; $s$ for $hh + lx + mxx$, it becomes $x : y + np : qq + ax\sqrt{r} + yy : \sqrt{s}$ equals 0, which is the *second* equation. Now from my calculus it comes out that $d, x : y$ is $+xdy + ydx, : yy$, and similarly that $d, np : qq$ is $(\pm)2npdq(\mp)q\,\overline{ndp + pdn} : q^3$, and $d, ax\sqrt{r}$ is $[+]axdr : 2\sqrt{r} + adx\sqrt{r}$, and $d, yy : \sqrt{s}$ is $((\pm))yyds((\mp))4ysdy : 2[s]\sqrt{s}$, all of which differential quantities from $d, x : y$ to $d, yy : \sqrt{s}$ added together make 0, and in this way give a *third* equation, in such a way that for terms of the second equation there are substituted their differential quantities. Now $dn$ is $bdx$, and $dp$ is $-2xdx$, and $dq$ is $edx + 2fxdx$, and $dr$ is $2ydy$, and $ds$ is $ldx + 2mdx$. From which values substituted in the third equation we have a *fourth* equation, where the differential quantities which alone remain, namely $dx$, $dy$, are always found outside the denominators or square roots, and each single term is affected either by $dx$ or $dy$, always keeping the law of homogeneity with respect to these two quantities, however complicated the calculations may be; whence one can always have the value of $dx : dy$, or the ratio $dx$ to $dy$, that is the sought line $DX$ to the given line $XY$, which ratio in my calculation will be (changing the fourth equation by analogy) as $+x : y + axy : \sqrt{r}((\mp))2y : \sqrt{s}$ is to $\mp 1 : y(\pm)2np\,\overline{e + 2fx} : q^3(\mp)\,\overline{-2nx + pb} : qq + a\sqrt{r}((\pm))yy\,\overline{l + 2mx} : 2s\sqrt{s}$. Further, $x$ and $y$ are given by the point $Y$, and so also are given the values of the above letters $n, p, q, r, s$, by means of $x$ and $y$. Therefore we have what is sought. And as this example is quite complicated I have written it at length, so that the method of using the above rules again in a more difficult calculation will be clear. Now it remains to show their use in examples more plain to understand.

Let there be given two points $C$ and $E$, and a line $SS$ in the same plane with them; there is sought a point $F$ in the line $SS$ thus taken, so that the meeting point of the lines $CF$, $CE$, makes the least possible sum of the products of $CF$ and a given line $h$, and of $FE$ and a given line $r$, that is if $SS$ separates different media, and $h$ represents the density of the medium, as of water, on the side of $C$, and $r$ the density of the medium, as of air, on the side of $E$, there is sought the point $F$ such that the path from $C$ to $E$ through $F$ is the easiest of all possible. Let us assume that all these possible sums of products, or all possible paths, [472] are represented by ordinates $KV$ of the curve $VV$, perpendicular to the line $GK$, which we call $w$, and there is to be found the minimum, $NM$. Because the points $C$ and $E$ are given, there will be given also the perpendiculars to $SS$, namely $CP$ (which we call $c$) and $EQ$ ($e$), and also $PQ$ ($p$), and $QF$ which is equal to $GN$ (or $AX$) we will call $x$, and $CF$, $f$, and $EF$, $g$; then $FP$ is $p - x$, and $f$ equals $\sqrt{cc + pp - 2px + xx}$, or more briefly, $\sqrt{l}$, and $g$ equals $\sqrt{ee + xx}$ or more briefly $\sqrt{m}$. Therefore we have $w$ equals $h\sqrt{l} + r\sqrt{m}$, of which equation the differential equation (supposing $dw$ to be 0, in case of a minimum) is 0 equal to $-hdl : 2\sqrt{l} - rdm : 2\sqrt{m}$ by the rules of my calculus already taught; now $dl$ is $2dx\,\overline{-p + x}$ and $dm$ is $2xdx$, therefore it becomes $h\,\overline{p - x} : f$ equals $rx : g$. Which if now this is adapted to dioptrics, and $f$ and $g$, or $CF$ and $FE$ are put equal, because the same refraction is maintained at $F$ whatever the length of the line $CF$, it becomes $h\,\overline{p - x} = rx$, or $h : r :: x : \overline{p - x}$, or $h$ to $r$ is as $QF$ to $FP$, that is the sines of the angles of incidence and refraction, $FP$ and $QF$, will be as reciprocals of $r$ and $h$, the densities of the media in which the incidence and refraction takes place. Which densities, however, are to be understood not with respect to ours, but with respect to the resistance they make to the rays of light. And thus there is a demonstration of the calculation, shown by me elsewhere in these *Acta*, when I have explained the general fundaments of optics, catoptrics, and dioptrics. As other very learned men have found in roundabout ways, what someone skilled in this calculus can show in three lines of magic.

———————————

# CHAPTER 5

# THE MATHEMATICS OF NATURE: NEWTON'S *PRINCIPIA*

Newton's *Philosophiae naturalis principia mathematica* (*The mathematical principles of natural philosophy*) was published in 1687, and it is hardly an exaggeration to say that it revolutionized the role of mathematics in our understanding of the physical world. Its main aim was a mathematical explanation of the motion of the planets, but it also touches on fluid flow, wave motion, the ebb and flow of tides, and paths of comets. Not all Newton's ideas stood the test of time, but his theory of gravity and planetary motion laid the foundations for what became the accepted view of the universe until the twentieth century. Beyond that, the attempt to match theory with observation, so strikingly seen in the *Principia*, is now integral to modern science.

Just as in his development of the calculus twenty years earlier, Newton was very much aware of the work of his predecessors, and in particular the astronomical laws of Johannes Kepler. By 1619 Kepler, working from the observations made by Tycho Brahe and others, had found three laws of planetary motion: (i) that planets move in elliptical orbits with the sun as focus; (ii) that the radial line from sun to planet sweeps out equal areas in equal times; and (iii) if $D$ is the average distance of a planet from the sun and $T$ its period of orbit, then $D^3$ is proportional to $T^2$. This was the beginning of a mathematical description, but there was no suggestion as to *why* such laws should hold. At the same time there were several other theories about the nature of the universe that were based on imagination rather than evidence. Towards the end of his life Kepler himself reverted to a model of the universe based on nested Platonic solids, while Descartes suggested that the planets were held in place by systems of vortices whirling in some celestial fluid.

In England by the late 1670s, mathematical speculation was beginning to replace philosophical speculation. Halley, Hooke, and other members of the Royal Society pondered on the possibility of an inverse square law of planetary attraction, and at some point Halley consulted Newton on the matter and was given the correct answer: that an inverse square law gives rise to elliptical orbits, just as Kepler had observed. Halley was so impressed that he persuaded Newton to write out and publish what he knew.

The *Principia*, greatly expanded from the initial calculations requested by Halley, was written in three Books, of which Book I is the most theoretical and the most mathematically demanding. After setting out basic axioms and principles, Newton showed that Kepler's second law (equal areas in equal times) must hold for motion under *any* centripetal force, but that the particular case of an elliptical orbit implies an inverse square law. He also claimed the more general converse result, that an inverse square law always gives rise to orbits that are conic sections. Book II discusses the motion of planets, pendulums, and other bodies, in a resisting medium, and can be read as an extended attack upon the theory of vortices. The most interesting section for modern readers is perhaps Newton's discussion of wave motion. In Book III, entitled 'De mundi systemate' ('The system of the world'), Newton demonstrated in more detail that an inverse square law could account for such disparate phenomena as Kepler's laws, the shape of the earth, the motion of the moon and the pattern of the tides, and the paths of comets. In this part Newton made extensive calculations and repeatedly checked them against experimental observations, so that the universe itself became for the first time the subject of scientific experiment.

The first uncomfortable surprise to the modern reader of the *Principia* is the style in which is written. Twenty years earlier Newton had discovered the laws of calculus, and his fluent quantities and fluxions seem ideally suited to descriptions of the physical world. One might therefore expect to find in the *Principia* the first applications of this new theory, but on the face of it there are none at all. Instead the *Principia* demands a deep understanding of classical geometry and the traditional language of ratio. It opens in Euclidean style, with a list of Definitions and Axioms, and continues in similar vein with a series of Propositions, each one built on those that precede it and proved by purely geometrical arguments. Euclid is not the only ancient geometer invoked: many of the propositions in the early part of the book rely on the advanced and difficult geometry of Apollonius.

In another sense though, and a very important one, Newton's new way of thinking *did* emerge: in his use of 'ultimate ratio', or the ratio between two diminishing quantities at the final moment before they vanish. Here Newton moved irrevocably away from anything that would have been acceptable to Greek geometers, and drew instead on ideas that he must have tested and refined through his years of work on fluxions. The formal concept of a limit was still a long way into the future, but Newton in many ways came very close to it. Certainly he had a clear intuitive idea both of the possibilities and the difficulties of handling vanishing quantities, and the first part of the *Principia* was devoted to establishing, as far as he was able, a viable theory of limits. The extracts below have been selected to illustrate his careful construction of these mathematical arguments in Book I.

The *Principia* was eventually reprinted and translated many times, and like all important but difficult mathematical texts accrued much commentary along the way. The second edition, with several revisions was published in 1713 by Richard Bentley, though the mathematical editing was done by Roger Cotes. A third edition, with Newton's final additions and corrections, was edited by Henry Pemberton and published in 1726, the year before Newton died. The extracts below have been taken from the first edition, to show how they were first presented to the world in 1687.


## 5.1 NEWTON'S *PRINCIPIA*, BOOK I


### 5.1.1 The axioms

The *Principia* opens with a series of definitions: of matter, motion, impressed force, centripetal force, acceleration, and so on. Continuing in the same Euclidean style, it goes on to offer three axioms (and their corollaries), which are now more commonly known as Newton's laws of motion.

## The laws of motion and a corollary
from Newton, *Principia*, 1687, Book I, Axioms 1–3 and Corollary 1

[ 12 ]

# AXIOMATA
## SIVE
# LEGES MOTUS

### Lex. I.

*Corpus omne perseverare in statu suo quiescendi vel movendi unifor-
miter in directum, nisi quatenus a viribus impressis cogitur statum
illum mutare.*

PRojectilia perseverant in motibus suis nisi quatenus a resisten-
tia aeris retardantur & vi gravitatis impelluntur deorsum.
Trochus, cujus partes cohærendo perpetuo retrahunt sese
a motibus rectilineis, non cessat rotari nisi quatenus ab aere re-
tardatur. Majora autem Planetarum & Cometarum corpora motus suos & progressivos & circulares in spatiis minus resistentibus
factos conservant diutius.

### Lex.    II.

*Mutationem motus proportionalem esse vi motrici impressæ, & fieri se-
cundum lineam rectam qua vis illa imprimitur.*

Si vis aliqua motum quemvis generet, dupla duplum, tripla tri-
plum generabit, sive simul & semel, sive gradatim & successive im-
pressa fuerit. Et hic motus quoniam in eandem semper plagam
cum vi generatrice determinatur, si corpus antea movebatur, mo-
tui ejus vel conspiranti additur, vel contrario subducitur, vel obli-
quo oblique adjicitur, & cum eo secundum utriusq; determinatio-
nem componitur. Lex. III.

[ 13 ]

## Lex. III.

*Actioni contrariam semper & æqualem esse reactionem : sive corporum duorum actiones in se mutuo semper esse æquales & in partes contrarias dirigi.*

Quicquid premit vel trahit alterum, tantundem ab eo premitur vel trahitur.    Siquis lapidem digito premit, premitur & hujus digitus a lapide.  Si equus lapidem funi allegatum trahit, retrahetur etiam & equus æqualiter in lapidem: nam funis utrinq; distentus eodem relaxandi se conatu urgebit Equum versus lapidem, ac lapidem versus equum, tantumq; impediet progressum unius quantum promovet progressum alterius.    Si corpus aliquod in corpus aliud impingens, motum ejus vi sua quomodocunq; mutaverit, idem quoque vicissim in motu proprio eandem mutationem in partem contrariam vi alterius ( ob æqualitatem pressionis mutuæ ) subibit.    His actionibus æquales fiunt mutationes non velocitatum sed motuum, ( scilicet in corporibus non aliunde impeditis : ) Mutationes enim velocitatum, in contrarias itidem partes factæ, quia motus æqualiter mutantur, sunt corporibus reciproce proportionales.

### Corol.  I.

*Corpus viribus conjunctis diagonalem parallelogrammi eodem tempore describere, quo latera separatis.*

Si corpus dato tempore, vi sola *M*, ferretur ab *A* ad *B*, & vi sola *N*, ab *A* ad *C*, compleatur parallelogrammum *ABDC*, & vi utraq; feretur id eodem tempore ab *A* ad *D*. Nam quoniam vis *N* agit secundum lineam 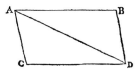 *AC* ipsi *BD* parallelam, hæc vis nihil mutabit velocitatem accedendi ad lineam illam *BD* a vi altera genitam.  Accedet igitur corpus eodem tempore ad lineam *BD* sive vis *N* imprimatur, sive non, atq; adeo in fine illius temporis reperietur alicubi in linea

illa

# AXIOMS
### OR
# LAWS OF MOTION

## Law I

*Every body persists in a state of rest or uniform motion in a direction, except in so far as it is moved by impressed forces to change that state.*

Projectiles persevere in their motion except in so far as they are retarded by the resistance of air, and impelled downwards by the force of gravity. A spinning top, whose parts by cohesion continually draw themselves away from rectilinear motion, does not cease to rotate except in so far as it is retarded by air. Moreover, the major bodies of the planets and comets conserve both their progressive and circular motion for longer in less resistant space.

## Law II

*The change in motion is proportional to the impressed motive force, and takes place along the straight line in which that force is impressed.*

If a different force generates some other motion, twice the force will generate twice, three times will generate three times, whether they are impressed all at once at the same time, or gradually and successively. And since this motion is fixed always in the same plane as the generating force, if the body was moving before, its motions if in the same direction are added, or if in the opposite direction subtracted, or if at an oblique angle are added obliquely, and compounded according to the direction of both.

[13]

## Law III

*Reactions are always equal and opposite to actions: or the actions of two bodies upon each other are always equal and aligned in opposite directions.*

Whatever pushes or pulls another body, is in the same way pushed or pulled by it. If someone pushes a stone with a finger, then the finger is also pushed by the stone. If a horse pulls a stone tied to a rope, the horse is also and equally pulled by the stone: for the rope stretched at each end in the same effort to relax will urge the horse towards the stone and the stone toward the horse, and will impede the progress of one as much as it helps the progress of the other. If some body impinges on another, it will change its momentum by its force; likewise it will in turn undergo the same change in its own momentum in the opposite direction by the force of the other (because of the mutually equal pressures). By these actions equal changes are made not to velocity but to momentum (clearly if the body is not impeded otherwise). For changes in velocity, made in contrary directions, because the momentum is equally changed, are reciprocally proportional to [the masses of] the bodies.

## Corollary I

*A body under joined forces describes the diagonal of a parallelogram in the same time as the sides under separate forces.*

If the body in a given time, by force *M* alone, is taken from *A* to *B*, and by force *N* alone from *A* to *C*, there is completed the parallelogram *ABDC*, and by the force of both it is taken in the same time from *A* to *D*. For since the force *N* acts along the line *AC* parallel to *BD*, this force will do nothing to change the velocity of motion along the line *BD*, generated by the other force. Therefore the body will will move along the line [14] *BD* in the same time whether the force *N* is applied or not; and therefore at the end of that time it will be found somewhere on the line *BD*. By the same argument at the end of the same time it will be found somewhere on the line *CD*, and accordingly it must be found at the meeting point *D* of both lines.

_____

## 5.1.2 Ultimate ratios

After the Euclidean style of the introduction, Book I of the *Principia* opens with a lemma that immediately carries the reader well beyond the bounds of Euclidean geometry. Fixed and stable figures are now replaced by quantities that change over time, as Newton lays the foundations for everything that follows by introducing the crucial concept of 'ultimate equality'.

Wallis in his *Arithmetica infinitorum* in 1656 had repeatedly asserted that two quantities whose difference can be made less than any assigned quantity can be considered equal, and Newton as a young man had read that book with close attention. Wallis had justified his claim by reference to Euclid X.1, but Newton in Lemma I now used a simple argument by contradiction.

**Ultimate equality**

from Newton, *Principia*, 1687, Book I, Lemmas 1 and 2

[ 26 ]

# DE

# MOTU CORPORUM

### Liber PRIMUS

## SECT I.

*De Methodo Rationum primarum & ultimarum, cujus ope sequentia demonstrantur.*

### LEMMA I.

QVantitates, ut & quantitatum rationes, quæ ad æqualitatem dato tempore constanter tendunt & eo pacto propius ad invicem accedere possunt quam pro data quavis differentia; fiunt ultimo æquales.

*Si* negas, fit earum ultima differentia *D*. Ergo nequeunt propius ad æqualitatem accedere quam pro data differentia *D*: contra hypothesin.

Lem-

[ 27 ]

## Lemma II.

*Si in figura quavis* A a c E *rectis* A a, A E, *& curva* A c E *comprehensa, inscribantur parallelogramma quotcunq;* A b, B c, C d, *&c. sub basibus* AB, BC, CD, *&c. æqualibus, & lateribus* B b, C c, D d, *&c. figuræ lateri* A a *parallelis contenta; & compleantur parallelogramma* a Kbl, bLcm, cMdn, *&c, Dein horum parallelogrammorum latitudo minuatur, & numerus augeatur in infinitum: dico quod ultimæ rationes, quas habent ad se invicem figura inscripta* AKbLcMdD, *circumscripta* A a l b m c n d o E, *& curvilinea* A a b c d E, *sunt rationes æqualitatis.*

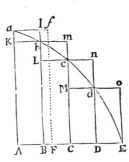

Nam figuræ inscriptæ & circumscriptæ differentia est summa parallelogrammorum $Kl + Lm + Mn + Do$, hoc est ( ob æquales omnium bases ) rectangulum sub unius basi $Kb$ & altitudinum summa $Aa$, id est rectangulum $ABla$. Sed hoc rectangulum, eo quod latitudo ejus $AB$ in infinitum minuitur, fit minus quovis dato. Ergo, per Lemma I, figura inscripta & circumscripta & multo magis figura curvilinea intermedia fiunt ultimo æquales. *Q. E. D.*

---

TRANSLATION

ON

# THE MOTION OF BODIES
## Book ONE
## SECTION I

*On the method of first and last ratios, by means of which what follows is demonstrated*

### Lemma I

*Quantities, as also ratios of quantities, which continually tend to equality in a given time, and by that means can approach each other more closely than by any given difference, become ultimately equal.*

Suppose you deny this, and let their ultimate difference be $D$. Therefore they do not approach equality more closely than by the given difference $D$; which contradicts the hypothesis. [27]

Lemma II

*Suppose in any figure AacE bounded by the lines Aa, AE, and the curve AcE, there are inscribed the contents of any number of parallelograms Ab, Bc, Cd, etc. on equal bases AB, BC, CD, etc. and with sides Bb, Cc, Dd, etc. parallel to the side Aa of the figure, and the parallelograms aKbl, bLcm, cMdn, etc. are completed. Then if the width of these parallelograms is diminished, and the number of them is increased indefinitely, I say that the ultimate ratios to each other of the inscribed figure, AKbLcMdD, the circumscribed figure AalbmcndoE, and the curvilinear figure AabcdE, are ratios of equality.*

For the difference of the inscribed and circumscribed figures is the sum of the parallelograms $Kl + Lm + Mn + Do$, that is (because of equal bases) the rectangle on one of the bases $Kb$ and of altitude the sum $Aa$, that is the rectangle $ABla$. But this rectangle, because its width $AB$ is diminished infinitely, becomes less than any given quantity. Therefore, by Lemma I, the inscribed and circumscribed figures and, even more so, the curvilinear figure between them, become ultimately equal. Which was to be demonstrated.

———————

### 5.1.3 Properties of small angles

Newton had discovered infinite series for sines and tangents some twenty years earlier, but did not introduce them into the *Principia*. Instead, in Book I, Lemma 7, he proved from basic geometry and his principle of ultimate equality that a quantity, its sine, and its tangent, become 'ultimately equal' as the quantity itself becomes very small.

## Properties of small angles

from Newton, *Principia*, 1687, Book I, Lemma 7

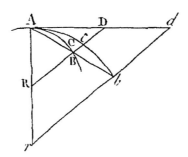

### Lemma. VII.

*Jifdem pofitis, dico quod ultima ratio arcus, chordæ & tangentis ad
invicem eft ratio æqualitatis.Vide* Fig. Lem. 6 *&* 8 *vi.*

Nam producantur A B & A D ad *b* & *d* & fecanti B D parallela agatur *b d*. Sitq; arcus A *b* fimilis arcui A B. Et punctis
A, B coeuntibus, angulus *d* A *b*, per Lemma fuperius, evanefcet;
adeoq; rectæ A *b*, A *d* & arcus intermedius A *b* coincident,& propterea æquales erunt. Unde & hilce femper proportionales rectæ
A B, A D, & arcus intermedius A B rationem ultimam habebunt
æqualitatis. *Q. E. D.*

*Corol.* 1. Unde fi per B ducatur tangenti parallela B F rectam
quamvis A F per A tranfeuntem
perpetuo fecans in F, hæc ultimo
ad arcum evanefcentem A B rationem habebit æqualitatis, eo quod
completo parallelogrammo A F B-
D, rationem femper habet æqualitatis ad A D.

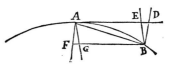

*Corol.* 2. Et fi per B & A ducantur plures rectæ B E, B D, A F,
A G, fecantes tangentem A D & ipfius parallelam B F, ratio ul-
tima abfciffarum omnium A D, A E, B F, B G, chordæq; & arcus
A B ad invicem erit ratio æqualitatis.

*Corol.* 3. Et propterea hæ omnes lineæ in omni de rationibus
ultimis argumentatione pro fe invicem ufurpari poffunt.

## Lemma VII

*With the same suppositions, I say that the ultimate ratios to each other of an arc, a chord, and a tangent are ratios of equality. See the figure for Lemma 6 and 8.*

For suppose AB and AD are extended towards b and d, and bd is drawn parallel to the cutting line BD. And let the Arc Ab be similar to the arc AB. And as the points A, B come together, the angle dAb, by the above lemma, vanishes; and therefore the lines Ab, Ad, and the intermediate arc Ab coincide, and are therefore equal. Whence also the lines AB, AD, and the intermediate arc AB, which are always proportional to these, have an ultimate ratio of equality. Which was to be demonstrated.

*Corollary 1.* Whence if through B there is drawn BF parallel to the tangent, always cutting at F some line AF passing through A, this ultimately will have a ratio of equality to the vanishing arc AB, because having completed the parallelogram AFDB, it will always have a ratio of equality to AD.

*Corollary 2.* And if through B and A there are drawn several lines BE, BD, AF, AG, cutting the tangent AD and its parallel BF, the ultimate ratios of all the segments AD, AE, BF, BG, and the chord, and the arc AB to each other will be ratios of equality.

*Corollary 3.* And therefore all these lines can be used in place of each other in any argument concerning ultimate ratios.

_____

## 5.1.4  Motion under a centripetal force

After a number of introductory but essential lemmas, Newton's study of motion begins properly at Book I, Proposition 1, with motion under a centripetal force. As yet the precise nature of the force remains unspecified. All we know is that it attracts the revolving body towards a fixed centre. From this simple definition, and using easy Euclidean geometry combined with the principle of ultimate equality, Newton derived Kepler's second law: that revolving bodies (moving in a plane) sweep out equal areas in equal times. In Proposition 2 he went on to prove the converse, that bodies moving in a plane, which sweep out equal areas in equal times, must be attracted to a central point (which may be either fixed or moving at constant speed).

## Motion under a centripetal force

from Newton, *Principia*, 1687, Book I, Proposition 1

[ 37 ]

### SECT. II.

*De Inventione Virium Centripetarum.*

#### Prop. I. Theorema. I.

*Areas quas corpora in gyros acta radiis ad immobile centrum virium ductis describunt, & in planis immobilibus consistere, & esse temporibus proportionales.*

Dividatur tempus in partes æquales, & prima temporis parte describat corpus vi insita rectam *A B.* Idem secunda temporis parte, si nil impediret, recta pergeret ad *c,* ( per Leg. I ) describens lineam *B c* æqualem ipsi *A B,* adeo ut radiis *A S,* B S, *c S* ad centrum actis, confectæ forent æquales areæ *A S B,* B S *c.* Verum ubi corpus venit ad B, agat vis centripeta impulsu unico sed magno, faciatq; corpus a recta B *c* deflectere & pergere in recta B *C.* Ipsi B *S* parallela agatur *c C* occurrens B *C* in

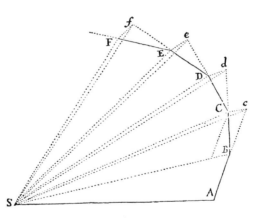

*C,* & completa secunda temporis parte, corpus ( per Legum Corol. I ) reperietur in *C,* in eodem plano cum triangulo A *S B.* Junge *S C,* & triangulum *S B C,* ob parallelas S B, C *c,* æquale erit triangulo *S B c,* atq; adeo etiam triangulo *S A B.* Simili argumento si
vis

**[ 38 ]**

vis centripeta fucceffive agat in *C, D, E,* &c. faciens ut corpus fingulis temporis particulis fingulas defcribat rectas *C D, D E E F,* &c. jacebunt hæ in eodem plano, & triangulum *S C D* triangulo *S B C* & *S D E* ipfi *S C D* & *S E F* ipfi *S D E* æquale erit. Æqualibus igitur temporibus æquales areæ in plano immoto defcribuntur: & componendo, funt arearum fummæ quævis *S A D S, S A F S* inter fe, ut funt tempora defcriptionum. Augeatur jam numerus & minuatur latitudo triangulorum in infinitum, & eorum ultima perimeter *A D F,*( per Corollarium quartum Lemmatis tertii ) erit linea curva; adeoq; vis centripeta qua corpus de tangente hujus curvæ perpetuo retrahitur, aget indefinenter; areæ vero quævis defcriptæ *S A D S, S A F S* temporibus defcriptionum femper proportionales, erunt iifdem temporibus in hoc cafu proportionales. *Q. E. D.*

TRANSLATION

## SECTION II
### *On finding centripetal forces*
### Proposition I. Theorem I

*The areas that bodies, made to move in orbits, describe by means of radii drawn to a fixed centre of force, are situated in fixed planes, and are proportional to the times.*

The time is divided into equal moments, and in the first moment of time let the body under its inherent force describe the straight line *AB*. Likewise in the second moment of time, if nothing impedes it, it would go straight through to *c* (by Law I), describing the line *Bc* equal to *AB*, so that by the radii *AS, BS, cS*, taken to the centre, there will be formed consecutive equal areas *ASB, BSc*. But where the body comes to *B*, the centripetal force delivers a single but large impulse, and causes the body to deflect from the line *Bc* and to move along the line *BC*. There is taken *cC* parallel to *BS* meeting *BC* at *C*, and at the completion of the second moment of time, the body (by the Corollary to Law I) is found at *C*, in the same plane as the triangle *ASB*. Join *SC*, and the triangle *SBc*, because of the parallels *SB, Cc*, will be equal to triangle *SBc*, and therefore also to triangle *SAB*. By a similar argument if [38] the centripetal force acts successively at *C, D, E*, etc. as though making the body describe each single line *CD, DE, EF*, etc. in each single moment of time, these will fall in the same plane, and the triangle *SCD* will be equal to the triangle *SBC*, and *SDE* to *SCD*, and *SEF* to *SCD*. Therefore in equal times there will be described equal areas in a fixed plane. And putting them together, any sums of those areas such as *SADS, SAFS*, will be to each other as the times of description. Now let the number of triangles be increased and the sides decreased indefinitely, and their ultimate perimeter *ADF* (by the fourth Corollary to the third Lemma) will be a curved line; and therefore the centripetal force by which the body is continually pulled back from the tangent to this curve, acts without restriction; but any described areas *SADS, SAFS*, always proportional to the times of description, will be in this case proportional to those times. Which was to be demonstrated.

### 5.1.5 Quantitative measures of centripetal force

In Book I, Proposition 4, Newton derived a quantitative law of centripetal force for circular motion. In modern notation, if the mass is $m$, the radius $r$, and the angular velocity $\omega$, the centripetal force is given by $mr\omega^2$, but Newton dealt only with ratios, so that the mass cancelled out. This law led to a number of important corollaries, one of which (Corollary 6) states that if Kepler's third law is taken to be correct then the planets are subject to an inverse square law of centripetal attraction.

---

### Quantitative measures of centripetal force

from Newton, *Principia*, 1687, Book I, Proposition 4, with Corollaries

---

Prop. IV. Theor. IV.

*Corporum quæ diverfos circulos æquabili motu defcribunt, vires cen-*
*tripetas ad centra eorundem circulorum tendere, & effe inter fe*
*ut arcuum fimul defcriptorum quadrata applicata ad circulorum ra-*
*dios.*

Corpora $B$, $b$ in circumferentiis circulorum $BD$, $bd$ gyran-
tia, fimul defcribant arcus $BD$, $bd$.  Quoniam fola vi infita de-
fcriberent tangentes $BC$, $bc$ his arcubus æquales, manifeftum
est quod vires centripetæ funt quæ
perpetuo retrahunt corpora de
tangentibus ad circumferentias
circulorum, atq; adeo hæ funt
ad invicem in ratione prima fpa-
tiorum nafcentium $CD$, $cd$: tendunt vero ad centra circulorum per Theor. II, propterea
quod areæ radiis defcriptæ po-
nuntur temporibus proportiona-
les.  Fiat figura $t\mathcal{k}b$ figuræ $D$
$CB$ fimilis, & per Lemma V,

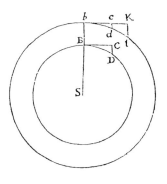

lineola $CD$ erit ad lineolam $\mathcal{k}t$ ut
arcus $BD$ ad arcum $bt$: nec non, per Lemma XI, lineola nafcens
$t\mathcal{k}$ ad lineolam nafcentem $dc$ ut $bt$ quad. ad $bd$ quad. & ex æ-
quo lineola nafcens $DC$ ad lineolam nafcentem $dc$ ut $BD \times bt$
ad $bd$ quad. feu quod perinde eft, ut $\dfrac{BD \times bt}{Sb}$ ad $\dfrac{bd\ quad.}{Sb}$, a-
deoq; ( ob æquales rationes $\dfrac{bt}{Sb}$ & $\dfrac{BD}{SB}$ ) ut $\dfrac{BD\ quad.}{SB}$ ad $\dfrac{bd}{Sb}$
quad.  Q. E. D.

Corol. 1. Hinc vires centripetæ funt ut velocitatum quadrata
applicata ad radios circulorum.

Corol. 2. Et reciproce ut quadrata temporum periodicorum ap-

G                                                                              pli-

[ 42 ]

plicata ad radios ita funt hæ vires inter fe.    Id eft ( ut cum Geometris loquar ) hæ vires funt in ratione compofita ex duplicata
ratione velocitatum directe & ratione fimplici radiorum inverfe :
necnon in ratione compofita ex ratione fimplici radiorum directe
& ratione duplicata temporum periodicorum inverfe.

*Corol.* 3. Unde fi tempora periodica æquantur, erunt tum vires centripetæ tum velocitates ut radii, & vice verfa.

*Corol.* 4. Si quadrata temporum periodicorum funt ut radii,
vires centripetæ funt æquales, & velocitates in dimidiata ratione
radiorum : Et vice verfa.

*Corol.* 5. Si quadrata temporum periodicorum funt ut quadrata radiorum, vires centripetæ funt reciproce ut radii, & velocitates æquales : Et vice verfa.

*Corol.* 6. Si quadrata temporum periodicorum funt ut cubi radiorum, vires centripetæ funt reciproce ut quadrata radiorum ;
velocitates autem in radiorum dimidiata ratione : Et vice verfa.

*Corol.* 7. Eadem omnia de temporibus, velocitatibus & viribus,
quibus corpora fimiles figurarum quarumcunq; fimilium, centraq;
fimiliter pofita habentium, partes defcribunt, confequuntur ex
Demonftratione præcedentium ad hofce cafus applicata.

*Scholium*

Cafus Corollarii fexti obtinet in corporibus cæleftibus ( ut fe-
orfum colligerunt etiam noftrates *Wrennus, Hookius & Halleus* )
& propterea quæ fpectant ad vim centripetam decrefcentem in
duplicata ratione diftantiarum a centris decrevi fufius in fequentibus exponere.

*Notation*

In keeping with his geometric style of writing, Newton retained the notation introduced by Viète
and modified by Oughtred, in which *AB quad* or *ABq* is used for *AB*-squared. This notation
persisted in geometric arguments for many years (see also 10.1.1, for example) despite the
introduction of superscript notation by Descartes in 1637.

TRANSLATION

## Proposition IV. Theorem IV

*For bodies that describe various circles in uniform motion, the centripetal forces tend to the
centre of those circles, and are to each other as the squares of the simultaneously described
arcs, to the radii of the circles.*

Bodies *B*, *b*, revolving on the circumferences of the circles *BD*, *bd*, simultaneously
describe the arcs *BD*, *bd*. Since under their own force alone they would describe tangents

*BC, bc*, to those equal arcs, it is clear that there are centripetal forces continuously pulling the bodies back from the tangents to the circumferences of the circles, and therefore that these are to each other in the first ratio of the the emerging spaces *CD, cd*; but tend towards the centre of the circles, by Theorem II, because the areas described by the radii are supposed proportional to the times. Let figure *tkb* be constructed similar to figure *DCB*, and by Lemma V, the small line *CD* will be to the small line *kt* as the arc *BD* to the arc *bt*; and also, by Lemma XI, the emerging small line *tk* to the emerging small line *dc* as $bt_q$ to $bd_q$, and from equality [of ratios] the emerging small line *DC* to the emerging small line *dc* as $BD \times bt$ to $bd_q$, or what comes to the same thing, as $\frac{BD \times bt}{Sb}$ to $\frac{bd_q}{Sb}$, and therefore (because of equal ratios $\frac{bt}{Sb}$ and $\frac{BD}{SB}$) as $\frac{BD_q}{SB}$ to $\frac{bd_q}{Sb}$.

Which was to be demonstrated.

*Corollary 1.* Hence the centripetal forces are as the squares of the velocities divided by the radii of the circles.

*Corollary 2.* And inversely as the squares of the periodic time [42] divided by the radii, so are these forces to one another. That is (as it is put by geometers) these forces are in a ratio composed from a duplicate direct ratio of the velocities and a simple inverse ratio of the radii; and also in a ratio composed from a simple direct ratio of the radii and a duplicate inverse ratio of the periodic times.

*Corollary 3.* Whence if the periodic times are equal, then both the centripetal forces and the velocities will be as the radii, and conversely.

*Corollary 4.* If the squares of the periodic times are as the radii, the centripetal forces are equal, and the velocities as the square roots of the radii, and conversely.

*Corollary 5.* If the squares of the periodic times are as the squares of the radii, the centripetal forces are as reciprocals of the radii, and the velocities are equal, and conversely.

*Corollary 6.* If the squares of the periodic times are as the cubes of the radii, the centripetal forces are as the reciprocals of the squares of the radii; moreover, the velocities are as the square roots of the radii, and conversely.

*Corollary 7.* When bodies describe similar parts of any similar figures, having similarly placed centres, everything concerning time, velocity, and force follows from the preceding demonstration applied to this case.

### *Commentary*

The case of the sixth Corollary holds for heavenly bodies (as our countrymen *Wren, Hooke*, and *Halley* have also separately discovered), and therefore what pertains to a centripetal force decreasing as the square of the distance from the centre I have decided to explain more fully in what follows.

———————————

### 5.1.6 The inverse square law for a parabola

In Book I, Proposition 11, Newton gave a further derivation of the inverse square law. His first derivation (Proposition 4, Corollary 6) had depended on Kepler's third law. Now he showed that it was only necessary to assume Kepler's first law, that a body moves in an elliptical orbit under a force directed towards one of the foci. His argument was based on the geometric properties of the ellipse and reveals a thorough understanding both of classical geometry and the principles of motion along a curve. Proposition 12 gave the corresponding arguments for a body moving along a hyperbola. Below we see the similar but rather easier argument that follows in Proposition 13, for a body moving along a parabola.

Newton claimed, in Corollary 1, that Propositions 11, 12, and 13 together give rise to the converse theorem: that bodies moving under an inverse square law necessarily move along one of the conic sections. Newton regarded this as 'obvious' and only in later editions did he give a sketchy justification of this important Corollary.[1]

---

1. For detailed discussion on this point see Cohen and Whitman 1999, 132–136.

# The inverse square law for a parabola

from Newton, *Principia*, 1687, Book I, Lemmas 13 and 14, Proposition 13 and Corollaries

### Lemma XIII.

*Latus rectum Parabolæ ad verticem quemvis pertinens, est quadru-
plum distantiæ verticis illius ab umbilico figuræ.* Patet ex Conicis.

### Lemma XIV.

*Perpendiculum quod ab umbilico Parabolæ ad tangentem ejus demit-
titur, medium est proportionale inter distantias umbilici a puncto
contactus & a vertice principali figuræ.*

Sit enim A P Q Parabola, S umbilicus ejus, A vertex princi-
palis, P punct-
um contact-
us, P O ordi-
natim applica
ta ad diame-
trum princi-
palem, P M
tangens dia-
metro princi-
pali occur-

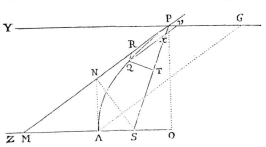

rens in M,& S N linea perpendicularis ab umbilico in tangentem.
Jungatur A N, & ob æquales M S & S P, M N & N P, M A &
A O, parallelæ erunt rectæ A N & O P, & inde triangulum S A N
rectangulum erit ad A & simile triangulis æqualibus S M N, S P N,
Ergo P S est ad S N ut S N ad S A. Q. E. D.

Corol. 1. P S q. est ad S N q. ut P S ad S A.

Corol. 2. Et ob datam S A, est S N q. ut P S.

Corol. 3. Et concursus tangentis cujusvis P M cum recta S N
quæ ab umbilico in ipsam perpendicularis est, incidit in rectam
A N, quæ Parabolam tangit in vertice principali.                Prop

[ 54 ]

## Prop. XIII. Prob. VIII.

*Moveatur corpus in perimetro Parabolæ: requiritur Lex vis centripe-
tæ tendentis ad umbilicum hujus figuræ.*

Maneat conftructio Lemmatis, fitq; P corpus in perimetro Parabolæ, & a loco *Q* in quem corpus proxime movetur, age ipfi S P
Parallelam *Q* R & perpendicularem *Q T*, necnon *Q v* tangenti parallelam & occurentem tum diametro *Y* P G in *v*, tum diftantiæ
S P in x.    Jam ob fimilia triangula P x *v*, M S P & æqualia unius
latera *S* M, S P, æqualia funt alterius latera P x feu *Q R* & P *v*.
Sed, ex Conicis, quadratum ordinatæ *Q v* æquale eft rectangulo
fub latere recto & fegmento diametri P *v*, id eft ( per Lem. XIII. )
rectangulo 4 P S x P *v* feu 4 P S x *Q* R; & punctis P & *Q* coeuntibus, ratio *Q v* ad *Q* x ( per Lem. 8. ) fit æqualitatis.   Ergo
*Q* x q. eo in
cafu, æquale
eft rectangu-
lo 4 P S x Q
R.   Eft au-
tem ( ob æ-
quales angu-
los *Q* x T, M
P S, P MO )
*Q*xq. ad QTq.

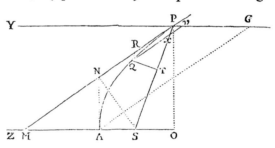

ut P S q. ad S Nq.  hoc eft ( per Corol. I. Lem. X IV. )ut P S ad
A S,  id eft ut 4 P S x *Q* R ad 4 A S x *Q* R,  & inde ( per Prop.
9. Lib. V Elem. ) Q T q. & 4 A S x Q R æquantur.   Ducantur
hæc æqualia in $\frac{SPq.}{QR}$, & fiet $\frac{SPq. \times QTq.}{QR}$ æquale S P q. x 4 A S :
& propterea ( per Corol. Theor. V. ) vis centripeta eft reciproce
ce ut *S* P q. x 4 A S,  id eft, ob datam 4 A S, reciproce in duplicata ratione diftantiæ S P. Q. E. I.

*Corol.*

[ 55 ]

*Corol.* I. Ex tribus noviſſimis Propoſitionibus conſequens eſt, quod ſi corpus quodvis P, ſecundum lineam quamvis rectam P R, quacunq; cum velocitate exeat de loco P, & vi centripeta quæ ſit reciproce proportionalis quadrato diſtantiæ a centro, ſimul agitetur; movebitur hoc corpus in aliqua ſectionum Conicarum umbilicum habente in centro virium; & contra.

*Corol.* II. Et ſi velocitas, quacum corpus exit de loco ſuo P, ea ſit, qua lineola P R in minima aliqua temporis particula deſcribi poſſit, & vis centripeta potis ſit eodem tempore corpus idem movere per ſpatium Q R : movebitur hoc corpus in Conica aliqua ſectione cujus latus rectum eſt quantitas illa $\frac{QT q.}{Q R}$ quæ ultimo ſit ubi lineolæ P R, Q R in infinitum diminuuntur.    Circulum in his Corollariis refero ad Ellipſin, & caſum excipio ubi corpus recta deſcendit ad centrum.

---

TRANSLATION

---

### Lemma XIII

*The latus rectum* [width at the focus] of a parabola belonging to any vertex, is four times the distance of that vertex from the focus of the figure. Clear from the *Conics* [of Apollonius].

### Lemma XIV

*A perpendicular dropped from the focus of a parabola to a tangent is a mean proportional between the distances to the focus from the point of contact and from the principal vertex of the figure.*

For suppose *APQ* is a parabola, *S* its focus, *A* its principal vertex, *P* a point of contact, *PO* an ordinate to the principal diameter, *PM* a tangent meeting the principal diameter at *M*, and *SN* a perpendicular from the focus to the tangent. Draw *AN*, and because *MS* and *SP*, *MN* and *NP*, *MA* and *AO*, are equal, the lines *AN* and *OP* will be parallel, and hence the triangle *SAN* will be right-angled at *A*, and similar to the equal triangles *SMN*, *SPN*. Therefore *PS* is to *SN* as *SN* to *SA*. Which was to be demonstrated.

Corollary 1. $PS_q$ is to $SN_q$ as *PS* to *SA*.

Corollary 2. And because *SA* is known, so is $SN_q$ to *PS*.

Corollary 3. And the meeting of any tangent *PM* with the line *SN* which is perpendicular to it from the focus, falls on the line *AN*, which touches the parabola at the principal vertex.

## Proposition XIII. Problem VIII

*Suppose a body is moved along the perimeter of a parbola; it is required to find the law of the centripetal force tending towards the focus of that figure.*

Keep the construction of the lemmas, and let $P$ be a body on the perimeter of the parabola, and from a place $Q$ into which the body is almost moved, take $QR$ parallel and $QT$ perpendicular to $SP$, and also $Qv$ parallel to the tangent and meeting the diameter $YPG$ at $v$, and the line $SP$ at $x$. Now because of similar triangles $Pxv$, $MSP$, and the equality of the sides of one, $SM$, $SP$, the sides of the other are also equal, $Px$ or $QR$ and $Pv$. But, from *Conics*, the square of the ordinate $Qv$ is equal to the product of the latus rectum and the segment $Pv$ of the diameter, that is (by Lemma XIII) the product $4PS \times Pv$ or $4PS \times QR$; and as the points $P$ and $Q$ come together, the ratio $Qv$ to $Qx$ (by Lemma 8) becomes one of equality. Therefore $Qx_q$ in this case is equal to the product $4PS \times QR$. Moreover (because of equal angles $QxT$, $MPS$, $PMO$) $Qx_q$ is to $QT_q$ as $PS_q$ to $SN_q$, that is (by Lemma XIV, Corollary I) as $PS$ to $AS$, that is as $4PS \times QR$ to $4AS \times QR$, and thence (by *Elements*, Book V, Proposition 9) $QT_q$ and $4AS \times QR$ are equal. Multiplying these equal quantities by $\frac{SP_q}{QR}$, then $\frac{SP_q \times QT_q}{QR}$ becomes equal to $SP_q \times 4AS$. And therefore (by the Corollary to Theorem V) the centripetal force is reciprocal to $SP_q \times 4AS$, that is, since $4AS$ is given, reciprocal to the square of the distance $SP$. Which was to be found.

*Corollary I.* From the three latest propositions the consequence is that if any body $P$ departs from a place $P$ with any velocity, and moves on any line $PR$, and is at the same time acted on by a centripetal force which is in inverse proportion to the square of the distance from the centre, this body will be moved along some conic section having its focus as the centre of force; and conversely.

*Corollary II.* And if the velocity with which the body leaves $P$ is such that the line segment $PR$ can be described in some least moment of time, and the centripetal force is able to make the same body move through the space $QR$ in the same time, then the body will move along some conic section whose *latus rectum* is that quantity $\frac{QT_q}{QR}$ which is the ultimate ratio when the line segments $PR$, $QR$, are diminished indefinitely. In these Corollaries I refer to a circle as an ellipse, and exclude the case where the body falls directly to the centre.

# CHAPTER 6

# EARLY NUMBER THEORY

N umber theory is concerned with the most basic elements of mathematics, the natural numbers, yet it also presents some of the most intractable problems. One of the most famous is Fermat's 'last theorem', which was concise enough to write down in a margin but took almost 400 years to prove. Many other claims about the natural numbers are equally simple to state, but even an approach to a proof still remains elusive. Most of modern number theory is beyond the scope of this book, and this chapter no more than touches upon its beginnings. Although several important results were discovered by Indian mathematicians as early as the sixth century AD, these were not translated into European languages until the nineteenth century or later, and in the meantime number theory had also begun to emerge in France and England from its classical roots in the writings of Euclid and Diophantus.

## 6.1 PERFECT NUMBERS

### 6.1.1 Euclid's theorem on perfect numbers, *c.* 250 BC

In Euclid's *Elements*, Book VII, we find perfect numbers defined as (whole) numbers that are the sum of their parts, or proper divisors (see 1.3.1). In Book IX, Euclid went on to state and prove a result that gave rise to much speculation later. In modern notation, if $1 + 2 + 4 + \cdots + 2^{n-1} (= 2^n - 1)$ is a prime $p$, then $p \times 2^{n-1}$ is a perfect number. As in Chapter 1, we will use Barrow's 1660 edition of Euclid to show the steps of the proof. Barrow offered the specific example $n = 5$ and $p = 31$, but the proof itself is quite general.

---

## Euclid's theorem on perfect numbers

from *Euclide's Elements*, edited by Barrow, 1660, Proposition IX.36

---

*Notation*
Margin notes refer to earlier propositions, thus 14.7 means Book VII, Proposition 14, and so on.

### P R o p. XXXVI.

1. A,2.  B,4.  C,8.  D,16.
E,31.  G,62.  H,124.  L,248.  F, 496.
M,31.          N,465.
P - - - -          Q - - -

*If from a unite be taken how many numbers soever*
1,A,B,C,D, *in double proportion continually, untill the*
*whole added together* E *be a prime number ; and if this*
*whole*

### E U C L I D E'S *Elements.*                    193

*whole* E *multiplying the last produce a number* F , *that*
*which is produced* F *shall be a perfect number.*

Take as many numbers E, G, H , L , likewise in
double proportion continually ; then *a* of equality     a 14.7.
A.D :: E.L.*b* therefore AL = DE *c* = F. *d* whence     b 19 7.
L = F. Wherefore E,G,H,L,F , are ÷ in double           c *hyp.*
$\frac{2}{2}$                                                            d 7.ax.7.
                                                         e 35. 9.
proportion. Let G — E be = M,and F — E = N ;            f 3.ax.1.
*e* then M.E :: N.E + G + H + L. *f* But M = E.           g 14. 5.
g therefore N = E + G + H + L. *h* therefore F           h 2.ax.1.
= 1 + B + C + D + E + G + H + L = E +
N.Moreover because D *k* measures DE(F)*l* therefore      k 7.ax.7.
every one, 1, A,B, C, *m* measuring D , as *m* also E,     l 11.ax.7.
G,H,L,does measure F.And further,no other num-          m 11.9.
ber measures the said F.   For if there do, let it be P,
which measures F by Q.*n* therefore PQ = F = D-         n 9.ax.7.
F. *o* therefore E. Q:: P. D. therefore seeing A  a      o 19.7.
prime number measures D, *p* and so no other P mea-     p 13. 9.
sures the same , *q* consequently E does not measure     q 20.def.9.
Q. Wherefore E being supposed a prime number,
*r* it shall be prime to Q. *s* wherefore E and Q are the   r 31.7.
least in their proportion ; *t* and so E measures P as    s 23. 7.
many times as Q does D ; *u* therefore Q is one of       t 21. 7.
them A,B,C. Let it be B. seeing then of equality B.     u 13.7.
D :: E H.*x* and so BH = DE = F = PQ.*x* and so          x 19.7.
also Q B :: H. P.*y* therefore H = P. therefore P is      y 14. 5.
also one of them A, B, C , &c. *against the Hypoth.*
Wherefore no other beside the foresaid numbers
measures F ,and *z* consequently F is a perfect num-     z 21. def.7.
ber. *Which was to be Demonstrated.*

*The End of the ninth Book.*

### 6.1.2  Mersenne primes, 1644

Euclid's definition of perfect numbers and his theorem that if $2^n - 1$ is prime then $(2^n - 1) \times 2^{n-1}$ is perfect, survived in the arithmetical treatises of Nicomachus ($c.$ 100 AD), and Boethius ($c.$ 486 AD), but with additional layers of speculation that would never have appeared in Euclid. It was suggested, for example, that perfect numbers, being few and far between, were to be compared to virtues, while all other numbers, in which the divisors sum to more or less than the original number, were classed as superabundant or deficient. It was also asserted that perfect numbers end alternately in six or eight (in Roman numerals, an alternating pattern of VI and VIII), and that they can be generated *only* by Euclid's rule. The first claim breaks down after the first few cases, and the second was proved correct (for even perfect numbers) only in 1749, by Euler. The question of whether odd perfect numbers exist at all remains undecided to this day.

Perfect numbers continued to exert their fascination into the sixteenth and seventeenth centuries, and led naturally to the search for primes of the form $2^n - 1$. Mersenne, in 1644 believed that $2^n - 1$ was prime for $n = 2, 3, 5, 7, 13, 17, 19, 31, 67, 127, 257$, but was unable to test the larger numbers. His list was offered as an alternative to one given by the catholic theologian Petrus Bungus in his *Numerorum mysteria* in 1599. There Bungus had demonstrated, amongst other things, the sinfulness of the number 11, and that the 666, the number of the Beast in the *Book of Revelation*, was to be associated not with the Pope, but with Martin Luther. He also provided a list of perfect numbers, most of which, as Mersenne scornfully pointed out, were completely wrong.

Mersenne's list was not accurate either. It was already known to Fermat that if $p$ and $q$ are prime and if $q$ divides $2^p - 1$, then $q$ must be of the form $2kp + 1$ for some integer $k$; this limits the number of divisors that need to be tested and was used by Euler to prove that $2^{31} - 1$ is divisible by 621. Mersenne's ninth number, $2^{67} - 1$, is also composite, as was proved by Edouard Lucas in 1867, although the actual factors ($193707721 \times 761838257287$) were not found until 1903, by Frank Nelson Cole. On the other hand, by the end of the nineteenth century, three further primes were found to be missing from Mersenne's list: $2^{61} - 1$, $2^{89} - 1$, and $2^{107} - 1$.

Perfect numbers are no longer charged with religious or moral significance, but the search for Mersenne primes is by no means over. Testing for divisors of $2^p - 1$ for large primes $p$ has become a standard measure of computing efficiency, and from time to time a new Mersenne prime is announced. The largest discovered to date can be found on the Mersenne prime website, http://primes.utm.edu/mersenne/

---

## Mersenne's list of primes

from Mersenne, *Cogitata physico-mathematica*, 1644, unpaginated preface, §XIX

---

Vbi fuerit operæpretium aduertere XXVIII numeros à Petro Bungo pro perfectis exhibitos, capite XXVIII. libri de Numeris, non esse omnes Perfectos, quippe 20 sunt imperfecti, adeovt solos octo perfectos habeat videlicet 6. 28. 496. 8128. 23550336. 8589869056. 137-43869328, & 2305843008139952128; qui sunt è regione tabulæ Bungi, 1, 2, 3, 4, 8, 10, 12, & 29 : quique soli perfecti sunt, vt qui Bungum habuerint, errori medicinam faciant.

Porrò numeri perfecti adeo rari sunt, vt vndecim dumtaxat potuerint hactenus inueniri : hoc est, alii tres à Bongianis differentes : neque enim vllus est alius perfectus ab illis octo, nisi superes exponentem numerum 62, progressionis duplæ ab 1 incipientis. Nonus enim perfectus est potestas exponentis 68 minus 1. Decimus, potestas exponentis 128, minus 1. Vndecimus denique, potestas 258, minus 1, hoc est potestas 257, vnitate decurtata, multiplicata per potestatem 256.

Qui vndecim alios repererit, nouerit se analysim omnem, quæ fuerit hactenus, superasse : memineritque interea nullum esse perfectum à 17000 potestate ad 32000; & nullum potestatum interuallum tantum assignari posse, quin detur illud absque perfectis. Verbi gratia, si fuerit exponens 050000, nullus erit numerus progressionis duplæ vsque ad 2090000, qui perfectis numeris seruiat, hoc est qui minor vnitate, primus existat.

Vnde clarum est quàm rari sint perfecti numeri, & quàm meritò viris perfectis comparentur; esseque vnam ex maximis totius Matheseos difficultatibus, præscriptam numerorum perfectorum multitudinum exhibere; quemadmodum & agnoscere num dati numeri 15, aut 20 caracteribus constantes, sint primi necne, cum nequidem sæculum integrum huic examini, quocumque modo hactenus cognito, sufficiat.

Here it will be worthwhile to draw to the attention that the 28 numbers exhibited by Peter Bungus as perfect, in chapter XXVIII of his book of numbers, are not all perfect, indeed 20 are imperfect, so that there are only eight perfect, clearly 6, 28, 496, 8128, 23550336, 8589869056, 137438691328, and 2305843008139952128, which are ranked in the table of Bungus as 1, 2, 3, 4, 8, 10, 12, and 29; which alone are perfect, so those who keep to Bungus practice medicine erroneously.

Beyond that the perfect numbers are indeed rare, so that it has so far been possible to find only eleven, that is, three others different from those of Bungus, for there is not one perfect other than those eight unless you raise the exponent beyond 62, in the progression of powers of two starting from 1. For the ninth perfect number the power has exponent 68 minus 1. For the tenth, the power has exponent 128 minus 1. Finally for the eleventh, the power [with exponent] 258 minus 1, that is, the 257th power, and having taken away unity, multiplied by the 256th power.

Anyone who will find others than these eleven must make himself exceed all analysis that has been done up to now; and he should remember meanwhile that there are no perfect numbers from the 17000th to the 32000th power; and it is not possible to assign such an interval of powers unless it is free of perfect numbers. For example, if there is an exponent 50000, there is no number in the progression of powers of two as far as 2090000 which can serve for a perfect number, that is, which reduced by one is a prime.

Whence it is clear how rare are the perfect numbers, and how rightly they are compared to perfect men; and that it is one of the most difficult of all mathematical problems to exhibit a list of a collection of perfect numbers; just as also to understand whether given numbers consisting of 15 or 20 digits, are prime or not, since not even a whole lifetime is sufficient to examine this, by any method so far known.

### 6.1.3  Fermat's little theorem, 1640

It was almost certainly the search for primes of the form $2^p - 1$ that led Fermat to the first formulation of his 'little theorem'. In its modern form, the theorem is as follows: given any number $a$, and prime $p$ such that $p$ does not divide $a$, then $a^{p-1} \equiv 1 \pmod{p}$. In October 1640 Fermat sent the theorem for the case $a = 2$ to Mersenne, and the more general case to his correspondent and rival Frenicle de Bessy, but declined to offer a proof to either. We may take him at his word that he could have done so if he had wished, but his 'little theorem', like so many other important mathematical results of the seventeenth-century, appears to have been derived in the first place from intuition, observation, and intelligent pattern-spotting.

# Fermat's little theorem (1)

from Fermat to Mersenne, October 1640, as published in Fermat, *Varia opera*, 1679, 177

Ce que j'eſtime le plus eſt cét abbregé pour l'invention des nombres parfaits, à quoy je ſuis reſolu de m'attacher, ſi Monſieur Frenicle ne me fait part de ſa methode. Voicy trois propoſitions que j'ay trouvées, ſur leſquelles j'eſpere de faire un grand baſtiment.

Les nombres moindres de l'unité que ceux qui procedent de la progreſſion double, comme

| 1 | 2 | 3 | 4 | 5 | 6 | 7 | 8 | 9 | 10 |
|---|---|---|---|---|---|---|---|---|---|
| 1 | 3 | 7 | 15 | 31 | 63 | 127 | 255 | 511 | 1023 |
| 11 | 12 | 13 | 2047 | 4095 | 8191 | &c. | | | |

Soient appellez les nombres parfaits, parceque toutes les fois qu'ils ſont premiers ils les produiſent. Mettez au deſſus de ces nombres, autant en progreſſion naturelle 1. 2. 3. &c. qui ſoient appellez leurs expoſans.

Cela ſuppoſé, je dis,

1. Que lors que l'expoſant d'un nombre radical eſt compoſé, ſon radical eſt auſſi compoſé, comme parceque 6. expoſant de 63. eſt compoſé, · je dis que 63. eſt auſſi compoſé.

2. Lors que l'expoſant eſt nombre premier, je dis que ſon radical moins l'unité eſt meſuré par le double de l'expoſant, comme parceque 7. expoſant de 127. eſt nombre premier, je dis que 126. eſt multiple de 14.

3. Lors que l'expoſant eſt nombre premier, je dis que ſon radical ne peut être meſuré par aucun nombre premier que par ceux qui ſont plus grands de l'unité qu'un multiple du double de l'expoſant, ou que le double de l'expoſant. Comme parce que 11. expoſant de 2047. eſt nombre premier, je dis qu'il ne peut être meſuré que par un nombre plus grand de l'unité que 22. comme 23. ou bien par un nombre plus grand de l'unité qu'un multiple de 22. en effet 2047. n'eſt meſuré que par 23. & par 89. duquel ſi vous ôtez l'unité, reſte 88. multiple de 22.

Voilà trois fort belles propoſitions que j'ay trouvées & prouvées non ſans peine. Je les puis appeller les fondements de l'invention des nombres parfaits. Je ne doute pas que Monſieur Frenicle ne ſoit allé plus avant, mais je ne fais que commencer, & ſans doute ces propoſitions paſſeront pour tres-belles dans l'eſprit de ceux qui n'ont pas beaucoup épluché ces matieres, & je ſeray bien aiſe d'apprendre le ſentiment de Monſieur de Roberval.

## TRANSLATION

What I esteem most is this short method for finding perfect numbers, to which I have resolved to devote myself, if Monsieur Frenicle does not share his method with me. Here are three propositions that I have found, on which I hope to build a great edifice.

The numbers one less than those that occur in a progression by doubling, such as

| 1 | 2 | 3 | 4 | 5 | 6 | 7 | 8 | 9 | 10 | 11 | 12 | 13 | |
|---|---|---|---|---|---|---|---|---|---|---|---|---|---|
| 1 | 3 | 7 | 15 | 31 | 63 | 127 | 255 | 511 | 1023 | 2047 | 4095 | 8191 | etc. |

may be called [roots of] perfect numbers, because whenever they are prime they produce them. Put above these numbers the natural progression 1, 2, 3, etc. which may be called their exponents.

That assumed, I say,

1. That when the exponent corresponding to a root is composite, the root itself is also composite, so because 6, the exponent of 63, is composite, I say that 63 is also composite.

2. When the exponent is prime, I say that the root less one is divisible by twice the exponent, so because 7, the exponent of 127, is prime, I know that 126 is a multiple of 14.

3. When the exponent is prime, I say that the root may not be divided by any prime number except by those that are greater by one than a multiple of twice the exponent, or than the double of the exponent. So, because 11, the exponent of 2047, is prime, I know that it may only be divided by a number greater by one than 22, namely 23, or rather, by a number greater by one than a multiple of 22. Indeed 2047 is only divisible by 23 and by 89, from which if you take one, there remains 88, a multiple of 22.

These are three very beautiful propositions that I have found and proved, not without difficulty. I may call them the foundations for the discovery of perfect numbers. I do not doubt that Monsieur Frenicle has gone further, but I have only begun, and without doubt these propositions will pass as excellent in the mind of those who have not immersed themselves much in these matters, and I will be very happy to learn the reaction of Monsieur Roberval.

---

## Fermat's little theorem (2)

from Fermat to Frenicle, 18 October 1640, as published in Fermat, *Varia opera*, 1679, 164

---

Tout nombre premier mesure infailliblement une des puissances − 1. de quelque progression que ce soit , & l'exposant de ladite puissance est soûs-multiple du nombre premier donné − 1. Et aprés qu'on a trouvé la premiere puissance qui satisfait à la question, toutes celles dont les exposans sont multiples de l'exposant de la premiere satisfont de méme à la question.

Exemple, soit la progression donnée ,

| 1 | 2 | 3 | 4 | 5 | 6 | |
|---|---|---|---|---|---|---|
| 3 | 9 | 27 | 81 | 243 | 729, | &c. |

Avec ses exposans au dessus.

Prenez , par exemple, le nombre premier 13. il mesure la troisiéme puissance − 1, de laquelle 3. exposant est soûsmultiple de 12. qui est moindre de l'unité que le nombre de 13. Et parce que l'exposant de 729. qui est 6. est multiple du premier exposant 3. il s'ensuit que 13. mesure aussi ladite puissance de 729 − 1. Et cette proposition est generalement vraye en toutes progressions & en tous nombres premiers. Dequoy je vous envoyerois la demonstration, si je n'apprehendois d'étre trop long.

Every prime number divides without fail one of the powers −1 of any progression whatever, and the exponent of the said power is a submultiple of the given prime number −1. And after one has found the first power that satisfies the question, all those in which the exponents are multiples of the exponent of the first satisfy the question in the same way.

For example, let the given progression be

$$
\begin{array}{ccccccc}
1 & 2 & 3 & 4 & 5 & 6 & \\
3 & 9 & 27 & 81 & 243 & 729 & \text{etc.}
\end{array}
$$

with its exponents above it.

Take, for example, the prime number 13. It divides the third power −1, of which 3, the exponent, is a divisor of 12, which is less by unity than the number 13. And because the exponent of 729, which is 6, is a multiple of the first exponent 3, it follows that 13 also divides the said power 729 − 1. And this proposition is generally true for all progressions and for all prime numbers. Of which I would send you the proof if I did not fear to go on too long.

## 6.2 'PELL'S' EQUATION

### 6.2.1 Fermat's challenge and Brouncker's response, 1657

Fermat's research into properties of the natural numbers continued for many years. He was particularly inspired by problems from the *Arithmetica* of Diophantus, which he read in the Latin edition published by Bachet in 1621. Fermat found many remarkable results but had little success in persuading his contemporaries to share his interest or even to understand what he was up to. Blaise Pascal, for example, had responded to him in 1655 as follows:[1]

I admire your method by divisors, rather more than I truly understand it, […] But, Monsieur, if I have gone along with you in that, seek elsewhere those who can follow you in your numerical discoveries, of which you have given me the honour of sending me the statements. For my part, I confess to you that this goes far past me; I am capable only of admiring them, and very humbly beg you to use your first leisure to complete them.

Finding no-one in France with whom to discuss his discoveries, Fermat looked further afield, and in 1657 tried to communicate them to Wallis in England. His first problem,

---

1. 'J'admire votre méthode par les parts, d'autant mieux que je l'entends fort bien, […] Mais, Monsieur, si j'ai concouru avec vous en cela, cherchez ailleurs qui vous suivre dans vos inventions numériques, dont vous m'avez fait la grâce de m'envoyer les énonciations. Pour moi, je vous confesse que cela me passe de bien loin; je ne suis capable que de les admirer, et vous supplie très humblement d'occuper votre premier loisir à les achever.' Fermat, 1891–1912, II, 314.

set in the form of an open challenge, was to find whole numbers $a$ and $b$ satisfying the equation $na^2 + 1 = b^2$, where $n$ is any prime integer.[2]

Given any non-square number, there are infinitely many squares which multiplied by the given number, and added to one, make a square. For example, take 3, a non-square number; multiplied by the square 1, and added to one, it makes 4, which is a square. Likewise the same 3 multiplied by 16, and added to one, makes 49, which is a square. And in place of 1 and 16, there may likewise be found infinitely many other squares. But we seek a general canon, given any non-square number. There is sought, for example, a square, which multiplied by 149, or 109, or 433, etc. and added to one, makes a square.

Wallis dismissed the question as trivial. Brouncker, however, offered the solution

$$a = \frac{2r}{r^2 - n},$$

where $a$ and $n$ are as in the equation above, and $r$ is an arbitrary integer. Brouncker's solutions was based on the identity

$$\frac{n(2r)^2}{(r^2 - n)^2} + 1 = \frac{(r^2 + n)^2}{(r^2 - n)^2}.$$

He failed to recognize what Fermat had implied but not made explicit, that he wanted solutions in integers. Once Brouncker understood what was needed, he tackled the problem more seriously, and came up with an elegant and general algebraic solution. He chose the particular case $n = 13$ to demonstrate his method, but clearly it could work for any value of $n$. Fermat was forced to admit, somewhat grudgingly, that Brouncker was correct, and never revealed his own solution.

There was little or no further interest in such problems during the rest of the seventeenth century, but in the 1720s Euler came across Brouncker's solution in Wallis's *Opera mathematica*.[3] Euler mistakenly attributed it to Pell (a simple substitution of one obscure English mathematician for another), but both he and later Lagrange went on to develop Brouncker's ideas considerably further.[4]

---

2. 'Dato quovis numero non-quadrato, dantur infiniti quadrati qui in datum numerum ducti, adscita unitate, conficiant quadratum. Exemplum. Datur 3, numerus non-quadratus; ille ductus in quadratum 1, adscita unitate, facit 49, qui est quadratus. Et loco 1 et 16, possunt alii infinitii quadrati idem praestantes inveniri. Sed Canonem Generalem, Dato quovis numero non-quadrato, inquirimus. Quaeratur, verbi gratia, quadratus, qui ductus in 149, aut 109, aut 433, etc. adscita unitate conficiat quadratum.' Fermat to Digby, February 1657; cited in Wallis 1658, letter 8; published in Fermat 1679, 190.

3. Wallis 1693–99, I, pp.          4. For details see Dickson 1919–23, 352–364.

---

## Brouncker's solution of 'Pell's equation'

from Brouncker to Wallis, November 1657, as published in Wallis, *A treatise of algebra*, 1685, 365

---

The Method is this.

Suppose we (for example) the Non-quadrate number proposed, $n = 13$, and the Square sought $aa$; and therefore $naa + 1 = 13aa + 1$, a Square number. Then is

$$13aa + 1 = 9aa + 6ab + bb$$

That is     $4aa + 1 = 6ab + bb =$

Therefore    $2b > a > b.$

Be it       $a = b + c.$ And therefore

$$4bb + 8bc + 4cc + 1 = 6bb + 6bc + bb$$

That is     $2bc + 4cc + 1 = 3bb =$

$$2c > b > c$$
$$b = c + d$$
$$2cc + 2cd + 4cc + 1 = 3cc + 6cd + 3dd$$
$$3cc + 1 = 4cd + 3dd =$$
$$2d > c > d$$
$$c = d + e$$
$$3dd + 6de + 3ee + 1 = 4dd + 4de + 3dd$$
$$2de + 3ee + 1 = 4dd =$$
$$2e > d > e$$
$$d = e + f$$
$$2ee + 2ef + 3ee + 1 = 4ee + 8ef + 4ff$$
$$ee + 1 = 6ef + 4ff =$$
$$7f > e > 6f$$
$$e = 6f + g$$
$$36ff + 12fg + gg + 1 = 36ff + 6fg + 4ff$$
$$6fg + gg + 1 = 4ff =$$
$$2g > f > g$$
$$f = g + h$$
$$6gg + 6gh + gg + 1 = 4gg + 8gh + 4hh$$
$$3gg + 1 = 2gh + 4hh =$$
$$2h > g > h$$
$$g = h + j$$
$$3hh + 6hj + 3jj + 1 = 2hh + 2hj + 4hh$$
$$4hj + 3jj + 1 = 3hh$$
$$2j = h$$
$$j = 1.$$

Therefore     
$$j = 1$$
$$h = 2$$
$$g = 3$$
$$f = 5$$
$$e = 33$$
$$d = 38$$
$$c = 71$$
$$b = 109$$
$$a = 180.$$

And in the like manner may we proceed for any other Non-quadrate number proposed.

## 6.3 FERMAT'S FINAL CHALLENGE

We can hardly leave seventeenth-century number theory without mentioning one of the most famous mathematical problems of all time, Fermat's 'last theorem'. Working on Proposition II.8 of the *Arithmetica* of Diophantus, Fermat observed that although it is indeed always possible to separate a square into two other squares, the same is not true for a cube or any higher power. He noted the 'theorem' in the margin of his copy of Bachet's 1621 edition of the *Arithmetica* (see 1.3.3).[5]

It is a rule that no cube into two cubes, nor a fourth power into two fourth powers, and generally no power at all beyond the square, can be separated into two of the same name, of which I have truly discovered a marvellous proof. Here the meagreness of the margin will not hold it.

The date of Fermat's annotation is not known, but in August 1657 he sent further number challenges to the mathematicians of England and the Netherlands, and one of them was to separate a given cube into two other cubes. Wallis replied somewhat casually that he was sure Brouncker could handle it; Fermat's reply in April 1658 was scathing.[6]

And to make him [Wallis] see that lack of knowledge in this sort of question makes him sometimes conceive a greater opinion of his strength than he rightly has, he says that he does not doubt at all that my Lord *Brouncker* can resolve the two questions *to separate a given cube number into two rational cubes*, and *to separate a given number composed of two cubes into two other rational cubes*. I reply to him that he may by chance be not mistaken in the second, although it is quite difficult, but for the first, it is one of my negative propositions, which neither he nor Lord Brouncker can perhaps demonstrate so easily; for I maintain,

*That there is no cube at all in numbers, that can be separated into two rational cubes.*

Wallis was not to be drawn, and Fermat's 'last theorem' was not taken up by any other mathematician in his own lifetime. In later years, however, his scribbled words in the margin of Diophantus became the focus of thousands of hours of effort by amateur and professional mathematicians alike. The theorem was finally proved by Andrew Wiles in 1995, but the proof used mathematics far beyond anything Fermat could have envisaged, and certainly beyond anything he could have written in his margin.

---

5. 'Cubum autem in duos cubos, aut quadratoquadratum in duos quadratoquadratos & generaliter nullam in infinitam ultra quadratum potestatem in duos eiusdem nominis fas est dividere cuius rei demonstrationem mirabilem sane detexi. Hanc marginis exiguitas non caperet.' Diophantus 1670, 61.

6. 'Et pour luy faire voir que le defaut de connoisance de cette sorte de questions luy fera quelquefois concevoir plus grande opinion de ses forces qu'il n'en doit raisonnablement avoir, il dit qu'il ne doute point que My Lord *Brouncker* ne resolve les deux questions, *datum numerum cubum in duos cubos rationales dividere*, Et *datum numerum ex duobus cubis compositum in duos alios cubos rationales dividere*, Ie luy répons qu'il pourra paradventure ne se mesconter pas en la seconde quoy quelle soit assez difficile, mais que pour la premiere, c'est de mes propositions negatives que ni luy ni le Seigneur Brouncker ne demontreront peut estre pas si aysement; car ie soutiens,
*Qu'il n'y a aucun cube en nombres qui puisse estre divisé en deux cubes rationaux.*' Fermat to Wallis, 7 April 1658, as published in Wallis 1658, 159–160.

# CHAPTER 7

# EARLY PROBABILITY

Combinatorial problems have appeared for centuries in many different guises: from Indian texts as early as the sixth century BC that posed and answered questions about combinations of tastes, or perfumes, or precious stones, to discussions by medieval Hebrew writers about combinations of letters of the alphabet. Lists of the possible numbers on the faces of two or three dice appeared in medieval European texts, but the first writer known to have offered a systematic calculation of probabilities was Girolamo Cardano. His treatise *Liber de ludo aleae* (*A book on the game of dice*) was written around 1526, though it was not published until 1663. By that time, the calculation of odds in gambling was becoming the foundation of the modern theory of probability.

## 7.1 THE MATHEMATICS OF GAMBLING

### 7.1.1 Pascal's correspondence with Fermat, 1654

Two particular problems arising from games of dice were already in circulation in the sixteenth century: (1) how many throws of two dice are needed to give an even chance of two sixes? (2) how should the stakes be fairly divided between two players if a game is interrupted before the end? The first was treated by Cardano in his *Liber de ludo aleae*, and a version of the second appeared in Luca Pacioli's *Summa de arithmetica* in 1494. Both questions were re-posed in 1654 by one Monsieur de Méré to Blaise Pascal, who discussed the second in correspondence with Fermat.

Here we give Fermat's solution to the problem of sharing out the stakes if a game of four rounds is interrupted after the first, second, or third round.

## Pascal's correspondence with Fermat
from Pascal to Fermat, 29 July 1654, from Fermat, *Varia opera*, 1679, 179–180

❦❦❦❦❦❦❦❦❦❦❦❦❦❦❦❦❦❦❦❦❦

### *Lettre de Monsieur Pascal à M. de Fermat.*

Le 29. Iuillet 1654.

MONSIEUR,

L'impatiance me prend aussi-bien qu'à vous, & quoy que je sois encore au lit, je ne puis m'empécher de vous dire que je receus hier au soir de la part de Mr. de Carcavi vôtre lettre sur les partis, que j'admire si fort que je ne puis vous le dire. Je n'ay pas le loisir de m'étendre, mais en un mot vous avez trouvé les deux partis des dez & des parties dans la parfaite justesse, j'en suis tout satisfait, car je ne doute plus maintenant que je ne sois dans la verité, apres la rencontre admirable où je me trouve avec vous; j'admire bien davantage la methode des parties que celle des dez. J'avois veu plusieurs personnes trouver celles des dez, comme Mr. le Chevalier de Meré, qui est celuy qui m'a proposé ces questions, & aussi Monsieur de Roberval, mais Mr. de Meré n'avoit jamais pû trouver la juste valeur des parties ny de biais pour y arriver, de sorte que je me trouvois seul qui eusse connu cette proportion. Vôtre methode est tres-seure, & est celle qui m'est la premiere venüe à la pensée dans cette recherche. Mais parce que la peine des combinaisons est excessive, j'en ay trouvé un Abbregé, & proprement une autre methode bien plus courte & plus nette que je voudrois vous pouvoir dire icy en peu de mots. Car je voudrois desormais vous ouvrir mon cœur s'il se pouvoit, tant j'ay de joye de voir nôtre rencontre. Je voy bien que la verité est la méme à Tolose & à Paris. Voicy à peu prés comme je fais pour sçavoir la valeur de chacune des parties, quand deux joüeurs joüent par exemple en trois parties, & chacun a mis 32. pistoles au jeu.

Posons que le premier en ait deux & l'autre une, ils joüent maintenant une partie, dont le sort est tel, que si le premier la gagne, il gagne tout l'argent qui est au jeu, sçavoir 64 pistoles; si l'autre la gagne, ils sont deux parties à deux parties; & par consequent s'ils veulent se separer, il faut qu'ils retirent chacun leur mise, sçavoir chacun 32. pistoles. Considerez donc, Monsieur, que si le premier gagne il luy appartient 64. s'il perd il luy appartient 32. Donc s'ils veulent ne point hazarder cette partie, & se separer sans la joüer, le premier doit dire, je suis seur d'avoir 32. pistoles, car la perte

Z 2

## 180                 Lettres

méme me les donne , mais pour les 32. autres, peut-étre je les auray , peut-étre vous les aurez, le hazard eſt égal, partageons donc ces 32 piſtoles par la moitié , & me donnez outre cela mes 32. qui me ſont ſeures , il aura donc 48. piſtoles & l'autre 16.

Poſons maintenant que le premier ait deux parties,& l'autre point , & ils commencent à joüer une partié , le ſort de cettte partie eſt tel , que ſi le premier la gagne il tire tout l'argent, 64. piſtoles, ſi l'autre la gagne les voilà revenus au cas precedent , auquel le premier aura deux parties , & l'autre une ; Or nous avons déja monſtré qu'en ce cas il appartient à celuy qui a les deux parties 48. piſtoles , donc s'ils veulent ne point joüer cette partie , il doit dire ainſi , ſi je la gagne , je gagneray tout, qui eſt 64. ſi je la perds , il m'appartiendra legitimement 48. Donc donnez - moy les 48. qui me ſont certaines , au cas méme que je perde , & partageons les 16. autres par la moitié , puis qu'il y a autant de hazard que vous les gagnez comme moy , ainſi il aura 48 & 8. qui ſont 56. piſtoles.

Poſons enfin que le premier n'ait qu'une partie & l'autre point.

Vous voyez, Monſieur, que s'ils commencent une partie nouvelle , le ſort en eſt tel , que ſi le premier la gagne , il aura deux parties à point , & partant par le cas precedent il luy appartient 56. s'il le perd ils ſont partie à partie , donc il luy appartient 32 piſtoles. Donc il doit dire ſi vous voulez ne la pas joüer donnez-moy 32. piſtoles qui me ſont ſeures , & partageons le reſte de 56. par la moitié, de 56. ôtez 32.reſte 24. partagez donc 24. par la moitié prenez en 12. & moy 12. qui avec 32. font 44.

Or parce moyen vous voyez par les ſimples ſouſtractions que pour la premiere par-tie il appartient ſur l'argent de l'autre 12. piſtoles , pour la ſeconde autres 12. & pour la derniere 8.

---

TRANSLATION
_____

29 July 1654

MONSIEUR,

Impatience overtakes me as well as you and, although I am still confined to bed, I cannot resist telling you that I received yesterday evening, by the hand of Monsieur de Carcavi, your letter on courses of action, which I admire more than I can tell you. I do not have leisure to speak at length, but, in a word, you have found the two courses of action, of the dice and of the participants, with perfect correctness; I am completely satisfied with it, and I now no longer doubt that I am right, after finding myself in such wonderful agreement with you. I admire rather more the method of participants rather than that of the dice. I have seen several people find that of the dice, like Monsieur le Chevalier de Méré, who is the one that proposed these questions to me, and also Monsieur Roberval: but Monsieur de Méré had never been able to find the correct value of the rounds, nor the basis for arriving at it, so that I found myself the only one who knew this proportion. Your method is very sound and it is the one that came to me first on thinking about this research. But, because the effort of combinations is excessive, I have found a shortcut, and strictly speaking another method, much shorter and clearer, that I would like to tell you here in a few words. For from now on I would like to open my heart to you, if

I may, so joyful am I to see our agreement. I see very well that the truth is the same in Toulouse and in Paris. Here is roughly what I do to find the value of each round, when two players play, for example, for three rounds, and each has put 32 pistoles into the game.

Let us suppose that the first has won two and the other one; they now play a round in such a way that if the first wins, he wins all the money that is in the game, namely 64 pistoles; if the other wins it, they are two rounds to two rounds, and consequently, if they want to separate, they must each take back their share, namely 32 pistoles each. Therefore consider, Monsieur, that if the first wins he gets 64; if he loses he gets 32. Therefore, if they do not want to chance this round, and separate without playing it, the first must say: I am sure of having 32 pistoles, for even losing [180] gives me that, but for the other 32, perhaps I will have them, perhaps you will have them, the chance is equal; therefore let us share these 32 pistoles half and half and give me, besides that, the 32 of which I am certain. He will therefore have 48 pistoles and the other 16.

Now suppose that the first has won two rounds, and the other none, and they begin to play a round; the nature of this round is such that if the first wins it, he takes all the money, 64 pistoles; if the other wins it, here they return to the previous case, in which the first would have won two rounds, and the other, one. Now, we have already shown that in this case there goes, to him who has two rounds, 48 pistoles; therefore, if they do not want to play this round at all, he must say thus: if I win it, I would win everything, which is 64; if I lose it, I will rightly get 48. Therefore give me the 48 of which I am certain, even in the case that I lose, and let us share the 16 others half and half, because there is as much chance that you would win them as I. Thus he would have 48 and 8, which is 56 pistoles.

Finally let us suppose that the first has won only one round and the other none.

You see, Monsieur, that if they begin a new round, the nature of it is such that if the first wins it, he will have two rounds to none, and on quitting, by the previous case, he will get 56; if he loses it, they will be round for round, therefore he gets 32 pistoles. Therefore he must say: if you do not want to play give me 32 pistoles of which I am certain, and let us share the remainder from 56, half and half, from 56 take 32, there remain 24, therefore share 24 half and half, of which you take 12, and to me 12 which with 32 make 44.

Now in this way you see by simple subtractions that for the first round he gets 12 pistoles of the money of the other, for the second another 12, and for the last 8.

---

### 7.1.2 Jacob Bernoulli's *Ars conjectandi*, 1713

Pascal's ideas were to be enormously influential. When Huygens visited Paris in 1655 he too became interested in the mathematics of gambling, and in 1657 published *De ratiociniis in aleae ludo* (*On reasoning in a game of dice*). In this short treatise he not only dealt with de Méré's problems but also showed, as Pascal had done, how to calculate the *valeur* or, as we should now say, the expected value of a game of chance.

Huygens' book remained the only general introduction to probability for the rest of the seventeenth century, and in 1713 it was republished, together with Jacob Bernoulli's commentary on it, as the first section of Bernoulli's posthumous *Ars conjectandi* (*The art of conjecture*), a book that Bernoulli had completed shortly before he died in 1705. There is a nice double meaning in its title: the Latin verb *coniectare* means literally 'to throw together', which may be taken to refer either to thoughts or to dice.

In the second section of the book Bernoulli discussed at some length the mathematics of permutations (*rerum variationes*, variations in things) and combinations (*rerum conjunctiones*, bringing together of things). A third section applied this teaching to games of chance, and a shorter and final fourth section applied it to civil, moral, and economic affairs.

Though Bernoulli's treatise was based primarily on games of chance, he also began to ask more general questions, for example, about the number of trials needed in order to be reasonably sure of an underlying probability. Since he was handling binomial distributions in which he needed to sum large numbers of terms, however, the answer was not easy to calculate except in the simplest cases.

## Bernoulli's treatment of combinations and permutations
### from Jacob Bernoulli, *Ars conjectandi*, 1713, 132–135

# CAP. · IX.

*Invenire numerum electionum rerum pluri-*
*um, quarum nonnullæ funt eædem, nulla*
*verò fæpiùs in electione affumi debet, quam*
*ipfa reperitur in toto rerum numero.*

HYpothefis hæc eft capitis fexti, nifi quòd ibi omnes diverfi or-
dines unius combinationis pro unâ eâdemque electione, hîc pro
totidem diverfis electionibus habendi funt. De Problemate hoc fen-
fu accepto nihil definitum invenio apud Auctores; ego quæfitum fe-
quenti modo exploro: Sunto ex. gr. combinandæ & permutandæ
modis omnibus literæ $a$, $b$, $c$, eâ lege, ut in nullâ combinatione $a$
fæpiùs quàm quater, $b$ quam ter, & $c$ quàm bis occurrat, hoc eft,
ut aliter enunciem, fint combinandæ & permutandæ omnifariam literæ $aaaabbbcc$ feu $a^4 b^3 c^2$, quarum 4 funt eædem, item tres aliæ,
& rurfum duæ aliæ eædem, fitque determinandus numerus harum
combinationum, tam fecundùm fingulos quàm fecundùm omnes
exponentes. Conftat, ante omnia electiones folius $a^4$, inclufo nul-
lione quem unitatis notâ defignamus, effe has quinque: $1$, $a$, $aa$, $a^3$, $a^4$.
Singulis harum applicetur litera $b$, primò femel, dein bis, tertiò
ter, ut fiant novæ electiones: $b$, $ab$, $aab$, $a^3 b$, $a^4 b$: nec non, $bb$, $abb$,
$aabb$, $a^3 bb$, $a^4 bb$: ut & $b^3$, $ab^3$, $aab^3$, $a^3 b^3$, $a^4 b^3$, planè ut
factum cap. 6. Sed harum electionum illæ, quas $b$ femel ingredi-
tur, per reg. 2, cap. 1 ordine infuper recipiunt permutationes $1, 2,$
$3, 4, 5$; prima vid. unam $b$, fecunda duas $ab$ & $ba$, tertia tres
$aab$, $aba$, $baa$ &c. Illæ verò, quas $b$ ingreditur bis, ordine permutationes admittunt $1, 3, 6, 10, 15$, juxta numeros fcil. trigonales; prima nempe unam $bb$; fecunda tres, $abb$, $bab$, $bba$; tertia
fex, $aabb$, $abab$, $abba$, $baab$, $baba$, $bbaa$. &c. Et illæ, in quibus $b$
ter occurrit, permutationes ordine capiunt $1, 4, 10, 20, 35$, juxta
numeros pyramidales: quemadmodùm etiam illæ, fi quæ darentur
electiones, in quibus $b$ fæpiùs adhuc recurrit, permutationes admit-
terent juxta alios & alios figuratos gradatim altiores in infinitum.
Hoc peracto, fingulis præcedentium electionum permutationibus $1$;
$a$, $b$; $aa$, $ab$, $ba$, $bb$; $a^3$, $aab$, $aba$, $baa$, $abb$, $bab$, $bba$, $b^3$; &c.
tertia porrò litera $c$ nunc femel nunc bis adjungi intelligatur; ita no-
væ prodibunt electiones, $c$; $ac$, $bc$; $aac$, $abc$, $bac$, $bbc$; $a^3 c$ &c.

**R 3**                                                    nec

134     *ARTIS CONJECTANDI*

nec non, $cc$; $acc$, $bcc$; $aacc$, $abcc$, $bacc$, $bbcc$; $a^3cc$ &c. quarum priores, quæ literam $c$ semel tantùm includunt, respectu hujusce literæ, ordine reliquarum non immutato, subeunt permutationes 1, 2, 3, 4, &c. juxta numeros naturales; nempe unio $c$ unam, singuli binionum $ac$, $bc$ duas; singuli ternionum $aac$, $abc$, $bac$, $bbc$, tres, & ita porrò: posteriores verò, quæ lit. $c$ bis continent, permutationes ordine patiuntur 1, 3, 6, 10 &c. secundùm trigonales; binio nempe $cc$ unam, ternionum $acc$, $bcc$ singuli tres; quaternionum $aacc$, $abcc$, $bacc$, $bbcc$ singuli sex, & ita consequenter. Dico, ordine reliquarum præter $c$ literarum non immutato; aliàs enim ex. gr. $abcc$ non 6, sed 12 permutationes admittit, at quarum dimidia pars redundat, utpote sequenti quaternioni $bacc$ attribuenda. Quòd si jam quarta adesset litera, ea similiter omnibus præcedentibus permutationibus secundum singulas suas dimensiones foret applicanda, ad formandum novas electiones, quæ denuò permutationes reciperent secundùm numeros vel laterales, vel trigonales, vel pyramidales, &c. prout accedens litera vel semel, vel bis, vel ter iis adjuncta esset. Quo pacto nulla optatarum combinationum nos fugiet, neque etiam ulla bis computabitur. Ex dictis verò facilè perspicitur ratio constructionis sequentis Tabellæ, quâ numerum talium combinationum secundùm exponentes tam singulos quàm universos expedite definio. Scribo ordine omnes exponentes combinationum, quas propositæ res $a^4 b^3 c^2$ suscipere possunt, à 0 usque ad 9; & sub eorum primis colloco tot unitates, quot prima litera habet dimensiones, & unam ampliùs, nempe quinque; quibus statim subjungo quinque numeros laterales 1, 2, 3, 4, 5; & his totidem trigonales 1, 3, 6, 10, 15, totidemque pyramidales 1, 4, 10, 20, 35; donec præter seriem unitatum tot habeam series, quot altera litera $b$ habet dimensiones, easq; gradatim dextrorsum promoveo, ut factum cap. 6. Tum addo terminos, qui in eodem sibi gradu perpendiculariter respondent, ut fiant numeri 1, 2, 4, 8, 15 &c. Hos confestim duco in totidem laterales 1, 2, 3, 4 &c. & trigonales 1, 3, 6, 10 &c. singulos ordine multiplicando per singulos, ut præter seriem 1, 2, 4, 8 &c. tot aliæ prodeant numerorum series, 1, 4, 12, 32 &c. & 1, 6, 24, 80 &c. quot tertia litera $c$ obtinet dimensiones, quas rursus gradatim dispono & addo, continuaturus eodem tenore ulteriùs, si plures literæ superper-

pereſſent . Sic tandem ex ultimâ additione prodibunt numeri, qui
multitudinem combinationum ſecundùm exponentes quiſque ſuos
indicant, adeoque ſimul collecti numerum omnium ſimpliciter combinationum produnt :

| Res Combi- nanda. | Exponentes Combinationum. | | | | | | | | | |
|---|---|---|---|---|---|---|---|---|---|---|
| | 0. | 1. | 2. | 3. | 4. | 5. | 6. | 7. | 8. | 9. |
| $a^4$ | I | I | I | I | I | | | | | |
| | | I | 2 | 3 | 4 | 5 | | | | |
| | | | I | 3 | 6 | 10 | 15 | | | |
| | | | | I | 4 | 10 | 20 | 35 | | |
| $a^4b^3$ | I | 2 | 4 | 8 | 15 | 25 | 35 | 35 | | |
| | | I | 4 | 12 | 32 | 75 | 150 | 245 | 280 | |
| | | | I | 6 | 24 | 80 | 225 | 525 | 980 | 1260 |
| $a^4b^3c^2$ | I | 3 | 9 | 26 | 71 | 180 | 410 | 805 | 1260 | 1260 |

Diſcimus ex hâc Tabellâ, quòd res propoſitæ $a^4b^3c^2$ contineant unum nullionem, tres uniones, 9 binarios, 26 ternarios, &c.
tandemque 1260 novenarios, & quòd ſumma omnium abſolutè combinationum ſit 4025 .

---

TRANSLATION

## Chap. IX.

*To find the greatest number of choices of things, of which none are the same, but none*
*must be taken more often in the choice than it appears in the total*
*number of things.*

This is the premise of the sixth chapter, except that there all the different arrangements
of one combination in one and the same choice, are here to be had as the same number
of different choices. Of the problem taken in this sense I find nothing prescribed in
other authors; I investigate what is sought in the following way. Let, for example, the
letters *a*, *b*, *c*, be combined and permuted in all ways, according to the rule that in
no combination *a* occurs more than four times, *b* more than three, or *c* more than
twice, that is, if I may put it another way, let there be all possible combinations and
permutations of the letters *aaaabbbcc* or $a^4b^3c^2$, of which 4 are the same, likewise three
others, and again two others the same, and let there be determined the number of these
combinations, according to each or to all exponents. First of all, for choices from $a^4$
only, including none, which we denote by the symbol of one, there are these five: 1, *a*,
*aa*, $a^3$, $a^4$. To each of these may be adjoined the letter *b*, first once, then twice, thirdly

three times, to make nine choices: $b$, $ab$, $aab$, $a^3b$, $a^4b$: and, $bb$, $abb$, $aabb$, $a^3bb$, $a^4bb$: as also $b^3$, $ab^3$, $aab^3$, $a^3b^3$, $a^4b^3$, plainly as done in Chapter 6. But those of these choices, which contain $b$ once, by Chapter 1, rule 2, take permutations beyond that from the progression 1, 2, 3, 4, 5; namely, first one, $b$, second two, $ab$ and $ba$, third three $aab$, $aba$, $baa$, etc. And those in which $b$ is contained twice, admit permutations from the progression 1, 3, 6, 10, 15, clearly following the triangular numbers; namely the first, one, $bb$; second, three, $abb$, $bab$, $bba$; third, six, $aabb$, $abab$, $abba$, $baab$, $baba$, $bbaa$, etc. And those in which $b$ occurs three times, take permutations from the progression 1, 4, 10, 20, 35, following the pyramidal numbers. In which manner those also, if choices are given in which $b$ occurs more often than this, admit permutations following some other figurate numbers of higher degrees, indefinitely. This accomplished, to each permutation of the preceding choices 1; $a$, $b$; $aa$, $ab$, $ba$, $bb$; $a^3$, $aab$, $aba$, $baa$, $abb$, $bab$, $bba$, $b^3$; etc. the third letter $c$ is next understood to be added first once, then twice; thus it produces new choices, $c$; $ac$, $bc$; $aac$, $abc$, $bac$, $bbc$; $a^3c$ etc. [134] and $cc$; $acc$, $bcc$; $aacc$, $abcc$, $bacc$, $bbcc$; $a^3cc$ etc. of which the former, which contain the letter $c$ only once, where I do not change the order of the rest with respect to this letter, yield 1, 2, 3, 4, etc. permutations, following the natural numbers: namely $c$ only, one; each pair $ac$, $bc$, two; each triple $aac$, $abc$, $bac$, $bbc$, three, and so on; but the latter, which contain the letter $c$ twice, yield permutations from the progression 1, 3, 6, 10 etc. following the triangular numbers; namely the pair $cc$, one; the triples $acc$, $bcc$, each three; quaternions $aacc$, $abcc$, $bacc$, $bbcc$, each six; and so on subsequently. I say that I do not change the order of the rest of the letters apart from $c$; for otherwise, for example, $abcc$ admits not 6 but 12 permutation, but half of them are redundant, in as much as they must be attributed to the next quaternion $bacc$. If there is now adjoined a fourth letter, this must similarly be applied to all the previous permutations according to each of their dimensions, to form new choices, which again take permutations following the natural, or triangular, or pyramidal numbers, etc. according to whether the letter is adjoined to them once, or twice, or three times. Having done this, none of the desired combinations can escape us, nor either will any be counted twice. And from what has been said there is easily seen the reason for the construction of the following table, in which I conveniently set out the number of such combinations according to the exponents, whether taken singly or together. I write all the exponents of the combinations, which the proposed entity $a^4b^3c^2$ can take, in order from 0 to 9; and under the first of them I place so many units as the first letter has dimensions, and one more, namely five; immediately under which I lay five natural numbers 1, 2, 3, 4, 5; and under these the same number of triangulars 1, 3, 6, 10, 15, the same number of pyramidals 1, 4, 10, 20, 35; until apart from the series of units, I have as many series as the next letter $b$ has dimensions, and these I move step by step to the right, as done in Chapter 6. Then I add terms, which correspond to each other in the same vertical, to make the numbers 1, 2, 4, 8, 15, etc. These I multiply immediately by the same number of laterals 1, 2, 3, 4, etc. and triangulars 1, 3, 6, 10, etc., multiplying each in order by each, so that besides the series 1, 2, 4, 8, etc. it produces as many other series of numbers, 1, 4, 12, 32, etc. and 1, 6, 24, 80, etc. as the third letter $c$ has dimensions, which again I place in steps and add, to be continued further in the same way, if there are to be more letters. [135] Thus at length from the final addition there are produced numbers which indicate the total number of combinations according to any exponents, and therefore collected together they give simply the number of all combinations:

| Things to be combined | Exponents of the combinations | | | | | | | | | |
|---|---|---|---|---|---|---|---|---|---|---|
| | 0. | 1. | 2. | 3. | 4. | 5. | 6. | 7. | 8. | 9. |
| $a^4$ | 1 | 1 | 1 | 1 | 1 | | | | | |
| | | 1 | 2 | 3 | 4 | 5 | | | | |
| | | | 1 | 3 | 6 | 10 | 15 | | | |
| | | | | 1 | 4 | 10 | 20 | 35 | | |
| $a^4b^3$ | 1 | 2 | 4 | 8 | 15 | 25 | 35 | 35 | | |
| | | 1 | 4 | 12 | 32 | 75 | 150 | 245 | 280 | |
| | | | 1 | 6 | 24 | 80 | 225 | 525 | 980 | 1260 |
| $a^4b^3c^2$ | 1 | 3 | 9 | 26 | 71 | 180 | 410 | 805 | 1260 | 1260 |

We learn from this table, that the proposed entity $a^4b^3c^2$ contains one null, three singletons, 9 pairs, 26 triples, etc. and at length 1260 nontuples, and that the total sum of all combinations is 4025.

### 7.1.3 De Moivre's calculation of confidence, 1738

Huygens' *De ratiociniis* was influential not only on the continent, but in England too. In 1692 John Arbuthnot, originally from Scotland but at the time working as a young mathematics teacher in London, produced an English translation of the text in a pocket-size edition entitled *Of the laws of chance, or, a method of calculation of the hazards of game*. Huygens' original and Arbuthnot's translation of it were the only books on probability available to Abraham de Moivre when he in turn took up the study of games of chance around 1709.

In 1711 de Moivre was persuaded by the Royal Society to publish some of his findings in the *Philosophical transactions*, and they were later written up at much greater length in *The doctrine of chances: or, a method of calculating the probability of events in play*, published in 1718, a book that contained theoretical methods as well as many applications to particular games and problems. A second edition, claiming to be 'fuller, clearer, and more correct than the first' was published in 1738 (with the word 'probability' in the title now changed to 'probabilities'). Two important additions to the text were a section on the 'Value of Lives', an early study of life insurance; and an answer to the question: 'What reasonable Conjectures may be derived from Experiments, or what are the Odds that after a certain number of Experiments have been made concerning the happening or failing of Events, the Accidents of Contingency will not afterwards vary from those of Observation beyond certain Limits?'[1]

---

1. De Moivre 1738, xiii.

De Moivre's answer to the second question was based on results he had found in 1730, when by clever use of infinite series he had discovered the formula

$$\sum_{1}^{n} \log m \approx \left(n + \frac{1}{2}\right) \log n - n + \text{constant}.$$

(The symbol $\approx$ is to be read as 'equals approximately'.) The value of the constant, $\log\sqrt{2\pi}$, was discovered by de Moivre's friend and correspondent James Stirling, and the whole is now known as Stirling's formula.[2] By a similar method, de Moivre was able to calculate logarithms of ratios of terms in a binomial expansion, and in particular found that the logarithm of the ratio of the middle term of $(1+1)^{2m}$ to a term at a distance $l$ from it is approximately

$$\left(m + l - \frac{1}{2}\right)\log(m + l - 1) + \left(m - l + \frac{1}{2}\right)\log(m - l + 1) - 2m\log m + \log\frac{m + l}{m}.$$

For large $m$, using the approximation

$$\log(m + \alpha) = \log m + \log\left(1 + \frac{\alpha}{m}\right) \approx \log m + \frac{\alpha}{m},$$

the above expression reduces to approximately $\frac{2l^2}{m}$.

Conversely, the logarithm of the ratio to the middle term of a term at distance $l$ is $-\frac{2l^2}{m}$, and the ratio itself is (in modern notation) $e^{-2l^2/m}$, which de Moivre was able to write as a power series. By Stirling's formula the middle term itself is approximately $\frac{2}{\sqrt{nc}}$, with $c = 2\pi$. Thus de Moivre could write each term of the binomial expansion as a power series, and he summed the terms from 0 to $\frac{1}{2}\sqrt{n}$ by calculating a definite integral. This gave him the probability that an event will occur between $\frac{1}{2}n + \frac{1}{2}\sqrt{n}$ and $\frac{1}{2}n - \frac{1}{2}\sqrt{n}$ times. Essentially what he had discovered was a normal approximation to the binomial distribution and a method of calculating confidence intervals.

A third edition of *The doctrine of chance*, corrected and augmented once again, was published in 1756, two years after de Moivre himself had died.

---

### De Moivre's approximation to the normal distribution
from de Moivre, *The doctrine of chance*, second edition, 1738, 236–238
Eighteenth Century Collection Online, Gale Digital Collection

---

*Notation*
The word 'into' as in '2/$\sqrt{nc}$ into $l$' is from the Latin *in* and indicates multiplication not, as in modern use, division. The 'number which answers to the hyperbolic logarithm $-2ll/n$' is the number whose natural logarithm is $-2ll/n$, namely $e^{-2ll/n}$.

II. I alfo found that the Logarithm of the Ratio which the middle Term of a high Power has to any Term diftant from it by an Interval denoted by *l*, would be denoted by a very near approximation,.

---

2. De Moivre 1730, supplement p. 10.

tion, (suppofing $m = \frac{1}{2}n$) by the Quantities $\overline{m + l - \frac{1}{2}} \times$ log.
$\overline{m + l - 1} + \overline{m - l + \frac{1}{2}} \times$ log. $\overline{m - l + 1} - 2m \times$ log. $m +$ log.
$\overline{\frac{m + l}{m}}$ .

### COROLLARY 1.

This being admitted, I conclude, that if $m$ or $\frac{1}{2}n$ be a Quantity infinitely great, then the Logarithm of the Ratio, which a Term diftant from the middle by the Interval $l$, has to the middle Term, is
$- \frac{2ll}{n}$ .

### COROLLARY 2.

The Number, which anfwers to the Hyperbolic Logarithm
$- \frac{2ll}{n}$ , being

$$1 - \frac{2ll}{n} + \frac{4l^4}{2nn} - \frac{8l^6}{6n^3} + \frac{16l^8}{24n^4} - \frac{32l^{10}}{120n^5} + \frac{64l^{12}}{720n^6} , \&c.$$

it follows, that the Sum of the Terms intercepted between the Middle, and that whofe diftance from it is denoted by $l$, will be

$$\frac{2}{\sqrt{nc}} \text{ into } l - \frac{2l^3}{1 \times 3n} + \frac{4l^5}{2 \times 5nn} - \frac{8l^7}{6 \times 7n^3} + \frac{16l^9}{24 \times 9n^4} - \frac{32l^{11}}{120 \times 11n^5}, \&c.$$

Let now $l$ be fuppofed $= s\sqrt{n}$, then the faid Sum will be ex-preffed by the Series

$$\frac{2}{\sqrt{c}} \text{ into } s - \frac{2s^3}{3} + \frac{4s^5}{2 \times 5} - \frac{8s^7}{6 \times 7} + \frac{16s^9}{24 \times 9} - \frac{32s^{11}}{120 \times 11} , \&c.$$

Moreover, if $s$ be interpreted by $\frac{1}{2}$ , then the Series will become

$$\frac{2}{\sqrt{c}} \text{ into } \frac{1}{2} - \frac{1}{3 \times 4} + \frac{1}{2 \times 5 \times 8} - \frac{1}{6 \times 7 \times 16} + \frac{1}{24 \times 9 \times 32} - \frac{1}{120 \times 11 \times 64}, \&c.$$

which converges fo faft, that by help of no more than feven or eight Terms, the Sum required may be carried to fix or feven places of Decimals: Now that Sum will be found to be 0.427812, inde-pendently from the common Multiplicator $\frac{2}{\sqrt{c}}$ , and therefore to the Tabular Logarithm of 0.427812, which is $\overline{9}.6312529$, adding the Logarithm of $\frac{2}{\sqrt{c}}$ , *viz.* $\overline{9}.9019400$, the Sum will be $\overline{19}.5331929$, to which anfwers the number 0.341344.

### LEMMA.

If an Event be fo dependent on Chance, as that the Probabilities of its happening or failing be equal, and that a certain given number $n$
of

of Experiments be taken to obferve how often it happens and fails, and alſo that $l$ be another given number, leſs than $\frac{1}{2}n$, then the Probability of its neither happening more frequently than $\frac{1}{2}n + l$ times, nor more rarely than $\frac{1}{2}n - l$ times, may be found as follows.

Let L and L be two Terms equally diſtant on both ſides of the middle Term of the Binomial $\overline{1+1}|^n$ expanded, by an Interval equal to $l$; let alſo $f$ be the Sum of the Terms included between L and L together with the Extreams, then the Probability required will be rightly expreſſed by the Fraction $\frac{f}{2^n}$, which being founded on the common Principles of the Doctrine of Chances, requires no Demonſtration in this place.

### COROLLARY 3.

And therefore, if it was poſſible to take an infinite number of Experiments, the Probability that an Event which has an equal number of Chances to happen or fail, ſhall neither appear more frequently than $\frac{1}{2}n + \frac{1}{2}\sqrt{n}$ times, nor more rarely than $\frac{1}{2}n - \frac{1}{2}n\sqrt{n}$ times, will be expreſs'd by the double Sum of the number exhibited in the ſecond Corollary, that is, by 0.682688, and conſequently the Probability of the contrary, which is that of happening more frequently or more rarely than in the proportion above aſſigned will be 0.317312, thoſe two Probabilities together compleating Unity, which is the meaſure of Certainty: Now the Ratio of thoſe Probabilities is in ſmall Terms 28 to 13 very near.

### COROLLARY 4.

But altho' the taking an infinite number of Experiments be not practicable, yet the preceding Concluſions may very well be applied to finite numbers, provided they be great, for Inſtance, if 3600 Experiments be taken, make $n = 3600$, hence $\frac{1}{2}n$ will be $= 1800$, and $\frac{1}{2}\sqrt{n} = 30$, then the Probability of the Event's neither appearing oftner than 1830 times, nor more rarely than 1770, will be 0.682688.

COROL-

## 7.2 MATHEMATICAL PROBABILITY THEORY

De Moivre's book, despite its initial concern with 'probabilities of events in play', had already transformed discussions of games of cards or dice into a much more generally applicable theory of confidence limits. By the mid eighteenth century probability theory was becoming a branch of mathematics in its own right, no longer tied to the theory of gambling. In this section we give just two examples of different ways in which probability theory was developed and applied, one theoretical, the other more practical. First, we have what is now called Bayes' theorem, from a paper of 1763. The second is an example from Laplace's great textbook on probability of 1812, far removed in content, style, and sheer size from the short treatises on gambling that had preceded it only a century earlier. The particular example chosen below illustrates the application of probability theory to statistical evidence.

### 7.2.1  Bayes' theorem, 1763

A simple form of what is now called Bayes' theorem appeared in a lengthy paper by the Reverend Thomas Bayes, read to the Royal Society in December 1763, two years after Bayes himself had died.

## Bayes' theorem

from Bayes, 'An essay towards solving a problem in the doctrine of chances', *Philosophical transactions of the Royal Society*, 1763, 378–379

### P R O P.  3.

The probability that two fubfequent events will both happen is a ratio compounded of the probability of the 1ft, and the probability of the 2d on fuppofition the 1ft happens.

Suppofe that, if both events happen, I am to receive N, that the probability both will happen is $\frac{P}{N}$, that the 1ft will is $\frac{a}{N}$ (and confequently that the 1ft will not is $\frac{N-a}{N}$) and that the 2d will happen upon fuppofition the 1ft does is $\frac{b}{N}$. Then (by definition 5) P will be the value of my expectation, which will become $b$ if the 1ft happens. Confequently if the 1ft happens, my gain by it is $b$—P, and if it fails my lofs is P. Wherefore, by the foregoing propofition, $\frac{a}{N}$ is to $\frac{N-a}{N}$, i. e. $a$ is to N—$a$ as P is to $b$—P. Wherefore (componendo inverfè) $a$ is to N as P is to $b$. But the ratio of P to N is compounded of the ratio of P to $b$, and that of $b$ to N. Wherefore the

5                                                                    fame

### [ 379 ]

fame ratio of P to N is compounded of the ratio of $a$ to N and that of $b$ to N, i. e. the probability that the two fubfequent events will both happen is compounded of the probability of the 1ft and the probability of the 2d on fuppofition the 1ft happens.

Corollary.  Hence if of two fubfequent events the probability of the 1ft be $\frac{a}{N}$, and the probability of both together be $\frac{P}{N}$, then the probability of the 2d on fuppofition the 1ft happens is $\frac{P}{a}$.

### 7.2.2 Laplace and an application of probability, 1812

The most important textbook on probability of the early nineteenth century was Laplace's *Théorie analytique des probabilités* (*Analytic theory of probabilities*) of 1812. Laplace not only provided a comprehensive treatment of the mathematics of probability, but also demonstrated many applications. As a preliminary, in Book I, he discussed two theories that he had first developed some thirty years earlier: the theory of generating functions, and approximations for functions of large numbers.[3] In Book II, Laplace developed a general mathematical theory of probability, with applications not only to the traditional subject of gambling, but to many other topics, such as the calculation of errors and confidence intervals, to population statistics, and, in a later supplement, to natural philosophy. Laplace later claimed that the theory of probability was only common sense reduced to calculation, but in his *Théorie analytique* he made heavy demands on the mathematical competence of his readers. Two years after its publication he discussed probability in a much more elementary way in his *Essai philosophique des probabilités* (1814), based on lectures given at the École Normale in 1795. The *Essai* is descriptive, and illustrated with plenty of examples, and did much to bring the theory of probability to the attention of a wider audience.

The extract below is from Chapter VI of the *Théorie analytique*, entitled 'De la probabilité des causes et des événemens futurs, tirée des événemens observés' ('On the probability of causes and of future events, drawn from observed events'). Here Laplace discussed a number of demographic questions, such as population predictions based on birth rates for a great empire such as France. In this extract he compares the ratios of male to female baptisms in London and Paris, and speculates upon a possible cause.

---

### Laplace's comparison of baptisms in London and Paris
from Laplace, *Théorie analytique des probabilités*, 1812, 381–384

29. On a vu qu'à Londres, le rapport observé des naissances des garçons à celles des filles, est égal à $\frac{19}{18}$, tandis qu'à Paris, celui des baptêmes des garçons à ceux des filles, n'est que $\frac{25}{24}$. Cela semble indiquer une cause constante de cette différence. Déterminons la probabilité de cette cause.

Soient $p$ et $q$ les nombres des baptêmes des garçons et des filles, faits à Paris dans l'intervalle du commencement de 1745 à la fin de 1784; en désignant par $x$, la possibilité du baptême d'un garçon,

---

3. It was in his discussion of functions of large numbers that Laplace found the formula $\int_0^\infty e^{-t^2} dt = \frac{1}{2}\sqrt{\pi}$. It was also here that he claimed that by 'the generality of analysis' ('la généralité de l'analyse') it was possible to extend some of his results to cases where $t$ was imaginary (see 15.2.2).

382     THÉORIE ANALYTIQUE

et faisant, comme dans le numéro précédent,

$$y = x^p . (1 - x)^q,$$

la valeur de $x$ la plus probable, sera celle qui rend $y$ un *maximum;*
elle est donc $\frac{p}{p+q}$ ; en supposant ensuite

$$x = \frac{p}{p+q} + \theta ;$$

la probabilité de la valeur de $\theta$ sera, par le n° 26, égale à

$$\frac{d\theta}{\sqrt{\pi}} . \sqrt{\frac{(p+q)^3}{2pq}} . c^{-\frac{(p+q)^3}{2pq}.\theta^2}$$

En désignant par $p'$, $q'$ et $\theta'$, ce que deviennent $p$, $q$ et $\theta$ pour
Londres, on aura

$$\frac{d\theta'}{\sqrt{\pi}} . \sqrt{\frac{(p'+q')^3}{2p'q'}} . c^{-\frac{(p'+q')^3}{2p'q'}.\theta'^2}$$

pour la probabilité de $\theta'$ ; le produit

$$\frac{d\theta.d\theta'}{\pi} . \sqrt{\frac{(p+q)^3.(p'+q')^3}{4pq.p'q'}} . c^{-\frac{(p+q)^3}{2pq}.\theta^2 - \frac{(p'+q')^3}{2p'q'}.\theta'^2}$$

de ces deux probabilités, sera donc la probabilité de l'existence
simultanée de $\theta$ et de $\theta'$. Faisons

$$\frac{p'}{p'+q'} + \theta' = \frac{p}{p+q} + \theta + t ;$$

la fonction différentielle précédente devient

$$\frac{d\theta.dt}{\pi} . \sqrt{\frac{(p+q)^3.(p'+q')^3}{4pq.p'q'}} . c^{-\frac{(p+q)^3}{2pq}.\theta^2 - \frac{(p'+q')^3}{2p'q'}.\left(\theta+t-\frac{p'q-pq'}{(p+q).(p'+q')}\right)^2} .$$

En l'intégrant pour toutes les valeurs possibles de $\theta$, et ensuite
pour toutes les valeurs positives de $t$; on aura la probabilité que
la possibilité des baptêmes des garçons est plus grande à Londres
qu'à Paris. Les valeurs de $\theta$ peuvent s'étendre depuis $\theta$ égal à $-\frac{p}{p+q}$

jusqu'à $\theta$ égal à $1 - \dfrac{p}{p+q}$; mais lorsque $p$ et $q$ sont de très-grands nombres, le facteur $c^{-\frac{(p+q)^3}{2pq} \cdot \theta^2}$ est si petit à ces deux limites, qu'on peut le regarder comme nul ; on peut donc étendre l'intégrale relative à $\theta$, depuis $\theta = -\infty$ jusqu'à $\theta = \infty$. On voit par la même raison, que l'intégrale relative à $t$, peut être étendue depuis $t = 0$ jusqu'à $t = \infty$. En suivant le procédé du n° 27 pour ces intégrations multiples, on trouvera facilement que si l'on fait

$$k^2 = \frac{(p+q)^3 \cdot (p'+q')^3}{2p'q'(p+q)^3 + 2pq \cdot (p'+q')^3},$$

$$h = \frac{p'q - pq'}{(p+q) \cdot (p'+q')},$$

$$\theta + \frac{2pq \cdot k^2}{(p+q)^3} \cdot (t-h) = t',$$

ce qui donne $d\theta = dt'$; la différentielle précédente intégrée d'abord par rapport à $t'$ depuis $t' = -\infty$ jusqu'à $t' = \infty$, et ensuite depuis $t = 0$ jusqu'à $t$ infini, donnera

$$\int \frac{k\,dt}{\sqrt{\pi}} \cdot c^{-k^2 \cdot (t-h)^2}$$

pour la probabilité qu'à Londres, la possibilité des baptêmes des garçons est plus grande qu'à Paris. Si l'on fait

$$k \cdot (t-h) = t'',$$

cette intégrale devient

$$\int \frac{dt''}{\sqrt{\pi}} \cdot c^{-t''^2},$$

l'intégrale étant prise depuis $t'' = -kh$ jusqu'à $t'' = \infty$; et il est visible qu'elle est égale à

$$1 - \int \frac{dt''}{\sqrt{\pi}} \cdot c^{-t''^2},$$

l'intégrale étant prise depuis $t'' = kh$ jusqu'à $t''$ infini. De là il suit, par le n° 27 du premier Livre, que si l'on suppose

$$i^2 = \frac{p'q' \cdot (p+q)^3 + pq \cdot (p'+q')^3}{(p+q) \cdot (p'+q') \cdot (p'q - pq')^2};$$

THÉORIE ANALYTIQUE

la probabilité que la possibilité des baptêmes des garçons est plus grande à Londres qu'à Paris, a pour expression,

$$1 - \frac{i \cdot c^{-\frac{1}{2i^2}}}{\sqrt{2\pi}} \cdot \cfrac{1}{1 + \cfrac{i^2}{1 + \cfrac{2i^2}{1 + \cfrac{3i^2}{1 + \cfrac{4i^2}{1 + \text{etc.}}}}}} \qquad (\mu)$$

En faisant dans cette formule,

$$p = 393386 \,, \quad q = 377555,$$
$$p' = 737629 \,, \quad q' = 698958,$$

elle devient

$$1 - \frac{1}{328269}.$$

Il y a donc 328268 à parier contre un, qu'à Londres, la possibilité des baptêmes des garçons est plus grande qu'à Paris. Cette probabilité approche tellement de la certitude, qu'il y a lieu de rechercher la cause de cette supériorité.

Parmi les causes qui peuvent la produire, il m'a paru que les baptêmes des enfans trouvés, qui font partie de la liste annuelle des baptêmes à Paris, devaient avoir une influence sensible sur le rapport des baptêmes des garçons à ceux des filles ; et qu'ils devaient diminuer ce rapport, si, comme il est naturel de le croire, les parens des campagnes environnantes, trouvant de l'avantage à retenir près d'eux les enfans mâles, en avaient envoyé à l'hospice des Enfans trouvés de Paris, dans un rapport moindre que celui des naissances des deux sexes. C'est ce que le relevé des registres de cet hospice m'a fait voir avec une très-grande probabilité. Depuis le commencement de 1745 jusqu'à la fin de 1809, on y a baptisé 163499 garçons et 159405 filles, nombre dont le rapport est $\frac{39}{38}$, et diffère trop du rapport $\frac{25}{24}$ des baptêmes des garçons et des filles à Paris, pour être attribué au simple hasard.

*Notation*
Laplace's $c$ is the constant we now denote by $e$.

TRANSLATION

29. One has seen that in London, the observed ratio of births of boys to those of girls, is equal to $\frac{19}{18}$, while in Paris that of baptisms of boys to those of girls, is only $\frac{25}{24}$. This seems to indicate a steady reason for this difference. Let us determine the probability of this cause.

Let $p$ and $q$ be the numbers of baptisms of boys and girls done in Paris in the interval from the beginning of 1745 to the end of 1784; on denoting by $x$ the possibility of baptism of a boy, and making, as in the previous section,

$$y = x^p \cdot (1 - x)^q,$$

the most probable value of $x$ will be that which makes $y$ a *maximum*; it is therefore $\frac{p}{p+q}$; and supposing further

$$x = \frac{p}{p + q} + \theta;$$

the probability of the value of $\theta$ will be, by section 26, equal to

$$\frac{d\theta}{\sqrt{\pi}} \cdot \sqrt{\frac{(p + q)^3}{2pq}} \cdot c^{-\frac{(p+q)^3}{2pq} \cdot \theta^2}.$$

On denoting by $p'$, $q'$ and $\theta'$, what $p$, $q$ and $\theta$ become for London, one will have

$$\frac{d\theta'}{\sqrt{\pi}} \cdot \sqrt{\frac{(p' + q')^3}{2p'q'}} \cdot c^{-\frac{(p'+q')^3}{2p'q'} \cdot \theta'^2}$$

for the probability of $\theta'$; the product

$$\frac{d\theta \cdot d\theta'}{\pi} \cdot \sqrt{\frac{(p + q)^3 \cdot (p' + q')^3}{4pq \cdot p'q'}} \cdot c^{-\frac{(p+q)^3}{2pq} \cdot \theta^2 - \frac{(p'+q')^3}{2p'q'} \cdot \theta'^2}$$

of these two probabilities, will therefore be the probability of the simultaneous existence of $\theta$ and of $\theta'$. Putting

$$\frac{p'}{p' + q'} + \theta' = \frac{p}{p + q} + \theta + t;$$

the previous differential function becomes

$$\frac{d\theta \cdot dt}{\pi} \cdot \sqrt{\frac{(p + q)^3 \cdot (p' + q')^3}{4pq \cdot p'q'}} \cdot c^{-\frac{(p+q)^3}{2pq} \cdot \theta^2 - \frac{(p'+q')^3}{2p'q'} \cdot \left(\theta + t - \frac{p'q - pq'}{(p+q) \cdot (p'+q')}\right)^2}.$$

On integrating for all possible values of $\theta$, and then for all positive values of $t$, one will have the probability that the possibility of baptisms of boys is greater in London than in Paris. The values of $\theta$ may extend from $\theta$ equal to $-\frac{p}{p+q}$ [383] to $\theta$ equal to $1 - \frac{p}{p+q}$; but when $p$ and $q$ are very large numbers, the factor $c^{-\frac{(p+q)^3}{2pq} \cdot \theta^2}$ is so small at these two limits, that one may regard it as zero; one may therefore extend the integral with respect to $\theta$, from $\theta = -\infty$ to $\theta = \infty$. One sees by the same reasoning, that the integral with respect to $t$, may be extended from $t = 0$ to $t = \infty$. Following the procedure of section 27 for these multiple integrations, one will easily find that if one makes

$$k^2 = \frac{(p+q)^3 \cdot (p'+q')^3}{2p'q'(p+q)^3 + 2pq(p'+q')^3},$$

$$h = \frac{p'q - pq'}{(p+q) \cdot (p'+q')},$$

$$\theta + \frac{2pq \cdot k^2}{(p+q)^3} \cdot (t - h) = t',$$

which gives $d\theta = dt'$, the previous differential integrated first with respect to $t'$ from $t' = -\infty$ to $t' = \infty$, and then from $t = 0$ to $t$ infinite, will give

$$\int \frac{kdt}{\sqrt{\pi}} \cdot c^{-k^2 \cdot (t-h)^2}$$

for the probability that in London, the possibility of baptisms of boys is greater than in Paris. If one makes

$$k \cdot (t - h) = t'',$$

this integral becomes

$$\int \frac{dt''}{\sqrt{\pi}} \cdot c^{-t''^2},$$

the integral being taken from $t'' = -kh$ to $t'' = \infty$; and it is clear that it is equal to

$$1 - \int \frac{dt''}{\sqrt{\pi}} \cdot c^{-t''^2},$$

the integral being taken from $t'' = kh$ to $t''$ infinite. From that it follows, by section 27 of the first Book, that if one assumes

$$i^2 = \frac{p'q' \cdot (p+q)^3 + pq \cdot (p'+q')^3}{(p+q) \cdot (p'+q') \cdot (p'q - pq')^2};$$

[384] the probability that the possibility of baptisms of boys is greater in London than in Paris, has for its expression,

$$1 - \frac{i \cdot c^{-\frac{1}{2i^2}}}{\sqrt{2\pi}} \cdot \cfrac{1}{1 + \cfrac{i^2}{1+ \cfrac{2i^2}{1+ \cfrac{3i^2}{1+ \cfrac{4i^2}{1+ \text{etc.}}}}}}$$

On putting in this formula,

$$p = 393386, q = 377555,$$
$$p' = 737629, q' = 698958,$$

it becomes

$$1 - \frac{1}{328269}.$$

There are therefore odds of 328268 to one, that in London, the possibility of baptisms of boys is greater than in Paris. This probability approaches so closely to certainty, that there are grounds for seeking the cause of this higher figure.

Among the causes that might produce it, it seemed to me that baptisms of abandoned infants, which form part of the annual list of baptisms in Paris, would have a noticeable influence on the ratio of baptisms of boys to those of girls; and that they would diminish this ratio, if, as it is natural to believe, parents in the surrounding countryside, finding some advantage in keeping male infants close to them, sent them to the hospice for abandoned infants in Paris in a ratio less than that of the births of the two sexes. This is what a reading of the register of this hospice made me see with very great probability. Since the beginning of 1745 to the end of 1809, there were baptized 163499 boys and 159405 girls, numbers of which the ratio is $\frac{39}{38}$, which differs too much from the ratio of $\frac{25}{24}$ of baptisms of boys and girls in Paris, to be attributed to simple chance.

# CHAPTER 8

# POWER SERIES

T he discovery that mathematical quantities such as logarithms, sines or tangents, or algebraic expressions like $\sqrt{1 - x^2}$, could be written as power series was one of the great mathematical achievements of the mid seventeenth century, as far-reaching in its implications as the calculus itself. In fact power series and the calculus were historically and mathematically inseparable: both appeared in Britain during the fruitful years between 1660 and 1670, arising practically simultaneously in the work of more than one mathematician and for more than one reason.[1]

The first published power series appeared in 1668 in the *Logarithmotechnia* of Nicolaus Mercator, who found by straightforward long division that (as he wrote it):

$$\frac{1}{1 + a} = 1 - a + aa - a^3 + a^4 \quad (\&c.)$$

This and Mercator's related work on the quadrature of the hyperbola (see 3.2.4) prompted Newton to disclose similar results and several further series obtained by him during the winter of 1664 to 1665, in a treatise entitled 'De analysi'. Newton sent 'De analysi' to Barrow in Cambridge and John Collins in London, and in 1670 Collins sent extracts to James Gregory in Edinburgh, who replied that he himself had also found several series. Assuming that Newton had priority, Gregory waited for him to publish first, but died in 1673 long before Newton did so. Consequently we have some idea of Gregory's achievements but very little insight into his methods.

The discovery of power series brought about a revolutionary change in mathematical thinking. Until the middle of the seventeenth century most of the important concepts in mathematics had arisen or been expressed geometrically: sines and tangents were

---

1. Some similar series were known in southern India in the mid sixteenth century but those discoveries remained unknown in Europe until the nineteenth century.

lines relating to a circle; logarithms were conceptualized as distances along a line, or as areas under a hyperbola. With the development of power series, trigonometric and logarithmic quantities could be handled algebraically, with little or no reference to geometric interpretations. Algebraic manipulation was faster, clearer, and more powerful, and mathematics began to depart irrevocably from the geometric language that (in western Europe) had been its mainstay, and entered instead into its modern algebraic incarnation.

## 8.1 DISCOVERIES OF POWER SERIES

### 8.1.1 Newton and the general binomial theorem, 1664–1665

It is hardly surprising that once he had glimpsed the possibility, power series emerged for Newton in a variety of apparently unrelated ways. Writing to Leibniz in 1676, Newton claimed that he had discovered at least three ways of finding such series: by numerical interpolation, by algebraic operations, and by solving equations. To Leibniz he offered only results, not methods, but later study of his manuscripts has confirmed that he did indeed work with all three methods in the mid 1660s.

Newton's initial discoveries came about as a direct result of reading Wallis's *Arithmetica infinitorum* in 1664, and the page below shows some of these important early findings. First, his discovery of the series for $(1+x)^{-1}$, by extrapolating 'Pascal's triangle' backwards. Since Newton assumed he could integrate term by term, this led him immediately to a power series for the area under a hyperbola, in modern terms, $\log(1 + x)$, and he entertained himself using the series to calculate $\log 1.1$ and $\log 1.01$ to many decimal places. Second, we have his method of interpolation by finite differences. In the extract below, a small finite difference table lies immediately to the right of the central table. Newton used this to find the coefficients in the series expansions of $(1 - x^2)^{-\frac{1}{2}}$, $(1 - x^2)^{\frac{1}{2}}, (1 - x^2)^{\frac{3}{2}}, (1 - x^2)^{\frac{5}{2}}, \ldots$, and the results are shown as columns of fractions in the table on the left. Integrating the second of these series term by term gives a power series for a partial area of a quadrant. Although Newton had by now improved considerably on Wallis's methods, he continued to use Wallis's way of writing coefficients as a sequence of multiplications, thus $1, \frac{1}{2}, -\frac{1}{8}, \ldots$ as $\frac{0}{0}, \frac{0}{0} \times \frac{1}{2}, \frac{0}{0} \times \frac{1}{2} \times -\frac{1}{4}, \ldots$, with no scruples about using Wallis's fraction $\frac{0}{0}$.

By carrying out many such interpolations, and observing the patterns of the coefficients, Newton eventually discovered a general rule, namely

$$(1 + Q)^{\frac{m}{n}} = 1 + \frac{m}{n}Q + \frac{m}{n}\frac{(m-n)}{2n}Q^2 + \frac{m}{n}\frac{(m-n)}{2n}\frac{(m-2n)}{3n}Q^3 + \cdots$$

or what we now know as the general binomial theorem. For Newton this result arose purely from experimental and numerical evidence. He gave no theoretical justification, nor did he discuss limitations on the size of $Q$ or any other questions of convergence.

---

### Newton and the general binomial theorem

from Newton's manuscript, CUL Add. MS 3958.3, f. 72

---

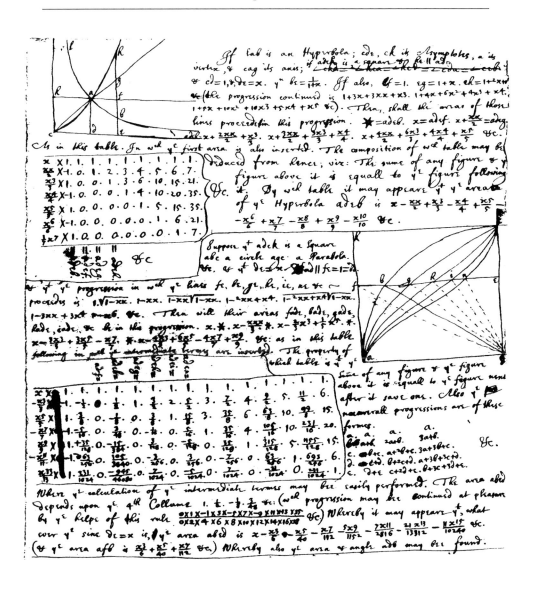

*Notation*

For ease of reading in the transcript below, Newton's seventeenth-century abbreviations and spelling have been replaced by their modern equivalents.

TRANSCRIPT

If *lab* is an Hyperbola; *cde, ck* its Asymptotes, *a* its vertex, and *cag* its axis; if *adck* is a square and *he* is parallel to *ad*, and $cd = 1$, and $de = x$, then $be = \frac{1}{1+x}$. If also, $ef = 1$, $eg = 1 + x$, $eh = 1 + 2x + x^2$ etc. (the progression continued is $1 + 3x + 3xx + x^3$, $1 + 4x + 6x^2 + 4x^3 + x^4$, $1 + 5x + 10x^2 + 10x^3 + 5x^4 + x^5$ etc). Then, shall the areas of those lines proceed in this progression. $* = adeb$, $x = adef$, $x + \frac{xx}{2} = adeg$, $adeh = x + \frac{2xx}{2} + \frac{x^3}{3}$, $x + \frac{3xx}{2} + \frac{3x^3}{3} + \frac{x^4}{4}$, $x + \frac{4xx}{2} + \frac{6x^3}{3} + \frac{4x^4}{4} + \frac{x^5}{5}$ etc. As in this table. In which the first area is also inserted. The composition of which table may be deduced from hence; viz: The sum of any figure and the figure above it is equal to the figure following it. By which table it may appear that the area of the Hyperbola *adeb* is $x - \frac{xx}{2} + \frac{x^3}{3} - \frac{x^4}{4} + \frac{x^5}{5} - \frac{x^6}{6} + \frac{x^7}{7} - \frac{x^8}{8} + \frac{x^9}{9} - \frac{x^{10}}{10}$ etc.

| | | | | | | | | | | |
|---|---|---|---|---|---|---|---|---|---|---|
| $x$ | × | 1 | 1 | 1 | 1 | 1 | 1 | 1 | 1 | 1 |
| $\frac{xx}{2}$ | × | −1 | 0 | 1 | 2 | 3 | 4 | 5 | 6 | 7 |
| $\frac{x^3}{3}$ | × | 1 | 0 | 0 | 1 | 3 | 6 | 10 | 15 | 21 |
| $\frac{x^4}{4}$ | × | −1 | 0 | 0 | 0 | 1 | 4 | 10 | 20 | 35 |
| $\frac{x^5}{5}$ | × | 1 | 0 | 0 | 0 | 0 | 1 | 5 | 15 | 35 |
| $\frac{x^6}{6}$ | × | −1 | 0 | 0 | 0 | 0 | 0 | 1 | 6 | 21 |
| $\frac{x^7}{7}$ | × | 1 | 0 | 0 | 0 | 0 | 0 | 0 | 1 | 7 |

Suppose that *adck* is a Square, *abc* a circle, *age* a Parabola, etc. and that $de = x$ and *ad* is parallel to $fe = 1 = bc$. And that the progression in which the lines *fe, be, ge, he, ie, ne*, etc. proceeds is $1, \sqrt{1 - xx}, 1 - xx, \overline{1 - xx}\sqrt{1 - xx}, 1 - 2xx + x^4$, $\overline{1 - 2xx + x^4}\sqrt{1 - xx}, 1 - 3xx + 3x^4 - x^6$, etc. Then will their areas *fade, bade, gade, hade, iade*, etc. be in this progression $x, *, x - \frac{xxx}{3}, *, x - \frac{2}{3}x^3 + \frac{1}{5}x^5, *, x - \frac{3x^3}{3} + \frac{3x^5}{5} - \frac{x^7}{7}$, $*, x - \frac{4x^3}{3} + \frac{6x^5}{5} - \frac{4x^7}{7} + \frac{x^9}{9}$, etc: as in this table following in which the indeterminate terms are inserted.

| | | | | | | | | | | | | | | | | |
|---|---|---|---|---|---|---|---|---|---|---|---|---|---|---|---|---|
| $x$ | × | 1 | 1 | 1 | 1 | 1 | 1 | 1 | 1 | 1 | 1 | 1 | 1 | 1 | 1 |
| $-\frac{x^3}{3}$ | × | −1 | $-\frac{1}{2}$ | 0 | $\frac{1}{2}$ | 1 | $\frac{3}{2}$ | 2 | $\frac{5}{2}$ | 3 | $\frac{7}{2}$ | 4 | $\frac{9}{2}$ | 5 | $\frac{11}{2}$ | 6 |
| $\frac{x^5}{5}$ | × | 1 | $\frac{3}{8}$ | 0 | $-\frac{1}{8}$ | 0 | $\frac{3}{8}$ | 1 | $\frac{15}{8}$ | 3 | $\frac{35}{8}$ | 6 | $\frac{63}{8}$ | 10 | $\frac{99}{8}$ | 15 |
| $-\frac{x^7}{7}$ | × | −1 | $-\frac{5}{16}$ | 0 | $\frac{3}{48}$ | 0 | $-\frac{1}{16}$ | 0 | $\frac{5}{16}$ | 1 | $\frac{35}{16}$ | 4 | $\frac{105}{16}$ | 10 | $\frac{231}{16}$ | 20 |
| $\frac{x^9}{9}$ | × | 1 | $\frac{35}{128}$ | 0 | $-\frac{15}{384}$ | 0 | $\frac{3}{128}$ | 0 | $-\frac{5}{128}$ | 0 | $\frac{35}{128}$ | 1 | $\frac{315}{128}$ | 5 | $\frac{1155}{128}$ | 15 |
| $-\frac{x^{11}}{11}$ | × | −1 | $-\frac{63}{256}$ | 0 | $\frac{305}{3840}$ | 0 | $-\frac{3}{256}$ | 0 | $\frac{3}{256}$ | 0 | $-\frac{7}{256}$ | 0 | $\frac{63}{256}$ | 1 | $\frac{693}{256}$ | 6 |
| $\frac{x^{13}}{13}$ | × | 1 | $\frac{231}{1024}$ | 0 | $-\frac{945}{46080}$ | 0 | $\frac{7}{1024}$ | 0 | $-\frac{5}{1024}$ | 0 | $\frac{7}{1024}$ | 0 | $-\frac{21}{1024}$ | 0 | $\frac{231}{1024}$ | 1 |

The property of which table is that the sum of any figure and the figure above it is equal to the figure next after it save one. Also the numeral progressions are of these forms.

$$
\begin{array}{llll}
a & a & a & a \\
b & a+b & 2a+b & 3a+b \\
c & b+c & a+2b+c & 3a+3b+c \\
d & c+d & b+2c+d & a+3b+3c+d \\
e & d+e & c+2d+e & b+3c+3d+e
\end{array}
$$

Where the calculation of the intermediate terms may be easily performed. The area *abed* depends upon the 4th column $1, \frac{1}{2}, -\frac{1}{8}, \frac{3}{48}$, etc. (which progression may be continued at pleasure by the help of this rule $\frac{0\times1\times-1\times3\times-5\times7\times-9\times11\times-13\times15}{0\times2\times4\times6\times8\times10\times12\times14\times16\times18}$ etc.) Whereby it may appear that, whatever the sine $de = x$ is, the area *abed* is $x - \frac{x^3}{6} - \frac{x^5}{40} - \frac{x^7}{112} - \frac{5x^9}{1152} - \frac{7x^{11}}{2816} - \frac{21x^{13}}{13312} - \frac{11x^{15}}{10240}$ etc. (and the area *afb* is $\frac{x^3}{6} + \frac{x^5}{40} + \frac{x^7}{112}$ etc.) Whereby also the area and angle *adb* may be found.

_____

## 8.1.2  Newton's 'De analysi', 1669

As Newton developed his initial findings he began to apply multiplication, division, and root extraction to power series, as a way both of checking his results and of finding new series. For Newton power series could be handled in the same way as finite expressions, and an equation involving power series was just an equation that happened to have an infinite number of terms, as useful and acceptable as the finite kind for solving problems. Ever since Viète had introduced the word 'analysis' in 1591 (see 2.3.1), it had been understood as a method of investigating problems by means of solving equations, so that to begin with 'analysis' and 'algebra' were practically synonymous. Newton was the first to see that 'analysis' could be extended to include 'infinite equations' as well. The full title of his first mathematical treatise, in 1669, was 'De analysi per aequationes numero terminorum infinitas' ('Analysis by means of equations with an infinite number of terms'), a decisive and significant shift towards the modern meaning of 'analysis'. Some examples of his treatment of infinite series in that treatise are given below.

---

### Series from Newton's 'De analysi'

from Newton, 'De analysi', 1669, as published in *Analysis per quantitatum series, fluxiones, ac differentias*, 1711, 6–7

---

## *Exempla Radicem Extrahendo.*

**Si** fit $\sqrt{aa+xx}\ =y$, Radicem fic extraho,

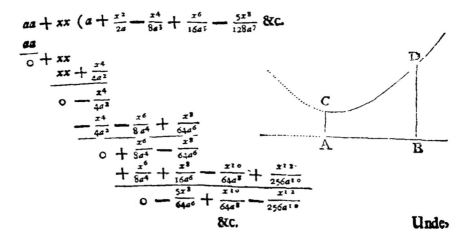

$aa + xx \ (a + \frac{x^2}{2a} - \frac{x^4}{8a^3} + \frac{x^6}{16a^5} - \frac{5x^8}{128a^7}$ &c.

$\dfrac{aa}{0} + xx$

$\qquad xx + \frac{x^4}{4a^2}$

$\qquad\quad 0 - \frac{x^4}{4a^2}$

$\qquad\qquad - \frac{x^4}{4a^2} - \frac{x^6}{8a^4} + \frac{x^8}{64a^6}$

$\qquad\qquad\quad 0 + \frac{x^6}{8a^4} - \frac{x^8}{64a^6}$

$\qquad\qquad\qquad + \frac{x^6}{8a^4} + \frac{x^8}{16a^6} - \frac{x^{10}}{64a^8} + \frac{x^{12}}{256a^{10}}$

$\qquad\qquad\qquad\quad 0 - \frac{5x^8}{64a^6} + \frac{x^{10}}{64a^8} - \frac{x^{12}}{256a^{10}}$

&c.                                                                    Unde,

---

### PER ÆQUATIONES INFINITAS.      7

**Unde,** pro Æquatione $\sqrt{aa+xx}=y$, nova producitur, viz.

$y = a + \frac{x^2}{2a} - \frac{x^4}{8a^3} + \frac{x^6}{16a^5} - \frac{5x^8}{128a^7}$ &c. Et ( per Reg. 2.) Area quæfita

ABDC erit $= ax + \frac{x^3}{6a} - \frac{x^5}{40a^3} + \frac{x^7}{112a^5} - \frac{5x^9}{1152a^7}$ &c.  Et hæc eft Quadratura Hyperbolæ.

Eodem modo, fi fit $\sqrt{aa-xx}= y$, ejus Radix erit

$a - \frac{x^2}{2a} - \frac{x^4}{8a^3} - \frac{x^6}{16a^5} - \frac{5x^8}{128a^7}$ &c.

Adeoque Area quæfita ABDC erit

æqualis $ax - \frac{x^3}{6a} - \frac{x^5}{40a^3} - \frac{x^7}{112a^5} - \frac{5x^9}{1152a^7}$ &c.

Et hæc eft Quadratura Circuli.

Vel fi ponas $\sqrt{x-xx}= y$; erit Radix æqualis infinitæ feriei.

$x^{\frac{1}{2}} - \frac{1}{2}x^{\frac{3}{2}} - \frac{1}{8}x^{\frac{5}{2}} - \frac{1}{16}x^{\frac{7}{2}} - \frac{5}{128}x^{\frac{9}{2}}$ &c.

Et Area quæfita ABD æqualis erit

$\frac{2}{3}x^{\frac{3}{2}} - \frac{1}{5}x^{\frac{5}{2}} - \frac{1}{28}x^{\frac{7}{2}} - \frac{1}{72}x^{\frac{9}{2}} - \frac{5}{704}x^{\frac{11}{2}}$ &c.

five $x^{\frac{1}{2}}$ in $\frac{2}{3}x - \frac{1}{5}x^2 - \frac{1}{28}x^3 - \frac{1}{72}x^4 - \frac{5}{704}x^5$ &c.

Et hæc eft Areæ Circuli Quadratura.

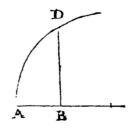

TRANSLATION

*Examples by the extraction of roots*

If $\sqrt{aa + xx} = y$, I extract the root thus,

$$aa + xx \left( a + \frac{x^2}{2a} - \frac{x^4}{8a^3} + \frac{x^6}{16a^5} - \frac{5x^3}{128a^7} \right. \quad \text{etc.}$$

$$\frac{aa}{0} + xx$$

$$xx + \frac{x^4}{4a^2}$$

$$0 - \frac{x^4}{4a^2}$$

$$- \frac{x^4}{4a^2} - \frac{x^6}{8a^4} + \frac{x^8}{64a^6}$$

$$0 + \frac{x^6}{8a^4} - \frac{x^8}{64a^6}$$

$$+ \frac{x^6}{8a^4} + \frac{x^8}{16a^6} - \frac{x^{10}}{64a^8} + \frac{x^{12}}{256a^{10}}$$

$$0 - \frac{5x^8}{64a^6} + \frac{x^{10}}{64a^8} - \frac{x^{12}}{256a^{10}}$$

Whence, by means of the equation $\sqrt{aa + xx} = y$, a new one is produced, namely $y = a + \frac{x^2}{2a} - \frac{x^4}{8a^3} + \frac{x^6}{16a^5} - \frac{5x^8}{128a^7}$ etc. And (by rule 2) the sought area $ABDC$ will be equal to $ax + \frac{x^3}{6a} - \frac{x^5}{40a^3} + \frac{x^7}{112a^5} - \frac{5x^9}{1152a^7}$ etc. And this is the quadrature of the hyperbola.

In the same way, if $\sqrt{aa - xx} = y$, the root of it will be
$a - \frac{x^2}{2a} - \frac{x^4}{8a^3} - \frac{x^6}{16a^5} - \frac{5x^8}{128a^7}$etc.

And therefore the sought area $ABDC$ will be equal to
$ax - \frac{x^3}{6a} - \frac{x^5}{40a^3} - \frac{x^7}{112a^5} - \frac{5x^9}{1152a^7}$etc.

And this is the quadrature of the circle.

Or if you put $\sqrt{x - xx} = y$, the root will be equal to the infinite series
$x^{\frac{1}{2}} - \frac{1}{2}x^{\frac{3}{2}} - \frac{1}{8}x^{\frac{5}{2}} - \frac{1}{16}x^{\frac{7}{2}} - \frac{5}{128}x^{\frac{9}{2}}$ etc.

And the sought area $ABD$ will be equal to
$\frac{2}{3}x^{\frac{3}{2}} - \frac{1}{5}x^{\frac{5}{2}} - \frac{1}{28}x^{\frac{7}{2}} - \frac{1}{72}x^{\frac{9}{2}} - \frac{5}{704}x^{\frac{11}{2}}$ etc.

or $x^{\frac{1}{2}}$ times $\frac{2}{3}x - \frac{1}{5}x^2 - \frac{1}{28}x^3 - \frac{1}{72}x^4 - \frac{5}{704}x^5$ etc.

And this is the quadrature of a part of a circle.

### 8.1.3 Newton's letters to Leibniz, 1676

'De analysi' was not published until 1711, but Newton's series became public before that through letters he wrote for Leibniz in June and October 1676. (The letters are sometimes known as the 'Epistola prior' and 'Epistola posterior', respectively.)

Newton began the June letter with a statement of the general binomial theorem, a result he said he had discovered some years ago (in fact, as we have seen, in the winter of 1664). In the October letter he acknowledged his debt to Wallis, who was not slow to notice the accolade, and quoted long extracts from the letters in *A treatise of algebra*, which he was then completing, though it was not published until 1685. The extracts below are Newton's examples I to III and VII as published by Wallis (the 'he' in the first line is Newton). Series I gives arcsin $x$ (in a circle of radius $r$); series II gives sin $z$ and the versed sine of $z$, that is $1 - \cos z$. In example III it is assumed that we know the ratio of a chord $x$ to the diameter $d$, namely the sine of an angle $\theta$; the series then gives the sine of any multiple, $n\theta$, of the same angle. Newton pointed out that for odd values of $n$ the series is finite, and gives the usual expressions for sines of multiple angles. Series IV, V, and VI are concerned with properties of an ellipse, and are omitted here. Series VII is for the antilogarithm of $z$, based on the quadrature of the hyperbola.

Power series from the *Epistola prior*

from Newton, *Epistola prior*, 13 June 1676, as published in Wallis, *A treatise of algebra*, 1685, 341–342, 343

# C H A P.  XCV.

*Examples of the Application thereof, in many Cafes.*

EXAMPLES of this kind he gives us many, (fome whereof I fhall here tranfcribe ;) in fome of which he makes ufe of the Letters A,B,C,D,&c; for the Firft, Second, Third, Fourth ; and the confequent Terms or Members of the Series found, (to fpare the repeating of it.)

Example I. From the Sine (right or verfed,) being given, to find the Arch. Suppofe the Radius $r$ ; the Right Sine $x$ : The Arch is

$$= x + \frac{x^3}{6rr} + \frac{3x^5}{40\,r^4} + \frac{5x^7}{112\,r^6} + \&c. \text{ That is,}$$

$$= x + \frac{1\times 1 \times x\,x}{2\times 3\times rr}A + \frac{3\times 3\times x\,x}{4\times 5\,rr}B + \frac{5\times 5\times x\,x}{6\times 7\,rr}C + \frac{7\times 7\times x\,x}{8\times 9\,rr}D + \&c.$$

Or, fuppofing the Diameter $d$ ; and the Verfed Sine $x$ : The Arch is,

$$= d^{\frac{1}{2}}x^{\frac{1}{2}} + \frac{x^{\frac{3}{2}}}{6d^{\frac{1}{2}}} + \frac{3\,x^{\frac{5}{2}}}{40d^{\frac{1}{2}}} + \frac{5\,x^{\frac{7}{2}}}{112d^{\frac{1}{2}}} + \&c. \text{ That is,}$$

$$= \sqrt{dx}, \text{ into } 1 + \frac{x}{6} + \frac{3\,xx}{40\,d} + \frac{5\,xxx}{112\,dd} + \&c.$$

(Note here, as hath been afore intimated, that $\frac{1}{2}, \frac{1}{2}, \frac{1}{2}$, &c, are here intended as Exponents of the Dimenfions of $x, d$, &c. And the like in divers other places where the like do fo occur.)

Examp. II. From the Arch given, to find the Sine ; Right or Verfed. Suppofe the Radius $r$, the Arch $z$ : The Right Sine is,

$$= z - \frac{z^3}{6rr} + \frac{z^5}{120\,r^4} - \frac{z^7}{5040\,r^6} + \frac{z^9}{36288\,r^8} - \&c. \text{ That is;}$$

$$= z - \frac{zz}{2\times 3\,rr}A - \frac{zz}{4\times 5\,rr}B - \frac{zz}{6\times 7\,rr}C - \frac{zz}{8\times 9\,rr}D - \&c.$$

And the Verfed Sine $= \frac{zz}{2r} - \frac{z^4}{24\,r^3} + \frac{z^6}{720\,r^5} - \frac{z^8}{4032\,r^7} + \&c. \text{ That is,}$

$$= \frac{zz}{1\times 2r} - \frac{zz}{3\times 4\,r^7}A - \frac{zz}{5\times 6\,rr}B - \frac{zz}{7\times 8\,rr} - \&c.$$

Examp. III. An Arch being given, to find another in a given Proportion. Suppofe the Diameter $d$ ; the Chord of the given Arch $x$ ; the Arch fought, to that given, as $n$ to 1. The Chord hereof is,

$= n x$

$$= n x + \frac{1 - nn}{2 \times 3\, dd} x x\, A + \frac{9 - nn}{4 \times 5\, dd} x x\, B + \frac{25 - nn}{6 \times 7\, dd} x x\, C + \frac{49 - nn}{8 \times 9\, dd} x x D$$

$$+ \frac{81 - nn}{10 \times 11\, dd} x x\, E + \&c.$$

Note here; that if *n* be an odd number, the Series will be finite; and the Refult the fame, as in the ordinary Algebra, for Multiplying a given Angle by the number *n*.

[...]

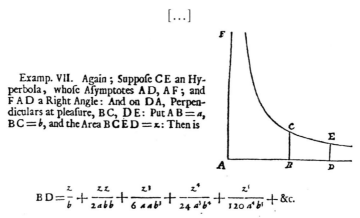

Examp. VII.  Again ; Suppofe C E an Hyperbola, whofe Afymptotes A D, A F ; and F A D a Right Angle: And on D A, Perpendiculars at pleafure, B C, D E: Put A B = *a*, B C = *b*, and the Area B C E D = *x*: Then is

$$B D = \frac{z}{b} + \frac{zz}{2a b b} + \frac{z^3}{6\, aab^3} + \frac{z^4}{24\, a^3 b^4} + \frac{z^5}{120\, a^4 b^5} + \&c.$$

Where the Coefficients of the Denominators, arife by continual Multiplication of this Arithmetical Progreffion; 1, 2, 3, 4, 5, &c.
Hence, a Logarithm being given, we may find the Number to which it belongs.

## 8.1.4 Gregory's binomial expansion, 1670

In March 1670 John Collins sent Newton's series for the quadrature of the circle to James Gregory in Edinburgh, and Gregory replied on 23 November with some further series of his own, saying: 'I suppose these series I send you here enclosed, may have some affinity with those inventions you advertise me that Mr. Newton had discovered.'[2] Unfortunately, we do not have Gregory's original letter, only extracts copied, possibly not always accurately, by Collins. They were published almost two centuries later by Stephen Jordan Rigaud in an invaluable collection of letters entitled *Correspondence of scientific men of the seventeenth century* (1841).

Since Gregory's words are sparse, the first extract below requires some explanation. Essentially Gregory has created a logarithmic scale on some unspecified base by fixing $\log b = e$ and $\log(b + d) = e + c$. He then wants to know what number will correspond to any other logarithm of the form $e + a$ (note that $e$ here is *not* the base of natural logarithms).

From the information given we have

$$e = \log b$$

$$c = \log(b + d) - \log b$$

---

2. Rigaud 1841, II, 203.

Thus

$$e + a = e + \frac{a}{c}c$$

$$= \log b + \frac{a}{c}(\log(b + d) - \log b)$$

$$= \log b + \frac{a}{c}\log\left(1 + \frac{d}{b}\right)$$

Hence, on Gregory's scale, the number whose logarithm is $e + a$ must be $b\left(1 + \frac{d}{b}\right)^{\frac{a}{c}}$. The binomial expansion of this last expression is precisely the series given by Gregory, as may easily be checked by making the appropriate substitutions for $\frac{f}{c}$, $\frac{g}{c}$, etc.

---

### Gregory's binomial expansion
from Gregory to Collins, 23 November 1670, as published in Rigaud, *Correspondence*, 1841, II, 209–210

---

## To find the number of a logarithm.

## Sint duo numeri, primus $b$, secundus $b + d$, logarith-

mus numeri $b$ sit $e$, et logarithmus numeri $b + d$ sit $e + c$, quæritur numerus cujus logarithmus $e + a$.
    Sit series continue proportionalium,

$$b,\ d,\ \frac{d^2}{b},\ \frac{d^3}{b^2},\ \&c.\ ;$$

et alia series $\frac{a}{c}$, $\frac{a - c}{2c}$, $\frac{a - 2c}{3c}$, $\frac{a - 3c}{4c}$, &c. ;

fiatque productum ex duobus primis hujus seriei ter- minis $\frac{f}{c}$, ex tribus primis $\frac{g}{c}$, ex quatuor primis $\frac{h}{c}$, ex

quinque $\frac{i}{c}$, &c. ; erit numerus logarithmi $e + a =$

$$b + \frac{ad}{c} + \frac{fd^2}{cb} + \frac{gd^3}{cb^2} + \frac{hd^4}{cb^3} + \frac{id^5}{cb^4} + \frac{kd^6}{cb^5} + \&c.$$

Hinc adhibita quadam industria nullo negotio resolvi- tur quævis æquatio pura.

*Note* A 'pure' equation is one whose highest power is not 'affected' by any lower power, that is, it takes the simplest possible form, $x^n = k$.

To find the number of a logarithm.

Let there be two numbers, the first $b$, the second $b + d$; let the logarithm of the number $b$ be $e$, and the logarithm of the number $b + d$ be $e + c$; there is sought the number whose logarithm is $e + a$.

Let there be a series of continued proportionals, $b$, $d$, $\frac{d^2}{b}$, $\frac{d^3}{b^2}$, etc.;

and another series $\frac{a}{c}$, $\frac{a-c}{2c}$, $\frac{a-2c}{3c}$, $\frac{a-3c}{4c}$, etc.

and let the product made by the first two terms of this series be $\frac{f}{c}$, and by the first three $\frac{g}{c}$, and by the first four $\frac{h}{c}$, and by five $\frac{i}{c}$, etc.; then the number with logarithm $e + a$

$$= b + \frac{ad}{c} + \frac{fd^2}{cb} + \frac{gd^3}{cb^2} + \frac{hd^4}{cb^3} + \frac{id^5}{cb^4} + \frac{kd^6}{cb^5} + \text{etc.}$$

Hence applying a certain amount of work, any pure equation can be solved without any trouble.

---

In February 1671 Gregory sent Collins further examples of power series, this time for arctan $t$, tan $a$, sec $a$, and others.[3] As with the binomial expansion he had sent three months earlier, Gregory stated his new results without any explanation. The only clue as to his methods comes from some jottings on the back of an envelope, or to be more precise, on the back of a letter from Gideon Shaw, an Edinburgh bookseller. The letter is dated 29 January 1671, and it is clear that the notes on the back of the letter and the results Gregory sent to Collins a few days later are related because the same numerical slip appears in both. The notes are too terse, however, to be construed as the development of new ideas, and are more likely to have been Gregory's reminders to himself of results he had previously worked out more fully elsewhere.

The fragments show some remarkable achievements on Gregory's part. Essentially he seems to have been finding an ordinate to a curve by a method of successive approximations, very similar to what later came to be called the Newton–Raphson method. He applied this to trigonometric curves involving sines, tangents, or secants, and so needed to understand rates of change of trigonometric quantities. He did, and wrote such relationships algebraically, so that where $q$ was the tangent, for instance, he wrote its rate of change as $1 + q^2$.

A second remarkable feature of Gregory's notes is that he seems to have understood the relationship we would now write as

$$\frac{\mathrm{d}}{\mathrm{d}x} f(q) = \frac{\mathrm{d}f}{\mathrm{d}q} \cdot \frac{\mathrm{d}q}{\mathrm{d}\theta} \cdot \frac{\mathrm{d}\theta}{\mathrm{d}x}.$$

In the cases Gregory was handling the last two multipliers were constant, so he could find successive 'derivatives' of $f(q)$ with respect to $x$ by 'differentiating' with respect

---

3. Gregory 1939, 170.

to $q$ and multiplying by the required factor. This describes his procedure in modern language, because we do not know how he described or thought of it himself, but careful scrutiny of his working shows that he was certainly carrying out some such process. Once again the few small errors in his working are historically valuable, because they enable us to see more clearly what he was trying to do and where he went wrong.[4]

This brief discussion of Gregory's results has been included as a further example of the way similar mathematical ideas can emerge almost simultaneously but independently in the minds of more than one person. It also illustrates the difficulties of historical reconstruction: for Newton we have detailed evidence of his thought processes, but for Gregory we have virtually none.

## 8.2 TAYLOR SERIES

### 8.2.1 Taylor's increment method, 1715

In 1715 the English mathematician Brook Taylor published a slim volume entitled *Methodus incrementorum*, in which he explained how to predict the behaviour of a changing quantity from the rate of change of its increments. Along the way he arrived at one of the most important mathematical discoveries of the early eighteenth century: Taylor series.

Taylor's original notation with its plethora of dots, is not easy to follow. If we use the modern symbol $\delta$ to indicate a small change in the variable that follows it, then we may say that a variable $x$ increases to $x + \delta x$ over time $\delta t$. Its value after a further time $\delta t$ will be $x + \delta x + \delta(x + \delta x)$, or more simply, $x + 2\delta x + \delta(\delta x)$. This is how Taylor began to build up his series (see his table under the word *DEMONSTRATIO*). His dependent variable was $x$, and his independent variable, assumed to increase uniformly with time, was $z$. In modern notation $\dot{x}, \ddot{x}$ may be replaced by $\delta x, \delta(\delta x)$, and so on, while $\dot{z} = \delta z$ is a constant, and $\ddot{z}$ and all higher rates of change are zero. First, Taylor showed by an extension of the argument above that, after $n$ increments, the new value of $x$ is (in $\delta$ notation)

$$
\begin{aligned}
x &+ \frac{n}{1}\delta x + \frac{n(n-1)}{1.2}\delta(\delta x) + \frac{n(n-1)(n-2)}{1.2.3}\delta(\delta(\delta x)) + \cdots \\
&= x + \delta x \frac{n\delta z}{1\delta z} + \delta(\delta x)\frac{n\delta z \cdot (n-1)\delta z}{1.2(\delta z)^2} + \delta(\delta(\delta x))\frac{n\delta z \cdot (n-1)\delta z \cdot (n-2)\delta z}{1.2.3(\delta z)^3} + \cdots.
\end{aligned}
$$

---

4. For further details see Gregory 1939, 350–359, but be aware of the modern interpretations sometimes made by the editor, H W Turnbull.

Passing from increments to fluxions in Corollary 2, Taylor assumed (i) that in the numerators each term $(n - k)\delta z$ can be replaced by $n\delta z = v$, a constant; (ii) that elsewhere $x$ can be replaced by $\dot{x}$, $z$ by $\dot{z}$, and so on. A modern form of this argument would be that $\frac{\delta x}{\delta z}$ tends to $\frac{dx}{dz}$, $\frac{\delta(\delta x)}{(\delta z)^2}$ tends to $\frac{d^2x}{dz^2}$, and so on (which shows why we write $\frac{d^n x}{dz^n}$ for the $n^{\text{th}}$ derivative). So now the series of terms above becomes

$$x + \frac{dx}{dz} \cdot \frac{v}{1} + \frac{d^2x}{dz^2} \cdot \frac{v^2}{1.2} + \frac{d^3x}{dz^3} \cdot \frac{v^3}{1.2.3} + \cdots .$$

---

### Taylor's series
from Taylor, *Methodus incrementorum*, 1715, 21–23

---

# PROP. VII.  THEOR. III.

*Sint* z *&* x *quantitates duæ variabiles, quarum* z *uniformiter*

*augetur per data incrementa* z, *& fit* nz $=v$, $v - \dot{z} = \dot{v}$,

$\dot{v} - \ddot{z} = \ddot{v}$, *& fic porrò.   Tum dico quod quo tem-*

*pore* z *crefcendo fit* z $+$ v, x *item crefcendo fiet*

$$x + x\frac{v}{1z} + x\frac{v\dot{v}}{1.2z^2} + x\frac{v\,\dot{v}.\ddot{v}}{1.2.3z^3} + \&c.$$

$$( \ 22 \ )$$

## DEMONSTRATIO.

| $x$ | | $x$ | | $x$ | | $x$ | $x$ | &c. |
|---|---|---|---|---|---|---|---|---|
| $x+x$ | | $x+x$ | | $x+x$ | | $x+x$ | &c. | |
| $x+2x+x$ | | $x+2\ x+x$ | | $x+2\ x+x$ | | &c. | | |
| $x+3\ x+3\ x+x$ | | $x+3\ x+3\ x+x$ | | &c. | | | | |
| $x+4\ x+6\ x+4\ x+x$ | &c. | | | | | | | |
| &c. | | | | | | | | |

Valores fucceffivi ipfius $x$ per additionem continuam collecti funt $x$, $x+x$, $x+2x+x$, $x+3x+3x+x$, &c. ut patet per operationem in tabula annexa expreffam. Sed in his valoribus $x$ coefficientes numerales terminorum $x$, $x$, $x$, &c. eodem modo formantur, ac coefficientes terminorum correfpondentium in dignitate binomii. Et (per Theorema *Newtonianum*) fi dignitatis index fit $n$, coefficientes erunt $1, \dfrac{n}{1}, \dfrac{n}{1} \times \dfrac{n-1}{2}, \dfrac{n}{1} \times \dfrac{n-1}{2} \times \dfrac{n-2}{3}$, &c. Ergò quo tempore $z$ crefcendo fit $z + nz$, hoc eft $z + v$, fiet $x$ æqualis feriei $x + \dfrac{n}{1}x + \dfrac{n}{1} \times \dfrac{n-1}{2}x + \dfrac{n}{1} \times \dfrac{n-1}{2} \times \dfrac{n-2}{3} + x$ &c.

Sed funt $\dfrac{n}{1} = \left( \dfrac{nz}{z} = \right) \dfrac{v}{z}$, $\dfrac{n-1}{2} = \left( \dfrac{nz-z}{2z} = \right) \dfrac{v}{2z}$, $\dfrac{n-2}{3} =$

## ( 23 )

$$\left(\frac{n\dot{z}-2\dot{z}}{3\dot{z}} = \right) \frac{\overset{\shortmid\shortmid}{v}}{\overset{\centerdot}{z}}, \text{ &c.}$$ Proinde quo tempore $z$ crefcendo fit $z+v$,

eodem tempore $x$ crefcendo fiet $x + x\dfrac{\overset{\centerdot}{v}}{\underset{\centerdot}{1\dot{z}}} + x\dfrac{\overset{\centerdot}{v}\overset{\centerdot\centerdot}{v}}{\underset{\centerdot}{1.2\dot{z}^2}} + x\dfrac{\overset{\centerdot}{v}\overset{\centerdot\centerdot}{v}\overset{\shortmid\shortmid}{v}}{\underset{\centerdot}{1.2.3\dot{z}^3}} +$

$+$ &c.

### C O R O L L. I.

Et ipfis $z$, $x$, $\overset{\centerdot}{x}$, $\overset{\centerdot\centerdot}{x}$, &c. iifdem manentibus, mutato figno ipfius $v$, quo tempore $z$ decrefcendo fit $z - v$, eodem tempore $x$ decrefcen-

do fiet $x - x\dfrac{\overset{\centerdot}{v}}{\underset{\centerdot}{1\dot{z}^2}} + x\dfrac{\overset{\centerdot}{v}\overset{\centerdot}{v}}{\underset{\centerdot}{1.2\dot{z}^2}} - x\dfrac{\overset{\centerdot}{v}\overset{\centerdot}{v}\overset{\centerdot\centerdot}{v}}{\underset{\centerdot}{1.2.3\dot{z}^3}}$ &c. vel juxta notatio-

nem noftram $x - x\dfrac{v}{\underset{\centerdot}{1\dot{z}}} + x\dfrac{\overset{\centerdot}{vv}}{\underset{\centerdot}{1.2\dot{z}^2}} - x\dfrac{\overset{\centerdot}{v}\overset{\centerdot}{v}\overset{\shortmid\shortmid}{v}}{\underset{\centerdot}{1.2.3\dot{z}^3}}$ &c. ipfis $\overset{\centerdot}{v},\overset{\shortmid\shortmid}{v}$,&c.

converfis in $-\underset{\shortmid}{v}$, $-\underset{\shortmid\shortmid}{v}$, &c.

### C O R O L L. II.

Si pro Incrementis evanefcentibus fcribantur fluxiones ipfis pro-portionales, factis jam omnibus $\overset{\shortmid\shortmid}{v}$, $\overset{\centerdot}{v}$, $v$, $\underset{\shortmid}{v}$, $\underset{\shortmid\shortmid}{v}$, &c. æqualibus

quo tempore $z$ uniformiter fluendo fit $z + v$ fiet $x$, $x + \overset{\centerdot}{x}\dfrac{v}{1\dot{z}} +$

$\overset{\centerdot\centerdot}{x}\dfrac{v^2}{1.2\dot{z}^2} + \overset{\centerdot\centerdot\centerdot}{x}\dfrac{v^3}{1.2.3\dot{z}^3}$ &c. vel mutato figno ipfius $v$, quo tem-

pore $z$ decrefcendo fit $z - v$, $x$ decrefcendo fiet $x - \overset{\centerdot}{x}\dfrac{y}{1\dot{z}} +$

$\overset{\centerdot\centerdot}{x}\dfrac{v^2}{1.2\dot{z}^2} - \overset{\centerdot\centerdot\centerdot}{x}\dfrac{v^3}{1.2.3\dot{z}^3} +$ &c.     G        P R O P.

TRANSLATION

PROPOSITION VII. THEOREM III.

*Let $z$ and $x$ be two variable quantities, of which $z$ is uniformly increased by a given increment $\dot{z}$, and let $nz = v, v - z = \dot{v}, \dot{v} - z = \ddot{v}$, and so on. Then I say that in the time that $z$ increasing becomes $z + v$, $x$ likewise increasing becomes $x + \dot{x}\frac{v}{1\dot{z}} + \ddot{x}\frac{v\dot{v}}{1.2\dot{z}^2} + \dddot{x}\frac{v\dot{v}\ddot{v}}{1.2.3\dot{z}^3} + $ etc.*

DEMONSTRATION

| | | | | |
|---|---|---|---|---|
| $x$ | $\dot{x}$ | $\ddot{x}$ | $\dddot{x}$ | $\ddddot{x}$ etc. |
| $x + \dot{x}$ | $\dot{x} + \ddot{x}$ | $\ddot{x} + \dddot{x}$ | $\dddot{x} + \ddddot{x}$ etc. | |
| $x + 2\dot{x} + \ddot{x}$ | $\dot{x} + 2\ddot{x} + \dddot{x}$ | $\ddot{x} + 2\dddot{x} + \ddddot{x}$ etc. | | |
| $x + 3\dot{x} + 3\ddot{x} + \dddot{x}$ | $\dot{x} + 3\ddot{x} + 3\dddot{x} + \ddddot{x}$ etc. | | | |
| $x + 4\dot{x} + 6\ddot{x} + 4\dddot{x} + \ddddot{x}$ etc. | | | | |
| etc. | | | | |

The successive values of $x$ by continued addition, brought together, are $x, x + \dot{x}, x+2\dot{x}+\ddot{x}, x+3\dot{x}+3\ddot{x}+\dddot{x}$, etc as is clear from the working shown in the adjoined table.

But in these values of $x$ the numerical coefficients of the terms $x, \dot{x}, \ddot{x}$, etc are formed in the same way as the coefficients of the corresponding terms in powers of binomials. And (by the *Newtonian* theorem) if the index of the power is $n$, the coefficients will be 1, $\frac{n}{1}, \frac{n-1}{2}, \frac{n}{1} \times \frac{n-1}{2} \times \frac{n-2}{3}$, etc. Therefore in the time that $z$ increasing becomes $z+nz$, which is $z + v$, $x$ will become equal to the series $x + \frac{n}{1}\dot{x} + \frac{n}{1} \times \frac{n-1}{2}\ddot{x} + \frac{n}{1} \times \frac{n-1}{2} \times \frac{n-2}{3}\dddot{x}$ etc.

But $\frac{n}{1} = \left(\frac{nz}{\dot{z}} = \right)\frac{v}{\dot{z}}, \frac{n-1}{2} = \left(\frac{nz-z}{2\dot{z}} = \right)\frac{\dot{v}}{2\dot{z}}, \frac{n-2}{3} = \left(\frac{nz-2z}{3\dot{z}} = \right)\frac{\ddot{v}}{3\dot{z}}$, etc. [23] Whence in the time that $z$ increasing becomes $z + v$, in the same time $x$ increasing becomes

$$x + \dot{x}\frac{v}{1\dot{z}} + \ddot{x}\frac{v\dot{v}}{1.2\dot{z}^2} + \dddot{x}\frac{v\dot{v}\ddot{v}}{1.2.3\dot{z}^3} + \text{etc.}$$

And keeping $z$, $x$, $\dot{x}$, $\ddot{x}$, etc. the same, but changing the sign of $v$, in the time that $z$ decreasing becomes $z - v$, in the same time $x$ decreasing becomes

$$x - \dot{x}\frac{v}{1\dot{z}} + \ddot{x}\frac{v\dot{v}}{1.2\dot{z}^2} - \dddot{x}\frac{v\dot{v}\ddot{v}}{1.2.3\dot{z}^3}, \text{ etc., or using our notation } x - \dot{x}\frac{v}{1\dot{z}} + \ddot{x}\frac{v\overset{v}{v}}{1.2\dot{z}^2} + \dddot{x}\frac{v\overset{v}{v}\overset{vv}{v}}{1.2.3\dot{z}^3}$$

etc. with $\dot{v}$, $\ddot{v}$, etc. changed into $-\overset{v}{v}$, $-\overset{v}{v}$, etc.

If instead of the increasing increments there are written fluxions proportional to them, now making all $\dot{v}$, $\ddot{v}$, $v$, $\overset{v}{v}$, $\overset{vv}{v}$, etc. equal, in the time that $z$ flowing uniformly becomes $z+v$,

$x$ will become $x + \dot{x}\frac{v}{1\dot{z}} + \ddot{x}\frac{v^2}{1.2\dot{z}^2} + \dddot{x}\frac{v^3}{1.2.3\dot{z}^3}$ etc. or changing the sign of $v$, in the time that $z$ decreasing becomes $z-v$, $x$ decreasing will become $x - \dot{x}\frac{v}{1\dot{z}} + \ddot{x}\frac{v^2}{1.2\dot{z}^2} - \dddot{x}\frac{v^3}{1.2.3\dot{z}^3} +$ etc.

---

## 8.2.2 Maclaurin's series, 1742

Colin Maclaurin's *A treatise of fluxions* was written as a response to those who criticized the methods of the calculus (see 10.2), and most of Book I is devoted to demonstrating the validity of the calculus using traditional geometric standards of rigour. In Book II Maclaurin went on to show what could be achieved by the calculus of fluxions.

His derivation of Taylor series was somewhat easier than Taylor's because he began by assuming the existence of the series and then needed only to calculate the coefficients. He did warn against the case where one of the derivatives becomes infinite, but otherwise there is no discussion of convergence.

## Maclaurin's series
from Maclaurin, *A treatise of fluxions*, 1742, II, 610

751. The following theorem is likewife of great ufe in this doctrine. Suppofe that $y$ is any quantity that can be expreffed by a feries of this form $A + Bz + Cz^2 + Dz^3 + \&c.$ where $A, B, C, \&c.$ reprefent invariable coefficients as ufual, any of which may be fuppofed to vanifh. When $z$ vanifhes, let $E$ be the value of $y$, and let $\dot{E}, \ddot{E}, \overset{...}{E}, \&c.$ be then the refpective values of $\dot{y}, \ddot{y}, \overset{...}{y}, \&c.$ $z$ being fuppofed to flow uniformly.

Then $y = E + \dfrac{\dot{E}z}{\dot{z}} + \dfrac{\ddot{E}z^2}{1\times2\,\dot{z}^2} + \dfrac{\overset{...}{E}z^3}{1\times2\times3\,\dot{z}^3} + \dfrac{\overset{....}{E}z^4}{1\times2\times3\times4\,\dot{z}^4} +$ &c. the law of the continuation of which feries is manifeft. For fince $y = A + Bz + Cz^2 + Dz^3 + \&c.$ it follows that when $z = o$, A is equal to $y$; but (by the fuppofition) E is then equal to $y$; confequently $A = E$. By taking the fluxions, and dividing by $\dot{z}$, $\dfrac{\dot{y}}{\dot{z}} = B + 2Cz + 3Dz^2 + \&c.$ and when $z = o$, B is equal to $\dfrac{\dot{y}}{\dot{z}}$, that is to $\dfrac{\dot{E}}{\dot{z}}$. By taking the fluxions a-gain, and dividing by $\dot{z}$, (which is fuppofed invariable) $\dfrac{\ddot{y}}{\dot{z}^2} =$ $2C + 6Dz + \&c.$ let $z = o$, and fubftituting $\ddot{E}$ for $\ddot{y}$, $\dfrac{\ddot{E}}{\dot{z}^2} =$ $2C$, or $C = \dfrac{\ddot{E}}{2\dot{z}^2}$. By taking the fluxions again, and dividing by $\dot{z}$, $\dfrac{\overset{...}{y}}{\dot{z}^3} = 6D + \&c.$ and by fuppofing $z = o$, we have $D = \dfrac{\overset{...}{E}}{6\dot{z}^3}$ Thus it appears that $y = A + Bz + Cz^2 + Dz^3 + \&c. =$ $E + \dfrac{\dot{E}z}{\dot{z}} + \dfrac{\ddot{E}z^2}{1\times2\,\dot{z}^2} + \dfrac{\overset{...}{E}z^3}{1\times2\times3\,\dot{z}^3} + \dfrac{\overset{....}{E}z^4}{1\times2\times3\times4\,\dot{z}^4} + \&c.$ This pro-pofition may be likewife deduced from the binomial theorem.

### 8.2.3  Functions as infinite series, 1748

In 1748, Euler incorporated power series into his definition of functions, and indeed believed not only that *all* functions could be expressed in this way, but that it was the best means of understanding them.

---

### Functions as infinite series
from Euler, *Introductio in analysin infinitorum*, 1748, I, §59

---

## C A P U T   I V.

### *De explicatione Functionum per series infinitas.*

59.  CUm Functiones fractæ atque irrationales ipsius $z$ non in forma integra $A + Bz + Cz^2 + Dz^3 + \&c.$ continentur, ita ut terminorum numerus sit finitus, quæri solent hujusmodi expressiones in infinitum excurrentes, quæ valorem cujusvis Functionis sive fractæ sive irrationalis exhibeant. Quin etiam natura Functionum transcendentium melius intelligi censetur, si per ejusmodi formam, etsi infinitam, exprimantur. Cum enim natura Functionis integræ optime perspiciatur, si secundum diversas potestates ipsius $z$ explicetur, atque adeo ad formam $A + Bz + Cz^2 + Dz^3 + \&c.$ reducatur, ita eadem forma aptissima videtur ad reliquarum Functionum omnium indolem menti repræsentandam, etiamsi terminorum numerus sit revera infinitus.  Perspicuum autem est nullam Functionem non integram ipsius $z$ per numerum hujusmodi terminorum $A + Bz + Cz^2 + \&c.$ finitum exponi posse; eo ipso enim

*PER SERIES INFINITAS.*      47

Functio foret integra; num vero per hujusmodi terminorum seriem infinitam exhiberi possit, si quis dubitet, hoc dubium per ipsam evolutionem cujusque Functionis tolletur.  Quo autem hæc explicatio latius pateat, præter potestates ipsius $z$ exponentes integros affirmativos habentes, admitti debent potestates quæcunque.  Sic dubium erit nullum quin omnis Functio ipsius $z$ in hujusmodi expressionem infinitam transmutari possit: $Az^\alpha + Bz^\beta + Cz^\gamma + Dz^\delta + \&c.$ denotantibus exponentibus $\alpha, \beta, \gamma, \delta,$ &c. numeros quoscunque.

CAP.IV.

TRANSLATION

CHAPTER IV

*On expressing functions by means of infinite series*

59. Since fractional or irrational functions of $z$ are not confined to complete forms $A + Bz + Cz^2 + Dz^3 +$ etc. where the number of terms is finite, it is usual to seek expressions of this kind carrying on to infinity, which exhibit the value of the function whether fractional or irrational. And indeed the nature of transcendental functions is thought to be better understood if expressed in this kind of form, even though infinite. For since the nature of complete functions is best seen if they are expressed according to various powers of $z$, and therefore reduced to the form $A + Bz + Cz^2 + Dz^3 +$ etc., so the same form seems most appropriate for representing to the mind the nature of all remaining functions, although the number of terms may be truly infinite. Moreover it is obvious that no non-complete function in $z$ can be expressed by a finite number of terms of this kind, $A + Bz + Cz^2 +$ etc., for by this itself [47] the function would become complete; but then it may be exhibited by an infinite series of terms of this kind, and if anyone should doubt it, this doubt will be removed by the expansion of that function. Moreover, this exposition extends further: besides powers of $z$ having positive integer exponents, there must be admitted any powers at all. Thus there will be no doubt but that every function of $z$ may be transformed into this kind of infinite expression: $Az^\alpha + Bz^\beta + Cz^\gamma + Dz^\delta +$ etc., the exponents $\alpha, \beta, \gamma, \delta$, etc. denoting any powers whatever.

---

## 8.3 CONVERGENCE OF SERIES

The discovery of power series during the seventeenth century opened up such promising new possibilities that, to begin with, questions of convergence were scarcely considered. Newton was sure-footed enough to operate only with series that *did* converge, though he was sometimes concerned with *rate* of convergence, claiming on one occasion that he could reduce the time required for a particular calculation from 1000 years to three or four days.[5] Brouncker in 1668 had tried to show, by summing groups of terms, that his series for logarithms must converge (see 3.2.2), and in 1682 Leibniz argued for the convergence of $1 - \frac{1}{3} + \frac{1}{5} - \frac{1}{7} + \ldots$ as follows:[6]

---

5. Newton to Leibniz, 24 October 1676, in Newton *Correspondence*, 139.
6. 'Eritque valor justo major 1 errore tamen existente infra $\frac{1}{3}$

$$\text{minor } \tfrac{1}{1} - \tfrac{1}{3} \ldots\ldots\ldots \tfrac{1}{5}$$
$$\text{major } \tfrac{1}{1} - \tfrac{1}{3} + \tfrac{1}{5} \ldots\ldots \tfrac{1}{7}$$
$$\text{minor } \tfrac{1}{1} - \tfrac{1}{3} + \tfrac{1}{5} - \tfrac{1}{7} \ldots \tfrac{1}{9} \text{ etc.}$$

Tota ergo series continet omnes appropinquationes simul, sive valores justo majores & justo minores: prout enim longe continuata intelligitur, erit error minor fractione data, ac proinde & minor data quavis quantitate. Quare tota series exactum exprimit valorem.' Leibniz 1682, 44.

The value 1 will be greater than the correct value, nevertheless by an error less than $\frac{1}{3}$

$\frac{1}{1} - \frac{1}{3}$ will be smaller by an error less than $\frac{1}{5}$

$\frac{1}{1} - \frac{1}{3} + \frac{1}{5}$ will be greater by an error less than $\frac{1}{7}$

$\frac{1}{1} - \frac{1}{3} + \frac{1}{5} - \frac{1}{7}$ will be smaller by an error less than $\frac{1}{9}$

etc.

Therefore the series as a whole contains all approximations at once, or values greater than correct and less than correct: for according to how far it is understood to be continued, the error will be smaller than a given fraction, and therefore also less than any given quantity. Therefore the series as a whole expresses the exact value.

It was not until the second half of the eighteenth century, however, that more general questions of convergence began to be taken seriously.

### 8.3.1  D'Alembert's ratio test, 1761

One of the first mathematicians to be concerned about convergence of series was d'Alembert. His memoir *Réflexions sur les suites* (*Reflections on series*), published in 1761, opened with a statement of what later came to be called d'Alembert's ratio test, but initially only for the binomial expansion, $(1 + \mu)^m$, and without any proof. He went on to investigate the application of this rule to several possible cases, and eventually observed that if the series converges and the $n^{\text{th}}$ term is $A$, then the sum of the remaining terms is less than $A + A\mu + A\mu^2 + A\mu^3 + \cdots$, which gave him an estimate of the error term if the series is cut short.

Towards the end of the memoir he extended the ratio test without comment or proof also to the sine series. The subsequent discussion displays both confusion and caution and serves as a useful reminder of just how far from being properly understood such series still were.

## D'Alembert's ratio test

from D'Alembert, 'Réflexions sur les Suites & sur les Racines imaginaires', *Opuscules* V,
1761, 171, 182–184

### §. I.

*Réflexions sur les suites divergentes ou convergentes.*

1. SI on éleve $1 + \mu$ à la puiſſance $m$, le terme $n^e$ de
la ſerie ſera $\mu^{n-1} \times \dfrac{m(m-1)\ldots(m-n+2)}{2 \cdot 3 \cdot 4 \ldots n-1}$, & le ſuivant,
c'eſt-à-dire le $(n+1)^e$, ſera $\mu^n \times \dfrac{m(m-1)\ldots(m-n+2)(m-n+1)}{2 \cdot 3 \cdot 4 \ldots n-1 \cdot n}$;
donc le rapport du $(n+1)^e$ terme au $n^e$ ſera $\dfrac{\mu(m-n+1)}{n}$;
or pour que la ſerie ſoit convergente, il faut que ce rapport ( abſtraction faite du ſigne qu'il doit avoir ) ſoit $<$
que l'unité.

[...]

31. Ces réflexions ſur la divergence des ſeries en
pluſieurs cas, paroiſſent mériter attention de la part des
Géometres dans les démonſtrations qu'ils donnent de
certaines vérités. Je n'en citerai qu'un exemple. On ſait
que l'expreſſion du ſinus $\zeta$ d'un angle $x$, eſt $\zeta = x -$
$\dfrac{x^3}{2 \cdot 3} + \dfrac{x^5}{2 \cdot 3 \cdot 4 \cdot 5} - \dfrac{x^7}{2 \cdot 3 \cdot 4 \cdot 5 \cdot 7}$, &c. Il eſt évident
que cette expreſſion, à laquelle on peut parvenir par dif-
férentes routes, ne peut être cenſée exacte, qu'autant
qu'elle eſt convergente, au moins dans ſes derniers ter-
mes; or le $n^e$ terme de cette ſuite étant $\dfrac{x^{2n+1}}{2 \cdot 3 \ldots 2n+1}$;
eſt au précédent comme $\dfrac{x^2}{2n(2n+1)}$ eſt à l'unité; d'où
il eſt viſible que ſi on prend $x =$ à un arc très-grand $k\pi$,
$\pi$ étant la demi-circonférence, & $k$ un nombre très-grand,
entier ou rompu, la ſerie ſera divergente, juſqu'à ce
qu'on arrive à un terme $\dfrac{x^{2n+1}}{2 \cdot 3 \ldots 2n+1}$, où $k^2 \pi^2$ ſoit
plus petit que $2n(2n+1)$. De-là il s'enſuit, que comme
on peut toujours arriver à un pareil terme, la ſerie dont
il s'agit exprimera toujours le ſinus d'un arc quelconque
$x$, pourvu qu'on la pouſſe à un très-grand nombre de
termes ſi $x$ eſt fort grand; mais ſi on veut avoir une ſerie

182    *RÉFLEXIONS.*

très-convergente dès les premiers termes, il faudra, fi *x* eft plus grand que la circonférence, fubftituer dans la formule au lieu de *x*, *x* — 2 *n* π, *n* exprimant un nombre entier pofitif, & 2 *n* π un arc égal à la circonférence, prife tant de fois qu'on voudra, de maniere que 2 *n* π foit < *x*, & (2 *n* + 1) π > *x*; & fi *x* — 2 *n* π eft > 90 degrés (car les arcs *x* & 180 — *x* ont le même finus), il faudra mettre dans cette derniere formule 180 — *x* + 2 *n* π, au lieu de *x* — 2 *n* π.

32. La démonftration que M. Bernoulli a donnée dans fes Œuvres, Tome IV, pages 20 & 21, de la fomme de la ferie $1 + \frac{1}{4} + \frac{1}{9} + \frac{1}{16} + \frac{1}{25}$, &c. eft fondée fur l'expreffion $x - \frac{x^3}{2.3}$, &c. du finus par l'arc; il étoit, ce me femble, néceffaire pour n'avoir aucun fcrupule fur cette démonftration, d'être affuré que cette expreffion, pouffée à l'infini, donne en effet la valeur de l'arc; précaution que M. Bernoulli, & perfonne que je fache, n'avoit encore prife. Elle étoit néanmoins d'autant plus effentielle, que l'expreffion de l'arc par le finus, fondée fur la ferie connue qui eft l'intégrale de $\frac{dx}{\sqrt{(1 - xx)}}$, ne peut être regardée comme exacte, c'eft-à-dire comme repréfentant à-la-fois tous les arcs qui ont le même finus; puifque cette ferie ne repréfente évidemment qu'un feul des arcs qui répondent au finus dont il s'agit, favoir le plus petit de ces arcs, celui qui eft inférieur ou tout au plus égal à 90 degrés. Cependant c'eft d'un autre côté une forte de paradoxe remarquable, que l'expreffion de l'arc

*SUR   LES   SUITES.*    183

par le finus ne repréfentant qu'un feul arc de 90 degrés
au plus , l'expreffion du finus par l'arc , qu'on peut déduire ( par la méthode du retour des fuites ) , de l'expreffion de l'arc par le finus , repréfente exactement , étant
pouffée à l'infini , le finus de tous les arcs poffibles , plus
petits ou plus grands que 90° , & même que la circonférence ou demi-circonférence prife tant de fois qu'on
voudra. Je laiffe à d'autres Géometres le foin d'éclaircir
ce myftere , ainfi que plufieurs autres qui peuvent fe
rencontrer dans la théorie des fuites ; théorie qui me
paroît encore très-imparfaite , & quant à la partie analytique , & quant à la partie métaphyfique. Pour moi , j'a-
voue que tous les raifonnemens & les calculs fondés fur
des feries qui ne font pas convergentes, ou qu'on peut fuppofer ne pas l'être , me paroîtront toujours très-fufpects ,
même quand les réfultats de ces raifonnemens s'accor-
deroient avec des vérités connues d'ailleurs.

TRANSLATION

### xxxvth MEMOIR

*Reflections on series and on imaginary roots*

### §1
*Reflections on divergent and convergent series*

1. If one raises $1 + \mu$ to the power $m$, the $n^{\text{th}}$ term of the series will be
$\mu^{n-1} \times \frac{m(m-1)\cdots(m-n+2)}{2.3.4.....n-1}$, and the next, that is to say the $(n+1)^{\text{th}}$, will be $\mu^n \times$
$\frac{m(m-1)...(m-n+2)(m-n+1)}{2.3.4.....n-1.n}$; therefore the ratio of the $(n+1)^{\text{th}}$ term to the $n^{\text{th}}$ will be
$\frac{\mu(m-n+1)}{n}$; now for the series to be convergent, it must be that the ratio (separated from
the sign that it might have) is $<$ than one.

$$[\ldots]$$

[181]

31. These reflections on the divergence of series in several cases seem to merit attention on the part of Geometers in the demonstration that they give of certain truths. I
will cite only one example. One knows that the expression for the sine $z$ of an angle $x$
is $z = x - \frac{x^3}{2.3} + \frac{x^5}{2.3.4.5} - \frac{x^7}{2.3.4.5.7}$, etc. It is clear that this expression, at which one may
arrive by different routes, can only be thought exact insofar as it is convergent, at least
in the later terms; now the $n^{\text{th}}$ term of this series, being $\frac{x^{2n+1}}{2.3.....2n+1}$, is to the preceding

one as $\frac{x^2}{2n(2n+1)}$ is to one; from which it is obvious that if one takes $x$ equal to a very large arc $k\pi$, $\pi$ being the semi-circumference, and $k$ a very large number, whole or fractional, the series will be divergent, until one arrives at a term $\frac{x^{2n+1}}{2.3.....2n+1}$, where $k^2\pi^2$ is smaller than $2n(2n+1)$. From which it follows that, since one may always arrive at such a term, the series of which we speak will always express the sine of any arc $x$, provided that one extends it to a very great number of terms if $x$ is quite large; but if one wants to have a series [182] rapidly convergent from the first terms, one must, if $x$ is greater than the circumference, substitute in the formula instead of $x$, $x - 2n\pi$, $n$ standing for a whole positive number, and $2n\pi$ for an arc equal to the circumference taken as many times as one wishes, in such a way that $2n\pi$ is $< x$ and $(2n+1)\pi > x$; and if $x - 2n\pi$ is $> 90$ degrees one must put in this last formula $180 - x - 2n\pi$ instead of $x - 2n\pi$ (for the arcs $x$ and $180 - x$ have the same sines).

32. The demonstration that Monsieur Bernoulli has given in his *Oeuvres*, volume IV, pages 20 and 21, of the sum of the series $1 + \frac{1}{4} + \frac{1}{9} + \frac{1}{16} + \frac{1}{25}$, etc. is based on the expression $x - \frac{x^3}{2.3}$, etc. of the sine in terms of the arc; it would be necessary, it seems to me, in order to have no scruple about this demonstration, to be sure that this expression, taken to infinity, indeed gives the value of the arc; a precaution that Monsieur Bernoulli, or anyone that I know, has not yet taken. For all that, it is all the more essential that the expression for the arc in terms of the sine, based on the known series which is the integral of $\frac{dx}{\sqrt{(1-xx)}}$, should not be regarded as exact, that is to say as representing simultaneously all the arcs which have the same sines; because this series clearly represents only a single one of the arcs that correspond to the sine in question, that is, the smallest of these arcs, that which is less than or at most equal to 90 degrees. Meanwhile, it is on the other hand a remarkable kind of paradox that while the expression for the arc [183] in terms of the sine represents only a single arc of 90 degrees at most, the expression for the sine in terms of the arc, which one can deduce (by the method of inversion of series) from the expression for the arc in terms of the sine, represents exactly, being taken to infinity, the sines of all possible arcs, less than or greater than 90°, and even than the circumference or semi-circumference taken as many times as one pleases. I leave to other Geometers the trouble of clarifying this mystery, just as several others may engage in the theory of series; a theory that seems to me very imperfect, as much in the analytic part as in the metaphysical part. For myself, I assert that all reasoning and calculations based on series that do not converge, or that one may suppose do not, always seems to me extremely suspect, even when the results of this reasoning agree with truths known in other ways.

————————

### 8.3.2 Lagrange and the remainder term, 1797

So closely linked were Taylor series and the differential calculus that Lagrange set out to establish the principles of calculus purely on the basis of power series, without any reference to infinitely small or vanishing quantities (for the details see 14.1.2). He published his ideas in 1797 in a lengthy paper entitled *Théorie des fonctions analytiques* and revised and extended them in a second edition, by now book length, in 1813. Most of the extracts in this present book are taken from the first edition, despite the sometimes poor quality of the reproductions, to illustrate Lagrange's original thinking.

For Lagrange an 'analytic function' was any function defined by the usual algebraic operations of addition and subtraction, multiplication and division, raising to powers and extraction of roots. He took it for granted that any such function was infinitely differentiable and could be expressed as a convergent power series. He wanted to know, however, how many terms one needed to take. If one stopped after some finite number of terms, what would be the value of the neglected remainder? This, he claimed, was one of the most important problems in the theory of series (Lagrange 1797, §46).

Lagrange's estimate for the 'remainder' was calculated in his sections §49 to §53. In §47 he had already supposed that for any analytic function $f$, the general value $f(x)$, which he denoted simply by $fx$, could be written as

$$f(x) = f(x - xz) + xzf'(x - xz) + \frac{x^2 z^2}{2} f''(x - xz) + \text{etc.}$$

and had defined $P$, $Q$, $R$, to be functions (of $z$) satisfying the following equations:

$$f(x) = f(x - xz) + xP$$
$$f(x) = f(x - xz) + xzf'(x - xz) + x^2 Q$$
$$f(x) = f(x - xz) + xzf'(x - xz) + \frac{x^2 z^2}{2} f''(x - xz) + x^3 R.$$

Differentiating these equations with respect to $z$ yields:

$$P' = f'(x - xz)$$
$$Q' = zf''(x - xz)$$
$$R' = \frac{z^2}{2} f'''(x - xz).$$

and Lagrange's objective was now to find upper and lower bounds for $P, Q, R, \ldots$.

Lagrange's introduction of yet another new function, $F(z)$, with derivative of the form $F'(z) = z^m Z$, at first seems arbitrary, but Lagrange's intention was to equate $F(z)$ later to $P, Q, R$, etc. in turn.

The lemma to which Lagrange referred at the beginning of his argument had been proved in §48: if the first derivative $f'$ of a function $f$ is strictly positive for $a < x < b$ then $f(b) - f(a) > 0$ (see 11.2.3). Later he also assumed (in the final part of §51) a version of the intermediate value theorem.

---

## Lagrange's error term

from Lagrange, *Théorie des fonctions analytiques*, 1797, §49–§53

---

49. A l'aide de ce lemme, on peut trouver des limites en plus et en moins de toute fonction primitive dont on connaît la fonction prime.

Soit la fonction primitive $F\zeta$ dont la fonction prime $F'\zeta$ soit exprimée par $\zeta^m Z$, $Z$ étant une fonction donnée de $\zeta$. Soit $M$ la plus grande, et $N$ la plus petite valeur de $Z$ pour toutes les valeurs de $\zeta$ comprises entre les quantités $a$ et $b$, en regardant comme plus grandes les négatives moindres, et comme moindres les négatives plus grandes, ce qui est conforme à la marche du calcul, puisque, par exemple, $-1 > -2$, $-5 > -7$, et de même $-2 < -1$, et ainsi des autres. Donc les quantités $M - Z$ et $Z - N$ seront toujours positives depuis $\zeta = a$ jusqu'à $\zeta = b$, et il en sera de même des quantités $\zeta^m (M - Z)$ et $\zeta^m (Z - N)$.

Donc, 1.°, si on fait $f'\zeta = \zeta^m (M - Z)$, on aura par le lemme précédent $fb - fa > 0$; or, $\zeta^m Z$ étant $F'\zeta$, sa fonction primitive sera $F\zeta$, et comme $M$ est une quantité constante, la fonction primitive de $M\zeta^m$ est $\dfrac{M\zeta^{n+1}}{m+1}$, puisque la fonction prime de celle-ci est, par la règle

## DES FONCTIONS ANALYTIQUES.    47

générale ( $n.°\ 18$ ), $\dfrac{(m+1)\,M\,\zeta^{m}}{m+1} = M\,\zeta^{m}$. Donc on aura $f\zeta =$

$\dfrac{M\zeta^{m+1}}{m+1} - F\zeta$ ; et faisant successivement $\zeta = a$ et $\zeta = b$ , l'équation

$fb - fa > 0$ donnera

$$\frac{Mb^{m+1}}{m+1} - Fb - \frac{Ma^{m+1}}{m+1} + Fa > 0 \ ;$$

d'où l'on tire

$$Fb < Fa + \frac{M\left(b^{m+1} - a^{m+1}\right)}{m+1}.$$

2.° Si on fait , $f'\zeta = \zeta^{m}(Z - N)$, on aura aussi $fb - fa > 0$ , et l'on

trouvera , comme ci-dessus , $f\zeta = F\zeta - \dfrac{N\zeta^{m+1}}{m+1}$ ; donc faisant successi-

vement $\zeta = a$ et $= b$ , l'équation $fb - fa > 0$ , donnera $Fb - \dfrac{Nb^{m+1}}{m+1}$

$- Fa + \dfrac{Na^{m+1}}{m+1} > 0$ ; d'où l'on tire

$$Fb > Fa + \frac{N\left(b^{m+1} - a^{m+1}\right)}{m+1}.$$

50. Appliquons ces résultats aux quantités $P$ , $Q$ , $R$ , &c. du n.° 47.

Comme ces quantités sont regardées comme des fonctions de $\zeta$ , nous supposerons d'abord $P = F\zeta$ , et par conséquent $P' = F'\zeta = f'(x - x\zeta)$ ; donc , puisqu'on a supposé $F'\zeta = \zeta^{m}Z$ , prenant $m = 0$ , on aura $Z = f'$ $(x - x\zeta)$. Supposons maintenant $a = 0$ , et $b = 1$ , la condition de la fonction $P$ , qui doit être nulle lorsque $\zeta = 0$ , donnera $Fa = 0$ , et alors $Fb$ sera la valeur de $P$ , répondant à $\zeta = 1$.

Donc , si $M$ et $N$ sont la plus grande et la plus petite valeur de $f'(x - x\zeta)$ , relativement à toutes les valeurs de $\zeta$ depuis $\zeta = 0$ jusqu'à $\zeta = 1$ , on aura $Fb < M$ et $> N$. Par conséquent $M$ et $N$ seront les deux limites de la quantité $P$ , en y faisant $\zeta = 1$.

Supposons , en second lieu , $Q = F\zeta$ , on aura $Q' = F'\zeta = \zeta f''(x - x\zeta)$ ; donc , faisant $m = 1$ , on aura $Z = f''(x - x\zeta)$. Soit pareillement $a = 0$ et $b = 1$ , on aura aussi par la condition de la fonction $Q$ , qui doit être nulle lorsque $\zeta$ est nul , $Fa = 0$ et alors $Fb$ sera égale à la valeur de $Q$ , répondant à $\zeta = 1$.

48                    T H É O R I E

Donc, si $M1$ et $N1$ sont la plus grande et la plus petite valeur de $f''(x - x\zeta)$ pour toutes les valeurs de $\zeta$ depuis $\zeta = 0$ jusqu'à $\zeta = 1$, on aura $Fb < \dfrac{M1}{2}$ et $> \dfrac{N1}{2}$. De sorte que $\dfrac{M1}{2}$ et $\dfrac{N1}{2}$ seront les limites de la valeur de $Q$, lorsque $\zeta$ y est $= 1$.

Supposons, en troisième lieu, $R = F\zeta$, on aura $R' = F'\zeta = -\dfrac{\zeta^2}{2} f'''(x - x\zeta)$; donc, faisant $m = 2$, $a = 0$, $b = 1$, on trouvera de la même manière que si $M2$ et $N2$ sont la plus grande et la plus petite valeur de $\dfrac{1}{2} f'''(x - x\zeta)$, en donnant à $\zeta$ toutes les valeurs depuis zéro jusqu'à l'unité, on aura $\dfrac{M2}{3}$ et $\dfrac{N2}{3}$ pour les limites de la valeur de la quantité $R$, lorsqu'on y fait $\zeta = 1$.

Et ainsi de suite.

51. Maintenant il est clair qu'en donnant à $\zeta$, dans une fonction de $x(1 - \zeta)$, toutes les valeurs depuis $\zeta = 0$ jusqu'à $\zeta = 1$, les valeurs que recevra cette fonction seront les mêmes que celles que recevrait une pareille fonction de $u$, en donnant successivement à $u$ toutes les valeurs depuis $u = 0$ jusqu'à $u = x$; car faisant $x(1 - \zeta) = u$, $\zeta = 0$ donne $u = x$, $\zeta = 1$ donne $u = 0$, et les valeurs intermédiaires de $\zeta$ donneront des valeurs de $u$ intermédiaires entre celles-ci. D'où il est aisé de conclure que les quantités $M$ et $N$ seront la plus grande et la plus petite valeur de $f'u$, relativement à toutes les valeurs de $u$ depuis $u = 0$ jusqu'à $u = x$; et que par conséquent toute valeur intermédiaire entre $M$ et $N$ pourra être exprimée par $f'u$, en donnant à $u$ une valeur intermédiaire entre $0$ et $x$. Donc la valeur de la quantité $P$ relative à $\zeta = 1$ pourra être exprimée par $f'u$, $u$ étant une quantité entre $0$ et $x$. On en conclura de même que la valeur de $Q$ répondant à $\zeta = 1$, pourra être exprimée par $\dfrac{1}{2} f''u$, en donnant à $u$ une valeur intermédiaire entre $0$ et $x$;

Et pareillement que la valeur de $R$ relative à $\zeta = 1$ pourra être exprimée par $\dfrac{1}{2 \cdot 3} f'''u$, en prenant pour $u$ une quantité entre $0$ et $x$.

Et ainsi de suite.

## DES FONCTIONS ANALYTIQUES.    49

'52. D'où résulte enfin ce théorème nouveau et remarquable par sa simplicité et sa généralité , qu'en désignant par $u$ une quantité inconnue , mais renfermée entre les limites o et $x$ , on peut développer successivement toute fonction de $x$ et d'autres quantités quelconques suivant les puissances de $x$ , de cette manière

$$fx = f. + xf^{\prime} u ,$$
$$= f. + xf^{\prime}. + \frac{x^2}{2} f^{\prime\prime} u ,$$
$$= f. + xf^{\prime}. + \frac{x^2}{2} f^{\prime\prime}. + \frac{x^3}{2.3} f^{\prime\prime\prime} u ,$$
$$\&c.$$

les quantités $f. , f^{\prime}. , f^{\prime\prime}. , \&c.$ , étant les valeurs de la fonction $fx$ et de ses dérivées $f^{\prime}x , f^{\prime\prime}x , \&c.$ , lorsqu'on y fait $x = o$.

53. Ainsi , pour le développement de $f( z + x )$ suivant les puissances de $x$ , on aura $f. = fz , f^{\prime}. = f^{\prime}z , f^{\prime\prime}. = f^{\prime\prime}z , \&c.$ où l'on remarquera que les quantités $f^{\prime}z , f^{\prime\prime}z , \&c.$ sont également les fonctions primes , secondes , &c. de $fz$ , ce qui est évident , car il est visible que $f^{\prime}( z + x )$ , $f^{\prime\prime}( z + x ) , \&c.$ sont également les fonctions primes , secondes , &c. de $f( z + x )$ , soit qu'on les prenne relativement à $x$ ou relativement à $z$ , puisque l'augmentation de $z + x$ est la même en changeant $x$ en $x + i$ ou $z$ en $z + i$.

Prenant donc $f^{\prime}z , f^{\prime\prime}z , \&c.$ pour les fonctions dérivées de $fz$ , on aura

$$f( z + x ) = fz + xf^{\prime}( z + u ) ,$$
$$= fz + x f^{\prime}z + \frac{x^2}{2} f^{\prime\prime}( z + u ) ,$$
$$= fz + xf^{\prime}z + \frac{x^2}{2} f^{\prime\prime}z + \frac{x^3}{2.3} f^{\prime\prime\prime}( z + u ) ,$$
$$\&c.$$

où $u$ désigne une quantité indéterminée , mais renfermée entre les limites o et $x$.

En changeant $z$ en $x$ et $x$ en $i$ , on aura le développement de $f( x + i )$ suivant les puissances de $i$ ; et l'on voit que dans ce développement la série infinie , à commencer d'un terme quelconque , est toujours égale à la valeur de ce premier terme , en y mettant $x + j$ à la place de $x$ , $j$ étant une

G

50    T H E O R I E

quantité entre o et i ; que par conséquent la plus grande et la plus petite valeur de ce terme, relativement à toutes les valeurs de j depuis o jusqu'à i, seront les limites de la valeur du reste de la série continuée à l'infini.

Si on fait $f\gamma = \gamma^m$, on aura le développement du binome $(\gamma + x)^m$, et on en conclura que la somme de tous les termes, à commencer d'un terme quelconque $\dfrac{m(m-1)\ldots\ldots\ldots(m-n+1)}{1.2.\ldots n}\gamma^{m-n}x^n$, sera renfermée entre ces limites $\dfrac{m(m-1)\ldots\ldots(m-n+1)}{1.2.\ldots n}\gamma^{m-n}x^n$ et $\dfrac{m(m-1)\ldots(m-n+1)}{1.2.\ldots n}(\gamma+x)^{m-n}x^n$; car il est évident que la plus grande et la plus petite valeur de $(\gamma+u)^{m-n}$ seront $(\gamma+x)^{m-n}$ et $\gamma^{m-n}$.

La perfecion des méthodes d'approximation dans lesquelles on emploie les séries, dépend non-seulement de la convergence des séries, mais encore de ce qu'on puisse estimer l'erreur qui résulte des termes qu'on néglige, et à cet égard on peut dire que presque toutes les méthodes d'approximation dont on fait usage dans la solution des problèmes géométriques et mécaniques, sont encore très-imparfaites. Le théorème précédent pourra servir dans beaucoup d'occasions à donner à ces méthodes la perfection qui leur manque, et sans laquelle il est souvent dangereux de les employer.

---

### TRANSLATION

49. With the aid of this lemma, one may find the upper and lower bounds of every primitive function for which one knows the first derived function.

Let the primitive function be $Fz$ for which the derived function $F'z$ may be expressed as $z^m Z$, $Z$ being a given function of $z$. Let $M$ be the greatest and $N$ the smallest value of $Z$, for all values of $z$ contained between the quantities $a$ and $b$, regarding the least negatives as greater, and the greater negatives as least, which conforms to the way of calculation, since, for example, $-1 > -2$, $-5 > -7$ and in the same way $-2 < -1$, and so on for others. Therefore the quantities $M - Z$ and $Z - N$ will be always positive from $z = a$ to $z = b$, and it will be the same for the quantities $z^m(M - Z)$ and $z^m(Z - N)$.

Therefore, 1st, if one makes $f'z = z^m(M - Z)$, one will have by the preceding lemma $fb - fa > 0$; now $z^m Z$ being $F'z$, its primitive function will be $Fz$, and since $M$ is a constant quantity, the primitive function of $Mz^m$ is $\frac{Mz^{m+1}}{m+1}$, because the first derived function of this is, by the [47] general rule (§18), $\frac{(m+1)Mz^m}{m+1} = Mz^m$. Therefore one will have $fz = \frac{Mz^{m+1}}{m+1} - Fz$; and putting successively $z = a$ and $z = b$, the equation $fb - fa > 0$ will give

$$\frac{Mb^{m+1}}{m+1} - Fb - \frac{Ma^{m+1}}{m+1} + Fa > 0;$$

from which one obtains

$$Fb < Fa + \frac{M(b^{m+1} - a^{m+1})}{m+1}.$$

2nd. If one puts $f'z = z^m(Z - N)$, one will also have $fb - fa > 0$, and one will find, as above, $fz = Fz - \frac{Nz^{m+1}}{m+1}$; therefore putting successively $z = a$ and $z = b$, the equation $fb - fa > 0$ will give $Fb - \frac{Nb^{m+1}}{m+1} - Fa + \frac{Na^{m+1}}{m+1} > 0$; from one which one obtains

$$Fb > Fa + \frac{N(b^{m+1} - a^{m+1})}{m+1}.$$

50. Let us apply these results to the quantities $P$, $Q$, $R$, etc. of §47.

Since these quantities are regarded as functions of $z$, we will suppose first that $P = Fz$, and consequently $P' = F'z = f'(x - xz)$; therefore, since one supposed that $F'z = z^mZ$, taking $m = 0$, one will have $Z = f'(x - xz)$. Now let us suppose $a = 0$ and $b = 1$; the nature of the function $P$, which must be zero when $z = 0$, will give $Fa = 0$, and then $Fb$ will be the value of $P$ corresponding to $z = 1$.

Therefore, if $M$ and $N$ are the greatest and least values of $f'(x - xz)$, relative to all the values of $z$, from $z = 0$ to $z = 1$, one will have $Fb < M$ and $> N$. Consequently $M$ and $N$ will be the two bounds of the quantity $P$, on making $z = 1$.

Supposing in the second place that $Q = Fz$, one will have $Q' = F'z = zf''(x - xz)$; therefore making $m = 1$, one will have $Z = f''(x - xz)$. Let $a = 0$ and at the same time $b = 1$, we will also have from the nature of the function $Q$, which must be zero when $z$ is zero, $Fa = 0$, and then $Fb$ will be equal to the value of $Q$ corresponding to $z = 1$. [48] Therefore if $M_1$ and $N_1$ are the greatest and least values of $f''(x - xz)$ for all values of $z$, from $z = 0$ to $z = 1$, one will have $Fb < \frac{M_1}{2}$ and $> \frac{N_1}{2}$, so that $\frac{M_1}{2}$ and $\frac{N_1}{2}$ will be the bounds of the value of $Q$ when $z = 1$.

Supposing in the third place that $R = Fz$, one will have $R' = F'z = \frac{z^2}{2}f'''(x - xz)$; therefore making $m = 2$, $a = 0$, $b = 1$, we will find in the same way that if $M_2$ and $N_2$ are the greatest and least values of $\frac{1}{2}f'''(x - xz)$, on giving $z$ all values from zero to one, we will have $\frac{M_2}{3}$ and $\frac{N_2}{3}$ for the bounds of the value of the quantity $R$, when one makes $z = 1$.

And so on.

51. Now it is clear that by giving to $z$, in a function of $x(1 - z)$, all values from $z = 0$ to $z = 1$, the values that the function will take will be the same as those which would be taken by a similar function of $u$, on giving successively to $u$ all values from $u = 0$ to $u = x$; for putting $x(1 - z) = u$, $z = 0$ gives $u = x$, $z = 1$ gives $u = 0$, and the intermediate values of $z$ will give the intermediate values of $u$ between these. From which it is easy to conclude that the quantities $M$ and $N$ will be the greatest and least values of $f'u$, relative to all values of $u$, from $u = 0$ to $u = x$; and that consequently every intermediate value between $M$ and $N$ can be expressed by $f'u$, by giving $u$ a value intermediate between 0 and $x$. Therefore the value of the quantity $P$ corresponding to $z = 1$ can be expressed by $f'u$, where $u$ is a quantity between 0 and $x$. One deduces in the same way that the value of $Q$ corresponding to $z = 1$ can be expressed as $\frac{1}{2}f''u$, by giving $u$ a value intermediate between 0 and $x$.

And similarly that the value of $R$ corresponding to $z = 1$ can be expressed as $\frac{1}{2.3}f'''u$, by taking for $u$ a quantity between 0 and $x$.

And so on.

[49] 52. From which there finally results this new theorem, remarkable for its simplicity and generality, that on denoting by $u$ an unknown quantity, contained between the bounds 0 and $x$, one may successively expand every function of $x$, and other quantities, in powers of $x$, in this way,

$$fx = f. + xf'u$$

$$= f. + xf'. + \frac{x^2}{2}f''u,$$

$$= f. + xf'. + \frac{x^2}{2}f''. + \frac{x^3}{2.3}f'''u,$$

etc.,

where the quantities $f., f'., f''.$, etc. are the values of the function $fx$ and its derivatives $f'x, f''x, f''x$, etc. when one makes $x = 0$.

53. Thus for the expansion of $f(z+x)$, in powers of $x$, one will have $f. = fz, f'. = f'z$, $f''. = f''z$, etc., where one notes that the quantities $f'z, f''z$, etc. are in the same way the first, second, etc. derivatives of $fz$, which is clear, for it is obvious that $f'(z + x)$, $f''(z+x)$, etc. are in the same way the first, second, etc. derivatives of $f(z+x)$, whether one takes them relative to $x$ or relative to $z$, because the increase of $z + x$ is the same on changing $x$ to $x + i$, or $z$ to $z + i$.

Therefore taking $f'z, f''z$, etc. for the derived functions of $fz$, one will have

$$f(x + z) = fz + xf'(z + u),$$

$$= fz + xf'z + \frac{x^2}{2}f''(z + u),$$

$$= fz + xf'z + \frac{x^2}{2}f''z + \frac{x^3}{2.3}f'''(z + u),$$

etc.,

where $u$ denotes an unknown quantity, contained between the limits 0 and $x$.

Changing $z$ to $x$ and $x$ to $i$, one will have the expansion of $f(x+i)$ in powers of $i$; and one sees that in this expansion the infinite series, beginning with any term whatever, is always equal to the value of this first term, on putting $x + j$ in place of $x$, $j$ being [50] a quantity between 0 and $i$; and that consequently the greatest and least values of this term, relative to all values of $j$, from 0 to $i$, will be the bounds for the value of the rest of the series continued to infinity.

If one puts $fz = z^m$, one will have the binomial expansion $(z + x)^m$, and one can conclude that the sum of all the terms, beginning from any term whatever $\frac{m(m-1)...(m-n+1)}{1.2...n}z^{m-n}x^n$, will be contained between the bounds $\frac{m(m-1)...(m-n+1)}{1.2...n}z^{m-n}x^n$ and $\frac{m(m-1)...(m-n+1)}{1.2...n}(z + x)^{m-n}x^n$; for it is clear that the greatest and least values of $(z + x)^{m-n}$ will be $(z + x)^{m-n}$ and $z^{m-n}$.

The perfection of methods of approximation in which one uses series depends not only on the convergence of the series, but also on being able to estimate the error that results from the terms one neglects; and in this respect one may say that nearly all the methods of approximation used in the solution of geometric and mechanical problems are still very imperfect. The preceding theorem may serve on many occasions to give these methods the perfection they are lacking, and without which it is often dangerous to make use of them.

_____

## 8.4 FOURIER SERIES

The most virtuoso handling of power series, and in some respects the culmination of naive analysis, came from Joseph Fourier in the early years of the nineteenth century. Drawing on the work of Wallis, Newton, Taylor, Maclaurin, and Euler, Fourier pushed the mathematics of intuition, common sense, and pattern recognition just about as far as it could go. Despite (or sometimes because of) his lack of rigour, his work was to lead to some of the most profound and far-reaching problems of nineteenth-century mathematics, many of which will be explored in subsequent chapters of this book. But for now, we will allow him to stand at the apex of early achievements with power series.

### 8.4.1 Fourier's derivation of his coefficients, 1822

The treatise on heat diffusion for which Fourier is now best remembered was presented to the Paris Academy for the first time in 1807, but was not published, due in part to objections from Lagrange. Over the next few years Fourier made revisions, and the mathematical part of his work was eventually published in his _Théorie analytique de la chaleur_ in 1822.

In the course of his investigations Fourier was led to explore functions $\varphi(x)$ of the form (§207)

$$\varphi(x) = a \sin x + b \sin 2x + c \sin 3x + d \sin 4x + \cdots \tag{1}$$

where each term $\sin nx$ can itself be expanded as an infinite series. Meanwhile, writing $\varphi(x)$ as a Taylor series gave him another series

$$\varphi(x) = x\varphi'(0) + \frac{x^2}{2}\varphi''(0) + \frac{x^3}{2.3}\varphi'''(0) + \ldots. \tag{2}$$

Fourier equated coefficients of $x$ in (1) and (2), giving rise to an infinite set of simultaneous equations. Undaunted, he pressed ahead, and after thirteen pages of calculation deduced the coefficients $a, b, c, d, \ldots$ in terms of the derivatives $\varphi(0), \varphi'(0), \varphi'''(0), \ldots$, and so on (the even derivatives being identically zero) (§215).

There were many unstated assumptions in all this: that $\varphi$ is infinitely differentiable; that the infinite sum on the right hand side of (1) converges to $\varphi(x)$ for the relevant values of $x$; that the Taylor series (2) is also convergent; and that (1) and (2) are identical for the same values of $x$. None of these questions troubled Fourier. Further, in (§217), he found a method of simplifying his results using Taylor series for $\varphi(\pi)$, $\varphi''(\pi)$, ..., and so on, but failed to observe that for $\varphi$ as defined by (1), $\varphi(\pi) = \varphi''(\pi) = \cdots = 0$, thus rendering all his coefficients zero and his equations meaningless. Rarely can such far-reaching results have been based on such insecure foundations.

Nevertheless, let us allow ourselves to return to an early nineteenth-century mindset and follow Fourier from the following set of equations (which he labelled (B)) for $\varphi(x)$:

$$\frac{1}{2}\pi\varphi(x) = \sin x \left\{ \varphi(\pi) - \frac{1}{1^2}\varphi''(\pi) + \frac{1}{1^4}\varphi^{\mathrm{IV}}(\pi) - \frac{1}{1^6}\varphi^{\mathrm{VI}}(\pi) + \ldots \text{etc.} \right\}$$

$$- \frac{1}{2}\sin 2x \left\{ \varphi(\pi) - \frac{1}{2^2}\varphi''(\pi) + \frac{1}{2^4}\varphi^{\mathrm{IV}}(\pi) - \frac{1}{2^6}\varphi^{\mathrm{VI}}(\pi) + \ldots \text{etc.} \right\}$$

$$+ \frac{1}{3}\sin 3x \left\{ \varphi(\pi) - \frac{1}{3^2}\varphi''(\pi) + \frac{1}{3^4}\varphi^{\mathrm{IV}}(\pi) - \frac{1}{3^6}\varphi^{\mathrm{VI}}(\pi) + \ldots \text{etc.} \right\}$$

$$- \frac{1}{4}\sin 4x \left\{ \varphi(\pi) - \frac{1}{4^2}\varphi''(\pi) + \frac{1}{4^4}\varphi^{\mathrm{IV}}(\pi) - \frac{1}{4^6}\varphi^{\mathrm{VI}}(\pi) + \ldots \text{etc.} \right\}$$

$$+ \text{etc.} \tag{B}$$

Fourier's next step was to put the general coefficient of $\frac{1}{n}\sin nx$ equal to $s$, and then to solve a differential equation for $s$. Differentiating with respect to $\pi$ as Fourier did is not to be recommended, but it is possible to get round the problem by substituting a general variable $x$ and replacing it by $\pi$ later. Fourier did not say how he knew or found the general solution to the differential equation $s + \frac{1}{n^2}\frac{d^2 s}{dx^2} = \varphi(x)$ but it can be checked and found correct by differentiation. The term $a \cos nx$ in this general solution is assumed to be zero (because $\varphi(x)$ is an odd function), and the required result then follows on putting $x = \pi$.

---

### Fourier's series

from Fourier, *Théorie analytique de la chaleur*, 1822, §219

---

**219.**

Nous avons supposé jusqu'ici que la fonction dont on demande le développement en séries de sinus d'arcs multiples, peut être développée en une série ordonnée, suivant les puissances de la variable $x$, et qu'il n'entre dans cette dernière série que des puissances impaires. On peut étendre les mêmes conséquences à des fonctions quelconques, même à celles

232    THÉORIE DE LA CHALEUR.

qui seraient discontinues et entièrement arbitraires. Pour
établir clairement la vérité de cette proposition, il est nécessaire de poursuivre l'analyse qui fournit l'équation précédente (B) et d'éxaminer quelle est la nature des coëfficents
qui multiplient $\sin.x$, $\sin. 2x$, $\sin. 3x$, $\sin. 4x$. En désignant
par $\frac{s}{n}$ la quantité qui multiplie dans cette équation $\frac{1}{n}\sin. nx$,
si $n$ est impair, et $-\frac{1}{n}\sin. nx$, si $n$ est pair; on aura

$$s = \varphi \pi - \frac{1}{n^2}\varphi'' \pi + \frac{1}{n^4}\varphi^{iv} \pi - \frac{1}{n^6}\varphi^{vi} \pi + \text{etc.}$$

Considérant $s$ comme une fonction de $\pi$, différentiant deux
fois, et comparant les résultats, on trouve $s + \frac{1}{n^2}\frac{d^2 s}{d\pi^2} = \varphi \pi$;
équation à laquelle la valeur précédente de $s$ doit satisfaire.
Or, l'équation $s + \frac{1}{n^2}\frac{d^2 s}{d x^2} = \varphi x$, dans laquelle $s$ est considérée
comme une fonction de $x$, a pour intégrale

$$s = a\cos. nx + b\sin. nx + n\sin. nx \int \cos. nx . \varphi x . dx$$
$$- n\cos. nx \int \sin. nx . \varphi x\, dx.$$

$n$ étant un nombre entier, et la valeur de $x$ étant égale à $\pi$,
on a $s = \pm n \int \varphi x . \sin. nx\, dx$. Le signe $+$ doit être choisi lorsque $n$ est impair, et le signe $-$ lorsque ce nombre est pair.
On doit supposer $x$ égal à la demi-circonférence $\pi$, après
l'intégration indiquée; ce résultat se vérifie, lorśqu'on développe au moyen de l'intégration par parties, le terme

$$\int \varphi x \sin. nx . dx$$

CHAPITRE III.                                    233

en remarquant que la fonction $\varphi x$ ne contient que des puissances impáires de la variable et en prenant l'intégrale depuis $x = 0$ jusqu'à $x = \pi$.

On en conclut immédiatement que ce terme équivaut à

$$\pm \left( \varphi \pi - \varphi'' \pi \cdot \frac{1}{n^2} + \varphi^{IV} \pi \cdot \frac{1}{n^4} - \varphi^{VI} \pi \cdot \frac{1}{n^6} + \varphi^{VIII} \pi \cdot \frac{1}{n^8} + \text{etc.} \right).$$

Si l'on substitue cette valeur de $\frac{s}{n}$ dans l'équation (B), en prenant le signe $+$ lorsque le terme de cette équation est de rang impair, et le signe $-$ lorsque $n$ est pair; on aura en général $S(\varphi x . \sin . n x . d x)$ pour le coëfficient de $\sin . n x$; on parvient de cette manière à un résultat très-remarquable exprimé par l'équation suivante :

$$\frac{1}{2} \pi \varphi x = \sin . x \, S \left( \sin . x . \varphi x . d x \right) + \sin . 2 x \, S \left( \sin . 2 x \, \varphi x \, d x \right)$$
$$+ \sin . 3 x \, S \left( \sin . 3 x . \varphi x \, d x \right) ..... + \sin . i x \, S \left( \sin . i x \, \varphi x \, d x \right) + \text{etc.} ;$$

$$(\mathbf{D})$$

le second membre donnera toujours le développement cherché de la fonction $\varphi x$, si l'on effectue les intégrations depuis $x = 0$, jusqu'à $x = \pi$.

*Notation*

There are some misprints in Fourier's text, and corrections are indicated in the translation by square brackets. Fourier sometimes used an ordinary letter $S$ as an integral sign, and to avoid confusion this has been replaced by the standard $\int$ sign (which he himself used elsewhere).

TRANSLATION

219.

We have assumed until now that the function for which one seeks the expansion as a series of sines of multiple arcs, may be expanded as an ordered series, in powers of the variable $x$, and that there enter into this last series only odd powers. One may extend the same results to any functions whatever, even to those [232] which are discontinuous and entirely arbitrary. To establish clearly the truth of this proposition, it is necessary to follow the analysis supplied by the above equation (B) and to examine the nature of the coefficients which multiply $\sin x$, $\sin 2x$, $\sin 3x$, $\sin 4x$. Denoting by $[s]$ the quantity which multiplies $\frac{1}{n} \sin nx$ in this equation, if $n$ is odd, or $-\frac{1}{n} \sin nx$, if $n$ is even, one will have

$$s = \varphi \pi - \frac{1}{n^2} \varphi^{II} \pi + \frac{1}{n^4} \varphi^{IV} \pi - \frac{1}{n^6} \varphi^{VI} \pi + \text{etc.}$$

Considering $s$ as a function of $\pi$, differentiating twice, and comparing the results, one finds $s + \frac{1}{n^2}\frac{d^2 s}{d\pi^2} = \varphi\pi$; an equation that the above value of $s$ must satisfy. Now, the equation $s + \frac{1}{n^2}\frac{d^2 s}{dx^2} = \varphi x$, in which $s$ is considered as a function of $x$, has for integral

$$s = a\cos nx + b\sin nx + n\sin nx \int \cos nx\,\varphi x\,dx - n\cos nx \int \sin nx\,\varphi x\,dx.$$

Making $n$ a whole number, and the value of $x$ equal to $\pi$, one has $s = \pm n \int \varphi x.\sin nx\,dx$. The sign $+$ must be chosen when $n$ is odd, and the sign $-$ when this number is even. One must assume that $x$ is equal to the semicircumference $\pi$ after the integration indicated; this result is verified when one expands, by means of integration by parts, the term

$$\int \varphi x\sin nx\,dx,$$

[233] on noting that the function $\varphi x$ contains only odd powers of the variable and on taking the integral from $x = 0$ to $x = \pi$.

One deduces from this immediately that this term is equivalent to

$$\pm(\varphi\pi - \varphi^{II}\pi\frac{1}{n^2} + \varphi^{IV}\pi\frac{1}{n^4} - \varphi^{VI}\pi\frac{1}{n^6} + \varphi^{VIII}\pi\frac{1}{n^8} + \text{etc.})$$

If one substitutes this value of $\frac{s}{n}$ in equation (B), taking the sign $+$ when the term in this equation is of odd rank, and the sign $-$ when $n$ is even, one will have in general $\int (\varphi x.\sin nx\,dx)$ for the coefficient of $\sin nx$. One arrives in this way at a very remarkable result expressed by the following equation:

$$\frac{1}{2}\pi\varphi x = \sin x \int (\sin x\,\varphi x\,dx) + \sin 2x \int (\sin 2x\,\varphi x\,dx) + \sin 3x \int (\sin 3x\,\varphi x\,dx)$$

$$+ \cdots + \sin ix \int (\sin ix\,\varphi x\,dx) + \text{etc.;}\quad (D)$$

the right hand side will always give the sought expansion of the function $\varphi x$, if one carries out the integrations from $x = 0$ to $x = \pi$.

———

# CHAPTER 9

# FUNCTIONS

The concept of a function, now so central to mathematics, emerged only slowly from the beginning of the eighteenth century onwards. In this chapter we will see how and why it changed, from the first published definition in 1706, to the modern formal definition that was in place by the late nineteenth century.

In the central section of this chapter we will also see how mid eighteenth-century mathematicians, Euler in particular, recognized the close connections between circular and logarithmic functions, but moved steadily away from the older geometric definitions towards a unified theory based on algebraic manipulation of infinite series.

## 9.1 EARLY DEFINITIONS OF FUNCTIONS

### 9.1.1 Johann Bernoulli's definition of function, 1718

One of the early challenge questions that tested the new-found power of the calculus was the *isoperimeter* (equal length) problem, proposed by Jacob Bernoulli to his younger brother Johann through the pages of the *Acta eruditorum* in May 1697. The problem was as follows:[1]

There is sought from all isoperimetric curves, constructed on a common base *BN*, that one *BFN* (Fig. VII), which does not itself contain the maximum space, but makes that [space] contained

---

1. 'Quaeritur ex omnibus Isoperimetris, super communi base *BN* constitutis illa *BFN*, (Fig. VII) quae non ipsa quidem maximum comprehendat spatium, sed faciat, ut aliud curva *BZN* comprehensum sit maximum, cujus applicata *PZ* ponitur esse ratione quavis multiplicata vel submultiplicata rectae *PF* vel arcus *BF*.' Jacob Bernoulli, *Acta eruditorum* (1697), 214.

by another curve *BZN* the maximum, whose ordinates *PZ* may be put in any ratio, multiple or submultiple, to the lines *PF* or the arcs *BF*.

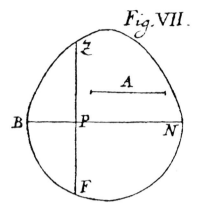

**Figure 9.1** Jacob Bernoulli's diagram, *Acta eruditorum*, 1697, Fig VII

The problem was described verbally and geometrically, not even in terms of co-ordinate geometry, though $(x, y)$ co-ordinates were soon introduced by both Bernoullis as an aid to solution. The word *applicata*, here translated as 'ordinates', was simply a standard description of parallel lines with their ends along a common line (in Latin, *applicare* is to lay ships along a quayside). More importantly for the present discussion, the problem was expressed in the classical language of ratio and proportion: the lines *PZ* were allowed to be in any *ratio* to the lines *PF*. For the modern reader this may need some explanation, because such descriptions have disappeared almost entirely from modern mathematics. Lines *PZ* in duplicate or triplicate ratio to lines *PF* are not twice or three times as long, but as the *squares* or *cubes* of those lines: these are 'multiple ratios'. On the other hand lines *PZ* in subduplicate or subtriplicate ratio to lines *PF* are as the square or cube roots: these are 'submultiple ratios'. Clearly then what Bernoulli had in mind was that the lengths *PZ* should be, as we would say, any integer or fractional power of the lengths *PF*.

Johann Bernoulli responded a few months later and his solution was published in French in the *Journal des savans* in December 1697, with a shorter version in Latin in the *Acta eruditorum* in January 1698. His re-statement of the problem was almost exactly as Jacob had originally posed it, but now he explicitly replaced ratios by powers (*puissances*):[2]

---

2. 'La première question est telle: *D'entre toutes les Courbes isopérimétres constituées sur un axe déterminé BN, on demande celle, comme BFN, qui ne comprenne pas elle même le plus grand espace; mais qui fasse qu'un autre compris par la Courbe BZN soit le plus grand, après avoir prolongé l'appliquée EP [sic], de sorte que PZ soit en raison quelconque multipliée, ou sous multipliée, de l'appliquée PF, ou de l'arc BF; c'est-à-dire, que PZ soit la tantième proportionelle que l'on voudra d'une donnée A, & de l'appliquée PF, ou de l'arc BF. Le sens de cette question est de déterminer la Courbe BFN entre une infinité d'autres de même longueur qu'elle, dont les appliquées PF ou les arcs BF élevés à une puissance donnée, & exprimés par d'autres appliquées PZ, fassent le plus grand espace BZN.'* Johann Bernoulli, *Opera*, I, 208.

The first question is this: *From all isoperimetric curves constructed on a given axis BN, one seeks that one BFN, which does not itself contain the greatest space; but which would make another [space] contained by the curve BZN the greatest, after having lengthened the ordinates [F]P, in such a way that PZ is in any ratio, multiple or submultiple, to the ordinate PF, or to the arc BF; that is to say, that PZ is in whatever proportion one wants to a given quantity A, and the ordinate PF, or the arc BF. The meaning of this question is, to determine the curve BFN from an infinity of others of the same length, whose ordinates PF or arcs BF raised to a given power and expressed as other ordinates PZ, will make the greatest space BZN.*

The word 'function' has not yet appeared, but during the years 1694 to 1698 Johann Bernoulli and Leibniz had already begun to use it (Latin *functio*; French *fonction*) in their correspondence with each other. In June 1698 Johann Bernoulli sent Leibniz a new solution of the isoperimeter problem in which he had now broadened the terms of reference to include not just simple powers of the ordinates but 'les fonctions quelconques' ('any functions whatever'). Johann requested that his solution should not be printed before his brother Jacob had presented his own, and it was eventually published after Jacob's death, in the *Mémoires* of the Paris Academy in 1706.[3]

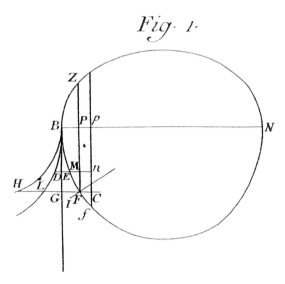

Figure 9.2  Johann Bernoulli's diagram of 1706

*From all isoperimetric curves described on the same given axis BN, find the curve BFN such that its ordinates FP raised to a given power, or generally such that any functions whatsoever of the ordinates, expressed as other ordinates PZ, form or fill up a space BZN, which is the greatest of all that can be formed in the same way.*

3. 'De toutes les Courbes isopérimétres décrites sur un même axe déterminé BN, trouver la Courbe BFN telle, que ses appliquées FP élevées à une puissance donnée, ou generalement telle, que les fonctions quelconques de ces appliqées, exprimées par d'autres appliqués PZ, forment ou remplissent un espace BZN, qui soit le plus grand de tous ceux qui peuvent être formés de la même maniere.' Johann Bernoulli, *Opera*, I, 424.

Although the formulation of the problem now included the new word 'function', Johann Bernoulli did not define what he meant by it, and was not entirely consistent in his use of the term. In the passage above and elsewhere, he used 'functions' (plural) to mean new ordinates, or lengths, calculated from the original ones by a fixed rule. In this sense a function was strictly speaking a *quantity*, represented by length, not the *rule* for finding the quantity. At other times, however, Bernoulli used the term 'function' (singular) to refer to the rule itself. The ambiguous use of 'functions' (plural) to mean 'quantities' and 'function' (singular) to mean a 'rule' is seen, for example, in this paragraph, where both forms appear:[4]

One must observe carefully that the difference between the functions of two lines such as $RO$, $RT$, which exceed one another by an infinitely small quantity of the second order, $TO$, is found by simply differentiating the function of $RO$, and multiplying by $TO$ that which arises, ...

For Johann Bernoulli in 1698, differentiation was defined only for sums and differences, products and quotients, powers and roots, and so his functions were necessarily restricted to combinations of these operations. When he came to write a comprehensive treatment of the isoperimeter problem in 1718, he gave the first published definition of a function, as follows:[5]

DEFINITION

Here one calls a *function* of a variable magnitude, a quantity composed in any manner possible from this variable magnitude and constants.

Bernoulli had now explicitly defined a function as a *quantity* and yet it is clear that what really mattered was the fixed *rule* for finding that quantity for each ordinate. Later in the same paper he introduced the symbol $\phi$ to represent the required function, writing, for example, $\phi Pb + \phi Rc = \phi Pg + \phi Ri$, and in this way he began to bring together the ideas of rule and quantity: for each ordinate, $Pb$ say, there is an associated *quantity*, or length $\phi Pb$, but the symbol $\phi$ reinforces the idea that the *rule* for finding the quantity is the same in every case.

The isoperimeter problem, stated so simply by Jacob Bernoulli in 1697, eventually resulted in a new branch of mathematics, the calculus of variations. For us, it also provides a fascinating case-study in the evolution of mathematical language and presentation as the problem was rephrased and developed over the first twenty years of its existence. The diagrams alone, drawn afresh for each new solution, illustrate an increasingly sophisticated approach: compare the diagram published with Johann Bernoulli's paper in 1706 (Figure 9.2) with Jacob Bernoulli's original from 1697 (Figure 9.1). But the

---

4. 'Il faut bien remarquer que la différence des fonctions de deux lignes comme $RO$, $RT$, qui se surpassant d'une quantité $TO$ infiniment petite du second genre, se trouve en différentiant simplement la fonction de $RO$, & en multipliant par $TO$ ce qui en vient, ....' Johann Bernoulli, *Opera*, I, 426.

5. 'DEFINITION. On Appelle ici *Fonction* d'une grandeur variable, une quantité composée de quelque maniére que ce soit de cette grandeur variable & de constantes.' Johann Bernoulli, *Opera*, II, 241–242.

mathematical language also changed dramatically. In January 1698, Johann Bernoulli began by describing the problem exactly as Jacob had done, in traditional terms of multiple or submultiple ratios (*raisons*); but even in the same paragraph he also used the more modern language of powers (*puissances*). Only six months later he had moved much further, from simple powers to functions (*fonctions*). Given the rapidity of change it is hardly surprising that Bernoulli's use of 'function' was somewhat ambiguous. By 1718 he recognized the need for a formal definition, but in fact what helped most to clarify his ideas to his readers was his use of yet another kind of language, mathematical symbolism: Bernoulli's symbol $\phi$ represented his concept so concisely and so well that it has, in only slightly modified form, remained in use ever since, even though the concept of function itself has continued to change and develop.

## 9.1.2 Euler's definition of a function (1), 1748

Leonhard Euler gave a definition of a function right at the beginning of his *Introductio in analysin infinitorum* of 1748, preceded only by even more fundamental definitions of known and unknown quantities. Euler had been taught by Johann Bernoulli, and so it is not surprising that his definition was closely related to Bernoulli's: an algebraic expression composed in any way of known and unknown quantities. Where Bernoulli had primarily regarded functions as a set of quantities or values, however, Euler now emphasized the expression, or rule, by which the values were found. In practice the distinction was less clear than it might seem since Euler, like Bernoulli, moved freely from one to the other. Only one paragraph after the definition, Euler's 'analytic expression' already becomes a 'variable quantity'. This lack of separation between rule and quantity allowed him to apply descriptions such as 'algebraic', 'transcendental', 'rational', and 'irrational', which had previously applied only to numbers, also to operations and functions.

   Euler's definition did not rule out multiple-valued functions; the expression $\sqrt{(9-z^2)}$ is double-valued, but Euler seems to have assumed that only the positive value would be considered. Expressions such as $z^0$ and $1^z$, however, whose value never varies, were excluded from his definition.

## Euler's definition of a function, 1748

from Euler, *Introductio in analysin infinitorum*, 1748, I, §4–§8

4. *Functio quantitatis variabilis , est expressio analytica quomo-docunque composita ex illa quantitate variabili, & numeris seu quantitatibus constantibus.*

Omnis ergo expressio analytica , in qua præter quantitatem variabilem $z$ omnes quantitates illam expressionem componentes sunt constantes , erit Functio ipsius $z$: Sic $a + 3z$; $az - 4zz$; $az + b \sqrt{(aa - zz)}$; $c^z$ ; &c. sunt Functiones ipsius $z$.

5. *Functio ergo quantitatis variabilis ipsa erit quantitas variabilis.*

Cum enim loco quantitatis variabilis omnes valores determinatos substituere liceat, hinc Functio innumerabiles valores determinatos induet; neque ullus valor determinatus excipietur, quem Functio induere nequeat, cum quantitas variabilis quoque valores imaginarios involvat. Sic etsi hæc Functio $\sqrt{(9 - zz)}$, numeris realibus loco $z$ substituendis, nunquam valorem ternario majorem recipere potest; tamen ipsi $z$ valores imaginarios tribuendo

tribuendo ut $5\sqrt{} - 1$, nullus affignari poterit valor determinatus C A P. I.
quin ex formula $\sqrt{(9 - zz)}$ elici queat. Occurrunt autem nonnunquam Functiones tantum apparentes, quæ, utcunque quantitas variabilis varietur, tamen ufque eumdem valorem retinent,

ut $z^0$; $1^z$; $\frac{aa - az}{a - z}$, quæ, etfi fpeciem Functionis mentiuntur,

tamen revera funt quantitates conftantes.

6. *Præcipuum Functionum difcrimen in modo compofitionis, quo
ex quantitate variabili & quantitatibus conftantibus formantur, po-
fitum eft.*

Pendet ergo ab Operationibus quibus quantitates inter fe com-
poni & permifceri poffunt: quæ Operationes funt Additio &
Subtractio; Multiplicatio & Divifio: Evectio ad Poteftates &
Radicum Extractio; quo etiam Refolutio Æquationum eft refe-
renda. Præter has Operationes, quæ algebraïcæ vocari folent,
dantur complures aliæ tranfcendentes, ut Exponentiales, Loga-
rithmicæ, atque innumerabiles aliæ, quas Calculus integralis
fuppeditat.

Interim fpecies quædam Functionum notari poffunt; ut mul-
tipla $2z$; $3z$; $\frac{z}{5}z$; $az$; &c. & Poteftates ipfius $z$, ut $z^z$;
$z^3$; $z^{\frac{5}{2}}$; $z^{-1}$; &c. quæ, uti ex unica operatione funt defum-
tæ, ita expreffiones quæ ex operationibus quibufcunque nafcun-
tur, Functionum nomine infigniuntur.

7. *Functiones dividuntur in Algebraïcas & Tranfcendentes; illæ
funt, quæ componuntur per operationes algebraïcas folas, hæ vero
in quibus operationes tranfcendentes infunt.*

Sunt ergo multiplæ ac Poteftates ipfius $z$ Functiones algebraïcæ; atque omnes omnino expreffiones, quæ per operationes algebraïcas ante memoratas formantur, cujufmodi eft

$\frac{a + bz^n - c\sqrt{(2z - zz)}}{aaz - 3bz^3}$. Quin-etiam Functiones algebraïcæ

fæpenumero nequidem explicite exhiberi poffunt, cujufmodi
Functio ipfius $z$ eft $Z$, fi definiatur per hujufmodi æquationem;
$Z^5 = azzZ^3 - bz^4Z^2 + cz^3Z - 1$. Quanquam enim hæc

A 3                          æquatio

**LIB. I.** æquatio refolvi nequit ; tamen conftat $Z$ æquari expreffioni cui-
piam ex variabili $z$ & conftantibus compofitæ ; ac propterea fore $Z$ Functionem quamdam ipfius $z$.     Cæterum de Functionibus tranfcendentibus notandum eft, eas demum fore tranfcendentes, fi operatio tranfcendens non folum ingrediatur, fed
etiam quantitatem variabilem afficiat. Si enim operationes tranfcendentes tantum ad quantitates conftantes pertineant, Functio
nihilominus algebraïca eft cenfenda : uti fi $c$ denotet circumfe-
rentiam Circuli, cujus radius fit $= 1$, erit utique $c$ quantit.:
tranfcendens, verumtamen hæ expreffiones $c + z$ ; $cz^2$ ; $4z^c$ &c.
erunt Functiones algebraïcæ ipfius $z$. Parvi quidem eft momenti
dubium quod a quibufdam movetur, utrum ejufmodi expreffiones $z^c$ Functionibus algebraïcis annumerari jure poffint, necne ; quinetiam Poteftates ipfius $z$, quarum exponentes fint numeri irrationales, uti $z^{\sqrt{2}}$ nonnulli maluerunt Functiones inter-
fcendentes quam algebraïcas appellare.

    8. *Functiones algebraïcæ fubdividuntur in Rationales & Irrationa-
les : illæ funt, fi quantitas variabilis in nulla irrationalitate invol-
vitur ; hæ vero, in quibus figna radicalia quantitatem variabilem
afficiunt.*

    In Functionibus ergo rationalibus aliæ operationes præter Ad-
ditionem, Subtractionem, Multiplicationem, Divifionem, &
Evectionem ad Poteftates, quarum exponentes fint numeri in-
tegri, non infunt : erunt adeo $a + z$ ; $a - z$ ; $az$ ; $\dfrac{aa + zz}{a + z}$ ;
$az^2 - bz^3$ ; &c. Functiones rationales ipfius $z$. At hujufmodi
expreffiones $\sqrt{z}$ ; $a + \sqrt{(aa - zz)}$ ; $\sqrt[3]{(a - 2z + zz)}$ :
$\dfrac{aa - z\sqrt{(aa + zz)}}{a + z}$ erunt Functiones irrationales ipfius $z$.

    *Hæ commode diftinguntur in Explicitas & Implicitas.*

    Explicitæ funt, quæ per figna radicalia funt evolutæ, cujuf-
modi exempla modo funt data. Implicitæ vero Functiones irrationales funt quæ ex refolutione æquationum ortum habent.
Sic $Z$ erit Functio irrationalis implicita ipfius $z$, fi per hujufmodi
æqua-

æquationem $Z^7 = az\, Z^2 - bz^3$ definiatur ; quoniam va-CAP.
lorem explicitum pro $Z$, admiffis etiam fignis radicalibus, exhibere non licet ; propterea quod Algebra communis nondum
ad hunc perfectionis gradum eft evecta.

4. *A function of a variable quantity is an analytic expression composed in any way from that variable quantity and from numbers or constant quantities.*

Therefore every analytic expression, in which apart from the variable quantity $z$ all quantities composing that expression are constant, will be a function of $z$. Thus $a + 3z$; $az - 4zz$; $az + b\sqrt{(aa - zz)}$; $c^z$; etc. are functions of $z$.

5. *Therefore a function of a variable quantity will itself be a variable quantity.*

For since in place of a variable quantity one may substitute all known values, this function may take on innumerable known values; nor is any known value excluded, which a function may not take on, since the variable quantity may also involve imaginary values. Thus even though the function $\sqrt{(9 - zz)}$ with real numbers substituted in place of $z$ never takes values greater than three, nevertheless by giving $z$ imaginary values, [5] such as $5\sqrt{-1}$, there can be no given value that cannot be elicited from the formula $\sqrt{(9 - zz)}$. But it sometimes happens that there are apparent functions which, however the variable quantity changes, always keep the same value, like $z^0$; $1^z$; $\dfrac{aa - az}{a - z}$; which, although imitating a kind of function, are really constant quantities.

6. *Here is laid down the principle thing that distinguishes functions, in the manner of composition by which they are formed, from a variable quantity and constant quantities.*

This depends on the operations by which the quantities may be composed and mixed together. The operations are addition and subtraction; multiplication and division; raising to powers and extraction of roots; by which also the solving of equations is carried out. Besides these operations, which are usually called algebraic, there are are several others that go beyond them [*transcendentes*], such as exponentials, logarithms, and innumerable others, which integral calculus supplies.

Meanwhile, certain notation for functions may be noted, such as multiples $2z$, $3z$; $\frac{3}{5}z$; $az$; etc. and powers of $z$, such as $z^2$; $z^3$; $z^{\frac{1}{2}}$; $z^{-1}$; etc., which have been chosen for use in particular operations; thus expressions which arise from any such operations are given the name of functions.

7. *Functions are divided into algebraic and transcendental; the former are those composed by algebraic operations alone, but the latter are those in which transcendental operations are involved.*

Thus multiples and powers of $z$ are algebraic functions; also all expressions whatever which are formed from the algebraic operations formerly mentioned, of which kind is

$$\frac{a + bz^n - c\sqrt{(2z - zz)}}{aaz - 3bz^3}.$$

Although it is also very often the case that algebraic functions may not be exhibited explicitly; of this kind is the function $Z$ of $z$ if it is defined by an equation of the kind: $Z^5 = azzZ^3 - bz^4Z^2 + cz^3Z - 1$. For although here [6] the equation may not be solved, nevertheless $Z$ stands equal to some expression composed from the variable $z$ and constants, and therefore $Z$ is some function of $z$. Something else must be noted of transcendental functions; they become immediately transcendental if a transcendental operation is not only involved, but also affects the variable quantity. For if transcendental operations pertain just to the constant quantities, the function is to be thought of as more or less algebraic: as when $c$ denotes the circumference of a circle whose radius $= 1$, and so $c$ is a transcendental quantity, however these expressions $c + z$; $czz$; $4z^c$; etc. will be algebraic functions of $z$. One will be moved by only a small moment of doubt as to whether or not expressions of the kind $z^c$ may truly be counted algebraic functions; all the same, powers of $z$ in which the exponents are irrational numbers, such as $z^{\sqrt{2}}$, some may prefer to call 'interscendent' rather than algebraic.

8. *Algebraic functions are subdivided into rational and irrational: the former are those where the variable quantity involves no irrationality; but the latter where root signs affect the variable quantity.*

Thus in rational functions there are no other operations besides addition, subtraction, multiplication, division, and raising to powers where the exponents are whole numbers. Hence $a + z$; $a - z$; $az$; $\frac{aa+zz}{a+z}$; $az^3 - bz^5$; etc. will be rational functions of $z$. But expressions of this kind $\sqrt{z}$; $a + \sqrt{(aa - zz)}$; $\sqrt[3]{(a - 2z + zz)}$; $\dfrac{aa - z\sqrt{(aa + zz)}}{a + z}$ will be irrational functions of $z$.

*Here we may conveniently distinguish explicit and implicit [irrational functions].*

Explicit are those arising from root signs, of which kind alone examples have been given. Implicit, however, are irrational functions, which arise from the solving of equations. Thus $Z$ will be an implicit function of $z$ if it is defined by this kind of [7] equation: $Z^7 = azZ^2 - bz^5$, because it is not possible to exhibit an explicit value of $Z$, even using root signs, because general algebra has not yet risen to this degree of perfection.

---

### 9.1.3 Euler's definition of a function (2), 1755

In Volume I of the *Introductio*, as we have seen in 9.1.2 (and 8.2.3), Euler considered a function to be a finite (or infinite) algebraic expression. By the time he came to write Volume II, however, his view had changed radically. In §1 to §7 of Volume II, he described carefully how any function of $x$ gives rise to a *curve*:[6]

Thus, any function of $x$ translated by this means into geometry, determines a certain line, either straight or curved, whose nature will depend on the nature of the function $y$.

The surprise comes in §8 where Euler makes the converse assertion, that any curve, however generated, can be regarded as a function:[7]

Although many curved lines can be described mechanically by the continuous motion of a point, by which means the whole curve is at once offered to the eye, nevertheless we may best consider these curves to originate from Functions, this being all the more analytic and more general, and much better suited to calculus. Therefore, any function of $x$ will give a line, whether straight or curved, whence in turn curved lines may be regarded as functions.

---

6. 'Quare, quaelibet ipsius $x$ Functio, hoc modo ad Geometriam translata, certam determinabit lineam, sive rectam sive curvam, cujus natura a natura Functionis $y$ pendebit.' Euler, *Introductio*, II, §6.

7. 'Quanquam complures lineae curvae per motum puncti continuum mechanice describi possunt, quo pacto tota linea curva simul oculis offertur, tamen hanc linearum curvarum ex Functionibus originem hic potissimum contemplabimur, tanquam magis analyticam latiusque patentem, atque ad calculum magis accomodatam. Quaelibet ergo Functio ipsius $x$ suppeditabit lineam quandam, sive rectam sive curvam, unde vicissim lineas curvas ad Functiones revocare licebit.' Euler, *Introductio*, II, §8.

Euler's change of view, from functions defined by expressions to functions defined by curves, had been brought about by one of the deepest problems faced by mid eighteenth-century mathematicians, the solution of the wave equation. In 1747 d'Alembert had published his discovery of the relationship

$$\frac{\partial^2 y}{\partial x^2} = \frac{1}{c^2}\frac{\partial^2 y}{\partial t^2}$$

(see 10.1.2). The questions now was: what kind of functions could satisfy such an equation? D'Alembert insisted that they should be differentiable in the eighteenth-century sense, that is, that it should be possible to apply to them the rules of differentiation laid down by Leibniz. Such functions were by definition, he claimed, the only kind of functions to which calculus was relevant. Euler almost immediately took issue with d'Alembert on this point. The initial position of a plucked string, for example, forced him to consider functions whose curves might have awkward joins or corners, and which were *not* everywhere differentiable (Euler described them as 'discontinuous', see 11.2.2).

The controversy forced a fundamental reassessment of what kind of functions were permissible. The argument between Euler and d'Alembert can be seen as part of a lengthy and difficult transition from regarding a function as an algebraic formula, to a fully analytic understanding (in the modern sense) of functions and differentiability. Euler, with his deep mathematical intuition, recognized the shortcomings of the former, but did not have at his disposal the ideas that could carry him towards the latter. Nevertheless, by the time he came to write his *Institutiones calculi differentialis* in 1755, his concept of a function had changed significantly since the period before d'Alembert's discovery. Now he defined a function as *any* relationship where one quantity changes with another: it was no longer necessary to be able to write down an explicit algebraic formula connecting them. This fundamental re-thinking about what began as a purely mathematical concept had been brought about by the attempt to match mathematical descriptions to the physical world.

## Euler's definition of a function, 1755

from Euler, *Institutiones calculi differentialis*, 1755, Preface, iv–vi

*Quoniam haec differentia inter quantitates constantes & variabiles exemplo maxime illustrabitur, consideremus iactum globi ex tormento bellico vi pulveris pyrii explosi; siquidem hoc exemplum ad rem dilucidandam imprimis idoneum videtur.    Plures igitur hic occurrunt quantitates, quarum ratio in ista inuestigatione est habenda: primo scilicet quantitas pulueris pyrii; tum eleuatio tormenti supra horizontem; tertio longitudo iactus super plano horizontali; quarto tempus, quo globus explosus in aere versatur: ac nisi xperimenta eodem tormento instituantur, insuper eius longitudo cum pondere globi in computum trahi deberet.    Verum hic a varietate tormenti & globi animum remoueamus, ne in quaestiones nimium implicatas incidamus.    Quodsi ergo seruata perpetuo eadem*

*pul-*

### PRAEFATIO.   v

pulueris pyrii quantitate, eleuatio tormenti continuo immutetur, iactusque longitudo cum tempore transitus globi per aerem requiratur; in hac quaestione copia pulueris seu vis impulsus erit quantitas constans, eleuatio autem tormenti cum longitudine iactus eiusque duratione ad quantitates variabiles referri debebunt; siquidem pro omnibus eleuationis gradibus has res definire velimus, vt inde innotescat, quantae mutationes in longitudine ac duratione iactus ab omnibus eleuationis variationibus oriantur. Alia autem erit quaestio, si seruata eadem tormenti eleuatione, quantitas pulueris pyrii continuo mutetur, & mutationes, quae inde in iactum redundant, definiri debeant: hic enim eleuatio tormenti erit quantitas constans, contra vero quantitas pulueris pyrii, & longitudo ac duratio iactus quantitates variabiles. Sic igitur patet, quomodo mutato quaestionis statu eadem quantitas modo inter constantes, modo inter variabiles numerari queat: simul autem hinc intelligitur, ad quod in hoc negotio maxime est attendendum, quomodo quantitates variabiles aliae ab aliis ita pendeant, vt mutata vna reliquae necessario immutationes recipiant. Priori scilicet casu, quo quantitas pulueris

A 3

pyrii

VI. *PRAEFATIO.*

*pyrii eadem manebat, mutata tormenti eleuatione etiam longitudo & duratio iactus mutantur; funtque ergo longitudo & duratio iactus quantitates variabiles pendentes ab eleuatione tormenti, hacque mutata fimul certas quasdam mutationes patientes: pofteriori vero cafu pendent a quantitate pulueris pyrii, cuius mutatio in illis certas mutationes producere debet. Quae autem quantitates hoc modo ab aliis pendent, vt his mutatis etiam ipfae mutationes fubeant, eae harum functiones appellari folent; quae denominatio latiffime patet, atque omnes modos, quibus vna quantitas per alias determinari poteft, in fe complectitur. Si igitur x denotet quantitatem variabilem, omnes quantitates, quae vtcunque ab x pendent, feu per eam determinantur, eius functiones vocantur; cuiusmodi funt quadratum eius x x, aliaeue potentiae quaecunque, nec non quantitates ex his vtcunque compofitae; quin etiam transcendentes, & in genere quaecunque ita ab x pendent, vt aucta vel diminuta x ipfae mutationes recipiant.*

Because this difference between constant and variable quantities is best illustrated by an example, let us consider the flight of a ball expelled from a cannon by the force of gunpowder, since this example seems especially suited to clarifying the matter. There occur here, then, several quantities, of which the relationship is to be found in this investigation: first, of course, the quantity of gunpowder; then the elevation of the cannon above the horizon; third, the length of the flight over the horizontal plane; fourth, the time in which the expelled ball is turned in the air. And above all, unless experiments are carried out with the cannon, its length and the weight of the ball must be brought into the calculation. Truly here we must take our mind off the variety of cannons and balls, lest we fall into far too complicated questions. And therefore keeping the quantity of powder always the same, [v] as the elevation of the cannon is continually changed, there is required the length of flight with the time passed in the air by the ball; in this question the amount of powder or force of expulsion will be constant quantities, while the elevation of the cannon, and the length of flight and its duration must be regarded as variable quantities, since for all degrees of elevation we wish to define these things, that hence it will be known, how great are the changes in length and duration of flight arising from all variations in elevation. While another question will be if, keeping the elevation of the cannon the same, the quantity of gunpowder is continually changed, and we need to define the changes that hence affect the flight: for here the elevation of the cannon will be constant, while the quantity of gunpowder, and the length and duration of the flight are variable quantities. Thus it is clear, therefore, how by changing the nature of the question, it is possible to count quantities only amongst the constants or only amongst the variables. At the same time moreover, it is to be understood, what in this matter is most wanted, how variable quantities depend on each other, so that changes in one necessarily bring about changes in the others. First it is taken to be the case that the quantity of gunpowder [vi] is held the same, and by a change in elevation of the cannon the length and duration of flight are both changed; and therefore the length and duration of flight are variable quantities depending on the elevation of the cannon, changes in the latter showing at once certain definite changes [in the former]. But in the next case, those things depend on the quantity of gunpowder, a change in which must produce definite changes in those. Moreover, the quantities that depend in this way on others, so that the latter having changed, they themselves also undergo change, are usually called functions; which name opens up most generally all the ways in which one quantity may be determined from others involved with it. If therefore $x$ denotes a variable quantity, then all quantities which in any way depend on $x$, or are determined by it, are called functions of it; of this kind are the square of it, $xx$, or any other power whatever, and also quantities in any way composed from these; but also transcendental quantities, of any kind depending on $x$, such that by increase or decrease in $x$ they themselves are changed.

## 9.2 LOGARITHMIC AND CIRCULAR FUNCTIONS

An understanding of the relationship between circle measurement and logarithms was rooted, like so much of early modern mathematics, in a deep understanding of classical geometry. While sines, tangents, and secants were defined using circles, logarithms were intimately related to the hyperbola and areas bounded by it; and everyone knew that the circle and the hyperbola were intimately related as conic sections. Maclaurin described the relationship in some detail in Book II of his *Treatise of fluxions*, in a chapter entitled 'Of the analogy betwixt circular arches and logarithms':[8]

The properties of the circle and ellipse often suggest similar properties of the hyperbola, and reciprocally the properties of hyperbolic areas (which are sometimes more easily discovered because of their analogy to the properties of logarithms described in *book* I. *chap.* 6.) are of use for discovering the analogous properties of circular and elliptic areas.

It was Euler, however, who really clarified the deep connection between logarithmic and trigonometric functions, defining all of them algebraically, and linking them by astonishingly simple equations in his *Introductio* of 1748. One may question Euler's hand-waving treatment of infinitely small and infinitely large quantities but one cannot dismiss the range and quality of his results, nor his achievement in bringing so much fundamental mathematical material together.

### 9.2.1  A new definition of logarithms, 1748

In Chapter IV of the *Introductio*, Euler investigated properties of $y$ defined by $y = a^z$ (for fixed $a$) and defined $z$ as the *logarithm* of $y$, and $a$ as the *base*. Mathematically speaking this comes to the same thing as Napier's definition of 1614 (where a certain distance along the line $\alpha\omega$ represents the quantity $y$, and distance along the line $AO$ represents the exponent $z$) but conceptually it is very different: moving points (as in 2.1.2), or areas under a hyperbola (as in 3.2.4), have been replaced by a simple algebraic formula. Now observe what could come of such a formula in the hands of Euler.

---

8. Maclaurin 1742, II, §758.

## The exponential series

from Euler, *Introductio in analysin infinitorum*, 1748, I, §114–§116

## C A P U T   V I I.

### *De quantitatum exponentialium ac Logarithmorum per Series explicatione.*

**114.** QUia eft $a^0 = 1$, atque crefcente Exponente ipfius $a$ fimul valor Poteftatis augetur, fi quidem $a$ eft numerus unitate major; fequitur fi Exponens infinite parum cyphram excedat, Poteftatem ipfam quoque infinite parum unitatem effe fuperaturam. Sit $\omega$ numerus infinite parvus, feu Fractio tam exigua, ut tantum non nihilo fit æqualis, erit

$a^\omega = 1 + \psi$, exiftente $\psi$ quoque numero infinite parvo. Ex præcedente enim capite conftat nifi $\psi$ effet numerus infinite parvus, neque $\omega$ talem effe poffe. Erit ergo vel $\psi = \omega$, vel $\psi > \omega$, vel $\psi < \omega$, quæ ratio utique a quantitate litteræ $a$ pendebit, quæ cum adhuc fit incognita, ponatur $\psi = k\omega$, ita ut fit $a^\omega = 1 + k\omega$; &, fumta $a$ pro bafi Logarithmica, erit $\omega = l(1 + k\omega)$.

### E X E M P L U M.

Quo clarius appareat, quemadmodum numerus $k$ pendeat a bafi $a$, ponamus effe $a = 10$; atque ex tabulis vulgaribus quæramus Logarithmum numeri quam minime unitatem fupe-

L 3                                      rantis,

LIB. I. rantis, puta $1 + \frac{1}{1000000}$, ita ut fit $k\omega = \frac{1}{1000000}$ ; erit

$l(1 + \frac{1}{1000000}) = l\frac{1000001}{1000000} = 0,00000043429 = \omega$. Hinc,

ob $k\omega = 0,0000100000$, erit $\frac{1}{k} = \frac{43429}{100000}$ & $k = $

$\frac{100000}{43429} = 2,30258$ : unde patet $k$ effe numerum finitum pendentem a valore bafis $a$. Si enim alius numerus pro bafi $a$ ftatuatur, tum Logarithmus ejufdem numeri $1 + k\omega$ ad priorem datam tenebit rationem, unde fimul alius valor litteræ $k$ prodiret.

115. Cum fit $a^\omega = 1 + k\omega$, erit $a^{i\omega} = (1 + k\omega)^i$ , quicunque numerus loco $i$ fubftituatur. Erit ergo $a^{i\omega} = 1 + $
$\frac{i}{1} k\omega + \frac{i(i-1)}{1.2} k^2\omega^2 + \frac{i(i-1)(i-2)}{1.2.3} k^3\omega^3 + $ &c.
Quod fi ergo ftatuatur $i = \frac{z}{\omega}$, & $z$ denotet numerum quemcunque finitum, ob $\omega$ numerum infinite parvum, fiet $i$ numerus infinite magnus, hincque $\omega = \frac{z}{i}$, ita ut fit $\omega$ Fractio denominatorem habens infinitum, adeoque infinite parva, qualis eft affumta. Subftituatur ergo $\frac{z}{i}$ loco $\omega$, eritque $a^z = (1 + $
$\frac{kz}{i})^i = 1 + \frac{1}{1} kz + \frac{1(i-1)}{1.2i} k^2 z^2 + \frac{1(i-1)(i-2)}{1.2i.3i} k^3 z^3 + $
$\frac{1(i-1)(i-2)(i-3)}{1.2i.3i.4i} k^4 z^4 + $ &c. , quæ æquatio erit vera fi pro $i$ numerus infinite magnus fubftituatur. Tum vero eft $k$ numerus definitus ab $a$ pendens, uti modo vidimus.

116. Cum autem $i$ fit numerus infinite magnus, erit $\frac{i-1}{i} = 1$; patet enim quo major numerus loco $i$ fubftituatur, eo propius valorem Fractionis $\frac{i-1}{i}$ ad unitatem effe acceffurum, hinc fi

$i$ fit

*AC LOGARITHM. TER SERIES EXPLICAT.* 87

$i$ fit numerus omni affignabili major. Fractio quoque $\frac{i---1}{i}$ Cap. VII.

ipfam unitatem adæquabit. Ob fimilem autem rationem erit

$\frac{i---2}{i} = 1$; $\frac{i---3}{i} = 1$; & ita porro; hinc fequitur fore

$\frac{i---1}{2i} = \frac{1}{2}$; $\frac{i---2}{3i} = \frac{1}{3}$; $\frac{i---3}{4i} = \frac{1}{4}$; & ita porro. His

igitur valoribus fubftitutis, erit $a^z = 1 + \frac{kz}{1} + \frac{k^2z^2}{1.2} + \frac{k^3z^3}{1.2.3} +$

$\frac{k^4z^4}{1.2.3.4} +$ &c. in infinitum. Hæc autem æquatio fimul re-

lationem inter numeros $a$ & $k$ oftendit, pofito enim $z = 1$,

erit $a = 1 + \frac{k}{1} + \frac{k^2}{1.2} + \frac{k^3}{1.2.3} + \frac{k^4}{1.2.3.4} +$ &c., atque

ut $a$ fit $= 10$, neceffe eft ut fit circiter $k = 2,30258$, uti

ante invenimus.

[...]

122. Quoniam ad fyftema Logarithmorum condendum ba-

fin $a$ pro lubitu accipere licet, ea ita affumi poterit ut fiat

$k = 1$. Ponamus ergo effe $k = 1$, eritque per Seriem fupra

Euleri *Introduct. in Anal. infin. parv.* M (116)

90 *DE QUANTITATUM EXPONENTIALIUM*

LIB. I. (116) inventam, $a = 1 + \frac{1}{1} + \frac{1}{1.2} + \frac{1}{1.2.3} + \frac{1}{1.2.3.4} +$ &c.,

qui termini, fi in fractiones decimales convertantur atque

actu addantur, præbebunt hunc valorem pro $a =$

2,718281828459045235360281, cujus ultima adhuc nota ve-

ritati eft confentanea. Quod fi jam ex hac bafi Logarithmi

conftruantur, ii vocari folent Logarithmi *naturales* feu *hyperbo-

lici*, quoniam quadratura hyperbolæ per iftiufmodi Logari-

thmos exprimi poteft. Ponamus autem brevitatis gratia pro

numero hoc 2,718281828459 &c. conftanter litteram $e$, quæ

ergo denotabit bafin Logarithmorum naturalium feu hyperbo-

licorum, cui refpondet valor litteræ $k = 1$; five hæc littera $e$

quoque exprimet fummam hujus Seriei $1 + \frac{1}{1} + \frac{1}{1.2} +$

$\frac{1}{1.2.3} + \frac{1}{1.2.3.4} +$ &c. in infinitum.

# CHAPTER VII

*On exponential and logarithmic quantities*
*expressed by series*

114. Because $a^0 = 1$ and, as the exponent increases, the value of the power of $a$ grows, if indeed $a$ is a number greater than one, it follows that if the exponent exceeds zero by an infinitely small amount, the power itself will also be greater than one by an infinitely small amount. Let $\omega$ be an infinitely small number, or a fraction so tiny that it is almost equal to nothing; then we will have $a^\omega = 1 + \psi$, with $\psi$ also being an infinitely small number. For from what was considered in the preceding chapter, unless $\psi$ is infinitely small, $\omega$ cannot be so either. Therefore we will have either $\psi = \omega$, or $\psi > \omega$, or $\psi < \omega$, which relationship will depend on the letter $a$, and since it [the relationship] is so far supposed unknown, put $\psi = k\omega$, so that $a^\omega = 1 + k\omega$, then taking $a$ for the logarithmic base we will have $\omega = l(1 + k\omega)$.

*Example*

So that it will appear more clearly how the number $k$ depends on the base $a$, we put $a = 10$; and from a common table of logarithms we seek the logarithm of the number exceeding unity by the smallest amount, [86] thus $1 + \dfrac{1}{1000000}$, so that $k\omega = \dfrac{1}{1000000}$; we will have $l\left(1 + \dfrac{1}{1000000}\right) = l\dfrac{1000001}{1000000} = 0.00000043429 = \omega$. Here, since $k\omega = 0.00000100000$, we will have $\dfrac{1}{k} = \dfrac{43429}{100000}$ and $k = \dfrac{100000}{43429} = 2.30258$: whence it is clear that $k$ is a finite number depending on the value of the base $a$. For if another number stands in for the base $a$, then the logarithm of the number $1 + k\omega$ will have a ratio to the first number given, whence at the same time there will arise another value of the letter $k$.

115. Since $a^\omega = 1 + k\omega$, we will have $\alpha^{i\omega} = (1 + k\omega)^i$, whatever number is substituted in place of $i$. Therefore we will have $a^{i\omega} = 1 + \dfrac{i}{1}k\omega + \dfrac{i(i-1)}{1.2}k^2\omega^2 + \dfrac{i(i-1)(i-2)}{1.2.3}k^3\omega^3 +$ etc. If, therefore, there is put $i = \dfrac{z}{\omega}$ and $z$ denotes some finite number, since $\omega$ is an infinitely small number, $i$ will be an infinitely large number, and hence $\omega = \dfrac{z}{i}$, so that $\omega$ is a fraction having an infinite denominator, and therefore infinitely small, as was assumed. Therefore substituting $\dfrac{z}{i}$ in place of $\omega$, we will have $a^z = \left(1 + \dfrac{kz}{i}\right)^i = 1 + \dfrac{1}{1}kz + \dfrac{1(i-1)}{1.2i}k^2z^2 + \dfrac{1(i-1)(i-2)}{1.2i.3i}k^3z^3 + \dfrac{1(i-1)(i-2)(i-3)}{1.2i.3i.4i}k^4z^4 +$ etc., which equation is true if an infinitely large number is substituted for $i$. But then $k$ is a fixed number depending on $a$, as we have seen.

116. Moreover since $i$ is an infinitely large number, we will have $\dfrac{i-1}{i} = 1$; for it is clear that the greater the number substituted in place of $i$, the more nearly the value of the fraction $\dfrac{i-1}{i}$ will approach one; hence if [87] $i$ is a number greater than any assignable quantity, the fraction $\dfrac{i-1}{i}$ will also approximate to one itself. Moreover, for similar reasons, we will have $\dfrac{i-2}{i} = 1$; $\dfrac{i-3}{i} = 1$; and so on; hence it follows that

$$\frac{i-2}{2i} = \frac{1}{2}; \ \frac{i-2}{3i} = \frac{1}{3}; \ \frac{i-3}{4i} = \frac{1}{4};$$ and so on. Therefore, substituting these values,

we will have $a^z = 1 + \dfrac{kz}{1} + \dfrac{k^2z^2}{1.2} + \dfrac{k^3z^3}{1.2.3} + \dfrac{k^4z^4}{1.2.3.4} +$ etc. indefinitely. Moreover, this

equation at the same time shows the relationship between the numbers $a$ and $k$, for

putting $z = 1$, we will have $a = 1 + \dfrac{k}{1} + \dfrac{k^2}{1.2} + \dfrac{k^3}{1.2.3} + \dfrac{k^4}{1.2.3.4} +$ etc. and if $a = 10$,

it must be that $k$ will be about 2.30258, as we have already found.

[…]

[89] 122. Because we may freely choose any base $a$ for constructing a system of logarithms, we may take that which makes $k = 1$. Therefore let us put $k = 1$, and from the series above [90] (§116), $a = 1 + \dfrac{1}{1} + \dfrac{1}{1.2} + \dfrac{1}{1.2.3} + \dfrac{1}{1.2.3.4} +$ etc., whose terms, if converted into decimal fractions and added, give a value $a = 2.71828182845904523536028$, the last digit of which agrees with what is so far known to be correct. Logarithms constructed on this base are usually called *natural* or *hyperbolic* because the quadrature of the hyperbola can be expressed by logarithms of this kind. Moreover, we will always put for brevity the letter $e$ for this number 2.718281828459 …, which therefore denotes the base for natural or hyperbolic logarithms, which corresponds to the value $k = 1$; or also this letter $e$ expresses the sum of this series $a = 1 + \dfrac{1}{1} + \dfrac{1}{1.2} + \dfrac{1}{1.2.3} + \dfrac{1}{1.2.3.4} +$ etc. taken infinitely.

### 9.2.2 Series for sine and cosine, 1748

In Chapter VIII of the *Introductio* Euler moved on to trigonometric quantities, and in the opening paragraphs set out the basic properties of sine, cosine, and tangent. His discussion was based on elementary properties of arcs and circles (Euler worked with arcs where we would now speak of angles), but there are no diagrams in his text. His work was based entirely on the manipulation of formulae, and he listed a great many identities: for sines and cosines of sums and differences, for example, or for sums and products of sines and cosines. Then, starting only from the simple property that $\sin z^2 + \cos z^2 = 1$, Euler derived power series for both sine and cosine. Note that he had no qualms about invoking the imaginary quantity $\sqrt{-1}$ when he needed it. Observe too that he asserted a form of what is now known as de Moivre's Theorem, but based only on calculations for $n = 2$ and $n = 3$.

---

### Series for sine and cosine

from Euler, *Introductio in analysin infinitorum*, 1748, I, §132–§134

---

132. Cum fit $(\textit{fin. } z)^2 + (\textit{cof. } z)^2 = 1$ erit, Factoribus fumendis, $(\textit{cof. } z + \sqrt{-1} . \textit{fin. } z)(\textit{cof. } z - \sqrt{-1} . \textit{fin.} z) = 1$; qui Factores, etfi imaginarii, tamen ingentem præftant ufum in Arcubus combinandis & multiplicandis. Quæratur enim productum horum Factorum $(\textit{cof. } z + \sqrt{-1} . \textit{fin. } z)(\textit{cof. } y + \sqrt{-1} . \textit{fin. } y.)$ ac reperietur $\textit{cof. } y . \textit{cof. } z - \textit{fin. } y . \textit{fin. } z + (\textit{cof. } y . \textit{fin. } z + \textit{fin. } y . \textit{cof. } z)$

Euleri *Introduct. in Anal. infin. parv.*           N           $\sqrt{}$

98    *DE QUANTITATIBUS TRANSCENDENT.*

LIB. I. $\sqrt{}$ — 1. Cum autem fit *cof. y. cof. z* — *fin. y. fin. z* = *cof.* $(y+z)$ & *cof. y. fin. z* + *fin. y. cof. z* = *fin.* $(y+z)$ erit hoc productum
$(cof. y. + \sqrt{} —1. fin. y)(cof. z + \sqrt{} —1. fin. z) = cof. (y+z) + \sqrt{} —1. fin. (y+z)$

& fimili modo

$(cof. y — \sqrt{} —1. fin. y)(cof. z —\sqrt{} —1. fin. z) = cof. (y+z) — \sqrt{} —1. fin. (y+z)$

item

$( cof. x \pm \sqrt{} —1. fin. x )( cof. y \pm \sqrt{} —1. fin. y )( cof. z \pm \sqrt{} —1. fin. z ) = cof. (x+y+z) \pm \sqrt{} —1. fin. (x+y+z).$

133. Hinc itaque fequitur fore $( cof. z \pm \sqrt{} —1. fin z)^2 = cof. 2z \pm \sqrt{} —1. fin. 2z$, & $( cof. z \pm \sqrt{} —1. fin. z)^3 = cof. 3z \pm \sqrt{} —1. fin. 3z.$

ideoque generaliter erit $( cof. z \pm \sqrt{} —1. fin. z)^n = cof. nz \pm \sqrt{} —1. fin. nz.$

Unde, ob fignorum ambiguitatem, erit

$$cof. nz = \left( \frac{cof. z + \sqrt{} —1. fin. z)^n + (cof. z —\sqrt{} —1. fin. z)^n}{2} \right) \&$$

$$fin. nz = \frac{( cof. z + \sqrt{} —1. fin. z)^n — ( cof. z —\sqrt{} —1. fin. z)^n}{2 \sqrt{} —1}$$

Evolutis ergo binomiis hifce erit per Series:

$$cof. nz = ( cof. z)^n — \frac{n(n—1)}{1.2} ( cof. z)^{n—2} ( fin. z )^2 +$$

$$\frac{n(n—1)(n—2)(n—3)}{1. \quad 2. \quad 3. \quad 4} ( cof. z)^{n—4} ( fin. z )^4 —$$

$$\frac{n(n—1)(n—2)(n—3)(n—4)(n—5)}{1.2.3.4.5.6} ( cof. z)^{n—6}$$

$( fin. z )^6$ + &c., &

$$fin. nz = \frac{n}{1} ( cof. z)^{n—1} fin. z — \frac{n(n—1)(n—2)}{1. \quad 2. \quad 3}$$

$$( cof. z )^{n—3} ( fin. z)^3 + \frac{n(n—1)(n—2)(n—3)(n—4)}{1.2.3.4.5}$$

$( cof. z )^{n—5} ( fin. z )^5 —$ &c.

134.

134. Sit Arcus *z* infinite parvus, erit *fin. z* $=$ *z* & *cof. z* C A P.
$=$ I : fit autem *n* numerus infinite magnus, ut fit Arcus *n z* V I I I.

finitæ magnitudinis, puta, *nz* $=$ *v*; ob *fin. z* $=$ *z* $=$ $\frac{v}{n}$ erit

$$\text{cof. } v = 1 - \frac{v^2}{1.2} + \frac{v^4}{1.2.3.4} - \frac{v^6}{1.2.3.4.5.6} + \&c., \&$$

$$\text{fin. } v = v - \frac{v^3}{1.2.3} + \frac{v^5}{1.2.3.4.5} - \frac{v^7}{1.2.3.4.5.6.7} + \&c.$$

<hr>

TRANSLATION

132. Since $(\sin z)^2 + (\cos z)^2 = 1$ we will have, after taking factors, $(\cos z + \sqrt{-1}\sin z)(\cos z - \sqrt{-1}\sin z) = 1$; which factors, although imaginary, are nevertheless of very great use in combining and multiplying arcs. For if there is sought the product of these factors $(\cos z + \sqrt{-1}\sin z)(\cos y + \sqrt{-1}\sin y)$ there is found $\cos y . \cos z - \sin y . \sin z + (\cos y . \sin z + \sin y . \cos z)\sqrt{-1}$. [98] Moreover, since $\cos y . \cos z - \sin y . \sin z = \cos(y+z)$ and $\cos y . \sin z + \sin y . \cos z = \sin(y+z)$ we will have this product $(\cos y + \sqrt{-1}\sin y)(\cos z + \sqrt{-1}\sin z) = \cos(y+z) + \sqrt{-1}\sin(y+z)$ and similarly $(\cos y - \sqrt{-1}\sin y)(\cos z - \sqrt{-1}\sin z) = \cos(y+z) - \sqrt{-1}\sin(y+z)$ and likewise $(\cos x \pm \sqrt{-1}\sin x)(\cos y \pm \sqrt{-1}\sin y)(\cos z \pm \sqrt{-1}\sin z) = \cos(x+y+z) \pm \sqrt{-1}\sin(x+y+z)$.

133. Hence it follows that $(\cos z \pm \sqrt{-1}\sin z)^2 = \cos 2z \pm \sqrt{-1}\sin 2z$, and $(\cos z \pm \sqrt{-1}\sin z)^3 = \cos 3z \pm \sqrt{-1}\sin 3z$; and therefore generally we will have $(\cos z \pm \sqrt{-1}\sin z)^n = \cos nz \pm \sqrt{-1}\sin nz$.

Whence, from the ambiguity of the signs, we will have

$$\cos nz = \frac{(\cos z + \sqrt{-1}\sin z)^n + (\cos z - \sqrt{-1}\sin z)^n}{2} \quad \text{and}$$

$$\sin nz = \frac{(\cos z + \sqrt{-1}\sin z)^n - (\cos z - \sqrt{-1}\sin z)^n}{2\sqrt{-1}}.$$

Therefore expanding these binomials we will have as series:

$$\cos nz = (\cos z)^n - \frac{n(n-1)}{1.2}(\cos z)^{n-2}(\sin z)^2 + \frac{n(n-1)(n-2)(n-3)}{1.2.3.4}(\cos z)^{n-4}(\sin z)^4$$

$$- \frac{n(n-1)(n-2)(n-3)(n-4)(n-5)}{1.2.3.4.5.6}(\cos z)^{n-6}(\sin z)^6 + \text{etc., and}$$

$$\sin nz = \frac{n}{1}(\cos z)^{n-1}\sin z - \frac{n(n-1)(n-2)}{1.2.3}(\cos z)^{n-3}(\sin z)^3$$

$$+ \frac{n(n-1)(n-2)(n-3)(n-4)}{1.2.3.4.5}(\cos z)^{n-5}(\sin z)^5 - \text{etc.}$$

[99] 134. Supposing the arc $z$ is infinitely small, we will have $\sin z = z$ and $\cos z = 1$. Moreover suppose $n$ is an infinitely large number, so that the arc $nz$ is of finite magnitude, thus, $nz = v$; since $\sin z = z = \frac{v}{n}$ we will have

$$\cos v = 1 - \frac{v^2}{1.2} + \frac{v^4}{1.2.3.4} - \frac{v^6}{1.2.3.4.5.6} + \text{etc., and}$$

$$\sin v = v - \frac{v^3}{1.2.3} + \frac{v^5}{1.2.3.4.5} - \frac{v^7}{1.2.3.4.5.6.7} + \text{etc.}$$

### 9.2.3 Euler's unification of elementary functions, 1748

Towards the end of his chapter on circular functions Euler demonstrated how sines and cosines are related to the exponential function he had defined in Chapter VII. Substituting $v = \pi$ in Euler's penultimate identity below leads to the remarkable fact that $e^{i\pi} = -1$, a discovery usually attributed to Euler, though he did not actually write it down in the *Introductio*.

---

### Euler's unification of elementary functions

from Euler, *Introductio in analysin infinitorum*, 1748, I, §138

---

**138.** Ponatur denuo in formulis §. 133, Arcus $z$ infinite parvus, & fit $n$ numerus infinite magnus $i$, ut $iz$ obtineat valorem finitum $v$. Erit ergo $nz = v$; & $z = \frac{v}{i}$, unde *fin.* $z = \frac{v}{i}$ & *cof.* $z = 1$; his fubftitutis fit *cof.* $v =$

LIB. I.

$$\frac{\left(1 + \frac{v\sqrt{-1}}{i}\right)^i + \left(1 - \frac{v\sqrt{-1}}{i}\right)^i}{2} ; \text{ atque } \text{fin. } v =$$

$$\frac{\left(1 + \frac{v\sqrt{-1}}{i}\right)^i - \left(1 - \frac{v\sqrt{-1}}{i}\right)^i}{2\sqrt{-1}}. \text{ In Capite autem}$$

præcedente vidimus effe $\left(1 + \frac{z}{i}\right)^i = e^z$, denotante $e$ bafin Logarithmorum hyperbolicorum : fcripto ergo pro $z$ partim $+ v\sqrt{-1}$ partim $- v\sqrt{-1}$ erit *cof.* $v =$

$$\frac{e^{+v\sqrt{-1}} + e^{-v\sqrt{-1}}}{2} \quad \& \textit{fin.} v = \frac{e^{+v\sqrt{-1}} - e^{-v\sqrt{-1}}}{2\sqrt{-1}}.$$

Ex quibus intelligitur quomodo quantitates exponentiales imaginariæ ad Sinus & Cofinus Arcuum realium reducantur. Erit vero $e^{+v\sqrt{-1}} = \textit{cof.} v + \sqrt{-1}.\textit{fin.} v$ & $e^{-v\sqrt{-1}} = \textit{cof.} v - \sqrt{-1}.\textit{fin.} v$.

138. Again let $z$ be an infinitely small arc in the formulae of §133, and let $n$ be an infinitely large number $i$, so that $iz$ takes the finite value $v$. Therefore we will have $nz = v$, and $z = \frac{v}{i}$, whence $\sin z = \frac{v}{i}$ and $\cos z = 1$; making these substitutions, [104] $\cos v = \dfrac{\left(1 + \frac{v\sqrt{-1}}{i}\right)^i + \left(1 - \frac{v\sqrt{-1}}{i}\right)^i}{2}$

and $\sin v = \dfrac{\left(1 + \frac{v\sqrt{-1}}{i}\right)^i - \left(1 - \frac{v\sqrt{-1}}{i}\right)^i}{2\sqrt{-1}}$. Moreover, in the preceding chapter we have

seen that $\left(1 + \frac{z}{i}\right)^i = e^z$, with $e$ denoting the base of hyperbolic logarithms: therefore

writing for $z$ first $+v\sqrt{-1}$ and then $-v\sqrt{-1}$ we will have $\cos v = \dfrac{e^{+v\sqrt{-1}} + e^{-v\sqrt{-1}}}{2}$,

and $\sin v = \dfrac{e^{+v\sqrt{-1}} - e^{-v\sqrt{-1}}}{2\sqrt{-1}}$. From which it may be understood how imaginary exponential quantities may be reduced to real sines and cosines. Indeed we will have $e^{+v\sqrt{-1}} = \cos v + \sqrt{-1}\sin v$ and $e^{-v\sqrt{-1}} = \cos v - \sqrt{-1}\sin v$.

---

## 9.3 NINETEENTH-CENTURY DEFINITIONS OF FUNCTION

Euler's 1755 definition of a function, as *any* relationship between two quantities, was by no means universally accepted even for much of the nineteenth century. Lagrange, for example, in the introduction to his *Théorie des fonctions analytiques* in 1813, offered something very close to Euler's 1748 definition of a function as a formal expression (and it was clear from his context that it might be finite or infinite, see 10.2.4). Augustin-Louis Cauchy, rightly credited as one of the first mathematicians to establish analysis on secure foundations, was innovative in very many ways, but was also an adept borrower, and in his 1821 textbook *Cours d'analyse*, he too adopted Euler's definition of 1748, relying on an *expression* that connects the variables:[9]

When variable quantities are so disposed amongst themselves that, the value of one of them being given, one may deduce the values of all the others, one generally conceives the various quantities to be expressed in terms of one of them, which thus takes the name of *independent variable*; and the other quantities expressed in terms of that independent variable are what one calls functions of that variable.

9. 'Lorsque des quantités variables sont tellement liées entre elles que, la valeur de l'une d'elles étant donnée, on puisse en conclure les valeurs de toutes les autres, on conçoit d'ordinaire ces diverses quantités exprimées au moyen de l'une d'entre elles, qui prend alors le nom de *variable indépendente* et les autres quantités exprimées au moyen de la variable indépendent sont ce qu'on appelle des fonctions de cette variable.' Cauchy 1821, §1.

Cauchy's examples immediately afterwards show that he had in mind functions very similar to those offered by Euler: $\log x$, $\sin x$, $x + y$, $x^y$, and so on. Like Euler, he distinguished between explicit and implicit functions, and also allowed multiple-valued functions, for which he invented a special double-bracket notation, for example, $\text{arcsin}((x))$ to indicate all possible values of $\text{arcsin}\, x$.

The same definition of a function as an expression was still in circulation very much later in the nineteenth century. It appeared, for example, in Eduard Heine's 'Die Elemente der Functionenlehre' ('The elements of function theory') in 1872, though by now multiple values had finally been eliminated:[10]

*Definition.   A single-valued function* of a variable $x$ is an expression, which is unambiguously defined for every rational or irrational value of $x$.

Other mathematicians, however, preferred Euler's 1755 definition. The French text-book writer Silvestre François Lacroix, writing in 1797, was keenly aware of the recent history of mathematics, and on the opening page of his *Traité du calcul*, succinctly summarized the changes of thought that had taken place in the previous century, and gave an up-to-date definition.[11]

The older analysts understood in general under the name of *functions* of a quantity, all the powers of that quantity. Following that, one understood the meaning of this word as applying to the result of various algebraic operations: thus one still called a *function* of one or more quantities every algebraic expression involving in any way sums, products, quotients, power and roots of these quantities. Finally, new ideas brought about by the progress of analysis, have given place to the following definition of functions:

*Every quantity of which the value depends on one or more other quantities, is said to be a* function *of these others, whether one knows or is ignorant of the operations one must carry out to create the former from the latter.*

Despite the huge influence of Cauchy, the most important of the mid-nineteenth-century definitions (for example, those given by Dirichlet in 1837 and by Weierstrass in 1861)[12] were usually closer to Euler's 1755 definition than to Cauchy's. Fourier's various definitions make a particularly interesting case study because they display a medley of contemporary concepts. To begin with, Fourier assumed, like Euler in 1748 (see 9.1.3),

---

10. '*Definition. Einwerthige Function* einer Veränderlichen $x$ heisst ein Ausdruck, der für jeden einzelnen rationalen oder irrationalen Werth von $x$ eindeutig definirt ist.' Heine 1872, 180.

11. 'Les anciens Analystes comprenaient en général sous la dénomination de *fonctions* d'une quantité, toutes les puissances de cette quantité. Dans la suite on a étendu le sens de ce mot, en l'appliquant aux résultats des diverses opérations algébriques: ainsi on a encore appelé *fonction* d'une ou de plusieurs quantités, toute expression algébrique renfermant d'une manière quelconque des sommes, des produits, des quotiens, des puissances et des racines de ces quantités. Enfin de nouvelles idées, amenées par les progrès de l'analyse, ont donnée lieu à la définition suivante des fonctions.

*Toute quantité dont la valeur dépend d'une ou de plusieurs autres quantités, est dite* fonction *de ces dernières, soit qu'on sache ou qu'on ignore par quelles opérations il faut passer pour remonter de celles-ci à la première.'* Lacroix, *Traité du calcul*, 1797, I, 1.

12. For Dirichlet see Youschkevitch 1967, 78; for Weierstrass see Dugac 1973, 63.

that any curve could be regarded as a function, but at the same time he set out to find a single expression that would represent it:[13]

... the line that bounds the ordinates proportional to the temperatures at different points will continually change its form. The problem is to express the variable form of this curve by an equation, and thus to contain in a single formula all the successive states of the solid.

Fourier used the language of functions throughout his *Théorie analytique de la chaleur*, expecting the reader to understand the terminology without any need for definition. Only in the final pages of the book, when it had become clear that his trigonometric series could represent some very strange-looking 'curves', did he introduce the following description, now widely quoted but for Fourier himself something of an afterthought:[14]

In general, the function $f(x)$ represents a series of values, or ordinates, each of which is arbitrary. The abscissa may take an infinite number of values, and there are the same number of ordinates $f(x)$. All have *for the time being* numerical values, positive, negative, or zero. One does not at all suppose that the ordinates are subject to a common law: they succeed each other in any manner whatsoever, and each is given as if it were a single quantity.

From all this it can be concluded that for most of the nineteenth century, definitions of function, though varying considerably from writer to writer, were based almost entirely on those offered by Euler in the mid-eighteenth century, with very little essential change. Only very late in the nineteenth century did a definition appear that looks to us more modern and more precise, and it emerged in a new context, that of defining real numbers (of which we shall see much more in Chapter 16).

### 9.3.1 A definition from Dedekind, 1888

The final definition of function in this chapter is taken from Dedekind's seminal essay *Was sind und was sollen die Zahlen?* (*What are numbers and what should they be?*) of 1888 (see also 16.3.2 and 18.2.2). Dedekind's description is very close to the modern idea of a function as a mapping: a literal translation of *Abbildung* is 'image', or 'representation', a very different and much more precise concept than the loosely defined relationship between quantities envisaged by Euler and his successors. For Dedekind, an element and its image do not even need to be quantities; they may be objects or simply names. Nevertheless, there is a strong sense of historical continuity in Dedekind's notation for the image of an element, essentially the same as that invented by Johann Bernoulli 170 years earlier.

---

13. '... la ligne qui termine les ordonnées proportionelles aux températures des différents points, changera continuellement de forme. La question consiste à exprimer, par une équation, la forme variable de cette courbe, et à comprendre ainsi dans une seule formule tous les états successifs du solide.' Fourier 1822, §3.

14. 'En général, la fonction $f(x)$ réprésente une suite de valeurs, ou ordonneés, dont chacune est arbitraire. L'abscisse se pouvant recevoir une infinité des valeurs, il y a un pareil nombre d'ordonées $f(x)$. Toutes ont des valeurs numériques *actuelles*, ou positives, ou négatives, ou nulles. On ne suppose point que ces ordonneés soient assujetties à une loi commune: elles se succèdent d'une manière quelconque, et chacune d'elles est donnée comme le serait une seule quantité.' Fourier 1822, §417.

# Dedekind's definition of a function

from Dedekind, *Was sind und was sollen die Zahlen?*, 1888; from *Gesammelte mathematische Werke*, 1930–32, III, 348

— 348 —

§ 2.

Abbildung eines Systems.

21. Erklärung\*). Unter einer Abbildung φ eines Systems $S$ wird ein Gesetz verstanden, nach welchem zu jedem bestimmten Element $s$ von $S$ ein bestimmtes Ding gehört, welches das Bild von $s$ heißt und mit φ$(s)$ bezeichnet wird; wir sagen auch, daß φ$(s)$ dem Element $s$ entspricht, daß φ$(s)$ durch die Abbildung φ aus $s$ entsteht oder erzeugt wird, daß $s$ durch die Abbildung φ in φ$(s)$ übergeht. Ist nun $T$ irgendein Teil von $S$, so ist in der Abbildung φ von $S$ zugleich eine bestimmte Abbildung von $T$ enthalten, welche der Einfachheit wegen wohl mit demselben Zeichen φ bezeichnet werden darf und darin besteht, daß jedem Elemente $t$ des Systems $T$ dasselbe Bild φ$(t)$ entspricht, welches $t$ als Element von $S$ besitzt; zugleich soll das System, welches aus allen Bildern φ$(t)$ besteht, das Bild von $T$ heißen und mit φ$(T)$ bezeichnet werden, wodurch auch die Bedeutung von φ$(S)$ erklärt ist. Als ein Beispiel einer Abbildung eines Systems ist schon die Belegung seiner Elemente mit bestimmten Zeichen oder Namen anzusehen. Die einfachste Abbildung eines Systems ist diejenige, durch welche jedes seiner Elemente in sich selbst übergeht; sie soll die identische Abbildung des Systems heißen. Der Bequemlichkeit halber wollen wir in den folgenden Sätzen 22, 23, 24, die sich auf eine beliebige Abbildung φ eines beliebigen Systems $S$ beziehen, die Bilder von Elementen $s$ und Teilen $T$ entsprechend durch $s'$ und $T'$ bezeichnen; außerdem setzen wir fest, daß kleine und große lateinische Buchstaben ohne Akzent immer Elemente und Teile dieses Systems $S$ bedeuten sollen.

## §2.
### *Mapping a system*

21. *Explanation.* By a *mapping* $\varphi$ of a system $S$ we understand a law, by which to every determined element $s$ of $S$ there *belongs* a determined object, which is called the *image* of $s$ and will be denoted by $\varphi(s)$; we say also, that $\varphi(s)$ *corresponds* to the element $s$, that $\varphi(s)$ *results* or *is produced* from $s$ by the mapping $\varphi$, that $s$ is *transformed* to $\varphi(s)$ by the mapping $\varphi$. If now $T$ is an arbitrary part of $S$, then in the mapping $\varphi$ of $S$ there is at the same time contained a determined mapping of $T$, which for the sake of simplicity may be denoted by the same symbol $\varphi$ and consists of this, that to every element $t$ of the system $T$ there corresponds the same image $\varphi(t)$, which $t$ has as an element of $S$; at the same time the system that consists of all images $\varphi(t)$ will be called the *image* of $T$ and will be denoted by $\varphi(T)$, by which the meaning of $\varphi(S)$ is also explained. As an example of a mapping of a system we may already regard the association of its elements with determined symbols or names. The simplest mapping of a system is that by which each of its elements is transformed into itself; this will be called the *identical* mapping of the system. For convenience in the following theorems, 22, 23, 24, which refer to an arbitrary mapping $\varphi$ of an arbitrary system $S$, the images of elements $s$ and parts $T$ will be denoted respectively by $s'$ and $T'$; in addition we will specify that small and capital italic letters without accent will always signify elements and parts of this system $S$.

CHAPTER 10

# MAKING CALCULUS WORK

There is deliberate double meaning in the title of this chapter, in an attempt to capture both the usefulness and the vulnerability of calculus as it was understood and used in the eighteenth century. Almost as soon as it was created, calculus was seen as an invaluable tool for handling physical problems, and as familiarity with it grew it was put to use in a wide variety of ways, many of them far removed from the tangent and quadrature questions that had first given rise to it. In the first half of this chapter, there are two important examples of such applications, and to these may be added several others to be found elsewhere in this book: Leibniz's refraction problem in his very first paper on the calculus in 1684 (4.2.1); de Moivre's calculation of confidence intervals in 1738 (7.2.1); Laplace's model of planetary perturbation in 1787 (17.1.3); and Fourier's theory of heat diffusion in 1822 (8.4.1).

The sheer usefulness of calculus helped to drive it forward, but at the same time it was widely recognized that the foundations were not secure. The arguments that went on in the seventeenth century as to whether infinitely small quantities were 'something' or 'nothing', and the evasion of those arguments by those who found them too abstruse, spilled over into the eighteenth century and began to cause controversy even outside mathematics. Hence, the second half of this chapter, and the second interpretation of its title: the struggle to establish calculus as an indisputably rigorous method.

## 10.1 USES OF CALCULUS

### 10.1.1 Jacob Bernoulli's curve of uniform descent, 1690

The power of the Leibnizian calculus became apparent within just a few years of its first publication, through a series of challenge problems discussed between Huygens and the Bernoulli brothers, Jacob and Johann, in the pages of the *Acta eruditorum*. The solutions put forward by Huygens were generally of a traditional geometric kind, but the Bernoullis rapidly learned to apply the methods of differential and integral calculus. The first of these problems was posed by Leibniz himself: to find the curve traced by a body falling under gravity through equal vertical distances in equal times. Jacob Bernoulli's solution, given below, was published in the *Acta eruditorum* in May 1690.

---

**Jacob Bernoulli's curve of uniform descent**

from Jacob Bernoulli, 'Analysis problematis antehac propositi',
*Acta eruditorum* (1690), 217–219

---

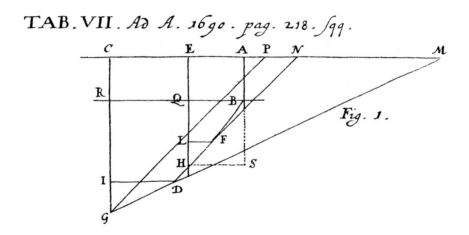

TAB. VII. *Ad A. 1690 . pag. 218 . ∫qq .*

*Fig. 1.*

*J.B. ANALYSIS PROBLEMATIS ANTEHAC PROPOSITI,
de inventione lineæ defcenfus a corpore gravi percurrendæ uniformiter, fic ut temporibus æqualibus æquales altitudines emetiatur: & alterius cujusdam Problematis Propofitio.*

Ec                                                  Solu-

218
## ACTA ERUDITORUM

SOlutionem Problematis nudam dedit Ill. Hugenius in Nov. Rote-rod. Hanc poftea excepit in Act.Lipf. A.1689. p. 195. fqq. celeb. Auctoris Demonftratio Synthetica. Analyfin, quam fuppreffit uterq;, ipfius Auctoris calculo differentiali inftitutam nunc pando, eum in finem, ut Virum Cel. ad par officii genus publico præftandum, tentandamque fua Methodo Problematis deinceps proponendi folutionem invitem.

TAB.VII.      Intelligatur grave demiffum ab A per curvam quæfitam BFG,
Fig. 1.  in qua fumtæ fint particulæ infinite parvæ, adeoque pro rectis habendæ DG, FH, altitudinum æqualium GI, HL, eæque producantur in M, N, ut fiant Tangentes GM, HN, ipfique HN parallela ducatur GP. Celeritates gravis acquifitæ in G & H eædem funt, cum iis quas acquireret defcendendo perpendiculariter ab eadem linea horizontali AC, per rectas CG, EH, quæ quidem funt Quadrata ipfarum celeritatum, ut notum. Quibus pofitis,

CG. EH :: Quad. Celerit. in G. Quad. Cel. in H :: DGq. FHq :: DGq. GIq ✛ GIq (HLq). FHq :: GMq. GCq ✛ HEq. HNq :: GMq. GCq ✛ GCq. GPq :: GMq. GPq. Unde Problema ad puram Geometriam reductum huc redit: Datis pofitione recta AC & puncto A invenire curvam BHG, talem ut applicata CG ad applicatam EH rationem habeat duplicatâ ejus, quam habet tangens GM ad rectam GP parallelam tangenti HN. Patet autem, rectam AC, ad quam applicantur CG, EH, non poffe effe axem curvæ, nec A verticem; cum alias applicata ad punctum A evanefceret, ac proinde applicatarum ratio fieret infinite magna, ejufdem fubduplicata manente finita.

q.e.a. | HL.    HF    :: GC. GP    | a. y :: bbdyq. aadxq ✛
Anal. CG=a | dy. $\sqrt{dxq \mathbin{\text{✛}} dyq}$ :: a.a $\sqrt{dxq \mathbin{\text{✛}} dyq}$ | aadyq,
   GM=b |           $\frac{}{dyq}$ | bb y d y q = a³ d x q ✛
   AE=x | CG. EH :: GMq. GPq | a³ d y q,
     |    | bb y d y q — a³ d y q =
   EH=y | a . y :: bb . aadxq ✛ aadyq | a³dxq,
   |       $\frac{}{dyq}$ | dy $\sqrt{bby-a^3}$ =dx $\sqrt{a^3}$

Ergo & horum Integralia æquantur, np. $\frac{2bby - 2a3}{3bb} \sqrt{bby - a^3} = x$

$\sqrt{a^3}$; pofitoque $y - \frac{a^3}{bb} = Z$, habetur $\frac{2}{3} Z \sqrt{bbz} = x \sqrt{a^3}$ | $\frac{4}{9} bb z^3 =$

                            a³xx

## MENSIS MAJI A. M DC LXXXX.    219

$$a^3xx \mid z\,3 = \frac{9\,a^3\,xx}{4\,bb} :$$ quare demiſſa ex A perpendiculari A B $= \frac{a^3}{bb}$, du-

ctaque BR parallela ipſi AC, ſi vertice B, axe BR & latere recto $\frac{9\,a^3}{4bb}$

ſeu $\frac{9}{4}$ AB, deſcribatur Curva Paraboloidica BHG ejus naturæ, ut ſo-
lidum ex latere recto in Quadratum abſciſſæ æquetur cubo applicatæ, habetur quæſitum.    Porro quia per curvam BHG deſcendens
grave temporibus æqualibus æquales altitudines percurrit, tantundem eſt quoad deſcenſus altitudinem, ac ſi celeritate in B acquiſita
deinceps uniformiter deſcenderet per BS; quo caſu conſtat, eodem
tempore duplo plus ſpatii confici, quam conficitur motu a quiete
æqualiter accelerato; adeoque ſi BS dupla ſumatur ipſius AB, fore tempus deſcenſus per BH poſt AB = tempori per AB.
    Problema viciſſim proponendum hoc eſto:
*Invenire, quam curvam referat funis laxus & inter duo puncta fixa
libere ſuſpenſus.* Sumo autem, funem eſſe lineam in omnibus ſuis
partibus facillime flexilem.

*Notation*

Bernoulli used Oughtred's notation for squares, for example, $DGq$ for $DG$-squared, and also
for ratios, for example, $A.B :: C.D$ where we would now write $A : B = C : D$. To a modern
reader the most unfamiliar (and confusing) of Bernoulli's symbols is his large $+$ to indicate
multiplication of ratios: what Bernoulli wrote as $A.B + C.D$ would now be written as $\frac{A}{B} \times \frac{C}{D}$. To
avoid confusion with the $+$ sign as used for addition (which also appears in Bernoulli's paper),
I have replaced his large $+$ where appropriate by $[\times]$.

### TRANSLATION

*ANALYSIS BY J. B. OF A PROBLEM PREVIOUSLY PROPOSED, for finding the line of
descent of a body falling uniformly under gravity, in such a way that in equal times it
measures out equal distances: and the proposition of another problem of this kind.*
[218] The illustrious Huygens gave an outline solution to this problem in November.
That celebrated author afterwards showed it by a synthetic [geometric] demonstration
in the *Acta*, 1689, p. 195 onwards. I now offer an analytic foundation, which he sup-
pressed in both cases, for the differential calculus of that author, in order that I might
invite that celebrated man to perform the same kind of public duty, persuading by the
method of the problem after proposing the solution.

TAB. VII.
*Fig. 1.*

    There is to be understood [a body] falling under gravity starting from $A$ along the
sought curve $BFG$, in which there are taken infinitely small parts, represented by the
lines $DG$, $FH$, of equal altitudes $GI$, $HL$; and these are produced to $M$, $N$, to give
tangents $GM$, $HN$; and $GP$ is drawn parallel to $HN$. The speeds acquired under gravity
at $G$ and $H$ are the same as those it would acquire descending perpendicularly from

the same horizontal line *AC*, along the lines *CG*, *EH*, which indeed are the squares of those speeds, as is known. Given which,

*CG.EH* :: square of speed at *G*. square of speed at *H* :: *DGq.FHq* :: *DGq.GIq*[×] *GIq*([=]*HLq*).*FHq* :: *GMq.GCq*[×]*HEq.HNq* :: *GMq.GCq*[×]*GCq.GPq* :: *GMq.GPq*. Whence the problem is now reduced to pure geometry: given the position of the line *AC* and the point *A*, find the curve *BHG* such that the ratio of the ordinate *CG* to the ordinate *EH* is the square of that of the tangent *GM* to the line *GP*, parallel to the tangent *HN*. Moreover, it is clear that the line *AC*, to which are applied the ordinates *CG*, *EH*, cannot be the axis of the curve, nor *A* its vertex; since otherwise the ordinate at the point *A* would vanish, and hence the ratio of the ordinates would become infinitely large, while its square root remained finite.
What is to be analysed.

*Analysis*

$$CG = a$$

$$GM = b$$

$$AE = x$$

$$EH = y$$

$$HL.HF :: GC.GP$$

$$dy.\sqrt{dx_q + dy_q} :: a.a\sqrt{\frac{dx_q + dy_q}{dy_q}}$$

$$CG.EH :: GMq.GPq$$

$$a.y :: bb.\frac{aadx_q + aady_q}{dy_q},$$

$$a.y :: bbdy_q.aadx_q + aady_q,$$

$$bbydy_q = a^3 dx_q + a^3 dy_q,$$

$$bbydy_q - a^3 dy_q = a^3 dx_q,$$

$$dy\sqrt{bby - a^3} = dx\sqrt{a^3}.$$

Therefore also the integrals of these are equal, thus

$$\frac{2bby - 2a^3}{3bb}\sqrt{bby - a^3} = x\sqrt{a^3};$$

and putting $y - \dfrac{a^3}{bb} = z$ we have

$$\frac{2}{3}z\sqrt{bbz} = x\sqrt{a^3}$$

$$\frac{4}{9}bbz^3 = a^3xx$$

$$z^3 = \frac{9a^3xx}{4bb}$$

[219] whence taking a perpendicular $AB = \dfrac{a^3}{bb}$ from $A$ and taking $BR$ parallel to $AC$,

if the vertex is $B$, the axis $BR$ and the *latus rectum* $\dfrac{9a^3}{4bb}$ or $\frac{9}{4}AB$, there is described a parabolic curve $BHG$, of such a kind that the solid formed from the *latus rectum* multiplied by the square of the abscissa equals the cube of the ordinates, and we have what is sought. Then because descending by gravity along the curve $BHG$, [the body] runs through equal altitudes in equal times, it is just as if it falls vertically, and as if from the speed acquired at $B$ it then falls uniformly through $BS$; which being so, in the same time it completes twice as much distance as in the motion under uniform acceleration from rest; therefore if $BS$ is taken to be twice $AB$, then the time of descent along $BH$ after $AB =$ time along $AB$.

The problem proposed in turn is this:

*To find the curve given by a loose rope hanging freely between two fixed points.* I take the rope to be a line perfectly flexible throughout.

---

### 10.1.2  D'Alembert and the wave equation, 1747

In 1747 Jean le Rond d'Alembert published the first derivation of the wave equation. For a point on a vibrating string at distance $s$ from the origin and at time $t$, the displacement may be written as $y = \varphi(t, s)$. D'Alembert deduced that the accelerating force $\dfrac{\partial^2 y}{\partial t^2}$ is proportional to $\dfrac{\partial^2 y}{\partial s^2}$. He also observed that, when the constant of proportionality is made equal to 1, the solution must be of the general form

$$y = \Psi(t + s) + \Gamma(t - s).$$

for arbitrary functions $\Psi$ and $\Gamma$, and he showed that for a stopped string this is a periodic solution.

D'Alembert used a number of partial derivatives without explaining them as such, so it may be helpful to interpret his notation as follows: $p = \dfrac{\partial \varphi}{\partial t}$, $q = \dfrac{\partial \varphi}{\partial s}$, $\alpha = \dfrac{\partial^2 \varphi}{\partial t^2}$, and $\beta = \dfrac{\partial^2 \varphi}{\partial s^2}$. Euler's theorem, as referred to by d'Alembert in §II, is that $\dfrac{\partial^2 \varphi}{\partial s \partial t} = \dfrac{\partial^2 \varphi}{\partial t \partial s}$ (= d'Alembert's $v$). D'Alembert's form of the wave equation (in §V) is that $\alpha$ is proportional to $\beta$.

The importance of d'Alembert's work was recognized immediately, and within a year Euler had confirmed both the equation and the solution, by a rather more sophisticated derivation.[1] The vibrating string problem and its solutions had important repercussions far beyond the practical implications, leading to a much deeper understanding both of the nature of functions (see 9.1.3) and of continuity and differentiability (see 11.2.2). Here, however, we give only the mechanical derivation.

---

1. Euler 1748b.

## D'Alembert's derivation of the wave equation

from D'Alembert, 'Recherches sur la courbe que forme une corde tendüe mise en vibration', *Histoire de l'Académie des Sciences à Berlin*, (1747), 214–217

# RECHERCHES

## SUR LA COURBE QUE FORME UNE CORDE

### TENDUË MISE EN VIBRATION,

### PAR MR. D'ALEMBERT.

## I.

Je me propofe de faire voir dans ce Memoire, qu'il y a une infinité d'autres courbes que *la Compagne de la Cycloide allongée*, qui fatisfont au Probleme dont il s'agit. Je fuppoferay toujours 1<sup>mo</sup>, que les excurfions ou vibrations de la corde font fort petites, enforte que les arcs A M de la courbe qu'elle forme, puiffent toujours être fuppofés fenfiblement égaux aux abfciffes correfpondantes A P. 2°. que la corde eft uniformement epaiffe dans toute fa longueur: 3°. que la force F de la tenfion eft au poids de la corde, en raifon conftante, c. a. d. comme *m* à 1; d'où il s'enfuit que fi on nomme *p* la gravité, & *l* la longueur de la corde, on pourra fuppofer $F = p m l$; 4°. que fi on nomme A P ou A M, *s*; P M, *y*; & qu'on faffe *d s* conftante, la force acceleratrice du point M fuivant M P, eft $- \dfrac{F \, d \, d \, y}{d \, s^2}$, fi la

*Fig. 1.*

courbe eft concave vers A C, ou $\dfrac{F \, d \, d \, y}{d \, s^2}$ fi elle eft convexe. *Voyez Taylor Meth. Incr.*

II. Cela

✳  215  ✳

*Fig. 2.*

II. Cela posé, imaginons que M $m$, $m$ $n$, soyent deux côtés consecutifs de la courbe dans un instant quelconque, & que P $p$ = $p$ $\pi$, c. à. d. que $ds$ soit constant. Soit $t$ le tems écoulé depuis que la corde a commencé à entrer en vibration: il est certain que l'ordonnée P M ne peut etre exprimée que par une fonction du tems $t$, & de l'abscisse ou de l'arc correspondant $s$ ou A P. Soit donc P M = $\varphi$ $(t, s,)$ c. à. d. egale à une fonction inconnuë de $t$, & de $s$; on fera $d[\varphi (t, s,] = p\,dt + q\,ds$, $p$, & $q$ etant pareillement des fonctions inconnuës de $t$ & de $s$; or il est evident par le Theor. de Mr. Euler, Tom. VII. des Mem. de Petersb. p. 177, que le coëfficient de $ds$ dans la differentielle de $p$ doit etre egal au coëfficient de $dt$ dans la differentielle de $q$; soit donc $dp = \alpha\,dt + v\,ds$, on aura $dq = v\,dt + b\,ds$, $\alpha$, $v$, $\beta$, etant encore des fonctions inconnuës de $t$ & de $s$.

III. De là il s'ensuit, que comme les cotés M $m$, $m$ $n$, appartiennent à la même courbe, on aura $p$ $m$ — P M egale à la difference de $\varphi (t, s,)$ en ne faisant varier que $s$, c. à. d. que $p$ $m$ — P M = $q\,ds = ds$ . $q$; & que la quantité que nous avons nommé cy-dessus $ddy$, c. a. d. la difference seconde de P M, prise en ne faisant varier que $s$, sera $ds$ . $b\,ds$, on aura donc $\dfrac{F\,ddy}{ds^2} = F \beta$.

*Fig. 3.*

IV. Imaginons presentement que les points M, $m$, $n$ viennent en M$'$, $m'$, $n'$; il est certain que l'excés de P M$'$ sur P M sera egal à la difference de $\varphi (t, s,)$ prise en ne faisant varier que $t$, c. à. d. que P M$'$ — P M = $p\,dt = dt$ . $p$; & que la difference seconde de P M prise en ne faisant varier que $t$, c. à. d. la difference de M M$'$, ou ce qui est la même chose, l'espace parcouru par le point M en vertu de la force acceleratrice qui l'anime, sera = $\alpha\,dt$.

V. Cela posé, soit $a$ l'espace qu'un corps pesant animé de la gravité $p$, parcourreroit dans un tems donné & constant $\theta$: il est evident que l'on aura (par le Lem. XI. Sect. I. Liv. I. Princ. Math.) $\alpha\,ds^2$:

## 🕸 216 🕸

$$\alpha\, d t^2 : 2a = F\beta\, d t^2 : p\,\theta^2, \text{ donc } \alpha = \frac{2\,a\,F\,\beta}{p\,\vartheta^2} = \frac{2\,a\,p\,m\,l\,\beta}{p\,\vartheta^2} =$$

$$\beta \quad . \quad \frac{2\,a\,m\,l}{\vartheta^2}.$$

VI. Nous remarquerons d'abord, que l'on peut repréfenter le tems donné $\theta$ par une ligne conftante de telle grandeur que l'on voudra : il faudra feulement avoir foin de prendre, pour exprimer les parties variables & indeterminées du tems, des lignes $t$ qui foyent à la ligne qu'on aura prife pour marquer $\theta$, dans le rapport de ces parties variables du tems au tems conftant & donné, pendant lequel un corps pefant parcourt l'efpace $a$. On pourra donc fuppofer $\theta$ telle, que $\vartheta^2 = 2\,a\,m\,l$ : & en ce cas on aura $\alpha = \beta$. Donc puis-que $d p = \alpha\, d t + v\, d s$, il faut que $d q$ ou $v\, d t + \beta\, d s$ foit $= v\, d t + \alpha\, d s$.

VII. Pour déterminer par ces conditions les quantités $\alpha$ & $v$, on remarquera, que comme $d p = \alpha\, d t + v\, d s$, & $d q = v\, d t + \alpha\, d s$, on aura $d p + d q = (\alpha + v) . (d t + d s)$; & $d p - d q = (\alpha - v) . (d t - d s)$. d'où il s'enfuit

$1^o$, que $\alpha + v$ eft egale à une fonction de $t + s$, & que $\alpha - v$ eft egal a une fonction de $t - s$.

$2^o$. Que par confequent on aura $p = \dfrac{\Phi\,(t+s) + \Delta\,(t-s)}{2}$

ou fimplement $= \Phi\,(t+s) + \Delta\,(t-s)$; & $q = \Phi\,(t+s) - \Delta\,(t-s)$, d'où l'on tire P M ou $s\,(p\, d t + q\, d s) = \psi\,(t+s) + \Gamma\,(t-s)$, $\psi\,(t+s)$ & $\Gamma\,(t-s)$ exprimant des fonctions encore inconnuës de $t+s$ & de $t-s$.
l'equation generale de la courbe eft donc

$$y = \psi\,(t+s) + \Gamma\,(t-s).$$

VIII.

❈  217  ❈

VIII. Or il est aisé de voir que cette equation renferme une
infinité de courbes.  Pour le faire voir, ne prenons icy qu'un cas
particulier, savoir celui, où $y = o$, quand $s = o$; c. à. d. supposons que la corde, lorsqu'elle commence à entrer en vibration, soit
etenduë en ligne droite, & qu'elle soit forcée à sortir de son etat de
repos, par l'action de quelque cause que ce puisse etre; il est evident
que l'on aura $\psi s + \Gamma - s = o$, donc $\Gamma - s = - \psi s$.
De plus, comme la corde passe toujours par les points fixes A & B,
il faut que $s = o$, & $s = l$, rendent $y = o$, quelle que soit $t$;
donc 1°. $\psi t + \Gamma t = o$, & $\Gamma t = - \psi t$; donc $\Gamma (t - s) = -$
$\psi (t - s)$; donc on aura $y = \psi (t + s) - \psi (t - s)$; donc il faut
que $- \psi - s = \Gamma s = - \psi s$; donc $\psi s$ doit etre une fonction de $s$
dans laquelle il n'entre que des puissances paires, lorsqu'on l'aura
reduite en serie.  2°. De plus la condition de $y = o$ lorsque $s = l$,
donne $\psi (t + l) - \psi (t - l) = o$.  Il faut donc trouver une
quantité $\psi (t + s)$, telle, que $\psi s - \psi - s = o$ & $\psi (t + l)$
$- \psi (t - l) = o$.

IX. Pour y parvenir, imaginons la courbe $t o$ T, dont les     Fig. 4.
coordonnées soyent T R $= u$, Q R $= z$, & qui soyent telles,  que
$u = \psi z$; cela posé puisque $\psi s - \psi - s$ doit etre egale à zero,
il est evident qu'en prenant Q $r =$ Q R, il faut que $r t =$ R T; &
qu'ainsi la courbe $t o$ T aura, de part & d'autre du point $o$, des portions semblables & egales, $t o$, $o$ T.  De plus, comme $\psi (t + l)$
doit etre $=$ à $\psi (t - l)$ & que la difference de $t + l$ & de $t - l$ est $2l$,
il est evident que la courbe $t o$ T doit etre telle, qu'etant supposée en-
tierement decrite, deux ordonnées quelconques distantes l'une de
l'autre de la quantité $2l$, soyent egales entr'elles.  Donc si on suppose
Q R $= l$, on verra que la partie T K doit etre egale & semblable
à $t$ O; que la partie K X doit etre aussi egale & semblable à $o$ T &c.;
& comme les parties $t$ O, $o$ T, sont deja semblables & egales, il
s'ensuit que la courbe cherchée s'etend à l'infini des   deux
côtes du point $o$, & qu'elle est composée de parties toutes egales &
semblables à la partie $o$ T K, dont l'abscisse Q V $= 2l$, &  qui est

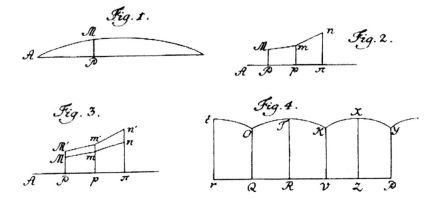

Fig. 1.

Fig. 2.

Fig. 3.

Fig. 4.

*Notation*

D'Alembert sometimes used $s$ as an integral sign, even though it was also in use as a variable; in the translation below, $s$ as an integral sign has been replaced by the symbol $\int$. Also, where we would now write $\Psi(-s)$, D'Alembert wrote $\Psi - s$; to avoid ambiguity in such cases I have inserted square brackets, thus, $\Psi[-s]$.

TRANSLATION

RESEARCH ON THE CURVE FORMED BY A TAUT STRING
SET IN VIBRATION,
BY MONSIEUR D'ALEMBERT.

I.

I propose to show in this Memoir, that there is an infinity of curves other than the *collection of elongated cycloids*, which satisfy the problem in question. I will always suppose, first, that the movements or vibrations of the string are very small, so that the arcs $AM$ of the curve that is formed may always be supposed essentially equal to the corresponding abscissas $AP$. Second, that the string is uniformly thick along its whole length. Third, that the tension force $F$ is in a constant ratio to the weight of the string, that is, as $m$ to 1; from which it follows that if one calls gravity $p$, and the length of the string $l$, one may suppose $F = pml$. Fourth, that if one denotes $AP$ or $AM$ by $s$, and $PM$ by $y$, and makes $ds$ constant, the accelerating force at the point $M$ in the direction $MP$ is $-\dfrac{Fddy}{ds^2}$, if the curve is concave towards $AC$, or $\dfrac{Fddy}{ds^2}$ if it is convex. *See Taylor Meth.[odus] Incr.[ementorum].* [215] II. That said, let us imagine that $Mm$, $mn$, are two consecutive segments of the curve at any instant, and that $Pp = p\pi$, that is to say, that $ds$ is constant. Let $t$ be the time passed since the string began to vibrate; certainly the ordinate $PM$ can be expressed as a function of the time $t$ and the abscissa or corresponding arc $s$ or $AP$, only. Therefore let $PM = \varphi(t, s, )$, that is to say, equal to an unknown function of $t$ and $s$; put $d[\varphi(t, s, )] = pdt + qds$, where $p$ and $q$ are in the same way unknown functions of $t$ and $s$; now it is clear from the Theorem of Monsieur Euler, Vol. VII. of the Memoirs of St Petersburg, p. 177, that the coefficient of $ds$ in the differential of $p$ must be equal to the coefficient of $dt$ in the differential of $q$; therefore if $dp = \alpha dt + v ds$, one will have $dq = v dt + \beta ds$, with $\alpha, v, \beta$, being again unknown functions of $t$ and of $s$.

III. From this it follows that, since the segments $Mm$, $mn$, belong to the same curve, one will have $pm - PM$ equal to the difference of $\varphi(t, s, )$ letting only $s$ vary, that is to say, that $pm - PM = qds = ds.q$; and that the quantity that we have called until now $ddy$, that is to say, the second difference of $PM$, taken by letting only $s$ vary, will be $ds.\beta ds$; one will therefore have $\dfrac{Fddy}{ds^2} = F\beta$.

IV. Let us now imagine that the points $M$, $m$, $n$ become $M'$, $m'$, $n'$; certainly the excess of $PM'$ over $PM$ will be equal to the difference of $\varphi(t, s, )$ taken by letting only $t$ vary, that is to say, that $PM' - PM = p\,dt = dt.p$; and that the second difference of $PM$, taken by letting only $t$ vary, that is to say, the difference $MM'$ or, what is the same

*Fig. 1.*

*Fig. 2.*

*Fig. 3.*

thing, the distance travelled by the point $M$ by virtue of the accelerating force acting on it, will be equal to $\alpha\, dt$.

V. That said, let $a$ be the distance that a weighted body, moving under gravity $p$, will travel in a given and constant time $\theta$: it is clear that one will have (by Principia mathematica Book I. Section I. Lemma XI.) [216]

$$\alpha\, dt^2 : 2a = F\beta\, dt^2 : p\theta^2, \text{ therefore } \alpha = \frac{2aF\beta}{p\theta^2} = \frac{2apml\beta}{p\theta^2} = \beta.\frac{2aml}{\theta^2}.$$

VI. We will note first, that one may represent the given time $\theta$ by a constant line of whatever length one pleases: one must only take care, in expressing the variable and unknown moments of time, to take lines $t$ which, to the line taken to represent $\theta$, are in the ratio of these variable moments of time, to the constant and given time during which a weighted body passes through the distance $a$. One may therefore take $\theta$ so that $\theta^2 = 2aml$; and in that case one will have $\alpha = \beta$. Therefore since $dp = \alpha\, dt + v\, ds$, it must be that $dq$ or $v\, dt + \beta\, ds$ is equal to $v\, dt + \alpha\, ds$.

VII. To determine from these conditions the quantities $\alpha$ and $v$, one observes that since $dp = \alpha\, dt + v\, ds$, and $dq = v\, dt + \alpha\, ds$, one will have $dp + dq = (\alpha + v).(dt + ds)$; and $dp - dq = (\alpha - v).(dt - ds)$, from which it follows

1. that $\alpha + v$ is equal to a function of $t + s$, and that $\alpha - v$ is equal to a function of $t - s$.

2. that consequently one will have $p = \dfrac{\varphi(t + s) + \Delta(t - s)}{2}$ or simply $\varphi(t + s) + \Delta(t - s)$; and $q = \varphi(t + s) - \Delta(t - s)$, from which one deduces that $PM$ or $\int (pdt + qds) = \Psi(t + s) + \Gamma(t - s)$, where $\Psi(t + s)$ and $\Gamma(t - s)$ again express unknown functions of $t + s$ and $t - s$.

The general equation of the curve is therefore

$$y = \Psi(t + s) + \Gamma(t - s).$$

[217]

VIII. Now it is easy to see that this equation includes an infinity of curves. To show this, we here take only a particular case, namely that where $y = 0$ when $t = 0$; that is, let us suppose that the string, when it starts to vibrate, is extended in a straight line, and that it is forced to depart from that state of rest by the action of some cause whatever it may be; it is clear that one will have $\Psi s + \Gamma[-s] = 0$, therefore $\Gamma[-s] = -\Psi s$. Further, since the string always passes through the fixed points $A$ and $B$, it must be that $s = 0$ and $s = l$ make $y = 0$, whatever the value of $t$; therefore, first, $\Psi t + \Gamma t = 0$ and $\Gamma t = -\Psi t$; therefore $\Gamma(t - s) = -\Psi(t - s)$; therefore one will have $y = \Psi(t + s) - \Psi(t - s)$; therefore it must be that $-\Psi[-s] = \Gamma s = -\Psi s$; therefore $\Psi s$ must be a function of $s$ in which there are only even powers when one reduces it to a series. Second, further, the condition $y = 0$ when $s = l$ gives $\Psi(t + l) - \Psi(t - l) = 0$. One must therefore find a quantity $\Psi(t + s)$ such that, $\Psi s - \Psi[-s] = 0$ and $\Psi(t + l) - \Psi(t - l) = 0$.

IX. To arrive at this, let us imagine the curve $toT$, of which the ordinates are $TR = u$, $QR = z$, and which are such that $u = \Psi z$; that said, since $\Psi s - \Psi[-s]$ must be equal to zero, it is clear that by taking $Qr = QR$ we must have $rt = RT$, and that thus the curve $toT$ will have, on one side and the other of the point $o$, similar and equal portions, $to$, $oT$. Further, since $\Psi(t + l)$ must be equal to $\Psi(t - l)$ and the difference

*Fig. 4.*

of $t + l$ and $t − l$ is $2l$, it is clear that the curve $toT$, assuming it is completely described, must be such that any two ordinates distant one from the other by a quantity $2l$ must be equal to each other. Therefore, if one supposes $QR = l$, one will see that the part $TK$ must be equal and similar to $tO$; that the part $KX$ must also be equal and similar to $oT$ etc.; and since the parts $tO$, $oT$, are already similar and equal, it follows that the sought curve extends to infinity from the two sides of the point $o$, and that is is composed of parts everywhere equal and similar to the part $oTK$, of which the abscissa $QV = 2l$, and which is [218] divided by its mid point $T$ into two similar and equal parts.

—————————

## 10.2 FOUNDATIONS OF THE CALCULUS

For as long as mathematicians had attempted to work with infinitely small quantities, from the late 1620s onwards, there had been doubts and disputes as to the validity of their methods. Such questions troubled some more than others: Cavalieri tried hard to put his work on firm foundations, but many of those who came after him, notably Torricelli and Wallis, had fewer scruples, leading to scathing criticisms of their methods even in the seventeenth century (see 2.4.2).

The calculus, whether derived by Newtonian or Leibnizian principles, ultimately relied on the disappearance of infinitely small quantities. Newton's $o$ method, for example, like Fermat's maximum/minimum method before it (see 3.1.1, 4.1.2, 4.1.3), was based on division by a quantity that was then set to zero. Newton justified his intuitions by appealing to 'prime and ultimate ratios' (see 5.1.2), an approach that was not improved upon for many years, but begged the question of how one defines a first or last moment of time. The Leibnizian calculus appeared to circumvent such problems by treating differentiation and integration simply as a set of formal algebraic rules, but that merely obscured the fact that the rules themselves were ultimately based on the vanishing of 'momentary differences', the infinitely small quantities $dx$, $dy$, $dt$, and so on (see 4.2.1).

Mathematicians from the beginning of the eighteenth century onwards were well aware of the criticisms, and repeatedly attempted to justify their methods, but without any convincing success. The extracts in this section have been chosen to illustrate what the difficulties were perceived to be, and to show how mathematicians even of the stature of Euler and Lagrange struggled with them and attempted in very different ways to overcome them.

## 10.2.1 Berkeley and *The analyst*, 1734

The most sustained polemic against the methods of the calculus was delivered not by a mathematician but by a theologian. In 1734 George Berkeley, Bishop of Cloyne in Ireland, published *The analyst, or, a discourse addressed to an infidel mathematician*, in which he delivered an onslaught of closely-argued criticisms and protested that mathematical beliefs were no more securely founded than religious faith. (The 'infidel' mathematician to whom all this was addressed is believed to be Edmund Halley.)

---

**Berkeley's objections to calculus**
from Berkeley, *The analyst*, 1734, 17–18
Eighteenth Century Collection Online, Gale Digital Collection

---

VI. And yet in the *calculus differentialis*, which Method serves to all the same Intents and Ends with that of Fluxions, our modern Analysts are not content to consider only the Differences of finite Quantities: they also consider the Differences of those Differences, and the Differences of the Differences of the first Differences. And so on *ad infinitum*. That is, they consider Quantities infinitely less than the least discernible Quantity; and others infinitely less than those infinitely small ones; and still others infinitely less than the preceding Infinitesimals, and so on without End or Limit. Insomuch that we are to admit an infinite Succession of Infinitesimals, each infinitely less than the foregoing, and infinitely greater than the following. As there are first, second, third, fourth, fifth, &c. Fluxions, so there are Differences, first, second, third, fourth &c. in an infinite Progression towards nothing; which you still approach and never arrive at.

C                              And

18 *The* Analyſt.

And (which is moſt ſtrange) although you ſhould take a Million of Millions of theſe Infiniteſimal, each whereof is ſuppoſed infinitely greater than ſome other real Magnitude, and add them to the leaſt given Quantity, it ſhall be never the bigger. For this is one of the modeſt *poſtulata* of our modern Mathematicians, and is a Corner-ſtone or Ground-work of their Speculations.

VII. All theſe Points, I ſay, are ſuppoſed and believed by certain rigorous Exactors of Evidence in Religion, Men who pretend to believe no further than they can ſee. That Men, who have been converſant only about clear Points, ſhould with Difficulty admit obſcure ones might not ſeem altogether unaccountable. But he who can digeſt a ſecond or third Fluxion, a ſecond or third Difference, need not, methinks, be ſqueamiſh about any Point in Divinity. There is a natural Preſumption that Mens Faculties are made alike. It is on this Suppoſition that they attempt to argue and convince one another. What, therefore, ſhall appear evidently impoſſible and repugnant to one, may be preſumed the ſame to another. But with what Appearance of Reaſon ſhall any Man preſume to ſay, that Myſteries may not be Objects of Faith, at the ſame time that he himſelf admits ſuch obſcure Myſteries to be the Object of Science?

VIII. It

### 10.2.2 Maclaurin's response to Berkeley, 1742

The quasi-theological nature of the debate that followed the publication of Berkeley's book can be gauged from the title of an immediate response from James Jurin: *Geometry no friend to infidelity* (1734). A more mathematically based argument came from Colin Maclaurin in Edinburgh, whose *Treatise of fluxions* was written primarily as a response to Berkeley's criticisms, and became the most important English calculus text of the mid eighteenth century (see also 8.2.2).

Maclaurin's *Treatise* is in two volumes, and in the first he set out to establish calculus on the kind of rigorous geometric foundations that would be acceptable to any adherent of Greek mathematics, carefully proving his statements by the traditional method of double *reductio ad absurdum*. The problem with proof by contradiction, however, as readers of Greek mathematics also knew, and for which they had all too often criticized ancient writers, is that it gives no insight into how results have been discovered in the first place. Maclaurin's work was open to the same charge. It was after all not the *results* of the calculus that were in question but its *methods*.

In the first chapter of the second volume, Maclaurin turned to the method of infinitesimals and attempted to show by a purely geometric argument why it was that no error arose from the neglect of infinitely small quantities. There is no algebra here at all; indeed his diagram and opening argument are very similar to those used by Napier in constructing logarithms over a century earlier.

## Maclaurin's treatment of infinitesimals

from Maclaurin, *A treatise of fluxions*, 1742, II, §496

496. In general suppose as in art. 66. that while the point P  **FIG. 220.**
describes the right line A*a* with an uniform motion, the point
M sets out from L with a velocity that is to the constant velocity of P as L*c* to D*g*, and proceeds in the right line E*e* with a
motion continually accelerated or retarded, that LS any space
described by M is always to DG the space described in the same
time by P as L*f* to D*g*, that *cx* is to D*g* as the difference of the
velocities of M at S and L to the constant velocity of P, and
that LS is always to LC as L*f* to L*c*. Then LS being always
expressed by LC ∓ CS, it is manifest that (since LC is to DG
as L*c* to D*g*, or as the velocity of M at L to the velocity of P)
LC is what would have been described by M if its motion had
continued uniformly from L, and that CS arises in this expression in consequence of the acceleration or retardation of the
motion of the point M while it describes LS. But if LS and
DG be supposed infinitely small increments of EL and AD, *cx*
will be infinitely less than D*g*; and since *cf* is less than *cx* by
what was shewn in art. 66. it follows that *cf* will be infinitely
less than L*c*, and CS infinitely less than LC. Therefore when
the increment LS is supposed infinitely small, and its expression
is resolved into two parts LC and CS, of which the former LC
is always in the same ratio to DG (the simultaneous increment
of AD) while the increments vary, and the latter CS is infinitely less than the former LC, we may conclude that the part CS
is that which arises in consequence of the variation of the motion of M while it describes LS, and is therefore to be neglected in measuring the motion of M at L or the fluxion of the right
line EL. Thus the manner of investigating the differences or
fluxions of quantities in the method of infinitesimals may be de-

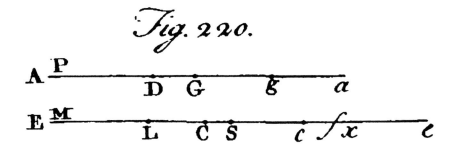

**4I6**        *Of the method of Infinitesimals.*        Book **I**.

duced from the principles of the method of fluxions demonstrated above.   For instead of neglecting CS because it is infinitely less than LC, (according to the usual manner of reasoning in
that method,) we may reject it, because we may thence conclude
that it is not produced in consequence of the generating motion
at L but of the subsequent variations of this motion.   And it
appears why the conclusions in the method of infinitesimals are
not to be represented as if they were only near the truth, but
are to be held as accurately true.

### 10.2.3  Euler and infinitely small quantities, 1755

We have already seen Euler's practical handling of the infinitely small and the infinitely
large in his development of exponential and trigonometric series (9.2.1 to 9.2.3). Seven
years later in his *Institutiones calculi differentialis* (*Foundations of differential calculus*)
of 1755 he engaged at some length in a theoretical discussion of the difficulties, and
gave the following definitions of infinitely large and infinitely small quantities.

## Euler on the infinitely large and the infinitely small
from Euler, *Institutiones calculi differentialis*, 1755, §82–§86

*C A P U T   I I I.*   77

82.   Verum vt ad propofitum reuertamur, etiamſi quis neget in mundo numerum infinitum reuera exiſtere; tamen in ſpeculationibus mathematicis ſaepiſſime occurrunt quaeſtiones, ad quas, niſi numerus infinitus admittatur, reſponderi non poſſet.   Sic, ſi quaeratur ſumma omnium numerorum, qui hanc ſeriem $1 + 2 + 3 + 4 + 5 + \&c.$ conſtituunt; quia iſti numeri ſine fine progrediuntur, atque creſcunt, eorum omnium ſumma certe finita eſſe non poterit: quo ipſo efficitur, eam eſſe infinitam.   Hinc, quae quantitas tanta eſt, vt omni quantitate finita ſit maior, ea non infinita eſſe nequit.   Ad huiusmodi quantitatem deſignandam Mathematici vtuntur hoc ſigno $\infty$, quo denotatur quantitas omni quantitate finita, ſeu aſſignabili, maior.   Sic cum Parabola ita definiri queat, vt dicatur eſſe Ellipſis infinite longa, recte affirmare poterimus axem Parabolae eſſe Lineam rectam infinitam.

83.   Haec autem Infiniti doctrina magis illuſtrabitur, ſi, quid ſit infinite paruum Mathematicorum, expoſuerimus.   Nullum autem eſt dubium, quin omnis quantitas eousque diminui queat, quoad penitus euaneſcat, atque in nihilum abeat.   Sed quantitas infinite parua nil aliud eſt niſi quantitas euaneſcens, ideoque reuera erit $= 0$.   Conſentit quoque ea infinite paruorum definitio, qua dicuntur omni quantitate aſſignabili minora: ſi enim quantitas tam fuerit parua, vt omni quantitate aſſignabili ſit minor, ea certe non poterit non eſſe nulla; namque niſi eſſet $= 0$, quantitas aſſignari poſſet ipſi aequalis, quod eſt contra hypotheſin.   Quaerenti ergo, quid ſit quantitas

K 3

infi-

*CAPUT III.*

infinite parua in Mathefi, refpondemus eam effe reuera
$=$ o : neque ergo in hac idea tanta Myfteria latent, quanta vulgo putantur, & quae pluribus calculum infinite par-
vorum admodum fufpeɕum reddiderunt.   Interim tamen
dubia, fi quae fupererunt, in fequentibus, vbi hunc calculum fumus tradituri, funditus tollentur.

84.   Cum igitur oftenderimus, quantitatem infinite
paruam reuera effe cyphram, primum occurrendum eft
obieɕioni, cur quantitates infinite paruas non perpetuo
eodem charaɕere o defignemus, fed peculiares notas ad
eas defignandas adhibeamus.   Quia enim omnia nihila
funt inter fe aequalia, fuperfluum videtur variis fignis ea
denotare.   Verum quamquam duae quaeuis cyphrae ita
inter fe funt aequales, vt earum differentia fit nihil: tamen, cum duo fint modi comparationis, alter arithme-
ticus, alter geometricus; quorum illo differentiam, hoc
vero quotum ex quantitatibus comparandis ortum fpeɕa-
mus; ratio quidem arithmetica inter binas quasque cyphras eft aequalitatis, non vero ratio geometrica.   Facillime hoc perfpicietur ex hac proportione geometrica
$2 : 1 = o : o$, in qua terminus quartus eft $= o$, vti tertius.   Ex natura autem proportionis, cum terminus primus duplo fit maior quam fecundus, neceffe eft, vt &
tertius duplo maior fit quam quartus.

85.   Haec autem etiam in vulgari Arithmetica funt
planiffima: cuilibet enim notum eft, cyphram per quemvis numerum multiplicatam dare cyphram, effeque $n. o = o$,

ficque

## *C A P U T   III.*    79

ficque fore $n : 1 = 0 : 0$. Vnde patet fieri poſſe, vt duae cyphrae quamcunque inter ſe rationem geometricam teneant, etiamſi, rem arithmetice ſpeĉtando, earum ratio ſemper ſit aequalitatis.     Cum igitur inter cyphras ratio quaecunque intercedere poſſit, ad hanc diuerſitatem indicandam conſulto varii charaĉteres vſurpantur; praeſertim tum, cum ratio geometrica, quam cyphrae variae inter ſe tenent, eſt inueſtiganda.     In calculo autem infinite paruorum nil aliud agitur, niſi vt ratio geometrica inter varia infinite parua indagetur, quod negotium propterea, niſi diuerſis ſignis ad ea indicanda vteremur, in maximam confuſionem illaberetur, neque vllo modo expediri poſſet.

86. Si ergo, prouti in Analyſi infinitorum modus ſignandi eſt receptus, denotet $dx$ quantitatem infinite parvam, erit vtique tam $dx = 0$, quam $adx = 0$, denotante $a$ quantitatem quamcunque finitam.     Hoc tamen non obſtante erit ratio geometrica $adx : dx$ finita, nempe vt $a : 1$; & hanc obrem haec duo infinite parua $dx$ & $adx$, etiamſi vtrumque ſit $= 0$, inter ſe confundi non poſſunt, ſi quidem eorum ratio inueſtigetur.     Simili modo, ſi diuerſa occurrunt infinite parua $dx$ & $dy$, etiamſi vtrumque ſit $= 0$, tamen eorum ratio non conſtat.     Atque in inueſtigatione rationis inter duo quaeque huiusmodi infinite parua omnis vis calculi differentialis verſatur.     Vſus autem huius comparationis, etiamſi primo intuitu admodum exiguus videatur, tamen ampliſſimus deprehenditur, atque adhuc indies magis elucet.

---

### TRANSLATION

82. But to return to the problem, although some may deny that an infinite number truly exists in the world, nevertheless in mathematical speculations there very often occur questions, to which, unless an infinite number is admitted, it is not possible to

respond. Thus, if there is sought the sum of all the numbers that constitute this series $1 + 2 + 3 + 4 + 5+$ etc., since these numbers progress without end, and increase, the sum of all of them could certainly not be finite; and therefore it comes about that it must be infinite. Hence, such a quantity, that is greater than any finite quantity, cannot be said not to be infinite. To denote a quantity of this kind mathematicians use this sign $\infty$, by which is meant a quantity greater than any finite, or assignable, quantity. Thus when a parabola is defined in such a way that it is said to be an infinitely long ellipse, we could correctly assert that the axis of the parabola is an infinitely long straight line.

83. Moreover, this teaching on the infinite will be better illustrated, if we explain what would mathematically be infinitely small. There is no doubt that every quantity can be decreased so far that it simply vanishes, and goes to nothing. But an infinitely small quantity is nothing other than a vanishing quantity, and is therefore really equal to 0. This definition of the infinitely small also fits those quantities that are said to be less than every assignable quantity: for if a quantity becomes so small, that it is less than any assignable quantity, it certainly cannot be other than nothing; for unless it were 0, it would be possible to assign a quantity equal to it, which is against the hypothesis. Therefore, to those asking [78] what an infinitely small quantity is in mathematics, we reply that it is really 0; therefore, there are not so many mysteries hidden in this as are commonly thought, and which to many render the calculus of the infinitely small in some way suspect. Meanwhile, if they ignore them in what follows, where we teach this calculus, their doubts will be completely removed.

84. Therefore since we have shown an infinitely small quantity to be really zero, the first objection is: why do we not always denote infinitely small quantities by the sign 0, but employ special signs to denote them? For since all nothings are equal amongst themselves, it seems superfluous to denote them by different signs. But although any two zeros are equal amongst themselves, so that their difference becomes nothing, nevertheless, when the two are compared in some way, either arithmetically or geometrically, there we see a difference between them, in fact the quantity arising from the comparison; indeed the arithmetic ratio between two such zeros is equality, but not the geometric ratio. This is very easily seen from the geometric proportion $2 : 1 = 0 : 0$, in which the fourth term is 0, as is the third. Moreover from the nature of proportions, since the first term is twice as great as the second, it must also be that the third is twice as great as the fourth.

85. Moreover this is also very plain in common arithmetic; for it is known to everyone that zero multiplied by any number gives zero, and that $n.0 = 0$, [79] and thus it will be that $n : 1 = 0 : 0$. Whence it is clear that it is possible for two zeros to have any geometric proportion between them, although looking at the thing arithmetically, their ratio is always one of equality. Therefore since it is possible to introduce any ratio between zeros, different symbols are used to indicate this diversity, since usually it is the geometric ratio between different zeros that is to be investigated. Indeed, in the calculus of the infinitely small we are concerned with nothing other than geometric ratios between different infinitely small quantities, and in this matter, therefore, unless we use different signs to indicate them, we will be led into great confusion, and with no way to escape from it.

86. If, therefore, as is the accepted way of writing in the analysis of infinites, $dx$ denotes an infinitely small quantity, we will have both $dx = 0$ and $a\,dx = 0$, where $a$ denotes

any finite quantity. This is so notwithstanding that the geometric ratio $a\,dx : dx$ is finite, namely as $a : 1$; and here, on account of that, these two infinitely small quantities $dx$ and $a\,dx$, although both are equal to 0, should not be confused with each other, if indeed their ratio is is to be investigated. Similarly, if there occur different infinitely small quantities $dx$ and $dy$, although both are equal to 0, nevertheless their ratio is not constant. And to the investigation of ratios between two infinitely small quantities of this kind, there is applied all the power of the differential calculus. Moreover the use of such comparisons, although it may seem at first sight very limited, is nevertheless found to be exceedingly broad, as from here on will appear much more clearly.

--------

### 10.2.4  Lagrange's attempt to avoid the infinitely small, 1797

Lagrange was very often inspired by Euler, but on the subject of the infinitely small he parted company from him decisively. Rather than tolerate vague and unsatisfactory definitions of the kind Euler had given, Lagrange attempted to abandon infinitely small quantities altogether. His aim instead was to establish differential calculus on the foundation of Taylor series, together with algebraic manipulation of finite quantities only. He first explained his ideas in his *Théorie des fonctions analytiques* in 1797, but within two years he was already planning a longer and more detailed version, and the second edition, corrected and augmented, and with the material now separated into chapters, was eventually published in 1813. The extract below is from the Introduction to the second edition, where Lagrange gave the reasons for his new approach, in a perceptive and articulate account of different historical approaches to calculus and the problems with each of them.

Lagrange's basic assumption was that any function could be expanded as a power series (such a function he called a 'primitive function', $f$). He then defined its derivatives (or 'derived functions', $f'$, $f''$, ...) as the coefficients of the respective powers of the variable, and was able to show that these correspond to the usual understanding of $\frac{df}{dx}$, $\frac{d^2f}{dx^2}$, and so on. For the details of his derivation see 14.1.2.

There are several problems with this approach. It assumes, first, that for any required function a power series exists; and second, that it is well behaved over an indefinite range of values. Further, there is no way of discovering the 'derived functions' except by the usual rules of calculus. Nevertheless, Lagrange's approach was enormously influential. When Charles Babbage, George Peacock, and John Herschel translated Lacroix's *Traité élémentaire du calcul* into English in 1816, they complained that Lacroix had 'substituted the method of limits of D'Alembert, in the place of the more correct and natural method of Lagrange', and Peacock wrote extensive notes 'to enable the Student to make use of the principle of Lagrange'.[2] Ten years later, in 1826, Cauchy began to establish the calculus of residues on precisely the principles Lagrange had advocated (see 15.2.3).

--------

2. Lacroix 1816, iii and iv.

**Lagrange's avoidance of the infinitely small**

from Lagrange, *Théorie des fonctions*, from the second edition, 1813, 1–5

# THÉORIE

## DES

# FONCTIONS ANALYTIQUES,

### CONTENANT

*Les Principes du Calcul différentiel, dégagés de toute considération d'infiniment petits, d'évanouissans, de limites et de fluxions, et réduits à l'analyse algébrique des quantités finies.*

# INTRODUCTION.

*Des Fonctions en général. Des Fonctions primitives et dérivées. Des différentes manières dont on a envisagé le Calcul différentiel. Objet de cet Ouvrage.*

ON appelle *fonction* d'une ou de plusieurs quantités, toute expression de calcul dans laquelle ces quantités entrent d'une manière quelconque, mêlées ou non avec d'autres quantités qu'on regarde comme ayant des valeurs données et invariables, tandis que les quantités de la fonction peuvent recevoir toutes les valeurs possibles. Ainsi, dans les fonctions, on ne considère que les quantités qu'on suppose variables, sans aucun égard aux constantes qui peuvent y être mêlées.

Le mot *fonction* a été employé par les premiers analystes pour désigner en général les puissances d'une même quantité. Depuis, on a étendu la signification de ce mot à toute quantité formée

I

2                    THÉORIE DES FONCTIONS.

d'une manière quelconque d'une autre quantité. *Leibnitz* et les
*Bernoulli* l'ont employé les premiers dans cette acception générale,
et il est aujourd'hui généralement adopté.

Lorsqu'à la variable d'une fonction on attribue un accroissement quelconque, en ajoutant à cette variable une quantité indéterminée, on peut par les règles ordinaires de l'algèbre, si la
fonction est algébrique, la développer suivant les puissances de
cette indéterminée. Le premier terme du développement sera la
fonction proposée qu'on appellera *fonction primitive;* les termes
suivants seront formés de différentes fonctions de la même variable,
multipliées par les puissances successives de l'indéterminée. Ces
nouvelles fonctions dépendront uniquement de la fonction primitive dont elles dérivent, et pourront s'appeler *fonctions dérivées.*
En général, quelle que soit la fonction primitive, algébrique ou
non, elle peut toujours être développée ou censée developpée de
la même manière, et donner ainsi naissance à des fonctions dérivées. Les fonctions considérées sous ce point de vue, constituent
une analyse d'un genre supérieur à l'analyse ordinaire, par sa généralité et ses nombreux usages ; et l'on verra dans cet ouvrage que
l'analyse qu'on appelle vulgairement *transcendante* ou *infinitésimale,*
n'est au fond que l'analyse des fonctions primitives et dérivées, et
que les calculs différentiel et intégral ne sont, à proprement
parler, que le calcul de ces mêmes fonctions.

Les premiers géomètres qui ont employé le calcul différentiel,
*Leibnitz,* les *Bernoulli,* l'*Hopital,* etc. l'ont fondé sur la considération
des quantités infiniment petites de différens ordres, et sur la supposition qu'on peut regarder et traiter comme égales, les quantités qui
ne diffèrent entre elles que par des quantités infiniment petites à leur
égard. Contens d'arriver par les procédés de ce calcul d'une manière
prompte et sûre à des résultats exacts, ils ne se sont point occupés
d'en démontrer les principes. Ceux qui les ont suivis, *Euler,* d'*Alem-*
*bert,* etc., ont cherché à suppléer à ce défaut, en faisant voir, par des
applications particulières, que les différences qu'on suppose infiniment petites, doivent être absolument nulles, et que leurs rapports,
seules quantités qui entrent réellement dans le calcul, ne sont autre
chose que les limites des rapports des différences finies ou indéfinies.

## INTRODUCTION.                              5

Mais il faut convenir que cette idée, quoique juste en elle-même, n'est pas assez claire pour servir de principe à une science dont la certitude doit être fondée sur l'évidence, et surtout pour être présentée aux commençans; d'ailleurs, il me semble que comme dans le calcul différentiel, tel qu'on l'emploie, on considère et on calcule en effet les quantités infiniment petites ou supposées infiniment petites elles-mêmes, la véritable métaphysique de ce calcul consiste en ce que l'erreur résultant de cette fausse supposition est redressée ou compensée par celle qui naît des procédés mêmes du calcul, suivant lesquels on ne retient dans la différentiation que les quantités infiniment petites du même ordre. Par exemple, en regardant une courbe comme un polygone d'un nombre infini de côtés chacun infiniment petit, et dont le prolongement est la tangente de la courbe, il est clair qu'on fait une supposition erronée; mais l'erreur se trouve corrigée dans le calcul par l'omission qu'on y fait des quantités infiniment petites. C'est ce qu'on peut faire voir aisément dans des exemples, mais dont il serait peut-être difficile de donner une démonstration générale.

*Newton*, pour éviter la supposition des infiniment petits, a considéré les quantités mathématiques comme engendrées par le mouvement, et il a cherché une méthode pour déterminer directement les vitesses ou plutôt le rapport des vitesses variables avec lesquelles ces quantités sont produites; c'est ce qu'on appelle, d'après lui, la *méthode des fluxions* ou *le calcul fluxionnel*, parce qu'il a nommé ces vitesses *fluxions* des quantités. Cette méthode ou ce calcul s'accorde pour le fond et pour les opérations, avec le calcul différentiel, et n'en diffère que par la métaphysique qui paraît en effet plus claire, parce que tout le monde a ou croit avoir une idée de la vitesse. Mais, d'un côté, introduire le mouvement dans un calcul qui n'a que des quantités algébriques pour objet, c'est y introduire une idée étrangère, et qui oblige à regarder ces quantités comme des lignes parcourues par un mobile; de l'autre, il faut avouer qu'on n'a pas même une idée bien nette de ce que c'est que la vitesse d'un point à chaque instant, lorsque cette vitesse est variable; et on peut voir par le savant Traité des fluxions de *Maclaurin*, combien il est difficile de démon-

4                   THÉORIE DES FONCTIONS.

trer rigoureusement la méthode des fluxions , et combien d'artifices particuliers il faut employer pour démontrer les différentes parties de cette méthode.

Aussi *Newton* lui-même , dans son livre des Principes , a préféré, comme plus courte , la méthode des dernières raisons des quantités évanouissantes ; et c'est aux principes de cette méthode que se réduisent en dernière analyse les démonstrations relatives à celle des fluxions. Mais cette méthode a , comme celle des limites dont nous avons parlé plus haut, et qui n'en est proprement que la traduction algébrique, le grand inconvénient de considérer les quantités dans l'état où elles cessent, pour ainsi dire, d'être quantités ; car quoiqu'on conçoive toujours bien le rapport de deux quantités tant qu'elles demeurent finies, ce rapport n'offre plus à l'esprit une idée claire et précise, aussitôt que ses termes deviennent l'un et l'autre nuls à-la-fois.

C'est pour prévenir ces difficultés, qu'un habile Géomètre anglais, qui a fait dans l'analyse des découvertes importantes , a proposé dans ces derniers temps, de substituer à la méthode des fluxions jusqu'alors suivie scrupuleusement par tous les géomètres anglais, une autre méthode purement analytique , et analogue à la méthode différentielle, mais dans laquelle , au lieu de n'employer que les différences infiniment petites ou nulles des quantités variables, on emploie d'abord des valeurs différentes de ces quantités, qu'on égale ensuite, après avoir fait disparaître par la division, le facteur que cette égalité rendrait nul. Par ce moyen, on évite à la vérité les infiniment petits et les quantités évanouissantes ; mais les procédés et les applications du calcul sont embarrassans et peu naturels , et on doit convenir que cette manière de rendre le calcul différentiel plus rigoureux dans ses principes , lui fait perdre ses principaux avantages , la simplicité de la méthode et la facilite des opérations. *Voyez* l'ouvrage intitulé : *the residual analysis a new branch of the Algebric art* , *by* John Landen , *London*, 1764, ainsi que le discours publié par le même auteur , en 1758, sur le même objet.

Ces variations dans la manière d'établir et de présenter les principes du calcul différentiel, et même dans la dénomination de ce

calcul, montrent, ce me semble, qu'on n'en avait pas saisi la véritable théorie, quoiqu'on eût trouvé d'abord les règles les plus
simples et les plus commodes pour le mécanisme des opérations.

On trouvera de nouvelles considérations sur cet objet dans la
première leçon sur le Calcul des fonctions.

Dans un mémoire imprimé parmi ceux de l'Académie de Berlin,
de 1772, et dont l'objet était l'analogie entre les différentielles et
les puissances positives, et entre les intégrales et les puissances
négatives, j'avançai que la théorie du développement des fonctions en série, contenait les vrais principes du calcul différentiel,
dégagés de toute considération d'infiniment petits ou de limites,
et je démontrai par cette théorie le théorème de *Taylor*, qui est
le fondement de la méthode des séries, et qu'on n'avait encore
démontré que par le secours de ce calcul, ou par la considération
des différences infiniment petites.

Depuis, *Arbogast* a présenté à l'Académie des Sciences, un
Mémoire où la même idée est exposée avec des développemens
et des applications qui lui appartiennent. Mais l'auteur n'ayant encore
rien publié sur ce sujet (*), et m'étant trouvé engagé par des
circonstances particulières à développer les principes généraux de
l'analyse, j'ai rappelé mes anciennes idées sur ceux du calcul
différentiel, et j'ai fait de nouvelles réflexions tendantes à les con-
firmer et à les généraliser; c'est ce qui a occasionné cet Ecrit,
que je ne me détermine à publier que par la considération de
l'utilité dont il peut être à ceux qui étudient cette branche impor-
tante de l'analyse.

TRANSLATION

## THEORY OF ANALYTIC FUNCTIONS,
### CONTAINING

*The principles of differential calculus, free from all considerations of the infinitely small,
vanishing quantities, limits or fluxions, and reduced to algebraic analysis of finite
quantities.*

## INTRODUCTION

*Functions in general. Primitive and derived functions. The different ways in which the
differential calculus has been envisaged. Subject of this work.*

One calls a *function* of one or more quantities every expression of calculus in which the quantities enter in any manner, mixed or not with other quantities that one regards as having given and fixed values, as long as the quantities in the function may receive every possible value. Thus, in functions, one considers only the quantities that one supposes variable, without any regard to constants which may be mixed with them.

The word *function* was employed by the first analysts to denote, in general, powers of the same quantity. Since then, one has understood this word to mean every quantity formed [2] in any manner whatever from another quantity. *Leibniz* and the *Bernoullis* employed it first in this general sense, and it is today generally accepted.

When the variable of a function is given any increase, on adjoining to that variable an unknown quantity, one may by the ordinary rules of algebra, if the function is algebraic, expand it in powers of the unknown. The first term of the expansion will be the proposed function, which one calls the *primitive function*; the following terms will be formed from different functions of the same variable, multiplied by successive powers of the unknown. These new functions will depend uniquely on the primitive function from which they derive, and may be called *derived functions*. In general, whatever the primitive function is, algebraic or not, it may always be expanded or regarded as expanded in the same way, and thus to give rise to derived functions. Functions considered from this point of view constitute analysis of a kind superior to ordinary analysis in the generality of its numerous uses; and one will see in this work that the analysis that is commonly called *transcendental* or *infinitesimal* is at root nothing other than the analysis of primitive and derived functions, and that the differential and integral calculus are nothing other, properly speaking, than the calculus of these same functions.

The first geometers who employed the differential calculus, *Leibniz*, the *Bernoullis*, *l'Hôpital*, etc. founded it on the consideration of infinitely small quantities of different orders, and on the supposition that one may regard and treat as equal quantities that do not differ amongst themselves except by quantities infinitely small with respect to them. Content to arrive by the procedures of this calculus in a prompt and sure way at correct results, they were not at all worried about demonstrating the principles. Those who followed them, *Euler*, *d'Alembert*, etc. sought to supply this defect, making it seem, through particular applications, that the differences one supposed infinitely small must be absolutely nothing, and that their ratios, the only quantities that really entered into the calculus, were nothing other than the limits of ratios of finite or indefinite differences. [3] But one must agree that this idea, however correct in itself, is not clear enough to serve as a principle for a science in which certainty must be founded on evidence, and above all for it to be presented to beginners; besides, it seems to me that since in the differential calculus, however one uses it, one indeed considers and calculates quantities infinitely small or assumed infinitely small, the true justification of this calculus is that the error resulting from this false supposition is redressed or compensated by what arises from the same procedures of the calculus, according to which one retains in differentiation only infinitely small quantities of the same order. For example, in regarding a curve as a polygon with an infinite number of sides, each infinitely small, it is clear that one makes an erroneous supposition; but the error is found to be corrected in the calculation by the omission that one makes there of infinitely small quantities. This is what one can easily see in these examples, but of which it would be difficult to give a general demonstration.

Newton, to avoid the supposition of infinitely small quantities, considered mathematical quantities to be generated by movement, and he sought a method of determining directly the speeds or more often the ratio of variable speeds with which these quantities were produced; this is what one calls, after him, the *method of fluxions* or *the fluxional calculus*, because he named these speeds *fluxions* of quantities. This method or this calculus agrees in its principles and in its operations with the differential calculus, and differs from it only in the justification, which seems indeed clearer, because everyone has or believes they have an idea of speed. But, on the one hand, to introduce movement into a calculation which has only algebraic quantities for its objects is to introduce a foreign idea, and one which obliges us to regard these quantities as lines traced by a moving point; on the other, one must admit that one has not even the barest idea of what is meant by the speed of a point at each instant, when this speed is variable; and one may see from the learned *Treatise of fluxions* of *Maclaurin*, how difficult it is to [4] demonstrate the method of fluxions rigorously, and how many particular artifices one must employ to demonstrate the different parts of this method.

Also *Newton* himself, in his book of *Principia*, preferred, as being shorter, the method of ultimate ratios of vanishing quantities; and it is to the principles of this method that, in the last analysis, are reduced demonstrations relating to the matter of fluxions. But this method has, like that of limits of which we spoke above and which is not properly in the tradition of algebra, the great inconvenience of considering quantities in the state where they cease, as one might say, to be quantities; for although one easily conceives the ratio of two quantities as long as they remain finite, the ratio no longer offers to the mind any clear or precise idea as soon as the terms become, both one and the other, at once nothing.

It was to prevent these difficulties that an able English geometer, who had made some important discoveries in analysis, proposed in his later years to substitute for the method of fluxions, until then followed scrupulously by all English geometers, another method, purely analytic, and analogous to the differential method, but in which, instead of employing only infinitely small or null differences of the variable quantities, one uses instead different values of these quantities, which one then puts equal, after having eliminated by division the factor that renders the equality null. By this means, one indeed avoids infinitely small or vanishing quantities; but the procedures and applications of this calculus are crude and not very natural, and one must agree that this manner of rendering the differential calculus more rigorous in its principles, makes it lose its principle advantages, the simplicity of its method and the ease of its operations. *See* the work entitled *The residual analysis a new branch of the algebraic art* by John Landen, *London* 1764, as well as the discourse published by the same author, in 1758, on the same subject.

These variations in the manner of establishing and presenting the principles of differential calculus, and even in the name of [5] the calculus, show, it seems to me, that one one does not know the true theory, even though one has found instead the simplest rules and those most convenient for the mechanism of the operations.

One will find new considerations on this subject in the first lesson on the calculus of functions.

In a memoir published among those of the Academy of Berlin for 1772, and in which the subject was the analogy between differentials and positive powers, and between integrals and negative powers, I suggested that the theory of expansion of functions in series contains the true principles of differential calculus, disengaged from all considerations of infinitely small quantities or limits, and I demonstrated by that theory the theorem of *Taylor*, which is the foundation of the method of series, and which had never yet been demonstrated except with the aid of the calculus, or from consideration of infinitely small differences.

Since then, *Arbogast* has presented to the Academy of Sciences, a memoir where the same idea is shown with developments and applications that pertain to it. But the author having as yet published nothing more on this subject, and having found myself engaged through particular circumstances in developing the general principles of analysis, I have recalled my old ideas on those of the differential calculus, and have had new thoughts tending to confirm and generalize them; it is this that has occasioned this writing, which I mean to publish only on account of the use it may be to those who study this important branch of analysis.

———————

# CHAPTER 11

# LIMITS AND CONTINUITY

Differential calculus was developed without any explicit definition of either limits or continuity, but with an intuitive assumption that both could in some sense be taken for granted. Widespread use of the calculus during the eighteenth century led to more careful consideration of such matters, but it was not until the early nineteenth century that Bolzano and Cauchy arrived at what are more or less the modern definitions. In this chapter we trace the history of both ideas up to the early 1820s.

## 11.1 LIMITS

### 11.1.1 Wallis's 'less than any assignable', 1656

The first writer to work with the concept of a limit in something like the modern sense was Wallis, who in his *Arithmetica infinitorum* in 1656 repeatedly claimed that two quantities whose difference could be made less than any assignable quantity could ultimately be considered equal (see, for example, 3.2.3). In 1656 Wallis stated this as a self-evident fact, but thirty years later, in his *Treatise of algebra*, he attempted to justify it by appealing to Euclidean ratio theory. In the *Elements* Book V (Definition V) Euclid had stated a special property of homogeneous magnitudes (that is, magnitudes of the same kind): given any pair of such quantities, the smaller of them, however tiny, can always be multiplied to exceed the greater. Wallis argued the converse, namely, that if a quantity is (or becomes) so small that it *cannot* be made to exceed a larger quantity, no matter many times it is multiplied, it must be regarded as 'no quantity' or nothing:[1]

And whatever is so little or nothing in any kind, as that it cannot by Multiplication, become so great or greater than any proposed Quantity of that kind, is (as to that kind of Quantity,) *None at all.*

Wallis then went on to claim something rather stronger: if a difference between two quantities is less than any assignable quantity, then by definition it cannot be multiplied to exceed some given quantity, and therefore by the previous argument it is nothing, and the two original quantities are equal. Again, Wallis claimed Euclid as his authority:[2]

…he [Euclid] takes this for a Foundation of his Process in such Cases: That *those Magnitudes* (or Quantities,) *whose Difference may be proved to be Less than any Assignable are equal.* For if unequal, their Difference, how small soever, may be so Multiplied, as to become Greater than either of them: And if not so, then it is nothing.

Though he attributed his arguments to Euclid, Wallis was stretching them considerably further than Euclid or any other Greek author had ever done. The first proposition of Book X of the *Elements* makes the following claim: if from a given quantity there is repeatedly subtracted a half (or more), then what remains will eventually be less than any preassigned quantity. This was crucial to the method of exhaustion; it enables one to prove, for instance, that the space between a circle and an inscribed polygon can be made as small as one pleases by repeatedly doubling the number of sides of the polygon. Nowhere, however, did Euclid or any other Greek mathematician claim that this steadily diminishing quantity could be considered non-existent, or zero. Instead, Proposition X.1 was used in proofs by double contradiction to show, for example, that the space inside a circle was neither greater nor less than some predetermined quantity (see 1.2.3).

Wallis's insight may not have had the classical authority he claimed for it but, like several of his ideas in the *Arithmetica infinitorum*, it was put to particularly good use by Newton.

### 11.1.2  Newton's first and last ratios, 1687

In the *Principia* in 1687 Newton gave Wallis's idea of 'ultimate equality' the status of a proposition, indeed he made it the opening Lemma of Book I, Section I (see 5.1.2).

At the very end of Section I, Newton introduced the Latin word *limes*, in the everyday sense of a boundary which may not be crossed, just as Barrow had done in 1660 (see 1.2.1). He used 'limes' in a similar sense again in the final sentence when he spoke of quantities decreasing *sine limite*, that is, without end, or indefinitely. Newton also observed that a quantity may approach such a boundary as closely as one pleases; by Lemma I this was equivalent to 'ultimate equality'.

---

1. Wallis 1685, 281.     2. Wallis 1685, 282.

# Newton's idea of a limit

from Newton, *Principia mathematica*, 1687, I, 35–36

[ 35 ]

contenta. Præmiſi vero hæc Lemmata ut effugerem tædium deducendi perplexas demonſtrationes, more veterum Geometrarum, ad abſurdum. Contractiores enim redduntur demonſtrationes per methodum indiviſibilium. Sed quoniam durior eſt indiviſibilium Hypotheſis; & propterea Methodus illa minus Geometrica cenſetur, malui demonſtrationes rerum ſequentium ad ulcimas quantitatum evaneſcentium ſummas & rationes, primaſq; naſcentium, id eſt, ad limites ſummarum & rationum deducere, & propterea limitum illorum demonſtrationes qua potui breuitate præmittere. His enim idem præſtatur quod per methodum indiviſibilium; & principiis demonſtratis jam tutius utemur.   Proinde in ſequentibus, ſiquando quantitates tanquam ex particulis conſtantes conſideravero, vel ſi pro rectis uſurpavero lineolas curvas, nolim indiviſibilia ſed evaneſcentia diviſibilia, non ſummas & rationes partium determinatarum, ſed ſummarum & rationum limites ſemper intelligi, vimq; talium demonſtrationum ad methodum præcedentium Lemmatum ſemper revocari.

Objectio eſt, quod quantitatum evaneſcentium nulla ſit ultima proportio; quippe quæ, antequam evanuerunt, non eſt ultima, ubi evanuerunt, nulla eſt.   Sed & eodem argumento æque contendi poſſet nullam eſſe corporis ad certum locum pergentis velocitatem ultimam. Hanc enim, antequam corpus attingit locum, non eſſe ultimam, ubi attigit, nullam eſſe. Et reſponſio facilis eſt.   Per velocitatem ultimam intelligi eam, qua corpus movetur neq; antequam attingit locum ultimum & motus ceſſat, neq; poſtea, ſed tunc cum attingit, id eſt illam ipſam velocitatem quacum corpus attingit locum ultimum & quacum motus ceſſat.   Et ſimiliter per ultimam rationem quantitatum evaneſcentium intelligendam eſſe rationem quantitatum non antequam evaneſcunt, non poſtea, ſed quacum evaneſcunt.   Pariter & ratio prima naſcentium eſt ratio quacum naſcuntur.   Et ſumma prima & ultima eſt quacum eſſe ( vel augeri & minui ) incipiunt & ceſſant. Extat limes quem velocitas in fine motus attingere poteſt, non autem tranſgredi.

F 2                              Hæc

[ 36 ]

Hæc eſt velocitas ultima. Et par eſt ratio limitis quantitatum &
proportiorum omnium incipientium & ceſſantium. Cumq; hic limes ſit certus & definitus, Problema eſt vere Geometricum eun-
dem determinare. Geometrica vero omnia in aliis Geometricis
determinandis ac demonſtrandis legitime uſurpantur.

    Contendi etiam poteſt, quod ſi dentur ultimæ quantitatum e-
vaneſcentium rationes, dabuntur & ultimæ magnitudines; & ſic
quantitas omnis conſtabit ex indiviſibilibus, contra quam *Euclides*
de incommenſurabilibus, in libro decimo Elementorum, demon-
ſtravit. Verum hæc Objectio falſæ innititur hypotheſi. Ultimæ
rationes illæ quibuſcum quantitates evaneſcunt, revera non ſunt
rationes quantitatum ultimarum, ſed limites ad quos quantitatum
ſine limite decreſcentium rationes ſemper appropinquant, & quas
propius aſſequi poſſunt quam pro data quavis differentia, nunquam vero tranſgredi, neq; prius attingere quam quantitates diminuuntur in infinitum. Res clarius intelligetur in infinite magnis.
Si quantitates duæ quarum data eſt differentia augeantur in infinitum, dabitur harum ultima ratio, nimirum ratio æqualitatis,
nec tamen ideo dabuntur quantitates ultimæ ſeu maximæ quarum
iſta eſt ratio. Igitur in ſequentibus, ſiquando facili rerum ima-
ginationi conſulens, dixero quantitates quam minimas, vel eva-
neſcentes vel ultimas, cave intelligas quantitates magnitudine de-
terminatas, ſed cogita ſemper diminuendas ſine limite.

### TRANSLATION

I have put forward these lemmas at the beginning, in order to avoid the tedium of
composing intricate demonstrations by contradiction in the manner of the ancient
geometers. For the demonstrations are rendered more concise by the method of indivisibles. But since the hypothesis of indivisibles is cruder, and that method therefore
judged less geometrical, I have preferred to deduce the demonstrations of what follows
by means of first or last sums and ratios of nascent or vanishing quantities, that is,
to limits of sums and ratios, and therefore to put forward demonstrations of those
limits as briefly as I could. For the same can be shown by these as by the method of
indivisibles, and the principles having been demonstrated, we may now more safely
use them. Consequently in what follows, whenever I have considered quantities as if
consisting of particles, or if I have used little curved lines for straight lines, I do not
mean indivisibles but vanishing divisibles, and there should always be understood not
sums and ratios of the known parts but the limits of sums and ratios, and the validity
of such demonstrations is always to be based on the method of the preceding lemmas.

    The objection is that the ultimate ratio of vanishing quantities might not exist; since
before they vanish, it is not ultimate; and where they have vanished, it is non-existent.
But by the same argument it could equally be contended that the ultimate velocity

of a body arriving at a certain place does not exist. For in this case, before the body reaches the place, the velocity is not ultimate; where it reaches it, it does not exist. And the answer is easy. By the ultimate velocity is to be understood that with which the body moves, not before it reaches the final place and the motion ceases, nor after, but as it reaches it; that is, that same velocity with which the body reaches the final place and with which the motion ceases. And similarly by the ultimate ratio of vanishing quantities there must be understood the ratio of quantities not before they vanish, nor after, but with which they vanish. And equally the first ratio of nascent quantities is the ratio with which they originate. And the first or ultimate sum is that with which they begin or cease to be (according as they are increasing or decreasing). There exists a limit which at the end of the motion the velocity may attain, but not exceed. [36] This is the ultimate velocity. And likewise for the limiting ratio of all quantities and proportions beginning or ceasing to be. And since this limit is fixed and definite, the problem is to determine it correctly geometrically. Indeed anything geometric can legitimately be used to determine or demonstrate other things geometrically.

It may also be contended that if ultimate ratios of vanishing quantities are given, so are the ultimate magnitudes; and thus every quantity will consist of indivisibles, contrary to what *Euclid* proved of incommensurables in the tenth book of the *Elements*. But this objection is based on a false hypothesis. Those ultimate ratios with which quantities vanish, are not actually ratios of ultimate quantities, but limits to which the ratios of quantities decreasing without limit always approach, and which they may attain more closely than by any given difference, but never exceed, nor attain before the quantities are infinitely diminished. This may be more clearly understood for the infinitely large. If two quantities, whose difference is given, are infinitely increased, their ultimate ratio will be given, namely the ratio of equality, but nevertheless there will not thereby be given the ultimate or greatest quantities of which this is the ratio. Therefore whenever in what follows, to make things easier to imagine, I speak of quantities as the smallest, or vanishing, or ultimate, avoid thinking of quantities of finite magnitude, but always consider that they are to be decreased without limit.

———————————

## 11.1.3 Maclaurin's definition of a limit, 1742

Maclaurin, writing some sixty years after Newton, continued to use the word 'limit' in much the same sense, as a bound that may be approached as closely as one wishes. Stung by the criticisms of Berkeley and others (see 10.2.2) he took great pains to show that limits were well defined, but his words 'it is manifest …' did nothing to avoid or disguise the fundamental problem of neglecting *o* after dividing by it.

## Maclaurin's definition of a limit

from Maclaurin, *A treatise of fluxions*, 1742, I, §502–§503

502. But however safe and convenient this method may be, some will always scruple to admit infinitely little quantities, and infinite orders of infinitesimals, into a science that boasts of the most evident and accurate principles as well as of the most rigid demonstrations; and therefore we chose to establish so extensive and useful a doctrine in the preceeding chapters on more unexceptionable *postulata*. In order to avoid such suppositions, Sir ISAAC NEWTON considers the simultaneous increments of the flowing quantities as finite, and then investigates the ratio which is the limit of the various proportions which those increments bear to each other, while he supposes them to decrease together till they vanish; which ratio is the same with the ratio of the fluxions by what was shewn in art. 66, 67 and 68. In order to discover this limit, he first determines the ratio of the increments in general, and reduces it to the most simple terms so as that (generally speaking) a part at least of each term may be independent of the value

Chap. XII.    *Of the limits of Ratios.*    421

value of the increments themselves; then by supposing the increments to decrease till they vanish, the limit readily appears.

503. For example, let $a$ be an invariable quantity, $x$ a flowing quantity, and $o$ any increment of $x$; then the simultaneous increments of $xx$ and $ax$ will be $2xo + oo$ and $ao$, which are in the same ratio to each other as $2x + o$ is to $a$. This ratio of $2x + o$ to $a$ continually decreases while $o$ decreases, and is always greater than the ratio of $2x$ to $a$ while $o$ is any real increment, but it is manifest that it continually approaches to the ratio of $2x$ to $a$ as its limit; whence it follows that the fluxion of $xx$ is to the fluxion of $ax$ as $2x$ is to $a$. If $x$ be supposed to flow uniformly, $ax$ will likewise flow uniformly, but $xx$ with a motion continually accelerated : The motion with which $ax$ flows may be measured by $ao$, but the motion with which $xx$ flows is not to be measured by its increment $2xo + oo$, (by ax. 1.) but by the part $2xo$ only, which is generated in consequence of that motion; and the part $oo$ is to be rejected because it is generated in consequence only of the acceleration of the motion with which the variable square flows, while $o$ the increment of its side is generated : And the ratio of $2xo$ to $ao$ is that of $2x$ to $a$, which was found to be the limit of the ratio of the increments $2xo + oo$ and $ao$.

## 11.1.4 D'Alembert's definition of a limit, 1765

When d'Alembert wrote and edited the mathematical sections of the great *Encyclopédie* of Denis Diderot, published between 1751 and 1765, he provided new and useful definitions of many recent mathematical concepts. His definition of 'limit' in Volume IX was close to Newton's idea of a limit as a bound that could be approached as closely as one chose, and because d'Alembert, like Newton, worked with examples that were primarily geometric, there was still no obvious need to consider quantities that might oscillate from one side of a limit to the other.

---

### D'Alembert's definition of a limit
from Diderot and d'Alembert, *Encyclopédie*, 1751–65, IX, 542

---

#### TRANSLATION

---

LIMIT (*Mathematics*). One says that a magnitude is the *limit* of another magnitude, when the second may approach the first more closely than by a given quantity, as small as one wishes, moreover without the magnitude which approaches being allowed ever to surpass the magnitude that it approaches; so that the difference between such a quantity and its *limit* is absolutely unassignable.

For example, suppose we have two polygons, one inscribed in a circle and the other circumscribed; it is clear that one may increase the number of sides as much as one wishes, and in that case each polygon will approach ever more closely to the circumference of the circle; the perimeter of the inscribed polygon will increase and that of the circumscribed polygon will decrease, but the perimeter or edge of the first will never surpass the length of the circumference, and that of the second will never be smaller than that same circumference; the circumference of the circle is therefore the *limit* of the increase of the first polygon and of the decrease of the second.

1. If two magnitudes are the *limit* of the same quantity, the two magnitudes will be equal to each other.

2. Suppose $A \times B$ is the product of two magnitudes $A, B$. Let us suppose that $C$ is the *limit* of the magnitude $A$, and $D$ the *limit* of the quantity $B$; I say that $C \times D$, the product of the *limits*, will necessarily be the *limit* of $A \times B$, the product of the magnitudes $A, B$.

These two propositions, which one will find demonstrated exactly in the *Institutions de Géométrie*, serve as principles for demonstrating rigorously that one has the area of a circle from multiplying its semicircumference by its radius. *See the work cited, p. 331 and following in the second volume.*

The theory of *limits* is the foundation of the true justification of the differential calculus. *See* DIFFERENTIAL, FLUXION, EXHAUSTION, INFINITE. Strictly speaking, the *limit* never coincides, or never becomes equal to the quantity of which it is the *limit*, but the latter approaches it ever more closely, and may differ from it as little as one wishes. The circle, for example, is the *limit* of the inscribed and circumscribed polygons; for strictly it never coincides with them, although they may approach it indefinitely. This notion may serve to clarify several mathematical propositions. For example, one says that the sum of a decreasing geometric progression in which the first term is $a$ and the second $b$, is $\dfrac{aa}{a-b}$; this value is never strictly the sum of the progression, it is the *limit* of that sum, that is to say, the quantity which it may approach as closely as one wishes, without ever arriving at it exactly. For if $e$ is the last term in the progression, the exact value of the sum is $\dfrac{aa-be}{a-b}$, which is always less than $\dfrac{aa}{a-b}$ because even in a decreasing geometric progression, the last term $e$ is never 0; but as this term continually approaches zero, without ever arriving at it, it is clear that zero is its *limit*, and that consequently the *limit* of $\dfrac{aa-be}{a-b}$ is $\dfrac{aa}{a-b}$, supposing $e=0$, that is to say, on putting in place of $e$ its *limit*. See SEQUENCE or SERIES, PROGRESSION, etc.

---

## 11.1.5 Cauchy's definition of a limit, 1821

Cauchy's definition of a limit, first given in his *Cours d'analyse* in 1821, imitated that of d'Alembert and combined the same basic ideas: the existence of a fixed value, and the possibility of approaching it as closely as one wishes. The same definition was repeated, with further examples, at the beginning of his *Résumé des leçons* in 1823.

Cauchy established the concept of a limit as the starting point of textbook expositions of analysis but in most respects his definition was no clearer than Newton's 150 years earlier, for there was still no precise discussion of what it meant to approach a fixed value 'indefinitely', nor of whether a variable quantity might actually attain or even at times surpass its limit. Cauchy offered the well worn illustration of a circle and polygons, but also produced a new and more interesting example, of an irrational number approached by rationals; he did not yet suggest, however, that a limit could be approached from both sides simultaneously.

## Cauchy's definition of a limit, 1821

from Cauchy, *Cours d'analyse*, 1821, 4–5

On nomme quantité *variable* celle que l'on considère comme devant recevoir successivement plusieurs valeurs différentes les unes des autres. On désigne une semblable quantité par une lettre prise ordinairement parmi les dernières de l'alphabet. On appelle au contraire quantité *constante*, et on désigne ordinairement par une des premières lettres de l'alphabet toute quantité qui reçoit une valeur fixe et déterminée. Lorsque les valeurs successivement attribuées à une même variable s'approchent indéfiniment d'une valeur fixe, de manière à finir par en différer aussi peu que l'on voudra, cette dernière est appelée la *limite* de toutes les autres. Ainsi, par exemple, un nombre irrationnel est la limite des diverses fractions qui en fournissent des valeurs de plus en plus approchées. En géométrie, la surface du cercle est la limite vers laquelle convergent les surfaces des polygones inscrits, tandis que le nombre de leurs côtés croît de plus en plus ; &c. . . .

Lorsque les valeurs numériques successives d'une même variable décroissent indéfiniment, de manière à s'abaisser au-dessous de tout nombre donné, cette variable devient ce qu'on nomme un *infiniment petit* ou une quantité *infiniment petite*. Une variable de cette espèce a zéro pour limite.

Lorsque les valeurs numériques successives

d'une même variable croissent de plus en plus, de
manière à s'élever au-dessus de tout nombre donné,
on dit que cette variable a pour limite *l'infini positif*,
indiqué par le signe ∞, s'il s'agit d'une variable
positive, et *l'infini négatif*, indiqué par la notation
— ∞, s'il s'agit d'une variable négative. Les infinis
positif et négatif sont désignés conjointement sous
le nom de *quantités infinies*.

---

TRANSLATION

One calls a *variable* quantity one that is considered to take successively several values
different from each other. One denotes such a quantity by a letter usually taken from
amongst the last in the alphabet. On the other hand one calls a *constant* quantity every
quantity that takes a fixed and known value, and one usually denotes it by one of the
first letters of the alphabet. When the values successively attributed to the same variable
approach indefinitely to a fixed value, in such a way as to end by differing from it as
little as one wishes, this last is called the *limit* of all the others. Thus, for example,
an irrational number is the limit of various fractions that furnish values more and
more closely approaching it. In geometry, the area of a circle is the limit towards which
converge the areas of inscribed polygons, when the number of their sides increases
more and more; etc....

When the successive numerical values of the same variable decrease indefinitely, in
such a way as to fall below every given number, this variable becomes what one calls an
*infinitesimal* or an *infinitely small* quantity. A variable of this kind has zero for its limit.

When the successive numerical values [5] of the same variable increase more and
more, in such a way as to rise above every given number, one says that this variable has
for its limit *positive infinity*, indicated by the sign ∞, if one is dealing with a positive
variable, and *negative infinity*, indicated by the notation −∞, if one is dealing with a
negative variable. Positive and negative infinities are known jointly under the name of
*infinite quantities*.

---

## 11.2 CONTINUITY

### 11.2.1 Wallis and smooth curves, 1656

The concept of continuity arises most naturally from the consideration of curves: intuitively a continuous curve is one that can be drawn without the pen leaving the paper.
This idea was first made explicit by Wallis in the *Arithmetica infinitorum* of 1656, where
he defined a smooth curve (*aequabilis curva*) as one that does not jump about (*non
subsultans*). For Wallis this was a property that allowed him to interpolate intermediate values in a reliable way. Thus he was instinctively using what was later called the
'intermediate value theorem', which states that if a function (or its associated curve) is
continuous between two finite values then it must pass through all intermediate values.

---

### Wallis's smooth curve

from Wallis, *Arithmetica infinitorum*, 1656, Proposition 192

---

**PROP. CXCII.** *Theorema.*

SI fit æquabilis Curva(non hinc inde fubfultans)VC,
cujus Axis VX, & Tangens invertice VT; unde
ductis ad curvam rectis axi parallelis, & ab invicem
æqualibus diftantiis remotis, harum Secunda, Quarta, Sexta, Octava, &c. ( in locis paribus. ) fint ut
1,6,30,140, &c. (qui numeri fiunt ex continuâ mul-
tiplicatione horum, $1 \times \frac{6}{1} \times \frac{10}{2} \times \frac{14}{3} \times \frac{11}{4}$ &c.) Erit, ut Secunda ad Tertiam (hoc eft, ut 1 ad numerum ipfis 1,
6, interponendum,) fic Semicirculus ad Quadratum
Diametri.

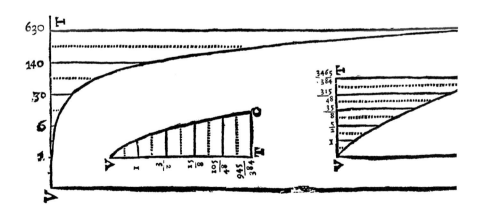

## PROPOSITION 192

*Theorem*

Suppose there is a smooth curve *VC* (not jumping about from here to there), whose axis is *VX*, and with tangent *VT* to the vertex, and such that, taking lines from [the tangent] to the curve, parallel to the axis and equally spaced from each other, the second, fourth, sixth, eighth of them, etc. (in the even places) are as 1, 6, 30, 140, etc. (which numbers arise from continued multiplication of these, $1 \times \frac{6}{1} \times \frac{10}{2} \times \frac{14}{3} \times \frac{18}{4}$, etc.). Then the second to the third (that is, 1 to the number that must be interposed between 1 and 6) is as a semicircle to the square of its diameter.

### 11.2.2 Euler's definition of continuity, 1748

During the eighteenth century, continuity in the sense of 'smoothness' was taken for granted for curves defined by an algebraic relationship between the variables. As with the concept of 'function', however, the analysis of vibrating strings threw ideas about continuity into some confusion. By 1748 it was clear that d'Alembert's wave equation

$$\frac{\partial^2 y}{\partial x^2} = \frac{1}{c^2} \frac{\partial^2 y}{\partial t^2}$$

was satisfied by *any* function of the form $y = \Phi(x + ct) + \Gamma(x - ct)$ (see 10.1.2), and the problem that now arose was the nature of the functions $\Phi$ and $\Gamma$. The difficulty was that a plucked string in its starting position could have one or more 'corners'. To Euler it was clear that functions with joins and corners must be allowed into the analysis of the problem. For d'Alembert, on the other hand, because such functions were not differentiable, they had to be excluded.

   This was the background to Euler's definition of continuity in Volume II of his *Introductio* in 1748, where he distinguished between curves that could be expressed along their entire length by a single function (as d'Alembert required), and those that had to be defined piecewise (which Euler wished to include). For Euler only the first kind counted as 'continuous', not just unbroken, but with no sudden changes of direction. Thus, Euler described as 'continuous' what we now describe as 'differentiable', a much stronger condition.

# Euler's definition of continuity

from Euler, *Introductio in analysin infinitorum*, 1748, II, §9, here from the second
edition, 1797, 6

9. Ex hac linearum curvarum idea ſtatim ſequitur earum diviſio in *continuas* & *diſcontinuas* ſeu *mixtas*. Linea ſcilicet curva *continua* ita eſt comparata, ut ejus natura per unam ipſius *x* Functionem definitam exprimatur. Quod ſi autem linea curva ita ſit comparata, ut variæ ejus portiones *BM*, *MD*, *DM* &c., per varias ipſius *x* Functiones exprimantur; ita ut, poſtquam ex una Functione portio *BM* fuerit definita, tum ex alia Functione portio *MD* deſcribatur; hujuſmodi lineas curvas *diſcontinuas* ſeu *mixtas* & *irregulares* appellamus: propterea quod non ſecundum unam legem conſtantem formantur, atque ex portionibus variarum curvarum continuarum componuntur.

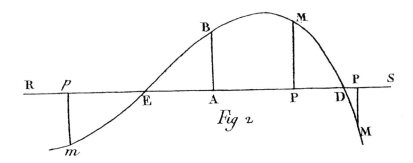

*Fig 2*

## TRANSLATION

9. From this idea of curved lines there immediately follows a separation of them into *continuous* and *discontinuous* or *mixed*. Clearly a curve is *continuous* if it is established in such a way, that its character is expressed by a single fixed function of *x*. But if the curve is so established, that the various portions of it *BM*, *MD*, *DM*, etc. are expressed by different functions of *x*, in such a way that after the portion *BM* has been defined by one function, then the portion *MD* is described by another function, curves of this kind we call *discontinuous* or *mixed*, also *irregular*, because they are not formed according to one constant law, but are composed from portions of different continuous curves.

### 11.2.3 Lagrange's arbitrarily small intervals, 1797

It was not until very late in the eighteenth century that there began to emerge more precise ideas of what it meant for a function to be continuous, in Wallis's sense of 'not jumping about', by considering values at points arbitrarily close together. One of the first mathematicians to investigate changes in a function over small intervals was Lagrange in his *Théorie des fonctions* of 1797. As a prerequisite to calculating the error term in a Taylor series (see 8.3.2), Lagrange established the following lemma: if the first derivative of a function $f$, defined on an interval $[a, b]$, is strictly positive, then $f(b) - f(a) > 0$.

His proof is not altogether sound: in the second paragraph below, he fixes $i$ for a particular value of $z$, but in the third paragraph allows $z$ to take a whole range of values from $a$ to $b$. Unfortunately, there is no guarantee that one single value of $i$ will serve for all these values of $z$ at once. The main purpose of reproducing the proof here, however, is to demonstrate Lagrange's use of arbitrarily small intervals, a technique that was to be profoundly influential later.

---

### Lagrange's arbitrarily small intervals

from Lagrange, *Théorie des fonctions analytiques*, 1797, §48

---

Pour cela·, nous allons établir ce lemme général.

Si une fonction prime de $z$, telle que $f'z$ est toujours positive pour toutes les valeurs de $z$, depuis $z = a$ jusqu'à $z = b$, $b$ étant $> a$, la différence des fonctions primitives qui répondent à ces deux valeurs de $z$, savoir, $fb - fa$, sera nécessairement une quantité positive.

Considérons la fonction $f(z + i)$, dont le développement est $fz + if'z + \frac{i^2}{2} f''z + \&c.$, nous avons vu qu'on peut toujours prendre la quantité $i$ assez petite pour qu'un terme quelconque de cette série devienne plus grand que la somme de tous ceux qui le suivent ( $n.° 14$ ). Ainsi le terme $if'z$ pourra devenir plus grand que le reste de la série ; par conséquent si $f'z$ est une quantité positive, on pourra prendre $i$ positif et assez petit pour que toute la série $if'z + \frac{i^2}{2} f''z + \&c.$ ait nécessairement une valeur positive ; mais cette série est $= f'(z + i) - fz$ ; donc, si $f'z$ est une quantité positive, on pourra prendre pour $i$ une quantité positive et assez petite pour que la quantité $f(z + i) - fz$ soit nécessairement positive.

Mettons successivement à la place de $z$ les quantités $a$, $a + i$, $a + 2i$, $a + 3i$, &c., $a + ni$, il en résultera que l'on peut prendre $i$ positif et assez petit pour que toutes les quantités $f(a + i) - fa$, $f(a + 2i) - f(a + i)$, $f(a + 3i) - f(a + 2i)$, jusqu'à $f[a + (n + 1)i] - f(a + ni)$, soient nécessairement positives, si les quantités $f'a$, $f'(a + i)$, $f'(a + 2i)$, &c. jusqu'à $f'(a + ni)$ le sont. Donc aussi,

46                    T H É O R I E

dans ce cas, la somme des premières quantités, c'est-à-dire, la quantité $f[a + (n + 1)i] - fa$, sera positive.

Faisons maintenant $a + (n + 1)i = b$, on aura $i = \dfrac{b - a}{n + 1}$, et l'on

en conclura que la quantité $fb - fa$ sera necessairement positive, si

toutes les quantités $f'a, f'(a + \dfrac{b - a}{n + 1}), f'(a + \dfrac{2(b - a)}{n + 1}) f'(a +$

$\dfrac{3(b - a)}{n + 1})$, &c., jusqu'à $f'(a + \dfrac{n(b - a)}{n + 1})$, sont positives, en

prenant $n$ aussi grand qu'on voudra.

Donc, à plus forte raison, la quantité $fb - fa$ sera positive, si $f'z$ est
toujours une quantité positive, en donnant à $z$ toutes les valeurs possibles
depuis $z = a$, jusqu'à $z = b$, puisque parmi ces valeurs se trouveront

nécessairement les valeurs $a, a + \dfrac{b - a}{n + 1}, a + \dfrac{2(b - a)}{n + 1}$, &c.

$a + \dfrac{n(b - a)}{n + 1}$, en prenant $n$ aussi grand qu'on voudra.

---

TRANSLATION

For that [calculation of bounds], we will establish this general lemma:
If a first derived function of $z$, such as $f'z$, is always positive for all values of $z$ from $z = a$
to $z = b$, with $b > a$, the difference between the primitive functions corresponding to
these two values of $z$, namely, $fb - fa$ will necessarily be a positive quantity.

Let us consider the function $f(z + i)$ of which the expansion is $fz + if'z + \dfrac{i^2}{2}f''z +$
etc.; we have seen that one may always take the quantity $i$ small enough that any term
of this series becomes greater than the sum of all those that follow (§14). Thus the term
$if'z$ may become greater than the rest of the series; consequently if $f'z$ is a positive
quantity, one may take $i$ positive and small enough that the whole series $if'z + \dfrac{i^2}{2}f''z +$
etc. necessarily has a positive value; but this series is $f(z + i) - fz$; therefore, if $f'z$ is
a positive quantity, one may take for $i$ a positive quantity so small that the quantity
$f(z + i) - fz$ is necessarily positive.

Let us put successively in place of $z$ the quantities $a, a + i, a + 2i, a + 3i$, etc. to $a + ni$;
it will then come about that one may take $i$ positive and so small that all the quantities
$f(a + i) - fa, f(a + 2i) - f(a + i), f(a + 3i) - f(a + 2i)$, to $f[a + (n + 1)i)] - f(a + ni)$
will necessarily be positive, if the quantities $f'a, f'(a + i), f'(a + 2i)$ etc. to $f'(a + ni)$
are so. Therefore also, [46] in this case, the sum of the former quantities, that is to say,
the quantity, $f[a + (n + 1)i] - fa$ will be positive.

Now putting $a + (n+1)i = b$, we will have $i = \dfrac{b-a}{n+1}$, and from that one concludes that the quantity $fb - fa$ will necessarily be positive if all the quantities $f'a, f'\left(a + \frac{b-a}{n+1}\right)$, $f'\left(a + \frac{2(b-a)}{n+1}\right), f'\left(a + \frac{3(b-a)}{n+1}\right)$, etc. to $f'\left(a + \frac{n(b-a)}{n+1}\right)$ are positive, on taking $n$ as large as one wants.

Therefore, for even stronger reason, the quantity $fb - fa$ will be positive if $f'z$ is always a positive quantity, on giving $z$ all possible values from $z = a$ to $z = b$, since among those values will necessarily be found the values $a$, $a + \frac{b-a}{n+1}$, $a + \frac{2(b-a)}{n+1}$ etc. to $a + \frac{n(b-a)}{n+1}$, on taking $n$ as large as one wants.

_____

### 11.2.4 Bolzano's definition of continuity, 1817

In 1817, the Prague mathematician Bernard Bolzano published a short pamphlet with a very long title: *Rein analytischer Beweis des Lehrsatzes, dass zwischen je zwey Werthen, die ein entgegengesetztes Resultat gewähren, wenigstens eine reelle Wurzel der Gleichung liege* (*Purely analytic proof of the theorem that between any two values which give results of opposite sign, there lies at least one real root of the equation*). His paper, exactly as its title suggests, attempted to prove the intermediate value theorem, namely the theorem that a continuous function that is positive at one point and negative at another must be zero at some point in between. The theorem is, of course, valid only for continuous functions, and until then most proofs had relied on a common sense understanding of smooth curves. Bolzano was severely critical of such approaches, arguing that any proof must rest on properly analytic foundations, and was thus led to the first formal definition of continuity.[3] Bolzano's paper marks such an important transition from intuitive notions of continuity to an analytic definition that it is quoted here at some length. For further important theorems from the same paper see 16.1.1 and 16.3.1.

_____

3. Steve Russ, editor and translator of Bolzano's papers, has pointed out that Bolzano distinguished between continuity of a curve (for which he used *continuirlich*) and continuity of a function (for which he used *stetig*, literally 'steady'), and made no explicit connection between the two except to note that continuity of a curve could not be used to prove continuity of a function; see Russ 2004, 254 note *a*.

# Bolzano's definition of continuity

from Bolzano, *Rein analytischer Beweis*, 1817, 6–14, as translated by Steve Russ in Bolzano 2004, 254–257

6

I. Bey der gewöhnlichsten Beweisart stüzt man sich auf eine aus der Geometrie entlehnte Wahrheit: daß nähmlich eine jede continuirliche Linie von einfacher Krümmung, deren Ordinaten erst positiv, dann negativ sind (oder umgekehrt), die Abscissenlinie nothwendig irgendwo in einem Puncte, der zwischen jenen Ordinaten liegt, durchschneiden müsse. Gegen die Richtigkeit sowohl, als auch gegen die Evidenz dieses geometrischen Satzes ist gar nichts einzuwenden. Aber eben so offenbar ist auch, daß es ein nicht zu duldender Verstoß gegen die gute Methode sey, Wahrheiten der reinen (oder allgemeinen) Mathematik (d. h. der Arithmetik, Algebra oder Analysis) aus Betrachtungen herleiten zu wollen, welche in einen bloß angewandten (oder speciellen) Theil derselben, nahmentlich in die Geometrie gehören. Und hat man die Unschicklichkeit einer dergleichen μεταβασις εἰς ἄλλο γένος nicht längst schon gefühlt und anerkannt? hat man sie nicht schon in hundert andern Fällen, wo man ein Mittel gewußt, vermieden, und diese Vermeidung sich zum Verdienste angerechnet? *) Muß man sich also nicht, wenn man anders folgerecht seyn will, dieses auch hier zu thun

*) Ein Beyspiel geben die vorhin angeführten Abhandlungen des Hrn. Prof. Gauß.

7

thun bestreben? — Denn in der That, wer immer bedenket, daß die Beweise in der Wissenschaft keinesswegs bloße Gewißmachungen, sondern vielmehr Begründungen d. h. Darstellungen jenes objectiven Grundes, den die zu beweisende Wahrheit hat, seyn sollen: dem leuchtet von selbst ein, daß der echt wissenschaftliche Beweis, oder der objective Grund einer Wahrheit, welche von allen Größen gilt, gleich viel, ob sie im Raume oder nicht im Raume sind, unmöglich in einer Wahrheit liegen könne, die bloß von Größen, welche im Raume sind, gilt. Bey Festhaltung dieser Ansicht begreift man vielmehr, daß ein dergleichen geometrischer Beweis, wie in den meisten Fällen, so auch in dem gegenwärtigen, ein wirklicher Zirkel sey. Denn ist gleich die geometrische Wahrheit, auf die man sich hier beruft, (wie wir schon eingestanden haben) höchst evident, und bedarf sie also keines Beweises als Gewißmachung; so bedarf sie nichts desto weniger doch einer Begründung. Denn sichtbar sind die Begriffe, aus denen sie besteht, so zusammengesetzt, daß man nicht einen Augenblick anstehen kann, zu sagen, sie gehöre keineswegs zu jenen einfachen Wahrheiten, welche man eben deßhalb, weil sie nur Grund von andern, selbst keine Folgen sind, Grundsätze oder Grundwahrheiten nennet; sie sey vielmehr ein Lehrsatz oder eine Folgewahrheit, d. h. eine solche Wahrheit, die ihren Grund in gewissen andern hat, und daher auch in der Wissenschaft durch Herlei-

## TRANSLATION

I. The *most common* kind of proof [of the intermediate value theorem] depends on a truth borrowed from *geometry, namely: that every continuous line of simple curvature of which the ordinates are first positive and then negative* (or conversely) *must necessarily intersect the abscissa-line somewhere at a point lying between these ordinates.* There is certainly nothing to be said against the *correctness*, nor against the *obviousness* of this geometrical proposition. But it is also equally clear that it is an unacceptable breach of *good method* to try to derive truths of *pure* (or general) mathematics (i.e. arithmetic, algebra, analysis) from considerations which belong to a merely *applied* (or special) part of it, namely *geometry*. Indeed, have we not long felt, and acknowledged, the impropriety of such a crossing to another kind? Are there not a hundred other cases where a method

**8**

leitung aus denselben, dargethan werden muß. *)
Nun denke, wer da will, dem objectiven Grunde
nach, warum eine Linie unter den vorhin erwähnten
Umständen ihre Abscissenlinie durchschneide: so wird
gewiß jeder sehr bald gewahr werden, daß dieser
Grund in nichts Anderm liege, als in jener allgemeinen Wahrheit, zufolge deren jede stetige Function
von x, welche für einen Werth von x positiv, für
einen andern negativ wird, für irgend einen dazwi-
schen liegenden Werth von x zu Null werden muß.
Und dieß ist eben die Wahrheit, die hier bewiesen
werden soll. Weit gefehlt also, daß diese letztere aus
jener hergeleitet werden dürfte (wie dieß in der Beweisart, die wir jetzt prüfen, geschieht): muß vielmehr umgekehrt diese von jener abgeleitet werden, wenn
man die Wahrheiten in der Wissenschaft eben so darstellen will, wie sie nach ihrem objectiven Zusammen-
hange mit einander verbunden sind.

II. Nicht minder verwerflich ist der Beweis,
den Einige aus dem Begriffe der Stetigkeit einer
Function, mit Einmengung der Begriffe von Zeit
und

---

*) Man vergleiche über dieß Alles meine Beyträge
zu einer begründeteren Darstellung der
Mathematik. Ite Lieferung. Prag 1810. II.
Abthl. §§. 2. 10. 20. 21, wo man die logi-
schen Begriffe, welche ich hier als bekannt voraus
setze, entwickelt findet.

**9**

und Bewegung, führten. „Wenn sich zwey Functionen f x und φ x, sagen sie, nach dem Gesetze der
Stetigkeit ändern, und wenn .für x = α,
f α < φ α; für x = β aber f β > φ β ist: so muß es
irgend einen zwischen α und β liegenden Werth u
geben, für welchen f u = φ u ist. Denn wenn
man sich vorstellt, daß die veränderliche Größe x in
diesen beyden Functionen nach und nach alle zwischen
α und β liegende Werthe, und in demselben Au-
genblicke immer beyderseits denselben Werth annimmt:
so ist im Anfange dieser stetigen Werthveränderung
von x, f x < φ x, und am Ende f x > φ x.
Da aber beyde Functionen vermöge ihrer Stetigkeit
erst alle mittleren Werthe durchgehen müssen, bevor
sie zu einem höheren gelangen können; so muß es
irgend einen mittleren Augenblick geben, in
welchem beyde einander gleich waren." — Dieses
versinnlicht man noch durch das Beyspiel der Bewegung zweyer Körper, deren der eine anfangs hin-
ter dem andern war, zuletzt ihm vorgeeilt ist,
und folglich nothwendig einmahl bey ihm vorbey
gegangen seyn muß. —

Niemand wird wohl in Abrede stellen, daß der
Begriff der Zeit, und vollends jener der Bewegung in der allgemeinen Mathematik eben so fremd-
artig sey, als der des Raumes. Gleichwohl, wenn
diese zwey Begriffe hier nur der Erläuterung wegen eingemengt wären, hätten wir nichts dagegen zu
er-

of avoiding this has been discovered, and where the avoidance was considered a virtue? So if we were to be consistent must we not strive to do the same here? [7] In fact, anyone who considers that scientific proofs should not merely be *confirmations*, but rather *groundings*, i.e. presentations of the objective reason of the truth to be proved, realizes at once that the strictly scientific proof, or the objective reason of a truth, which holds equally for *all* quantities, whether in space or not, cannot possibly lie in a truth which holds merely for quantities which are in *space*. If we adhere to this view we see instead that such a *geometrical* proof is, in this as in most cases, really circular. For which the geometrical truth to which we refer here is (as we have already admitted) extremely *obvious* and therefore needs no *proof* in the sense of *confirmation*, it none the less does need a *grounding*. For it is apparent that the concepts of which it consists are so combined that we cannot hesitate for a moment to say that it cannot possibly be one of those *simple* truths, which are called *axioms*, or *basic truths*, because they are the *basis* for other truths and are not themselves consequences. On the contrary, it is a *theorem of consequent truth*, i.e. a kind of truth that has its basis in certain other truths and therefore, in science, [8] must be proved by a derivation from these other truths. Now

10

11

erinnern. Denn auch wir sind keineswegs einem so übertriebenen Purismus zugethan, der, um die Wissenschaft von allem Fremdartigen rein zu erhalten, verlangt, daß man in ihrem Vortrage nicht einmahl einen aus fremdem Gebiethe entlehnten Ausdruck, auch nur in uneigentlicher Bedeutung, und in der Absicht aufnehme, um eine Sache so kürzer und klärer zu bezeichnen, als es durch eine in lauter eigenthümlichen Benennungen abgefaßte Beschreibung geschehen kann, oder nur, um den Übelklang der steten Wiederholung der nähmlichen Worte zu meiden, oder um durch den bloßen Nahmen, den man der Sache beylegt, schon an ein Beyspiel zu erinnern, das zur Bestätigung der Behauptung dienen kann. Hieraus ersieht man zugleich, daß wir auch Beyspiele und Anwendungen nicht im Geringsten für etwas Solches halten, das der Vollkommenheit des wissenschaftlichen Vortrages Abbruch thue. Nur dieses fordern wir dagegen strenge: daß man die Beyspiele nie statt der Beweise aufstelle, und auf bloß uneigentlich gebrauchte Redensarten, und auf die Nebenvorstellungen, die sie mit sich führen, niemahls die Wesenheit des Schlusses selbst gründe, so daß der letztere wegfällt, sobald man jene ändert.

Nach diesen Ansichten dürfte sich also noch allenfalls die Einmengung des Begriffes der Zeit in obigem Beweise entschuldigen lassen; weil auf die Redensarten, die von ihm hergenommen sind, kein Schluß

Schluß gegründet wird, der nicht auch ohne ihn gälte. Keineswegs aber kann die zuletzt gegebene Versinnlichung durch die Bewegung eines Körpers für etwas Mehreres angesehen werden, als für ein bloßes Beyspiel, das den Satz selbst nicht beweiset, vielmehr durch ihn erst bewiesen werden muß.

a. Halten wir uns also mit Weglassung dieses Beyspiels nur an das übrige Raisonnement. Bemerken wir zuförderst, daß in demselben ein unrichtiger Begriff der Stetigkeit zu Grunde gelegt sey. Nach einer richtigen Erklärung nähmlich versteht man unter der Redensart, daß eine Function fx für alle Werthe von x, die inner- oder außerhalb gewisser Grenzen liegen *), nach dem Gesetze der Stetigkeit sich ändre, nur so viel, daß, wenn x irgend ein solcher Werth ist, der Unterschied f(x + ω) — fx kleiner als jede

---

*) Es gibt Functionen, welche für alle Werthe ihrer Wurzel stetig veränderlich sind, z. B. $\alpha x + \beta x$. Allein es gibt auch andre, die sich nur inner- oder außerhalb gewisser Grenzwerthe ihrer Wurzel nach dem Gesetze der Stetigkeit ändern. So ändert sich $x + \sqrt{(1 - x)(2 - x)}$ nur für alle Werthe von x, die $< + 1$, oder $> + 2$ sind, stetig; nicht aber für die Werthe, die zwischen $+ 1$ und $+ 2$ liegen.

consider, if you will, the objective reason why a line, as described above, intersects its abscissae-line. Surely everyone will soon see that this reason lies in nothing other than that general truth, as a result of which every continuous function of $x$ which is positive for one value of $x$, and negative for another, must be zero for some intermediate value of $x$. And this is precisely the truth which is to be proved here. It is therefore quite wrong to have allowed the latter to be derived from the former (as happens in the kind of proof we are now examining). Rather, conversely, the former must be derived from the latter if we intend to represent the truths in science exactly as they are related to each other in their objective connection.

II. The proof which some people have produced from the concept of the *continuity* of a function mixed up with the concepts of *time* [9] and *motion*, is no less objectionable. 'If two functions $fx$ and $\phi x$', they say, 'vary according to the law of continuity and if for $x = \alpha, f\alpha < \phi\alpha$, but for $x = \beta, f\beta > \phi\beta$, then there must be some value $u$, lying between $\alpha$ and $\beta$, for which $fu = \phi u$. For if we imagine that the variable quantity $x$ in both these functions successively takes all values between $\alpha$ and $\beta$, and in both always takes the same value at the same moment, then at the *beginning* of this continuous

**12**

be gegebene Größe gemacht werden kön=
ne, wenn man ω so klein, als man nur
immer will, annehmen kann; oder es sey
(nach den Bezeichnungen, die wir im §. 14. des
binomischen Lehrsatzes u. s. w. Prag 1816.
eingeführt) $f(x+\omega) = fx + \Omega$. Daß aber, wie
man in diesem Beweise annimmt, die stetige Function
niemahls zu einem höheren Werthe gelange, ohne erst
alle niedrigeren durchgegangen zu seyn, d. h. daß
$f(x+n\Delta x)$ jeden zwischen $fx$ und $f(x+\Delta x)$ lie=
genden Werth annehmen könne, wenn man n nach
Belieben zwischen o und + 1 nimmt: das ist wohl
eine sehr wahre Behauptung, aber sie kann nicht
als Erklärung des Begriffes der Stetigkeit angesehn
werden, sondern ist vielmehr ein Lehrsatz über den=
selben; und zwar ein solcher, der sich nur erst nach
Voraussetzung des Satzes selbst beweisen läßt, zu
dessen Beweise man ihn hier anwenden will. Denn
wenn M irgend eine zwischen $fx$ und $f(x+\Delta x)$ lie=
gende Größe bedeutet; so ist die Behauptung, daß
es irgend einen zwischen o und + 1 liegenden Werth
von n gebe, für welchen $f(x+n\Delta x) = M$ ist,
nur ein besonderer Fall von der allgemeinen
Wahrheit, daß, wenn $fx < \varphi x$ und
$f(x+\Delta x) > \varphi(x+\Delta x)$ ist, es irgend einen
mittleren Werth $x + n\Delta x$ geben müsse, für welchen
$f(x+n\Delta x) = \varphi(x+n\Delta x)$ ist. Aus die=
ser allgemeinen Wahrheit nähmlich ergibt sich jene erstere
Be=

**13**

Behauptung in dem besondern Falle, wo die Function
$\varphi x$ in eine constante Größe M übergeht.

b. Aber gesetzt auch, man könnte diesen Satz
auf einem andern Wege darthun: doch würde der Be=
weis, den wir prüfen, noch einen andern Fehler ha=
ben. Daraus nähmlich, daß $fx > \varphi x$ und $f\beta < \varphi\beta$
ist, würde nur folgen, daß wenn u irgend ein
zwischen α und β liegender Werth ist, bey welchem
$\varphi u > \varphi \alpha$ aber $< \varphi\beta$ ist; so werde $fx$ bevor es
aus $f\alpha$ in $f\beta$ übergeht, d. h. bey irgend einem x,
das zwischen α und β liegt, ebenfalls $= \varphi u$. Ob
aber dieses bey eben demselben Werthe von x,
der $= u$ ist, geschehe; d. h. (weil u jeden beliebi=
gen Werth zwischen α und β bedeuten kann, der
$\varphi u > \varphi \alpha$ und $< \varphi\beta$ macht) ob es irgend einen
zwischen α und β liegenden Werth von x gibt, bey
welchem beyde Functionen $fx$ und $\varphi x$ einander
gleich werden: das würde noch immer nicht folgen.

c. Das Täuschende des ganzen Beweises be=
ruhet überhaupt nur auf der Einmengung des Be=
griffes der Zeit. Denn wenn man diesen wegläßt,
so zeigt sich alsbald, daß der Beweis nichts anders,
als eine Wiederholung des zu beweisenden Satzes selbst
mit andern Worten ist. Denn sagen, daß die Func=
tion $fx$, bevor sie aus ihrem Zustande des Kleinerseyns
in den des Größerseyns übergeht, erst durch den des
Gleichseyns mit $\varphi x$ hindurch gehen müsse; heißt
ohne

**14**

ohne Zeitbegriffe sagen, daß unter den Werthen, die
$fx$ annimmt, wenn man für x jeden beliebigen Werth
zwischen α und β setzt, auch einer sey, der $fx = \varphi x$
macht; was der zu beweisende Satz selbst ist.

change in the value of x, $fx < \phi x$, and at the *end*, $fx > \phi x$. But since both functions,
by virtue of their continuity, must first go through all intermediate values before they
can reach a higher value, there must be some *intermediate moment* at which they were
both equal to one another.' This is further illustrated by the example of the *motion* of
two bodies, of which one is initially *behind* the other and later *ahead* of the other. It
necessarily follows that at one time it must have *passed* the other.

No one will want to deny that the concept of *time*, as well as that of *motion*, is just as
alien to general mathematics as the concept of *space*. Nevertheless we would have no
objection if these two concepts were only introduced here for the sake of *clarification*.
[10] For we are in no way party to a *purism* so exaggerated, that it demands, in order
to keep the science free from everything alien, that in its exposition one cannot even
use an *expression* borrowed from another field, even if only in a figurative sense and

with the purpose of describing a fact more briefly and clearly than could be done in a description involving purely specialist terms. Nor [do we object to such use] if it is just to avoid the monotony of constant repetition of the same word, or to remind us, by the mere name given to a thing, of an example which could serve to confirm a claim. It follows immediately that we do not regard *examples* and *applications* as detracting in the least from the perfection of a scientific exposition. There is only one thing that we do strictly require: that examples never be put forward instead of *proofs*, and that the essence of a deduction never be based on the merely figurative use of phrases or on associated ideas, so that the deduction itself becomes void as soon as these are changed.

In accordance with these views, the inclusion of the concept of *time* in the above proof may still perhaps be excused, because no conclusion is based on phrases containing it, [11] which would not also hold without it. But the last *illustration* using the *motion* of a body cannot be regarded as anything more than a mere *example* which does not prove the proposition itself, but instead must first be proved by it.

(a) Therefore let us leave this example and concentrate on the rest of the reasoning. *First of all*, let us notice that this is based on an incorrect concept of *continuity*. According to a *correct definition*, the expression *that a function fx varies according to the law of continuity for all values of x inside or outside certain limits* means only that, *if x is any such value the difference $f(x+\omega) - fx$ can be made smaller than* [12] *any given quantity, provided $\omega$ can be taken as small as we please*, or (in the notation we introduced in §14 of *Der binomische Lehrsatz* etc., Prague, 1816), $f(x + \omega) = fx + \Omega$. But, as assumed in this proof, the continuous function is one which never reaches a higher value without having first gone through all lower values, i.e. $f(x + n\Delta x)$ can take every value between $fx$ and $f(x + \Delta x)$ if $n$ is taken arbitrarily between 0 and $+1$. That is indeed a very *true* assertion, but it cannot be regarded as a *definition* of the concept of continuity: it is rather a *theorem* about continuity. In fact it is a theorem which can only itself be proved on the assumption of the proposition to whose proof one wishes to apply it here. For if $M$ denotes any quantity between $fx$ and $f(x + \Delta x)$, then the assertion that there is some value of $n$ between 0 and $+1$ for which $f(x + n\Delta x) = M$ is only a special case of the general truth that if $fx < \phi x$ and $f(x + \Delta x) > \phi(x + \Delta x)$, then there must be some intermediate value $x + n\Delta x$ for which $f(x + n\Delta x) = \phi(x + n\Delta x)$. The first assertion follows from this general truth [13] in the special case when the function $\phi x$ becomes a constant quantity $M$.

(b) But even supposing one could prove this proposition in another way, the proof which we are examining would have yet another defect. That is, from the fact that $f\alpha > \phi\alpha$ and $f\beta < \phi\beta$ it would only follow that, if $u$ is any value lying between $\alpha$ and $\beta$ for which $\phi u > \phi\alpha$ but $< \phi\beta$, then $fx$ becomes equal to $\phi u$ in going from $f\alpha$ to $f\beta$, i.e. for *some x* lying between $\alpha$ and $\beta$, $fx = \phi u$. But whether this happens for *exactly the same* value of $x$ which $= u$, that is (since $u$ can be any arbitrary value lying between $\alpha$ and $\beta$ which makes $\phi u > \phi\alpha$ and $< \phi\beta$) whether there is some value of $x$ lying between $\alpha$ and $\beta$ for which *both* functions $fx$ and $\phi x$ are equal to one another would still not follow.

(c) The deceptive nature of the whole proof really rests on the fact that the concept of *time* has been involved in it. For if this were omitted it would soon be seen that the proof is nothing but a re-statement in different words of the proposition to be proved. For to say that the function $fx$, before it passes from the state of being smaller than $\phi x$ to that of being greater, must first go through the state of being equal to $\phi x$, is to say, [14] without the concept of time, that among the values that $fx$ takes if $x$ is given every arbitrary value between $\alpha$ and $\beta$, there is one that makes $fx = \phi x$, which is exactly the proposition to be proved.

---

## 11.2.5  Cauchy's definition of continuity, 1821

One of the books that Cauchy studied during his years in Cherbourg between 1810 and 1812 was Lagrange's *Théorie des fonctions analytiques*, in which Lagrange had explored properties of $f(z + i) - f(z)$ as $i$ becomes very small (see 11.2.3), and this may have led Cauchy to think along the same lines. The definition of continuity that Cauchy eventually gave in his *Cours d'analyse* of 1821, however, was also strikingly similar to Bolzano's of 1817. Whether Cauchy had ever seen Bolzano's definition is not known. The *Rein analytischer Beweis*, though initially published as a pamphlet, was also reprinted in the *Abhandlungen der königliche Böhmische Gesellschaft der Wissenschaften* (*Proceedings of the Royal Bohemian Society of Sciences*), which from 1817 onwards was available in the Bibliothèque Impériale (now the Bibliothèque Nationale) in Paris, so it is not impossible that Cauchy had at least glanced at it. Throughout his life he was quick to take up interesting new ideas, but was generally more concerned to develop his own version of them than to acknowledge other people's; whether that is what happened here is impossible to say.

## Cauchy's definition of continuity
from Cauchy, *Cours d'analyse*, 1821, 34–35

——————

§. 2.ᵉ *De la continuité des Fonctions.*

Parmi les objets qui se rattachent à la considération des infiniment petits, on doit placer les notions relatives à la continuité ou à la discontinuité des fonctions. Examinons d'abord sous ce point de vue les fonctions d'une seule variable.

Soit $f(x)$ une fonction de la variable $x$, et supposons que, pour chaque valeur de $x$ intermédiaire entre deux limites données, cette fonction admette constamment une valeur unique et finie. Si, en partant d'une valeur de $x$ comprise entre ces limites, on attribue à la variable $x$ un accroissement infiniment petit $\alpha$, la fonction elle-même recevra pour accroissement la différence

$$f(x+\alpha)-f(x),$$

qui dépendra en même temps de la nouvelle variable $\alpha$ et de la valeur de $x$. Cela posé, la fonction $f(x)$ sera, entre les deux limites assignées à la variable $x$, fonction *continue* de cette variable, si, pour chaque valeur de $x$ intermédiaire entre ces limites, la valeur numérique de la différence

$$f(x+\alpha)-f(x)$$

décroît indéfiniment avec celle de $\alpha$. En d'autres termes, *la fonction $f(x)$ restera continue par rap-*

*port à x entre les limites données , si , entre ces limites, un accroissement infiniment petit de la variable produit toujours un accroissement infiniment petit de la fonction elle-même.*

On dit encore que la fonction $f(x)$ est, dans le voisinage d'une valeur particulière attribuée à la variable $x$, fonction continue de cette variable, toutes les fois qu'elle est continue entre deux limites de $x$, même très-rapprochées , qui renferment la valeur dont il s'agit.

Enfin, lorsqu'une fonction $f(x)$ cesse d'être continue dans le voisinage d'une valeur particulière de la variable $x$, on dit qu'elle devient alors *discontinue*, et qu'il y a pour cette valeur particulière *solution de continuité*.

D'après ces explications , il sera facile de reconnaitre entre quelles limites une fonction donnée de la variable $x$ est continue par rapport à cette variable. Ainsi , par exemple , la fonction sin. $x$, admettant pour chaque valeur particulière de la variable $x$ une valeur unique et finie, sera continue entre deux limites quelconques de cette variable, attendu que la valeur numérique de sin. $\left(\frac{1}{2}a\right)$, et par suite celle de la différence

$$\text{sin.}\,(x+a) - \text{sin.}\,x = 2\,\text{sin.}\left(\tfrac{1}{2}a\right)\text{cos.}\left(x+\tfrac{1}{2}a\right),$$

décroissent indéfiniment avec celle de $a$, quelle que soit d'ailleurs la valeur finie que l'on attribue à $x$.

TRANSLATION

## §2 On the continuity of functions

Among the subjects that depend on the consideration of infinitely small quantities, one must place ideas relating to the continuity or discontinuity of functions. Let us first examine from this point of view functions of a single variable.

Let $f(x)$ be a function of the variable $x$, and let us suppose that, for each value of $x$ between two given limits, this function always takes a unique and finite value. If, starting from a value of $x$ included between these limits, one gives to the variable $x$ an infinitely small increment $\alpha$, the function itself will receive as an increment the difference

$$f(x + \alpha) - f(x),$$

which will depend at the same time on the new variable $\alpha$ and on the value of $x$. This said, the function $f(x)$ will be, between the two assigned limits of the variable $x$, a *continuous* function of this variable, if, for each value of $x$ intermediate between these limits, the numerical value of the difference

$$f(x + \alpha) - f(x)$$

decreases indefinitely with that of $\alpha$. In other words, *the function $f(x)$ will remain continuous with respect* [35] *to $x$ between the given limits, if, between those limits, an infinitely small increase in the variable always produces an infinitely small increase in the function itself.*

One also says that the function $f(x)$ is, in the neighbourhood of a particular value given to the variable $x$, a continuous function of that variable, whenever it is continuous between two limits for $x$, even very close together, which enclose the value one is dealing with.

Finally, when the function $f(x)$ ceases to be continuous in the neighbourhood of a particular value of the variable $x$, one says that it then becomes *discontinuous*, and that it has for that particular value a *break in continuity*.

After these explanations, it will be easy to recognize the limits between which a given function of the variable $x$ is continuous with respect to that variable. Thus, for example, the function $\sin x$, taking for each particular value of the variable $x$ a unique and finite value, will be continuous between any two limits of that variable, seeing that the numerical value of $\sin(\frac{1}{2}\alpha)$, and consequently that of the difference

$$\sin(x + \alpha) - \sin x = 2 \sin\left(\tfrac{1}{2}\alpha\right) \cos\left(x + \tfrac{1}{2}\alpha\right),$$

decreases indefinitely with that of $\alpha$, whatever finite value one may give to $x$.

### 11.2.6 Cauchy and the intermediate value theorem, 1821

Cauchy gave his first statement of the intermediate value theorem in the second chapter of his *Cours d'analyse* in 1821, and the proof he offered there was based on precisely the kind of intuitive geometric reasoning of which Bolzano, writing four years earlier, had been so critical. But as an afterthought Cauchy referred the reader to a second proof, to be found in additional material at the end of the book, and his description of the supplementary proof as 'purely analytic' ('purement analytique') perhaps suggests at least some familiarity with Bolzano's paper of the same title.

Cauchy's Note III at the end of the *Cours d'analyse* does indeed contain a proof of the intermediate value theorem, but almost incidentally. Its main aim is the numerical solution of equations. With this in mind Cauchy set out to find the root of an equation $f(x) = 0$, when it is known that $f(x)$ changes sign between $x = x_0$ and $x = X$, by pinning down the root inside smaller and smaller nested intervals. This is a *constructive* proof of the intermediate value theorem, showing exactly how to locate the required value.

Cauchy's proof is sound in almost every respect, except that he made one fundamental and as yet unproved assumption: that a monotonic bounded sequence converges to a limit. Cauchy took this to be self-evident, but in fact it relies on (or is equivalent to) completeness of the real numbers, to which we shall return in Chapter 16.

---

**Cauchy and the intermediate value theorem (1)**
from Cauchy, *Course d'analyse*, 1821, 43–44

---

4.$^e$ THÉORÈME. *Si la fonction $f(x)$ est continue par rapport à la variable $x$ entre les limites $x=x_0$, $x=X$, et que l'on désigne par $b$ une quantité intermédiaire entre $f(x_0)$ et $f(X)$, on pourra toujours satisfaire à l'équation*

$$f(x) = b$$

*par une ou plusieurs valeurs réelles de $x$ comprises entre $x_0$ et $X$.*

**44**          COURS D'ANALYSE.

*DÉMONSTRATION.* Pour établir la proposition précédente, il suffit de faire voir que la courbe qui a pour équation

$$y = f(x)$$

rencontrera une ou plusieurs fois la droite qui a pour équation

$$y = b$$

dans l'intervalle compris entre les ordonnées qui correspondent aux abscisses $x_0$ et $X$ : or c'est évidemment ce qui aura lieu dans l'hypothèse admise. En effet, la fonction $f(x)$ étant continue entre les limites $x = x_0$, $x = X$, la courbe qui a pour équation $y = f(x)$, et qui passe 1.° par le point correspondant aux coordonnées $x_0$, $f(x_0)$, 2.° par le point correspondant aux coordonnées $X$ et $f(X)$, sera continue entre ces deux points : et, comme l'ordonnée constante $b$ de la droite qui a pour équation $y = b$ se trouve comprise entre les ordonnées $f(x_0)$, $f(X)$ des deux points que l'on considère, la droite passera nécessairement entre ces deux points, ce qu'elle ne peut faire sans rencontrer dans l'intervalle la courbe ci-dessus mentionnée.

On peut, au reste, comme on le fera dans la note III, démontrer le 4.ᵉ théorème par une méthode directe et purement analytique, qui a même l'avantage de fournir la résolution numérique de l'équation

$$f(x) = b.$$

4. THEOREM. *If the function f(x) is continuous with respect to the variable x between the limits $x = x_0$ and $x = X$, and one denotes by b an intermediate quantity between $f(x_0)$ and $f(X)$, one can always satisfy the equation*

$$f(x) = b$$

*by one or more real values of x contained between $x_0$ and $X$.*

[44] PROOF. To establish the preceding proposition it is sufficient to show that the curve which has for its equation

$$y = f(x)$$

will meet once or several times the straight line that has for its equation

$$y = b$$

in the interval contained between the ordinates that correspond to the abscissae $x_0$ and $X$: but it is clear that this will happen under the supposed hypothesis. Indeed, the function $f(x)$ being continuous between the limits $x = x_0, x = X$, the curve which has for its equation $y = f(x)$, and which passes, first, through the point corresponding to the coordinates $x_0, f(x_0)$, second, through the point corresponding to coordinates $X, f(X)$, will be continuous between these two points; and, since the constant ordinate $b$ of the straight line that has for its equation $y = b$ is found contained between the ordinates $f(x_0)$ and $f(X)$ of the two points one is considering, the straight line will necessarily pass between these two points, which it cannot do without meeting the above mentioned curve within the interval.

One may, besides, as we will do in note III, demonstrate the 4th theorem by a direct and purely analytic method, which at the same time has the advantage of supplying the numerical solution of the equation

$$f(x) = b.$$

Cauchy and the intermediate value theorem (2)

from Cauchy, *Course d'analyse*, 1821, 460–462

**460**

## NOTE III.

*Sur la Résolution numérique des Équations.*

RÉSOUDRE *numériquement* une ou plusieurs équations, c'est trouver les valeurs en nombres des inconnues qu'elles renferment ; ce qui exige évidemment que les constantes comprises dans les équations dont il s'agit soient elles-mêmes réduites en nombres. Nous nous occuperons seulement ici des équations qui renferment une inconnue, et nous commencerons par établir à leur égard les théorèmes suivans.

1.$^{er}$ THÉORÈME. *Soit* $f(x)$ *une fonction réelle de la variable* $x$, *qui demeure continue par rapport à cette variable entre les limites* $x = x_0$, $x = X$. *Si les deux quantités* $f(x_0)$, $f(X)$ *sont de signes contraires, on pourra satisfaire à l'équation*

$$(1) \qquad f(x) = 0$$

*par une ou plusieurs valeurs réelles de* $x$ *comprises entre* $x_0$ *et* $X$.

*DÉMONSTRATION.* Soit $x_0$ la plus petite des deux quantités $x_0$, $X$. Faisons

$$X - x_0 = h \, ;$$

et désignons par $m$ un nombre entier quelconque supérieur à l'unité. Comme des deux quantités $f(x_0)$, $f(X)$, l'une est positive, l'autre négative, si l'on forme la suite

$$f(x_0), \ f\left(x_0 + \frac{h}{m}\right), \ f\left(x_0 + 2\frac{h}{m}\right), \ldots f\left(X - \frac{h}{m}\right), f(X),$$

et que dans cette suite on compare successivement· le premier terme avec le second, le second avec le troisième, le troisième avec le quatrième, &c..., on finira nécessairement par trouver une ou plusieurs fois deux termes consécutifs qui seront de signes contraires. Soient

$$f(x_{,}), \quad f(X'),$$

deux termes de cette espèce, $x_{,}$ étant la plus petite des deux valeurs correspondantes de $x$. On aura évidemment

$$x_{\bullet} < x_{,} < X' < X,$$

et

$$X' - x_{,} = \frac{h}{m} = \frac{1}{m}(X - x_{o}).$$

Ayant déterminé $x_{,}$ et $X'$ comme on vient de le dire, on pourra de même, entre ces deux nouvelles valeurs de $x$, en placer deux autres $x_{2}$, $X''$ qui, substituées dans $f(x)$, donnent des résultats de signes contraires, et qui soient propres à vérifier les conditions

$$x_{,} < x_{2} < X'' < X',$$

$$X'' - x_{2} = \frac{1}{m}(X' - x_{,}) = \frac{1}{m^{2}}(X - x_{o}).$$

En continuant ainsi, on obtiendra, 1.° une série de valeurs croissantes de $x$, savoir,

$$(2) \qquad x_{o}, \quad x_{,}, \quad x_{2}, \quad \&c\ldots,$$

2.° une série de valeurs décroissantes

$$(3) \qquad X, \quad X', \quad X'', \quad \&c\ldots,$$

qui, surpassant les premières de quantités respectivement égales aux produits

**462**                    NOTE III.

$$\mathbf{1} \times (X - x_\bullet) , \quad \frac{1}{m} \times (X - x_0) , \quad \frac{1}{m^2} \times (X - x_0) , \quad \&c.,$$

finiront par différer de ces premières valeurs aussi peu que l'on voudra. On doit en conclure que les termes généraux des séries ( 2 ) et ( 3 ) convergeront vers une limite commune. Soit $a$ cette limite. Puisque la fonction $f(x)$ reste continue depuis $x = x_0$ jusqu'à $x = X$, les termes généraux des séries suivantes ,

$$f(x_0) , \quad f(x_1) , \quad f(x_2) , \quad \&c \ldots ,$$
$$f(X) , \quad f(X') , \quad f(X'') , \quad \&c \ldots$$

convergeront également vers la limite commune $f(a)$ ; et , comme en s'approchant de cette limite ils resteront toujours de signes contraires , il est clair que la quantité $f(a)$ , nécessairement finie , ne pourra différer de zéro. Par conséquent on vérifiera l'équation

$$(1) \qquad f(x) = 0 ,$$

en attribuant à la variable $x$ la valeur particulière $a$ comprise entre $x_0$ et $X$. En d'autres termes ,

$$(4) \qquad x = a$$

sera une *racine* de l'équation ( 1 ).

<hr/>

TRANSLATION

<hr/>

## NOTE III

*On the numerical solution of equations*

To solve *numerically* one or several equations is to find the values in numbers of the unknowns that they contain; this clearly requires that the constants contained in the equations one is dealing with are themselves reduced to numbers. We will be occupied here solely with equations that contain one unknown, and we will begin by establishing the following theorems in respect to them.

1. THEOREM *Let $f(x)$ be a real function of the variable $x$, which remains continuous with respect to this variable between the limits $x = x_0$, $x = X$. If the two quantities $f(x_0)$, $f(X)$ are of contrary sign, one may satisfy the equation*

(1)
$$f(x) = 0$$

*with one or several real values of $x$ contained between $x_0$ and $X$.*

PROOF. Let $x_0$ be the smaller of the two quantities $x_0$, $X$. We put

$$X - x_0 = h,$$

and denote by $m$ any whole number greater than one. Since of the two quantities $f(x_0)$, $f(X)$, one is positive, the other negative, if one forms the sequence

$$f(x_0), f\left(x_0 + \tfrac{h}{m}\right), f\left(x_0 + 2\tfrac{h}{m}\right), \ldots f\left(X - \tfrac{h}{m}\right), f(X),$$

[461] and if in this sequence one compares successively the first term with the second, the second with the third, the third with the fourth, etc., one will necessarily end by finding once or several times two consecutive terms that will be of contrary sign. Let

$$f(x_1), f(X'),$$

be two terms of this kind, $x_1$ being the smaller of the two corresponding values of $x$. Clearly one will have

$$x_0 < x_1 < X' < X,$$

and

$$X' - x_1 = \frac{h}{m} = \frac{1}{m}(X - x_0).$$

Having determined $x_1$ and $X'$ as we have just said, one may do the same between these two new values of $x$, there placing two others $x_2$, $X''$, which, substituted into $f(x)$, give results of contrary sign, and which correctly satisfy the conditions

$$x_1 < x_2 < X'' < X',$$

$$X'' - x_2 = \frac{1}{m}(X' - x_1) = \frac{1}{m^2}(X - x_0).$$

Continuing in this way, one will obtain, first, a sequence of increasing values of $x$, namely,

(2)
$$x_0, x_1, x_2, \text{etc.} \ldots,$$

second, a sequence of decreasing values

(3)
$$X, X', X'', \text{etc.} \ldots,$$

which, exceeding the former by quantities respectively equal to the products [462]

$$1 \times (X - x_0), \frac{1}{m} \times (X - x_0), \frac{1}{m^2} \times (X - x_0), \text{etc.},$$

will end by differing from these former values by as little as one wishes. One must therefore conclude that the general terms of series (2) and (3) will converge towards a common limit. Let $a$ be that limit. Since the function $f(x)$ remains continuous from $x = x_0$ to $x = X$, the general terms of the following series,

$$f(x_0), f(x_1), f(x_2), \text{etc.} \dots$$
$$f(X), f(X'), f(X''), \text{etc.} \dots$$

will converge in the same way towards the common limit $f(a)$; and, since in approaching that limit they remain always of contrary sign, it is clear that the quantity $f(a)$, necessarily finite, cannot differ from zero. Consequently one can satisfy the equation

(1) $$f(x) = 0$$

by giving the variable $x$ the particular value $a$ contained between $x_0$ and $X$. In other words,

(4) $$x = a$$

will be a *root* of equation (1).

————————

# CHAPTER 12

# SOLVING EQUATIONS

I n this chapter we take up once again the story of solving equations (see 1.4), and follow it through two further centuries, from Cardano in 1545 to Lagrange in 1771.

## 12.1 CUBICS AND QUARTICS

### 12.1.1 Cardano and the *Ars magna*, 1545

By the early sixteenth century, quadratic equations in a variety of manifestations were well understood.[1] Attempts to find the right recipe for cubic equations, however, met with rather less success. The breakthrough came in northern Italy around 1520 when Scipione Ferreo in Bologna discovered a method for cubic equations without a square term (in modern notation, $x^3 + px = q$). The same method was rediscovered by Niccolo Tartaglia in 1535 in the course of a contest with Antonio Maria Fiore (a pupil of Ferreo), and he in turn passed it on in 1539 to Girolamo Cardano. Tartaglia gave the solution in the form of a verse which neatly encapsulated the method for those who already understood it, but was cryptic enough to be meaningless to the uninitiated (and therefore not unlike a modern mathematical formula):[2]

> When the cube with the things next after
> Together equal some number apart
> Find two others that by this differ
> And this you will then keep as a rule

---

1. It was recognized, for example, that an equation between a sixth power, cubes, and numbers was a form of quadratic.
2. 'Quando chel cubo con le cose apresso / Se aguaglia à qualche numero discreto / Trovan dui altri differenti in esso/ Dapoi terrai questo per consueto / Ch'el lor' produtto sempre fia equale / Al terzo cubo delle cose neto / El residuo poi suo generale / Delli lor lati cubi ben sottratti / Varra la tua cosa principale.' Tartaglia 1546, 124.

> That their product will always be equal
> To a third cubed of the number of things
> The difference then in general between
> The sides of the cubes subtracted well
> Will be your principal thing.

For an equation of the form $x^3 + px = q$, Tartaglia's verse instructs us to find two numbers we may call $u$ and $v$, such that $v - u = q$ and $uv = (p/3)^3$. Then, he tells us, the required solution will be $x = \sqrt[3]{u} - \sqrt[3]{v}$, which is easily checked and found to be correct. Cardano published the rule in 1545 in *De artis magnis, sive regulis algebrae* (*On the great art, or the rules of algebra*), more commonly known then and now as the *Ars magna*.

---

### Cardano's rule for cubic equations
from Cardano, *Ars magna*, 1545, 30

---

R E G V L A.

Deducito tertiam partem numeri rerum ad cubum, cui addes quadratum dimidij numeri æquationis, & totius accipe radicem, scili cet quadratam, quam seminabis, uniç dimidium numeri quod iam in se duxeras, adijcies, ab altera dimidium idem minues, habebisç Bi nomium cum sua Apotome, inde detracta ℞ cubica Apotomæ ex ℞ cubica sui Binomij, residuū quod ex hoc relinquitur, est rei æstimatio. Exemplum.cubus & 6 positiones, æquan tur 20,ducito 2 , tertiam partem 6 , ad cu bum,fit 8,duc 10 dimidium numeri in se, fit 100,iunge 100 & 8,fit 108,accipe radi cem quæ est ℞ 108, & eam geminabis, alte ri addes 10,dimidium numeri,ab altero mi nues tantundem,habebis Binomiū ℞ 108 p:10,& Apotomen ℞ 108 m:10 , horum accipe ℞ᵃ cubᵃ & minue illam que est Apo tomæ,ab ea quæ est Binomij, habebis rei æstimationem, ℞ v: cub: ℞ 108 p: 10 m:℞ v: cubica ℞ 108 m:10.

| |
|---|
| cub⁹ p:6 reb⁹ æqlis 20 |
| 2           20 |
| 8 ————— 10 |
| 108 |
| ℞ 108 p:10 |
| ℞ 108 m:10 |
| ℞ v: cu.℞ 108 p:10 |
| m:℞ v:cu.℞ 108 m:10 |

*Notation*

Cardano wrote 'p:' for plus, 'm:' for minus, and '℞' for a square root. '℞v:' means *radix universalis*, or universal root, that is, the root of several connected terms; the scope of '℞v:' has to be understood from the context. Similarly, '℞v: cub:' or '℞V: cu:' are universal cube roots.

## Rule

Having raised a third part of the number of things to a cube, to which you add the square of half the number in the equation and take the root of the total, consider the square [root], which you will take twice; and to one of them you add half the number which you have already multiplied by itself, from the other you will subtract half of the same, and you will have the binome with its apotome, whence taking the cube root of the apotome from the cube root of its binome, the difference that comes from this, is the value of the thing.

For example, a cube and 6 things are equal to 20; raise 2, the third part of 6, to its cube, which makes 8; multiply 10, half the number, by itself, which makes 100; add 100 and 8, which makes 108; take the root which is $\mathcal{R}$ 108 and replicate it; to one add 10, half the number, from the other take just the same; you will have the binome $\mathcal{R}$ 108 p: 10, and the apotome $\mathcal{R}$ 108 m: 10; take the cube roots of these, and subtract that of the apotome from that of the binome; you will have the value of the thing, $\mathcal{R}$v:cube: $\mathcal{R}$ 108 p: 10 m: $\mathcal{R}$v:cube $\mathcal{R}$ 108 m: 10.

Cardano had gleaned from Tartaglia his first clues about solving cubics of a certain kind, but in the *Ars magna* he went very much further, and provided rules for all possible cubics and, with his pupil Ludovico Ferrari, for some quartic equations as well. In trying to understand and solve cubic equations, Cardano drew on images of cubes and other rectangular solids, but for fourth degree equations such physical representations are impossible, and in Cardano's text the diagrams become more sparse. A significantly greater difficulty in dealing with quartics is that the method requires the introduction of a second unknown quantity, which in Cardano's exposition is not easy to distinguish from the first since he used the single term *positio*, or 'supposed quantity' for both.

As an example of Cardano's method of working, here is his solution of the equation we can write as $x^4 = x + 2$, given first in modern notation, followed by the key passages in his own words. The letter $x$ stands for his first *positio*, or supposed quantity, and we will use $y$ for the second. To the left-hand side of the equation Cardano added the quantity we may write as $2yx^2 + y^2$, thus ensuring that this side of the equation remains a perfect square. Balancing the two sides we therefore have

$$x^4 + 2yx^2 + y^2 = 2yx^2 + x + (2 + y^2). \tag{1}$$

The right-hand side is quadratic in $x$, and by judicious choice of $y$ can also be made into a perfect square. The condition for this (equivalent to '$b^2 = 4ac$' in the usual quadratic formula) is that:

$$\tfrac{1}{4}x^2 = 2y(2 + y^2)x^2 \tag{2}$$

or

$$\tfrac{1}{4} = 2y^3 + 4y \tag{3}$$

and (3) is a cubic equation in $y$, of a form that Cardano could solve.

Making use of any value of $y$ that satisfies (3), Cardano had now reduced (1) to an equation between two squares. The left-hand side is the square of

$$x^2 + y, \tag{4}$$

and the right hand side is the square of

$$x\sqrt{2y} + \sqrt{2 + y^2}. \tag{5}$$

Equating (4) and (5), Cardano therefore had

$$x^2 = x\sqrt{2y} + \sqrt{2 + y^2} - y,$$

a straightforward quadratic equation which can be solved in the usual way.

Now here is Cardano's version of equations (1) to (3), with his solution:[3]

since therefore by adding 2 supposed numbers [of squares] plus 1 square of the number of squares to 1 supposed thing plus 2, it makes a total of 2 supposed numbers of squares plus 1 supposed thing plus 2 plus 1 square of the number of squares, and this has a root, it must be that the square of half the middle quantity, which is 1 supposed thing, equals the product of the extremes, therefore $\tfrac{1}{4}$ of the square will equal the square [times] 2 of the cubes plus 4 of the first supposed number, whence throwing away the squares on both sides, it makes $\tfrac{1}{4}$ equal to 2 cubes plus 4 supposed numbers, and $\tfrac{1}{8}$ equal to 1 cube plus 2 supposed numbers, whence the value of the thing is $\mathcal{R}$v: cube $\mathcal{R}$ $\tfrac{2075}{6912}$ p: $\tfrac{1}{16}$ m: $\mathcal{R}$v: cube $\mathcal{R}$ $\tfrac{2075}{6912}$ m: $\tfrac{1}{16}$; this therefore is the number of squares to be added to each side and doubled, and the square of this is the number to be added to both sides.

Although Ferrari and Cardano solved only this and a few other examples, it is clear that the method can be generalized to any fourth degree equation. Carried through as above, with only the most rudimentary notation, it is a stunning *tour de force*.

The *Ars magna*, however, contains much more than a set of labyrinthine rules for solving particular equations. It is one of the great mathematical texts of the Renaissance, full of far-reaching insights. Until then, for instance, no one had taken any interest in negative roots because the geometric imagery that had always been associated with equation-solving, and which al-Khwārizmī, Leonardo Pisano, and Cardano had all relied upon, rendered negative roots at best irrelevant and at worst meaningless.

---

3. 'quia igitur additis 2 positionibus p: 1 quadrato numeri quadratorum, ad 1 positionem p: 2, fit totum 2 positiones numeri quadratorum p; 1 pos. p: 2, p: 1 quadrato numeri quadratorum, and hoc habet radicem, oportet ut quadratum dimidij mediae quantitatis, quae est 1 positio, aequetur [75v] ductui extremorum, igitur $\tfrac{1}{4}$ quadrati, aequabitur quadrato, 2 cuborum p: 4 positionibus numeri prioris, quare abiectis quadratis utrinque, fiet $\tfrac{1}{4}$ aequalis 2 cubis p: 4 positionibus, and $\tfrac{1}{8}$ aequalis 1 cubo p: 2 positionibus, quare rei aestimatio est $\mathcal{R}$v: cubica $\mathcal{R}$ $\tfrac{2075}{6912}$ p: $\tfrac{1}{16}$ m: $\mathcal{R}$v: cubica $\mathcal{R}$ $\tfrac{2075}{6912}$ m: $\tfrac{1}{16}$, hic igitur est numerus quadratorum addendus utrique parti, and duplicatur, and quadratum huius erit numerus addendus ad utramque partem.' Cardano 1545, 75–75v.

Cardano showed that negative roots were valid in principle, even if not much use in practice, and in some of his demonstrations he worked quite explicitly with negative quantities, which he denoted by the postfix 'm:' (thus '$BC$m:' for what we now write as $-BC$). He came across the possibility of imaginary roots too, but failed to pursue them.

Cardano's most profound discovery, however, was what he called the *transformation of equations* (*aequationum transmutatio*). In Chapter VI of the *Ars magna*, he demonstrated something quite new: that equations could be changed by simple substitutions from one form to another. He gave the particular example of finding two numbers whose sum is the square of one of them and whose product is 8. Denoting the numbers by $x$ and $y$, we thus have $x + y = x^2$ and $xy = 8$. Eliminating $y$ yields $x^3 = x^2 + 8$, but eliminating $x$ yields $y^3 + 8y = 64$. For Cardano these equations were of different types (the first lacks a linear term, the second lacks a square), yet either is easily transformed to the other by the simple relationship $x = 8/y$. This was an insight of enormous importance, the first departure from the 'recipe' approach towards the understanding that equations could be investigated and manipulated without necessarily being solved. In the *Ars magna*, Cardano showed how to carry out a number of other useful transformations, by adding a carefully chosen constant to the unknown quantity, for example, or multiplying it by some appropriate number.

Very soon after the *Ars magna* was published, Cardano's ideas were taken up by another citizen of Bologna, Rafael Bombelli, who presented them in systematic and clearer form in his *L'algebra*, mostly written before 1560 but not published until 1572. A few years later Simon Stevin, an admirer of Bombelli, repeated much the same material in his *L'arithmetique ... aussi l'algebre* of 1585. As a result, Cardano's insights and techniques fairly rapidly became an established part of the equation-solving repertoire.

---

### Cardano on the transformation of equations
from Cardano, *Ars magna*, 1545, 15v–16

---

**4**      Eſt etiam tranſmutationis uia, qua ante demonſtrationem uniuer
                                                                    ſalia
DE ARITHMETICA    LIB. X.                                    16

ſalia capitula multa inueni, atcp inter reliqua, cubi æqualis qdratis &
numero, & cubi cum qdratis, æqualis numero, uelut cu conamur hanc
ſoluere quæſtionem, duos inuenias numeros, quorum aggregatum
æquale ſit alterius qdrato, & ex uno in alterum ducto, producatur 8,
una enim uia peruenies ad 1 cubum æqualem 1 qdrato p: 8, alia, ad 1
cubum p: 8 rebus, æqualem 64, hac igitur inuenta æſtimatione, ſi diui
ſeris 8 per eam, prodibit reliqua equatio, ex qua in capituli illius cogi
tationem perueni. Quæſtiones igitur alio ingenio cognitas ad igno⸗
tas transfer poſitiones, nec capituloru inuentio finem eſt habitura, nõ
tamen extra hæc, ex una quæſtione, generalia poteris aſſequi.

---

#### TRANSLATION

4      There is also the way of transformation, by which I discovered many general rules before
their demonstration, [16] and among the rest a cube equal to a square and number,
and a cube with a square equal to a number, as when we tried to solve this problem,
where you find two numbers of which the sum is equal to the square of one of them,
and from one multiplied by the other there is produced 8, for by one way you arrive
at 1 cube equal to 1 square p: 8, by another at 1 cube p: 8 things equal to 64, therefore
having found the value, if you divide 8 by it, it will produce the other equation, from
which I arrived at the idea for the rule for that one. Therefore substitute problems that
are by some ingenuity understood, for those that are not, and there will be no end to the
discovery of rules, and beyond this, from one question you will be able to understand
general rules.

---

## 12.2 FROM CARDANO TO LAGRANGE

Lagrange, writing in 1771, more than two centuries after the publication of the *Ars
magna*, claimed that there had been hardly any advance in solving polynomial equations
since the time of Cardano. In one sense, he was correct. The rules for solving cubics
and quartics had since been set out more clearly and in more general form, but were
essentially no different from those published in the *Ars magna* in 1545. Meanwhile there
had been no progress at all in solving equations of higher degree. On the other hand,

there had been some important advances in understanding the structure of equations, and a few other ideas that seemed promising. In this section we discuss just a few of them: Harriot's discovery of the multiplicative structure of polynomials around 1600; Hudde's rule for repeated roots, published in 1657; the attempt of Tschirnhaus to extend Cardano's methods to equations of fifth-degree or higher in 1683; and Lagrange's own investigation and summary of the existing methods in 1770.

## 12.2.1 Harriot and the structure of polynomials, *c*. 1600

Viète's *De aequationum recognitione et emendatione tractatus duo* (*Two treatises on the understanding and amendment of equations*), written in the 1590s though not published until 1615, took up many of the methods and insights of the *Ars magna*. Viète's most important contribution to the understanding of polynomial equations, however, was something quite new and different: an iterative *numerical* method for finding roots where algebraic methods failed. This was published in 1600 in *De numerosa potestatum ad exegesin resolutione* (*On the numerical resolution of powers for the purpose of showing* [*the root*]), a book that was read with close attention shortly afterwards by Thomas Harriot in England.

To use Viète's iterative method effectively, one needed to know the best place to start, and this led both Viète and Harriot to use the coefficients of equations to estimate upper and lower bounds for the roots. It seems that investigations of this kind led Harriot to his most significant insight: that polynomials could be created by multiplication of appropriate factors. Thus $(a - b)(a - c)$ gives rise to a quadratic; while $(a - b)(a - c)(a + d)$ and $(a - b)(aa - cd)$ give rise to cubics; and so on. The composition reveals immediately the number of positive or negative roots in each case and also, more significantly, various important and useful relationships between roots and coefficients.

Harriot's discovery was a major contribution to the structural understanding of polynomial equations. When he began his work he was interested, like all earlier mathematicians, only in positive roots, but as he progressed he began to recognize and accept the existence of negative and even complex roots, and systematically solved cubics for all three roots, and quartics for all four. Unfortunately when some of his papers were published posthumously in the *Artis analyticae praxis* (*The practice of the analytic art*) in 1631 the editors reverted to treating only positive roots, so that the full richness of Harriot's insights was lost to his immediate successors. The example below is from the *Praxis* and gives Harriot's derivation (more or less)[4] of the 'reciprocal equation' $a^3 - ba^2 + cda - bcd = 0$ ('reciprocal' being Viète's description of an equation in which the product of the outer terms is the same as the product of the inner terms). In his manuscripts Harriot recognized $a = \sqrt{-cd}$ as a possible root of this equation, but this was a step too far for the editors of the *Praxis* who restricted themselves to the (positive) root $a = b$ only.

---

4. See Stedall 2002, 157–159 and 124 for the original derivation.

## Harriot's construction of a cubic

from Harriot, *Artis analyticae praxis*, 1631, 19

*Reciprocarum Cubici ordinis deriuatio.*

### PROPOSITIO 6.

Æquatio reciproca . . . $aaa - baa + cda$ ══ $+ bcd$.  ab originali
$a - b$ ══ $aaa - baa + cda - bcd$.  poſito $b$. ipſi $a$. æquali de-
$aa + cd$ |
  riuata eſt.

Nam ſi ponatur  $b$ ══ $a$.  erit $a - b$ ══ $o$.

Poſito igitur $b$ ══ $a$.  eſt  $a - b$ | ══ $o$.
                               $aa + cd$ |

Eſt autem ex geneſi  $a - b$ | ══ $aaa - baa + cda - bcd$.  quæ eſt æqua-
                     $aa + cd$ |
  tio originalis hic deſignata.

Ergo . . . $aaa - baa + cda - bcd$ ══ $o$.

Ergo . . . $aaa - baa + cda$ ══ $+ bcd$.  quæ eſt æquatió reciprocá propó-
  ſita.

Deriuata eſt igitur æquatio reciproca propoſita ab originali deſignata, poſito $b$. ipſi $a$
  æquali. Vt eſt enunciatum.

---

### TRANSLATION

*Derivation of reciprocal equations of cubic degree*

### PROPOSITION 6.

The reciprocal equation $aaa - baa + cda = + bcd$ is derived from the original equation

$$\left.\begin{array}{c} a - b \\ aa + cd \end{array}\right| = aaa - baa + cda - bcd$$

having put $b$ equal to $a$.

For if we put $b = a$ then $a - b = 0$.

Therefore putting $b = a$ then

$$\left.\begin{array}{c} a - b \\ aa + cd \end{array}\right| = 0$$

Moreover,

$$\left.\begin{array}{c} a - b \\ aa + cd \end{array}\right| = aaa - baa + cda - bcd$$

which is the original equation here signified.

Therefore $aaa - baa + cda - bcd = 0$.

Therefore $aaa - baa + cda = + bcd$, which is the proposed reciprocal equation.

Therefore the proposed reciprocal equation is derived from the signified original
equation by putting $b$ equal to $a$. As we said.

## 12.2.2 Hudde's rule, 1657

Although he spent most of his life as a civic official in Amsterdam, Jan Hudde was recognized by his contemporaries as a mathematician of considerable ability. Unfortunately very little of his work has survived, apart from some correspondence and some short pieces published by his teacher, Frans van Schooten. Hudde's 'De reductione aequationum' ('On the reduction of equations'), written in the form of a letter to van Schooten in July 1657, was printed in van Schooten's second, extended, edition of Descartes' *Geometria* in 1659.

In his efforts to solve polynomials of degree five or six, Hudde discovered a rule for identifying the existence of double roots, which then enabled him to reduce the degree of the original equation. The rule was this: multiply the terms of the polynomial by numbers from any arithmetic progression, first term by first number, second by second, and so on; then a double root of the original equation will also be a root of the new one, and the common root can be found using the Euclidean algorithm. If the chosen progression is . . . , 4, 3, 2, 1, 0, the effect of multiplication is the same as that of differentiating (apart from a factor of $x$); thus, to take Hudde's own example, $x^3 - 4xx + 5x - 2$ becomes $3x^3 - 8xx + 5$, but differentiation as a formal process was not yet known.

---

### Hudde's rule for finding double roots

from Hudde, *De reductione aequationum*, 1657, as published in van Schooten 1659, I, 433–434

---

### X. REGVLA,

*Quæ modum docet reducendi omnem æquationem, sive literalem, sive numeralem, cujus incognita quantitas, (vel alia litera, quæ tanquam incognita considerari potest) duos vel plures æquales habet valores.*

Primò si in Proposita æquatione duæ æquales radices existant, multiplico eam per Arithmeticam Progressionem pro libitu assumptam: nimirum, $1^{\text{mum}}$ terminum æquationis per $1^{\text{mum}}$ terminum progressionis, $2^{\text{dum}}$ terminum æquationis per $2^{\text{dum}}$ terminum progressionis, & sic deinceps; & Productum, quod inde fit, erit $\infty$ o. Deinde, cum sic duas habeam æquationes,

I i i                                              quæ-

434   Iohannis Huddenii Epist. I.

quæro, per Methodum superiùs explicatam, maximum earum communem divisorem; atque hujus ope æquationem Propositam toties divido, quoties id fieri potest.

Exempli gratiâ, proponatur hæc æquatio $x^3 - 4xx + 5x - 2\infty0$, in qua duæ sunt æquales radices. Multiplico ergo ipsam per Arithmeticam Progressionem qualemcunque, hoc est, cujus incrementum vel decrementum sit vel 1, vel 2, vel 3, vel alius quilibet numerus; & cujus primus terminus sit vel 0, vel +, vel — quam 0 : Ita ut semper ejus ope talis terminus æquationis tolli possit, qualem quis voluerit, collocando tantùm sub eo 0.

Ut si, exempli causâ, ultimum ejus terminum auferre velim, multiplicatio fieri potest ipsius   $x^3 - 4xx + 5x - 2\infty\infty$

per hanc progressionem   3.   2.   1.   0

fietque $\overline{3x^3 - 8xx + 5x \quad * \quad \infty0.}$

Maxima autem communis divisor hujus & Propositæ æquationis est $x - 1\infty0$, per quam Proposita bis dividi potest; ita ut ejusdem radices sint 1, 1, & 2.

Sic si cupiam 1$^{mum}$ æquationis terminum auferre, multiplicatio institui potest ipsius   $x^3 - 4xx + 5x - 2\infty0$

per hanc progressionem 0.   1.   2.   3.

& fit $\overline{* \quad -4xx + 10x - 6\infty0.}$

Cujus quidem ac Propositæ æquationis maximus communis divisor, ut antea, est $x - 1\infty0$.

Similiter si 2$^{dum}$ terminum tollere lubeat, multiplicatio fieri potest, hoc pacto :   $x^3 - 4xx + 5x - 2\infty0$

+ 1.   0.   — 1. — 2

& prodibit $x^3 \quad * \quad \overline{-5x + 4\infty0.}$

Cujus item & Propositæ maximus communis divisor est $x - 1\infty0$.

Ubi notandum, non necessarium esse, semper uti Progressione cujus excessus sit 1, quanquam ea communiter sit optima.

TRANSLATION

## X. RULE

*Which teaches a method of reducing every equation, whether* [the coefficients are] *letters or numbers, whose unknown quantity (or another letter, which may be considered unknown) has two or more equal values.*

First, if in the proposed equation there exist two equal roots, I multiply it by an arithmetic progression taken at will: thus, the first term of the equation by the first term of the progression, the second term of the equation by the second term of the progression, and so on; and the product which thence arises will equal 0. Then, since I thus have two equations, [434] I seek, by the method explained above [the Euclidean Algorithm], their greatest common divisor; and by the aid of this I divide the proposed equation as often as it may be done.

For example, there is proposed this equation, $x^3 - 4xx + 5x - 2 = 0$, in which there are two equal roots. Therefore I multiply this by any arithmetic progression whatever, that is, whose increment or decrement is either 1, or 2, or 3, or any other number you please, and whose first term is either 0, or greater than or less than 0. Thus it is always possible to take away such terms of the equation as one wishes, by combining them as 0.

If, for example, I wish to take away the last term, I may multiply

|  | $x^3$ | $-$ | $4xx$ | $+$ | $5x$ | $-$ | $2$ | $=$ | $0$ |
|---|---|---|---|---|---|---|---|---|---|
| by this progression | 3 | | 2 | | 1 | | 0 | | |
| and it makes | $3x^3$ | $-$ | $8xx$ | $+$ | $5x$ | | $*$ | $=$ | $0.$ |

Moreover, the greatest common divisor of this and the proposed equation is $x - 1 = 0$, by which the proposed equation can be divided twice; so that its roots are 1, 1, and 2.

If I wish to take away the first term of the equation, I may carry out the multiplication of

|  | $x^3$ | $-$ | $4xx$ | $+$ | $5x$ | $-$ | $2$ | $=$ | $0$ |
|---|---|---|---|---|---|---|---|---|---|
| by this progression | 0 | | 1 | | 2 | | 3 | | |
| and it makes | $*$ | $-$ | $4xx$ | $+$ | $10x$ | $-$ | $6$ | $=$ | $0.$ |

whose greatest common divisor with the propsed equation, as before, is $x - 1 = 0$.

Similarly, if it is desired to take away the second term, the multiplication may be done in this way:

|  | $x^3$ | $-$ | $4xx$ | $+$ | $5x$ | $-$ | $2$ | $=$ | $0$ |
|---|---|---|---|---|---|---|---|---|---|
| | $+1$ | | $0$ | | $-1$ | | $-2$ | | |
| and it will produce | $x^3$ | | $*$ | $-$ | $5x$ | $+$ | $4$ | $=$ | $0.$ |

whose greatest common divisor with the proposed equation is likewise $x - 1 = 0$.

Where it must be noted that it is not necessary always to use a progression whose increment is 1, although this may generally be best.

————————

## 12.2.3 Tschirnhaus transformations, 1683

Ehrenfried Walter von Tschirnhaus was never more than a moderately competent mathematician but gave his name to what have come to be called 'Tschirnhaus transformations', the systematic removal of terms from a polynomial equation. If the process can be carried far enough, he argued, an equation is easily solved, but he himself failed to press the method to its conclusion and so never discovered the difficulties of applying it to a fifth degree equation.

## Tschirnhaus transformations

from Tschirnhaus, *Acta eruditorum*, 1683, 204–206

### 204     ACTA ERUDITORUM
*METHODUS AUFERENDI OMNES TER-*
*minos intermedios ex data æquatione,*
*per D. T.*

EX Geometria Dn. Des Cartes' notum eft, qua ratione femper fecundus terminus ex data æquatione poffit auferri; quoad plures terminos intermedios auferendos, hactenus nihil inventum vidi in Arte Analytica, imo non paucos offendi, qui crediderunt, id nulla arte perfici poffe.     Quapropter hic quædam circa hoc negotium aperire conftitui, verum faltem pro iis, qui Artis Analyticæ apprime gnari, cum aliis tam brevi explicatione vix fatisfieri poffit: reliqua, quæ hic defiderari poffent, alii tempori refervans.

Primo itaque loco, ad hoc attendendum; fit data aliqua æquatio cubica $x^3 - pxx + qx - r = o$, in qua x radices hujus æquationis defignat; p, q, r, cognitas quantitates repræfentant: ad auferendum jam fecundum terminum fupponatur $x = y + a$; jam ope harum duarum æquationum inveniatur tertia, ubi quantitas x abfit, & erit

$y^3 + 3ayy + 3aay + a^3 = o$     Ponatur nunc fecundus terminus æqua-
$\quad - pyy - 2pay - paa$         lis nihilo (quia hunc auferre noftra in-
$\quad\quad + qy \quad\quad + qa$         tentio) eritque $3ayy - pyy = o$. Unde
$\quad\quad\quad - r$               $a = \frac{p}{3}$: id quod indicat, ad auferendum

fecundum terminum in æquatione Cubica, fupponendum effe loco $x = y + a$ (prout modo fecimus) $x = y + \frac{p}{3}$. Hæc jam vulgata admodum funt, nec hic referuntur aliam ob caufam, quam quia fequentia admodum illuftrant, dum hifce bene intellectis, eo facilius, quæ modo proponam, capientur.

Sint jam fecundo in æquatione data auferendi duo termini: dico, quod fupponendum fit, $xx = bx + y + a$; fi tres, $x^3 = cxx + bx + y + a$; fi quatuor, $x^4 = dx^3 + cxx + bx + y + a$, atque fic in infinitum.     Vocabo autem has *æquationes affumtas*, ut eas diftinguam ab æquatione, quæ ut data confideratur. Ratio autem horum eft: quod eadem ratione, prout ope æquationis $x = y + a$ faltem unicus terminus poterat auferri, quia nimirum unica faltem indeterminata hic exiftit a, fic eadem ratione ope hujus $xx = bx + y + a$, non nifi duo termini poffunt auferri, quia duæ indeterminatæ a & b adfunt;

## MENSIS MAJI A. M DC LXXXIII.                205

adfunt; ac fic porro ope fequentis x³ = c x x ✠ b x ✠ y ✠ a, non plures
tribus auferri poffunt, quia tres tantum indeterminatæ a, b, c.   Ut autem intelligatur, qua ratione hoc affequi liceat, oftendam qua ratione
duo termini ex data æquatione ope affumptæ x x = b x ✠ y ✠ a fint auferendi: hinc enim (cum ubique eadem Methodus fit procedendi) facile conftabit, quomodo in hac re progrediendum, quousque quis ve-
lit.   Sit itaque

Tertio, Æquatio Cubica x³ — p x x ✠ q x — r = o, ex qua auferendi duo intermedii termini: auferatur primo fecundus terminus (id
quod equidem non opus eft, fed faltem hic ob nimiam prolixitatem
evitandam fit) tunc hinc obtinebimus æquationem fimilem huic
y³ — q y — r = o. Jam fit affumta æquatio (juxta fecundam annotatio-
nem) y y = b y ✠ z ✠ a, & fiat porro hinc tertia æquatio (procedendo
juxta cognita Analyfeos præcepta) ubi quantitas y penitus abfit, & ob-
nebitur

z³ ✠ 3 a z z ✠ 3 a a z ✠ a³ = o       Ponantur jam in hac æquatione Cu-
  — 2 q z z — 4 q a z — 2 q a a       bica fecundus & tertius terminus æqua-
  ✠ q q z ✠ q q a                    les o (quia hos duos intermedios aufer-
  — q b b z — q b b a                  re noftrum propofitum) & orientur
  ✠ 3 r b z ✠ 3 r b a                  hinc duæ æquationes 3 a z z — 2 q z z = o, &
  — r r                                3 a a z — 4 q a z ✠ q q z — q b b z ✠ 3rbz = o,
  — q r b                              quarum ope duæ indeterminatæ deter-
  ✠ r b³                               minantur: invenitur fiquidem a = $\frac{2q}{3}$

& b = $\frac{3}{q}$ multiplicatum in $\frac{r}{2} \pm \sqrt{\frac{rr}{4} - \frac{q^3}{27}}$.   Si itaque loco a & b modo
inventæ quantitates fubftituantur in æquatione y y = b y ✠ z ✠ a, ejus
ope, in æquatione data Cubica, duo termini poterunt auferri; feu
quod eo recidit, data æquatio Cubica ope hujus æquationis y y = b y ✠
z ✠ a, in aliam Cubicam æquationem transmutabitur, ubi duo intermedii termini ablati erunt.   Et fic idem proceffus obfervatur ad tres,
quatuor, quinque &c. terminos auferendos.   Cum enim data æquatio femper ope affumptæ ad aliam redigatur, quæ æque altas dimen-
fiones obtinet (veluti unico intuitu patet hic fieri) in hac tertia, tres,
quatuor, quinque &c. termini poterunt æquales poni nihilo, atque
hinc totidem femper æquationes habebimus, quot indeterminatæ ad-
Cc 3                                          funt,

206            ACTA ERUDITORUM
funt, ut proinde hæ femper ope harum æquationum poffint determinari.

TRANSLATION

<h2>METHOD OF REMOVING ALL INTERMEDIATE TERMS</h2>

*from a given equation,*

*by D. T.*

It is known from the Geometria of Monsieur Descartes by what method the second term can always be removed from a given equation; but as to the removal of more terms I have seen nothing discovered up to now in the Analytic Art; on the contrary, I have offended not a few who believed this could not be achieved by any technique. And therefore I have contrived here to open up certain things around this matter, or at least for those who are especially knowledgeable in the Analytic Art, since others can scarcely be satisfied by such a brief explanation; reserving to another time the rest, which may here be lacking.

Therefore this must be observed in the first place. Let there be given any cubic equation $x^3 - pxx + qx - r = 0$, in which $x$ denotes the roots of the equation, and $p$, $q$, $r$, represent known quantities. To remove the second term it may be supposed that $x = y + a$; now by means of these two equations there may be found a third, where the quantity $x$ is absent, and it will be

$$
\begin{array}{rcrcrcrcl}
y^3 & + & 3ayy & + & 3aay & + & a^3 & = & 0 \\
    & - & pyy  & - & 2pay & - & paa & & \\
    & + &      &   & qy   & + & qa  & & \\
    &   &      &   &      & - & r   & &
\end{array}
$$

Now putting the second term equal to nothing (because here our intention is to remove it) we will have $3ayy - pyy = 0$. Whence $a = \frac{p}{3}$, which indicates that, to remove the second term in a cubic equation, there must be put in place of $x = y + a$ (in the way we did) $x = y + \frac{p}{3}$. These things are already generally well known, nor are they mentioned here for any other reason than because they illustrate what follows; as long as these things are well understood, the more easily will be grasped what I put forward in a moment.

Now, second, suppose there are two terms to be removed from the given equation: I say that there must be put $xx = bx + y + a$; if three, $x^3 = cxx + bx + y + a$; if four, $x^4 = dx^3 + cxx + bx + y + a$, and thus indefinitely. Moreover I call these *assumed equations*, to distinguish them from the equation that is considered as given. Moreover, the reason for these is the same reason that a single term may be removed by means of the equation $x = y + a$, namely because there exists a single unknown $a$; so for the same reason by means of this, $xx = bx + y + a$, only two terms may be removed, because there are two unknowns $a$ and $b$; [205] and so on by means of the next, $x^3 = cxx + bx + y + a$, no more than three may be removed, because there are three unknowns, $a$, $b$, $c$. Moreover, that it might be understood how this may be continued, I show how two terms are removed from the given equation by means of the assumed equation $xx = bx + y + a$; for here it is easily established how to proceed in this thing, as far as one wishes (since the method may be carried out in the same way everywhere). Therefore let there be:

Third, a cubic equation $x^3 - pxx + qx - r = 0$, from which are to be removed two intermediate terms; first there is removed the second term (which we do not need to do, at least here, to avoid being too lengthy), then we will obtain an equation similar to this, $y^3 - qy - r = 0$. Now let the assumed equation be $yy = by + z + a$ (according to the second notation), and (proceeding according to the known precepts of Analysis) there then arises the third equation where the quantity $y$ is completely absent, and we will obtain

$$
\begin{array}{rcrcrcrcl}
z^3 & + & 3azz & + & 3aaz & + & a^3 & = & 0 \\
 & - & 2qzz & - & 4qaz & - & 2qaa & & \\
 & & & + & qqz & + & qqa & & \\
 & & & - & qbbz & - & qbba & & \\
 & & & + & 3rbz & + & 3rba & & \\
 & & & & & - & rr & & \\
 & & & & & - & qrb & & \\
 & & & & & + & rb^3 & &
\end{array}
$$

Now the second and third terms in this cubic equation are put equal to 0 (because our proposal is to remove these two intermediate terms) and there arise here two equations $3azz - 2qzz = 0$ and $3aaz - 4qaz + qqz - qbbz + 3rbz = 0$, by means of which the two unknowns are determined: indeed there is found $a = \frac{2q}{3}$ and $b = \frac{3}{q}$ multiplied by $\frac{r}{2} \pm \sqrt{\frac{rr}{4} - \frac{q^3}{27}}$. If therefore in place of $a$ and $b$ the quantities now found are substituted into the equation $yy = by + z + a$, two terms may be removed by means of this in the given cubic equation; or, what amounts to the same thing, the given cubic equation will be transformed by means of the equation $yy = by + z + a$ into another cubic equation, where the two intermediate terms will be removed. And thus the same procedure is observed to remove three, four, five terms, etc. For since the given equation is always reduced by means of an assumed equation to another, which retains equally high degree (just as the single case worked here shows), in this third equation, three, four, five terms, etc. may be put equal to nothing, and hence we will always have as many equations, as there are unknowns, [206] so that thence these may always be determined by means of these equations.

---

### 12.2.4  Lagrange and reduced equations, 1771

In 1771 Lagrange produced a paper almost 200 pages long entitled 'Réflexions sur la résolution algébrique des équations' ('Reflections on the algebraic solution of equations'). It was here that he remarked that the subject had hardly advanced since the time of Cardano; nevertheless, he reviewed and systematized the various procedures put forward by his predecessors: Ferreo, Tartaglia, Cardano, Hudde, Tschirnhaus, Euler, Cramer, and Bezout. His most important insight in the early part of the paper was the recognition of a reduced equation which, following Descartes, he called *la réduite*, and which must be solved first in order to solve the original equation. The extracts below show Lagrange's identification of the reduced equation for cubics and quartics.

## The reduced equation for a cubic

from Lagrange, 'Réflexions sur la résolution algébrique des équations', *Mémoires de l'Académie des Sciences* (1770), 135–137, 138–139, 140

---

### SECTION PREMIERE.

*De la résolution des équations du troisieme degré.*

1. Comme la résolution des équations du second degré est très facile, & n'est d'ailleurs remarquable que par son extreme simplicité, j'entrerai d'abord en matiere par les équations du troisieme degré, lesquelles deman-

dent pour être résolues des artifices particuliers qui ne se présentent pas naturellement.

Soit donc l'équation générale du troisieme degré

$$x^3 + m x^2 + n x + p = 0$$

& comme on sait qu'on peut toujours faire disparoitre le second terme de toute équation en augmentant ses racines du coëfficient du second terme divisé par l'exposant du premier, on pourra supposer d'abord pour plus de simplicité $m = 0$, ce qui réduira la proposée à la forme

$$x^3 + n x + p = 0.$$

C'est dans cet état que les équations du troisieme degré ont été d'abord traitées par Scipio Ferreo & par Tartalea à qui on doit leur résolution; mais on ignore le chemin qui les y a conduits; la méthode la plus naturelle pour y parvenir me paroit celle que Hudde a imaginée, & qui consiste à représenter la racine par la somme de deux indéterminées qui permettent de partager l'équation en deux parties propres à faire en sorte que les deux indéterminées ne dépendent que d'une équation résoluble à la maniere de celles du second degré.

Suivant cette méthode on fera donc $x = y + z$, ce qui étant substitué dans la proposée la réduira à celle-ci:

$$y^3 + 3 y^2 z + 3 y z^2 + z^3 + n (x + y) + p = 0$$

qu'on peut mettre sous cette forme plus simple

$$y^3 + z^3 + p + (x + y)(3 y z + n) = 0.$$

Qu'on fasse maintenant ces deux équations séparées

$$y^3 + z^3 + p = 0$$
$$3 y z + n = 0$$

l'on aura $z = -\dfrac{n}{3y}$; & substituant dans la premiere, $y^3 - \dfrac{n^3}{27 y^3} + p = 0$ c'est à dire

$$y^6 + p y^3 - \frac{n^3}{27} = 0.$$

Cette équation est à la vérité du sixieme degré, mais comme elle ne renferme que deux différentes puissances de l'inconnue, dont l'une a un exposant double

double de celui de l'autre, il est clair qu'elle peut se résoudre comme celles du second degré.    En effet on aura d'abord

$$y^3 = -\frac{p}{2} \pm V\left(\frac{p^2}{4} + \frac{n^3}{27}\right)$$

& de là

$$y = \sqrt[3]{\left(-\frac{p}{2} \pm V\left(\frac{p^2}{4} + \frac{n^3}{27}\right)\right)}.$$

Ainsi on connoîtra $y$ & $z$ & de là on aura $x = y + z = y - \frac{n}{3y}$.

$$[\ldots]$$

3. Puis donc que parmi les six valeurs de $y$ il n'y en a que trois qui donnent des valeurs différentes de $x$, il s'agit maintenant de distinguer ces valeurs.    Pour cela il faut trouver l'expression particulière de chacune des six valeurs de $y$; & si on nomme $1$, $\alpha$ & $\beta$ les trois racines cubiques de l'unité, c'est à dire, les trois racines de l'équation $x^3 - 1 = 0$, il est facile de voir que les six valeurs de $y$ seront, (en faisant pour abréger $\frac{p^2}{4} + \frac{n^3}{27} = q$) $\sqrt[3]{\left(-\frac{p}{2} \pm V\ q\right)}$, $\alpha\sqrt[3]{\left(-\frac{p}{2} \pm V\ q\right)}$,

$\beta\sqrt[3]{\left(-\frac{p}{2} \pm V\ q\right)}$; de là les valeurs correspondantes de $z = -\frac{n}{3y}$

seront, à cause de $\sqrt[3]{\left(-\frac{p}{2} \pm V\ q\right)} \times \sqrt[3]{\left(-\frac{p}{2} \mp V\ q\right)}$

$= \sqrt[3]{\left(\frac{p^2}{4} - q\right)} = -\frac{n}{3}$, & par conséquent $\sqrt[3]{\left(-\frac{p}{2} \mp V\ q\right)}$

$$[\ldots]$$

$$= - \frac{n}{\sqrt[3]{\left(-\frac{p}{2} \pm \sqrt{q}\right)}},$$ ces valeurs feront, dis-je,

$$\sqrt[3]{\left(-\frac{p}{2} \mp \sqrt{q}\right)}, \frac{1}{\alpha} \sqrt[3]{\left(-\frac{p}{2} \mp \sqrt{q}\right)}, \frac{1}{\beta} \sqrt[3]{\left(-\frac{p}{2} \mp \sqrt{q}\right)}.$$

Or fans connoître même les valeurs de $\alpha$ & $\beta$, il eft facile de s'affurer que $\alpha \beta$ doit être $= 1$; car puifque $1$, $\alpha$ & $\beta$ font les trois racines de l'équation $x^3 - 1 = 0$, on aura donc leur produit $1 . \alpha . \beta =$ au dernier terme $1$; donc $\alpha \beta = 1$; donc $\frac{1}{\alpha} = \beta$ & $\frac{1}{\beta} = \alpha$; de forte que les trois valeurs ci-deffus deviendront

$$\sqrt[3]{\left(-\frac{p}{2} \mp \sqrt{q}\right)}, \beta \sqrt[3]{\left(-\frac{p}{2} \mp \sqrt{q}\right)}, \alpha \sqrt[3]{\left(-\frac{p}{2} \mp \sqrt{q}\right)}.$$

Donc puifque $x = y + \gamma$, on aura, en ajoutant enfemble les valeurs correfpondantes de $y$ & $\gamma$,

$$\sqrt[3]{\left(-\frac{p}{2} \pm \sqrt{q}\right)} + \sqrt[3]{\left(-\frac{p}{2} \mp \sqrt{q}\right)},$$

$$\alpha \sqrt[3]{\left(-\frac{p}{2} \pm \sqrt{q}\right)} + \beta \sqrt[3]{\left(-\frac{p}{2} \mp \sqrt{q}\right)},$$

$$\beta \sqrt[3]{\left(-\frac{p}{2} \pm \sqrt{q}\right)} + \alpha \sqrt[3]{\left(-\frac{p}{2} \mp \sqrt{q}\right)},$$

où il eft facile de voir que des fignes ambigus de $\sqrt{q}$, foit qu'on prenne le fupérieur, ou l'inférieur, on aura toujours les trois mêmes valeurs de $x$.

De là il s'enfuit donc que l'on peut prendre indifféremment le radical $\sqrt{q}$ en plus ou en moins, & que les trois racines de l'équation propofée réfulteront immédiatement des trois valeurs du radical cubique

$$\sqrt[3]{\left(-\frac{p}{2} \pm \sqrt{q}\right)}.$$

[...]

5. L'équation du fixieme degré $y^6 + p y^3 - \frac{n^3}{27} = 0$ s'appelle la *réduite* du troifieme degré, parce que c'eft à fa réfolution que fe réduit celle de la propofée $x + n x + p = 0$. Or nous avons déja vu plus haut comment les racines de cette derniere équation dépendent des racines de celle-là; voyons réciproquement comment les racines de la *réduite* dépendent de celles de la propofée;

TRANSLATION

# FIRST SECTION
*On the solution of equations of third degree*

1. Since the solution of equations of second degree is very easy, and is furthermore remarkable only for its extreme simplicity, I will enter first into the matter of of equations

of third degree, those [136] requiring for their solution special methods which do not present themselves naturally.

Let there be therefore a general equation of the third degree

$$x^3 + mx^2 + nx + p = 0,$$

and as one knows that one may always make the second term disappear from any equation by increasing its roots by the coefficient of the second term divided by the power of the first, one may suppose first, for greater simplicity, that $m = 0$, which will reduce the proposed equation to the form

$$x^3 + nx + p = 0.$$

It is in this form that equations of third degree were first treated by Scipio Ferreo and by Tartaglia, to whom one owes their solution, but one does not know the path that led them to it. The most natural method of arriving at it seems to me that which Hudde imagined, and which consists of representing the root by the sum of two unknowns which allow the separation of the equation into two distinct parts, so that the two unknowns depend only on an equation solvable in the same way as those of second degree.

Following this method one therefore makes $x = y + z$, which being substituted into the proposed equation reduces it to this

$$y^3 + 3y^2z + 3yz^2 + z^3 + n(y + z) + p = 0$$

which one may put into this simpler form

$$y^3 + z^3 + p + (y + z)(3yz + n) = 0.$$

If one now makes these two separate equations

$$y^3 + z^3 + p = 0$$

$$3yz + n = 0$$

one will have $z = -\dfrac{n}{3y}$; and substituting into the first, $y^3 - \dfrac{n^3}{27y^3} + p = 0$, that is to say,

$$y^6 + py^3 - \frac{n^3}{27} = 0.$$

This equation is in fact of sixth degree, but since it contains only two different powers of the unknown, of which one has an exponent [137] double that of the other, it is clear that it may be solved like those of second degree. Indeed one will have first

$$y^3 = -\tfrac{p}{2} \pm \sqrt{\left(\tfrac{p^2}{4} + \tfrac{n^3}{27}\right)}$$

and from that

$$y = \sqrt[3]{\left(-\tfrac{p}{2} \pm \sqrt{\left(\tfrac{p^2}{4} + \tfrac{n^3}{27}\right)}\right)}.$$

Thus one will know $y$ and $z$ and from that one will have $x = y + z = y - \dfrac{n}{3y}$.

[...]

In §2 Lagrange observed that since $y$ is the solution of an equation of sixth degree it can have six possible values, and therefore so can $x$; but we know that $x$ is the solution of an equation of third degree, and can therefore take only three values. Therefore the six different values of $y$ must give rise to just three different values of $x$, each of which must arise twice.

[...]

[138] 3. Since therefore among the six values of $y$ there are only three which give different values of $x$, it is now a matter of distinguishing these values. For this one must find the specific formula for each of the six values of $y$; and if one calls $1, \alpha$ and $\beta$ the three cube roots of unity, that is to say, the three roots of the equation $x^3 - 1 = 0$, it is easy to see that the six values of $y$ will be (on putting for brevity $\frac{p^2}{4} + \frac{n^3}{27} = q$),

$$\sqrt[3]{\left(-\tfrac{p}{2} \pm \sqrt{q}\right)}, \quad \alpha\sqrt[3]{\left(-\tfrac{p}{2} \pm \sqrt{q}\right)}, \quad \beta\sqrt[3]{\left(-\tfrac{p}{2} \pm \sqrt{q}\right)};$$ from which the corresponding

values of $z = \frac{n}{3y}$ will be, since $\sqrt[3]{\left(-\tfrac{p}{2} \pm \sqrt{q}\right)} \times \sqrt[3]{\left(-\tfrac{p}{2} \mp \sqrt{q}\right)} = \sqrt[3]{\left(\tfrac{p^2}{4} - q\right)} = -\tfrac{n}{3}$,

and consequently $\sqrt[3]{\left(-\tfrac{p}{2} \mp \sqrt{q}\right)}$ [139] $= -\dfrac{n}{3\sqrt[3]{\left(-\tfrac{p}{2} \pm \sqrt{q}\right)}}$, these values will be, I say,

$$\sqrt[3]{\left(-\tfrac{p}{2} \mp \sqrt{q}\right)}, \quad \tfrac{1}{\alpha}\sqrt[3]{\left(-\tfrac{p}{2} \mp \sqrt{q}\right)}, \quad \tfrac{1}{\beta}\sqrt[3]{\left(-\tfrac{p}{2} \mp \sqrt{q}\right)}.$$ Then, without even knowing

the values of $\alpha$ and $\beta$, it is easy to assure oneself that $\alpha\beta$ must be $= 1$; for since $1, \alpha$ and $\beta$ are the three roots of the equations $x^3 - 1 = 0$, one will therefore have their product $1.\alpha.\beta = $ the last term $1$; therefore $\alpha\beta = 1$; therefore $\tfrac{1}{\alpha} = \beta$ and $\tfrac{1}{\beta} = \alpha$; so that the three values above become

$$\sqrt[3]{\left(-\tfrac{p}{2} \mp \sqrt{q}\right)}, \quad \beta\sqrt[3]{\left(-\tfrac{p}{2} \mp \sqrt{q}\right)}, \quad \alpha\sqrt[3]{\left(-\tfrac{p}{2} \mp \sqrt{q}\right)}.$$

Therefore since $x = y + z$, one will have, on adding together the corresponding values of $y$ and $z$,

$$\sqrt[3]{\left(-\tfrac{p}{2} \pm \sqrt{q}\right)} + \sqrt[3]{\left(-\tfrac{p}{2} \mp \sqrt{q}\right)},$$

$$\alpha\sqrt[3]{\left(-\tfrac{p}{2} \pm \sqrt{q}\right)} + \beta\sqrt[3]{\left(-\tfrac{p}{2} \mp \sqrt{q}\right)},$$

$$\beta\sqrt[3]{\left(-\tfrac{p}{2} \pm \sqrt{q}\right)} + \alpha\sqrt[3]{\left(-\tfrac{p}{2} \mp \sqrt{q}\right)},$$

from which it is easy to see that, whether one takes the upper or lower of the ambiguous signs of $\sqrt{q}$, one will always have the same three values of $x$.

From this it follows therefore that one may indifferently take the root $\sqrt{q}$ either positive or negative, and that the three roots of the proposed equation will result immediately from the three values of the cube root $\sqrt[3]{\left(-\tfrac{p}{2} \pm \sqrt{q}\right)}$.

$$[\ldots]$$

[140] 5. The equation of sixth degree $y^6 + py^3 - \dfrac{n^3}{27} = 0$ is called the *reduced equation* of the third degree, because it is to the solution of this that the solution of the proposed equation $x^3 + nx + p = 0$ is reduced. Now we have already seen above how the roots of this last equation depend on the roots of the former; conversely, we see how the roots of the *reduced equation* depend on those of the original equation.

——————————

---

## The reduced equation for a quartic

from Lagrange, 'Réflexions sur la résolution algébrique des équations', *Mémoires de l'Académie des Sciences* (1770), 173–174

---

Je suppose d'abord avec Ferrari que l'équation du quatrieme degré qu'il s'agit de résoudre soit privée de son second terme, ce qu'on fait d'ailleurs être toujours possible, en sorte que cette équation soit représentée ainsi

$$x^4 + n x^3 + p x + q = 0.$$

Qu'on fasse passer dans le second membre tous les termes excepté le premier, & qu'ensuite on ajoute à l'un & l'autre membre la quantité $2 y x^2 + y^2$, $y$ étant une indéterminée, l'on aura

$$x^4 + 2 y x^2 + y^2 = (2 y - n) x^2 - p x + y^2 - q$$

équation où le premier membre est évidemment le carré de $x^2 + y$, de sorte qu'il ne s'agira plus que de rendre aussi carré le second; or pour cela il faut, comme l'on fait, que le carré de la moitié du coëfficient du second terme $- p x$, soit égal au produit des coëfficiens des deux autres; ce qui donne cette condition

$$\frac{p^2}{4} = (2 y - n) (y^2 - q)$$

laquelle produit l'équation cubique

$$y^3 - \frac{n}{2} y^2 - q y + \frac{4 n q - p^2}{8} = 0;$$

supposant donc la résolution de cette équation en sorte qu'on connoisse une valeur de $y$, le second membre de la proposée deviendra

$$(2 y - n) \left( x - \frac{p}{2 (2 y - n)} \right)^2;$$

donc tirant la racine carrée des deux membres on aura

$$x^2 + y = \left( x - \frac{p}{2 (2 y - n)} \right) \sqrt{(2 y - n)}$$

équation où l'inconnue $x$ ne monte qu'au second degré, & qui n'a par conséquent plus de difficulté.

---

### TRANSLATION

I suppose first with Ferrari that the equation of fourth degree that one is concerned to solve is deprived of its second term, since one knows that this is always possible, so that this equation may be represented thus

$$x^4 + nx^2 + px + q = 0.$$

When one transfers to the right hand side all the terms except the first, and then adjoins to both sides the quantity $2yx^2 + y^2$, where $y$ is an unknown quantity, one will have

$$x^4 + 2yx^2 + y^2 = (2y - n)x^2 - px + y^2 - q$$

an equation where the left hand side is clearly the square of $x^2 + y$, so that it remains only to make the right hand side a square also; and for that it must be, as one knows, that the square of half the coefficient of the second term, $-px$, must be equal to the product of the coefficients of the two others; which gives this condition [174]

$$\frac{p^2}{4} = (2y - n)(y^2 - q)$$

which produces the cubic equation

$$y^3 - \frac{n}{2}y^2 - qy + \frac{4nq - p^2}{8} = 0;$$

Assuming therefore that this equation is solved in such a way that one knows one value of $y$, the right hand side of the proposed equation will become

$$(2y - n)\left(x - \tfrac{p}{2(2y-n)}\right)^2 ;$$

therefore, taking the square root of the two sides, one will have

$$x^2 + y = \left(x - \tfrac{p}{2(2y-n)}\right)\sqrt{(2y - n)},$$

an equation where the unknown $x$ appears only to the second degree, and which consequently holds no further difficulty.

————————

The alternative signs for $\sqrt{(2y - n)}$ give two different equations here, each of which (because quadratic) has two solutions, giving altogether four possible values for $x$. In paragraph §27 Lagrange stated that he would henceforth call the cubic equation for $y$,

$$y^3 - \frac{n}{2}y^2 - qy + \frac{4nq - p^2}{8} = 0,$$

the *reduced equation* (*la réduite*) and went on to observe (in §28) that it will have three possible roots. By substituting each of these in turn one is led not just to four but to *twelve* possible values of $x$. Lagrange was able to show that these are equal in triples, so that $x$ in fact takes only four values, as one would expect.

Lagrange had clearly established the role and importance of the reduced equation for cubics and quartics. In fact he had done much more: he had shown that the degree of the reduced equation was in both cases *higher* than that of the original equation but that special relationships, or symmetries, between the roots lowered the degree to a manageable level. One might suspect, though, that the reduced equation for a polynomial of fifth degree would present even greater difficulties, and so it turned out to be.

## 12.3 HIGHER DEGREE EQUATIONS

### 12.3.1 Lagrange's theorem, 1771

In Section 3 of the 'Réflexions' Lagrange finally turned to equations of fifth degree or higher. Reviewing the work of Tschirnhaus, Euler, and Bezout, he observed that in each case their methods led to problems more intractable than the original equation, and he began to voice some doubt as to whether equations of fifth degree (or higher) were amenable to such approaches at all:[5]

> The result of these reflections is that it is very doubtful that the methods of which we have just spoken can give the complete solution of equations of the fifth degree, and for even stronger reasons those of higher degree, and this uncertainty, together with the length of the calculations that the methods display, must put off in advance all those who might be tempted to make use of them to solve one of the most celebrated and important problems in Algebra. Also we see that even the authors of these methods content themselves with making applications to the third or fourth degree, and that no-one has yet tried to push their work further.

Lagrange's study of reduced equations for cubics and quartics had already led him to see that the roots of the reduced equation were functions of the roots of the original equation, and that those functions could therefore take only a limited number of values as the roots of the original equation are permuted amongst themselves. (This is precisely the property that keeps the degree of the reduced equations for cubics or quartics low enough to handle.) This led Lagrange to a more general investigation of functions that remain unchanged under permutations of their arguments. The function $x + y + z^2$, for instance, is invariant under an exchange of $x$ and $y$ but not under an exchange of $x$ or $y$ with $z$. A function $f(x_1, x_2, \ldots, x_n)$ with $n$ arguments $x_1, x_2, \ldots, x_n$ can in general take $n!$ values as the arguments are permuted amongst themselves. Lagrange discovered that if the function remains invariant under certain permutations, then the number of possible values it can take must divide $n!$ His proof was by example, and unfortunately he introduced some trivial mistakes: by cyclically permuting three of the arguments, for example, he should have obtained not two equal values but three. Nevertheless, his theorem was essentially correct and later on, in the context of group theory, it became known as Lagrange's Theorem; but in 1771 group theory was still half a century into the future.

---

5. 'Il résulte de ces réflexions qu'il est très douteux que les méthodes dont nous venons de parler puissent donner la résolution complette des équations du cinquieme degré, & à plus forte raison celle des degrés supérieurs; et cette incertitude, jointe à la longueur des calculs que ces méthodes exigent, doit rebuter d'avance tous ceux qui pourroient être tentés d'en faire usage pour résoudre un des problemes les plus célebres & les plus importans de l'Algebre. Aussi voyons-nous que les Auteurs mêmes de ces méthodes se sont contentés d'en faire l'application au troisième & au quatrieme degré, & que personne n'a encore entrepris de pousser leur travail plus loin.' Lagrange 1771, 140.

# The first statement of Lagrange's theorem

from Lagrange, 'Réflexions sur la résolution algébrique des équations', *Mémoires de l'Académie des Sciences* (1771), 202–203

97. Quoique l'équation $\Theta = 0$ doive être en général du degré 1. 2. 3 --- $\mu = \pi$, qui est égal au nombre des permutations dont les $\mu$ racines $x'$, $x''$, $x'''$ &c. sont susceptibles; cependant s'il arrive que la fonction proposée soit telle qu'elle ne reçoive aucun changement par quelqu'une ou quelques-unes de ces permutations, alors l'équation dont il s'agit s'abaissera nécessairement à un degré moindre.

DES SCIENCES ET BELLES-LETTRES.    203

Car supposons, par exemple, que la fonction $f : (x')\,(x'')\,(x''')\,(x'^{v})$ --- soit telle qu'elle conserve la même valeur en échangeant $x'$ en $x''$, $x''$ en $x'''$, & $x'''$ en $x'$, en sorte que l'on ait

$$f : (x')\,(x'')\,(x''')\,(x'^{v}) - - - = f : (x'')\,(x''')\,(x')\,(x'^{v}) - - -,$$

il est clair que l'équation $\Theta = 0$ aura déjà deux racines égales; mais je vais prouver que dans cette hypothese toutes les autres racines seront aussi égales deux à deux. En effet, considérons une racine quelconque de la même équation, laquelle soit représentée par la fonction $f : (x'^{v})\,(x''')\,(x')\,(x'')$ - - - -, comme celle-ci dérive de la fonction $f : (x')\,(x'')\,(x''')\,(x'^{v})$ - - - -, en échangeant $x'$ en $x'^{v}$, $x''$ en $x''$, $x'''$ en $x'$, $x'^{v}$ en $x''$, il s'ensuit qu'elle devra garder aussi la même valeur en y changeant $x'^{v}$ en $x'''$, $x'''$ en $x'$ & $x'$ en $x'^{v}$; de sorte qu'on aura aussi

$$f : (x'^{v})\,(x''')\,(x')\,(x'') - - - = f : (x''')\,(x')\,(x'^{v})\,(x'').$$

Donc, dans ce cas, la quantité $\Theta$ sera égale à un carré $\theta^2$, & par conséquent l'équation $\Theta = 0$ se réduira à celle-ci, $\theta = 0$, dont la dimension sera $\frac{\pi}{2}$.

On démontrera de la même maniere que, si la fonction $f : (x')\,(x')\,(x'')\,(x'^{v})$ - - - est de sa propre nature telle qu'elle conserve la même valeur en faisant deux ou trois ou un plus grand nombre de permutations différentes entre les racines $x'$, $x''$, $x'''$, $x'^{v}$ &c., les racines de l'équation $\Theta = 0$ seront égales trois à trois ou quatre à quatre ou &c.; en sorte que la quantité $\Theta$ sera égale à un cube $\theta^3$ ou à un carré-carré $\theta^4$ ou &c., & que par conséquent l'équation $\Theta = 0$ se réduira à celle-ci, $\theta = 0$, dont le degré sera $= \frac{\pi}{3}$ ou $= \frac{\pi}{4}$ ou &c.

*Notation*

The values of the function $f : (x')(x'')(x''') \ldots$ under all possible permutations of the $\mu$ arguments $x'$, $x''$, $\ldots$, are the roots of an equation $\Theta = 0$. In relation to the previous discussion, $x'$, $x''$, $x'''$, $\ldots$ are the roots of the original equation and $\Theta = 0$ is the reduced equation.

TRANSLATION

97. Although the equation $\Theta = 0$ must be in general of degree $1.2.3 \ldots \mu = \pi$, which is equal to the number of permutations to which the $\mu$ roots $x'$, $x''$, $x'''$ etc. are susceptible, meanwhile if it happens that the proposed function is such that it is not changed in any way by one or some of these permutations, then the equation in question is necessarily reduced to one of lower degree.

[203] For let us suppose, for example, that the function $f : (x')(x'')(x''')(x^{IV}) \ldots$ is such that it keeps the same value on changing $x'$ to $x''$, $x''$ to $x'''$, and $x'''$ to $x'$, so that one has

$$f : (x')(x'')(x''')(x^{IV}) \cdots = f : (x'')(x''')(x')(x^{IV}) \ldots,$$

it is clear that the equation $\Theta = 0$ will already have two equal roots; but I am going to prove that under this hypothesis all the other roots will also be equal two by two. Indeed, let us consider any root whatever of the same equation, which may be represented by the function $f : (x^{IV})(x''')(x')(x'') \ldots$; as this latter derives from the function $f : (x')(x'')(x''')(x^{IV}) \ldots$ on changing $x'$ to $x^{IV}$, $x''$ to $x'''$, $x'''$ to $x'$, $x^{IV}$ to $x''$, it follows that it must also keep the same value on changing $x^{IV}$ to $x'''$, $x'''$ to $x'$ and $x'$ to $x^{IV}$; so that one will also have

$$f : (x^{IV})(x''')(x')(x'') \cdots = f : (x''')(x')(x^{IV})(x'').$$

Therefore, in this case, the quantity $\Theta$ will be equal to a square $\theta^2$, and consequently the equation $\Theta = 0$ will reduce to this, $\theta = 0$, of which the degree is $\frac{\pi}{2}$.

One may demonstrate in the same way that, if the function $f : (x')(x'')(x''')(x^{IV}) \ldots$ is strictly of such a kind that it keeps the same value on making two or three or a greater number of different permutations between the roots $x'$, $x''$, $x'''$, $x^{IV}$ etc., the roots of the equation $\Theta = 0$ will be equal three by three or four by four or etc.; so that the quantity $\Theta$ will be equal to a cube $\theta^3$ or to a square-square $\theta^4$ or etc., and that consequently the equation $\Theta = 0$ will reduce to this, $\theta = 0$, of which the degree will be equal to $\frac{\pi}{3}$ or $\frac{\pi}{4}$ or etc.

## 12.3.2 Aftermath: the unsolvability of quintics

The problem in trying to solve a quintic equation is that the degree of the reduced equation in its most general form is 120, and although, as for cubics and quartics, this can be reduced by certain symmetries, one is still left with an equation very much worse than one of degree 5. As Lagrange had begun to suspect, it is *not* in general possible to solve quintic equations by algebraic operations alone. This was first proved by the Italian mathematician Paolo Ruffini, who published his demonstration in his *Teoria generale delle equazioni* in 1799 (and again with attempted repairs in *Riflessioni intorno alla soluzione delle equazioni algebriche generali* in 1813), but Ruffini's exposition was (and remains) obscure, and it was not entirely clear that he had actually proved the result he claimed.

Ruffini's work was unknown to Abel in Norway, who took up the same problem before 1820 while he was still at school. When Abel returned to the problem in 1823 he was able to prove that there is *no* general method of solving equations of degree five (or higher) by algebra alone. His proof relied on ideas first suggested in Lagrange's paper of 1770–71, concerning functions that remain invariant under permutations of the roots, together with further work published by Cauchy in 1815 on the number of values such functions could take (see 13.1.1). Abel's results were compressed into a 6-page paper, 'Mémoire sur les équations algébriques où on démontre l'impossibilité de la résolution de l'équation générale du cinquième degré' ('Memoir on algebraic equations in which there is demonstrated the impossibility of solving a general equation of fifth degree'), written in French and published at Abel's own expense in 1824. Two years later an expanded version of the paper was published in German (along with several other papers by Abel) in the first volume of *Crelle's Journal*.

Abel's argument goes beyond the scope of this book, and in any case we do not need to follow the story of polynomial equations further, because the effort to find more powerful methods of solution by algebraic methods alone had finally run into the ground. In mathematics, however, what is impossible in one direction often opens up new and unexpected prospects in another, and that was just what happened here. Lagrange's paper failed to produce a solution for quintics, but proved to be an inspiration not only to Abel, but to two of the most innovative mathematical thinkers of the early nineteenth century, Cauchy and Galois.

# CHAPTER 13

# GROUPS, FIELDS, IDEALS, AND RINGS

O ne of the most fundamental changes in mathematics from the eighteenth century to the nineteenth was the emergence of abstract algebra: the study of structures such as groups, fields, or vector spaces. The initial ideas almost always arose in the context of specific problems so that, to begin with, the elements of a group, for example, were always permutations, and the elements of vector spaces were directed quantities. Gradually it came to be understood that the underlying structures were relevant in many other situations, and could be studied in their own right. By the end of the nineteenth century, the process of abstraction had reached its culmination in the axiomatization of the essential properties, which is how such concepts are generally introduced today. This chapter traces some of the early history of groups, fields, and ideals, while vector spaces are dealt with in Chapter 17.

## 13.1 GROUPS

The origins of group theory are to be found in the independent work of the two most creative French mathematicians of the early nineteenth century, Augustin-Lous Cauchy, and Évariste Galois. It would be hard to find two more contrasting figures: Galois a rebel, Cauchy an extreme conservative who spent much of his life in the Paris institutions from which Galois and his work were turned away. Cauchy in his lifetime published almost 800 mathematical papers on a wide range of subjects, while Galois at his early death in 1832 left behind only a handful of papers and some hastily scribbled notes. Both of them, however, were inspired to take up the work of Lagrange on functions of the roots of equations, and the number of values such a function might take under permutation of the roots (see 12.3.1). Initially their ideas moved in different directions, but eventually came together in the 1860s to form the modern subject of group theory.

### 13.1.1 Cauchy's early work on permutations, 1815

Cauchy took up Lagrange's ideas on permuting the roots of an equation in one of his very earliest mathematical papers, written in 1812 when he was 23 years old, though it was not published until 1815. Cauchy distinguished initially between 'permutations' and 'substitutions': the former were simply arrangements of letters, the latter were the operations that take one arrangement to another. One of several important features of Cauchy's paper was that he regarded such operations as mathematical objects in their own right, each labelled by a single capital letter, and capable of composition amongst themselves to form 'products' or 'powers'. This was the first time such notions, derived from arithmetic, had been extended to anything other than numerical quantities.

**Cauchy's first paper on permutations**

from Cauchy, 'Mémoire sur le nombre des valeurs qu'une fonction peut acquérir ...',
*Journal de l'École Polytechnique*, 10 (1815), 1–5

# JOURNAL

# DE L'ÉCOLE POLYTECHNIQUE.

# MÉMOIRE

*Sur le Nombre des Valeurs qu'une Fonction peut acquérir, lorsqu'on y permute de toutes les manières possibles les quantités qu'elle renferme;*

PAR A. L. CAUCHY, INGÉNIEUR DES PONTS ET CHAUSSÉES.

MM. *LAGRANGE* et *VANDERMONDE* sont, je crois, les premiers qui aient considéré les fonctions de plusieurs variables relativement au nombre de valeurs qu'elles peuvent obtenir, lorsqu'on substitue ces variables à la place les unes des autres. Ils ont donné plusieurs théorèmes intéressans relatifs à ce sujet, dans deux mémoires imprimés en 1771, l'un à Berlin, l'autre à Paris. Depuis ce temps, quelques géomètres italiens se sont occupés avec succès de cette matière, et particulièrement M. *Ruffini,* qui a consigné le résultat de ses recherches dans le tome XII des Mémoires de la Société italienne, et dans sa Théorie des équations numériques. Une des conséquences les plus remarquables des travaux de ces divers géomètres, est qu'avec un nombre donné de lettres on ne peut pas toujours former une fonction qui ait un nombre déterminé de valeurs. Les caractères par lesquels cette

*XVII.ᵉ Cahier.*                                           A

**2**                    A N A L Y S E.

impossibilité se manifeste, ne sont pas toujours faciles à saisir ; mais
on peut du moins, pour un nombre donné de lettres, assigner des
limites que le nombre des valeurs ne peut dépasser, et déterminer en
outre un grand nombre de cas d'exclusion. Je vais exposer dans ce
mémoire ce qu'on avait déjà trouvé de plus important sur cet objet,
et ce que mes propres recherches m'ont permis d'y ajouter. J'examinerai
plus particulièrement le cas où le nombre des valeurs d'une fonction
est supposé plus petit que le nombre des lettres, parce que les fonctions de cette nature sont celles dont la connaissance est la plus utile
en analyse.

———————

Considérons une fonction de plusieurs quantités, et supposons que
l'on échange entre elles ces mêmes quantités une ou plusieurs fois
de suite. Si la fonction est du genre de celles qu'on appelle *symétriques*,
elle ne changera pas de valeur par suite des transpositions opérées
entre les quantités qu'elle renferme ; mais si elle n'est pas symétrique,
elle pourra obtenir, en vertu de ces mêmes transpositions, plusieurs
valeurs différentes les unes des autres, dont le nombre se trouvera
déterminé par la nature de la fonction dont il s'agit. Si l'on partage
les fonctions en divers ordres, suivant le nombre des quantités qu'elles
renferment, en sorte qu'une fonction du second ordre soit celle qui renferme deux quantités, une fonction du troisième ordre celle qui en
renferme trois, &c...., il sera facile de reconnaître qu'il existe une
liaison nécessaire entre le nombre des valeurs que peut obtenir une
fonction non symétrique et l'ordre de cette même fonction. Ainsi, par
exemple, une fonction du second ordre ne pourra jamais obtenir que
deux valeurs que l'on déduira l'une de l'autre par la transposition des
deux quantités qui la composent. De même, une fonction du troisième
ordre ne pourra obtenir plus de six valeurs ; une fonction du quatrième
ordre plus de vingt-quatre valeurs, &c.... En général, le *maximum* du
nombre des valeurs que peut obtenir une fonction de l'ordre $n$ sera

ANALYSE.

3

évidemment égal au produit

$$1 \cdot 2 \cdot 3 \ldots n;$$

car ce produit représente le nombre des manières différentes dont on peut disposer à la suite les unes des autres, les quantités dont la fonction se compose. On a donc déjà, par ce moyen, une limite que le nombre des valeurs en question ne peut dépasser : mais il s'en faut de beaucoup que dans chaque ordre on puisse former des fonctions dont le nombre des valeurs soit égal à l'un des nombres entiers situés au-dessous de cette limite. Un peu de réflexion suffit pour faire voir qu'aucun nombre au-dessous de la limite ne peut remplir la condition exigée, à moins qu'il ne soit diviseur de cette limite. On peut s'en assurer facilement à l'aide des considérations suivantes.

Soit $K$ une fonction quelconque de l'ordre $n$, et désignons par $a_1$, $a_2 \ldots a_n$ les quantités qu'elle renferme. Si l'on écrit à la suite les unes des autres les quantités dont il s'agit, ou, ce qui revient au même, les indices qui les affectent, dans l'ordre où ils se présentent, lorsqu'on les passe en revue en allant de gauche à droite, et en ayant soin de n'écrire qu'une seule fois chaque indice, on aura une permutation de ces mêmes indices, qui aura une relation nécessaire avec la fonction $K$. Par exemple, si la fonction $K$ était du quatrième ordre, et égale à

$$a_1 \, a_2{}^m \cos. \, a_4 + a_4 \, \sin. \, a_3 ,$$

la permutation relative à $K$ serait

$$1 \cdot 2 \cdot 4 \cdot 3.$$

Si, au-dessous de la permutation relative à $K$, on écrit une autre permutation formée avec les indices $1$, $2$, $3 \ldots n$, et que l'on remplace successivement dans la fonction $K$, chacun des indices qui composent la permutation supérieure par l'indice correspondant de la permutation inférieure, on aura une nouvelle valeur de $K$ qui sera ou ne sera pas équivalente à la première, et la permutation relative à cette nouvelle valeur de $K$ sera évidemment la permutation inférieure dont

A 2

4                          A N A L Y S E.

on vient de parler. On pourra obtenir, par ce moyen, les valeurs de $K$ relatives aux diverses permutations que l'on peut former avec les indices $1, 2, 3 \ldots n$; et si l'on représente par

$$K, \ K', \ K'', \ \&c. \ldots$$

les valeurs dont il s'agit, leur nombre sera égal au produit

$$1 \cdot 2 \cdot 3 \ldots n \, ,$$

et leur ensemble fournira toutes les valeurs possibles de la fonction $K$. Pour déduire deux de ces valeurs l'une de l'autre, il suffira de former les permutations relatives à ces deux valeurs, et de substituer aux indices de la première permutation les indices correspondans pris dans la seconde. Pour indiquer cette *substitution*, j'écrirai les deux permutations entre parenthèses, en plaçant la première au-dessus de la seconde: ainsi, par exemple, la substitution

$$\begin{pmatrix} 1.2.4.3 \\ 2.4.3.1 \end{pmatrix}$$

indiquera que l'on doit substituer dans $K$, l'indice 2 à l'indice 1, l'indice 4 à l'indice 2, l'indice 3 à l'indice 4, et l'indice 1 à l'indice 3. Si donc on supposait, comme ci-dessus,

$$K = a_1 \, a_2{}^m \, \cos. \, a_4 + a_4 \, \sin. \, a_3 ,$$

en désignant par $K'$ la nouvelle valeur de $K$ obtenue par la substitution

$$\begin{pmatrix} 1.2.4.3 \\ 2.4.3.1 \end{pmatrix} ,$$

on aurait

$$K' = a_2 \, a_4{}^m \, \cos. \, a_3 + a_3 \, \sin. \, a_1 .$$

Afin d'abréger, je représenterai dans la suite les permutations elles-mêmes par des lettres majuscules. Ainsi, si l'on désigne la permutation

$$1.2.4.3 \qquad \text{par} \qquad A_1 ,$$

et la permutation

$$2.4.3.1 \qquad \text{par} \qquad A_2 ,$$

A N A L Y S E.                                              5

la substitution

$$\begin{pmatrix} 1.2.4.3 \\ 2.4.3.1 \end{pmatrix}$$

se trouvera indiquée de la manière suivante,

$$\begin{pmatrix} A_1 \\ A_2 \end{pmatrix} .$$

# MEMOIR

*On the number of values that a function may take, when one permutes in
all possible ways the quantities that it contains;*

BY A. L. CAUCHY, ENGINEER OF BRIDGES AND ROADS.

Messieurs LAGRANGE and VANDERMONDE are, I believe, the first who have considered
functions of several variables with respect to the number of values that they may take,
when one substitutes these variables in place of one another. They have given several
interesting theorems relating to this subject, in two memoirs printed in 1771, one in
Berlin, the other in Paris. Since that time, some Italian geometers have engaged them-
selveswith success in this matter, and particularly Monsieur *Ruffini*, who has deposited
the result of his research in volume XII of the Memoirs of the Italian Society, and in
his *Theory of numerical equations*. One of the most remarkable results of the work of
these various geometers is that with a given number of letters one may not always form
a function which has a certain number of values. The formulae in which this [2] impossibility manifests itself are not always easy to know; but one can at least, for a given
number of letters, assign limits that the number of values may not exceed and, besides,
determine a great number of excluded cases. I am going to explain in this memoir
the most important things that have already been found on this subject, and what my
own researches permit me to add. I will examine most particularly the case where the
number of values of a function is assumed smaller than the number of letters, because
it is knowledge of functions of this kind that is most useful in analysis.

––––––––––––

Let us consider a function of several quantities, and let us suppose that one exchanges
these same quantities with each other once or several times in succession. If the function
is of a kind that one calls *symmetric*, it will not change its value following transpositions
carried out between the quantities it contains; but if it is not symmetric it may take, by
virtue of these same transpositions, several values different from each other, the number
of which may be determined by the nature of the function in question. If one separates
functions into various orders, according to the number of quantities they contain, so
that a function of the second order is one that contains two quantities, a function of the
third order is one that contains three, etc., it will be easy to recognize that there exists
a necessary relationship between the number of values that a non-symmetric function
can take and the order of that same function. Thus, for example, a function of the
second order can never take more than two values, which may be derived from each
other by a transposition of the two quantities it contains. In the same way, a function
of the third order cannot take more than six values; a function of the fourth order no
more than twenty-four values, etc. In general, the *maximum* number of values that a
function of order $n$ can take will [3] clearly be equal to the product

$$1.2.3 \ldots n;$$

for this product represents the number of different ways in which one may arrange one after another the quantities of which the function is composed. One has therefore already, in this way, a bound that the number of values in question may not exceed; but it must further be the case that for each order one may form functions for which the number of values is equal to a whole number below this bound. A little reflection suffices to show that a number below the bound may not satisfy the required condition, at least if it is not a divisor of that limit. One may easily assure oneself of this by means of the following considerations.

Let $K$ be any function of order $n$, and let us denote by $a_1, a_2 \ldots a_n$ the quantities it contains. If one writes one after the other the quantities in question, or, which comes to the same thing, the indices that belong to them, in the order in which they present themselves when one reviews them from left to right, and taking care to write each index only once, one will have an arrangement of these same indices, which will have a necessary relationship with the function $K$. For example, if the function $K$ was of fourth order, and equal to

$$a_1 a_2^m \cos a_4 + a_4 \sin a_3,$$

the arrangement relating to $K$ would be

$$1.2.4.3.$$

If below the arrangement relating to $K$ one writes another arrangement formed from the indices $1, 2, 3 \ldots n$ and, in the function $K$, successively replaces each of the indices that make up the upper arrangement by the the corresponding index of the lower arrangement, one will have a new value of $K$ which may or may not be equal to the first, and the arrangement relating to this new value of $K$ will clearly be the lower arrangement of which [4] we have just spoken. One may obtain, by this means, values of $K$ relating to various arrangements that one may form with the indices $1, 2, 3 \ldots n$; and if one represents by

$$K, K', K'', \text{etc.} \ldots$$

the values in question, their number will be equal to the product

$$1.2.3 \ldots n,$$

and together they will supply all possible values of the function $K$. To derive two of these values from one another, it will suffice to form the arrangements relating to these two values, and to substitute for the indices of the first arrangement the corresponding indices taken from the second. To indicate this *substitution*, I will write the two arrangements between parentheses, placing the first above the second: thus, for example, the substitution

$$\left( \begin{array}{c} 1.2.4.3 \\ 2.4.3.1 \end{array} \right)$$

will indicate that in $K$ one must substitute index 2 for index 1, index 4 for index 2, index 3 for index 4, and index 1 for index 3. If therefore one supposes, as above,

$$K = a_1 a_2^m \cos a_4 + a_4 \sin a_3,$$

and, denoting by $K'$ the new value of $K$ obtained by the substitution

$$\begin{pmatrix} 1.2.4.3 \\ 2.4.3.1 \end{pmatrix},$$

one will have

$$K' = a_2 a_4^m \cos a_3 + a_3 \sin a_1.$$

Finally, for brevity, I will represent the arrangements themselves by capital letters. Thus, if one denotes the arrangement

$$1.2.4.3 \quad \text{by} \quad A_1,$$

and the arrangement

$$2.4.3.1 \quad \text{by} \quad A_2,$$

[5] the substitution

$$\begin{pmatrix} 1.2.4.3 \\ 2.4.3.1 \end{pmatrix}$$

will be indicated in the following manner,

$$\begin{pmatrix} A_1 \\ A_2 \end{pmatrix}.$$

---

## 13.1.2 The *Premier mémoire* of Galois, 1831

When Cauchy wrote his paper on permutations in 1812, Galois was only a year old, but only seventeen years later he too took up Lagrange's work on the solvability of equations. He had read Cauchy's paper, and from the opening paragraphs would have known also of Ruffini's interest in the subject, but was as yet unaware of Abel's proof of the general unsolvability of quintics. In any case Galois' work led him in a rather different direction, towards distinguishing precisely *which* equations are algebraicially solvable and which are not. An equation is algebraically solvable if its roots can be expressed in terms of its coefficients using only the operations of addition, subtraction, multiplication, division, and root extraction (as, for example, in the usual formula for quadratic equations, and Cardano's rule for cubics). This is what Galois and other early nineteenth-century writers described as 'solution by radicals', meaning that it required no operation beyond the extraction of roots, or radicals.

Galois submitted two papers on the solvability of equations by radicals to the Paris Academy in May and June 1829, and they passed through the hands of Cauchy who possibly advised him to rework them. Galois resubmitted his ideas in a new paper in February 1830. This time it was given to Fourier, and unfortunately could not be found after Fourier's death three months later. Galois re-wrote the paper and submitted it for a third time in January 1831, but on 4 July of that year it was rejected by the new referees, Poisson and Lacroix, on the grounds that his reasoning was not clear, and that he did not yet appear to have given a criterion for solvability that could be easily applied. They were right on both counts, and if Galois had lived long enough he might have been persuaded to give a fuller and clearer exposition.

By this time, however, Galois was increasingly involved in revolutionary politics, and spent eight months in prison from July 1831 to March 1832. More tragically, he died needlessly as the result of a duel at the end of May 1832. During the night before he went out to fight, he wrote a letter to his friend Auguste Chevalier outlining his main mathematical findings. He also added some corrections and clarifications to the paper that had been returned to him by Poisson, which afterwards became known as his 'Premier mémoire'. In 1830 Galois had also written what has become known as his 'Seconde mémoire', a further and much more difficult exposition of his ideas on equations and groups. The two *mémoires* and the eleventh-hour letter to Chevalier are all we have of Galois' own thinking on the theory that came to be named after him.

Galois saw that the solvability of an equation depends on the properties of the group of permutations of its roots (its Galois group), a remarkable insight for a young man who was largely self-taught and not yet twenty. His writing was dense and difficult, however, and we give here only a short extract from the 'Premier mémoire' to give some idea of his style and approach. We begin with a note on substitutions added by Galois to the opening definitions of the 'Premier mémoire' on the night that he wrote his final letter to Chevalier.[1]

Substitutions are the passage from one arrangement to another.
The arrangement from which one begins in order to indicate the substitutions is completely arbitrary, when one is concerned with functions; for there is no reason why, in a function of several letters, one letter occupies one place rather than another.
Meanwhile, since one can hardly form an idea of a substitution without forming that of an arrangement, we shall frequently speak of arrangements, and we shall consider substitutions only as the passage from one arrangement to another.
When we wish to group substitutions, we will make them all arise from the same arrangement. Since we are always concerned with questions where the original disposition of the letters has no influence at all on the groups we are considering, one must have the same substitutions, whatever arrangement one starts from. Therefore, if in the same group one has substitutions $S$ and $T$, one is sure to have the substitution $ST$.
Which are the definitions we thought should be recalled to mind.

To show how Galois related properties of the group of substitutions to the solvability of an equation, we give part of his Proposition I.

---

1. Galois 1846, 419.

# A proposition from Galois' 'Premier mémoire'

from Galois, 'Mémoire sur les conditions de résolubilité des équations par radicaux', 1831;
as printed in *Journal de mathématiques pures et appliquées*, 11 (1846), 421–423

## PROPOSITION I.

Théorème. « Soit une équation donnée, dont $a$, $b$, $c$, ... sont les
» $m$ racines. Il y aura toujours un groupe de permutations des lettres
» $a$, $b$, $c$,... qui jouira de la propriété suivante :

» 1°. Que toute fonction des racines, invariable [*] par les substi-
» tutions de ce groupe, soit rationnellement connue ;

» 2°. Réciproquement, que toute fonction des racines, déterminable
» rationnellement, soit invariable par les substitutions. »

---

équation soient des fonctions rationnelles les unes des autres ; car l'équation auxiliaire
en V est dans ce cas.

Au surplus, cette remarque est purement curieuse. En effet, une équation qui a
cette propriété n'est pas, en général, plus facile à résoudre qu'une autre.

[*] Nous appelons ici invariable non-seulement une fonction dont la forme est
invariable par les substitutions des racines entre elles, mais encore celle dont la valeur
numérique ne varierait pas par ces substitutions. Par exemple, si $Fx = 0$ est une équation, $Fx$ est une fonction des racines qui ne varie par aucune permutation.

Quand nous disons qu'une fonction est rationnellement connue, nous voulons dire
que sa valeur numérique est exprimable en fonction rationnelle des coefficients de l'é-
quation et des quantités adjointes.

(Dans le cas des équations algébriques, ce groupe n'est autre chose que l'ensemble des $1.2.3\dots m$ permutations possibles sur les $m$ lettres, puisque, dans ce cas, les fonctions symétriques sont seules déterminables rationnellement.)

(Dans le cas de l'équation $\frac{x^n-1}{x-1}=0$, si l'on suppose $a=r$, $b=r^g$, $c=r^{g^2},\dots$, $g$ étant une racine primitive, le groupe de permutations sera simplement celui-ci :

$$abcd\ \dots\ \dots\ k$$
$$bcd\ \dots\ \dots\ ka$$
$$cd.\ \dots\ \dots\ kab$$
$$\dots\ \dots\ \dots\ \dots$$
$$kabc\ \dots\ \dots\ i;$$

dans ce cas particulier, le nombre des permutations est égal au degré de l'équation, et la même chose aurait lieu dans les équations dont toutes les racines seraient des fonctions rationnelles les unes des autres.)

DÉMONSTRATION. Quelle que soit l'équation donnée, on pourra trouver une fonction rationnelle V des racines, telle que toutes les racines soient fonctions rationnelles de V. Cela posé, considérons l'équation irréductible dont V est racine (lemmes III et IV). Soient V, V′. V″,..., $V^{(n-1)}$ les racines de cette équation.

Soient $\varphi V$, $\varphi_1 V$, $\varphi_2 V$, ..., $\varphi_{m-1} V$ les racines de la proposée.

Écrivons les $n$ permutations suivantes des racines

| (V) | $\varphi V,$ | $\varphi_1 V,$ | $\varphi_2 V,\dots,$ | $\varphi_{m-1} V,$ |
|---|---|---|---|---|
| (V′) | $\varphi V′,$ | $\varphi_1 V′,$ | $\varphi_2 V′,\dots,$ | $\varphi_{m-1} V′,$ |
| (V″) | $\varphi V″,$ | $\varphi_1 V″,$ | $\varphi_2 V″,\dots,$ | $\varphi_{m-1} V″;$ |
| $\dots$ | $\dots$ | $\dots$ | $\dots$ | $\dots$ |
| $(V^{(n-1)})$ | $\varphi V^{(n-1)},$ | $\varphi_1 V^{(n-1)},$ | $\varphi_2 V^{(n-1)},\dots,$ | $\varphi_{m-1} V^{(n-1)}:$ |

je dis que ce groupe de permutations jouit de la propriété énoncée.

En effet, $1°$ toute fonction F des racines, invariable par les substitutions de ce groupe, pourra être écrite ainsi : $F = \psi V$, et l'on aura

$$\psi V = \psi V′ = \psi V″ = \dots = \psi V^{(n-1)}.$$

La valeur de F pourra donc se déterminer rationnellement.

2°. *Réciproquement*. Si une fonction F est déterminable rationnellement, et que l'on pose F = ψV, on devra avoir

$$\psi V = \psi V' = \psi V'' = \ldots = \psi V^{(n-1)},$$

puisque l'équation en V n'a pas de diviseur commensurable et que V
satisfait à l'équation F = ψV, F étant une quantité rationnelle. Donc
la fonction F sera nécessairement invariable par les substitutions du
groupe écrit ci-dessus.

Ainsi, ce groupe jouit de la double propriété dont il s'agit dans le
théorème proposé. Le théorème est donc démontré.

Nous appellerons groupe de l'équation le groupe en question.

TRANSLATION

## PROPOSITION I

THEOREM. " Suppose there is given an equation of which $a, b, c, \ldots$ are the $m$ roots.
There will always be a group of permutations of the letters $a, b, c, \ldots$, which will display
the following property:

1st. That every function of the roots, invariant* under the substitutions of the group,
may be rationally known;

2nd. Conversely, that every function of the roots, rationally determinable, is invariant
under these substitutions."
[422] (In the case of algebraic equations, this group is nothing other than the set of
$1.2.3 \ldots m$ possible permutations on the $m$ letters, because in this case, the symmetric
functions alone are rationally determinable.)

(In the case of the equation $\frac{x^n-1}{x-1} = 0$, if one assumes $a = r, b = r^g, c = r^{g^2}, \ldots$,
where $g$ is a primitive root, the group of permutations will be simply this:

$$abcd \ldots \ldots k$$
$$bcd \ldots \ldots ka$$
$$cd \ldots \ldots kab$$
$$\ldots \ldots \ldots \ldots$$
$$kabc \ldots \ldots i;$$

in this particular case, the number of permutations is equal to the degree of the equation,
and the same thing will hold in equations in which all the roots are rational functions
of one another.)

PROOF. Whatever the given equation, one may find a rational function $V$ of the
roots, such that all the roots are rational functions of $V$. That said, let us consider

---

* We call here invariant not only a function of which the form is invariant under the substitutions of roots
amongst themselves, but one whose numerical value also does not change under these substitutions. For
example, if $Fx = 0$ is an equation, $Fx$ is a function of the roots which does not vary under any permutation.

When we say that a function is rationally known, we mean that the numerical value is expressible as a
rational function of the coefficients of the equation and its adjoint quantities.

the irreducible equation of which $V$ is a root (lemmas III and IV). Let $V$, $V'$, $V''$, …, $V^{(n-1)}$ be the roots of this equation.

Let $\varphi V, \varphi_1 V, \varphi_2 V, …, \varphi_{m-1} V$ be the roots of the proposed equation.

Let us write the following $n$ arrangements of the roots.

$$
\begin{array}{c|ccccc}
(V) & \varphi V, & \varphi_1 V, & \varphi_2 V, …, & \varphi_{m-1} V, \\
(V') & \varphi V', & \varphi_1 V', & \varphi_2 V', …, & \varphi_{m-1} V', \\
(V'') & \varphi V'', & \varphi_1 V'', & \varphi_2 V'', …, & \varphi_{m-1} V'', \\
… & … & … & … & … \\
(V^{(n-1)}) & \varphi V^{(n-1)}, & \varphi_1 V^{(n-1)}, & \varphi_2 V^{(n-1)}, …, & \varphi_{m-1} V^{(n-1)} :
\end{array}
$$

I say that this group of permutations has the stated property.

Indeed, first, every function $F$ of the roots, invariant under the substitutions of the group, can be written thus: $F = \psi V$, and one will have

$$\psi V = \psi V' = \psi V'' = \cdots = \psi V^{(n-1)}.$$

The value of $F$ will therefore be rationally determined.

[423] Second, *conversely*. If a function $F$ is rationally determinable, and one puts $F = \psi V$, one must have

$$\psi V = \psi V' = \psi V'' = \cdots = \psi V^{(n-1)},$$

because the equation in $V$ has no commensurable divisor and because $V$ satisfies the equation $F = \psi V$, where $F$ is a rational quantity. Therefore the function $F$ will necessarily be invariant under the substitutions of the group set out above.

Thus, this group displays the double property we are dealing with in the theorem proposed. The theorem is thus proved.

We will call the group in question the group of the equation.

———————

### 13.1.3 Cauchy's return to permutations, 1845

In March 1845 the young mathematician Joseph Bertrand submitted to the Paris Academy a paper entitled 'Mémoire sur le nombre de valeurs que peut prendre une fonction quand on y permute les lettres qu'elle renferme' ('Memoir on the number of values that a function can take when one permutes the letters that it contains'). In it he referred to Cauchy's paper of 1815, and went a considerable way towards a proof of a conjecture that Cauchy had made there. Cauchy was one of the referees for Bertrand's paper and, it seems, was inspired by it to resume his own work on the subject, because from September 1845 to January 1846 he produced a weekly flow of papers on the subject of 'substitutions' for the *Comptes rendus*. Bertrand's paper, meanwhile, was not published until November 1848.

At the same time Cauchy produced a longer paper entitled 'Mémoire sur les arrangements que l'on peut former avec des lettres données et sur les permutations ou substitutions a l'aide desquelles on passe d'un arrangement a un autre' ('Memoir on the arrangements one can form with given letters and on the permutations or substitutions by means of which one passes from one arrangement to another'), and published it in his own journal, *Exercices d'analyse et de physique mathématique*, in instalments from December 1845 to May 1846.[3]

In the first of his papers for the *Comptes rendus*, Cauchy defined a 'système de substitutions conjuguées' ('system of combined substitutions'), equivalent to what Galois had called a 'groupe', but described very differently.

---

### Cauchy's systems of combined substitutions

from Cauchy, 'Sur le nombre des valeurs égales ou inégales que peut acquérir une fonction', *Comptes rendus*, 21 (1845), 593–596, 605

---

ANALYSE MATHÉMATIQUE. — *Sur le nombre des valeurs égales ou inégales que peut acquérir une fonction de* n *variables indépendantes, quand on permute ces variables entre elles d'une manière quelconque; par* M. AUGUSTIN CAUCHY.

« Je m'étais déjà occupé, il y a plus de trente années, de la théorie des permutations, particulièrement du nombre des valeurs que les fonctions peuvent acquérir; et dernièrement, comme je l'expliquerai plus en détail dans une prochaine séance, M. Bertrand a joint quelques nouveaux théorèmes à ceux qu'on avait précédemment établis, à ceux que j'avais moi-même obtenus. Mais à la proposition de Lagrange, suivant laquelle le nombre des valeurs d'une fonction de *n* lettres est toujours un diviseur du produit 1.2.3...*n*, on avait jusqu'ici ajouté presque uniquement des théorèmes concernant l'impossibilité d'obtenir des fonctions qui offrent un certain nombre de valeurs. Dans un nouveau travail, j'ai attaqué directement les deux questions qui consistent à savoir : 1° quels sont les nombres de valeurs que peut acquérir une fonction de *n* lettres; 2° comment on peut effectivement former des fonctions pour lesquelles les nombres de valeurs distinctes soient

---

3. Issues of the *Exercices* from 1844 to 1846 were later bound together to form Volume III, which carries the date 1844 on its title page. This has led to confusion about the dating of Cauchy's work, but careful study of both external and internal evidence shows that Cauchy's papers on substitutions were written *after* Bertrand's paper of March 1845 (see Neumann 1989). The 'Mémoire' in the *Exercices* and the early papers in the *Comptes rendus* series contain much the same material.

( 594 )

les nombres trouvés. Mes recherches sur cet objet m'ont d'ailleurs conduit à des formules nouvelles relatives à la théorie des suites, et qui ne sont pas sans intérêt. Je me propose de publier, dans les *Exercices d'Analyse et de Physique mathématique,* les résultats de mon travail avec tous les développements qui me paraîtront utiles ; je demanderai seulement à l'Académie la permission d'en insérer des extraits dans le *Compte rendu,* en indiquant quelques-unes des propositions les plus remarquables auxquelles je suis parvenu.

**ANALYSE.**

§ I$^{er}$ — *Considérations générales.*

″ Soit $\Omega$ une fonction de $n$ variables

$$x, \ y, \ z, \ \dots$$

Ces variables pourront être censées occuper, dans la fonction, des places déterminées ; et, si on les déplace, en substituant les unes aux autres, la fonction $\Omega$ prendra successivement diverses valeurs

$$\Omega', \ \Omega'', \ \dots,$$

dont l'une quelconque $\Omega'$ pourra être ou égale à $\Omega$, quelles que soient les valeurs attribuées aux variables $x, \ y, \ z, \ \dots$ supposées indépendantes, ou généralement distincte de la valeur primitive $\Omega$, à laquelle elle ne deviendra égale que pour certaines valeurs particulières de $x, \ y, \ z, \ \dots$ propres à vérifier l'équation

$$\Omega' = \Omega.$$

″ Dans ce qui suit, je m'occuperai uniquement des propriétés dont les fonctions jouissent, en raison de leur forme, et non pas en raison des systèmes de valeurs que les variables peuvent acquérir. En conséquence, quand il sera question des valeurs *égales* entre elles que la fonction $\Omega$ peut acquérir quand on déplace les variables $x, \ y, \ z, \ \dots$, il faudra toujours se souvenir que ces valeurs sont celles qui restent égales, quelles que soient les valeurs attribuées aux variables $x, \ y, \ z, \ \dots$. Ainsi, par exemple, si l'on a

$$\Omega = x + y,$$

les deux valeurs que pourra prendre la fonction $\Omega$, quand on déplacera les

( 595 )

deux variables, savoir,

$$x + y \quad \text{et} \quad y + x,$$

seront *égales* entre elles, quelles que soient d'ailleurs les valeurs attribuées à $x$ et à $y$. Mais si l'on avait

$$\Omega = x + 2y,$$

les deux valeurs de la fonction, savoir,

$$x + 2y \quad \text{et} \quad y + 2x,$$

seraient deux valeurs *distinctes,* qu'on ne pourrait plus appeler *valeurs égales,* attendu qu'elles seraient le plus souvent inégales, et ne deviendraient égales que dans le cas particulier où l'on aurait $y = x$.

» Si l'on numérote les places occupées par les diverses variables $x, y, z, \ldots$ dans la fonction $\Omega$, et si l'on écrit à la suite les unes des autres ces variables $x, y, z, \ldots$ rangées d'après l'ordre de grandeur des numéros assignés aux places qu'elles occupent, on obtiendra un certain *arrangement*

$$x\,y\,z \ldots,$$

et quand les variables seront déplacées, cet arrangement se trouvera remplacé par un autre, qu'il suffira de comparer au premier pour connaître la nature des déplacements. Cela posé, ces diverses valeurs d'une fonction de $n$ lettres correspondront évidemment aux divers arrangements que l'on pourra former avec ces $n$ lettres. D'ailleurs, le nombre de ces arrangements est, comme l'on sait, représenté par le produit

$$1.2.3\ldots n.$$

Si donc l'on pose, pour abréger,

$$N = 1.2.3\ldots n,$$

$N$ sera le nombre des valeurs diverses, égales ou distinctes, qu'une fonction de $n$ variables acquerra successivement quand on déplacera de toutes les manières, en les substituant l'une à l'autre, les variables dont il s'agit.

» On appelle *permutation* ou *substitution* l'opération qui consiste à déplacer les variables, en les substituant les unes aux autres, dans une valeur

( 596 )

donnée de la fonction Ω, ou dans l'arrangement correspondant.

[...]

„ Considérons maintenant plusieurs substitutions

$$\begin{pmatrix} B \\ A \end{pmatrix}, \quad \begin{pmatrix} D \\ C \end{pmatrix}, \quad \begin{pmatrix} F \\ E \end{pmatrix}, \cdots$$

relatives aux $n$ lettres $x, y, z, \ldots$. J'appellerai substitutions *dérivées* toutes celles que l'on pourra déduire des substitutions données, multipliées une ou plusieurs fois les unes par les autres ou par elles-mêmes dans un ordre quelconque, et les substitutions données, jointes aux substitutions dérivées, formeront ce que j'appellerai un *système de substitutions conjuguées*. L'ordre de ce système sera le nombre total des substitutions qu'il présente, y compris la substitution qui offre deux termes égaux et se réduit à l'unité. Si l'on désigne par I cet ordre, et par

$$i, \ i', \ i'', \ldots$$

les ordres des substitutions données, I sera toujours divisible par chacun des nombres $i$, $i'$, $i''$, .... D'ailleurs I sera toujours un diviseur du produit

$$N = 1.2\ldots n.$$

Ajoutons qu'étant donné un système de substitutions conjuguées, on reproduira toujours les mêmes substitutions, rangées seulement d'une autre manière, si on les multiplie séparément par l'une quelconque d'entre elles, ou bien encore si l'une quelconque d'entre elles est séparément multipliée par elle-même et par toutes les autres.

---

### TRANSLATION

MATHEMATICAL ANALYSIS.—*On the number of equal or unequal values, that a function of n independent variables may take, when one permutes these variables between themselves in any way whatever;* by MONSIEUR AUGUSTIN CAUCHY.

I was already concerned, more than thirty years ago, with the theory of permutations, particularly with the number of values that functions may take; and latterly, as I will explain in more detail at a future meeting, Monsieur Bertrand has added several new theorems to those that were previously established and to those that I myself had obtained. But to the proposition of Lagrange, according to which the number of values of a function of $n$ letters is always a divisor of the product $1.2.3.\ldots.n$, there had until now been added almost entirely theorems concerning the impossibility of obtaining functions that offer a certain number of values. In new work, I have directly attacked two problems, which consist of finding, first, what are the numbers of values that a function of $n$ letters may take; second, how can one effectively form functions for which the numbers of distinct values are [594] the numbers found. My researches on this subject have led me besides to new formulas relating to the theory of series, and which are not without interest. I propose to publish the results of my work in the *Exercices d'Analyse et de Physique mathématique* with all the details that appear to me useful; I will only ask of the Academy permission to insert extracts in the *Compte rendu*, indicating some of the more remarkable propositions I have arrived at.

ANALYSIS

§1.—*General considerations.*

Let $\Omega$ be a function of $n$ variables

$$x, y, z, \ldots.$$

These variables may be thought to occupy definite places in the function; and, if one displaces them, by substituting one for another, the function $\Omega$ will successively take various values

$$\Omega', \Omega'', \ldots,$$

of which any one $\Omega'$ may be either equal to $\Omega$, whatever the values attributed to the variables $x, y, z, \ldots$, assumed independent, or generally distinct from the original value $\Omega$, to which it will not become equal except for certain particular values of $x, y, z, \ldots$ which correctly satisfy the equation

$$\Omega' = \Omega.$$

In what follows, I will be concerned only with properties that the functions display by reason of their form, and not by reason of the set of values that the variables may take. Consequently, when it is a question of values *equal* amongst themselves that the function $\Omega$ may take when one displaces the variables $x, y, z, \ldots$, one must always recall that these values are those that remain equal, whatever the values given to the variables $x, y, z, \ldots.$. Thus, for example, if one has

$$\Omega = x + y,$$

the two values that the function $\Omega$ may take when one interchanges [595] the two variables, that is,

$$x + y \quad \text{and} \quad y + x$$

will be *equal* to each other, whatever the values given to $x$ and $y$ besides. But if one had

$$\Omega = x + 2y,$$

the two values of the function, that is,

$$x + 2y \quad \text{and} \quad y + 2x,$$

will be two *distinct* values, which one may not call *equal values*, seeing that they will be more often unequal, and will not become equal except in the particular case where one has $y = x$.

If one numbers the places occupied by the different variables $x, y, z, \ldots$ in the function $\Omega$, and if one writes these variables $x, y, z, \ldots$ one after another, ranked in order of size of the numbers assigned to the places they occupy, one will obtain a certain *arrangement*

$$x \, y \, z \ldots,$$

and when the variables are displaced, this arrangements will be replaced by another, which it will suffice to compare with the first to know the nature of the displacements. That said, the various values of a function of $n$ letters clearly correspond to various arrangements that one may form with these $n$ letters. Besides, the number of these arrangements is, as one knows, represented by the product

$$1.2.3.\ldots.n.$$

If therefore one puts for brevity,

$$N = 1.2.3.\ldots.n,$$

$N$ will be number of values, equal or distinct, that a function of $n$ variables will take successively when one displaces the variables in question in all possible ways, by substituting one for another.

One calls *permutation* or *substitution* the operation that consists of displacing the variables, by substituting one for another, in a given value [596] of the function $\Omega$, or in the corresponding arrangement. …

$$[\ldots]$$

[605] Let us now consider several substitutions

$$\begin{pmatrix} B \\ A \end{pmatrix}, \quad \begin{pmatrix} D \\ C \end{pmatrix}, \quad \begin{pmatrix} F \\ E \end{pmatrix}, \ldots$$

with respect to the $n$ letters $x, y, z, \ldots$. I will call *derived* substitutions all those that one may deduce from the given substitutions, multiplied one or several times by one another or by themselves in any order, and the given substitutions together with the derived substitutions will form what I will call a *system of combined substitutions*. The *order* of this system will be the total number of substitutions that it offers, including the substitution that has two equal terms and is reduced to an identity. If one denotes this order by $I$, and by

$$i, i', i'', \ldots$$

the orders of the given substitutions, $I$ will always be divisible by each of the numbers $i, i', i'', \ldots$. Besides, $I$ will always be a divisor of the product

$$N = 1.2.\ldots.n.$$

Let us add that a system of combined substitutions being given, one may always reproduce the same substitutions, only arranged in another way, if one multiplies them one
by one, by any one of the others, or rather, again, if any one of them is multiplied one
by one by itself and by all the others.

———————————

Cauchy's flow of papers on substitutions in the autumn of 1845 dried up in early
1846 with three papers in January, one in February, and the last in April. That same
year, however, the surviving papers of Galois were finally published by Liouville in
his *Journal des mathématiques pures et appliquées*, leading to the understanding and
acceptance of Galois' remarkable discoveries, and eventually to a merging of his ideas
and Cauchy's. Further impetus came from the 1860 *Grand Prix* competition of the Paris
Academy, for which the subject, announced in 1857, was precisely that of Cauchy's 1845
papers:[4]

What may be the number of values of well defined functions containing a given number of
letters, and how may one form the functions for which there exists a given number of values?

Cauchy was on the committee that proposed the problem, but died before any submissions were received. In the end no prize was awarded, but two of the entrants, Émile
Mathieu and more especially Camille Jordan, went on to make significant contributions
to group theory.

In 1866 the third edition of Alfred Serret's *Cours d'algèbre supérieure* contained a
new chapter entirely devoted to the work of Galois, though Serret used Cauchy's word
'système' rather than Galois' 'groupe'. Thus within twenty years of publication Galois'
ideas had already entered the curriculum for students of higher algebra.

———————————

4. 'Quels peuvent être les nombres de valeurs des fonctions bien définies qui contiennent un nombre donné de lettres,
et comment peut-on former les fonctions pour lesquelles il existe un nombre donné de valeurs?' *Comptes rendus*, 44
(1857), 793–795.

### 13.1.4 Cayley's contribution to group theory, 1854

In 1853 Arthur Cayley was working on the properties of the curve known as a 'caustic', commonly seen in the patterns of light across a surface bounded by a reflecting circle. He let $(\xi, \eta)$ be the coordinates of a radiant point, $c$ the radius of the circle, and $\mu$ the index of refraction (the technicalities are not important here), and observed that the transformation

$$\xi' = \frac{c^2}{\xi}, \quad c' = \frac{c}{\mu}, \quad \mu' = \frac{c}{\xi} \qquad (\alpha)$$

yielded the same curve. He found six such transformations, which he denoted by $1$, $\alpha$, $\beta$, $\gamma$, $\delta$, $\epsilon$. He then observed that the composition of any two of them gave rise to one of the others, and indicated that he was treating these relationships further in a paper entitled 'On the theory of groups'. The fact that he referred to his six elements as a 'group' suggests that he recognized the structure identified by Galois, but now arising in a quite different context, and this may have led him to think about other examples and to try to abstract the crucial properties that all examples of groups had in common.

Cayley published his paper on the caustic towards the end of 1853, and followed it early in 1854 with 'On the theory of groups, as depending on the symbolic equation $\theta^n = 1$'. Here he defined a group as follows:[5]

A set of symbols,

$$1, \quad \alpha, \quad \beta \quad \ldots$$

all of them different, and such that the product of any two of them (no matter in what order), or the product of any one of them into itself, belongs to the set, is said to be a *group*.

This was a property Galois had noted with respect to substitutions (see 13.1.2), and in a footnote at this point Cayley made his one and only reference to Galois:

The idea of a group as applied to permutations or substitutions is due to Galois, and the introduction of it may be considered as marking an epoch in the progress of the theory of algebraical equations.

Cayley's groups, however, were apparently more general than those of Galois, because for him the members need not be permutations: $\theta$, an arbitrary element of a group, was what Cayley called simply a 'symbol of operation'. The first result he stated (without proof) was that if $\theta$ belongs to a group with $n$ elements then it must satisfy the equation $\theta^n = 1$, where 1 is the identity operation. He next set up what are now known as Cayley tables, for groups of order 4, and gave simple examples of such groups from the theory of elliptic functions, quadratic forms, and matrices. He carried out a similar procedure (see the extract below) to investigate groups of order 6, this time giving as his examples

---

5. Cayley 1854, 41.

a group of substitutions 1, $(abc)$, $(acb)$, $(bc)$, $(ca)$, $(ab)$, and the operations $1, \alpha, \beta, \ldots, \epsilon$ from his paper on the caustic.

Apart from a short additional note later the same year, and another in 1859 (on groups of order 8), that was all Cayley had to say on the subject in the 1850s. Only in 1878 did he return to the theory of groups in three further papers, but for the most part went little further than he had in 1854. He recognized that any (finite) group is in fact a permutation group, now known as Cayley's theorem.[6] He also stated (twice) that: 'A group is defined by means of the laws of combinations of its symbols', a dictum for which he also became well known.[7]

Cayley failed to pursue his ideas beyond a few easy examples and never came anywhere near the depth or sophistication of Cauchy or Galois. Nevertheless it was he who first recognized the existence of group structures in several disparate branches of mathematics, thus paving the way for a more general and axiomatic theory of groups later in the nineteenth century. (For a further comparison of Cayley with his continental contemporaries, see 17.3.2).

---

### Cayley and groups of order 6

from Cayley, 'On the theory of groups, as depending on the symbolic equation $\theta^n = 1$', *Philosophical magazine*, (4) 6 (1854), 43–46

---

I proceed to the case of a group of six symbols,

$$1, \alpha, \beta, \gamma, \delta, \epsilon,$$

which may be considered as representing a system of roots of the symbolic equation

$$\theta^6 = 1.$$

It is in the first place to be shown that there is at least one

---

6. Cayley 1878b.    7. Cayley 1878b, 1878c.

root which is a prime root of $\theta^3 = 1$, or (to use a simpler expression) a root having the index 3. It is clear that if there were a prime root, or root having the index 6, the square of this root would have the index 3, it is therefore only necessary to show that it is impossible that *all* the roots should have the index 2. This may be done by means of a theorem which I shall for the present assume, viz. that if among the roots of the symbolic equation $\theta^n = 1$, there are contained a system of roots of the symbolic equation $\theta^p = 1$ (or, in other words, if among the symbols forming a group of the order there are contained symbols forming a group of the order $p$), then $p$ is a submultiple of $n$. In the particular case in question, a group of the order 4 cannot form part of the group of the order 6. Suppose, then, that $\gamma$, $\delta$ are two roots of $\theta^6 = 1$, having each of them the index 2; then if $\gamma\delta$ had also the index 2, we should have $\gamma\delta = \delta\gamma$; and 1, $\gamma$, $\delta$, $\delta\gamma$, which is part of the group of the order 6, would be a group of the order 4. It is easy to see that $\gamma\delta$ must have the index 3, and that the group is, in fact, 1, $\gamma\delta$, $\delta\gamma$, $\gamma$, $\delta$, $\gamma\delta\gamma$, which is, in fact, one of the groups to be presently obtained; I prefer commencing with the assumption of a root having the index 3. Suppose that $\alpha$ is such a root, the group must clearly be of the form

$$1,\ \alpha,\ \alpha^2,\ \gamma,\ \alpha\gamma,\ \alpha^2\gamma,\quad (\alpha^3 = 1);$$

and multiplying the entire group by $\gamma$ as nearer factor, it becomes $\gamma$, $\alpha\gamma$, $\alpha^2\gamma$, $\gamma^2$, $\alpha\gamma^2$, $\alpha^2\gamma^2$; we must therefore have $\gamma^2 = 1$, $\alpha$, or $\alpha^2$. But the supposition $\gamma^2 = \alpha^2$ gives $\gamma^4 = \alpha^4 = \alpha$, and the group is in this case 1, $\gamma$, $\gamma^2$, $\gamma^3$, $\gamma^4$, $\gamma^5$ ($\gamma^6 = 1$); and the supposition $\gamma^2 = \alpha$ gives also this same group. It only remains, therefore, to assume $\gamma^2 = 1$; then we must have either $\gamma\alpha = \alpha\gamma$ or else $\gamma\alpha = \alpha^2\gamma$. The former assumption leads to the group

$$1,\ \alpha,\ \alpha^2,\ \gamma,\ \alpha\gamma,\ \alpha^2\gamma,\quad (\alpha^3 = 1,\ \gamma^2 = 1,\ \gamma\alpha = \alpha\gamma),$$

which is, in fact, analogous to the system of roots of the ordinary equation $x^6 - 1 = 0$; and by putting $\alpha\gamma = \lambda$, might be exhibited in the form 1, $\lambda$, $\lambda^2$, $\lambda^3$, $\lambda^4$, $\lambda^5$, ($\lambda^6 = 1$), in which this system has previously been considered. The latter assumption leads to the group

$$1,\ \alpha,\ \alpha^2,\ \gamma,\ \alpha\gamma,\ \alpha^2\gamma,\quad (\alpha^3 = 1,\ \gamma^2 = 1,\ \gamma\alpha = \alpha^2\gamma).$$

And we have thus two, and only two, essentially distinct forms of a group of six. If we represent the first of these two forms, viz. the group

$$1,\ \alpha,\ \alpha^2,\ \gamma,\ \alpha\gamma,\ \alpha^2\gamma,\quad (\alpha^3 = 1,\ \gamma^2 = 1,\ \gamma\alpha = \alpha\gamma)$$

by the general symbols

$$1,\ \alpha,\ \beta,\ \gamma,\ \delta,\ \epsilon,$$

we have the table

*as depending on the Symbolic Equation* $\theta^n = 1$.     45

|    | 1, | $\alpha$, | $\beta$, | $\gamma$, | $\delta$, | $\epsilon$ |
|----|----|-----------|----------|-----------|-----------|------------|
| 1 | 1 | $\alpha$ | $\beta$ | $\gamma$ | $\delta$ | $\epsilon$ |
| $\alpha$ | $\alpha$ | $\beta$ | $\gamma$ | $\delta$ | $\epsilon$ | 1 |
| $\beta$ | $\beta$ | $\gamma$ | $\delta$ | $\epsilon$ | 1 | $\alpha$ |
| $\gamma$ | $\gamma$ | $\delta$ | $\epsilon$ | 1 | $\alpha$ | $\beta$ |
| $\delta$ | $\delta$ | $\epsilon$ | 1 | $\alpha$ | $\beta$ | $\gamma$ |
| $\epsilon$ | $\epsilon$ | 1 | $\alpha$ | $\beta$ | $\gamma$ | $\delta$ |

while if we represent the second of these two forms, viz. the group

$$1,\ \alpha,\ \alpha^2,\ \gamma,\ \alpha\gamma,\ \alpha^2\gamma,\quad (\alpha^3=1,\ \gamma^2=1,\ \gamma\alpha=\alpha^2\gamma),$$

by the same general symbols

$$1,\ \alpha,\ \beta,\ \gamma,\ \delta,\ \epsilon,$$

we have the table

|    | 1 | $\alpha$ | $\beta$ | $\gamma$ | $\delta$ | $\epsilon$ |
|----|----|----------|---------|----------|----------|------------|
| 1 | 1 | $\alpha$ | $\beta$ | $\gamma$ | $\delta$ | $\epsilon$ |
| $\alpha$ | $\alpha$ | $\beta$ | 1 | $\epsilon$ | $\gamma$ | $\delta$ |
| $\beta$ | $\beta$ | 1 | $\alpha$ | $\delta$ | $\epsilon$ | $\gamma$ |
| $\gamma$ | $\gamma$ | $\delta$ | $\epsilon$ | 1 | $\alpha$ | $\beta$ |
| $\delta$ | $\delta$ | $\epsilon$ | $\gamma$ | $\beta$ | 1 | $\alpha$ |
| $\epsilon$ | $\epsilon$ | $\gamma$ | $\delta$ | $\alpha$ | $\beta$ | 1 |

or, what is the same thing, the system of equations

$$1 = \beta\alpha = \alpha\beta = \gamma^2 = \delta^2 = \epsilon^2$$
$$\alpha = \beta^2 = \delta\gamma = \epsilon\delta = \gamma\epsilon$$
$$\beta = \alpha^2 = \epsilon\gamma = \gamma\delta = \delta\epsilon$$
$$\gamma = \delta\alpha = \epsilon\beta = \beta\delta = \alpha\epsilon$$
$$\delta = \epsilon\alpha = \gamma\beta = \alpha\gamma = \beta\epsilon$$
$$\epsilon = \gamma\alpha = \delta\beta = \beta\gamma = \alpha\delta.$$

An instance of a group of this kind is given by the permutation of three letters ; the group

$$1, \ \alpha, \ \beta, \ \gamma, \ \delta, \ \epsilon$$

may represent a group of substitutions as follows :—

$$abc, \ cab, \ bca, \ acb, \ cba, \ bac$$

$$abc \ \ abc \ \ abc \ \ abc \ \ abc \ \ abc.$$

Another singular instance is given by the optical theorem proved in my paper " On a property of the Caustics by refraction of a Circle."

## 13.2 FIELDS, IDEALS, AND RINGS

Groups were the first kind of structured set to be identified and named, but by the end of the nineteenth century there were many others: domains, rings, ideals, fields, and so on. These concepts came from a variety of different directions. Fields, and later rings arose, like groups, out of the study of equations, whereas ideals came out of number theory and the study of cyclotomic integers (complex numbers of the form $a_0 + a_1\omega + a_2\omega^2 + \cdots + a_{n-1}\omega^{n-1}$ where $a_0, a_1, \ldots, a_{n-1}$ are ordinary integers and $\omega^n = 1$). By the end of the century many of these concepts were unified and systematized by Dedekind. some of the first hints, however, had already appeared in the work of Galois.

### 13.2.1 'Galois fields', 1830

In 1830, following the first submissions of his work on the solvability of equations to the Paris Academy, Galois published a paper entitled 'Sur la théorie des nombres' in the *Bulletin des sciences mathématiques, physiques et chimiques*, sometimes known as the *Bulletin de Férussac* after its editor. Writing to Chevalier on the night before the duel Galois described this paper as 'a lemma to the theory of primitive equations solvable by radicals', and it is clear from its final paragraphs that he believed he had found a necessary and sufficient condition for solvability of primitive equations.[8] Galois was mistaken in his conclusion, but on the way to reaching it he had succeeded in outlining much of the theory of what later became known as finite fields.

Galois took as his basic element any root of an irreducible polynomial of degree $\nu$, considered as a congruence modulo $p$ (a prime). He then investigated the non-zero elements generated from it by the usual algebraic operations. He argued that these must be $p^{\nu} - 1$ in number (though the text mistakenly has $p^{\nu-1}$). He also claimed, rather than proved, the existence of a 'primitive element' that generates such a set by repeated multiplication.

---

8. Primitive equations are equations of degree $N$ that cannot be decomposed in a regular way into $m$ factors of degree $n$ for any $m, n$ such that $N = mn$, where $m \neq 1$ and $n \neq 1$.

## Galois' construction of a finite field

from Galois, 'Sur la théorie des nombres', *Bulletin des sciences mathématiques, physiques et chimiques*, 13 (1830), 428–429

428                          *Mathématiques.*

218. Sur la théorie des nombres; par M. Galois.

( Ce mémoire fait partie des recherches de M. Galois sur la théorie des permutations et des équations algébriques ).

Quand on convient de regarder comme nulles toutes les quantités qui, dans les calculs algébriques, se trouvent multipliées par un nombre premier donné $p$, et qu'on cherche dans cette convention les solutions d'une équation algébrique $F\,x = o$, ce que M. Gauss désigne par la notation $F\,x \equiv o$, on n'a coutume de considérer que les solutions entières de ces sortes de questions. Ayant été conduit par des recherches particulières à considérer les solutions incommensurables, je suis parvenu à quelques résultats que je crois nouveaux.

Soit une pareille équation ou congruence, $F\,x = o$ et $p$ le module. Supposons d'abord, pour plus de simplicité, que la congruence en question n'admette aucun facteur commensurable, c'est-à-dire qu'on ne puisse pas trouver 3 fonctions $\varphi\,x$, $\psi\,x$, $\chi\,x$ telles que

$$\varphi\,x\,.\,\psi\,x = F\,x + p\,\chi\,x.$$

Dans ce cas, la congruence n'admettra donc aucune racine entière, ni même aucune racine incommensurable du degré inférieur. Il faut donc regarder les racines de cette congruence comme des espèces de symboles imaginaires, puisqu'elles ne satisfont pas aux questions de nombres entiers, symboles dont l'emploi dans le calcul sera souvent aussi utile que celui de l'imaginaire $\sqrt{-1}$ dans l'analyse ordinaire.

C'est la classification de ces imaginaires et leur réduction au plus petit nombre possible, qui va nous occuper.

Appelons $i$ l'une des racines de la congruence $F\,x = o$, que nous supposerons du degré $\nu$.

Considérons l'expression générale

$$a + a_1\,i + a_2\,i_2 + \ldots\ldots + a_{\nu-1}\,i^{\nu-1}\ \text{(A)}$$

où $a\ a_1\ a_2 \ldots a_{\nu-1}$ représentent des nombres entiers. En donnant à ces nombres toutes les valeurs, l'expression (A) en acquiert $p^\nu$, qui jouissent, ainsi que je vais le faire voir, des mêmes propriétés que les nombres naturels dans la *théorie des résidus des puissances*.

Ne prenons des expressions (A) que les $p^\nu - 1$, valeurs où $a$ $a_1\ a_2 \ldots a_{\nu-1}$ ne sont pas toutes nulles : soit $\alpha$ l'une de ces expressions.

Si l'on élève successivement $\alpha$ aux puissances $2^e$ $3^e$..., on aura une suite de quantités de même forme ( parce que toute fonction de $i$ peut se réduire au $\nu\text{-}1^e$ degré ). Donc on devra avoir $\alpha^n = 1$, $n$ étant un certain nombre, soit $n$ le plus petit nombre qui soit tel que l'on ait $\alpha^n = 1$. On aura un ensemble de $n$ expressions toutes différentes entr'elles.

$$1 \quad \alpha \quad \alpha^2 \quad \alpha^3 \quad . \quad . \quad . \quad \alpha^{n-1}$$

Multiplions ces $n$ quantités par une autre expression $\beta$ de la même forme. Nous obtiendrons encore un nouveau groupe de quantités toutes différentes des premières et différentes entr'elles. Si les quantités (A) ne sont pas épuisées, on multipliera encore les puissances de $\alpha$ par une nouvelle expression $\gamma$, et ainsi de suite. On voit donc que le nombre $n$ divisera nécessairement le nombre total des quantités (A). Ce nombre étant $p_\nu - 1$, on voit que $n$ divise $p^\nu - 1$. De là, suit encore que l'on aura

$$\alpha^{p^\nu - 1} = 1 \qquad \text{ou bien} \qquad \alpha^{p^\nu} = \alpha \ .$$

Ensuite on prouvera, comme dans la théorie des nombres, qu'il y a des racines primitives $\alpha$ pour lesquelles on ait précisément $p^\nu - 1 = n$, et qui reproduisent par conséquent, par l'élévation aux puissances, toute la suite des autres racines.

---

### TRANSLATION

### 218. ON THE THEORY OF NUMBERS; by MONSIEUR GALOIS.

(This memoir forms part of the researches of Monsieur Galois on the theory of permutations and algebraic equations.)

When one agrees to regard as zero all quantities which, in algebraic calculations, are multiplied by a given prime number $p$, and one seeks under this convention the solutions of an algebraic equation $Fx = 0$, that which Monsieur Gauss denotes by the notation $Fx \equiv 0$, one usually considers only integer solutions to these kinds of questions. Having been led by particular investigations to consider non-rational solutions, I have arrived at some results that I believe to be new.

Suppose there is such an equation or congruence, $Fx = 0$, with $p$ as modulus. Let us assume first of all, for greater simplicity, that the congruence in question does not have any rational factor, that is to say, that one may not find 3 functions $\phi x$, $\psi x$, $\chi x$ such that

$$\phi x . \psi x = Fx + p \chi x.$$

In this case, the congruence will not have any integer root, nor even any non-rational root of lesser degree. One must therefore regard the roots of this congruence as kinds of imaginary symbols, because they do not satisfy problems of whole numbers, symbols whose use in calculation will often be as useful as that of the imaginary $\sqrt{-1}$ in ordinary analysis.

It is the classification of these imaginaries and their reduction to the least number possible that is going to occupy us.

Let us call $i$ one of the roots of the congruence $Fx = 0$, which we suppose of degree $\nu$.

Let us consider the general expression

$$a + a_1 i + a_2 i^{[2]} + \cdots + a_{\nu-1} i^{\nu-1} \quad (A)$$

where $a \; a_1 \; a_2 \; \ldots \ldots \; a_{\nu-1}$ represent whole numbers. By giving these numbers all their values, the expression $(A)$ takes $p^\nu$ [values], which, as I am going to show, display the same properties as the natural numbers in the *theory of residues of powers*.

Let us take only the $[p^\nu - 1]$ expressions $(A)$ where $a \; a_1 \; a_2 \; \ldots \ldots \; a_{\nu-1}$ are not all zero: let $\alpha$ be one of these expressions. [429] If one raises $\alpha$ successively to its 2nd, 3rd, $\ldots$, powers, one will have a sequence of quantities of the same form (because every function of $i$ may be reduced to the $\nu - 1^{th}$ degree). Therefore one must have $\alpha^n = 1$, for a certain number $n$; let $n$ be the smallest number there is such that one has $\alpha^n = 1$. One will have a set of $n$ expressions all different from each other,

$$1 \; \alpha \; \alpha^2 \; \alpha^3 \ldots \alpha^{n-1}.$$

Let us multiply these $n$ quantities by another expression $\beta$ of the same form. We will again obtain a new group of quantities all different from the first and different from each other. If the quantities $(A)$ are not exhausted, one may multiply the powers of $\alpha$ again by a new expression $\gamma$, and so on. One sees therefore that the number $n$ will necessarily divide the total number of quantities $(A)$. This number being $p^\nu - 1$, one sees that $n$ divides $p^\nu - 1$. From that, it then follows that one will have

$$\alpha^{p^\nu - 1} = 1 \quad \text{or rather} \quad \alpha^{p^\nu} = \alpha.$$

Further one may prove, as in the theory of numbers, that there are primitive roots $\alpha$ for which one has precisely $p^\nu - 1 = n$, and which consequently reproduce, by raising to powers, the whole sequence of other roots.

---

### 13.2.2 Kummer and ideal numbers, 1847

In 1844, Ernst Kummer, professor of mathematics at the University of Breslau, published what was possibly the last significant mathematical paper to be composed in Latin: 'De numeris complexis, qui radicibus unitatis et numeris integris realibus constant' ('On complex numbers, which consist of roots of unity and real whole numbers'). In it Kummer demonstrated that the property of unique factorization, which so conveniently holds for the ordinary integers, breaks down in certain subsets of the complex numbers.

This may be illustrated by an example rather simpler than those Kummer was dealing with, by considering numbers of the form $a + b\sqrt{-5}$, where $a$ and $b$ are ordinary integers; this is a set we now denote by $\mathbb{Z}[\sqrt{-5}]$. In this set, the integer 6 can be factorized in two ways, as $6 = 2 \times 3$ and $6 = (1 + \sqrt{-5})(1 - \sqrt{-5})$. Further, it is not difficult to show that, within the same set, 2, 3, $(1 + \sqrt{-5})$, and $(1 - \sqrt{-5})$ do not have any further factors (ignoring changes of sign) other than themselves and 1, that is to say, they are 'irreducible'. This is a property that in ordinary integers we associate with primes, but technically 'prime' is defined in a different way: suppose that $p$ has the property that if it divides $ab$ then it divides $a$ or it divides $b$; in this case $p$ is said to be 'prime'. In the ordinary integers it can be shown that 'prime' and 'irreducible' are equivalent properties, but in $\mathbb{Z}[\sqrt{-5}]$ they are not: 2 divides 6 but it does not divide either $(1 + \sqrt{-5})$ or $(1 - \sqrt{-5})$, so it is *not* prime; on the other hand it has no factors except $\pm 2$ and $\pm 1$ and so it *is* irreducible. Furthermore, the property of unique factorization breaks down in $\mathbb{Z}[\sqrt{-5}]$, as the above example shows. In fact unique factorization holds if and only if all irreducibles are primes.

Kummer recognized this problem in 1844 in the context of working with cyclotomic integers. These are the numbers he described in his title, of the form $a_0 + a_1\omega + a_2\omega^2 + \cdots + a_{n-1}\omega^{n-1}$, where $a_0, a_1, \ldots, a_{n-1}$ are ordinary integers and $\omega^n = 1$. This last property relates the numbers to circle division, hence the name 'cyclotomic'. Over the next two or three years Kummer tried to find a way of restoring the property of unique factorization, and arrived at the concept of 'ideal complex numbers'. For the example above, for instance, the 'ideal' complex numbers are analogous to highest common factors of, say, 2 and $(1 \pm \sqrt{-5})$, or of 3 and $(1 \pm \sqrt{-5})$. Once such numbers are assumed to exist, 2, 3, $(1 + \sqrt{-5})$, and $(1 - \sqrt{-5})$ become reducible, and unique factorization is restored.

The details of the theory developed by Kummer are beyond the scope of this book, but in 1845 he published a brief preliminary notice of his findings in the proceedings of the Berlin Academy for 1845. This notice was reprinted in Crelle's journal in 1847, and its opening passage is reproduced here to illustrate the style and context of Kummer's work.

Note that in his third paragraph Kummer put forward the idea of an imaginary common chord of two non-intersecting circles as an analogy to the concept of an ideal common divisor of any two composite numbers. Previously, Newton, d'Alembert, Cauchy, and others had repeatedly used a circle inscribed and circumscribed by polygons as the standard geometric representation of a limit, and it is interesting to observe that even as late as 1847 Kummer was still using a geometric image as an example, and to some extent a justification, for a new idea in algebra.

## Kummer's ideal numbers

from Kummer, 'Zur Theorie der complexen Zahlen', *Journal für die reine und angewandte Mathematik*, 35 (1847), 319–320

# 15.
# Zur Theorie der complexen Zahlen.

### (Von dem Herrn Prof. *Kummer* in Breslau.)

#### ( Auszug aus den Berichten der Königl. Akad. der Wiss. zu Berlin vom März 1845.)

Es ist mir gelungen, die Theorie derjenigen complexen Zahlen, welche aus höheren Wurzeln der Einheit gebildet sind und welche bekanntlich in der Kreistheilung, in der Lehre von den Potenzresten und den Formen höherer Grade eine wichtige Rolle spielen, zu vervollständigen und zu vereinfachen; und zwar durch Einführung einer eigenthümlichen Art imaginärer Divisoren, welche ich *ideale complexe Zahlen* nenne; worüber eine kurze Mittheilung zu machen ich mir erlaube.

Wenn $\alpha$ eine imaginäre Wurzel der Gleichung $\alpha^\lambda = 1$, $\lambda$ eine Primzahl ist und $a, a_1, a_2$, etc. ganze Zahlen sind, so ist $f(\alpha) = a + a_1\alpha + a_2\alpha^2 + \ldots + a_{\lambda-1}\alpha^{\lambda-1}$ eine complexe ganze Zahl. Eine solche complexe Zahl kann entweder in Factoren derselben Art zerlegt werden; oder auch nicht. Im ersten Fall ist sie eine zusammengesetzte Zahl: im andern Fall ist sie bisher eine complexe Primzahl genannt worden. Ich habe nun aber bemerkt, dafs, wenn auch $f(\alpha)$ auf keine Weise in complexe Factoren zerlegt werden kann, sie deshalb noch nicht die wahre Natur einer complexen Primzahl hat, weil sie schon gewöhnlich der ersten und wichtigsten Eigenschaft der Primzahlen ermangelt: nämlich, dafs das Product zweier Primzahlen durch keine von ihnen verschiedene Primzahl theilbar ist. Es haben vielmehr solche Zahlen $f(\alpha)$, wenn gleich sie nicht in complexe Factoren zerlegbar sind, dennoch die Natur der zusammengesetzten Zahlen; die Factoren aber sind alsdann nicht wirkliche, sondern *ideale complexe Zahlen.* Der Einführung solcher idealen complexen Zahlen liegt derselbe einfache Gedanke zu Grunde, wie der Einführung der imaginären Formeln in die Algebra und Analysis; namentlich bei der Zerfällung der ganzen rationalen Functionen in ihre einfachsten Factoren, die linearen. Ferner ist es auch dasselbe Bedürfnifs, durch welches genöthigt, *Gaufs* bei den Untersuchungen über die biquadratischen Reste (weil hier alle Primfactoren von der Form $4m + 1$ die Natur zusammengesetzter Zahlen zeigen) die complexen Zahlen von der Form $a + b\sqrt{-1}$ zuerst einführte.

320                    *15. Kummer, zur Theorie der complexen Zahlen.*

Um nun zu einer festen Definition der wahren (gewöhnlich idealen)
Primfactoren der complexen Zahlen zu gelangen, war es nöthig, die unter
allen Umständen bleibenden Eigenschaften der Primfactoren complexer Zahlen
zu ermitteln, welche von der Zufälligkeit, ob die wirkliche Zerlegung Statt
habe, oder nicht, ganz unabhängig wären: ungefähr eben so, wie man, wenn
in der Geometrie von der gemeinschaftlichen Sehne zweier Kreise gesprochen
wird, auch dann, wenn die Kreise sich nicht schneiden, eine wirkliche Definition dieser idealen gemeinschaftlichen Sehne sucht, welche für alle Lagen
der Kreise pafst. Dergleichen bleibende Eigenschaften der complexen Zahlen,
welche geschickt sind, als Definitionen der idealen Primfactoren benutzt zu werden, giebt es mehrere, welche im Grunde immer auf dasselbe Resultat führen
und von denen ich eine als die einfachste und allgemeinste gewählt habe.

TRANSLATION

On the theory of complex numbers
(by Prof. *Kummer* of Breslau)
(Excerpt from the proceedings of the Royal Academy of Sciences at Berlin for March 1845.)

I have succeeded in completing and simplifying the theory of those complex numbers
which are constructed from higher roots of unity and which, as is well known, play an
important role in circle division, as well as in the theory of residues and of forms of
higher degree; indeed by introducing a particular kind of imaginary divisors which I
call *ideal complex numbers*; about which I hereby wish to make a short communication.

If $\alpha$ is an imaginary root of the equation $\alpha^\lambda = 1$, where $\lambda$ is a prime number, and
$a, a_1, a_2$, etc. are whole numbers, then $f(\alpha) = a + a_1\alpha + a_2\alpha^2 + \cdots + a_{\lambda-1}\alpha^{\lambda-1}$ is a
complex integer. Such a complex integer can either be decomposed into factors of the
same kind; or it can not. In the first case it is a composite number; in the other case it
has until now been called a complex prime number. But I have now noticed that, even if
$f(\alpha)$ can in no way be decomposed into complex factors, it still need not have the true
nature of a complex prime number, because usually it lacks the first and most important
property of prime numbers: namely, that the product of two prime numbers is divisible
by no prime number that is different from them. Frequently, such numbers $f(\alpha)$, even
if they are not decomposable into complex factors, nevertheless have the nature of
composite numbers; but the factors are then not actual, but *ideal complex numbers*.
The introduction of such ideal complex numbers therefore rests on the same basic
thinking as the introduction of imaginary formulas in Algebra and Analysis; namely
on the decomposition of polynomial functions into their simplest factors, the linear
ones. Further, it was the same need by which *Gauss* was driven in his investigation of
biquadratic residues (because here all prime factors of the type $4m+1$ display the nature
of composite numbers) to introduce for the first time complex numbers of the form

$a + b\sqrt{-1}$. [320] In order to obtain a clear definition of the true (usually ideal) prime factors of complex numbers, it was necessary to determine those properties of prime factors of complex numbers which persist in all cases and which would be completely independent of the fortuitousness of whether the real decomposition took place or not; almost as, when in geometry one speaks of the common chord of two circles, even if the circles do not intersect, one seeks a genuine definition of this ideal common chord, which holds for all positions of the circles. Likewise, there exist several such persistent properties of complex numbers, which are suitable for use in the definition of ideal prime factors, which basically always lead to the same result and from them I have chosen one as the simplest and most general.

———————

### 13.2.3 Dedekind on fields of finite degree, 1877

Dedekind unified the basic theory of fields, ideals, and rings during the 1870s, and published his ideas in a paper entitled 'Sur la théorie des nombres entiers algébriques' ('On the theory of algebraic integers'), which appeared in five parts in the *Bulletin des sciences mathématiques et astronomiques* in 1876 and 1877. Here Dedekind discussed *modules* (closed under addition and subtraction); *domaines* (closed under addition, subtraction, and multiplication, and later called rings); *corps* (closed under addition, subtraction, multiplication, and division, and later called fields); and *idéaux* (ideals).

In Part III of the paper, entitled 'Propriétés générales des nombres algébriques entiers' ('General properties of algebraic integers'), Dedekind defined *algebraic integers* to be real or complex numbers satisfying an equation

$$\theta^n + a_1\theta^{n-1} + a_2\theta^{n-2} + \cdots + a_{n-1} + a_n = 0$$

with integer coefficients. He proved that the algebraic integers are closed under addition, subtraction, and multiplication, so that they form a domain (or ring), and then went on to discuss divisibility. He pointed out that algebraic integers can be decomposed into factors in infinitely many ways. The number $\alpha$, for instance, can be written as $\alpha = \sqrt{\alpha}\sqrt{\alpha}$, or as $\alpha = \beta_1\beta_2$, where $\beta_1$ and $\beta_2$ are the two roots of the equation $\beta^2 - \beta + \alpha = 0$, and that $\sqrt{\alpha}, \beta_1, \beta_2$ are also algebraic integers. From here he went on to define a *field of finite degree* (*corps fini*).

---

### Dedekind's fields of finite degree

from Dedekind, 'Sur la théorie des nombres entiers algébriques', *Bulletin des sciences mathématiques et astronomiques* (2), 1 (1877), 148–151

---

§ 15. — *Corps finis.*

La propriété d'être décomposables d'une infinité de manières, que nous venons de signaler et qui se présente dans le domaine comprenant tous les nombres entiers, disparaît de nouveau dès que l'on se borne à considérer les nombres entiers renfermés dans un *corps fini*. Il faut d'abord définir l'étendue et la nature d'un tel corps.

Tout nombre algébrique $\theta$, que ce soit ou non un nombre entier, satisfait évidemment à une infinité d'équations différentes à coefficients rationnels, c'est-à-dire qu'il y a une infinité de fonctions entières $F(t)$ d'une variable $t$ qui s'évanouissent pour $t = \theta$, et dont les coefficients sont rationnels. Mais, parmi toutes ces fonctions $F(t)$, il doit nécessairement y en avoir une $f(t)$ dont le degré $n$ soit *le plus petit possible*, et de la méthode connue de la division de ces sortes de fonctions il résulte immédiatement que chacune des fonctions $F(t)$ doit être divisible algébriquement par cette fonction $f(t)$, et que $f(t)$ ne peut être divisible par aucune fonction entière de degré moindre à coefficients rationnels. Pour cette raison, la fonction $f(t)$ et aussi l'équation $f(\theta) = 0$ seront appelées *irréductibles*, et il est clair, en même temps, que les $n$ nombres $1, \theta^1, \theta^2, \ldots, \theta^{n-1}$ formeront un *système irréductible* (§ 4, 1°).

Considérons maintenant l'ensemble $\Omega$ de tous les nombres $\omega$ de la forme $\varphi(\theta)$, en désignant par

$$\varphi(t) = x_0 + x_1 t + x_2 t + \ldots + x_{n-1} t^{n-1}$$

toute fonction entière quelconque de $t$ à coefficients rationnels, entiers ou fractionnaires, $x_0, x_1, x_2, \ldots, x_{n-1}$, dont le degré est $< n$, et remarquons d'abord que tout nombre de cette espèce $\omega = \varphi(\theta)$, en vertu de l'irréductibilité de $f(t)$, ne peut se mettre sous cette forme que d'une seule manière. On fait voir ensuite aisément que ces nombres $\omega$ se reproduisent toujours par les *opérations rationnelles*, c'est-à-dire par addition, soustraction, multiplication et division. Pour les deux premières opérations, cela résulte évidemment de la forme commune $\varphi(\theta)$ de tous les nombres $\omega$, et pour la multiplication il suffit de remarquer que tout nombre de la forme $\psi(\theta)$, $\psi(t)$ étant une fonction entière de degré *quelconque*, à coefficients rationnels, est également un nombre $\omega$; car, si l'on divise $\psi(t)$ par $f(t)$, le reste de la division sera une fonction $\varphi(t)$ de l'espèce indiquée plus haut, et l'on aura en même temps $\psi(\theta) = \varphi(\theta)$. Pour traiter enfin le cas de la division, on n'a plus qu'à faire voir encore que, si $\omega = \varphi(\theta)$ est différent de zéro, sa valeur réciproque $\omega^{-1}$ appartient aussi au système $\Omega$; or $\varphi(t)$ n'ayant aucun diviseur commun avec la fonction irréductible $f(t)$, la méthode par laquelle on chercherait le plus grand commun diviseur des fonctions $f(t)$, $\varphi(t)$ fournit, comme on sait, deux fonctions entières $f_1(t)$, $\varphi_1(t)$, à coefficients rationnels, qui satisfont à l'identité

$$f(t) f_1(t) + \varphi(t) \varphi_1(t) = 1,$$

d'où résulte, pour $t = 0$, la vérité de l'énoncé précédent.

J'appellerai *corps* tout système A de nombres $a$ (ne s'annulant pas tous), tel que les sommes, les différences, les produits et les quotients de deux quelconques de ces nombres $a$ appartiennent au système A. L'exemple le plus simple d'un corps est celui du système de tous les nombres rationnels, et il est aisé de reconnaître que ce corps est contenu dans tout autre corps A; car, si l'on choisit à volonté un nombre $a$ du corps A, différent de zéro, il faut, suivant la définition, que le quotient $1$ des deux nombres $a$ et $a$ appartienne également au corps A, d'où résulte immédiatement la proposition énoncée, tous les nombres rationnels pouvant être engendrés au moyen du nombre $1$ par des additions, des soustractions, des multiplications et des divisions répétées.

D'après ce que nous avons démontré plus haut relativement aux nombres $\omega = \varphi(\theta)$, notre système $\Omega$ formera donc aussi un corps; les nombres rationnels se tirent de $\varphi(\theta)$, en annulant tous les coefficients $x_1, x_2, \ldots, x_{n-1}$ qui suivent $x_0$. Un corps $\Omega$ qui est produit, de la manière indiquée, par une équation irréductible $f(\theta) = 0$ du degré $n$, nous l'appellerons un corps *fini* [1], et le nombre $n$ sera dit son *degré*. Un tel corps $\Omega$ contient $n$ nombres indépendants entre eux, par exemple, les nombres $1, \theta, \theta^2, \ldots, \theta^{n-1}$, tandis que $n + 1$ nombres quelconques du corps formeront évidemment un système réductible (§ 4, 1°); cette propriété, jointe à la notion de corps, pourrait aussi servir de définition pour un corps $\Omega$ du $n^{\text{ième}}$ degré; je n'entrerai pas toutefois dans la démonstration de cette assertion.

Si l'on choisit maintenant arbitrairement $n$ nombres

$$\omega_1 = \varphi_1(\theta), \quad \omega_2 = \varphi_2(\theta), \ldots, \quad \omega_n = \varphi_n(\theta)$$

---

[1] Si l'on entend par diviseur d'un corps A tout corps B dont tous les nombres sont contenus aussi dans A, un corps fini pourra être encore défini comme un corps qui ne possède qu'un nombre fini de diviseurs. En employant ici le mot *diviseur* (et le mot *multiple*) dans un sens directement opposé à celui que nous lui avons attaché, en parlant des modules et des idéaux, il ne pourra sûrement en résulter aucune confusion.

du corps $\Omega$, ces nombres (d'après le § 4, 2°) formeront toujours, et
seulement alors, un système irréductible, lorsque le déterminant
formé avec les $n^2$ coefficients rationnels $x$ sera différent de zéro; dans
ce cas, nous appellerons le système des $n$ nombres $\omega_1$, $\omega_2$, ..., $\omega_n$,
une *base du corps* $\Omega$; alors il est évident que tout nombre $\omega = \varphi(\theta)$
peut toujours, et d'une seule manière, se mettre sous la forme

$$\omega = h_1\omega_1 + h_2\omega_2 + \ldots + h_n\omega_n,$$

les coefficients $h_1$, $h_2$, ..., $h_n$ étant des nombres rationnels, entiers
ou fractionnaires, et réciproquement, tous les nombres $\omega$ de cette
forme sont contenus dans $\Omega$; les coefficients rationnels $h_1$, $h_2$, ...,
$h_n$ seront dits les *coordonnées du nombre* $\omega$ par rapport à cette
base.

---

TRANSLATION

## §15 *Fields of finite degree*

The property of being decomposable in infinitely many ways that we have just indicated
and which presents itself in the domain containing all rational integers, disappears again
as soon as one confines oneself to considering rational integers contained in a *field of
finite degree*. One must first of all define the extent and the nature of such a field.

Every algebraic number $\theta$, whether or not it is an algebraic integer, clearly satisfies
infinitely many different equations with rational coefficients, that is to say, that there
are infinitely many polynomial functions [149] $F(t)$ of a variable $t$ which would vanish
for $t = \theta$, and of which the coefficients are rational. But, amongst all these functions
$F(t)$, there must necessarily be one $f(t)$ of which the degree $n$ is *the smallest possible*,
and by the known method of division for these kinds of function it results immediately
that each of the functions $F(t)$ must be algebraically divisible by this function $f(t)$, and
that $f(t)$ may not be divisible by any polynomial function of lesser degree with rational
coefficients. For this reason, the function $f(t)$ and also the equation $f(x) = 0$ will be
called *irreducible*, and it is clear, at the same time, that the $n$ numbers $1, \theta^1, \theta^2, ..., \theta^{n-1}$
will form an *irreducible system* (§4, 1).

Let us consider now the set $\Omega$ of all numbers $\omega$ of the form $\varphi(\theta)$, denoting by

$$\varphi(t) = x_0 + x_1 t + x_2 t^2 + \cdots + x_{n-1} t^{n-1}$$

any polynomial function whatever of $t$ with rational coefficients, integers or fractions,
$x_0, x_1, x_2, \ldots, x_{n-1}$, of which the degree is $< n$, and we note first that every number
of this kind $\omega = \varphi(\theta)$, by virtue of the irreducibility of $f(t)$, can be put into this
form in only one way. One then shows easily that these numbers $\omega$ always reproduce
themselves by *rational operations*, that is to say by addition, subtraction, multiplication
and division. For the two first operations, this clearly results from the common form

$\varphi(\theta)$ of all the numbers $\omega$, and for multiplication it suffices to note that every number of the form $\psi(\theta)$, where $\psi(t)$ is a polynomial function of *any* degree, with rational coefficients, is equally a number $\omega$; for, if one divides $\psi(t)$ by $f(t)$, the remainder in the division will be a function $\varphi(t)$ of the kind indicated above, and at the same time one will have $\psi(\theta) = \varphi(\theta)$. Finally to treat the case of division, one has to do no more than show again that, if $\omega = \varphi(\theta)$ is different from zero, its reciprocal value $\omega^{-1}$ belongs also to the system $\Omega$; now $\varphi(t)$ having no common divisor with the irreducible function $f(t)$, the method by which one would seek the greatest common divisor of the functions $f(t), \varphi(t)$ will supply, as one knows, two polynomial functions $f_1(t), \varphi_1(t)$, with rational coefficients, which satisfy the identity [150]

$$f(t)f_1(t) + \varphi(t)\varphi_1(t) = 1,$$

from which follows, for $t = \theta$, the fact stated previously.

I will call a *field* every system $A$ of numbers $a$ (not all zero), such that the sums, differences, products and quotients of any two of these numbers $a$ belong to the system $A$. The simplest example of a field is that of the system of all rational numbers, and it is easy to recognize that this field is contained in every other field $A$; for, if one chooses at will a number $a$ in the field $A$, different from zero, it must be, following the definition, that the quotient 1 of the two numbers $a$ and $a$ equally belongs to the field $A$, from which there results immediately the stated proposition, since all rational numbers can be generated from the number 1 by repeated additions, subtractions, multiplications and divisions.

After what we have shown above with respect to the numbers $\omega = \varphi(\theta)$, our system $\Omega$ will therefore also form a field; the rational numbers arise from $\varphi(\theta)$ by annulling all the coefficients $x_1, x_2, \ldots, x_{n-1}$ which follow $x_0$. A field $\Omega$ which is produced, in the manner indicated, by an irreducible equation $f(\theta) = 0$ of degree $n$, we will call a *finite* field, and the number $n$ will be said to be its *degree*. Such a field $\Omega$ contains $n$ numbers independent from each other, for example, the numbers $1, \theta, \theta^2, \ldots, \theta^{n-1}$, while any $n + 1$ numbers of the field will clearly form a reducible system (§4, 1); this property, together with the notion of a field, may also serve as a definition for a field of $n^{\text{th}}$ degree; I will not enter immediately into the demonstration of this assertion.

If one now chooses arbitrarily $n$ numbers

$$\omega_1 = \varphi_1(\theta), \omega_2 = \varphi_2(\theta), \ldots, \omega_n = \varphi_n(\theta)$$

[151] of the field $\Omega$, these numbers (by §4, 2) would form an irreducible system always and only when the determinant formed with the $n^2$ rational coefficients $x$ is different from zero; in this case we call the system of $n$ numbers $\omega_1, \omega_2, \ldots, \omega_n$ a *base of the field* $\Omega$; then it is clear that every number $\omega = \varphi(\theta)$ may always, and in only one way, be put in the form

$$\omega = h_1\omega_1 + h_2\omega_2 + \cdots + h_n\omega_n,$$

where the coefficients $h_1, h_2, \ldots, h_n$, are rational numbers, integers or fractions, and conversely all numbers $\omega$ of this form are contained in $\Omega$; the rational coefficients $h_1, h_2, \ldots, h_n$ will be called the *co-ordinates of the number $\omega$* with respect to this base.

### 13.2.4  Dedekind's definition of ideals, 1877

Working on quadratic forms in the early 1870s, Dedekind extended Kummer's concept of 'ideal' so that the word became no longer an adjective, describing a hypothetical quantity, but a noun, naming a mathematical entity that could be shown to exist. His first definition of an ideal appeared in 1871, in a supplement to the second edition of Dirichlet's *Vorlesungen über Zahlentheorie*, but he later presented what he claimed was a slightly simpler, if not shorter, version of the theory in his 1876–77 paper *Sur la théorie des nombres entiers algébriques*. Ideals were treated first in Part II, under the heading 'Le germe de la théorie des idéaux', but more fully in Part IV, 'Élements de la théorie des idéaux'.

## Dedekind's ideals

from Dedekind, 'Sur la théorie des nombres entiers algébriques', *Bulletin des sciences mathématiques et astronomiques*, (2) 1 (1877), 208–210

### § 19. — *Les idéaux et leur divisibilité.*

Soient, comme dans la Section précédente, $\Omega$ un corps fini du degré $n$, et $\mathfrak{o}$ le domaine de tous les nombres entiers $\omega$ contenus dans $\Omega$. Nous entendons par un *idéal* de ce domaine $\mathfrak{o}$ tout système $\mathfrak{a}$ de nombres $\alpha$ du domaine $\mathfrak{o}$ qui possède les deux propriétés suivantes :

I. Les sommes et les différences de deux nombres $\alpha$ quelconques du système $\mathfrak{a}$ appartiennent au même système $\mathfrak{a}$, c'est-à-dire que $\mathfrak{a}$ est un module.

II. Tout produit $\alpha\omega$ d'un nombre $\alpha$ du système $\mathfrak{a}$ par un nombre $\omega$ du système $\mathfrak{o}$ est un nombre du système $\mathfrak{a}$.

Signalons d'abord un cas particulièrement important de cette conception d'*idéal*. Soit $\mu$ un nombre déterminé ; le système $\mathfrak{a}$ de tous les nombres $\alpha = \mu\omega$ divisibles par $\mu$ formera un idéal. Nous appellerons un tel idéal un *idéal principal,* et nous le désignerons par $\mathfrak{o}(\mu)$, ou plus simplement par $\mathfrak{o}\mu$ ou $\mu\mathfrak{o}$ ; il est évident que cet idéal ne sera pas altéré si l'on remplace $\mu$ par un nombre associé, c'est-à-dire par un nombre de la forme $\varepsilon\mu$, $\varepsilon$ désignant une unité. Si $\mu$ est lui-même une unité, on aura $\mathfrak{o}\mu = \mathfrak{o}$, puisque tous les nombres contenus dans $\mathfrak{o}$ sont divisibles par $\mu$. Il est encore facile de reconnaître qu'aucun autre idéal ne peut contenir d'unité ; car si l'unité $\varepsilon$ est contenue dans l'idéal $\mathfrak{a}$, alors (d'après II) tous les produits $\varepsilon\omega$, et par suite aussi tous les nombres $\omega$ de l'idéal principal $\mathfrak{o}$ sont contenus dans $\mathfrak{a}$, et comme, par définition, tous les nombres de l'idéal $\mathfrak{a}$ sont également contenus dans $\mathfrak{o}$, on aura $\mathfrak{a} = \mathfrak{o}$. Cet idéal $\mathfrak{o}$ joue le même rôle parmi les idéaux que le nombre $1$ parmi les nombres rationnels entiers. Dans la notion d'un idéal principal $\mathfrak{o}\mu$ est compris aussi le cas singulier où $\mu = 0$, et où par conséquent l'idéal se compose du seul nombre zéro ; toutefois nous exclurons ce cas dans ce qui va suivre.

Dans le cas de $n = 1$, où notre théorie se change dans l'ancienne théorie des nombres, tout idéal est évidemment un idéal principal, c'est-à-dire un module de la forme $[m]$, $m$ étant un nombre rationnel entier (§§ 1 et 5) ; il en est également de même des corps quadratiques spéciaux, qui ont été considérés dans la Section II (§ 6 et commencement du § 7). Dans tous ces cas, où tout idéal du corps $\Omega$ est un idéal principal, règnent les mêmes lois de la divisibilité des nombres que dans la théorie des nombres rationnels entiers, puisque tout nombre *indécomposable* possède aussi le caractère d'un *nombre premier* (*voir* l'Introduction et le § 7). C'est de quoi l'on pourra aisément se convaincre dans ce qui doit suivre ; mais je présente dès maintenant cette remarque pour recommander au lecteur de faire la comparaison continuelle avec les cas spéciaux mentionnés et principalement avec l'ancienne théorie des nombres rationnels, parce que sans aucun doute cela facilitera beaucoup l'intelligence de notre théorie générale.

Puisque tout idéal (en vertu de I) est un module, nous transporterons immédiatement aux idéaux la notion de la divisibilité des modules (§ 1). On dit qu'un idéal $\mathfrak{m}$ est *divisible* par un idéal $\mathfrak{a}$, ou qu'il est un *multiple* de $\mathfrak{a}$, quand tous les nombres contenus dans $\mathfrak{m}$ sont aussi contenus dans $\mathfrak{a}$ ; on dit en même temps que $\mathfrak{a}$ est un *diviseur* de $\mathfrak{m}$. D'après cela, tout idéal est divisible par l'idéal $\mathfrak{o}$. Si $\alpha$ est un nombre de l'idéal $\mathfrak{a}$, l'idéal principal $\mathfrak{o}\alpha$ sera (d'après II) divisible par $\mathfrak{a}$ ; nous dirons, pour cette raison, que le *nombre* $\alpha$, et par suite tout nombre contenu dans $\mathfrak{a}$, est *divisible* par l'idéal $\mathfrak{a}$.

Nous dirons de même qu'un idéal $\mathfrak{a}$ est *divisible* par le *nombre* $\eta$, quand $\mathfrak{a}$ sera divisible par l'idéal principal $\mathfrak{o}\eta$ ; alors tous les nombres $\alpha$ de l'idéal $\mathfrak{a}$ seront de la forme $\eta\rho$, et il est facile de voir que le système $\mathfrak{r}$ de tous les nombres $\rho = \dfrac{\alpha}{\eta}$ formera un idéal. Réciproquement, si $\rho$ devient égal successivement à tous les nombres d'un idéal quelconque $\mathfrak{r}$, tandis que $\eta$ désigne un nombre déterminé, différent de zéro, tous les produits $\eta\rho$ formeront encore un idéal divisible par $\mathfrak{o}\eta$ ; un tel idéal, formé au moyen de l'idéal $\mathfrak{r}$ et du nombre $\eta$, et nous le désignerons, pour abréger, par $\mathfrak{r}\eta$ ou $\eta\mathfrak{r}$ ; on aura évidemment $(\mathfrak{r}\eta)\,\eta' = \mathfrak{r}\,(\eta\eta') = (\mathfrak{r}\eta')\,\eta$, et $\eta\mathfrak{r}'$ sera toujours divisible par $\eta\mathfrak{r}$ dans le cas, et seulement dans ce cas, où $\mathfrak{r}'$ sera divisible par $\mathfrak{r}$ ; donc l'équation $\eta\mathfrak{r}' = \eta\mathfrak{r}$ entraîne l'équation $\mathfrak{r}' = \mathfrak{r}$. La notion d'un idéal principal $\mathfrak{o}\mu$ se déduit de celle de $\mathfrak{r}\mu$, lorsqu'on suppose $\mathfrak{r} = \mathfrak{o}$.

Enfin il est à remarquer que la divisibilité de l'idéal principal

oμ par l'idéal principal oη est complétement identique avec la divisibilité du *nombre* μ par le *nombre* η; les lois de la divisibilité des
*nombres* de o sont donc entièrement contenues dans les lois de la
divisibilité des *idéaux*.

---

TRANSLATION

---

### §19 *Ideals and their divisibility*

Suppose, as in the preceding section, that $\Omega$ is a finite field of degree $n$ and $o$ the
domain of all algebraic integers $\omega$ contained in $\Omega$. We understand by an *ideal* of this
domain $o$ every system $a$ of numbers $\alpha$ of the domain $o$ that possesses the two following
properties:

I. The sum and the difference of any two numbers $\alpha$ of the system $a$ belong to the
same system $a$, that is to say, that $a$ is a module.

II. Every product $\alpha\omega$ of a number $\alpha$ of the system $a$ by a number $\omega$ of the system $o$
is a number of the system $a$.

Let us first indicate a particularly important case of this concept of an *ideal*. Let $\mu$
be a fixed number; the system $a$ of all the numbers $\alpha = \mu\omega$ divisible by $\mu$ will form
an ideal. We will call such an ideal a *principal ideal*, and we will designate it by $o(\mu)$, or
more simply by $o\mu$ or $\mu o$; it is clear that this ideal will not be altered if one replaces $\mu$
by an associated number, that is to say, by a number of the form $\varepsilon\mu$, where $\varepsilon$ denotes
a unit. If $\mu$ is itself a unit, one will have $o\mu = o$, because all the numbers contained
in $o$ are divisible by $\mu$. It is again easy to recognize that no other ideal can contain a
unit; for if the unit $\varepsilon$ is contained in the ideal $a$, then (by II) all the products $\varepsilon\omega$, and
consequently also all the numbers $\omega$ of the principal ideal $o$ are contained in $a$, and
since, by definition, all the numbers of the ideal $a$ are equally contained in $o$, one will
have $a = o$. This ideal $o$ plays the same role amongst ideals as the number 1 amongst
the rational integers. In the notion of a principal ideal $o\mu$ is contained also the special
case where $\mu = 0$, and where consequently the ideal contains only the number zero;
we will always exclude this case in what follows.

In the case $n = 1$, where our theory changes into the old theory of numbers, every
ideal is clearly a principal ideal, [200] that is to say, a module of the form $[m]$, where
$m$ is a rational integer (§1 and §5); it is equally the same for the special quadratic
fields that were considered in Section II (§6 and the beginning of §7). In all these
cases, where every ideal of the field $\Omega$ is a principal ideal, there hold the same laws
of divisibility of numbers as in the theory of rational integers, because every *irreducible* number possesses also the character of a *prime number* (see the Introduction
and §7). It is of this that one can easily convince oneself in what must follow; but I
offer this remark now to recommend that the reader makes a continual comparison
with the special cases mentioned and especially with the old theory of rational numbers, because without doubt this will greatly facilitate an understanding of our general
theory.

Because every ideal (by virtue of I) is a module, we will carry over immediately to ideals the notion of divisibility of modules (§1). One says that an ideal $\mathfrak{m}$ is *divisible* by an ideal $\mathfrak{a}$, or that it is a *multiple* of $\mathfrak{a}$, when all the numbers contained in $\mathfrak{m}$ are also contained in $\mathfrak{a}$; one says at the same time that $\mathfrak{a}$ is a *divisor* of $\mathfrak{m}$. From that, every ideal is divisible by the ideal $\mathfrak{o}$. If $\alpha$ is a number of the ideal $\mathfrak{a}$, the principal ideal $\mathfrak{o}\alpha$ will be (by II) divisible by $\mathfrak{a}$; we will say, for this reason, that the *number* $\alpha$, and consequently every number contained in $\mathfrak{a}$, is *divisible* by the ideal $\mathfrak{a}$.

We will say in the same way that an ideal $\mathfrak{a}$ is *divisible* by the *number* $\eta$, when $\mathfrak{a}$ is divisible by the principal ideal $\mathfrak{o}\eta$; then all the numbers $\alpha$ of the ideal $\mathfrak{a}$ will be of the form $\eta\rho$, and it is easy to see that the system $\mathfrak{r}$ of all the numbers $\rho = \dfrac{\alpha}{\eta}$ will form an ideal. Conversely, if $\rho$ becomes successively equal to all the numbers of any ideal $\mathfrak{r}$, while $\eta$ denotes a certain number different from zero, all the products $\eta\rho$ will again form an ideal divisible by $\mathfrak{o}\eta$; such an ideal, formed by means of the ideal $\mathfrak{r}$ and the number $\eta$, we will denote, for short, by $\mathfrak{r}\eta$ or $\eta\mathfrak{r}$; one will clearly have $(\mathfrak{r}\eta)\eta' = \mathfrak{r}(\eta\eta') = (\mathfrak{r}\eta')\eta$, and $\eta\mathfrak{r}'$ will be divisible by $\eta\mathfrak{r}$ when, and only when, $\mathfrak{r}'$ is divisible by $\mathfrak{r}$; therefore the equation $\eta\mathfrak{r}' = \eta\mathfrak{r}$ implies the equation $\mathfrak{r}' = \mathfrak{r}$. The notion of a principal ideal $\mathfrak{o}\mu$ is derived from $\mathfrak{r}\mu$ when one assumes that $\mathfrak{r} = \mathfrak{o}$.

Finally, it remains to note that the divisibility of a principal ideal [210] $\mathfrak{o}\mu$ by the principal ideal $\mathfrak{o}\eta$ is completely identical to the division of the *number* $\mu$ by the *number* $\eta$; the laws of divisibility of *numbers* in $\mathfrak{o}$ are therefore entirely contained in the laws of divisibility of *ideals*.

---

# CHAPTER 14

# DERIVATIVES AND INTEGRALS

In Chapter 4 we saw how the discoverers of the calculus, Newton and Leibniz, conceptualized the process of differentiation. For Newton it involved a vanishing small quantity $o$; for Leibniz it was based on finite quantities $dx$, $dy$, $du$, $dv$, …, which at some appropriate point in the calculation could be neglected. There was no escape by either route from quantities that were sometimes zero, sometimes non-zero, as circumstances required; a paradox that gave rise, as we saw in 10.1, to deep concerns about the validity of the calculus itself. In the first half of this chapter we look at some eighteenth- and early nineteenth-century attempts to define differentiation more securely, and in the second half we see some later developments in the concept of integration.

## 14.1 DERIVATIVES

### 14.1.1 Landen's algebraic principle, 1758

John Landen, an East Anglian surveyor and later a Fellow of the Royal Society, is now hardly remembered, but in the eighteenth century his efforts to base the fluxional calculus on purely algebraic principles were noted by both Lagrange and Lacroix. Landen's first book, *A discourse concerning the residual analysis*, published in 1758, was just 44 pages long, but offered a method of differentiation that avoided (or so Landen thought) any recourse to the infinitely small and could be successfully applied to the usual range of problems solved by calculus: tangents to curves, and maxima and minima. Landen followed it with a longer treatise on the same subject, *The residual analysis*, in 1764.

## Landen's algebraic principle

from Landen, *A discourse concerning the residual analysis*, 1758, 4–7
Eighteenth Century Collection Online, Gale Digital Collection

Yet, notwithſtanding the method of fluxions is ſo greatly applauded, I am induced to think, it is not the moſt natural method of reſolving many problems to which it is uſually applied.—The operations therein being chiefly performed with algebraic quantities, it is, in faɛt, a branch of the algebraic art, or an improvement thereof, made by the help of ſome peculiar principles borrowed from the doɛtrine of motion : which principles, I muſt confeſs, to me ſeem not ſo properly applicable to algebra as thoſe on which that art was, before, very naturally founded.   We may indeed very naturally conceive a line to be generated by motion; but there are quantities of various kinds, which we cannot conceive to be ſo generated.   It is only in a figurative ſenſe, that an algebraic quantity can be ſaid to increaſe or decreaſe with ſome velocity or degree of ſwiftneſs; and, by the fluxion of a quantity of that kind, we muſt, I preſume, to have a clear idea of its meaning, underſtand, the velocity of a point ſuppoſed to deſcribe a line denoting ſuch quantity.   Fluxions therefore are not immediately applicable to algebraic quantities; but in fluxionary computations made by means of ſuch quantities, we, to proceed with perſpicuity, muſt have recourſe to the ſuppoſition of lines being put to denote thoſe quantities,   and the generation of thoſe lines by motion.   It therefore, to me, ſeems more proper, in the inveſtigation of propoſitions by algebra, to proceed upon the *anciently-received* principles of that art, than to introduce therein, without any neceſſity, the new fluxionary principles, derived from a conſideration of motion; and the rather, as the introduɛtion of thoſe new principles is not attended with any peculiar advantage.—That the borrowing principles from the doɛtrine of motion, with a view to improve the analytic art, was done, not only without any neceſſity, but even without any peculiar advantage, will appear by ſhewing, that whatever can be done by the method of computation, which is
founded

# RESIDUAL ANALYSIS. 5

founded on thofe borrowed principles, may be done, as well, by another method founded entirely on the *anciently-received* principles of algebra: And that I fhall endeavour to fhew, as foon as I have leifure, in the treatife I lately propofed to pub- lifh by fubfcription.—In the mean time, this effay is intended to give the inquifitive reader fome notion of the new method of computation, which is the fubject of that treatife.—Which method I call the *Refidual Analyfis* ; becaufe, in all the enquiries wherein it is made ufe of, the conclufions are obtained by means of refidual quantities.

In the application of the *Refidual Analyfis*, a geometrical or phyfical problem is naturally reduced to another purely a₁ge- braical; and the folution is then readily obtained, without any fuppofition of motion, and without confidering quantities as compofed of infinitely fmall particles.

It is by means of the following theorem, *viz.*

$$\frac{x^{\frac{m}{n}} - v^{\frac{m}{n}}}{x - v} = x^{\frac{m}{n} - 1} \times \frac{1 + \frac{v}{x} + \left(\frac{v}{x}\right)^{2} + \left(\frac{v}{x}\right)^{3}}{1 + \left(\frac{v}{x}\right)^{\frac{m}{n}} + \left(\frac{v}{x}\right)^{\frac{2m}{n}} + \left(\frac{v}{x}\right)^{\frac{3m}{n}}} \quad \begin{array}{c} (m) \\ \\ (n) \end{array},$$

(where *m* and *n* are any integers,) that we are enabled to perform all the principal operations in our faid Analyfis; and I am not a little furprized, that a theorem fo obvious, and of fuch vaft ufe, fhould fo long efcape the no- tice of algebraifts !

I have no objection againft the truth of the method of fluxions, being fully fatisfied, that even a problem purely alge- braical may be very clearly refolved by that method, by bring- ing into confideration lines, and their generation by motion. But I muft own, I am inclined to think, fuch a problem would be more naturally refolved by pure algebra, without any fuch confideration of lines and motion. — Suppofe it re- quired to invefigate the binomial theorem; *i. e.* to expand $\overline{1 + x}^{\frac{m}{n}}$ into a feries of terms of *x*, and known coefficients.

**To**

To do this by the method of fluxions, we firſt aſſume

$$\overline{1+x}^{\frac{m}{n}} = 1 + ax + bx^2 + cx^3 + dx^4 \ \&c.$$

We, to proceed with perſpicuity, are next to conceive *x*, and each term of that aſſumed equation, to be denoted by ſome line, and that line to be deſcribed by the motion of a point: Then, ſuppoſing $\dot{x}$ to be the velocity of the point deſcribing the line *x*, and taking, by the rules taught by thoſe who have treated of the ſaid method, the ſeveral contemporary velocities of the other deſcribing points, or the fluxions of the ſeveral terms in the ſaid equation, we get

$$\frac{m}{n} \times \overline{1+x}^{\frac{m}{n}-1} \times \dot{x} = a\dot{x} + 2bx\dot{x} + 3cx^2\dot{x} + 4dx^3\dot{x} \ \&c.$$

becauſe, when the ſpace deſcribed by a motion is always equal to the ſum of the ſpaces deſcribed in the ſame time by any other motions, the velocity of the firſt motion is always equal to the ſum of the velocities of the other motions.

From which laſt equation, by dividing by $\dot{x}$, or ſuppoſing $\dot{x}$ equal to unity, we have

$$\frac{m}{n} \times \overline{1+x}^{\frac{m}{n}-1} = a + 2bx + 3cx^2 + 4dx^3 \ \&c.$$

Conſequently, multiplying by $1 + x$, we have

$$\frac{m}{n} \times \overline{1+x}^{\frac{m}{n}},$$ or its equal $\frac{m}{n} + \frac{m}{n}ax + \frac{m}{n}bx^2 + \frac{m}{n}cx^3 \ \&c.$

$$= a + {2b \brace a} x + {3c \brace 2b} x^2 + {4d \brace 3c} x^3 \ \&c.$$

From whence, by comparing the homologous terms, the co-eﬃcients *a*, *b*, *c*, &c. will be found.

The ſame theorem is inveſtigated by the *Reſidual Analyſis*, in the following manner.

Aſſuming,

## RESIDUAL ANALYSIS.    7

Aſſuming, as above,

$$\overline{1+x}^{\frac{m}{n}} = 1 + ax + bx^2 + cx^3 \ \&c.$$

we have $\overline{1+y}^{\frac{m}{n}} = 1 + ay + by^2 + cy^3 \ \&c.$

and, by ſubtraction,

$$\overline{1+x}^{\frac{m}{n}} - \overline{1+y}^{\frac{m}{n}} = a \cdot \overline{x-y} + b \cdot \overline{x^2-y^2} + c \cdot \overline{x^3-y^3} + d \cdot \overline{x^4-y^4}$$

&c.

If, now, we divide by the reſidual $x - y$, we ſhall get

$$\overline{1+x}^{\frac{m}{n}-1} \times \frac{1 + \frac{1+y}{1+x} + \overline{\left(\frac{1+y}{1+x}\right)}^2 + \overline{\left(\frac{1+y}{1+x}\right)}^3 \quad (m) \ *}{1 + \overline{\left(\frac{1+y}{1+x}\right)}^{\frac{m}{n}} + \overline{\left(\frac{1+y}{1+x}\right)}^{\frac{2m}{n}} + \overline{\left(\frac{1+y}{1+x}\right)}^{\frac{3m}{n}} \quad (n)}$$

$$= a + b \cdot \overline{x+y} + c \cdot \overline{x^2+xy+y^2} + d \cdot \overline{x^3+x^2y+xy^2+y^3} \ \&c.$$

which equation muſt hold true let $y$ be what it will: From whence, by taking $y$ equal to $x$, we find, as before,

$$\frac{m}{n} \times \overline{1+x}^{\frac{m}{n}-1} = a + 2bx + 3cx^2 + 4dx^3 \ \&c.$$

The reſt of the operation will therefore be as above ſpecified.

Now, as to either of theſe methods of inveſtigation, I ſhall not take upon me to ſay any thing in particular ; it is ſubmitted to the reader to compare one with the other, and judge which of the two is moſt natural.

### 14.1.2 Lagrange's derived functions, 1797

Lagrange, like Landen, was determined to avoid the difficulties of working with vanishing small quantities (see 10.2.4). Unlike most other eighteenth-century mathematicians, for example, Maclaurin, Euler, or Lacroix, all of of whom used differentiation to determine the coefficients in power series, Lagrange set out instead to make power series the starting point for his definition of derivatives.

## Lagrange's derived functions

from Lagrange, *Théorie des fonctions analytiques*, 1797, §16–§18

16. Après ces considérations générales sur le développement des fonctions, nous allons considérer en particulier la formule du n.º 3,

$$f(x + i) = fx + p.i + q\,i^2 + r\,i^3 + \&c.,$$

et chercher comment les fonctions dérivées $p$, $q$, $r$, &c. dépendent de la fonction primitive $fx$.

Pour cela, supposons que l'indéterminée $x$ devienne $x + o$, $o$ étant une quantité quelconque indéterminée et indépendante de $i$, il est visible que $f(x + i)$ deviendra $f(x + i + o)$; et l'on voit en même temps que l'on aurait le même résultat en mettant simplement $i + o$ à la place de $i$ dans $f(x + i)$. Donc aussi le résultat doit être le même, soit qu'on mette dans la série $fx + pi + q\,i^2 + r\,i^3 + \&c.$, $i + o$ à la place de $i$, soit qu'on y mette $x + o$ au lieu de $x$.

La première substitution donnera

$$fx + p\,(i + o) + q\,(i + o)^2 + r\,(i + o)^3 + \&c.\,;$$

savoir, en développant les puissances de $i + o$, et n'écrivant, pour plus de simplicité, que les deux premiers termes de chaque puissance, parce que la comparaison de ces termes suffira pour les déterminations dont nous avons besoin,

$$fx\; +\; p.i\; +\; q\,i^2\; +\; r\,i^3\; +\; s\,i^4\; +\; \&c.$$
$$+\; po\; +\; 2q i o\; +\; 3r\,i^2 o\; +\; 4s\,i^3 o\; +\; \&c.$$

**THÉORIE**

Pour faire l'autre substitution, soit $fx + f'x o + \&c., p + p'o + \&c.;$ $q + q'o + \&c. r + r'o + \&c.$, ce que deviennent les fonctions $fx$, $p$, $q$, $r$, &c. en y mettant $x + o$ pour $x$, et ne considérant dans le développement que les termes qui contiennent la première puissance de $o$, il est clair que la même formule deviendra

$$fx + p\,i + q\,i^2 + r\,i^3 + s\,i^4 + \&c.$$
$$+ f'x o + p'i o + q'i^2 o + r'i^3 o + \&c.$$

Comme ces deux résultats doivent être identiques, quelles que soient les valeurs de $i$ et de $o$, on aura, en comparant les termes affectés de $o$, de $io$, de $i^2 o$, &c. $p = f'x$, $2q = p'$, $3r = q'$, $4s = r'$, &c.

Maintenant, de même que $f'x$ est la première fonction dérivée de $fx$, il est clair que $p'$ est la première fonction dérivée de $p$, que $q'$ est la première fonction dérivée de $q$, $r'$ la première fonction dérivée de $r$, et ainsi de suite. Donc, si, pour plus de simplicité et d'uniformité, on dénote par $f'x$ la première fonction dérivée de $fx$, par $f''x$ la première fonction dérivée de $f'x$, par $f'''x$ la première fonction dérivée de $f''x$, et ainsi de suite, on aura $p = f'x$, et de-là $p' = f''x$; donc $q = \dfrac{p'}{2} = \dfrac{f'x}{2}$; donc $q' = \dfrac{f''x}{2}$, et de-là $r = \dfrac{q'}{3} = \dfrac{f'''x}{2 \cdot 3}$; donc $r' = \dfrac{f^{iv}x}{2 \cdot 3}$, et de-là $s = \dfrac{r'}{4} = \dfrac{f^{iv}x}{2 \cdot 3 \cdot 4}$, et ainsi de suite.

Donc, substituant ces valeurs dans le développement de la fonction $f(x + i)$, on aura

$$f(x + i) = fx + f'x\,i + \frac{f''x}{2}i^2 + \frac{f'''x}{2 \cdot 3}i^3 + \frac{f^{iv}x}{2 \cdot 3 \cdot 4}i^4 + \&c.$$

Cette nouvelle expression a l'avantage de faire voir comment les termes de la série dépendent les uns des autres, et sur-tout comment, lorsqu'on sait former la première fonction dérivée d'une fonction primitive quelconque, on peut former toutes les fonctions dérivées que la série renferme.

17. Nous appellerons la fonction $fx$, *fonction primitive*, par rapport aux fonctions $f'x$, $f'x$, &c. qui en dérivent, et nous appellerons celles-ci, *fonctions dérivées*, par rapport à celle-là. Nous nommerons de plus la première

DES FONCTIONS ANALYTIQUES.   15

fonction dérivée $f'x$, *fonction prime*; la seconde dérivée $f''x$, *fonction seconde*; la troisième fonction dérivée $f'''x$, *fonction tierce*, et ainsi de suite.

De la même manière, si $y$ est supposé une fonction de $x$, nous dénoterons ses fonctions derivées par $y'$, $y''$, $y'''$, &c., de sorte que $y$ étant une fonction primitive, $y'$ sera sa fonction *prime*, $y''$ en sera la fonction *seconde*, $y'''$ la fonction *tierce*, et ainsi de suite:

De sorte que $x$ devenant $x + i$, $y$ deviendra $y + y'i + \dfrac{y''i^2}{2} + \dfrac{y'''i^3}{2 \cdot 3} +$ &c.

18. Ainsi, pourvu qu'on ait un moyen d'avoir la fonction prime d'une fonction primitive quelconque, on aura, par la simple répétition des mêmes opérations, toutes les fonctions dérivées; et par conséquent tous les termes de la série qui résulte du développement de la fonction primitive.

Soit donc d'abord $fx = x^m$, on aura $f(x+i) = (x+i)^m$; or, il est facile de démontrer, soit par les simples règles de l'arithmétique, soit par les premières opérations de l'algèbre, que les deux premiers termes de la puissance $m$ du binome $x + i$ sont $x^m + m x^{m-1}i$, soit que $m$ soit un nombre entier ou fractionnaire, positif ou négatif; ainsi on aura $f'x = m x^{m-1}$. De-là on tirera de la même manière $f''x = m(m-1)x^{m-2}$; $f'''x = m(m-1)(m-2)x^{m-3}$, &c.; de sorte qu'on aura

$$(x+i)^m = x^m + m x^{m-1}i + \frac{m(m-1)}{2}x^{m-2}i^2 + \frac{m(m-1)(m-2)}{2 \cdot 3}x^{m-3}i^3 + \&c.;$$

ce qui est la formule connue du binome, laquelle se trouve ainsi démontrée pour toutes les valeurs de $m$.

---

TRANSLATION

16. After these general considerations on the expansion of functions, we are going to consider in particular the formula of §3:

$$f(x + i) = fx + pi + qi^2 + ri^3 + \text{etc.}$$

and investigate how the derived functions $p$, $q$, $r$, etc. depend on the primitive function $fx$.

For this, let us suppose that the unknown $x$ becomes $x + o$, where $o$ is some unknown quantity independent of $i$; it is clear that $f(x + i)$ becomes $f(x + i + o)$, and one sees at the same time that one would have the same result by putting simply $i + o$ in the place of $i$ in $f(x + i)$. Therefore, the result must also be the same, whether in the series $fx + pi + qi^2 + ri^3 +$ etc. one puts $i + o$ in place of $i$, or one puts $x + o$ in place of $x$.

The first substitution will give

$$fx + p(i + o) + q(i + o)^2 + r(i + o)^3 + \text{etc.};$$

that is, by expanding the powers of $i + o$, and writing, for greater simplicity, only the first two terms of each power, because the comparison of these terms will suffice for the determination of those we need,

$$
\begin{aligned}
fx \;+\;& pi \;+\; qi^2 \;+\; ri^3 \;+\; si^4 \;+\; \text{etc.;} \\
\;+\;& po \;+\; 2qio \;+\; 3ri^2o \;+\; 4si^3o \;+\; \text{etc.}
\end{aligned}
$$

[14] To make the other substitution, suppose $fx + f'xo+$ etc., $p + p'o+$ etc., $q + q'o+$ etc., $r + r'o+$ etc., are what the functions $fx, p, q, r$, etc. become on putting $x + o$ for $x$, and considering in the expansion only the terms that contain the first power of $o$, it is clear that the same formula must become

$$
\begin{aligned}
fx \;+\;& pi \;+\; qi^2 \;+\; ri^3 \;+\; si^4 \;+\; \text{etc.} \\
\;+\;& f'xo \;+\; p'io \;+\; q'i^2o \;+\; r'i^3o \;+\; \text{etc.}
\end{aligned}
$$

Since these two results must be identical, whatever the values of $i$ and $o$, one will have, on comparing the terms in $o$, $io$, $i^2o$, etc., $p = f'x, 2q = p', 3r = q', 4s = r'$, etc.

Now, just as $f'x$ is the first derived function of $fx$, it is clear that $p'$ is the first derived function of $p$, that $q'$ is the first derived function of $q$, $r'$ the first derived function of $r$, and so on. Therefore, if, for simplicity and uniformity, one denotes by $f'x$ the first derived function of $fx$, by $f''x$ the first derived function of $f'x$, by $f'''x$ the first derived function of $f''x$, and so on, one will have $p = f'x$, and from that $p' = f''x$; therefore

$$q = \frac{p'}{2} = \frac{f''x}{2}; \text{ therefore } q' = \frac{f'''x}{2}; \text{ and from that } r = \frac{q'}{3} = \frac{f'''x}{2.3}; \text{ therefore}$$

$$r' = \frac{f^{IV}x}{2.3}, \text{ and from that } s = \frac{r'}{4} = \frac{f^{IV}x}{2.3.4}, \text{ and so on.}$$

Therefore, substituting these values in the expansion of the function $f(x + i)$, one will have

$$f(x + i) = fx + f'xi + \frac{f''x}{2}i^2 + \frac{f'''x}{2.3}i^3 + \frac{f^{IV}x}{2.3.4}i^4 + \text{etc.}$$

This new expression has the advantage of showing how the terms of the series depend on one another, and above all how, when one knows how to form the first derived function of any primitive function, one may form all the derived functions that the series contains.

17. We will call the function $fx$ the *primitive function*, in relation to the functions $f'x$, $f''x$, etc. that derive from it, and we will call these the *derived functions*, in relation to the former. Further, we will name the first [15] derived function, $f'x$, the *first function*; the second derived function, $f''x$, the *second function*; the third derived function, $f'''x$, the *third function*, and so on.

In the same way, if $y$ is assumed to be a function of $x$, we will denote its derived functions by $y', y'', y'''$, etc. so that where $y$ is a primitive function, $y'$ will be its *first* function, $y''$ will be its *second* function, $y'''$ the *third* function, and so on.

So that on $x$ becoming $x + i$, $y$ will become $y + y'i + \frac{y''i^2}{2} + \frac{y'''i^3}{2.3} + \text{etc.}$

18. Thus, provided one has a means of finding the first function from any primitive function, one will have, by simple repetition of the same operations, all the derived functions, and consequently all the terms of the series that results from the expansion of the primitive function.

First, therefore, suppose $fx = x^m$, so one will have $f(x+i) = (x+i)^m$; now it is easy to demonstrate, whether by simple rules of arithmetic, or by the basic operations of algebra, that the first two terms of the $m^{th}$ power of the binomial $x + i$ are $x^m + mx^{m-1}i$, whether $m$ is a whole or fractional number, positive or negative; thus one will have $f'x = mx^{m-1}$. From there, one may obtain in the same way $f''x = m(m-1)x^{m-2}$; $f'''x = m(m-1)(m-2)x^{m-3}$, etc.; so that one will have

$$(x+i)^m = x^m + mx^{m-1}i + \frac{m(m-1)}{2}x^{m-2}i^2 + \frac{m(m-1)(m-2)}{2.3}x^{m-3}i^3 + \text{etc.}$$

which is the known binomial formula, which is thus demonstrated for all values of $m$.

---

### 14.1.3 Ampère's theory of derived functions, 1806

André-Marie Ampère is not generally thought of as a mathematician, but he was a lecturer at the École Polytechnique in the opening years of the nineteenth century and he, like Cauchy later, was required to teach analysis. In 1797 Lagrange had explored the behaviour of $f(x+i) - f(x)$ and its relationship to $if'(x)$ when $i$ is very small (11.2.3), and in 1806 Ampère published a paper in the *Journal de l'École Polytechnique* in which he attempted to establish a theory of derivatives based on the behaviour of the ratio

$$\frac{f(x+i) - f(x)}{i}$$

as $i$ approaches zero. In particular he was concerned to dispel the idea that this ratio will necessarily become zero (because the numerator tends to zero) or infinite (because the denominator tends to zero).

The opening of Ampère's proof is not easy to follow due to several negative suppositions and some faulty logic. He also incorrectly asserted (as Lagrange had done in 1797) that having found a set of 'sufficiently small' values of $i$, one could take a single value that would replace all of them. This is not the case unless convergence is uniform, a concept that was not yet even recognized. Nevertheless, the later part of Ampère's argument was correct and by a process of interval bisection he ended up with a proof of the mean value theorem. He himself was convinced that he had proved something more, that the ratio $\frac{f(x+i)-f(x)}{i}$ in general takes finite non-zero values as $i$ decreases, and was therefore, at least according to Ampère, a well-defined function of $x$.

Despite its many shortcomings, part of Ampère's proof is included here for two reasons. First, to illustrate the difficulties experienced by those who first tried to work with a definition of $f'(x)$ as a limit of a ratio. Second, to show that even a shaky proof can be influential. Lagrange referred to it in 1813 (in a revised proof of the lemma given in 11.2.3), as did Cauchy in 1823 (in his proof of the mean value theorem, 14.1.5). Cauchy also developed a similar method of repeated bisection in his second and more rigorous proof of the intermediate value theorem in 1821 (see 11.2.6).

---

## Ampère's theory of derived functions

from Ampère, 'Recherches sur quelques points de la théorie des fonctions dérivées ...',
*Journal de l'École Polytechnique*, 6 (1806), 150–154

---

Observons d'abord que pour qu'une fonction réelle (*) de $x$ et de $i$ devienne nulle ou infinie quand $i = 0$, il faut que cette fonction diminue ou augmente à mesure que $i$ diminue, de manière à devenir dans le premier cas et pour une valeur de $i$ assez petite, moindre que toute grandeur donnée, et à surpasser dans le second cas toute grandeur donnée, pourvu qu'on assigne à $i$ une valeur assez petite pour cela.

En sorte que si la propriété que nous venons de dire appartenir à la fonction

$$\frac{f(x + i) - f(x)}{i},$$

n'avait pas lieu pour toutes les valeurs de $x$, si ce n'est pour de certaines valeurs particulières et isolées de cette variable, on n'aurait qu'à donner successivement à $x$ deux valeurs $a$ et $k$, prises dans l'intervalle où cette propriété n'aurait pas lieu, pour que

$$\frac{f(x + i) - f(x)}{i}$$

diminuât ou crût à mesure que $i$ se rapprocherait de zéro, de manière à devenir moindre ou plus grande qu'une quantité prise à volonté.

Il s'ensuivrait donc qu'en donnant à $i$ une valeur plus petite que toutes les valeurs qu'il faudrait lui assigner pour cela depuis $x = a$ jusqu'à $x = k$,

---

(*) Une fonction pourrait passer d'une valeur finie à une valeur infinie ou nulle, sans croître ou diminuer indéfiniment si elle devenait imaginaire dans l'intervalle; mais cela ne saurait arriver à la fonction que nous considérons

$$\frac{f(x + i) - f(x)}{i},$$

qui ne peut devenir imaginaire que dans le cas où $f(x)$ cesserait aussi d'être réelle, et où il n'y aurait par conséquent plus lieu aux recherches qui sont l'objet de ce Mémoire.

aucune des valeurs de $x$ qui sont comprises dans cet intervalle, ne pourrait rendre la fonction que nous examinons, égale à cette quantité prise à volonté, et par conséquent si nous démontrons que cela n'est pas possible à l'égard de cette fonction

$$\frac{f(x + i) - f(x)}{i},$$

la propriété que nous avons dit lui appartenir sera complétement prouvée.

Soient $A$ et $K$ les valeurs de $f(x)$ correspondantes à $x = a$, et $x = k$, on pourra toujours supposer que $a$ et $k$ ont été pris de manière que $f(x)$ ne devienne point infini dans l'intervalle, et qu'on n'ait ni $A = K$, ni $a = k$, afin que

$$\frac{K - A}{k - a}$$

ne soit ni nul ni infini, et qu'on puisse prendre cette quantité pour celle au-dessus ou au-dessous de laquelle on pourrait toujours amener $\frac{f(x + i) - f(x)}{i}$, en donnant à $i$ une valeur assez petite pour cela.

Représentons par $B$, $C$, $D$, &c., les valeurs de $f(x)$ correspondantes aux valeurs de $x$, intermédiaires entre $a$ et $k$, que nous désignerons par $b$, $c$, $d$, &c., en supposant que l'ordre dans lequel nous les rangeons ici, est celui de leurs grandeurs; $e$, par exemple, étant intermédiaire entre $a$ et $k$, il sera d'abord aisé de s'assurer que des deux fonctions

$$\frac{K - E}{k - e} \text{ et } \frac{E - A}{e - a},$$

l'une est plus grande et l'autre plus petite que

$$\frac{K - A}{k - a};$$

car on a

$$\frac{K - E}{k - e} - \frac{K - A}{k - a} = \frac{aE - Ae + Ak - aK + eK - Ek}{(k - e)(k - a)},$$

et

$$\frac{K - A}{k - a} - \frac{E - A}{e - a} = \frac{aE - Ae + Ak - aK + eK - Ek}{(e - a)(k - a)},$$

valeurs qui ne diffèrent qu'en ce que l'une a au dénominateur le

152    ANALYSE.

facteur $k - e$, et l'autre a le facteur $e - a$, et qui sont par conséquent de même signe, tant que $e$ est intermédiaire entre $k$ et $a$; ce qui prouve que

$$\frac{K - A}{k - a}$$

l'est entre

$$\frac{K - E}{k - e} \text{ et } \frac{E - A}{e - a}.$$

Si l'on avait

$$aE - Ae + Ak - aK + eK - Ek = 0,$$

ces trois fractions seraient égales; mais cela ne changerait rien à la démonstration dont nous nous occupons ici; il faudrait seulement entendre par *quantité plus grande*, une quantité qui ne peut être qu'égale ou plus grande, et donner la même extension à cette expression, *quantité plus petite*. C'est ce que nous ferons toujours dans ce Mémoire.

$g$ étant intermédiaire entre $k$ et $e$, et $c$ entre $e$ et $a$, les deux fractions

$$\frac{K - E}{k - e} \text{ et } \frac{E - A}{e - a}$$

le seront respectivement entre

$$\frac{K - G}{k - g} \text{ et } \frac{G - E}{g - e} \text{, et entre } \frac{E - C}{e - c} \text{ et } \frac{C - A}{c - a}.$$

Parmi ces quatre dernières fractions, il y en aura donc nécessairement une plus grande que la plus grande de ces deux-ci,

$$\frac{K - E}{k - e} \text{ et } \frac{E - A}{e - a},$$

et par conséquent plus grande que

$$\frac{K - A}{k - a},$$

et il y en aura pour la même raison une plus petite que cette dernière quantité.

On démontrera de même que parmi les huit fractions

$$\frac{K-H}{k-h}, \frac{H-G}{h-g}, \frac{G-F}{g-f}, \frac{F-E}{f-e}, \frac{E-D}{e-d}, \frac{D-C}{d-c}, \frac{C-B}{c-b}, \frac{B-A}{b-a},$$

il

il y en a nécessairement une plus grande et une plus petite que

$$\frac{K - A}{k - a}.$$

En continuant de la même manière à intercaler des valeurs de $x$ entre les précédentes, on formera de nouvelles suites de fractions, parmi lesquelles il y en aura toujours une plus grande et une plus petite que

$$\frac{K - A}{k - a}.$$

Si l'on suppose dans ces opérations successives toutes les valeurs de $x$ équidifférentes entre elles, les dénominateurs des fractions d'une même suite seront égaux et de moitié plus petits que ceux de la suite précédente ; d'où il suit qu'on pourra les rendre aussi petits que l'on voudra. Après les avoir amenés à être moindres que la plus petite des valeurs de $i$ qu'on supposerait rendre

$$\frac{f(x + i) - f(x)}{i}$$

plus grande ou plus petite que la valeur finie

$$\frac{K - A}{k - a},$$

pour toutes les valeurs de $x$ comprises entre $k$ et $a$, il est évident que les diverses fractions de la suite où l'on serait parvenu, seraient autant de valeurs de

$$\frac{f(x + i) - f(x)}{i},$$

correspondantes à cet $i$, et à des valeurs de $x$ entre
constant dans une même suite, en faisant varier $x$
que nous considérons depuis $x = k$ jusqu'à $x = $ .
d'après ce que nous venons de voir, par une valeur plu
plus petite que

$$\frac{K - A}{k - a},$$

et par conséquent par une valeur égale à cette fract

*XIII.ᵉ Cahier.*

154    ANALYSE.

raisonnement (*) dont M. *Lagrange* s'est servi pour démontrer la réalité des racines irrationnelles des équations algébriques, où l'on trouve des changemens de signes dans les résultats que l'on obtient en substituant différens nombres à $x$. Cette conséquence étant contradictoire à la supposition d'où nous étions partis, que la valeur de $i$ avait été prise assez petite pour que toutes celles que prend

$$\frac{f(x+i) - f(x)}{i},$$

depuis $x = k$ jusqu'à $x = a$, fussent moindres ou plus grandes que

$$\frac{K - A}{k - a},$$

prouve que cette supposition était fausse, et qu'aucune valeur de $i$, quelque petite qu'elle soit, ne peut satisfaire à cette condition; d'où il suit qu'il est impossible que

$$\frac{f(x+i) - f(x)}{i},$$

augmente ou diminue indéfiniment, lorsqu'on rend $i$ de plus en plus petit pour toutes les valeurs de $x$ comprises dans l'intervalle que nous considérons; il faut donc, d'après ce qu'on a vu au commencement de ce mémoire, que cette fonction de $x$ et de $i$ se réduise, quand $i = 0$, à une fonction de $x$.

Puisque la fonction

$$\frac{f(x+i) - f(x)}{i},$$

devient égale à $f' x$ quand $i = 0$, on pourra la représenter en général par

$$f'(x) + I,$$

---

(*) Ce raisonnement ne pourrait être appliqué au cas présent, si

$$\frac{f(x+i) - f(x)}{i}$$

devenait infini dans l'intervalle de $k$ à $a$; mais la valeur de $i$ étant ici déterminée, quoique très-petite, cela ne saurait avoir lieu sans qu'une valeur de $f(x)$ fût infinie dans le même intervalle, ce qui est contraire aux suppositions d'où nous sommes partis, relativement aux valeurs $k$ et $a$ de $x$.

Let us observe first of all that for a real function* of $x$ and $i$ to become null or infinite when $i = 0$, it must be that the function decreases or increases as $i$ decreases, in such a way as to become, in the first case and for a small enough value of $i$, less than any given quantity, and in the second case to exceed any given quantity, provided that one assigns to $i$ a small enough value for that to happen.

So that if the property [of being finite and non-zero] that we have said must pertain to the function

$$\frac{f(x + i) - f(x)}{i}$$

did not hold for all values of $x$, except for certain particular and isolated values of that variable, one would only have to give successively to $x$ two values $a$ and $k$, taken in the interval where this property does not hold, for

$$\frac{f(x + i) - f(x)}{i}$$

to decrease or increase as $i$ approaches zero, in such a way as to become less than or greater than any quantity taken at will.

It follows therefore that by giving $i$ a value smaller than all the values one must assign for that from $x = a$ to $x = k$, [151] not one of the values of $x$ contained inside that interval can render the function that we are examining equal to that quantity taken at will, and consequently if we demonstrate that that is not possible with regard to this function

$$\frac{f(x + i) - f(x)}{i},$$

the property that we have said must pertain to it will be completely proved.

Let $A$ and $K$ be values of $f(x)$ corresponding to $x = a$ and $x = k$; one may always assume that $a$ and $k$ have been taken so that $f(x)$ never becomes infinite in the interval, and that one has neither $A = K$ nor $a = k$, so that

$$\frac{K - A}{k - a}$$

becomes neither null nor infinite, and that one may take this quantity for that above or below which one may always make $\dfrac{f(x + i) - f(x)}{i}$, by giving $i$ a small enough value for that to happen.

---

\* A function can pass from a finite value to an infinite value or zero without increasing or decreasing indefinitely if it becomes imaginary in the meantime; but this is supposed not to happen to the function we are considering

$$\frac{f(x + i) - fx}{i},$$

which cannot become imaginary except in the case where $f(x)$ also ceases to be real, and where consequently it has no further place in the researches that are the subject of this memoir.

Let us represent by $B$, $C$, $D$, etc. the values of $f(x)$ corresponding to values of $x$ intermediate between $a$ and $k$, which we will denote by $b$, $c$, $d$, etc. supposing that the order in which we arrange them here is that of size; where $e$, for example, is intermediate between $a$ and $k$, it will first be easy to assure ourselves that of the two functions

$$\frac{K - E}{k - e} \quad \text{and} \quad \frac{E - A}{e - a},$$

one is greater and the other is smaller than

$$\frac{K - A}{k - a};$$

for one has

$$\frac{K - E}{k - e} - \frac{K - A}{k - a} = \frac{aE - Ae + Ak - aK + eK - Ek}{(k - e)(k - a)},$$

and

$$\frac{K - A}{k - a} - \frac{E - A}{e - a} = \frac{aE - Ae + Ak - aK + eK - Ek}{(e - a)(k - a)},$$

values which differ only in that one has in the denominator [152] the factor $(k - e)$ and the other the factor $(e - a)$, and which are consequently of the same sign, since $e$ is intermediate between $k$ and $a$; which proves that

$$\frac{K - A}{k - a}$$

is between

$$\frac{K - E}{k - e} \quad \text{and} \quad \frac{E - A}{e - a}.$$

If one has

$$aE - Ae + Ak - aK + eK - Ek = 0,$$

these three fractions will be equal; but that changes nothing in the demonstration with which we are concerned here; one must only understand by *a greater quantity* a quantity that must be equal or greater, and give the same extended meaning to the expression *a smaller quantity*. This we will always do in this memoir.

Where $g$ is intermediate between $k$ and $e$, and $c$ between $e$ and $a$, the two fractions

$$\frac{K - E}{k - e} \quad \text{and} \quad \frac{E - A}{e - a}$$

will be, respectively, between

$$\frac{K - G}{k - g} \quad \text{and} \quad \frac{G - E}{g - e}, \quad \text{and between} \quad \frac{E - C}{e - c} \quad \text{and} \quad \frac{C - A}{c - a}.$$

Amongst these last four fractions, there will therefore necessarily be one greater than the greatest of these two

$$\frac{K-E}{k-e} \quad \text{and} \quad \frac{E-A}{e-a},$$

and consequently greater than

$$\frac{K-A}{k-a},$$

and for the same reason there will be one smaller than this last quantity.

One can demonstrate in the same way that among the eight fractions

$$\frac{K-H}{k-h}, \frac{H-G}{h-g}, \frac{G-F}{g-f}, \frac{F-E}{f-e}, \frac{E-D}{e-d}, \frac{D-C}{d-c}, \frac{C-B}{c-b}, \frac{B-A}{b-a},$$

[153] there is necessarily one greater and one smaller than

$$\frac{K-A}{k-a}.$$

Continuing in the same manner to interpolate values of $x$ between the preceding ones, one will form new sequences of fractions amongst which there will always be one greater and one smaller than

$$\frac{K-A}{k-a}.$$

If one assumes in these successive operations that all the values of $x$ are equally spaced from each other, the denominators of the fractions of the same sequence will be equal and half the size of those of the preceding sequence; from which it follows that one can make them as small as one wants. After having taken them to be less than the smallest value of $i$ that one assumes will render

$$\frac{f(x+i)-f(x)}{i}$$

greater or less than the finite value

$$\frac{K-A}{k-a},$$

for all values of $x$ contained between $k$ and $a$, it is clear that the various fractions of the sequence at which one has arrived will be the same as the values of

$$\frac{f(x+i)-f(x)}{i},$$

corresponding to this $i$, and to the values of $x$ between $k$ and $a$; but $i$ being constant in the same sequence, and making $x$ vary from $x = k$ to $x = a$ in the function we are considering, one will pass, as we have just seen, through values greater than and less than

$$\frac{K-A}{k-a},$$

and consequently through a value equal to that fraction, by virtue of [154] the reasoning* which Monsieur *Lagrange* has made use of to demonstrate the existence of irrational roots of algebraic equations, where one finds the changes of sign in the results one obtains by substituting various numbers for $x$. This consequence, contradicting the assumption from which we started, that the value of $i$ had been taken small enough so that all the values taken by

$$\frac{f(x+i) - f(x)}{i}$$

from $x = k$ to $x = a$ would be less than or greater than

$$\frac{K - A}{k - a},$$

proves that the assumption was false, and that no value of $i$, however small it may be, can satisfy this condition; from which it follows that it is impossible for

$$\frac{f(x+i) - f(x)}{i},$$

to increase or decrease indefinitely, when one makes $i$ smaller and smaller for all the values of $x$ contained in the interval we are considering; it must be, therefore, as we saw at the beginning of this memoir, that this function of $x$ and $i$ reduces, when $i = 0$ to a function of $x$.

_____

\* This reasoning cannot be applied in the present case if

$$\frac{f(x+i) - f(x)}{i}$$

becomes infinite in the interval from $k$ to $a$; but the value of $i$ being here finite, though very small, this is supposed not to happen unless a value of $f(x)$ is infinite in the same interval, which is contrary to the assumption we started from, with respect to the values $k$ and $a$ of $x$.

_____

### 14.1.4 Cauchy on derived functions, 1823

In the third lesson of his *Résumé des leçons …sur le calcul infinitésimal* of 1823, Cauchy finally brought together the ratio

$$\frac{f(x+i) - f(x)}{i}$$

and the concept of a limit to give what is essentially the standard modern definition of a derivative.

## Cauchy's definition of a derivative

from Cauchy, *Résumé des leçons*, 1823, Lesson 3

### TROISIÈME LEÇON.

*Dérivées des Fonctions d'une seule Variable.*

LORSQUE la fonction $y = f(x)$ reste continue entre deux limites données de la variable $x$, et que l'on assigne à cette variable une valeur comprise entre les deux limites dont il s'agit, un accroissement infiniment petit, attribué à la variable, produit un accroissement infiniment petit de la fonction elle-même. Par conséquent, si l'on pose alors $\Delta x = i$, les deux termes du *rapport aux différences*

$$(1) \qquad \frac{\Delta y}{\Delta x} = \frac{f(x+i) - f(x)}{i}$$

seront des quantités infiniment petites. Mais, tandis que ces deux termes s'approcheront indéfiniment et simultanément de la limite zéro, le rapport lui-même pourra converger vers une autre limite, soit positive, soit négative. Cette limite, lorsqu'elle existe, a une valeur déterminée, pour chaque valeur particulière de $x$ ; mais elle varie avec $x$. Ainsi, par exemple, si l'on prend $f(x) = x^m$, $m$ désignant un nombre entier, le rapport entre les différences infiniment petites sera

$$\frac{(x+i)^m - x^m}{i} = mx^{m-1} + \frac{m(m-1)}{1.2} x^{m-2} i + \ldots + i^{m-1}$$

et il aura pour limite la quantité $mx^{m-1}$, c'est-à-dire, une nouvelle fonction de la variable $x$. Il en sera de même en général ; seulement, la forme de la fonction nouvelle qui servira de limite au rapport $\frac{f(x+i) - f(x)}{i}$ dépendra de la forme de la fonction proposée $y = f(x)$. Pour indiquer cette dépendance, on donne à la nouvelle fonction le nom de *fonction dérivée*, et on la désigne, à l'aide d'un accent, par la notation

$$y' \quad \text{ou} \quad f'(x),$$

Dans la recherche des dérivées des fonctions d'une seule variable $x$, il est utile de distinguer les fonctions que l'on nomme *simples*, et que

10    COURS D'ANALYSE.

l'on considère comme résultant d'une seule opération effectuée sur cette variable, d'avec les fonctions que l'on construit à l'aide de plusieurs opérations et que l'on nomme *composées*. Les fonctions simples que produisent les opérations de l'algèbre et de la trigonométrie [ *voyez* la I.$^{re}$ partie du *Cours d'analyse*, ch. I.$^{er}$ ] peuvent être réduites aux suivantes

$$a + x, \quad a - x, \quad ax, \quad \frac{a}{x}, \quad x^a, \quad A^x, \quad L(x),$$

$$\sin x, \quad \cos x, \quad \arcsin x, \quad \arccos x,$$

$A$ désignant un nombre constant, $a = \pm A$ une quantité constante, et la lettre $L$ indiquant un logarithme pris dans le système dont la base est $A$. Si l'on prend une de ces fonctions simples pour $y$, il sera facile en général d'obtenir la fonction dérivée $y'$. On trouvera, par exemple,

pour $y = a + x$, $\dfrac{\Delta y}{\Delta x} = \dfrac{(a+x+i)-(a+x)}{i} = 1$, $\quad y' = 1$;

pour $y = a - x$, $\dfrac{\Delta y}{\Delta x} = \dfrac{(a-x-i)-(a-x)}{i} = -1$, $\quad y' = -1$;

pour $y = ax$, $\quad \dfrac{\Delta y}{\Delta x} = \dfrac{a(x+i)-ax}{i} = a$, $\quad y' = a$;

pour $y = \dfrac{a}{x}$, $\quad \dfrac{\Delta y}{\Delta x} = \dfrac{\frac{a}{x+i}-\frac{a}{x}}{i} = -\dfrac{a}{x(x+i)}$, $y' = -\dfrac{a}{x^2}$;

pour $y = \sin x$, $\dfrac{\Delta y}{\Delta x} = \dfrac{\sin \frac{1}{2}i}{\frac{1}{2}i}\cos\left(x+\frac{1}{2}i\right), y' = \cos x = \sin\left(x+\frac{\pi}{2}\right)$;

pour $y = \cos x$, $\dfrac{\Delta y}{\Delta x} = -\dfrac{\sin \frac{1}{2}i}{\frac{1}{2}i}\sin\left(x+\frac{1}{2}i\right), y' = -\sin x = \cos\left(x+\frac{\pi}{2}\right)$.

De plus, en posant $i = \alpha x$, $A^i = 1+\beta$ et $(1+\alpha)^a = 1+\gamma$, on trouvera

pour $y = L(x)$, $\dfrac{\Delta y}{\Delta x} = \dfrac{L(x+i)-L(x)}{i} = \dfrac{L(1+\alpha)}{\alpha x} = \dfrac{L(1+\alpha)^{\frac{1}{\alpha}}}{x}$, $y' = \dfrac{L(e)}{x}$;

pour $y = A^x$, $\dfrac{\Delta y}{\Delta x} = \dfrac{A^{x+i}-A^x}{i} = \dfrac{A^i-1}{i}A^x = \dfrac{A^x}{L(1+\beta)^{\frac{1}{\beta}}}$, $y' = \dfrac{A^x}{L(e)}$;

pour $y = x^a$, $\dfrac{\Delta y}{\Delta x} = \dfrac{(x+i)^a-x^a}{i} = \dfrac{(1+\alpha)^a-1}{\alpha}x^{a-1} = \dfrac{L(1+\alpha)^{\frac{1}{\alpha}}}{L(1+\gamma)^{\frac{1}{\gamma}}}ax^{a-1}, y' = ax^{a-1}$.

COURS D'ANALYSE.                                                    II

Dans ces dernières formules, la lettre $e$ désigne le nombre $2,718\dots$

qui sert de limite à l'expression $(1+\alpha)^{\frac{1}{\alpha}}$. Si l'on prend ce nombre pour base d'un système de logarithmes, on obtiendra les logarithmes *Népériens* ou *hyperboliques*, que nous indiquerons toujours à l'aide de la lettre $l$. Cela posé, on aura évidemment $l(e)=1$,

$$Le = \frac{Le}{LA} = \frac{le}{lA} = \frac{1}{lA} \, ;$$

et de plus on trouvera

pour    $y = l(x)$,    $y' = \dfrac{1}{x}$ ;

pour    $y = e^x$,    $y' = e^x$.

Les diverses formules qui précèdent étant établies seulement pour les valeurs de $x$ auxquelles correspondent des valeurs réelles de $y$, on doit supposer $x$ positive, dans celles de ces formules qui se rapportent aux fonctions $L(x)$, $l(x)$, et même à la fonction $x^a$, lorsque $a$ désigne une fraction de dénominateur pair, ou un nombre irrationnel.

Soit maintenant $z$ une seconde fonction de $x$, liée à la première $y = f(x)$ par la formule

$$(2) \qquad\qquad z = F(y).$$

$z$ ou $F(fx)$ sera ce qu'on appelle une *fonction de fonction* de la variable $x$; et, si l'on désigne par $\Delta x$, $\Delta y$, $\Delta z$, les accroissemens infiniment petits et simultanés des trois variables $x$, $y$, $z$, on trouvera

$$\frac{\Delta z}{\Delta x} = \frac{F(y+\Delta y)-F(y)}{\Delta x} = \frac{F(y+\Delta y)-F(y)}{\Delta y} \cdot \frac{\Delta y}{\Delta x} \, ,$$

puis, en passant aux limites,

$$(3) \qquad\qquad z' = y'.F'(y) = f'(x). F'(fx).$$

Par exemple, si l'on fait $z = ay$, et $y = l(x)$, on aura $z' = ay' = \dfrac{a}{x}$.

# THIRD LESSON

*Derivatives of functions of a single variable*

WHEN the function $y = f(x)$ remains continuous between two given limits of the variable $x$, and one assigns to that variable a value contained between the two limits in question, an infinitely small increase given to the variable produces an infinitely small increase in the function itself. Consequently, if one then puts $\Delta x = i$, the two terms of the *ratio of differences*

(1)
$$\frac{\Delta y}{\Delta x} = \frac{f(x+i) - f(x)}{i}$$

will be infinitely small quantities. But, while these two terms approach indefinitely and simultaneously to the limit zero, the ratio itself may converge towards another limit, perhaps positive, perhaps negative. This limit, when it exists, has a determined value for each particular value of $x$; but it varies with $x$. Thus, for example, if one takes $f(x) = x^m$, where $m$ denotes a whole number, the ratio between the infinitely small differences will be

$$\frac{(x+i)^m - x^m}{i} = mx^{m-1} + \frac{m(m-1)}{1.2}x^{m-2}i + \cdots + i^{m-1}$$

and it will have for its limit the quantity $mx^{m-1}$, that is to say, a new function of the variable $x$. It will be the same in general; the form of the new function that serves as the limit of the ratio $\dfrac{f(x+i) - f(x)}{i}$ will depend only on the form of the proposed function $f(x)$. To indicate this dependence, one gives the new function the name of *derived function*, and one denotes it, with the help of an accent, by the notation

$$y' \quad \text{or} \quad f'(x),$$

In seeking derivatives of a single variable $x$, it is useful to distinguish functions that one calls *simple*, and that [10] one regards as the result of a single operation carried out on that variable, from functions that one constructs by means of several operations and which one calls *compound*. The simple functions produced by the operations of algebra and trigonometry [see the 1st part of *Cours d'analyse*, chapter I] may be reduced to the following

$$a + x, \quad a - x, \quad ax, \quad \frac{a}{x}, \quad x^a, \quad A^x, \quad L(x),$$

$$\sin x, \quad \cos x, \quad \arcsin x, \quad \arccos x,$$

where $A$ denotes a constant number, $a = \pm A$ a constant quantity, and the letter $L$ indicating a logarithm taken in the system of which the base is $A$. If one takes one of these simple functions for $y$, it will be easy in general to obtain the derived function $y'$.

One will find, for example,

for $y = a + x$, $\quad \frac{\Delta y}{\Delta x} = \frac{(a+x+i)-(a+x)}{i} = 1$, $\quad y' = 1$;

for $y = a - x$, $\quad \frac{\Delta y}{\Delta x} = \frac{(a-x-i)-(a-x)}{i} = -1$, $\quad y' = -1$;

for $y = ax$, $\quad \frac{\Delta y}{\Delta x} = \frac{a(x+i)-ax}{i} = a$, $\quad y' = a$;

for $y = \frac{a}{x}$, $\quad \frac{\Delta y}{\Delta x} = \frac{\frac{a}{x+i}-\frac{a}{x}}{i} = -\frac{a}{x(x+i)}$, $\quad y' = -\frac{a}{x^2}$;

for $y = \sin x$, $\quad \frac{\Delta y}{\Delta x} = \frac{\sin \frac{1}{2}i}{\frac{1}{2}i} \cos\left(x + \frac{1}{2}i\right)$, $\quad y' = \cos x = \sin(x + \frac{\pi}{2})$;

for $y = \cos x$, $\quad \frac{\Delta y}{\Delta x} = -\frac{\sin \frac{1}{2}i}{\frac{1}{2}i} \sin\left(x + \frac{1}{2}i\right)$, $\quad y' = -\sin x = \cos(x + \frac{\pi}{2})$.

Further, putting $i = \alpha x$, $A^i = 1 + \beta$ and $(1+\alpha)^\alpha = 1 + \gamma$, one will find

for $y = L(x)$, $\quad \frac{\Delta y}{\Delta x} = \frac{L(x+i)-Lx}{i} = \frac{L(1+\alpha)}{\alpha x} = \frac{L(1+\alpha)^{\frac{1}{\alpha}}}{x}$, $\qquad y' = \frac{L(e)}{x}$;

for $y = A^x$, $\quad \frac{\Delta y}{\Delta x} = \frac{A^{x+i}-A^x}{i} = \frac{A^1-1}{i}A^x = \frac{A^x}{L(1+\beta)^{\frac{1}{\beta}}}$, $\qquad y' = \frac{A^x}{L(e)}$;

for $y = x^a$, $\quad \frac{\Delta y}{\Delta x} = \frac{(x+i)^a-x^a}{i} = \frac{(1+\alpha)^a-1}{\alpha}x^{a-1} = \frac{L(1+\alpha)^{\frac{1}{\alpha}}}{L(1+\gamma)^{\frac{1}{\gamma}}}ax^{a-1}$, $y' = ax^{a-1}$.

[11] In these last expressions the letter $e$ denotes the number $2.718\ldots$ which stands for the limit of the expression $(1+\alpha)^{\frac{1}{\alpha}}$. If one takes this number as the base of a system of logarithms, one will obtain *Naperian* or *hyperbolic* logarithms, which we will always indicate by means of the letter $l$. That said, one will clearly have $l(e) = 1$.

$$Le = \frac{Le}{LA} = \frac{le}{lA} = \frac{1}{lA};$$

and further, one will find

for $y = l(x)$, $\quad y' = \frac{1}{x}$;

for $y = e^x$, $\quad y' = e^x$.

The various preceding expressions being established only for the values of $x$ to which there correspond real values of $y$, one must assume $x$ positive, in those expressions that relate to the functions $L(x)$, $l(x)$, and the same for the function $x^a$, when $a$ denotes a fraction with an even denominator, or an irrational number.

Now suppose $z$ is a second function of $x$, linked to the first, $y = f(x)$, by the formula

(2) $$z = F(y).$$

$z$ or $F(fx)$ will be what one calls a *function of a function* of the variable $x$; and if one denotes by $\Delta x$, $\Delta y$, $\Delta z$, the infinitely small and simultaneous increments of the three variables $x$, $y$, $z$, one will find

$$\frac{\Delta z}{\Delta y} = \frac{F(y + \Delta y) - F(y)}{\Delta x} = \frac{F(y + \Delta y) - F(y)}{\Delta y} \cdot \frac{\Delta y}{\Delta x},$$

then, passing to the limits,

(3) $$z' = y' \cdot F'(y) = f'(x) \cdot F'(fx).$$

For example, if one makes $z = ay$, and $y = l(x)$, one will have $z' = ay' = \frac{a}{x}$.

### 14.1.5  The mean value theorem, and $\varepsilon$, $\delta$ notation, 1823

In the *Résumé des leçons* of 1823, Cauchy gave a more refined version of Ampère's theorem from 1806. For a continuous function $f$ defined between $x = x_0$ and $x = X$ Cauchy claimed that the ratio $\frac{f(X)-f(x_0)}{X-x_0}$ lies between the smallest value $A$, and the largest value $B$, of $f'(x)$ on the same interval. By appealing, as Ampère had, to the intermediate value theorem, Cauchy supposed that $f'(x)$ in fact passed through *all* values between $A$ and $B$. For him, the most immediate corollary of this was that there exists a value of $\theta$ between 0 and 1 for which $\frac{f(X)-f(x_0)}{X-x_0} = f'[x_0 + \theta(X - x_0)]$.

Cauchy persisted in the error that both Lagrange and Ampère had made before him (see 11.2.3 and 14.1.3): he assumed that for some small value of $\varepsilon$, the *same* small value of $i$ will ensure that $f(x) - \varepsilon < f(x + i) < f(x) + \varepsilon$ for *all* values of $x$ between $x_0$ and $X$. This is equivalent to an assumption not just of continuity but of *uniform* continuity, a concept that was still some way into the future. Nevertheless, Cauchy's error turned out to be useful, because it enabled him to replace the supposed small value of $i$ by the single symbol $\delta$, and thus he introduced the $\varepsilon$, $\delta$ notation that has since become synonymous with real analysis.

For Cauchy himself, this notation was simply a convenient working tool, and he never used it in any formal definition. Here, as so often, he helped to lay the foundations of Analysis, but also here, as so often, it was Weierstrass, teaching at the University of Berlin some thirty years later, who constructed much of the edifice. Unfortunately, however, there is no extract in this book from Weierstrass himself because he published no textbook, and we know of the contents of his lectures only from the notes and later writings his pupils.

---

### The mean value theorem and $\varepsilon$, $\delta$ notation
from Cauchy, *Résumé des leçons*, 1823, Lesson 7

---

Nous allons maintenant faire connaître une relation digne de remarque* qui existe entre la dérivée $f'(x)$ d'une fonction quelconque $f(x)$, et le rapport aux différences finies $\frac{f(x+h)-f(x)}{h}$. Si dans ce rapport on attribue à $x$ une valeur particulière $x_0$, et si l'on fait, en

---

* On peut consulter sur ce sujet un Mémoire de M. *Ampère*, inséré dans le 13.ᵉ cahier du *Journal de l'École polytechnique.*

outre, $x_0 + h = X$, il prendra la forme $\dfrac{f(X) - f(x_0)}{X - x_0}$. Cela posé, on établira sans peine la proposition suivante.

*Théorème. Si, la fonction $f(x)$ étant continue entre les limites $x = x_0$, $x = X$, on désigne par $A$ la plus petite, et par $B$ la plus grande des valeurs que la fonction dérivée $f'(x)$ reçoit dans cet intervalle, le rapport aux différences finies*

$$(4) \qquad \frac{f(X) - f(x_0)}{X - x_0}$$

*sera nécessairement compris entre $A$ et $B$.*

*Démonstration.* Désignons par $\delta$, $\varepsilon$, deux nombres très-petits, le premier étant choisi de telle sorte que, pour des valeurs numériques de $i$ inférieures à $\delta$, et pour une valeur quelconque de $x$ comprise entre les limites $x_0$, $X$, le rapport

$$\frac{f(x + i) - f(x)}{i}$$

reste toujours supérieur à $f'(x) - \varepsilon$, et inférieur à $f'(x) + \varepsilon$. Si, entre les limites $x_0$, $X$, on interpose $n - 1$ valeurs nouvelles de la variable $x$, savoir,

$$x_1, \quad x_2, \quad \ldots \quad x_{n-1},$$

de manière à diviser la différence $X - x_0$ en élémens

$$x_1 - x_0, \quad x_2 - x_1, \quad \ldots \quad X - x_{n-1},$$

qui, étant tous de même signe, aient des valeurs numériques inférieures à $\delta$; les fractions

$$(5) \qquad \frac{f(x_1) - f(x_0)}{x_1 - x_0}, \quad \frac{f(x_2) - f(x_1)}{x_2 - x_1}, \quad \ldots \quad \frac{f(X) - f(x_{n-1})}{X - x_{n-1}},$$

se trouvant comprises, la première entre les limites $f'(x_0) - \varepsilon$, $f'(x_0) + \varepsilon$, la seconde entre les limites $f'(x_1) - \varepsilon$, $f'(x_1) + \varepsilon$, &c.... seront toutes supérieures à la quantité $A - \varepsilon$, et inférieures à la quantité $B + \varepsilon$. D'ailleurs, les fractions (5) ayant des dénominateurs de même signe, si l'on divise la somme de leurs numérateurs par la somme de leurs dénominateurs, on obtiendra une fraction *moyenne*, c'est-à-dire, comprise entre la plus petite et la plus grande de celles que l'on considère [*voyez* l'Analyse algébrique, note II, 12.$^e$ théorème]. L'expression (4), avec laquelle cette moyenne coïncide, sera donc elle-même renfer-

28                    COURS D'ANALYSE.

mée entre les limites $A - \varepsilon$, $B + \varepsilon$; et, comme cette conclusion subsiste, quelque petit que soit le nombre $\varepsilon$, on peut affirmer que l'expression (4) sera comprise entre $A$ et $B$.

*Corollaire.* Si la fonction dérivée $f'(x)$ est elle-même continue entre
les limites $x = x_0$, $x = X$, en passant d'une limite à l'autre, cette fonction variera de manière à rester toujours comprise entre les deux valeurs
$A$ et $B$, et à prendre successivement toutes les valeurs intermédiaires.
Donc alors toute quantité moyenne entre $A$ et $B$ sera une valeur de $f'(x)$
correspondante à une valeur de $x$ renfermée entre les limites $x_0$ et
$X = x_0 + h$, ou, ce qui revient au même, à une valeur de $x$ de la forme

$$x_0 + \theta h = x_0 + \theta (X - x_0),$$

$\theta$ désignant un nombre inférieur à l'unité. En appliquant cette remarque
à l'expression (4), on en conclura qu'il existe, entre les limites o et 1,
une valeur de $\theta$ propre à vérifier l'équation

$$\frac{f(X) - f(x_0)}{X - x_0} = f'[x_0 + \theta(X - x_0)],$$

ou, ce qui revient au même, la suivante

(6)                $$\frac{f(x_0 + h) - f(x_0)}{h} = f'(x_0 + \theta h).$$

---

### TRANSLATION

We are now going to show a remarkable relationship* that exists between the derivative
$f'(x)$ of any function $f(x)$, and the ratio of finite differences $\dfrac{f(x + h) - f(x)}{h}$. If in
this ratio one gives $x$ a particular value $x_0$, and if, besides, one makes, [27] $x_0 + h = X$,
it will take the form $\dfrac{f(X) - f(x_0)}{X - x_0}$. That said, one may establish without difficulty the
following proposition.

Theorem. *If, the function $f(x)$ being continuous between the limits $x = x_0$, $x = X$,
one denotes by A the smallest and by B the largest, of the values that the derived function
$f'(x)$ takes in this interval, the ratio of finite differences*

(4)                       $$\frac{f(X) - f(x_0)}{X - x_0}$$

*will necessarily be contained between A and B.*

*Proof.* Denoting by $\delta$, $\varepsilon$, two very small numbers, the first being chosen so that for
numerical values of $i$ less than $\delta$, and for any value of $x$ contained between the limits

---

* One may consult on this subject a memoir of Monsieur Ampère, inserted into the 13th cahier of the
*Journal de l'École Polytechnique.*

$x_0$ and $X$, the ratio

$$\frac{f(x+i) - f(x)}{i}$$

remains always greater than $f'(x) - \varepsilon$ and less than $f'(x) + \varepsilon$. If, between the limits $x_0$ and $X$, one interposes $n-1$ new values of the variable $x$, say,

$$x_1, x_2, \ldots x_{n-1},$$

in such a way as to divide the difference $X - x_0$ into elements

$$x_1 - x_0, \; x_2 - x_1, \; \ldots \; X - x_{n-1},$$

which, being all of the same sign, have numerical values less than $\delta$, the fractions

(5) $$\frac{f(x_1) - f(x_0)}{x_1 - x_0}, \; \frac{f(x_2) - f(x_1)}{x_2 - x_1}, \; \ldots \; \frac{f(X) - f(x_{n-1})}{X - x_{n-1}},$$

being contained, the first between the limits $f'(x_0) - \varepsilon, f'(x_0) + \varepsilon$, the second between the limits $f'(x_1) - \varepsilon, f'(x_1) + \varepsilon$, etc. will all be greater than the quantity $A - \varepsilon$, and less than the quantity $B + \varepsilon$. Besides, the fractions (5) having denominators of the same sign, if one divides the sum of their numerators by the sum of their denominators, one will obtain a *mean* fraction, that is to say, contained between the smallest and the largest of those one is considering (see *L'analyse algébrique* [= *Cours d'analyse*], theorem 12, note II). Expression (4), with which that mean coincides, will therefore itself be contained [28] between the limits $A - \varepsilon, B + \varepsilon$; and, since that conclusion holds, however small the number $\varepsilon$, one can confirm that expression (4) will be contained between $A$ and $B$.

*Corollary.* If the derived function $f'(x)$ is itself continuous between the limits $x = x_0$, $x = X$, then in passing from one limit to the other, this function will vary in such a way as to remain always contained between the two values $A$ and $B$, and to take successively all the intermediate values. Therefore every intermediate quantity between $A$ and $B$ will be a value of $f'(x)$ corresponding to a value of $x$ contained between the limits $x_0$ and $X = x_0 + h$, or, which comes to the same thing, to a value of $x$ of the form

$$x_0 + \theta h = x_0 + \theta(X - x_0),$$

where $\theta$ denotes a number less than one. Applying this remark to expression (4), one may conclude that there exists, between the limits 0 and 1, a value of $\theta$ that correctly satisfies the equation

$$\frac{f(X) - f(x_0)}{X - x_0} = f'[x_0 + \theta(X - x_0)],$$

or, which comes to the same thing, the following

(6) $$\frac{f(x_0 + h) - f(x_0)}{h} = f'(x_0 + \theta h).$$

## 14.2 INTEGRATION OF REAL-VALUED FUNCTIONS

### 14.2.1 Euler's introduction to integration, 1768

Integration arose first and foremost as a means of finding areas contained by curves. Various ingenious methods had been invented from antiquity onwards for filling curved spaces with triangles or rectangles, and by the early seventeenth century it was recognized that several important results could be obtained by dividing areas into strips, together with the rule that we would now write as

$$\int_0^X x^n dx = \frac{X^{n+1}}{n+1}.$$

Integration of trigonometric and logarithmic functions followed later, by writing them as power series, or by using substitution or other special techniques.

Once the rules were established and it was accepted that integration and differentiation were inverse processes, geometric arguments could be discarded, and integration could be carried out by simply reversing the rules for differentiation (wherever that was possible). This was essentially how integration was regarded throughout the eighteenth century: as a formal, algebraic process, separated from any geometric interpretation. Euler, who did so much to create the eighteenth-century understanding of calculus, held steadfastly to an interpretation of integration as the inverse of differentiation, and pushed the rules of integration just about as far as they can be made to go: any function that *can* be integrated by algebra alone probably *was* so integrated by Euler. His *Institutiones calculi integralis* (*Foundations of integral calculus*) appeared in three large volumes between 1768 and 1780, with a fourth volume published posthumously in 1794. The first three volumes contain a comprehensive and detailed treatment of techniques of integration, and of solving both ordinary and partial differential equations. Below are two extracts, both from Volume I, to illustrate Euler's approach.

### Euler's introduction to integration

from Euler, *Institutiones calculi integralis*, 1768, I, Definitions 1 and 2, here from
the third edition, 1824

# PRAENOTANDA.

### DE

## CALCULO INTEGRALI

### IN GENERE.

#### Definitio 1.

**1.**

$C$*alculus integralis est methodus, ex data differentialium relatione inveniendi relationem ipsarum quantitatum: et operatio, qua hoc praestatur, integratio vocari solet.*

#### Corollarium 1.

2. Cum igitur calculus differentialis ex data relatione quantitatum variabilium, relationem differentialium investigare doceat: calculus integralis methodum inversam suppeditat.

#### Corollarium 2.

3. Quemadmodum scilicet in Analysi perpetuo binae operationes sibi opponuntur, veluti subtractio additioni, divisio multiplicationi, extractio radicum evectioni ad potestates, ita etiam simili ratione calculus integralis calculo differentiali opponitur.

#### Corollarium 3.

4. Proposita relatione quacunque inter binas quantitates variabiles $x$ et $y$, in calculo differentiali methodus traditur rationem differentialium $\partial y : \partial x$ investigandi: sin autem vicissim ex hac differentialium ratione ipsa quantitatum $x$ et $y$ relatio sit definienda, hoc opus calculo integrali tribuitur.

**1**

**2**                    DE CALCULO INTEGRALI

### Scholion 1.

5. In calculo differentiali iam notavi, quaestionem de differentialibus non absolute sed relative esse intelligendam, ita ut, si $y$ fuerit functio quaecunque ipsius $x$, non tam ipsum eius differentiale $\partial y$, quam eius ratio ad differentiale $\partial x$ sit definienda. Cum enim omnia differentialia per se sint nihilo aequalia, quaecunque functio $y$ fuerit ipsius $x$, semper est $\partial y = 0$, neque sie quicquam amplius absolute quaeri posset. Verum quaestio ita rite proponi debet, ut dum $x$ incrementum capit infinite parvum adeoque evanescens $\partial x$, definiatur ratio incrementi functionis $y$, quod inde capiet, ad istud $\partial x$: etsi enim utrumque est $= 0$, tamen ratio certa inter ea intercedit, quae in calculo differentiali proprie investigatur. Ita si fuerit $y = x x$, in calculo differentiali ostenditur esse $\frac{\partial y}{\partial x} = 2 x$, neque hanc incrementorum rationem esse veram, nisi incrementum $\partial x$, ex quo $\partial y$ nascitur, nihilo aequale statuatur. Verum tamen, hac vera differentialium notione observata, locutiones communes, quibus differentialia quasi absolute enunciantur, tolerari possunt, dummodo semper in mente saltem ad veritatem referantur. Recte ergo dicimus, si $y = xx$, fore $\partial y = 2x\partial x$, tam etsi falsum non esset, si quis diceret $\partial y = 3 x \partial x$, vel $\partial y = 4 x \partial x$, quoniam ob $\partial x = 0$ et $\partial y = 0$, hae aequalitates aeque subsisterent; sed prima sola rationi verae $\frac{\partial y}{\partial x} = 2 x$ est consentanea.

### Scholion 2.

6. Quemadmodum calculus differentialis apud Anglos methodus fluxionum appellatur, ita calculus integralis ab iis methodus fluxionum inuersa vocari solet, quandoquidem a fluxionibus ad quantitates fluentes revertitur. Quas enim nos quantitates variabiles vocamus, eas Angli nomine magis idoneo quantitates fluentes vocant, et earum incrementa infinite parva seu evanescentia fluxiones nominant, ita vt fluxiones ipsis idem sint, quod nobis differentialia. Haec diversitas loquendi ita iam usu invaluit, ut conciliatio vix unquam sit expectanda; equidem Anglos in formulis loquendi luben-

ter imitarer, sed signa quibus nos utimur, illorum signis longe an-
teferenda videntur. Verum cum tot iam libri utraque ratione con-
scripti prodierint, huiusmodi conciliatio nullum usum esset habitura.

### Definitio 2.

7. Cum functionis cuiuscunque ipsius $x$ differentiale huiusmodi
habeat formam $X \partial x$, proposita tali forma differentiali $X \partial x$, in
qua X sit functio quaecunque ipsius $x$, illa functio, cuius differentiale est $= X \partial x$, huius vocatur integrale, et praefixo signo $\int$
indicari solet: ita vt $\int X \partial x$ eam denotet quantitatem variabilem,
cuius differentiale est $= X \partial x$.

### Corollarium 1.

8. Quemadmodum ergo propositae formulae differentialis $X \partial x$
integrale, seu ea functio ipsius $x$, cuius differentiale est $= X \partial x$,
quae hac scriptura $\int X \partial x$ indicatur, investigari debeat, in calculo
integrali est explicandum.

### Corollarium 2.

9. Uti ergo littera $\partial$ signum est differentiationis, ita littera
$\int$ pro signo integrationis utimur, sicque haec duo signa sibi mutuo
opponuntur, et quasi se destruunt: scilicet $\int \partial X$ erit $= X$, quia
ea quantitas denotatur cuius differentiale est $\partial X$, quae utique est X.

### Corollarium 3.

10. Cum igitur harum ipsius $x$ functionum

$$x^2, \quad x^n, \quad \sqrt{(aa - xx)}$$

differentialia sint

$$2x \partial x, \quad n x^{n-1} \partial x, \quad \frac{-x \partial x}{\sqrt{(aa - xx)}}$$

signo integrationis $\int$ adhibendo, patet fore:

$$\int 2x \partial x = xx; \quad \int n x^{n-1} \partial x = x^n; \quad \int \frac{-x \partial x}{\sqrt{(aa-xx)}} = \sqrt{(aa-xx)}$$

unde usus huius signi clarius perspicitur.

*Notation*

Euler used the notation $\partial y, \partial x$ where we would now use $dy, dx$. For partial derivatives, later, he used parentheses, thus, $\left(\dfrac{\partial z}{\partial x}\right)$.

TRANSLATION

# PRELIMINARY NOTES
ON
### INTEGRAL CALCULUS
### IN GENERAL

## Definition 1

1. *Integral calculus is the method of finding, from a given relationship between differentials, a relationship between the quantities themselves: and the operation by which this is carried out is usually called integration.*

## Corollary 1

2. Therefore where differential calculus teaches us to investigate the relationship between differentials from a given relationship between variable quantities, integral calculus supplies the inverse method.

## Corollary 2

3. Clearly just as in Analysis two operations are always contrary to each other, as subtraction to addition, division to multiplication, extraction of roots to raising of powers, so also by similar reasoning integral calculus is contrary to differential calculus.

## Corollary 3

4. Given any relationship between two variable quantities $x$ and $y$, in differential calculus there is taught a method of investigating the ratio of the differentials, $\partial y : \partial x$; but if from this ratio of differentials there can in turn be determined the relationship of the quantities $x$ and $y$, this matter is assigned to integral calculus.

## Commentary 1

5. I have already noted that in differential calculus the question of differentials must be understood not absolutely but relatively, thus if $y$ is any function of $x$, it is not the differential $\partial y$ itself but its ratio to the differential $\partial x$ that is determined. For since all differentials in themselves are equal to nothing, whatever may be the function $y$ of $x$, always $\partial y = 0$, and thus it is not possible to search more generally for anything absolute. But the question must rightly be proposed thus, that while $x$ takes an infinitely small and therefore vanishing increment $\partial x$, there is defined a ratio of the increment of the function $y$, which it takes as a result, to $\partial x$; for although both are $= 0$, nevertheless there stands a definite ratio between them, which is correctly investigated by differential calculus. Thus if $y = xx$, it is shown by differential calculus that $\dfrac{\partial y}{\partial x} = 2x$, nor is this ratio of increments true unless the increment $\partial x$, from which $\partial y$ arises, is put equal to nothing. But nevertheless, having observed this truth about differentials, one can tolerate common language, in which differentials are spoken of as absolutes, while always at least in the mind referring to the truth. Properly, therefore, we say if $y = xx$ then $\partial y = 2x\partial x$, even though it would not be

false if anyone said $\partial y = 3x\partial x$, or $\partial y = 4x\partial x$, for since $\partial x = 0$ and $\partial y = 0$, these equalities would equally well stand; but only the first of the ratios, $\dfrac{\partial y}{\partial x} = 2x$, is agreed to be true.

## Commentary 2

6. In the same way that the differential calculus is called by the English the method of fluxions, so integral calculus is usually called by them the inverse method of fluxions, since indeed one reverts from fluxions to fluent quantities. For what we call variable quantities, the English more fitly call by the name of fluent quantities, and their infinitely small or vanishing increments they call fluxions, so that fluxions are the same to them as differentials to us. This variation in language is already established in use, so that a reconciliation is scarcely ever to be expected; indeed we imitate the English freely in forms of speech, [3] but the notation that we use seems to have been established a long time before their notation. And indeed since so many books are already published written either way, a reconciliation of this kind would be of no use.

## Definition 2

7. Since the differentiation of any function of $x$ has a form of this kind, $X\partial x$, when such a differential form $X\partial x$ is proposed, in which $X$ is any function of $x$, that function whose differential $= X\partial x$ called its integral, and is usually indicated by the prefix $\int$, so that $\int X\partial x$ denotes that variable quantity whose differential $= X\partial x$.

## Corollary 1

8. Therefore from the integral of the proposed differential $X\partial x$, or from the function of $x$ whose differential $= X\partial x$, both of which will be indicated by this notation $\int X\partial x$, there is to be investigated whatever is to be explained by integral calculus.

## Corollary 2

9. Therefore just as the letter $\partial$ is the sign of differentiation, so we use the letter $\int$ as the sign of integration, and thus these two signs are mutually contrary to each other, as though they destroy each other: certainly $\int \partial X = X$, because by the former is denoted the quantity whose differential is $\partial X$, which in both cases is $X$.

## Corollary 3

10. Therefore since the differentials of these functions of $x$

$$x^2, \quad x^n, \quad \sqrt{(aa - xx)}$$

are

$$2x\partial x, \quad nx^{n-1}\partial x, \quad \frac{-x\partial x}{\sqrt{(aa - xx)}}$$

then adjoining the sign of integration $\int$, they are seen to become:

$$\int 2x\partial x = xx; \quad \int nx^{n-1}\partial x = x^n; \quad \int \frac{-x\partial x}{\sqrt{(aa - xx)}} = \sqrt{(aa - xx)}$$

whence the use of this sign is more clearly seen.

---

### Euler's integration of a differential equation

from Euler, *Institutiones calculi integralis*, 1768, I, §865–§866, here from third edition, 1824

---

# CAPUT V.

### DE

## INTEGRATIONE AEQUATIONUM DIFFERENTIALIUM SECUNDI GRADUS, IN QUIBUS ALTERA VARIABILIS UNAM DIMEN-SIONEM NON SUPERAT, PER FACTORES.

### Problema 107.

### 865.

Sumto elemento $\partial x$ constante, si proponatur haec aequatio

$$\partial \partial y + A \partial x \partial y + B y \partial x^2 = X \partial x^2,$$

ubi X denotat functionem quamcunque ipsius $x$, invenire functionem ipsius $x$, per quam haec aequatio multiplicata fiat integrabilis.

### Solutio.

Ponatur $\partial y = p \partial x$, ut habeatur forma differentialis primi gradus

$$\partial p + A p \partial x + B y \partial x = X \partial x,$$

quae multiplicata per V, functionem quandam ipsius $x$, fiat integrabilis; scilicet

$$V \partial p + A V p \partial x + B V y \partial x = V X \partial x,$$

ubi cum posterius membrum $V X \partial x$ sit integrabile, idem in priori eveniat, necesse est. At primo perspicuum est ejus integralis partem fore $V p$, unde id ponatur $V p + S$ ut sit $V p + S = \int V X \partial x$, fietque

### 13

C A P A T   V.

$$\partial \, \mathrm{S} = - \, p \, \partial \, \mathrm{V} + \mathrm{A} \, \mathrm{V} \, p \, \partial \, x + \mathrm{B} \, \mathrm{V} \, y \, \partial \, x, \text{ seu}$$

$$\partial \, \mathrm{S} = \partial \, y \left( \mathrm{A} \, \mathrm{V} - \tfrac{\partial \, \mathrm{V}}{\partial \, x} \right) + \mathrm{B} \, \mathrm{V} \, y \, \partial \, x,$$

quae forma integrabilis reddi potest sumendo $\mathrm{V} = e^{\lambda x}$, erit enim

$$\partial \, \mathrm{S} = e^{\lambda x} [(\mathrm{A} - \lambda) \, \partial y + \mathrm{B} y \partial x] \text{ et } \mathrm{S} = (\mathrm{A} - \lambda) \, e^{\lambda x} y,$$

ubi $\lambda$ ita debet accipi, ut fiat

$$\mathrm{A} \lambda - \lambda \lambda = \mathrm{B} \text{ seu } \lambda \lambda - \mathrm{A} \lambda + \mathrm{B} = 0.$$

Tum ergo erit

$$e^{\lambda x} p + (\mathrm{A} - \lambda) \, e^{\lambda x} y = \int e^{\lambda x} \mathrm{X} \partial x, \text{ seu}$$

$$\partial y + (\mathrm{A} - \lambda) y \partial x = e^{-\lambda x} \partial x \int e^{\lambda x} \mathrm{X} \partial x,$$

quae jam per $e^{(\mathrm{A} - \lambda) x}$ multiplicata denuo fit integrabilis, datque

$$e^{(\mathrm{A} - \lambda) x} y = \int e^{(\mathrm{A} - 2\lambda) x} \partial x \int e^{\lambda x} \mathrm{X} \partial x.$$

Cum $\lambda$ sit una radix aequationis $\lambda \lambda - \mathrm{A} \lambda + \mathrm{B} = 0$, si ambas ejus radices ponamus $f$ et $g$, ut sit $\lambda = f$, erit $\mathrm{A} - \lambda = g$, et aequatio integralis

$$e^{g x} y = \int e^{(g - f) x} \partial x \int e^{f x} \mathrm{X} \partial x, \text{ seu}$$

$$e^{g x} y = \tfrac{1}{g - f} e^{(g - f) x} \int e^{f x} \mathrm{X} \partial x - \tfrac{1}{g - f} \int e^{g x} \mathrm{X} \partial x,$$

quae abit in formam supra inventam

$$y = \tfrac{1}{g - f} e^{-f x} \int e^{f x} \mathrm{X} \partial x - \tfrac{1}{g - f} e^{-g x} \int e^{g x} \mathrm{X} \partial x.$$

C o r o l l a r i u m   1.

866.  Aequatio ergo proposita seu inde nata

$$\partial p + \mathrm{A} p \partial x + \mathrm{B} y \partial x = \mathrm{X} \partial x$$

fit integrabilis si ducatur in $e^{\lambda x}$, existente $\lambda \lambda - \mathrm{A} \lambda + \mathrm{B} = 0$, sicque duplex habetur factor vel $e^{f x}$ vel $e^{g x}$.

TRANSLATION

# CHAPTER V
### ON THE INTEGRATION BY FACTORS OF DIFFERENTIAL EQUATIONS
### OF SECOND DEGREE, IN WHICH NO VARIABLE
### EXCEEDS ONE DIMENSION

### Problem 107

865.

Taking the element $\partial x$ to be constant, if there is proposed the equation

$$\partial\partial y + A\partial x\partial y + By\partial x^2 = X\partial x^2,$$

where $X$ denotes any function of $x$, find the function of $x$ by which this equation multiplied is made integrable.

### Solution

Put $\partial y = p\partial x$, so that we have a differential form of the first degree

$$\partial p + Ap\partial x + By\partial x = X\partial x,$$

which multiplied by $V$, some function of $x$, becomes integrable; thus

$$V\partial p + AVp\partial x + BVy\partial x = VX\partial x,$$

where when the second side $VX\partial x$ is integrable, it must comes about the same way in the first side. But for the first side it is clear that part of its integral will be $Vp$, whence it can be put as $Vp + S$ so that $Vp + S = \int VX\partial x$, and then [98]

$$\partial S = -p\partial V + AVp\partial x + BVy\partial x, \quad \text{or}$$

$$\partial S = \partial y\left(AV - \frac{\partial V}{\partial x}\right) + BVy\partial x,$$

which form can be rendered integrable taking $V = e^{\lambda x}$, for then

$$\partial S = e^{\lambda x}[(A - \lambda)\partial y + By\partial x] \quad \text{and} \quad S = (A - \lambda)e^{\lambda x}y,$$

where $\lambda$ must be taken so that it makes

$$A\lambda - \lambda\lambda = B \quad \text{or} \quad \lambda\lambda - A\lambda + B = 0.$$

Then, therefore,

$$e^{\lambda x}p + (A - \lambda)e^{\lambda x}y = \int e^{\lambda x}X\partial x, \quad \text{or}$$

$$\partial y + (A - \lambda)y\partial x = e^{-\lambda x}\partial x \int e^{\lambda x}X\partial x,$$

which now multiplied by $e^{(A-\lambda)x}$ becomes integrable, and gives

$$e^{(A-\lambda)x}y = \int e^{(A-2\lambda)x}\partial x \int e^{\lambda x}X\partial x.$$

Since $\lambda$ is one root of the equation $\lambda\lambda - A\lambda + B = 0$, if for both of the roots we put $f$ and $g$, so that if $\lambda = f$ then $A - \lambda = g$, then the integral equation is

$$e^{gx}y = \int e^{(g-f)x}\partial x \int e^{fx}X\partial x, \quad \text{or}$$

$$e^{gx}y = \frac{1}{g-f}e^{(g-f)x}\int e^{fx}X\partial x - \frac{1}{g-f}\int e^{gx}X\partial x,$$

which goes into the form found above

$$y = \frac{1}{g-f}e^{-fx}\int e^{fx}X\partial x - \frac{1}{g-f}e^{-gx}\int e^{gx}X\partial x.$$

Corollary 1

866. Therefore the equation given or arising from

$$\partial p + Ap\partial x + By\partial x = X\partial x$$

becomes integrable if multiplied by $e^{\lambda x}$, where $\lambda\lambda - A\lambda + B = 0$, and thus we have two factors, $e^{fx}$ and $e^{gx}$.

_____

### 14.2.2 Cauchy's definite integral, 1823

In his *Théorie analytique de la chaleur* of 1822, Fourier put forward the remarkable result that the coefficient of $\sin nx$ in the expansion

$$\varphi(x) = a\sin x + b\sin 2x + c\sin 3x + \dots$$

is given by $\int \varphi(x)\sin nx dx$ (see 8.4.1). It is not always possible, however, to integrate $\varphi(x)\sin nx$ by algebraic methods. Fourier gave some thought to this problem, and argued that it *is* always possible to draw the curve of $\varphi(x)$, and therefore of $\varphi(x)\sin nx$, and hence to find the integral as an area:[1]

One must imagine that for each abscissa $x$, to which corresponds a value of $\varphi x$, and a value of $\sin x$, one multiplies this last value by the first, and that at the same point of the axis one raises an ordinate proportional to the product $\varphi x \sin x$. One will form, by this continual operation, a third curve, whose ordinates are those of the trigonometric curve, reduced proportionally to ordinates of the arbitrary curve that represents $\varphi x$. This said, the area of the reduced curve taken from $x = 0$ to $x = \pi$, will give the exact value of the coefficient of $\sin x$.

_____

1. 'Il faut concevoir que pour chaque abscisse $x$, à laquelle répond une valeur de $\varphi x$, et une valeur de $\sin x$, on multiplie cette dernière valeur par la première, et qu'au même point de l'axe on élève une ordonnée proportionelle au produit $\varphi x. \sin x$. On formera, par cette opération continuelle, une troisième courbe, dont les ordonnées sont celles de la courbe trigonométrique, réduite proportionellement aux ordonnées de la courbe arbitrarire qui représente $\varphi x$. Cela posé, l'aire de la courbe réduite étant prise depuis $x = 0$ jusqu'à $x = \pi$, donnera la valeur exacte du coëfficient de $\sin x$.' Fourier 1822, §220.

Fourier thus returned integration to its seventeenth-century incarnation: integral as area. The following year, in his *Résumé des leçons*, Cauchy borrowed from Fourier both the idea and some useful notation, and gave the first textbook definition of a definite integral. Cauchy's (and Fourier's) use of the symbol $\int$ leads the reader naturally to assume that an integral obtained through calculation of area is the same as an integral obtained by reverse differentiation, but in 1823 this still remained to be proved. That the two methods lead to identical results is now known as the Fundamental Theorem of Calculus.

---

## Cauchy's definite integral
from Cauchy, *Résumé des leçons*, 1823, Lessons 21 and 23

---

### VINGT-UNIÈME LEÇON.
*Intégrales définies.*

SUPPOSONS que, la fonction $y = f(x)$ étant continue par rapport à la variable $x$ entre deux limites finies $x = x_0$, $x = X$, on désigne par $x_1$, $x_2, \ldots x_{n-1}$ de nouvelles valeurs de $x$ interposées entre ces limites, et qui aillent toujours en croissant ou en décroissant depuis la première limite jusqu'à la seconde. On pourra se servir de ces valeurs, pour diviser la différence $X - x_0$ en élémens

$$(1) \qquad x_1 - x_0, \; x_2 - x_1, \; x_3 - x_2, \; \ldots \; X - x_{n-1}$$

qui seront tous de même signe. Cela posé, concevons que l'on multiplie chaque élément par la valeur de $f(x)$ correspondante à l'*origine* de ce même élément, savoir, l'élément $x_1 - x_0$ par $f(x_0)$, l'élément $x_2 - x_1$ par $f(x_1)$, &c.., enfin l'élément $X - x_{n-1}$ par $f(x_{n-1})$; et soit

$$(2) \quad S = (x_1 - x_0) f(x_0) + (x_2 - x_1) f(x_1) + \ldots + (X - x_{n-1}) f(x_{n-1})$$

la somme des produits ainsi obtenus. La quantité $S$ dépendra évidemment, 1.° du nombre $n$ des élémens dans lesquels on aura divisé la différence $X - x_0$, 2.° des valeurs mêmes de ces élémens, et par conséquent du mode de division adopté. Or, il importe de remarquer que, si les valeurs numériques des élémens deviennent très-petites et le nombre $n$ très-considérable, le mode de division n'aura plus sur la valeur de $S$ qu'une influence insensible. C'est effectivement ce que l'on peut démontrer, comme il suit.

Si l'on supposait tous les élémens de la différence $X - x_0$ réduits à un seul qui serait cette différence elle-même, on aurait simplement

$$(3) \qquad\qquad S = (X - x_0) f(x_0).$$

Lorsqu'au contraire on prend les expressions (1) pour élémens de la différence $X - x_0$, la valeur de $S$, déterminée dans ce cas par l'équation (2), est égale à la somme des élémens multipliée par une moyenne entre les coefficiens

$$f(x_0), \; f(x_1), \; f(x_2), \; \ldots \; f(x_{n-1})$$

*Leçons de M. Cauchy.*                                                    V

82                    COURS D'ANALYSE.

[*voyez* dans les préliminaires du *Cours d'analyse*, le corollaire du 3.$^e$ théor.].

D'ailleurs, ces coefficiens étant des valeurs particulières de l'expression

$$f[x_0 + \theta(X - x_0)]$$

qui correspondent à des valeurs de $\theta$ comprises entre zéro et l'unité, on prouvera, par des raisonnemens semblables à ceux dont nous avons fait usage dans la 7.$^e$ leçon, que la moyenne dont il s'agit est une autre valeur de la même expression, correspondante à une valeur de $\theta$ comprise entre les mêmes limites. On pourra donc à l'équation (2) substituer la suivante

(4)              $$S = (X - x_0) f[x_0 + \theta(X - x_0)],$$

dans laquelle $\theta$ sera un nombre inférieur à l'unité.

Pour passer du mode de division que nous venons de considérer à un autre dans lequel les valeurs numériques des élémens de $X - x_0$ soient encore plus petites, il suffira de partager chacune des expressions (1) en de nouveaux élémens. Alors on devra remplacer, dans le second membre de l'équation (2), le produit $(x_1 - x_0) f(x_0)$ par une somme de produits semblables, à laquelle on pourra substituer une expression de la forme

$$(x_1 - x_0) f[x_0 + \theta_0(x_1 - x_0)],$$

$\theta_0$ étant un nombre inférieur à l'unité, attendu qu'il y aura entre cette somme et le produit $(x_1 - x_0) f(x_0)$ une relation pareille à celle qui existe entre les valeurs de $S$ fournies par les équations (4) et (3). Par la même raison, on devra substituer au produit $(x_2 - x_1) f(x_1)$ une somme de termes qui pourra être présentée sous la forme

$$(x_2 - x_1) f[x_1 + \theta_1(x_2 - x_1)],$$

$\theta_1$ désignant encore un nombre inférieur à l'unité. En continuant de la sorte, on finira par conclure que, dans le nouveau mode de division, la valeur de $S$ sera de la forme

(5)  $$S = (x_1 - x_0) f[x_0 + \theta_0(x_1 - x_0)] + (x_2 - x_1) f[x_1 + \theta_1(x_2 - x_1)] + \dots$$
$$+ (X - x_{n-1}) f[x_{n-1} + \theta_{n-1}(X - x_{n-1})].$$

Si l'on fait dans cette dernière équation

$$f[x_0 + \theta_0(x_1 - x_0)] = f(x_0) \pm \varepsilon_0, \; f[x_1 + \theta_1(x_2 - x_1)] = f(x_1) \pm \varepsilon_1, \dots$$
$$\dots\dots\dots\dots\dots\dots\dots\dots f[x_{n-1} + \theta_{n-1}(X - x_{n-1})] = f(x_{n-1}) \pm \varepsilon_{n-1},$$

on en tirera

COURS D'ANALYSE. 83

(6) $S = (x_1 - x_0)[f(x_0) \pm \varepsilon_0] + (x_2 - x_1)[f(x_1) \pm \varepsilon_1] + .. + (X - x_{n-1})[f(x_{n-1}) \pm \varepsilon_{n-1}]$

puis, en développant les produits,

(7) $S = (x_1 - x_0)f(x_0) + (x_2 - x_1)f(x_1) + ... + (X - x_{n-1})f(x_{n-1})$
$\pm \varepsilon_0 (x_1 - x_0) \pm \varepsilon_1 (x_2 - x_1) \pm ... \pm \varepsilon_{n-1} (X - x_{n-1}).$

Ajoutons que, si les élémens $x_1 - x_0, x_2 - x_1, ... X - x_{n-1}$ ont des valeurs numériques très-petites, chacune des quantités $\pm \varepsilon_0, \pm \varepsilon_1, ... \pm \varepsilon_{n-1}$ différera très-peu de zéro, et que par suite il en sera de même de la somme

$$\pm \varepsilon_0 (x_1 - x_0) \pm \varepsilon_1 (x_2 - x_1) \pm ..... \pm \varepsilon_{n-1} (X - x_{n-1}),$$

qui est équivalente au produit de $X - x_0$ par une moyenne entre ces diverses quantités. Cela posé, il résulte des équations (2) et (7) comparées entre elles qu'on n'altérera pas sensiblement la valeur de $S$ calculée pour un mode de division dans lequel les élémens de la différence $X - x_0$ ont des valeurs numériques très-petites, si l'on passe à un second mode dans lequel chacun de ces élémens se trouve subdivisé en plusieurs autres.

Concevons à présent que l'on considère à-la-fois deux modes de division de la différence $X - x_0$, dans chacun desquels les élémens de cette différence aient de très-petites valeurs numériques. On pourra comparer ces deux modes à un troisième tellement choisi, que chaque élément, soit du premier, soit du second mode, se trouve formé par la réunion de plusieurs élémens du troisième. Pour que cette condition soit remplie, il suffira que toutes les valeurs de $x$, interposées dans les deux premiers modes entre les limites $x_0$, $X$, soient employées dans le troisième, et l'on prouvera que l'on altère très-peu la valeur de $S$, en passant du premier ou du second mode au troisième, par conséquent, en passant du premier au second. Donc, lorsque les élémens de la différence $X - x_0$ deviennent infiniment petits, le mode de division n'a plus sur la valeur de $S$ qu'une influence insensible; et, si l'on fait décroître indéfiniment les valeurs numériques de ces élémens, en augmentant leur nombre, la valeur de $S$ finira par être sensiblement constante, ou, en d'autres termes, elle finira par atteindre une certaine limite qui dépendra uniquement de la forme de la fonction $f(x)$, et des valeurs extrêmes $x_0$, $X$ attribuées à la variable $x$. Cette limite est ce qu'on appelle une *intégrale définie*.

84                        COURS D'ANALYSE.

Observons maintenant que, si l'on désigne par $\Delta x = h = dx$ un accroissement fini attribué à la variable $x$, les differens termes dont se
compose la valeur de $S$, tels que les produits $(x_1 - x_0)f(x_0), (x_2 - x_1)f(x_1)$,
&c... seront tous compris dans la formule générale

(8)                        $h f(x) = f(x) \, dx$

de laquelle on les déduira l'un après l'autre, en posant d'abord $x = x_0$
et $h = x_1 - x_0$, puis $x = x_1$ et $h = x_2 - x_1$, &c... On peut donc énoncer que la quantité $S$ est une somme de produits semblables à l'expression (8); ce qu'on exprime quelquefois à l'aide de la caractéristique $\Sigma$
en écrivant

(9)                        $S = \Sigma h f(x) = \Sigma f(x) \, \Delta x.$

Quant à l'intégrale définie vers laquelle converge la quantité $S$, tandis que les élémens de la différence $X - x_0$ deviennent infiniment petits,
on est convenu de la représenter par la notation $\int h f(x)$ ou $\int f(x) \, dx$, dans
laquelle la lettre $\int$ substituée à la lettre $\Sigma$ indique, non plus une somme
de produits semblables à l'expression (8), mais la limite d'une somme
de cette espèce. De plus, comme la valeur de l'intégrale définie que
l'on considère dépend des valeurs extrêmes $x_0$, $X$ attribuées à la variable
$x$, on est convenu de placer ces deux valeurs, la première au-dessous,
la seconde au-dessus de la lettre $\int$, ou de les écrire à côté de l'intégrale,
que l'on désigne en conséquence par l'une des notations

(10)        $\int_{x_0}^{X} f(x) \, dx$,    $\int f(x) \, dx \begin{bmatrix} x_0 \\ X \end{bmatrix}$,    $\int f(x) \, dx \begin{bmatrix} x = x_0 \\ x = X \end{bmatrix}.$

La première de ces notations, imaginée par M. *Fourier*, est la plus simple.
Dans le cas particulier où la fonction $f(x)$ est remplacée par une quantité constante $a$, on trouve, quel que soit le mode de division de la différence $X - x_0$,            $S = a(X - x_0)$,            et l'on en conclut

(11)                        $\int_{x_0}^{X} a \, dx = a(X - x_0),$

Si, dans cette dernière formule on pose $a = 1$, on en tirera

(12)                        $\int_{x_0}^{X} dx = X - x_0.$

————————

[...]

Concevons à présent que, la limite $X$ étant supérieure à $x_0$, et la fonction $f(x)$ étant positive depuis $x=x_0$ jusqu'à $x=X$, $x, y$ désignent des coordonnées rectangulaires, et $A$ la surface comprise d'une part entre l'axe des $x$ et la courbe $y=f(x)$, d'autre part entre les ordonnées $f(x_0)$, $f(X)$. Cette surface, qui a pour base la longueur $X-x_0$ comptée sur l'axe des $x$, sera une moyenne entre les aires des deux rectangles construits sur la base $X-x_0$ avec des hauteurs respectivement égales à la plus petite et à la plus grande des ordonnées élevées par les différens points de cette base. Elle sera donc équivalente à un rectangle construit sur une ordonnée moyenne représentée par une expression de la forme $f[x_0+\theta(X-x_0)]$; en sorte qu'on aura

$$(8) \qquad A=(X-x_0)f[x_0+\theta(X-x_0)],$$

$\theta$ désignant un nombre inférieur à l'unité. Si l'on divise la base $X-x_0$ en élémens très-petits, $x_1-x_0$, $x_2-x_1, \dots X-x_{n-1}$, la surface $A$ se trouvera divisée en élémens correspondans dont les valeurs seront données par des équations semblables à la formule (8). On aura donc encore

$$(9) \quad A=(x_1-x_0)f[x_0+\theta_0(x_1-x_0)]+(x_2-x_1)f[x_1+\theta_1(x_2-x_1)]+\dots$$
$$\dots\dots\dots\dots\dots\dots+(X-x_{n-1})f[x_{n-1}+\theta_{n-1}(X-x_{n-1})],$$

$\theta_0, \theta_1, \dots \theta_{n-1}$, désignant des nombres inférieurs à l'unité. Si dans cette dernière équation on fait décroître indéfiniment les valeurs numériques des élémens de $X-x_0$, on en tirera, en passant aux limites,

$$(10) \qquad A=\int_{x_0}^{X}f(x)\,dx.$$

TRANSLATION

## TWENTY-FIRST LESSON

### Definite integrals

SUPPOSE that, the function $y=f(x)$ being continuous with respect to the variable $x$ between two finite limits $x=x_0$ and $x=X$, one denotes by $x_1, x_2, \dots x_{n-1}$ some new values of $x$ interposed between these limits, which always proceed by increasing or by decreasing from the first limit to the second. One may use these values to divide the difference $X-x_0$ into elements

$$(1) \qquad x_1-x_0, x_2-x_1, x_3-x_2, \dots X-x_{n-1}$$

which will be all of the same sign. That done, imagine that one multiplies each element by the value of $f(x)$ corresponding to the *beginning* of the same element, that is, the element $x_1-x_0$ by $f(x_0)$, the element $x_2-x_1$ by $f(x_1)$, etc., and finally the element $X-x_{n-1}$ by $f(x_{n-1})$; and let

(2)        $S = (x_1 - x_0)f(x_0) + (x_2 - x_1)f(x_1) + \cdots + (X - x_{n-1})f(x_{n-1})$

be the sum of the products thus obtained. The quantity $S$ will clearly depend, first, on the number $n$ of elements into which one will have divided the difference $X - x_0$, second, on the values themselves of these elements, and consequently on the method of division adopted. Now, it is important to remark that, if the absolute values of the elements become very small and the number $n$ very large, the method of division will have no more than a negligible influence on the value of $S$. This is effectively what one may demonstrate as follows.

If one supposed all the elements of the difference $X - x_0$ reduced to a single one, which would be this difference itself, one would have simply

(3)                        $S = (X - x_0)f(x_0)$.

When on the contrary one takes the expressions (1) for the elements of the difference $X - x_0$, the value of $S$, determined in this case by equation (2), is equal to the sum of the elements multiplied by a mean of the coefficients

$$f(x_0), f(x_1), f(x_2), \ldots f(x_{n-1})$$

[82] (*see* the preliminaries of the *Cours d'analyse*, corollary to the $3^{rd}$ theorem). Besides, these coefficients being particular values of the expression

$$f[x_0 + \theta(X - x_0)]$$

which correspond to values of $\theta$ contained between zero and one, we may prove, by reasoning similar to that of which we made use in the seventh lesson, that the mean with which we are concerned is another value of the same expression, corresponding to a value of $\theta$ contained between the same limits. One may therefore substitute the following in equation (2)

(4)                    $S = (X - x_0)f[x_0 + \theta(X - x_0)]$,

in which $\theta$ will be a number less than one.

To pass from the method of division we have just considered to another in which the absolute values of the elements $x - x_0$ are yet smaller, it will suffice to partition each of the expressions (1) into new elements. Then one must replace, in the second side of equation (2), the product $(x_1 - x_0)f(x_0)$ by a sum of similar products, for which one may substitute an expression of the form

$$(x_1 - x_0)f[x_0 + \theta_0(x_1 - x_0)],$$

where $\theta_0$ is a number less than one, seeing that between this sum and the product $(x_1 - x_0)f(x_0)$ there will be a similar relationship to that which exists between the values of $S$ given by equations (4) and (3). For the same reason, one must substitute for the product $(x_2 - x_1)f(x_1)$, a sum of terms which may be presented in the form

$$(x_2 - x_1)f[x_1 + \theta_1(x_2 - x_1)],$$

where $\theta_1$ again denotes a number less than one. Continuing in this way, one will end by concluding that, in the new method of division, the value of $S$ will be of the form

$$(5) \qquad S = (x_1 - x_0)f[x_0 + \theta_0(x_1 - x_0)] + (x_2 - x_1)f[x_1 + \theta_1(x_2 - x_1)] + \ldots$$

$$+ (X - x_{n-1})f[x_{n-1} + \theta_{n-1}(X - x_{n-1})].$$

If one puts in this last equation

$$f[x_0 + \theta_0(x_1 - x_0)] = f(x_0) \pm \varepsilon_0, f[x_1 + \theta_1(x_2 - x_1)] = f(x_1) \pm \varepsilon_1, \ldots$$

$$\ldots\ldots f[x_{n-1} + \theta_{n-1}(X - x_{n-1})] = f(x_{n-1}) \pm \varepsilon_{n-1},$$

one will obtain from it [83]

$$(6) \quad S = (x_1 - x_0)[f(x_0) \pm \varepsilon_0] + (x_2 - x_1)[f(x_1) \pm \varepsilon_1] + \ldots + (X - x_{n-1})[f(x_{n-1}) \pm \varepsilon_{n-1}]$$

then, by expanding the products,

$$(7) \qquad S = (x_1 - x_0)f(x_0) + (x_2 - x_1)f(x_1) + \cdots + (X - x_{n-1})f(x_{n-1})$$

$$\pm \varepsilon_0(x_1 - x_0) \pm \varepsilon_1(x_2 - x_1) \pm \cdots \pm \varepsilon_{n-1}(X - x_{n-1}).$$

We add that, if the elements $x_1 - x_0, x_2 - x_1, \ldots X - x_{n-1}$ have very small absolute values, each of the quantities $\pm\varepsilon_0, \pm\varepsilon_1, \cdots \pm \varepsilon_{n-1}$ will differ very little from zero, and consequently that it will be the same for the sum

$$\pm\varepsilon_0(x_1 - x_0), \pm\varepsilon_1(x_2 - x_1) \pm \cdots \pm \varepsilon_{n-1}(X - x_{n-1}),$$

which is equivalent to the product of $X - x_0$ by a mean of the various quantities. That said, it follows by comparing equations (2) and (7) that one will not noticeably change the value of $S$ calculated by a method of division in which the elements of the difference $X - x_0$ have very small absolute values, if one passes to a second method of division in which each of the elements is subdivided into several others.

Let us imagine for now that one is considering at the same time two methods of dividing the difference $X - x_0$, in each of which the elements of the difference have very small absolute values. One may compare these two methods with a third, so chosen that each element, whether of the first method or the second, is formed as the union of several elements of the third. For this condition to be satisfied, it will be sufficient that all the values of $x$ interposed in the first two methods between the limits $x_0$ and $X$, are used in the third, and one may prove that one alters the value of $S$ very little by passing from the first or second method to the third, and consequently by passing from the first to the second. Therefore, when the elements of the difference $X - x_0$ become infinitely small, the method of division has no more than a negligible influence on the value of $S$; and if one makes the absolute values of the elements decrease indefinitely, by increasing their number, the value of $S$ will end by being essentially constant, or, in other words, it will end by attaining a certain limit which will depend uniquely on the form of the function $f(x)$, and the extremes $x_0$ and $X$ given to the variable $x$. This limit is what one calls a *definite integral*. [84] Now observe that if one denotes by $\Delta x = h = dx$ a finite increase given to the variable $x$, the different terms of which the value of $S$ is composed, such as the products $(x_1 - x_0)f(x_0)$, $(x_2 - x_1)f(x_1)$, etc. will all be contained in the general formula

(8)                                    $hf(x) = f(x)dx$

from which one may deduce them one after the other, putting first $x = x_0$ and $h = x_1 - x_0$, then $x = x_1$ and $h = x_2 - x_1$, etc. One may therefore say that the quantity $S$ is a sum of products similar to expression (8); this is what one sometimes expresses by means of the symbol $\Sigma$ by writing

(9)                              $S = \Sigma hf(x) = \Sigma f(x)\Delta x.$

As to the definite integral towards which the quantity $S$ converges, as long as the elements of the difference $X - x_0$ become infinitely small, it is convenient to represent it by the notation $\int hf(x)$ or $\int f(x)dx$, in which the letter $\int$ substituted for the letter $\Sigma$ indicates no longer a sum of products similar to expression (8) but the limit of a sum of this kind. Further, since the value of the definite integral that one is considering depends on the extreme values $x_0$ and $X$ given to the variable $x$, it is convenient to place these two values, the first below the letter $\int$, the second above, or to write them at the side of the integral, which one consequently denotes by one of the notations

(10)        $\displaystyle\int_{x_0}^{X} f(x)dx, \quad \int f(x)dx \left[\begin{array}{c} x_0 \\ X \end{array}\right], \quad \int f(x)dx \left[\begin{array}{c} x = x_0 \\ x = X \end{array}\right].$

The first of these notations, created by Monsieur *Fourier*, is the simplest. In the particular case where the function $f(x)$ is replaced by a constant quantity $a$, one finds, whatever the method of division of the difference $X - x_0$,

$$S = a(X - x_0),$$

and one concludes from that

(11)                          $\displaystyle\int_{x_0}^{X} adx = a(X - x_0).$

If, in this last formula, one puts $a = 1$ one will obtain from it

(12)                          $\displaystyle\int_{x_0}^{X} dx = X - x_0.$

$$[\ldots]$$

[continuing, from the twenty-third Lesson]

Imagine now, the limit $X$ being greater than $x_0$, and the function $f(x)$ being positive from $x = x_0$ to $x = X$, that $x$, $y$, denote rectangular co-ordinates, and $A$ the area contained between the $x$-axis and the curve $y = f(x)$ in one direction, and between the ordinates $f(x_0)$ and $f(X)$ in the other. This area, which has for base the length $X - x_0$ taken along the $x$-axis, will be a mean between the areas of two rectangles constructed on the base $X - x_0$ with heights respectively equal to the smallest and the largest of the ordinates standing at different points on this base. It will therefore be equivalent to a rectangle constructed on a mean ordinate represented by an expression of the form $f[x_0 + \theta(X - x_0)]$; so that one will have

(8) $$A = (X - x) f[x_0 + \theta(X - x_0)],$$

where $\theta$ denotes a number less than one. If one divides the base $X - x_0$ into very small elements $x_1 - x_0, x_2 - x_1, \ldots X - x_{n-1}$, the area $A$ will be divided into corresponding elements, the values of which will be given by equations like formula (8). One will therefore again have

(9) $$A = (x_1 - x_0)f[x_0 + \theta_0(x_1 - x_0)] + (x_2 - x_1)f[x_1 + \theta_1(x_2 - x_1)] + \cdots$$
$$\cdots\cdots + (X - x_{n-1})f[x_{n-1} + \theta_{n-1}(X - x_{n-1})],$$

where $\theta_0, \theta_1 \ldots \theta_{n-1}$ denote numbers less than one. If in this last equation one makes the absolute values of the elements of $X - x_0$ decrease indefinitely, one will obtain from it, by passing to the limits,

(10) $$A = \int_{x_0}^{X} f(x)\,dx.$$

___

### 14.2.3 Cauchy and the fundamental theorem of calculus, 1823

In the twenty-sixth lesson of the *Résumé des leçons,* Cauchy was able to bring several of his previous results together to prove the Fundamental Theorem of Calculus, namely, that integration defined by taking the limit of a sum, and integration defined as the inverse of differentiation, were in fact identical (thereby justifying his earlier use of the symbol $\int$ for both).

## The fundamental theorem of the calculus
from Cauchy, *Résumé des leçons*, 1823, Lesson 26

COURS D'ANALYSE.                    101

## VINGT-SIXIÈME LEÇON.
### *Intégrales indéfinies.*

Si , dans l'intégrale définie $\int_{x_0}^{X} f(x)\,dx$ , on fait varier l'une des deux limites, par exemple , la quantité $X$ , l'intégrale variera elle-même avec cette quantité ; et, si l'on remplace la limite $X$ devenue variable par $x$ , on obtiendra pour résultat une nouvelle fonction de $x$ , qui sera ce qu'on appelle une intégrale prise à partir de *l'origine* $x = x_0$. Soit

(1) $$\mathscr{F}(x) = \int_{x_0}^{x} f(x)\,dx$$

cette fonction nouvelle. On tirera de la formule (19) [22.ᵉ leçon]

(2) $$\mathscr{F}(x) = (x - x_0) f[x_0 + \theta(x - x_0)], \quad \mathscr{F}(x_0) = 0 ,$$

$\theta$ étant un nombre inférieur à l'unité ; et de la formule (7) [23.ᵉ leçon]

$$\int_{x_0}^{x+a} f(x)\,dx - \int_{x_0}^{x} f(x)\,dx = \int_{x}^{x+a} f(x)\,dx = a\,f(x+\theta a), \quad \text{ou}$$

(3) $$\mathscr{F}(x+a) - \mathscr{F}(x) = a\,f(x+\theta a).$$

Il suit des équations (2) et (3) que , si la fonction $f(x)$ est finie et continue dans le voisinage d'une valeur particulière attribuée à la variable $x$ , la nouvelle fonction $\mathscr{F}(x)$ sera non-seulement finie, mais encore continue dans le voisinage de cette valeur , puisqu'à un accroissement infiniment petit de $x$ correspondra un accroissement infiniment petit de $\mathscr{F}(x)$. Donc , si la fonction $f(x)$ reste finie et continue depuis $x = x_0$ jusqu'à $x = X$, il en sera de même de la fonction $\mathscr{F}(x)$. Ajoutons que , si l'on divise par $a$ les deux membres de la formule (3), on en conclura , en passant aux limites ,

(4) $$\mathscr{F}'(x) = f(x).$$

Donc l'intégrale (1), considérée comme fonction de $x$ , a pour dérivée la fonction $f(x)$ renfermée sous le signe $\int$ dans cette intégrale. On prouverait de la même manière que l'intégrale $\int_{x}^{X} f(x)\,dx = -\int_{X}^{x} f(x)\,dx$ ,

*Leçons de M. Cauchy,*                              B b

## TWENTY-SIXTH LESSON
### *Indefinite integrals*

If in the definite integral $\int_{x_0}^X f(x)\,dx$ one makes one of the two limits vary, for example, the quantity $X$, the integral itself will vary with this quantity; and if one replaces the variable limit $X$ by $x$, one will obtain as a result a new function of $x$, which will be what one calls an integral taken from the *origin*, $x = x_0$. Let

$$(1) \qquad\qquad F = \int_{x_0}^x f(x)\,dx$$

be this new function. One will obtain from formula (19) ($22^{nd}$ lesson)

$$(2) \qquad F(x) = (x - x_0)f[x_0 + \theta(x - x_0)], \quad F(x_0) = 0,$$

where $\theta$ is a number less than one; and from formula (7) ($23^{rd}$ lesson)

$$\int_{x_0}^{x+\alpha} f(x)\,dx - \int_{x_0}^x f(x)\,dx = \int_x^{x+\alpha} f(x)\,dx = \alpha f(x + \theta\alpha), \quad \text{where}$$

$$(3) \qquad\qquad F(x + \alpha) - F(x) = \alpha f(x + \theta\alpha).$$

It follows from equations (2) and (3) that if the function $f(x)$ is finite and continuous in the neighbourhood of a particular value given to the variable $x$, the new function $F(x)$ will be not only finite but also continuous in the neighbourhood of that value, because an infinitely small increase in $x$ will correspond to an infinitely small increase in $F(x)$. Therefore, if the function $f(x)$ remains finite and continuous from $x = x_0$ to $x = X$, it will be the same for the function $F(x)$. We add that, if one divides the two sides of formula (3) by $\alpha$, one may conclude, by passing to the limits,

$$(4) \qquad\qquad F'(x) = f(x).$$

Therefore the integral (1), considered as a function of $x$, has for derivative the function $f(x)$ contained under the sign $\int$ in that integral.

------

## 14.2.4  Riemann integration, 1854

The mathematics of Bernhard Riemann is now collected in a single modest volume entitled *Gesammelte mathematische Werke* (1876), but this small quantity of published material is in no way commensurate with Riemann's influence on nineteenth-century mathematics, which was profound and long-lasting. His contribution to complex function theory is acknowledged by the attachment of his name to the Cauchy–Riemann equations and to Riemann surfaces; his quite different but equally important work on the distribution of primes is remembered through the Riemann $\zeta$-function and the Riemann hypothesis.

Some of Riemann's most important work was done in the earliest stages of his career, in his PhD thesis of 1851 and his *Habilitationschrift*, required for entry to university teaching, submitted in late 1853. The latter was on the subject of Fourier series, and in it Riemann took up the question Fourier had touched on in 1822: what are we to understand by the expression $\int_a^b f(x)\,dx$? His answer was a definition of integration far more precise than any that had been given previously. It was based on the one given by Cauchy in 1823 but with the additional requirement that the sums must converge for *all possible* partitions of the interval $[a, b]$ and *all possible* values of the variable that Cauchy called $\theta$ but Riemann called $\varepsilon$.

## Riemann integration

from Riemann, *Über die Darstellbarkeit einer Function durch eine trigonometrische Reihe*, 1854, §4–§5; from *Werke*, 1876, 225–227

### Ueber den Begriff eines bestimmten Integrals und den Umfang seiner Gültigkeit.

#### 4.

Die Unbestimmtheit, welche noch in einigen Fundamentalpunkten der Lehre von den bestimmten Integralen herrscht, nöthigt uns, Einiges voraufzuschicken über den Begriff eines bestimmten Integrals und den Umfang seiner Gültigkeit.

Also zuerst: Was hat man unter $\int_a^b f(x)\,dx$ zu verstehen?

Um dieses festzusetzen, nehmen wir zwischen $a$ und $b$ der Grösse nach auf einander folgend, eine Reihe von Werthen $x_1, x_2, \ldots, x_{n-1}$ an und bezeichnen der Kürze wegen $x_1 - a$ durch $\delta_1$, $x_2 - x_1$ durch $\delta_2, \ldots, b - x_{n-1}$ durch $\delta_n$ und durch $\varepsilon$ einen positiven ächten Bruch. Es wird alsdann der Werth der Summe

$$S = \delta_1\,f(a + \varepsilon_1\,\delta_1) + \delta_2\,f(x_1 + \varepsilon_2\,\delta_2) + \delta_3\,f(x_2 + \varepsilon_3\,\delta_3) + \cdots \\ + \delta_n\,f(x_{n-1} + \varepsilon_n\,\delta_n)$$

von der Wahl der Intervalle $\delta$ und der Grössen $\varepsilon$ abhängen. Hat sie nun die Eigenschaft, wie auch $\delta$ und $\varepsilon$ gewählt werden mögen, sich einer festen Grenze $A$ unendlich zu nähern, sobald sämmtliche $\delta$ unendlich klein werden, so heisst dieser Werth $\int_a^b f(x)\,dx$.

Hat sie diese Eigenschaft nicht, so hat $\int_a^b f(x)\,dx$ keine Bedeutung. Man hat jedoch in mehreren Fällen versucht, diesem Zeichen auch dann eine Bedeutung beizulegen, und unter diesen Erweiterungen des Begriffs eines bestimmten Integrals ist e i n e von allen Mathematikern angenommen. Wenn nämlich die Function $f(x)$ bei Annäherung des Arguments an einen einzelnen Werth $c$ in dem Intervalle $(a, b)$ unendlich gross wird, so kann offenbar die Summe $S$, welchen Grad von Kleinheit man auch den $\delta$ vorschreiben möge, jeden beliebigen

226        XII.  Ueber die Darstellbarkeit einer Function

Werth erhalten; sie hat also keinen Grenzwerth, und $\int_a^h \dot{f}(x)\,dx$ würde

nach dem Obigen keine Bedeutung haben.  Wenn aber alsdann

$$\int_a^{c-\alpha_1} \dot{f}(x)\,dx + \int_{c+\alpha_2}^h f(x)\,dx$$

sich, wenn $\alpha_1$ und $\alpha_2$ unendlich klein werden, einer festen Grenze

nähert, so versteht man unter $\int_a^b \dot{f}(x)\,dx$ diesen Grenzwerth.

Andere Festsetzungen von Cauchy über den Begriff des bestimmten Integrales in den Fällen, wo es dem Grundbegriffe nach ein solches nicht giebt, mögen für einzelne Klassen von Untersuchungen
zweckmässig sein; sie sind indess nicht allgemein eingeführt und dazu,
schon wegen ihrer grossen Willkürlichkeit, wohl kaum geeignet.

### 5.

Untersuchen wir jetzt zweitens den Umfang der Gültigkeit dieses
Begriffs oder die Frage: in welchen Fällen lässt eine Function eine
Integration zu und in welchen nicht?
Wir betrachten zunächst den Integralbegriff im engern Sinne,
d. h. wir setzen voraus, dass die Summe $S$, wenn sämmtliche $\delta$ unendlich klein werden, convergirt.  Bezeichnen wir also die grösste
Schwankung der Function zwischen $a$ und $x_1$, d. h. den Unterschied
ihres grössten und kleinsten Werthes in diesem Intervalle, durch $D_1$,
zwischen $x_1$ und $x_2$ durch $D_2$ ...., zwischen $x_{n-1}$ und $b$ durch $D_n$,
so muss

$$\delta_1 D_1 + \delta_2 D_2 + \cdots + \delta_n D_n$$

mit den Grössen $\delta$ unendlich klein werden.  Wir nehmen ferner an,
dass, so lange sämmtliche $\delta$ kleiner als $d$ bleiben, der grösste Werth,
den diese Summe erhalten kann, $\Delta$ sei; $\Delta$ wird alsdann eine Function
von $d$ sein, welche mit $d$ immer abnimmt und mit dieser Grösse unendlich klein wird.  Ist nun die Gesammtgrösse der Intervalle, in
welchen die Schwankungen grösser als $\sigma$ sind, $= s$, so wird der Beitrag dieser Intervalle zur Summe $\delta_1 D_1 + \delta_2 D_2 + \cdots + \delta_n D_n$ offenbar $\geqq \sigma s$.  Man hat daher

$$\sigma s \overline{\overline{\lessgtr}} \delta_1 D_1 + \delta_2 D_2 + \cdots + \delta_n D_n \overline{\overline{\lessgtr}} \Delta,\ \text{folglich}\ s \overline{\overline{\lessgtr}} \frac{\Delta}{\sigma}\,.$$

$\frac{\Delta}{\sigma}$ kann nun, wenn $\sigma$ gegeben ist, immer durch geeignete Wahl von *d* beliebig klein gemacht werden; dasselbe gilt daher von *s*, und es ergiebt sich also:

Damit die Summe *S*, wenn sämmtliche *δ* unendlich klein werden, convergirt, ist ausser der Endlichkeit der Function *f(x)* noch erforderlich, dass die Gesammtgrösse der Intervalle, in welchen die Schwankungen $> σ$ sind, was auch *σ* sei, durch geeignete Wahl von *d* beliebig klein gemacht werden kann.

Dieser Satz lässt sich auch umkehren:

Wenn die Function *f(x)* immer endlich ist, und bei unendlichem Abnehmen sämmtlicher Grössen *δ* die Gesammtgrösse *s* der Intervalle, in welchen die Schwankungen der Function *f(x)* grösser, als eine gegebene Grösse *σ*, sind, stets zuletzt unendlich klein wird, so convergirt die Summe *S*, wenn sämmtliche *δ* unendlich klein werden.

Denn diejenigen Intervalle, in welchen die Schwankungen $> σ$ sind, liefern zur Summe $δ_1 D_1 + δ_2 D_2 + \cdots + δ_n D_n$ einen Beitrag, kleiner als *s*, multiplicirt in die grösste Schwankung der Function zwischen *a* und *b*, welche (n. V.) endlich ist; die übrigen Intervalle einen Beitrag $< σ (b - a)$. Offenbar kann man nun erst *σ* beliebig klein annehmen und dann immer noch die Grösse der Intervalle (n. V.) so bestimmen, dass auch *s* beliebig klein wird, wodurch der Summe $δ_1 D_1 + \cdots + δ_n D_n$ jede beliebige Kleinheit gegeben, und folglich der Werth der Summe *S* in beliebig enge Grenzen eingeschlossen werden kann.

Wir haben also Bedingungen gefunden, welche nothwendig und hinreichend sind, damit die Summe *S* bei unendlichem Abnehmen der Grössen *δ* convergire und also im engern Sinne von einem Integrale der Function *f(x)* zwischen *a* und *b* die Rede sein könne.

Wird nun der Integralbegriff wie oben erweitert, so ist offenbar, damit die Integration durchgehends möglich sei, die letzte der beiden gefundenen Bedingungen auch dann noch nothwendig; an die Stelle der Bedingung, dass die Function immer endlich sei, aber tritt die Bedingung, dass die Function nur bei Annäherung des Arguments an einzelne Werthe unendlich werde, und dass sich ein bestimmter Grenzwerth ergebe, wenn die Grenzen der Integration diesen Werthen unendlich genähert werden.

### TRANSLATION

## On the concept of a definite integral and the extent of its validity

### 4.

The uncertainty that still prevails on some fundamental points of the theory of definite integrals requires us to begin with something about the concept of a definite integral and the extent of its validity.

So, first: What is one to understand by $\int_a^b f(x)dx$ ?

To establish this, we take a sequence of values $x_1, x_2, \ldots, x_{n-1}$, following one after another between $a$ and $b$ in order of size, and for the sake of brevity we denote $x_1 - a$ by $\delta_1$, $x_2 - x_1$ by $\delta_2$, $\ldots$, $b - x_{n-1}$ by $\delta_n$, and by $\varepsilon$ a proper fraction. Then the value of the sum

$$S = \delta_1 f(a + \varepsilon_1 \delta_1) + \delta_2 f(x_1 + \varepsilon_2 \delta_2) + \delta_3 f(x_2 + \varepsilon_3 \delta_3) + \cdots + \delta_n f(x_{n-1} + \varepsilon_n \delta_n)$$

will depend on the choice of the intervals $\delta$ and the quantities $\varepsilon$. If this now has the property that, however $\delta$ and $\varepsilon$ are chosen, it comes infinitely close to a fixed limit $A$ when all the $\delta$ become infinitely small, then this value is called $\int_a^b f(x)\,dx$.

If it does not have this property, then $\int_a^b f(x)\,dx$ has no meaning. But even then, there have been several attempts to attribute a meaning to this symbol, and among these extensions of the concept of a definite integral there is *one* accepted by all mathematicians. Namely, if the function $f(x)$ becomes infinitely large when the variable approaches a particular value $c$ in the interval $(a, b)$, then clearly the sum $S$, no matter what order of smallness one ascribes to $\delta$, can take any arbitrary [226] value; thus it has no limiting value, and $\int_a^b f(x)\,dx$ according to the above would have no meaning. But if then

$$\int_a^{c-\alpha_1} f(x)\,dx + \int_{c+\alpha_2}^b f(x)\,dx$$

approaches a fixed limit, as $\alpha_1$ and $\alpha_2$ become infinitely small, then one understands by this limit $\int_a^b f(x)\,dx$.

Other specifications by Cauchy of the concept of the definite integral in those cases where, according to the basic principles, no such thing exists, may serve some purpose in particular investigations; but they are not generally introduced and besides, because of their great arbitrariness, it is hardly appropriate to do so.

5.

Now, secondly, we investigate the extent of the validity of this concept, or the question: in which cases does a function permit integration and in which not?

First of all we consider the concept of an integral in a stricter sense, that is, we assume that the sum $S$ converges as all $\delta$ become infinitely small. If we denote the greatest variation of the function between $a$ and $x_1$, that is, the difference between its largest and smallest values in this interval, by $D_1$, between $x_1$ and $x_2$ by $D_2 \ldots$, between $x_{n-1}$ and $b$ by $D_n$, then

$$\delta_1 D_1 + \delta_2 D_2 + \cdots + \delta_n D_n$$

must become infinitely small with the quantities $\delta$. Further, we assume that, as long as all $\delta$ remain smaller than $d$, the largest value this sum can take will be $\Delta$; thus $\Delta$ will be a function of $d$, which always decreases with $d$ and becomes infinitely small with this quantity. Now if the total length of the intervals in which the variations are larger than $\sigma$ is equal to $s$, then the contribution of these intervals to the sum

$\delta_1 D_1 + \delta_2 D_2 + \cdots + \delta_n D_n$ will clearly be $\geq \sigma s$. Therefore one has

$$\sigma s \leq \delta_1 D_1 + \delta_2 D_2 + \cdots + \delta_n D_n \leq \Delta \quad \text{and consequently} \quad s \leq \frac{\Delta}{\sigma}.$$

Now $\frac{\Delta}{\sigma}$, if $\sigma$ is given, can always [227] be made as small as we like by appropriate choice of $d$; therefore the same holds for $s$, and it follows therefore that:

In order for the sum $S$ to converge, as all $\delta$ become infinitely small, it is necessary, in addition to the finiteness of the function $f(x)$, that the total length of the intervals in which the variations are $> \sigma$, whatever $\sigma$ is, can be made as small as we like by appropriate choice of $d$.

This proposition can also be reversed:

If the function $f(x)$ is always finite, and if, with the infinite decrease of all the quantities $\delta$, the total length $s$ of the intervals, in which the variation of the function $f(x)$ is larger than a given quantity $\sigma$, always in the end becomes infinitely small, then the sum $S$ converges as all $\delta$ become infinitely small.

For those intervals in which the variations are $> \sigma$ add to the sum $\delta_1 D_1 + \delta_2 D_2 + \cdots + \delta_n D_n$ a contribution which is smaller than $s$ multiplied by the largest variation of the function between $a$ and $b$, which (by hypothesis) is finite; the other intervals a contribution $< \sigma(b - a)$. Clearly we can now first take $\sigma$ as small as we like, and then still (by hypothesis) always take the length of the intervals so that $s$ also becomes as small as we like, by which means the sum $\delta_1 D_1 + \delta_2 D_2 + \cdots + \delta_n D_n$ can be made as small as we like, and consequently we can trap the value of the sum $S$ between limits as narrow as we please.

Thus we have found conditions which are necessary and sufficient for the sum $S$ to converge as the quantities $\delta$ decrease indefinitely, and thus one can speak in a stricter sense about an integral of the function $f(x)$ between $a$ and $b$.

If now the concept of the integral is extended as above, then clearly for the integration as a whole to be possible the second of the two conditions is still necessary; but the condition that the function is always finite will be replaced by the condition that the function is infinite *only* when the variable approaches *isolated* values, and that a definite limit results if the limits of integration approach these values infinitely closely.

———————

### 14.2.5  Lebesgue integration, 1902

Riemann's theory of integration, though much sounder than any that had preceded it, was still not without problems. The discovery, or invention, of increasingly 'pathological' functions during the nineteenth century led to functions that were not Riemann integrable, and whose existence even appeared to invalidate the fundamental theorem of the calculus itself. Such difficulties motivated the young Henri Lebesgue at the end of the century to reformulate the definition of integration once more, and his work not only resolved the outstanding problems but also led to an elegant simplification of the theory of integration.

Like Riemann, Lebesgue worked out the fundamentals of his theory at a very early stage of his career, for his doctoral thesis at the Sorbonne in 1902. An outline of his research was published in a series of five notes in the *Comptes rendus* of the Paris Academy between 1899 and 1901, and in the last of them (given below) he announced his new thoughts on integration. Lebesgue was then twenty-six; integration remained his key preoccupation and he continued to refine his theory for the next twenty years, by which time it had become an accepted part of modern mathematics.

A key component of Lebesgue's theory was the recent development of measure theory put forward in yet another important doctoral thesis, by Émile Borel in 1894. Lebesgue spent the years from 1897 to 1899 as a librarian at the École Normale Supérieure, where both he and Borel had been educated, and where he became familiar with Borel's *Leçons sur la théorie des fonctions*, published in 1898. Lebesgue extended and generalized Borel's ideas, and saw how to use measure theory in his new theory of integration. His basic idea was that instead of taking intervals on the $x$-axis, one should take intervals on the $y$-axis, and then consider the set of points $x$ such that $m < f(x) \leq M$ for some $m$ and $M$. If the measure of this set is $\lambda$, it clearly contributes a value between $\lambda m$ and $\lambda M$ to the integral. In fact the integral is defined as the limit (if it exists) of the sum of such terms, as all $m$ and $M$ become arbitrarily close.

A simply defined function over $[0, 1]$ that is integrable in Lebesgue's sense but not in Riemann's is

$$f(x) = \begin{cases} 0 & \text{if } x \text{ is rational} \\ 1 & \text{otherwise.} \end{cases}$$

The set of rationals, being of measure zero, contributes nothing to the Lebesgue integral, whose value over $[0, 1]$ is 1. Under Riemann's definition the function is not integrable at all.

For all its sophistication Lebesgue integration rests on very basic principles: the theories of inner and outer measure developed by Borel and Lebesgue in the 1890s are in some ways reminiscent of the most ancient approach to integration, the Archimedean method of pinning down a required quantity between upper and lower bounds. Integration pursued to its most advanced and general formulation returned in this sense to its earliest historical roots.

---

## Lebesgue integration

from Lebesgue, *Comptes rendus*, 132 (1901), 1025–1027

---

ANALYSE MATHÉMATIQUE. — *Sur une généralisation de l'intégrale définie.* Note de M. **H. Lebesgue**, présentée par M. Picard.

« Dans le cas des fonctions continues, il y a identité entre les notions d'intégrale et de fonction primitive. Riemann a défini l'intégrale de certaines fonctions discontinues, mais toutes les fonctions dérivées ne sont pas intégrables, au sens de Riemann. Le problème de la recherche des fonctions primitives n'est donc pas résolu par l'intégration, et l'on peut désirer une définition de l'intégrale comprenant comme cas particulier celle de Riemann et permettant de résoudre le problème des fonctions primitives (¹).

» Pour définir l'intégrale d'une fonction continue croissante

$$v(x)\,(a \leqq x \leqq b),$$

on divise l'intervalle $(a, b)$ en intervalles partiels et l'on fait la somme des quantités obtenues en multipliant la longueur de chaque intervalle partiel

---

(¹) Ces deux conditions imposées *a priori* à toute généralisation de l'intégrale sont évidemment compatibles, car toute fonction dérivée intégrable, au sens de Riemann, a pour intégrale une de ses fonctions primitives.

( 1026 )

par l'une des valeurs de $y$ quand $x$ est dans cet intervalle. Si $x$ est dans l'intervalle $(a_i, a_{i+1})$, $y$ varie entre certaines limites $m_i$, $m_{i+1}$, et réciproquement si $y$ est entre $m_i$ et $m_{i+1}$, $x$ est entre $a_i$ et $a_{i+1}$. De sorte qu'au lieu de se donner la division de la variation de $x$, c'est-à-dire de se donner les nombres $a_i$, on aurait pu se donner la division de la variation de $y$, c'est-à-dire les nombres $m_i$. De là deux manières de généraliser la notion d'intégrale. On sait que la première (se donner les $a_i$) conduit à la définition donnée par Riemann et aux définitions des intégrales par excès et par défaut données par M. Darboux. Voyons la seconde.

» Soit la fonction $y$ comprise entre $m$ et $M$. Donnons-nous

$$m = m_0 < m_1 < m_2 < \ldots < m_{p-1} < M = m_p;$$

$y = m$, quand $x$ fait partie d'un ensemble $E_0$; $m_{i-1} < y \leqq m_i$ quand $x$ fait partie d'un ensemble $E_i$.

» Nous définirons plus loin les mesures $\lambda_0$, $\lambda_i$ de ces ensembles. Considérons l'une ou l'autre des deux sommes

$$m_0\lambda_0 + \Sigma m_i\lambda_i; \quad m_0\lambda_0 + \Sigma m_{i-1}\lambda_i;$$

*si, quand l'écart maximum entre deux $m_i$ consécutifs tend vers zéro, ces sommes tendent vers une même limite indépendante des $m_i$ choisis. cette limite sera par définition l'intégrale des $y$ qui sera dite intégrable.*

» Considérons un ensemble de points de $(a, b)$; on peut d'une infinité de manières enfermer ces points dans une infinité dénombrable d'intervalles; la limite inférieure de la somme des longueurs de ces intervalles est la mesure de l'ensemble. Un ensemble $E$ est dit *mesurable* si sa mesure augmentée de celle de l'ensemble des points ne faisant pas partie de $E$ donne la mesure de $(a, b)$ ([1]). Voici deux propriétés de ces ensembles : une infinité d'ensembles mesurables $E_i$ étant donnée, l'ensemble des points qui font partie de l'un au moins d'entre eux est mesurable; si les $E_i$ n'ont deux à deux aucun point commun, la mesure de l'ensemble obtenu est la somme des mesures $E_i$. L'ensemble des points communs à tous les $E_i$ est mesurable.

» Il est naturel de considérer d'abord les fonctions telles que les ensembles qui figurent dans la définition de l'intégrale soient mesurables. On trouve que : *si une fonction limitée supérieurement en valeur absolue est*

---

([1]) Si l'on ajoute à ces ensembles des ensembles de mesures nulles convenablement choisis, on a des ensembles mesurables au sens de M. Borel (*Leçons sur la théorie des fonctions*).

( 1027 )

*⬛e que, quels que soient* A *et* B, *l'ensemble des valeurs de* x *pour lesquelles* ⬛a A $< y \leqq$ B *est mesurable, elle est intégrable* par le procédé indiqué. Une ⬛⬛e fonction sera dite *sommable.* L'intégrale d'une fonction sommable ⬛st comprise entre l'intégrale par défaut et l'intégrale par excès. De sorte ⬛ue, *si une fonction intégrable au sens de Riemann est sommable, l'intégrale* ⬛t *la même avec les deux définitions.* Or, *toute fonction intégrable au sens* ⬛ *Riemann est sommable,* car l'ensemble de ses points de discontinuité est ⬛e mesure nulle, et l'on peut démontrer que si, en faisant abstraction d'un ⬛nsemble de valeurs de x de mesure nulle, il reste un ensemble en chaque ⬛nt duquel une fonction est continue, cette fonction est sommable. ⬛ette propriété permet de former immédiatement des fonctions non inté-⬛ables au sens de Riemann et cependant sommables. Soient $f(x)$ et $\varphi(x)$ ⬛eux fonctions continues, $\varphi(x)$ n'étant pas toujours nulle; une fonction ⬛ui ne diffère de $f(x)$ qu'aux points d'un ensemble de mesure nulle partout ⬛nse et qui en ces points est égale à $f(x) + \varphi(x)$ est sommable sans être ⬛tégrable au sens de Riemann. *Exemple :* La fonction égale à o si x irra-⬛onnel, égale à 1 si x rationnel. Le procédé de formation qui précède ⬛ontre que l'ensemble des fonctions sommables a une puissance supé-⬛eure au continu. Voici deux propriétés des fonctions de cet ensemble.

⬛ » 1° *Si* f *et* φ *sont sommables,* $f + \varphi$ *et* $f\varphi$ *le sont* et l'intégrale de $f + \varphi$ ⬛t la somme des intégrales de f et de φ.

⬛ » 2° *Si une suite de fonctions sommables a une limite, c'est une fonction* ⬛ommable.

⬛ » L'ensemble des fonctions sommables contient évidemment $y = k$ et ⬛ = x; donc, d'après 1°, il contient tous les polynomes et comme, d'après ⬛°, il contient toutes ses limites, il contient donc toutes les fonctions con-⬛nues, toutes les limites de fonctions continues, c'est-à-dire les fonctions ⬛ première classe (voir Baire, *Annali di Matematica,* 1899), il contient ⬛outes celles de seconde classe, etc.

 » En particulier, *toute fonction dérivée, limitée supérieurement en valeur* ⬛bsolue, étant de première classe, *est sommable* et l'on peut démontrer que ⬛n *intégrale, considérée comme fonction de sa limite supérieure, est une de ses* *fonctions primitives.*

---

TRANSLATION

---

MATHEMATICAL ANALYSIS.—*On a generalization of the definite integral.* Note from Monsieur **H. Lebesgue**, presented by Monsieur Picard.

In the case of continuous functions, the notions of integral and of primitive function are identical. Riemann has defined the integral of certain discontinuous functions, but not all derived functions are integrable in the sense of Riemann. The problem of finding primitive functions is therefore not resolved by integration, and it would be desirable to have a definition of integral that comprises as a particular case that of Riemann, and permits the resolution of the problem of primitive functions.[1]

To define the integral of a continuous increasing function

$$v(x) \quad (a \leq x \leq b)$$

one divides the interval $(a, b)$ into partial intervals and one finds the sum of the quantities obtained by multiplying the length of each partial interval [1026] by one of the values of $y$ when $x$ is in that interval. If $x$ is in the interval $(a_i, a_{i+1})$, $y$ varies between certain limits $m_i, m_{i+1}$, and conversely if $y$ is between $m_i$ and $m_{i+1}$, then $x$ is between $a_i$ and $a_{i+1}$. So that instead of giving the division of the variation of $x$, that is to say, by giving the numbers $a_i$, one could give the division of the variation of $y$, that is to say the numbers $m_i$. From there, there are two methods of generalizing the notion of integral. One knows that the first (by giving the $a_i$) leads to the definition given by Riemann, and to definitions of integrals by excess and by defect given by Monsieur Darboux. Let us see the second.

Let the function $y$ be contained between $m$ and $M$. Let us give

$$m = m_0 < m_1 < m_2 < \cdots < m_{p-1} < M = m_p;$$

$y = m$ when $x$ belongs to a set $E_0$; and $m_{i-1} < y \leq m_i$ when $x$ belongs to a set $E_i$.

Further, we will define the measures $\lambda_0, \lambda_1$, of these sets. Let us consider one or other of the two sums

$$m_0\lambda_0 + \Sigma m_i\lambda_i; \quad m_0\lambda_0 + \Sigma m_{i-1}\lambda_i;$$

*if, when the maximum variation between two consecutive $m_i$ tends towards zero, these sums tend towards the same limit independently of the $m_i$ chosen, this limit will be by definition the integral of $y$, which will be said to be integrable.*

Let us consider a set of points of $(a, b)$; one may in infinitely many ways enclose these points in a denumerable infinity of intervals; the lower limit of the sum of the lengths of these intervals is the measure of the set. The set $E$ is said to be *measurable* if its measure added to that of the set of points not belonging to $E$ gives the measure of $(a, b)$.[2] Here are two properties of these sets: given an infinite number of measurable sets $E_i$, the set of points which belong to at least one of them is measurable; if no two of the $E_i$ have any point in common, the measure of the set obtained is the sum of the measures of $E_i$. The set of points common to all the $E_i$ is measurable.

It is natural to consider first those functions such that the sets which appear in the definition of the integral are measurable. One finds that: *if a function bounded above in absolute value is* [1027] *such that, whatever A and B are, the set of values of $x$ for which $A < y \leq B$ is measurable, it is integrable* by the procedure indicated. Such a function will be said to be *summable.* The integral of a summable function is contained between the integral by defect and the integral by excess. So that, *if a function integrable*

---

1. These two conditions imposed *a priori* on every generalization of the integral are clearly compatible, for any integrable derived function, in the sense of Riemann, has for integral one of its primitive functions.

2. If one adds to these sets, some sets of null measure conveniently chosen, one has measurable sets in the sense of Monsieur Borel (*Leçons sur la théorie des fonctions*).

*in the sense of Riemann is summable, the integral is the same for the two definitions.* Now, *every function integrable in the sense of Riemann is summable,* for the set of its points of discontinuity is of null measure, and one may demonstrate that if, on taking away a set of values of $x$ of null measure, there remains a set on each point of which a function is continuous, this function is summable. This property permits the immediate formation of functions non-integrable in the sense of Riemann but at the same time summable. Let $f(x)$ and $\phi(x)$ be two continuous functions, $\phi(x)$ being everywhere zero; a function that does not differ from $[\phi(x)]$ except at points on a set of zero measure that is everywhere dense, and which on these points is equal to $f(x) + \phi(x)$ is summable without being integrable in the sense of Riemann. *Example* : The function is equal to 0 if $x$ is irrational, and equal to 1 if $x$ is rational. The previous procedure for formation shows that the set of summable functions includes that of continuous functions. Here are two properties of functions of this set.

1. *If $f$ and $\phi$ are summable, so are $f + \phi$ and $f\phi$,* and the integral of $f + \phi$ is the sum of the integrals of $f$ and $\phi$.

2. *If a sequence of summable functions has a limit, it is a summable function.*

The set of summable functions clearly contains $y = k$ and $y = x$; therefore, by 1, it contains all polynomials and as, by 2, it contains all their limits, it therefore contains all continuous functions, and all the limits of continuous functions, that is to say, functions of the first class (see Baire, *Annali di Matematica,* 1899), and it contains all those of the second class, etc.

In particular, *every derived function, bounded above in absolute value,* being in the first class, *is summable* and one may show that *its integral, considered as a function of the upper limit, is one of its primitive functions.*

———————

# CHAPTER 15

# COMPLEX ANALYSIS

C omplex numbers were a relatively late addition to the mathematician's toolkit. They were tentatively first recognized in the mid-sixteenth century as possible solutions to quadratic or cubic equations (see 12.1). Cardano in 1545 observed, for example, that the problem of finding two numbers that add to 10 and multiply to 40 was satisfied by $5 + \sqrt{-15}$ and $5 - \sqrt{-15}$, but regarded the solution as both absurd and useless. Bombelli in his *Algebra* of 1572 carried out some simple calculations with what he called *meno di piu* ($\sqrt{-1}$) and *meno di meno* ($-\sqrt{-1}$), and showed that a root that seems 'impossible' might turn out to be acceptable because its imaginary parts cancel out, but he did not pursue the matter very far. Harriot, shortly after 1600, described imaginary numbers as 'noetic', and was the first mathematician to work with them systematically, but his findings remained unpublished. For the most part such roots were ignored: negative roots were described merely as 'false', but complex roots as 'impossible'. Only in the seventeenth century did imaginary numbers come to be accepted as legitimate, indeed necessary, roots of equations, and only during the nineteenth century did complex numbers come to be the subject of mathematical analysis in their own right.

## 15.1 THE COMPLEX PLANE

### 15.1.1 Wallis's representations, 1685

In *A treatise of algebra* Wallis proposed no fewer than ten geometric representations of complex numbers. In the first of them he suggested that the construction of the geometric mean of two positive numbers, which gives rise to a sine (see 1.2.2), could be replaced by a similar construction for the mean of a positive and a negative number, giving rise to a tangent. An alternative construction (see below) led him to observe that representations of imaginary numbers must move away from the real line and out into the plane.

Wallis's other ideas were mostly based on what to him were well-known properties of conic sections. He recognized, for example, that a hyperbola can be regarded as an 'imaginary' counterpart to a circle or ellipse. This is easy to see when the curves are described algebraically: a positive square in the standard equation of an ellipse is simply replaced by a negative square to give the corresponding equation of a hyperbola. Wallis in *De sectionibus conicis* in 1656 had derived algebraic equations for all the conic sections, and indeed had been one of the first mathematicians to argue that such curves could be treated algebraically, but he himself rarely used the equations in his subsequent work, and his arguments about imaginary numbers rested instead on older geometric insights.

---

### Wallis and imaginary numbers

from Wallis, *A treatise of algebra*, 1685, 266–267

WHAT hath been already faid of $\sqrt{-bc}$ in Algebra, (as a Mean Proportional between a Pofitive and a Negative Quantity:) may be thus Exemplified in Geometry.

If (for inftance,) Forward from A, I take $AB = +b$; and Forward from thence, $BC = +c$; (making $AC = +AB+BC = +b+c$, the Diameter of a Circle:) Then is the Sine, or Mean Proportional $BP = \sqrt{+bc}$.

But if Backward from A, I take $AB = -b$; and then Forward from that B, $BC = +c$; (making $AC = -AB+BC = -b+c$, the Diameter of the Circle:) Then is the Tangent or Mean Proportional $BP = \sqrt{-bc}$.

So that where $\sqrt{+bc}$ fignifies a Sine; $\sqrt{-bc}$ fhall fignify a Tangent, to the fame Arch (of the fame Circle,) AP, from the fame Point P, to the fame Diameter AC.

Suppofe now (for further Illuftration,) A Triangle ftanding on the Line AC (of indefinite length;) whofe one Leg $AP = 20$ is given; together with (the Angle PAB, and confequently) the Height $PC = 12$; and the length of the other Leg $PB = 15$: By which we are to find the length of the Bafe AB.

'Tis manifeft that the Square of AP being 400; and of PC, 144; their Difference 256 ($= 400 - 144$) is the Square of AC.

And therefore $AC (= \sqrt{256}) = +16$, or $-16$; Forward or Backward according as we pleafe to take the Affirmative or Negative Root. But we will here take the Affirmative.

Then, becaufe the Square of PB is 225; and of PC, 144; their Difference 81, is the Square of CB. And therefore $CB = \sqrt{81}$; which is indifferently, $+9$ or $-9$: And may therefore be taken Forward or Backward from C. Which gives a Double value for the length of AB; to wit, $AB = 16 + 9 = 25$, or $AB = 16 - 9 = 7$. Both Affirmative. (But if we fhould take, Backward from A, $AC = -16$; then $AB = -16 + 9 = -7$, and $AB = -16 - 9 = -25$. Both Negative)

## CHAP.LXVII.  *Of Negative Squares.*    267

Suppofe again, A P = 15, P C = 12, (and therefore
A C = √: 225 — 144: = √ 81 = 9,) P B = 20 (and
therefore B C = √: 400 — 144: = √ 256 = + 16, or
— 16:) Then is A B = 9 + 16 = 25, or A B = 9 — 16
= — 7. The one Affirmative, the other Negative. (The
fame values would be, but with contrary Signs, if we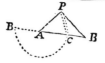
take A C = √ 81 = — 9: That is, A B = — 9 + 16 = + 7, A B = — 9 — 16
= — 25.)

In all which cafes, the Point B is found, (if not Forward, at leaft Backward,)
in the Line A C, as the Queftion fuppofeth.

And of this nature, are thofe Quadratick Equations, whofe Roots are Real,
(whether Affirmative or Negative, or partly the one, partly the other;) without any other Impoffibility than ( what is incident alfo to Lateral Equations,)
that the Roots (one or both) may be Negative Quantities.

But if we fhall Suppofe, A P = 20, P B = 12, P C = 15, (and therefore
A C = √ 175:) When we come to Subtract as before, the Square of P C (225,)
out of the Square P B ( 144,) to find the Square of B C, we find that cannot
be done without a Negative Remainder, 144 — 225 = — 81.

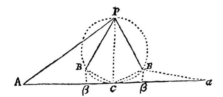

So that the Square of B C is (indeed) the Difference of the Squares of P B,
P C; but a defective Deference; (that of P C proving the greater, which was
fuppofed the Leffer; and the Triangle P B C, Rectangled, not as was fuppofed
at C, but at B:) And therefore B C = √ — 81.

Which gives indeed (as before) a double value of A B, √ 175, + √ — 81,
and √ 175, — √ — 81: But fuch as requires a new Impoffibility in Algebra,
(which in Lateral Equations doth not happen;) not that of a Negative Root,
or a Quantity lefs than nothing; (as before,) but the Root of a Negative
Square. Which in ftrictnefs of fpeech, cannot be: fince that no Real Root
(Affirmative or Negative,) being Multiplied into itfelf, will make a Negative
Square.

This Impoffibility in *Algebra*, argues an Impoffibility of the cafe propofed in
Geometry; and that the Point B cannot be had, (as was fuppofed,) in the Line
A C, however produced (forward or backward,) from A.

Yet are there Two Points defigned (out of that Line, but) in the fame Plain;
to either of which, if we draw the Lines A B, B P, we have a Triangle; whofe
Sides A P, P B, are fuch as were required: And the Angle P A C, and Altitude P C,
(above A C, though not above A B,) fuch as was propofed; And the Difference
of Squares of P B, P C, is that of C B.

And like as in the firft cafe, the Two values of A B (which are both Affirmative,) make the double of A C, (16 + 9; + 16 — 9, = 16 + 16 = 32:) So
here, √ 175 + √ — 81, + √ 175 — √ — 81, = 2 √ 175.

And (in the Figure,) though not the Two Lines themfelves, A B, A B, (as in
the Firft cafe, where they lay in the Line A C;) yet the Ground-lines on which
they ftand, A β, A β, are Equal to the Double of A C: That is, if to either of
thofe A B, we join B α, equal to the other of them, and with the fame Declivity;
A C α (the Diftance of A α) will be a Streight Line equal to the double of A C;
as is A C α in the Firft cafe.

The greateft difference is this; That in the firft Cafe, the Points B, B, lying
in the Line A C, the Lines A B, A B, are the fame with their Ground-Lines, but
not fo in this laft cafe, where B B are fo raifed above β β

## 15.1.2  Argand's representation, 1806

Wallis had based his representations of complex numbers on the familiar geometric concepts of his own time: mean proportionals and conic sections. Some 150 years later Argand, generally thought to be Jean Robert Argand (for despite his name having become commonplace we know almost nothing about him), based his representation on another kind of geometric intuition, that of quantities that have both magnitude and direction. Wallis had deliberately set out to represent complex numbers in two dimensions, but Argand seems to have fallen into the idea by accident. By thinking about the direction intermediate between that of $+1$ and $-1$ he came to see that it must be represented geometrically by a line at right angles to both of them, and algebraically by the quantity $\sqrt{-1}$, which for him, as for Wallis, was the mean proportional between $+1$ and $-1$.

Much of Argand's treatment of directed quantities, including his use of the notation $\overline{KA}$, reads like a modern elementary treatment of vectors. He showed, for instance, how to add and subtract such quantities, or decompose them in predetermined directions. Only later did he diverge from vector arithmetic, when he suggested that unit lengths could be multiplied by adding their angles.

Argand's original essay, entitled *Essai sur une manière de représenter les quantités imaginaires* (*Essay on a method of representing imaginary quantities*), was first published anonymously in 1806, but it was republished by Jules Hoüel in 1874. Observe that even in the late nineteenth century Hoüel still followed Argand in using the symbol :: introduced by Oughtred in 1631 for equality of ratios.

---

### Argand diagrams

from Argand, *Essai sur une manière de représenter les quantités imaginaires dans les constructions géométriques*; as published by Hoüel in 1874, 5–12

---

3. Maintenant, si, faisant abstraction du rapport des grandeurs absolues, on considère les différents cas que peut présenter le rapport des directions, on trouvera qu'ils se réduisent à ceux qu'offrent les deux proportions suivantes :

$$+1 : +1 :: -1 : -1,$$
$$+1 : -1 :: -1 : +1.$$

L'inspection de ces proportions et de celles qu'on formerait par le renversement des termes montre que les termes moyens sont de signes semblables ou différents, suivant que les extrêmes sont eux-mêmes de signes semblables ou différents.

Qu'on se propose actuellement de déterminer la moyenne proportionnelle géométrique entre deux quantités de signes

---

déterminé par ce qui précède : l'extension qu'on donne ici à leur signification ordinaire paraît permise, et d'ailleurs n'est pas absolument nouvelle. Ce qu'on appelle, en Optique, foyer imaginaire, par opposition au foyer réel, est le point de rencontre de rayons qui n'ont pas une existence physique, et qui peuvent, en quelque sorte, être considérés comme des rayons négatifs.

— 6 —

différents, c'est-à-dire la quantité $x$ qui satisfait à la proportion

$$+1 : +x :: +x : -1.$$

On est arrêté ici comme on l'a été en voulant continuer au delà de o la progression arithmétique décroissante, car on ne peut égaler $x$ à aucun nombre positif ou négatif; mais, puisqu'on a trouvé plus haut que la quantité négative, imaginaire lorsque la numération était appliquée à de certaines espèces de grandeurs, devenait réelle lorsque l'on combinait d'une certaine manière l'idée de *grandeur absolue* avec l'idée de *direction*, ne serait-il pas possible d'obtenir le même succès relativement à la quantité dont il s'agit, quantité réputée imaginaire par l'impossibilité où l'on est de lui assigner une place dans l'échelle des quantités positives ou négatives?

En y réfléchissant, il a paru qu'on parviendrait à ce but si l'on pouvait trouver un genre de grandeurs auquel pût s'allier l'idée de direction, de manière que, étant adoptées deux directions opposées, l'une pour les valeurs positives, l'autre pour les valeurs négatives, il en existât une troisième telle, que la direction positive fût à celle dont il s'agit comme celle-ci est à la direction négative.

4. Or, si l'on prend un point fixe K (*fig.* 1) et qu'on adopte pour unité positive la ligne KA considérée comme ayant sa direction de K en A, ce qu'on pourra désigner par $\overline{KA}$, pour distinguer cette quantité de la ligne KA dans laquelle on ne considère ici que la grandeur absolue, l'unité négative sera $\overline{KI}$, le trait supérieur ayant la même destination que celui qui est placé sur $\overline{KA}$, et la condi-

— 7 —

tion à laquelle il s'agit de satisfaire sera remplie par la ligne KE, perpendiculaire aux précédentes et considérée

Fig. 1.

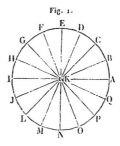

comme ayant sa direction de K en E, et qu'on exprimera également par $\overline{KE}$. En effet, la direction de $\overline{KA}$ est, à l'égard de la direction de $\overline{KE}$, ce que cette dernière est à l'égard de la direction de $\overline{KI}$. De plus, on voit que cette même condition est aussi bien remplie par $\overline{KN}$ que par $\overline{KE}$, ces deux dernières quantités étant entre elles comme $+1$ et $-1$, ainsi que cela doit être. Elles sont donc ce qu'on exprime ordinairement par $+\sqrt{-1}$, $-\sqrt{-1}$.

Par une marche analogue, on pourra insérer de nouvelles moyennes proportionnelles entre les quantités dont il vient d'être question. En effet, pour construire la moyenne proportionnelle entre $\overline{KA}$ et $\overline{KE}$, il faudra tirer la ligne CKL qui divise l'angle AKE en deux parties égales, et la moyenne cherchée sera $\overline{KC}$ ou $\overline{KL}$. La ligne GKP donnera également les moyennes entre $\overline{KE}$ et $\overline{KI}$ ou entre

TRANSLATION

3. If now, separately from the ratio of absolute magnitudes, one considers the different cases that the ratio of directions can present, one will find that they reduce to those offered by the two following proportions:

$$+1 : +1 :: -1 : -1,$$
$$+1 : -1 :: -1 : +1.$$

Inspection of these proportions and of those that one would form by reversal of terms shows that the mean terms are of similar or different sign, according to whether the extremes themselves are of similar or different sign.

So that one proposes in fact to determine the geometric mean proportional between two quantities of different sign, [6] that is to say the quantity $x$ that satisfies the proportion:

$$+1 : +x :: +x : -1.$$

One is halted here as one was in wanting to continue a decreasing arithmetic progression below 0, for one cannot make $x$ equal to any positive or negative number; but, since we found above that a negative quantity, imaginary when the name was applied to certain kinds of magnitudes, became real when one combined in a certain way the

— 8 —

$\overline{KA}$ et $\overline{KN}$. On obtiendra de même les quantités $\overline{KB}$, $\overline{KD}$, $\overline{KF}$, $\overline{KH}$, $\overline{KJ}$, $\overline{KM}$, $\overline{KO}$, $\overline{KQ}$ pour moyennes entre $\overline{KA}$ et $\overline{KC}$, $\overline{KC}$ et $\overline{KE}$,..., et ainsi de suite. On pourra pareillement insérer un plus grand nombre de moyennes proportionnelles entre deux quantités données, et le nombre des constructions qui pourront résoudre la question sera égal au nombre des rapports que présente la progression cherchée. S'il s'agit, par exemple, de construire deux moyennes, $\overline{KP}$, $\overline{KQ}$, entre $\overline{KA}$ et $\overline{KB}$, ce qui doit donner lieu aux trois rapports

$$\overline{KA} : \overline{KP} :: \overline{KP} : \overline{KQ} :: \overline{KQ} : \overline{KB},$$

il faut qu'on ait

$$\text{angle } \overline{AKP} = \text{angle } \overline{PKQ} = \text{angle } \overline{QKB},$$

le trait supérieur indiquant que ces angles sont en position homologue sur les bases AK, PK, QK. Or on peut y

Fig. 2.    Fig. 2 bis.

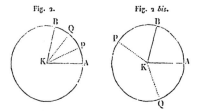

parvenir de trois manières, savoir, en divisant en trois parties égales : 1° l'angle AKB ; 2° l'angle AKB, plus une

circonférence ; 3° l'angle AKB, plus deux circonférences,

Fig. 2 ter.

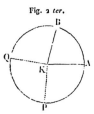

ce qui donnera les trois constructions représentées par les *fig.* 2, 2 *bis*, 2 *ter* (*).

**5.** Observons maintenant que, pour l'existence des relations qui viennent d'être établies entre les quantités $\overline{KA}$, $\overline{KB}$, $\overline{KC}$,..., il n'est pas nécessaire que le départ de la direction, qui constitue une partie de l'essence de ces quantités, soit fixé à un point unique K ; mais que

---

(*) Le principe sur lequel se fondent ces constructions, énoncé d'une manière générale, consiste en ce que le rapport de deux rayons $\overline{KP}$, $\overline{KQ}$, faisant entre eux un angle QKP, dépend de cet angle, lorsque l'on considère ces rayons comme tirés dans une certaine direction, et que ce rapport est le même que celui de deux autres rayons $\overline{KR}$, $\overline{KS}$, faisant entre eux le même angle ; mais, quoique ce principe soit, en quelque manière, une extension de celui sur lequel on établit le rapport géométrique entre une ligne positive et une ligne négative, on ne le présente ici que comme une hypothèse, dont il restera à établir la légitimité, et dont, jusque-là, les conséquences devront être confirmées par une autre voie.

---

idea of *absolute magnitude* with the idea of *direction*, will it not be possible to achieve the same success in relation to the quantity we are concerned with, a quantity reputed to be imaginary because of the impossibility one faces in assigning it a place on the scale of positive or negative quantities?

On reflecting on this, it appeared that one would arrive at this end if one could find a kind of magnitude with which there could be associated the idea of direction, in such a way that, having adopted two opposing directions, one for positive values, the other for negative values, there would exist a third, such that the positive direction would be to that we are concerned with as that itself is to the negative direction.

4. Now, if one takes a fixed point *K* (*fig.* 1) and adopts as a positive unit the line *KA* considered as having direction from *K* to *A*, one may denote this by $\overline{KA}$, to distinguish this quantity from the line *KA* for which one considers here only the absolute magnitude; the negative unit will be $\overline{KI}$, the overline having the same purpose as that which is placed over $\overline{KA}$, and the condition [6] one is concerned to satisfy will be fulfilled by the line *KE*, perpendicular to the preceding ones and considered as having direction from *K* to *E*, and which one may express in the same way by $\overline{KE}$. Indeed, the direction of $\overline{KA}$, with respect to the direction of $\overline{KE}$, is what the latter is with respect to the direction of $\overline{KI}$. Further, one sees that this same condition is as well satisfied by $\overline{KN}$ as by $\overline{KE}$,

— 10 —

ces relations ont également lieu, si l'on suppose que chaque expression, comme $\overline{\text{KA}}$, désigne en général une grandeur égale à KA, et prise dans la même direction, comme $\overline{\text{K}'\text{A}'}$, $\overline{\text{K}''\text{A}''}$, $\overline{\text{K}'''\text{A}'''}$, $\overline{\text{BK}}$,... (fig. 3).

Fig. 3.

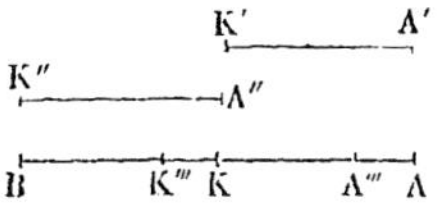

En effet, en suivant, à l'égard de cette nouvelle espèce de grandeurs, les raisonnements qui ont été faits plus haut, on verra que, si $\overline{\text{KA}}$, $\overline{\text{K}'\text{A}'}$, $\overline{\text{K}''\text{A}''}$,... sont des unités positives, $\overline{\text{AK}}$, $\overline{\text{A}'\text{K}'}$, $\overline{\text{A}''\text{K}''}$,... seront des unités négatives; que la moyenne proportionnelle entre $+\imath$ et $-\imath$ pourra être exprimée par une ligne quelconque, égale aux précédentes, perpendiculaire à leur direction, et qu'on pourra prendre à volonté dans l'un de ses deux sens, et ainsi de suite. On peut, pour aider les idées à se fixer, considérer un cas particulier, comme, par exemple, si l'on désigne par $\overline{\text{KA}}$ une force déterminée prise pour unité, et dont l'action s'exerce sur tous les points possibles, parallèlement à KA et dans le sens de K à A, cette unité pourra être exprimée par une ligne parallèle à KA, prise à partir d'un point quelconque. L'unité négative sera une force égale en action, et dont l'effet a lieu parallèlement à la même ligne, mais dans le sens de A à K, et pourra pareillement être exprimée par une ligne partant d'un point quelconque, laquelle sera prise en sens con-

— 11 —

traire de la précédente. Or il suffit que les qualités de positives et de négatives, que nous attribuons aux grandeurs d'une certaine espèce, dépendent de directions opposées entre lesquelles il en existe une moyenne, pour qu'on puisse y appliquer les idées développées ci-devant à l'égard des rayons partant d'un centre unique, et concevoir, entre toutes les lignes qui représenteront une telle espèce de grandeurs, les mêmes relations qu'ont offertes ces rayons.

6. En conséquence de ces réflexions, on pourra généraliser le sens des expressions de la forme $\overline{\text{AB}}$, $\overline{\text{CD}}$, $\overline{\text{KP}}$,..., et toute expression pareille désignera, par la suite, une ligne d'une certaine longueur, parallèle à une certaine direction, prise dans un sens déterminé entre les deux sens opposés que présente cette direction, et dont l'origine est à un point quelconque, ces lignes pouvant elles-mêmes être l'expression de grandeurs d'une autre espèce.

Comme elles doivent être le sujet des recherches qui vont suivre, il est à propos de leur appliquer une dénomination particulière. On les appellera *lignes en direction* ou, plus simplement, *lignes dirigées*. Elles seront ainsi distinguées des lignes *absolues*, dans lesquelles on ne considère que la longueur, sans aucun égard à la direction (*).

---

(*) L'expression de *lignes en direction* n'est qu'une abréviation de cette phrase : *lignes considérées comme appartenant à une certaine direction*. Cette remarque indique qu'on ne prétend point fonder de nouvelles dénominations, mais qu'on emploie cette façon de s'exprimer soit pour éviter la confusion, soit pour abréger le discours.

---

these last two quantities being between themselves like $+1$ and $-1$, just as they must be. They are therefore what one usually expresses by $+\sqrt{-1}, -\sqrt{-1}$.

By an analogous step, one may insert new mean proportionals between the quantities we were just concerned with. Indeed, to construct the mean proportional between $\overline{KA}$ and $\overline{KE}$, one must draw the line $CKL$ which divides the angle $AKE$ into two equal parts, and the sought mean will be $\overline{KC}$ or $\overline{KL}$. The line $GKP$ will in the same way give the means between $\overline{KE}$ and $\overline{KI}$ or between [8] $\overline{KA}$ and $\overline{KN}$. One will obtain in the same way the quantities $\overline{KB}, \overline{KD}, \overline{KF}, \overline{KH}, \overline{KJ}, \overline{KM}, \overline{KO}, \overline{KQ}$ as means between $\overline{KA}$ and $\overline{KC}$, $\overline{KC}$ and $\overline{KE}$, ..., and so on. One may similarly insert a greater number of mean proportionals between two given quantities, and the number of constructions which will resolve the question will be equal to the number of ratios that the sought progression presents. If one is concerned, for example, to construct two means, $\overline{KP}, \overline{KQ}$, between $\overline{KA}$ and $\overline{KB}$, which must give rise to three ratios:

$$\overline{KA} : \overline{KP} :: \overline{KP} : \overline{KQ} :: \overline{KQ} : \overline{KB},$$

one must have

$$\text{angle } \overline{AKP} = \text{angle } \overline{PKQ} = \text{angle } \overline{QKB},$$

— 12 —

7. En rapportant aux dénominations d'usage les diverses espèces de lignes en direction qui s'engendrent d'une unité primitive $\overline{KA}$, on voit que toute ligne parallèle à la direction primitive est exprimée par un nombre réel, que celles qui lui sont perpendiculaires sont exprimées par des nombres imaginaires ou de la forme $\pm a\sqrt{-1}$, et, enfin, que celles qui sont tracées dans une direction autre que les deux précédentes appartiennent à la forme $\pm a \pm b\sqrt{-1}$, qui se compose d'une partie réelle et d'une partie imaginaire.

Mais ces lignes sont des quantités tout aussi réelles que l'unité primitive; elles en dérivent par la combinaison de l'idée de la direction avec l'idée de la grandeur, et elles sont, à cet égard, ce qu'est la ligne négative, qui n'est nullement regardée comme imaginaire. Les noms de *réel* et d'*imaginaire* ne s'accordent donc pas avec les notions qui viennent d'être exposées. Il est superflu d'observer que ceux d'*impossible* et d'*absurde,* qu'on rencontre quelquefois, y sont encore plus contraires. On peut d'ailleurs s'étonner de voir ces termes employés dans les sciences exactes autrement que pour qualifier ce qui est contraire à la vérité (*).

Une quantité absurde serait celle dont l'existence en-

_____

(*) Il y a eu une époque où, conduits par la force de la vérité à admettre, dans les quantités abstraites, des valeurs négatives, les géomètres, ayant apparemment quelque difficulté à imaginer que *moins que rien* pût être quelque chose, donnèrent le nom de *fausses* aux valeurs dont il s'agit. Ce mot cessa d'être employé dans le sens qu'on y avait attaché, lorsqu'on eut rectifié les premières idées qui avaient donné lieu à cette dénomination vicieuse.

the overline indicating that these angles are in similar positions on the bases $AK$, $PK$, $QK$. Now one may arrive at this in three ways, namely, by dividing into three equal parts: 1. the angle $AKB$; 2. the angle $AKB$, plus one [9] circumference; 3. the angle $AKB$ plus two circumferences, which will give the three constructions represented by *figures 2, 2 bis, 2 ter*.

5. Now observe that, for the existence of the relationships that have just been established between the quantities $\overline{KA}$, $\overline{KB}$, $\overline{KC}$, ..., it is not necessary for the origin of the direction, which forms one part of the nature of these quantities, to be fixed at a unique point $K$; but that [10] these relationships are equally valid if one supposes that each expression, such as $\overline{KA}$, denotes in general a quantity equal to $KA$, and taken in the same direction, such as $\overline{K'A'}$, $\overline{K''A''}$, $\overline{K'''A'''}$, $\overline{BK}$, ...(*fig. 3*).

Indeed, by following the reasoning that has been carried out above with respect to this new kind of quantity, one will see that, if $\overline{KA}$, $\overline{K'A'}$, $\overline{K''A''}$, ...are positive units, $\overline{AK}$, $\overline{A'K'}$, $\overline{A''K''}$, ...will be negative units; that the mean proportional between $+1$ and $-1$ can be expressed by any line whatever, equal to the preceding ones, perpendicular to their direction, and which one may take at will in one of its two senses, and so on. One may, to help fix the ideas, consider a particular case, as, for example, if one denotes by $\overline{KA}$ a certain force taken as a unit, and whose action is exerted on all possible points, parallel to $KA$ and in the direction from $K$ to $A$; this unit may be expressed by a line parallel to $KA$, taken from any point whatever. The negative unit will be a force equal in action, whose effect occurs parallel to the same line, but in the direction from $A$ to $K$, and may similarly be expressed by a line departing from any point, which will be taken in the opposite direction [11] to the previous one. Now it suffices that the qualities of positive and negative, which we attribute to magnitudes of a certain kind, depend on opposite directions between which there exists a mean, for one to be able to apply the ideas developed above with respect to rays originating from a unique centre, and to conceive, between all the lines that represent such a kind of magnitude, the same relationships that these rays present.

6. As a consequence of these reflections, one can generalize the meaning of expressions of the form $\overline{AB}, \overline{CD}, \overline{KP}, \ldots$, and every similar expression will denote, in the same way, a line of a certain length, parallel to a certain direction, taken in a determined sense between the two opposing senses that the direction offers, and whose origin is at any point whatever; these lines may themselves be the expression of magnitudes of another kind.

Since they are to be the subject of the researches that are going to follow, it is proposed to give them a particular name. We will call them *lines with direction* or, more simply, *directed lines*. They will thus be distinguished from *absolute* lines, in which one considers only the length, without regard to direction. [12]

7. With respect to the names in use for various kinds of directed lines which arise from an original unit $\overline{KA}$, one sees that every line parallel to the original direction is expressed by a real number, that those that are perpendicular to it are expressed by imaginary numbers or by the form $\pm a\sqrt{-1}$, and, finally, that those that are drawn in a direction other than the two previous ones correspond to the form $\pm a \pm b\sqrt{-1}$, which is composed of a real part and an imaginary part.

But these lines are quantities altogether as real as the original unit; they derive from it through the combination of the idea of direction with the idea of magnitude, and they are, in this respect, what a negative line is, which is never regarded as imaginary. The names *real* and *imaginary* are therefore not in accordance with the notions just explained. It is superfluous to observe that *impossible* and *absurd*, which one sometimes meets, are even more contrary. One may besides be astonished to see these terms employed in the exact sciences other than to describe what is opposed to the truth.*

---

\* There was a time when, led by the force of truth to admit negative values amongst abstract quantities, geometers, apparently having some difficulty in imagining that *less than nothing* could be anything, gave the name *false* to the values concerned. This word ceased to be used in the sense then attached to it when they had corrected the earlier ideas that had given rise to this perverse name.

---

## 15.2 INTEGRATION OF COMPLEX FUNCTIONS

Most of this section is devoted to the work of Cauchy, who almost single-handedly developed the modern theory of complex analysis over a period of roughly twenty years, from 1814 to 1832. First, however, we will take a brief look at the eighteenth-century background to the problem of integrating complex functions.

### 15.2.1  Johann Bernoulli's transformations, 1702

As early as 1702 Johann Bernoulli showed how quotients of functions might be integrated by separating them into partial fractions, and he included some useful transformations which converted real integrals to imaginary ones, or conversely. At this point neither he nor anyone else had any compunction about swapping between real and imaginary in this way, especially since such transformations were extremely helpful.

As often happened with Bernoulli's work, his paper on integrals was published twice: in French in the *Mémoires* of the Paris Academy (1702), and in Latin (with fewer examples) in the *Acta eruditorum* (1703). Although the text was essentially the same in both cases, there were significant differences in notation. In the French version, the one that was eventually included in Bernoulli's collected works, we find, for example, $adt : 2bt$, where the Latin version has $\dfrac{adt}{2bt}$.

## Johann Bernoulli's transformations

from Johann Bernoulli, 'Problema exhibitum', *Acta eruditorum*, (1703), 29–31

*Probl. I.*

Trans-

30 **ACTA ERUDITORUM**

Transformare quantitatem differentialem $\frac{a\,dz}{bb-zz}$ in differen-

tialem Logarithmi $\frac{a\,dt}{2bt}$, & vice verfa.

Pone $z = \frac{t-1}{t+1}\,b$, & habebis $\frac{a\,dz}{bb-zz} = \frac{a\,dt}{2bt}$

Et vice verfa pone $t = \frac{+z+b}{-z+b}$ & habebis $\frac{a\,dt}{2bt} = \frac{a\,dz}{bb-zz}$

*Coroll.*

Eodem modo transformatur quantitas differentialis $\frac{a\,dt}{bb+zz}$

in differentialem Logarithmi imaginarii $\frac{-a\,dt}{2bt\sqrt{-1}}$ & viciffim.

*Probl. 2.*

Transformare quantitatem differentialem $\frac{a\,dz}{bb+zz}$ in dif-

ferentiale fectoris vel arcus Circularis $\frac{-a\,dt}{2\sqrt{t-bbtt}}$, & viciffim.

Pone $z = \sqrt{\frac{1}{t}-bb}$ & habebis $\frac{a\,dz}{bb+zz} = \frac{-a\,dt}{2\sqrt{t-bbtt}}$

Et vice verfa pone $t = \frac{1}{bb+zz}$, & habebis $\frac{-a\,dt}{2\sqrt{t-bbtt}} =$

$\frac{a\,dz}{bb+zz}$

*Probl. 3.*

Transformare Quantitatem differentialem $\frac{a\,dz}{bb-zz}$ in dif-

ferentiale Sectoris hyperbolici $\frac{a\,dt}{2\sqrt{t+bbtt}}$; & viciffim.

Pone $Z = \sqrt{\frac{1}{t}+bb}$, & deinde $t = \frac{1}{bb-zz}$; habebis

optatum.

*Probl.*

## MENSIS JANUARII A. MDCCIII.   31

*Probl. 4.*

Transformare quantitatem differentialem logarithmicam

■■■ in differentiale sectoris hyperbolici $\dfrac{a\,dr}{2\sqrt{r+bbrr}}$.

Pone $z = \dfrac{b + \sqrt{\dfrac{1}{r}+bb}}{b - \sqrt{\dfrac{1}{r}+bb}}$ ; habebis quæsitum:

*Coroll. 1.*

Eodem modo transformatur differentialis logarithmica i-

maginaria $\dfrac{a\,dt}{2bt\sqrt{-1}}$ In differentiale sectoris circuli realis. Po-

nendo enim $z = \dfrac{b\sqrt{-1}+\sqrt{\dfrac{1}{r}-bb}}{b\sqrt{-1}-\sqrt{\dfrac{1}{r}-bb}}$, habebitur $\dfrac{a\,dr}{2\sqrt{r-bbrr}}$.

*Coroll. 2.*

Cum ex probl. 2. $\int\dfrac{a\,dz}{bb+zz}$ dependeat a qradratura circu-

li, cum vero etiam $\dfrac{a\,dz}{bb+zz}$ fit $= \dfrac{\frac{1}{2}a\,dz}{bb+bz\sqrt{-1}} + \dfrac{\frac{1}{2}a\,dz}{bb-bz\sqrt{-1}}$,

quæ duo sunt differentialia logarithmi imaginarii : patet utique logarithmos imaginarios seu Sectores hyperbolicos imaginarios sumi debere pro sectoribus circularibus realibus. Hos enim in u-nam summam colligendo quantitates imaginariæ per mutuam compensationem se destruunt, ita ut nil nisi reale proveniat.

---

### TRANSLATION

There follow some short ways of reducing composite differentials to simple or logarithmic ones, and conversely; as also of imaginary simples to real composites or to lengths of arcs of a circle.

*Problem 1.*

[30] To transform the differential quantity $\dfrac{adz}{bb-zz}$ into a logarithmic differential $\dfrac{adt}{2bt}$, and conversely.

Put $z = \dfrac{t-1}{t+1}b$, and you will have $\dfrac{adz}{bb-zz} = \dfrac{adt}{2bt}$.

And conversely put $t = \dfrac{+z+b}{-z+b}$ and you will have $\dfrac{adt}{2bt} = \dfrac{adz}{bb-zz}$.

*Corollary*

In the same way the differential $\dfrac{adz}{bb + zz}$ is transformed into the differential of an imaginary logarithm $\dfrac{-adt}{2bt\sqrt{-1}}$ and conversely.

*Problem 2.*

To transform the differential quantity $\dfrac{adz}{bb + zz}$ into the differential of a sector or circular arc $\dfrac{-adt}{2\sqrt{t - bbtt}}$, and conversely.

Put $z = \sqrt{\dfrac{1}{t} - bb}$ and you will have $\dfrac{adz}{bb + zz} = \dfrac{-adt}{2\sqrt{t - bbtt}}$.

And conversely put $t = \dfrac{1}{bb + zz}$, and you will have $\dfrac{-adt}{2\sqrt{t - bbtt}} = \dfrac{adz}{bb + zz}$.

*Problem 3.*

To transform the differential quantity $\dfrac{adz}{bb - zz}$ into the differential of a hyperbolic sector $\dfrac{adt}{2\sqrt{t + bbtt}}$; and conversely.

Put $z = \sqrt{\dfrac{1}{t} + bb}$, and then $t = \dfrac{1}{bb - zz}$; you will have what was wanted. [31]

*Problem 4.*

To transform the logarithmic differential quantity $\dfrac{adt}{2bt}$ into the differential of a hyperbolic sector $\dfrac{adr}{2\sqrt{r + bbrr}}$.

Put $t = \dfrac{b + \sqrt{\dfrac{1}{r} + bb}}{b - \sqrt{\dfrac{1}{r} + bb}}$; and you will have what was sought.

*Corollary 1.*

In the same way the imaginary logarithmic differential $\dfrac{adt}{2bt\sqrt{-1}}$ may be transformed into the differential of a real circular arc. For putting

$t = \dfrac{b\sqrt{-1} + \sqrt{\dfrac{1}{r} - bb}}{b\sqrt{-1} - \sqrt{\dfrac{1}{r} - bb}}$, one will have $\dfrac{adr}{2\sqrt{r - bbrr}}$.

*Corollary 2.*

Since by problem 2, $\displaystyle\int \dfrac{adz}{bb + zz}$ depends on the quadrature of the circle, and since also $\dfrac{adz}{bb + zz}$ is $= \dfrac{\frac{1}{2}adz}{bb + bz\sqrt{-1}} + \dfrac{\frac{1}{2}adz}{bb - bz\sqrt{-1}}$, which are both differentials of an imaginary logarithm, it is clear that both imaginary logarithms or imaginary hyperbolic sectors must be taken for real circular sectors. For by collecting these into one sum, the imaginary quantities destroy each other by mutual cancellation, so that only a real quantity is produced.

---

### 15.2.2  Cauchy on definite complex integrals, 1814

By 1781 Euler had begun to evaluate real integrals by introducing complex variables and then separating out real and imaginary parts. Like Newton in his first discoveries of the calculus, Euler checked the validity of this venture by direct calculation, and remarked that the method was potentially useful, but the relevant paper, 'De valoribus integralium a termino variabilis $x = 0$ usque $x = \infty$ extensorum' ('On the values of integrals extended from the limit of the variable $x = 0$ to $x = \infty$'), was not published until 1794 in the posthumous Volume 4 of his *Institutiones calculi integralis*.

Meanwhile in 1782, Laplace too experimented with complex substitution, and his work was published before Euler's, in the *Mémoires* of the Paris Academy in 1785. Almost thirty years later, in 1812, he argued that the transition to imaginary variables ('le passage du réel à l'imaginaire') was justified by 'the generality of analysis' ('la généralité de l'analyse').[1] His colleague Poisson, however, expressed some doubts on the matter and insisted that all such results should be confirmed by direct methods.[2] It seems that Laplace suggested to Cauchy, then twenty-four years old, that he should try to resolve the argument, leading in 1814 to Cauchy's first lengthy paper on complex integration. The title, 'Mémoire sur les intégrales définies', was identical to that of a paper published by Poisson the previous year, and in Part I Cauchy took up Laplace's concept of the passage from real to imaginary.

In the opening section of the paper, Cauchy derived what have since become known as the Cauchy–Riemann equations for functions of a complex variable, and also showed that integrals along different paths are equal provided the function has no singularities. In the second section he went on to investigate what happens when the function *does* have a singularity, and showed that in this case a correction term is needed according to the path taken (see below).[3] Cauchy treated a general function $\phi(x, z)$ of two variables without requiring that it should satisfy the Cauchy–Riemann equations, but clearly what he had in mind was that $x$ and $z$ were the real and imaginary parts of a complex variable. Indeed, as an illustrative example he used the function $\phi(x, z) = \dfrac{z}{x^2 + z^2}$, which is the imaginary part of $\dfrac{1}{x + iz}$.

---

1. Laplace 1812, 96–97.    2. Poisson 1813
3. For a detailed analysis of this extract see Smithies 1997, 39–44.

Unfortunately, publication of the *Mémoires* was suspended around this time due to political upheavals in Paris, and Cauchy's paper did not appear in print until 1827. By that time, he had made significant further advances and added several footnotes, but in the extract below these have been omitted, leaving the paper closer to the form in which Cauchy wrote it in 1814.

---

### Integrals involving singularities
from Cauchy, 'Mémoire sur les Intégrales définies', 1814; *Oeuvres*, (1) 1, 389–391 and 394–395

---

PROBLÈME I. — *Soit* $K = \varphi(x, z)$ *une fonction de* $x$ *et de* $z$ *qui devienne indéterminée pour les valeurs* $x = X$, $z = Z$, *de ces deux variables. Concevons, de plus, que l'intégrale indéfinie*

$$\int \int \frac{\partial K}{\partial z} \, dx \, dz$$

*doive être prise entre les limites* $x = a'$, $x = a''$, $z = b'$, $z = b''$, *et que le système des valeurs* $x = X$, $z = Z$, *soit renfermé entre ces mêmes limites. On demande la valeur que reçoit l'intégrale dont il s'agit, lorsqu'on y substitue, dans tous les éléments à la fois, les valeurs de* $x$ *avant celles de* $z$.

*Solution.* — Supposons qu'en ayant égard aux signes des quantités, c'est-à-dire, en considérant une quantité négative plus grande comme plus petite qu'une autre quantité négative moindre, on ait

$$a' < a'', \quad b' < b''.$$

390                           MÉMOIRE

On aura, en général,

$$a' < X < a'', \quad b' < Z < b''.$$

Mais il pourra se faire aussi que X soit égal à l'une des limites $a'$, $a''$, et Z à l'une des limites $b'$, $b''$. Je commencerai par admettre cette dernière hypothèse, qui se partage naturellement en quatre autres, savoir :

$$X = a', \quad Z = b',$$
$$X = a', \quad Z = b'',$$
$$X = a'', \quad Z = b',$$
$$X = a'', \quad Z = b'';$$

et, pour plus de facilité, je supposerai d'abord que la fonction $K = \varphi(x, z)$ ne peut jamais devenir infinie entre les limites que l'on considère, ni même indéterminée, si ce n'est pour le système de valeurs

$$x = X, \quad z = Z.$$

Cela posé, soit en premier lieu

$$X = a', \quad Z = b'.$$

Pour obtenir la valeur de l'intégrale double $\int\int \frac{\partial K}{\partial z} dx\, dz$ entre les limites $x = a'$, $x = a''$, $z = b'$, $z = b''$, il suffira évidemment de chercher la valeur de la même intégrale entre les limites

$$x = a', \qquad x = a'',$$
$$z = b' + \zeta, \quad z = b'',$$

$\zeta$ étant une quantité très petite, et de supposer ensuite $\zeta = 0$. Mais, suivant que l'on fera évanouir $\zeta$ avant ou après l'intégration relative à $x$, on obtiendra la valeur que reçoit l'intégrale double cherchée, lorsqu'on y substitue, dans tous les éléments à la fois, les valeurs de $z$ avant celles de $x$, ou celle que reçoit la même intégrale, lorsqu'on effectue les substitutions en sens contraire. Entrons, à ce sujet, dans quelques détails.

L'intégrale indéfinie $\int \frac{\partial \mathbf{K}}{\partial z} dz$ étant représentée par

$$\mathbf{K} = \varphi(x, z) + \text{const.},$$

la même intégrale, prise entre les limites $z = b' + \zeta$, $z = b''$, sera

$$\int_{b'+\zeta}^{b''} \frac{\partial \mathbf{K}}{\partial z} dz = \varphi(x, b'') - \varphi(x, b' + \zeta).$$

Si l'on multiplie cette dernière par $dx$, et qu'on intègre le résultat entre les limites $x = a'$, $x = a''$, on aura

$$(9) \qquad \int_{a'}^{a''} \varphi(x, b'') dx - \int_{a'}^{a''} \varphi(x, b' + \zeta) dx,$$

pour la valeur de l'intégrale $\int_{a'}^{a''} \int_{b'+\zeta}^{b''} \frac{\partial \mathbf{K}}{\partial z} dx \, dz$. Si, dans l'expression précédente, on suppose, avant l'intégration relative à $x$, $\zeta = 0$, cette expression deviendra

$$(10) \qquad \int_{a'}^{a''} \varphi(x, b'') dx - \int_{a'}^{a''} \varphi(x, b') dx.$$

C'est la valeur de l'intégrale double cherchée, lorsqu'on y substitue les valeurs de $z$ avant celles de $x$. Mais, si l'on veut obtenir la valeur de la même intégrale double dans le cas où l'on fait les substitutions en sens contraire, il faudra à l'expression (10) ajouter une certaine quantité A dont la valeur sera déterminée par l'équation

$$(11) \qquad \mathbf{A} = \int_{a'}^{a''} [\varphi(x, b') - \varphi(x, b' + \zeta)] dx,$$

dans laquelle on ne doit supposer $\zeta = 0$ qu'après avoir fait l'intégration par rapport à $x$. En admettant cette valeur de A, on aura, pour la valeur de l'intégrale double cherchée dans le cas où l'on substitue les valeurs de $x$ avant celles de $z$,

$$\int_{a'}^{a''} \varphi(x, b'') dx - \int_{a'}^{a''} \varphi(x, b') dx + \mathbf{A}.$$

$$[\ldots]$$

*Exemple.* -- Soit $\mathrm{K} = \varphi(x, z) = \dfrac{z}{x^2 + z^2}$, et concevons que l'inté-grale

$$\int \int \frac{\partial \mathrm{K}}{\partial z} \, dx \, dz$$

doive être prise entre les limites $z = 0$, $z = 1$, $x = 0$, $x = 1$. Si l'on suppose les valeurs de $z$ substituées avant celles de $x$, on aura

$$\int_0^1 \frac{\partial \mathrm{K}}{\partial z} \, dz = \frac{1}{1 + x^2}, \quad \int_0^1 \int_0^1 \frac{\partial \mathrm{K}}{\partial z} \, dx \, dz = \int_0^1 \frac{dx}{1 + x^2} = \frac{\pi}{4}.$$

SUR LES INTÉGRALES DÉFINIES.    395

Mais, si l'on veut renverser l'ordre des substitutions, l'intégrale chan-gera de valeur; car la fonction $\dfrac{z}{x^2 + z^2}$ devient indéterminée, lorsqu'on suppose à la fois $x = 0$, $z = 0$. On a donc, dans le cas présent,

$$\mathrm{X} = a' = 0, \quad \mathrm{Z} = b' = 0.$$

Par suite, la quantité qu'il faut ajouter à la première valeur de l'inté-grale double pour obtenir la seconde sera

$$\mathrm{A} = -\int_0^1 \varphi(\xi, \zeta) \, d\xi = -\int_0^1 \frac{\zeta}{\xi^2 + \zeta^2} \, d\xi,$$

$\zeta$ devant être supposé nul après l'intégration relative à $\xi$. On a d'ail-leurs, en général,

$$\int \frac{\zeta}{\xi^2 + \zeta^2} \, d\xi = arc\ tang\ \frac{\xi}{\zeta} + \text{const.},$$

$arc\ tang\ \dfrac{\xi}{\zeta}$ désignant le plus petit des arcs qui ont $\dfrac{\xi}{\zeta}$ pour tangente. On aura donc

$$\int_0^1 \frac{\zeta}{\xi^2 + \zeta^2} \, d\xi = arc\ tang\ \frac{\varepsilon}{\zeta}.$$

Si, dans cette dernière expression, on fait $\zeta = 0$, elle deviendra égale à $\dfrac{\pi}{2}$. On a donc

$$\mathrm{A} = -\int_0^1 \frac{\zeta}{\xi^2 + \zeta^2} \, d\xi = -\frac{\pi}{2};$$

et, par suite,

$$\int_0^1 \int_0^1 \frac{\partial \mathrm{K}}{\partial z} \, dx \, dz = \frac{\pi}{4} + \mathrm{A} = -\frac{\pi}{4},$$

lorsqu'on substitue les valeurs de $x$ avant celles de $z$.

PROBLEM I.—*Let $K = \phi(x, z)$ be a function of $x$ and $z$ which becomes indeterminate for the values $x = X$, $z = Z$, of these two variables. Let us imagine, further, that the undetermined integral*

$$\int \int \frac{\partial K}{\partial z} \, dx dz$$

*is to be taken between the limits $x = a'$, $x = a''$, $z = b'$, $z = b''$, and that the set of values $x = X$, $z = Z$, is contained between the same limits. We seek the value taken by the integral in question, when one substitutes, into all the elements at the same time, the values of $x$ before those of $z$.*

*Solution.* Let us assume that having regard to the signs of the quantities, that is to say, by considering a greater negative quantity as smaller than another less negative quantity, one has

$$a' < a'', b' < b''.$$

[390] One will have, in general,

$$a' < X < a'', b' < Z < b''.$$

But it may also happen that $X$ is equal to one of the limits $a'$, $a''$, and $Z$ to one of the limits $b'$, $b''$. I will begin by assuming this last hypothesis, which separates naturally into four others, namely:

$$
\begin{aligned}
X &= a', & Z &= b' \\
X &= a', & Z &= b'' \\
X &= a'', & Z &= b', \\
X &= a'', & Z &= b'';
\end{aligned}
$$

and, for greater ease, I will suppose from the start that the function $K = \phi(x, z)$ may never become infinite between the limits one is considering, nor even indeterminate, except for the pair of values

$$x = X, z = Z.$$

That said, in the first place let

$$X = a', Z = b'.$$

To obtain the value of the double integral $\int \int \dfrac{\partial K}{\partial z} \, dx dz$ between the limits $x = a'$, $x = a''$, $z = b'$, $z = b''$, it will clearly suffice to seek the value of the same integral between the limits

$$
\begin{aligned}
x &= a', & x &= a'', \\
z &= b' + \zeta, & z &= b'',
\end{aligned}
$$

where $\zeta$ is a very small quantity, finally supposing $\zeta = 0$. But, depending whether one makes $\zeta$ vanish before or after integration with respect to $x$, one will obtain the value taken by the sought double integral when one substitutes, into all the elements at the same time, values of $z$ before those of $x$, or, taken by the same integral when one carries out the substitutions in the opposite order. Let us enter into some details on this subject.

[391] The indefinite integral $\int \dfrac{\partial K}{\partial z} dz$ being represented by

$$K = \phi(x, z) + \text{constant},$$

the same integral, taken between the limits $z = b' + \zeta$, $z = b''$, will be

$$\int_{b'+\zeta}^{b''} \frac{\partial K}{\partial z} dz = \phi(x, b'') - \phi(x, b' + \zeta).$$

If one multiplies this last by $dx$, and integrates the result between the limits $x = a'$, $x = a''$, one will have

$$(9) \qquad \int_{a'}^{a''} \phi(x, b'') dx - \int_{a'}^{a''} \phi(x, b' + \zeta) dx,$$

for the value of the integral $\int_{a'}^{a''} \int_{b'+\zeta}^{b''} \dfrac{\partial K}{\partial z} dx dz$. If, in the preceding expression one assumes, before integration with respect to $x$, that $\zeta = 0$, this expression will become

$$(10) \qquad \int_{a'}^{a''} \phi(x, b'') dx - \int_{a'}^{a''} \phi(x, b') dx.$$

This is the value of the sought double integral, when one substitutes the values of $z$ before the values of $x$. But if one wants to obtain the value of the same double integral in the case where one makes the substitutions in the opposite order, one must add to expression (10) a certain quantity $A$ whose value will be determined by the equation

$$(11) \qquad A = \int_{a'}^{a''} [\phi(x, b') - \phi(x, b' + \zeta)] dx,$$

in which one must not assume $\zeta = 0$ until after having carried out the integration with respect to $x$. By introducing this value of $A$, one will have, for the value of the sought double integral in the case where one substitutes the values of $x$ before those of $z$,

$$\int_{a'}^{a''} \phi(x, b'') dx - \int_{a'}^{a''} \phi(x, b') dx + A.$$

$$[\ldots]$$

Cauchy went on to show that the right hand side of (11) can be reduced to:

$$\int_{a'}^{a''} \phi(x, b') dx - \int_{a'}^{a''} \phi(x, b' + \zeta) dx = \int_0^\varepsilon \phi(a' + \xi, b' + \zeta) d\xi,$$

where $\varepsilon$ is a very small quantity and $\zeta = 0$ after integration, so that $A$ can be written in the alternative form

$$A = -\int_0^\varepsilon \phi(a' + \xi, b' + \zeta)d\xi.$$

To show how the method works in practice he gave the following example.

[...]

[394] *Example.*—Let $K = \phi(x, z) = \dfrac{z}{x^2 + z^2}$, and let us imagine that the integral

$$\int\int \frac{\partial K}{\partial z}dxdz$$

is to be taken between the limits $z = 0, z = 1, x = 0, x = 1$. If one supposes the values of $z$ substituted before those of $x$, one will have

$$\int_0^1 \frac{\partial K}{\partial z}dz = \frac{1}{1 + x^2}, \quad \int_0^1 \int_0^1 \frac{\partial K}{\partial z}dxdz = \int_0^1 \frac{dx}{1 + x^2} = \frac{\pi}{4}.$$

[395] But, if one wants to reverse the order of the substitutions, the integral will change in value; for the function $\dfrac{z}{x^2 + z^2}$ becomes indeterminate when one supposes $x = 0, z = 0$ at the same time. One therefore has in this case,

$$X = a' = 0, \quad Z = b' = 0.$$

It follows that the quantity one must add to the first value of the double integral to obtain the second will be

$$A = -\int_0^\varepsilon \phi(\xi, \zeta)d\xi = -\int_0^\varepsilon \frac{\zeta}{\xi^2 + \zeta^2}d\xi,$$

where $\zeta$ is supposed zero after integration with respect to $\xi$. One also has, in general,

$$\int \frac{\zeta}{\xi^2 + \zeta^2}d\xi = \arctan\frac{\xi}{\zeta} + \text{constant},$$

where $\arctan\dfrac{\xi}{\zeta}$ denotes the smallest of the arcs which have $\dfrac{\xi}{\zeta}$ for tangent. One will therefore have

$$\int_0^\varepsilon \frac{\zeta}{\xi^2 + \zeta^2}d\xi = \arctan\frac{\varepsilon}{\zeta}.$$

If, in this last expression, one makes $\zeta = 0$, it will become equal to $\dfrac{\pi}{2}$. One therefore has

$$A = -\int_0^\varepsilon \frac{\zeta}{\xi^2 + \zeta^2}d\xi = -\frac{\pi}{2};$$

and it follows that

$$\int_0^1 \int_0^1 \frac{\partial K}{\partial z}dxdz = \frac{\pi}{4} + A = -\frac{\pi}{4},$$

when one substitutes values of $x$ before those of $z$.

———————

### 15.2.3 The calculus of residues, 1826

In his 1814 paper on complex integrals, Cauchy still treated complex functions as sums of real and imaginary parts. Over the next ten years as he developed his ideas further he began to combine real and imaginary parts as a single complex integrand, leading not only to simpler equations but also to more powerful techniques. Then in 1826 he published a new and important paper entitled 'Sur un nouveau genre de calcul' ('On a new kind of calculus'), in which for the first time he defined the residue (*résidu*) of a function at a point where the function becomes infinite. Later in the same paper he defined the integral residue of the function as the sum of the residues at all such singularities.

His basic principle was to create series similar to Taylor series but now including a finite number of terms with *negative* powers of the increment $\varepsilon$. Just as Lagrange had defined derivatives as coefficients of $\dfrac{\varepsilon^n}{n!}$ for positive $n$ (see 10.2.4), Cauchy now defined residues as coefficients of $\dfrac{\varepsilon^{-n}}{n!}$, and treated them as the counterparts of derivatives in the ordinary calculus. Later he was able to show that the correction term $A$ in his paper of 1814 was just such a residue.

Cauchy deliberately worked by analogy to the ordinary calculus, and in doing so replicated not only its power but also the fragility of its foundations: like Newton and Leibniz before him, Cauchy was happy to work with infinitesimally small quantities which, once they had served their purpose, became zero. Nevertheless, his insights were no less significant than theirs had been. The immediate benefit was a powerful method of evaluating integrals as sums of residues; in the longer term Cauchy's work gave rise to an entire new theory of complex variables.

Cauchy's 1826 paper appeared in the first issue of his *Exercices de mathématiques*, essentially a monthly journal devoted to his own work, and many of the papers in which he went on to develop the theory over the next two years were published in subsequent issues of the *Exercices*.

## The calculus of residues

from Cauchy, 'Sur un nouveau genre de calcul', *Exercices de mathématiques*, 1826, 11–13

# SUR UN NOUVEAU GENRE DE CALCUL

## ANALOGUE AU CALCUL INFINITÉSIMAL.

On sait que le calcul différentiel, qui a tant contribué aux progrès de l'analyse, est fondé sur la considération des coefficients différentiels ou fonctions dérivées. Lorsqu'on attribue à une variable indépendante $x$ un accroissement infiniment petit $\varepsilon$, une fonction $f(x)$ de cette variable reçoit elle-même en général un accroissement infiniment petit dont le premier terme est proportionnel à $\varepsilon$, et le coefficient fini de $\varepsilon$ dans l'accroissement de la fonction est ce qu'on nomme le coefficient différentiel. Ce coefficient subsiste, quel que soit $x$, et ne peut s'évanouir constamment que dans le cas où la fonction proposée se réduit à une quantité constante. Il n'en est pas de même d'un autre coefficient dont nous allons parler, et qui est généralement nul, excepté pour des valeurs particulières de la variable $x$. Si, après avoir cherché les valeurs de $x$ qui rendent la fonction $f(x)$ infinie, on ajoute à l'une de ces valeurs, désignée par $x_{\prime}$, la quantité infiniment petite $\varepsilon$, puis, que l'on développe $f(x_{\prime} + \varepsilon)$ suivant les puissances ascendantes de la même quantité, les premiers termes du développement renfermeront des puissances négatives de $\varepsilon$, et l'un d'eux sera le produit de $\frac{1}{\varepsilon}$ par un coefficient fini, que nous appellerons le *résidu* de la fonction $f(x)$ relatif à la valeur particulière $x_{\prime}$ de la variable $x$. Les résidus de cette espèce se présentent naturellement dans plusieurs branches de l'analyse algébrique et de l'analyse infinitésimale. Leur considération fournit des méthodes simples et d'un usage facile, qui s'appliquent à un grand nombre de questions diverses, et des formules nouvelles qui paraissent mériter l'attention des géomètres. Ainsi, par exemple, on déduit immédiatement du calcul des résidus la formule d'interpolation de Lagrange, la décomposition des fractions rationnelles dans le cas des racines égales ou inégales, des formules générales propres à déterminer les valeurs des intégrales définies, la sommation d'une multitude de séries et particulièrement de séries périodiques, l'intégration des équations linéaires aux différences finies ou infiniment petites et à coefficients

( 12 )

constants, avec ou sans dernier terme variable, la série de Lagrange et d'autres séries du même genre, la résolution des équations algébriques ou transcendantes, etc. ...

La recherche des résidus d'une fonction $f(x)$ s'effectue d'ordinaire avec beaucoup de facilité. En effet, soit toujours $x_{\prime}$ l'une des valeurs de $x$ qui rendent cette fonction infinie, c'est-à-dire l'une des racines de l'équation

(1) $$\frac{1}{f(x)} = 0.$$

La valeur du produit $(x - x_{\prime})\, f(x)$, correspondante à $x = x_{\prime}$, se présentera sous une forme indéterminée. Mais en réalité, elle sera très-souvent une quantité finie. Adoptons d'abord cette hypothèse, et faisons

(2) $$(x - x_{\prime})\, f(x) = f(x).$$

On tirera de l'équation (2)

(3) $$f(x) = \frac{f(x)}{x - x_{\prime}},$$

et par suite

(4) $$f(x_{\prime} + \varepsilon) = \frac{f(x_{\prime} + \varepsilon)}{\varepsilon} = \frac{1}{\varepsilon}\, f(x_{\prime}) + f'(x_{\prime} + \theta\varepsilon),$$

$\theta$ désignant un nombre inférieur à l'unité. Par conséquent le résidu de la fonction $f(x)$, relatif à la valeur $x = x_{\prime}$, sera la quantité finie

(5) $$f(x_{\prime}),$$

ou, en d'autres termes, la valeur du produit

(6) $$\varepsilon f(x_{\prime} + \varepsilon)$$

correspondante à $\varepsilon = 0$. Dans le cas que nous venons de considérer, l'équation (1) est censée n'admettre qu'une seule racine égale à $x_{\prime}$.

On dit que l'équation (1) admet $m$ racines égales à $x_{\prime}$, $m$ désignant un nombre entier quelconque, lorsque le produit $(x - x_{\prime})^{m} f(x)$ obtient, pour $x = x_{\prime}$, une valeur finie différente de zéro. Soit, dans cette dernière hypothèse,

(7) $$(x - x_{\prime})^{m} f(x) = f(x).$$

( 13 )

f $(x_1)$ sera une quantité finie, et l'on aura

$$(8) \qquad f(x) = \frac{f(x)}{(x - x_1)^m},$$

puis l'on en conclura, en posant $x = x_1 + \varepsilon$,

$$(9) \qquad f(x_1 + \varepsilon) = \frac{f(x_1 + \varepsilon)}{\varepsilon^m}$$

$$= \frac{1}{\varepsilon^m} f(x_1) + \frac{1}{\varepsilon^{m-1}} \frac{f'(x_1)}{1} + \ldots + \frac{1}{\varepsilon} \frac{f^{(m-1)}(x_1)}{1.2.3\ldots(m-1)} + \frac{f^{(m)}(x_1 + \theta\varepsilon)}{1.2.3\ldots m},$$

$\theta$ désignant toujours un nombre inférieur à l'unité. Donc le résidu de la fonction $f(x)$, relatif à la valeur $x = x_1$, sera la quantité finie

$$(10) \qquad \frac{f^{(m-1)}(x_1)}{1.2.3\ldots(m-1)},$$

ou, en d'autres termes, ce que devient l'expression

$$(11) \qquad \frac{1.2.3\ldots(m-1)}{1} \frac{d^{m-1}[\varepsilon^m f(x_1 + \varepsilon)]}{d\varepsilon^{m-1}}$$

lorsqu'on pose, après les différentiations, $\varepsilon = 0$.

Pour abréger le discours, nous appellerons *résidu intégral* de la fonction $f(x)$ la somme des résidus de cette fonction relatifs aux diverses racines réelles ou imaginaires de l'équation (1), et *résidu intégral pris entre des limites données* la somme des résidus correspondants à des racines dans lesquelles les parties réelles et les coefficients de $\sqrt{-1}$ ne devront pas dépasser certaines limites. L'*extraction des résidus* sera l'opération par laquelle nous les déduirons de la fonction proposée. Nous indiquerons cette extraction à l'aide de la lettre initiale $\mathcal{E}$, qui sera considérée comme une nouvelle caractéristique, et, pour exprimer le résidu intégral de $f(x)$, nous placerons la lettre $\mathcal{E}$ devant la fonction entourée de doubles parenthèses, ainsi qu'il suit

$$(12) \qquad \mathcal{E}((f(x))).$$

Dans la notation (12), les doubles parenthèses, dont nous avons précédemment fait usage pour exprimer les valeurs multiples des fonctions [voyez la page 1],

I.                                                                                 3

## ON A NEW KIND OF CALCULUS
### ANALOGOUS TO INFINITESIMAL CALCULUS

One knows that the differential calculus, which has contributed so much to the progress of analysis, is based on the consideration of differential coefficients or derived functions. When one gives to an independent variable $x$ an infinitely small increment $\varepsilon$, a function $f(x)$ of that variable itself receives in general an infinitely small increment of which the first term is proportional to $\varepsilon$, and the finite coefficient of $\varepsilon$ in the increment of the function is what one calls the differential coefficient. This coefficient exists, whatever $x$ may be, and cannot vanish permanently except in the case where the proposed function is reduced to a constant quantity. It is not the same for another coefficient of which we are going to speak, and which is generally zero, except for particular values of the variable $x$. If, after having sought the values of $x$ which render the function $f(x)$ infinite, one adds to one of these values, denoted by $x_1$, the infinitely small quantity $\varepsilon$, then expands $f(x_1 + \varepsilon)$ in ascending powers of the same quantity, the first terms of the expansion will include negative powers of $\varepsilon$, and one of them will be the product of $\frac{1}{\varepsilon}$ and a finite coefficient, which we will call the *residue* of the function $f(x)$ with respect to a particular value $x_1$ of the variable $x$. Residues of this kind appear naturally in several branches of algebraic analysis and infinitesimal analysis. Consideration of them supplies simple methods, easy to use, which apply to a great number of different questions, and new formulas which would seem to merit the attention of geometers. Thus, for example, one deduces immediately from the calculus of residues Lagrange's interpolation formula, the decomposition of rational functions in the case of equal or unequal roots, general formulas suitable for finding the values of definite integrals, the summation of a multitude of series and particularly of periodic series, the integration of linear equations with finite or infinitely small differences and with constant coefficients, [12] with or without a final variable term, the series of Lagrange and other series of the same kind, the solution of algebraic or transcendental equations, etc.

Finding the residues of a function $f(x)$ is usually carried out with great ease. Indeed, let $x_1$ always be one of the values of $x$ which render this function infinite, that is to say, one of the roots of the equation

$$(1) \qquad \frac{1}{f(x)} = 0.$$

The value of the product $(x - x_1)f(x)$, corresponding to $x = x_1$, will appear in an indeterminate form. But in reality it will very often be a finite quantity. Let us adopt this hypothesis to begin with, and write

$$(2) \qquad (x - x_1)f(x) = \mathrm{f}(x).$$

One obtains from equation (2)

$$(3) \qquad f(x) = \frac{\mathrm{f}(x)}{x - x_1},$$

and it follows that

$$(4) \qquad f(x_1 + \varepsilon) = \frac{\mathsf{f}(x_1 + \varepsilon)}{\varepsilon} = \frac{1}{\varepsilon} \mathsf{f}(x_1) + \mathsf{f}'(x_1 + \theta \varepsilon),$$

where $\theta$ denotes a number less than one. Consequently the residue of the function $f(x)$, with respect to the value $x = x_1$, will be the finite quantity

$$(5) \qquad \mathsf{f}(x_1),$$

or, in other words, the value of the product

$$(6) \qquad \varepsilon f(x_1 + \varepsilon)$$

corresponding to $\varepsilon = 0$. In the case we have just considered, equation (1) is assumed to have only a single real root equal to $x_1$.

One says that equation (1) has $m$ roots equal to $x_1$, where $m$ denotes any whole number, when the product $(x - x_1)^m f(x)$ takes, for $x = x_1$, a finite value different from zero. Under this last hypothesis, let

$$(7) \qquad (x - x_1)^m f(x) = \mathsf{f}(x).$$

[13] $\mathsf{f}(x_1)$ will be a finite quantity, and one will have

$$(8) \qquad f(x) = \frac{\mathsf{f}(x)}{(x - x_1)^m},$$

from which one may infer, putting $x = x_1 + \varepsilon$,

$$(9) \qquad f(x_1 + \varepsilon) = \frac{\mathsf{f}(x_1 + \varepsilon)}{\varepsilon^m}$$

$$= \frac{1}{\varepsilon^m} \mathsf{f}(x_1) + \frac{1}{\varepsilon^{m-1}} \frac{\mathsf{f}'(x_1)}{1} + \cdots + \frac{1}{\varepsilon} \frac{\mathsf{f}^{(m-1)}(x_1)}{1.2.3 \ldots (m-1)} + \frac{\mathsf{f}^{(m)}(x_1 + \theta \varepsilon)}{1.2.3 \ldots m},$$

where $\theta$ always denotes a number less than one. Therefore the residue of the function $f(x)$, with respect to the value $x = x_1$, will be the finite quantity

$$(10) \qquad \frac{\mathsf{f}^{(m-1)}(x_1)}{1.2.3 \ldots (m-1)},$$

or, in other words, the value of the expression

$$(11) \qquad \frac{1.2.3 \ldots (m-1)}{1} \frac{d^{m-1}[\varepsilon^m f(x_1 + \varepsilon)]}{d\varepsilon^{m-1}}$$

when one puts, after the differentiations, $\varepsilon \, [=] \, 0$.

To shorten the discussion, we will call the sum of residues of this function with respect to the various real or imaginary roots of equation (1) the *integral residue* of the function $f(x)$, and the sum of residues corresponding to the roots in which the real parts and the coefficients of $\sqrt{-1}$ may not exceed certain limits, the *integral residue taken between given limits*. The *extraction of residues* will be the operation by which we will deduce them from the proposed function. We will indicate this extraction by means of the initial letter $\mathcal{E}$, which will be considered as a new symbol, and, to express the integral residue of $f(x)$, we will place the letter $\mathcal{E}$ in front of the function enclosed in double parentheses, thus as follows

$$\mathcal{E}((f(x))).$$

---

### 15.2.4 Cauchy's integral formulas, 1831

After further political upheavals in France in 1830, Cauchy exiled himself to Turin, where he became professor of theoretical physics. In 1831 he submitted to the Turin Academy a lengthy paper on celestial mechanics, and in the first part of it he gave proofs of what are now known as Cauchy's formulas. The relevant extract is given below. In the longer second part of the paper he went on to give applications to celestial mechanics.

In a second memoir presented to the Turin Academy later the same year Cauchy went on to establish the residue theorem for integrals around simple closed curves, thus bringing to an end a remarkable series of papers in which he had essentially established on his own the modern theory of complex analysis.

---

### Cauchy's integral formulas
from Cauchy, 'Résumé d'un mémoire sur la mécanique céleste', 1831; *Oeuvres*, (2) 12, 58–61

---

FORMULES POUR LE DÉVELOPPEMENT DES FONCTIONS EN SÉRIES.

*Calcul des limites* (¹).

Soient $p$ un arc réel et $n$ un nombre entier. On trouvera, en supposant $n > 0$,

(1)  $$\int_{-\pi}^{\pi} e^{np\sqrt{-1}}\, dp = \int_{-\pi}^{\pi} e^{-np\sqrt{-1}}\, dp = 0,$$

(¹) Le Mémoire qu'on va lire est une partie de celui qui a été lithographié à Turin

ET SUR LE CALCUL DES LIMITES.          59

et, en supposant $n = 0$,

$$(2) \qquad \int_{-\pi}^{\pi} dp = 2\pi.$$

Soit de plus

$$f(x) = a_0 + a_1 x + a_2 x^2 + \ldots + a_n x^n$$

une fonction entière de la variable $x$. Si l'on attribue à cette variable une valeur imaginaire $\overline{x}$ dont le module soit X, en sorte qu'on ait

$$\overline{x} = X e^{p\sqrt{-1}},$$

on tirera des formules $(1)$ et $(2)$

$$\int_{-\pi}^{\pi} f(\overline{x})\, dp = \int_{-\pi}^{\pi} f\left(\frac{1}{\overline{x}}\right) dp = 2\pi a_0 ;$$

on aura donc

$$(3) \qquad \int_{-\pi}^{\pi} f(\overline{x})\, dp = 2\pi f(0).$$

Il est d'ailleurs facile d'étendre la formule $(3)$ au cas où $f(\overline{x})$ cesse d'être une fonction entière de $x$. En effet, on a généralement

$$D_X f(\overline{x}) = \frac{1}{X\sqrt{-1}} D_p f(\overline{x}).$$

Or, si l'on intègre les deux membres de l'équation précédente : $1^\circ$ par rapport à X et à partir de $X = 0$; $2^\circ$ par rapport à $p$ entre les limites

en 1832. Nous le reproduisons ici tel qu'il a été publié à cette époque. Seulement, dans l'énoncé des conditions sous lesquelles subsiste la formule $(3)$ et, par suite, dans les énoncés des théorèmes II, III et VII, nous avons cru devoir, par la raison que nous avons déjà indiquée ailleurs (*voir*, dans le Tome I de cet Ouvrage, la fin de la Note *Sur l'intégration des équations différentielles des mouvements planétaires*, p. 32) [a], mentionner, avec les fonctions $f(x)$, $f(x, y)$, etc., leurs dérivées du premier ordre, et ajouter en conséquence au texte du Mémoire lithographié quelques mots que nous avons placés entre parenthèses. De plus, pour simplifier les notations, nous désignons souvent, comme nous l'avons fait dans plusieurs circonstances, les dérivées d'une fonction relatives à diverses variables $x, y, \ldots, p$, à l'aide des lettres caractéristiques $D_x$, $D_y$, ..., $D_p$, en écrivant, par exemple,

$$D_x f(x) \qquad \text{au lieu de} \qquad \frac{df(x)}{dx}.$$

[a] *Œuvres de Cauchy*, 2ᵉ série, t. XI, p. 50.

$p = -\pi$, $p = \pi$; et si l'on suppose que la fonction de X et de $p$, représentée par $f(\overline{x})$, reste finie et continue (avec sa dérivée), quel que soit $p$, pour la valeur attribuée à X et pour une valeur plus petite, on retrouvera précisément la formule (3).

D'autre part, comme on a $d\overline{x} = \overline{x}\, dp \sqrt{-1}$, si les fonctions dérivées $f'(\overline{x})$, $f''(\overline{x})$, ..., $f^{(n)}(\overline{x})$ restent elles-mêmes finies et continues pour la valeur attribuée à X et pour des valeurs plus petites, il suffira d'appliquer l'intégration par parties à l'intégrale

$$\int_{-\pi}^{\pi} \frac{f(\overline{x})}{\overline{x}^n}\, dp,$$

pour en conclure

$$\int_{-\pi}^{\pi} \frac{f(\overline{x})}{\overline{x}^n}\, dp = \frac{1}{n}\int_{-\pi}^{\pi} \frac{f'(\overline{x})}{\overline{x}^{n-1}}\, dp - \frac{1}{n(n-1)}\int_{-\pi}^{\pi} \frac{f''(\overline{x})}{\overline{x}^{n-2}}\, dp = \ldots,$$

et par suite

$$\int_{-\pi}^{\pi} \frac{f(\overline{x})}{\overline{x}^n}\, dp = \frac{1}{1.2.3\ldots n}\int_{-\pi}^{\pi} f^{(n)}(\overline{x})\, dp,$$

ou, en vertu de la formule (3),

$$(4) \qquad \frac{1}{2\pi}\int_{-\pi}^{\pi} \frac{f(\overline{x})}{\overline{x}^n}\, dp = \frac{f^{(n)}(0)}{1.2.3\ldots n}.$$

Si la fonction $f(\overline{x})$ s'évanouit pour une valeur nulle de $x$, l'équation (3) donnera simplement

$$(5) \qquad \int_{-\pi}^{\pi} f(\overline{x})\, dp = 0.$$

Des formules (3), (4), (5) on peut aisément déduire, comme on va le voir, celles qui servent à développer une fonction explicite ou implicite de la variable $x$ en une série ordonnée suivant les puissances ascendantes de cette variable.

Si, dans la formule (5), on remplace $f(\overline{x})$ par le produit

$$\overline{x}\,\frac{f(\overline{x}) - f(x)}{\overline{x} - x},$$

$x$ étant différent de $\bar{x}$, et le module de $x$ inférieur à X, on en conclura

$$\int_{-\pi}^{\pi} \frac{\bar{x}\,f(\bar{x})}{\bar{x}-x}\,dp = \int_{-\pi}^{\pi} \frac{\bar{x}\,f(x)}{\bar{x}-x}\,dp = f(x)\int_{-\pi}^{\pi}\left(1+\frac{x}{\bar{x}}+\frac{x^2}{\bar{x}^2}+\dots\right)dp = 2\pi f(x),$$

et par suite on retrouvera la formule connue

(6)
$$f(x) = \frac{1}{2\pi}\int_{-\pi}^{\pi} \frac{\bar{x}\,f(\bar{x})}{\bar{x}-x}\,dp.$$

L'équation (6) suppose, comme les équations (3) et (5), que la
fonction de X et de $p$ représentée par $f\left(\bar{x}\right)$ reste finie et continue pour
la valeur attribuée à X et pour des valeurs plus petites.

*Notation*
In this paper Cauchy wrote $D_x f(x)$ for $\dfrac{\mathrm{d}}{\mathrm{d}x}f(x)$.

### TRANSLATION

### FORMULAS FOR THE EXPANSION OF FUNCTIONS IN SERIES.
## Calculation of limits.

Let $p$ be a real arc and $n$ a whole number. One will find, assuming $n > 0$,

(1)
$$\int_{-\pi}^{\pi} e^{np\sqrt{-1}}\,dp = \int_{-\pi}^{\pi} e^{-np\sqrt{-1}}\,dp = 0,$$

[59] and assuming $n = 0$,

(2)
$$\int_{-\pi}^{\pi} dp = 2\pi.$$

Further, let

$$f(x) = a_0 + a_1 x + a_2 x^2 + \cdots + a_n x^n$$

be a polynomial function of the variable $x$. If one gives to this variable an imaginary
value $\bar{x}$ of which the modulus is $X$, in such a way that one has

$$\bar{x} = X e^{p\sqrt{-1}},$$

one will obtain from formulas (1) and (2)

$$\int_{-\pi}^{\pi} f(\bar{x})\,dp = \int_{-\pi}^{\pi} f\left(\frac{1}{\bar{x}}\right)dp = 2\pi a_0;$$

one will therefore have

(3)
$$\int_{-\pi}^{\pi} f(\bar{x})\,dp = 2\pi f(0).$$

Further it is easy to extend formula (3) to the case where $f(\bar{x})$ is no longer a polynomial function of $x$. Indeed, one has in general

$$D_X f(\bar{x}) = \frac{1}{X\sqrt{-1}} D_p f(\bar{x}).$$

Now, if one integrates the two sides of the preceding equation, first, with respect to $X$ and from $X = 0$, second, with respect to $p$ between the limits [60] $p = -\pi, p = \pi$; and if one assumes that the function of $X$ and $p$ represented by $f(\bar{x})$ remains finite and continuous (along with its derivative) for the value given to $X$ and for any smaller value, whatever $p$ may be, one will recover precisely formula (3).

On the other hand, since one has $d\bar{x} = \bar{x}\,dp\sqrt{-1}$, if the derived functions $f'(\bar{x}), f''(\bar{x}), \ldots, f^{(n)}(\bar{x})$ themselves remain finite and continuous for the value given to $X$ and for smaller values, it will suffice to apply integration by parts to the integral

$$\int_{-\pi}^{\pi} \frac{f(\bar{x})}{\bar{x}^n}\,dp,$$

to deduce

$$\int_{-\pi}^{\pi} \frac{f(\bar{x})}{\bar{x}^n}\,dp = \frac{1}{n}\int_{-\pi}^{\pi} \frac{f'(\bar{x})}{\bar{x}^{n-1}}\,dp = \frac{1}{n(n-1)}\int_{-\pi}^{\pi} \frac{f'',(\bar{x})}{\bar{x}^{n-2}}\,dp = \ldots,$$

and it follows that

$$\int_{-\pi}^{\pi} \frac{f(\bar{x})}{\bar{x}^n}\,dp = \frac{1}{1.2.3\ldots n}\int_{-\pi}^{\pi} f^{(n)}(\bar{x})\,dp,$$

or, by virtue of formula (3),

(4)
$$\frac{1}{2\pi}\int_{-\pi}^{\pi} \frac{f(\bar{x})}{\bar{x}^n}\,dp = \frac{f^{(n)}(0)}{1.2.3.\ldots.n}.$$

If the function $f(\bar{x})$ vanishes for a zero value of $x$, equation (3) will give simply

(5)
$$\int_{-\pi}^{\pi} f(\bar{x})\,dp = 0.$$

From formulas (3), (4), (5) one may easily deduce, as we will see, those that can be used to expand an explicit or implicit function of the variable $x$ in an ordered series of ascending powers of that variable.

If in formula (5) one replaces $f(\bar{x})$ by the product

$$\bar{x}\frac{f(\bar{x}) - f(x)}{\bar{x} - x},$$

[61] where $x$ is different from $\bar{x}$, and the modulus of $x$ is less than $X$, one infers that

$$\int_{-\pi}^{\pi} \frac{\bar{x}f(\bar{x})}{\bar{x} - x}\,dp = \int_{-\pi}^{\pi} \frac{\bar{x}f(x)}{\bar{x} - x}\,dp = f(x)\int_{-\pi}^{\pi} \left(1 + \frac{x}{\bar{x}} + \frac{x^2}{\bar{x}^2} + \ldots\right)dp = 2\pi f(x),$$

and consequently one recovers the known formula

(6)
$$f(x) = \frac{1}{2\pi} \int_{-\pi}^{\pi} \frac{\bar{x} f(\bar{x})}{\bar{x} - x} dp.$$

Equation (6) assumes, like equations (3) and (5), that the function of $X$ and $p$ represented by $f(\bar{x})$ remains finite and continuous for the value given to $X$ and for smaller values.

---

### 15.2.5  The Cauchy–Riemann equations, 1851

Cauchy wrote down what are now called the Cauchy–Riemann equations only in passing at the beginning of his investigations in 1814. Riemann's doctoral thesis of 1851 brought them to the heart of complex analysis, so that his name is now linked with Cauchy's. For Cauchy, who in general dealt with analytic functions, that is, functions defined by algebraic operations, these equations had simply been a useful general property, and only towards the end of his life did he begin to recognize their importance. Riemann, on the other hand, recognized the *necessity* of ensuring that the derivative of a complex function is well defined and independent of the path along which it is taken. Thus the equations were for him the essential starting point of his investigations.

In the first three paragraphs of his thesis Riemann discussed functions of a real variable but then moved on almost immediately to functions of a complex variable, which is where the extract below begins. At first he treated the complex variables $w$ and $z$ as sums of real and imaginary parts but by the end of section §1 was already starting to consider them as single quantities.

---

### The Cauchy–Riemann equations

from Riemann, *Grundlagen für eine allgemeine Theorie der Functionen einer veränderlichen complexen Grösse*, from §1 and §4, as published in 1867

---

Anders verhält es sich aber, wenn die Veränderlichkeit der Grösse z nicht auf reelle Werthe beschränkt wird, sondern auch complexe von der Form x + yi (wo $i = \sqrt{-1}$) zugelassen werden.

Es seien x + yi und x + yi + dx + dyi zwei unendlich wenig verschiedene Werthe der Grösse z, welchen die Werthe u + vi und u + vi + du + dvi der Grösse w entsprechen. Alsdann wird, wenn die Abhängigkeit der Grösse w von z eine willkührlich angenommene ist, das Verhältniss $\dfrac{du + dvi}{dx + dyi}$ sich mit den Werthen von dx und dy allgemein zu reden ändern, indem, wenn man $\quad d\,x \stackrel{\cdot}{+} d\,y\,i = \varepsilon\,e^{\varphi\,i}\quad$ setzt, $\quad\dfrac{d\,u + d\,v\,i}{d\,x + d\,y\,i}$

$$= \tfrac{1}{2}\left(\frac{d\,u}{d\,x} + \frac{d\,v}{d\,y}\right) + \tfrac{1}{2}\left(\frac{d\,v}{d\,x} - \frac{d\,u}{d\,y}\right)i + \tfrac{1}{2}\left[\frac{d\,u}{d\,x} - \frac{d\,v}{d\,y} + \left(\frac{d\,v}{d\,x} + \frac{d\,u}{d\,y}\right)i\right]\frac{d\,x - d\,y\,i}{d\,x + d\,y\,i}$$

$$= \tfrac{1}{2}\left(\frac{d\,u}{d\,x} + \frac{d\,v}{d\,y}\right) + \tfrac{1}{2}\left(\frac{d\,v}{d\,x} - \frac{d\,u}{d\,y}\right)i + \tfrac{1}{2}\left[\frac{d\,u}{d\,x} - \frac{d\,v}{d\,y} + \left(\frac{d\,v}{d\,x} + \frac{d\,u}{d\,y}\right)i\right]e^{-2\varphi\,i}$$

wird. Auf welche Art aber auch w als Function von z durch Verbindung der einfachen Grössenoperationen bestimmt werden möge, immer wird der Werth des Differentialquotienten $\dfrac{d\,w}{d\,z}$ von dem besondern Werthe des Differentials d z unabhängig sein *). Offenbar kann also auf diesem Wege nicht jede beliebige Abhängigkeit der complexen Grösse w von der complexen Grösse z ausgedrückt werden.

Das eben hervorgehobene Merkmal aller irgendwie durch Grössenoperationen bestimmbaren Functionen werden wir für die folgende Untersuchung, wo eine solche Function unabhängig von ihrem Ausdrucke betrachtet werden soll, zu Grunde legen, indem wir, ohne jetzt dessen Allgemeingültigkeit und Zulänglichkeit für den Begriff einer durch Grössenoperationen ausdrückbaren Abhängigkeit zu beweisen, von folgender Definition ausgehen:

Eine veränderliche complexe Grösse w heisst eine Function einer andern veränderlichen complexen Grösse z, wenn sie mit ihr sich so ändert, dass der Werth des Differentialquotienten $\dfrac{d\,w}{d\,z}$ unabhängig von dem Werthe des Differentials d z ist.

---

*) Diese Behauptung ist offenbar in allen Fällen gerechtfertigt, wo sich aus dem Ausdrucke von w durch z mittelst der Regeln der Differentiation ein Ausdruck von $\dfrac{d\,w}{d\,z}$ durch z finden lässt; ihre streng allgemeine Gültigkeit bleibt für jetzt dahin gestellt.

[...]

### 4.

Bringt man den Differentialquotienten $\dfrac{d\,u + d\,v\,i}{d\,x + d\,y\,i}$ in die Form

$$\frac{\left(\dfrac{d\,u}{d\,x} + \dfrac{d\,v}{d\,x}\,i\right)d\,x + \left(\dfrac{d\,v}{d\,y} - \dfrac{d\,u}{d\,y}\,i\right)d\,y\,i,}{d\,x + d\,y\,i}$$

so erhellt, dass er und zwar nur dann für je zwei Werthe von d x und d y denselben Werth haben wird, wenn

$$\frac{d\,u}{d\,x} = \frac{d\,v}{d\,y}\quad \text{und}\quad \frac{d\,v}{d\,x} = -\frac{d\,u}{d\,y}$$

ist. Diese Bedingungen sind also hinreichend und nothwendig, damit $w = u + v\,i$ eine Function von $z = x + y\,i$ sei. Für die einzelnen Glieder dieser Function fliessen aus ihnen die folgenden:

$$\frac{d^{2}u}{d\,x^{2}} + \frac{d^{2}u}{d\,y^{2}} = 0, \qquad \frac{d^{2}v}{d\,x^{2}} + \frac{d^{2}v}{d\,y^{2}} = 0,$$

welche für die Untersuchung der Eigenschaften, die Einem Gliede einer solchen Function einzeln betrachtet zukommen, die Grundlage bilden.

TRANSLATION

But it is quite another matter if the quantity $z$ is not restricted to varying over real values, but complex values of the form $x + yi$ (where $i = \sqrt{-1}$) are also permitted.

Let $x + yi$ and $x + yi + dx + dyi$ be two values of the quantity $z$, infinitely little different from each other, which correspond to the values $u + vi$ and $u + vi + du + dvi$ of the quantity $w$. Then, if the dependence of the quantity $w$ on $z$ is supposed arbitrary, the ratio $\dfrac{du + dvi}{dx + dyi}$ will in general vary according to the values of $dx$ and $dy$, [2] in that,

if one sets $dx + dyi = \varepsilon e^{\varphi i}$, then $\dfrac{du + dvi}{dx + dyi}$

$$= \frac{1}{2}\left(\frac{du}{dx} + \frac{dv}{dy}\right) + \frac{1}{2}\left(\frac{dv}{dx} - \frac{du}{dy}\right)i + \frac{1}{2}\left[\frac{du}{dx} - \frac{dv}{dy} + \left(\frac{dv}{dx} + \frac{du}{dy}\right)i\right]\frac{dx - dyi}{dx + dyi}$$

$$= \frac{1}{2}\left(\frac{du}{dx} + \frac{dv}{dy}\right) + \frac{1}{2}\left(\frac{dv}{dx} - \frac{du}{dy}\right)i + \frac{1}{2}\left[\frac{du}{dx} - \frac{dv}{dy} + \left(\frac{dv}{dx} + \frac{du}{dy}\right)i\right]e^{-2\varphi i}.$$

On the other hand, if $w$ can be determined as a function of $z$ by combining elementary operations in whatever way, the value of the differential quotient $\dfrac{dw}{dz}$ will always be independent of the particular values of the differentials $dz$.* Clearly not every arbitrary dependence of a complex quantity $w$ on a complex quantity $z$ can be expressed in this way.

The characteristic just emphasized of functions that may be determined in whatever way by means of elementary operations, we will lay as foundation in the following investigation, where we will regard such a function as independent of its expression; insofar as we will proceed from the following definition without at the moment proving its general validity and sufficiency for the concept of dependence expressible through operations:

A variable complex quantity $w$ is called a function of another variable complex quantity $z$, if it so varies with it, that the value of the differential quotient $\dfrac{dw}{dz}$ is independent of the value of the differential $dz$.

[...]

Next, in §2 and §3, Riemann digressed to discuss the underlying geometry, before returning to the equations.

[...]

If one brings the differential quotient $\dfrac{du + dvi}{dx + dyi}$ into the form

$$\frac{\left(\frac{du}{dx} + \frac{dv}{dx}i\right)dx + \left(\frac{dv}{dy} - \frac{du}{dy}i\right)dyi}{dx + dyi},$$

---

* This assertion is clearly correct in all cases where the expression for $w$ in terms of $z$ permits the finding of an expression for $\dfrac{dw}{dz}$ in terms of $z$ by means of the rules of differentiation; the strict general validity remains left aside for now.

4.

[4] then it becomes clear that it will have the same value for each two values of $dx$ and $dy$ if and only if

$$\frac{du}{dx} = \frac{dv}{dy} \quad \text{and} \quad \frac{dv}{dx} = -\frac{du}{dy}.$$

So these conditions are sufficient and necessary for $w = u + vi$ to be a function of $z = x + yi$. For the individual parts of this function there result from this the following:

$$\frac{d^2u}{dx^2} + \frac{d^2u}{dy^2} = 0, \quad \frac{d^2v}{dx^2} + \frac{d^2v}{dy^2} = 0,$$

which lay the foundation for the investigation of the properties of individual parts of such a function considered separately.

———————

# CHAPTER 16

# CONVERGENCE AND COMPLETENESS

We have already noted some seventeenth- and eighteenth-century discussions of convergence (or the lack of them) in 8.3, and in this chapter we take up the nineteenth-century continuation of the same story. One of the most powerful tools available to early nineteenth-century mathematicians investigating convergence turned out to be Cauchy sequences, and so that is where we shall begin.[1]

## 16.1 CAUCHY SEQUENCES

### 16.1.1 Bolzano and 'Cauchy sequences', 1817

Bolzano's ground-breaking paper of 1817 on the intermediate value theorem (see 11.2.4) also contained an entirely new approach to the question of convergence. Near the beginning of his proof, in §5, Bolzano remarked on a type of series with a special property:[2]

Particularly noteworthy [...] is the class of those series with the property that *change* in value (*increase* or *decrease*), *however far the continuation* of its terms is taken, always remains *smaller* than a certain quantity, which itself can be taken *as small as we please* provided the series has been continued far enough beforehand.

---

1. Nowadays we distinguish between a *sequence* (an ordered list of terms) and a *series* (the sum of a sequence) but in the early nineteenth century writers rarely made such a distinction. The German *Reihe* and French *série* were used for both, leaving the precise meaning to be understood from the context; in this chapter, therefore, these words have both been translated by 'series'.

2. 'Unter diesen ist besonder merkwürdig die Classe derjenigen Reihen, welche die Eigenschaft besitzen, daß die *Veränderung* (*Zu- oder Abnahme*), welche ihr Werth *durch eine auch noch so weit getriebene Fortsetzung* ihrer Glieder erleidet, immer *kleiner* verbleibt, als eine gewisse Größe, die wieder selbst *so klein, als man nur immer will,* angenommen werden kann, wenn man die Reihe schon vorher weit genug fortgesetzt hat.' Bolzano 1817, §5.

In the next two sections of the paper, §6 and §7, Bolzano attempted to prove that such series must always converge. It turned out to be more difficult than it might seem, and Bolzano was forced to introduce a fresh assumption the existence of a quantity $X$ to which the terms of the series approach as closely as we please. Such a hypothesis, Bolzano claimed 'contains nothing impossible' ('enthält auch gewiß nichts Unmögliches'), but it was precisely what he was trying to prove in the first place. The problem was deeper than Bolzano realized. Convergence of Cauchy sequences requires *completeness* of the real numbers or, simply speaking, that the number line is an unbroken continuum with no gaps. Convergence of Cauchy sequences is in fact mathematically *equivalent* to completeness: either must be assumed in order to prove the other. Without some such assumption, Bolzano was forced to introduce his hypothetical quantity $X$.

Bolzano's proof of the convergence of Cauchy sequences, though incorrectly argued, is given here because it was the *only* attempt at such a proof in the early nineteenth century, and illustrates the subtle and difficult nature of the problem. It is worth nothing his version of an argument used by Wallis and Newton 150 years earlier, that if $\omega$ can be made less than any given quantity it can be regarded as nothing.

# Bolzano and 'Cauchy sequences'

from Bolzano, *Rein analytischer Beweis*, 1817, §6–§7; as translated by Steve Russ in
Bolzano 2004, 266–268

35

Zuwachs soll der Voraussetzung nach so klein verbleiben können, als man nur immer will, wenn man erst n groß genug angenommen hat.

§. 7.

Lehrsatz. Wenn eine Reihe von Größen

$$\overset{1}{F}x, \overset{2}{F}x, \overset{3}{F}x, \dots, \overset{n}{F}x, \dots, \overset{n+r}{F}x, \dots$$

von der Beschaffenheit ist, daß der Unterschied zwischen ihrem nten Gliede $\overset{n}{F}x$ und jedem spätern $\overset{n+r}{F}x$, sey dieses von jenem auch noch so weit entfernt, kleiner als jede gegebene Größe verbleibt, wenn man n groß genug angenommen hat: so gibt es jedesmahl eine gewisse beständige Größe, und zwar nur eine, der sich die Glieder dieser Reihe immer mehr nähern, und der sie so nahe kommen können, als man nur will, wenn man die Reihe weit genug fortsetzt.

Beweis. Daß eine solche Reihe, wie sie der Lehrsatz beschreibt, möglich sey, erhellet aus §. 6. Die Annahme aber, daß eine Größe X vorhanden sey, der sich die Glieder dieser Reihe bey immer weiterer Fortsetzung so sehr, als man nur immer will, nähern, enthält auch gewiß nichts Unmögliches, wenn man noch nicht voraussetzt, daß diese Größe nur eine einzige und unveränderliche sey, Denn

C 2                                     wenn

§. 6.

5. Zusatz. Wenn man den Werth, welchen die Summe der ersten n, u + 1, n + 2, ..., n + r Glieder einer wie §. 5 beschaffenen Reihe hat, der Ordnung nach durch $\overset{n}{F}x, \overset{n+1}{F}x, \overset{n+2}{F}x, \dots, \overset{n+r}{F}x$ bezeichnet (§. 1): so stellen die Größen

$$\overset{1}{F}x, \overset{2}{F}x, \overset{3}{F}x, \dots, \overset{n}{F}x, \dots, \overset{n+r}{F}x, \dots$$

nun eine neue Reihe vor (die summatorische der vorigen genannt). Diese hat der gemachten Voraussetzung nach die besondre Eigenschaft, daß der Unterschied, der zwischen ihrem nten Gliede $\overset{n}{F}x$, und jedem spätern $\overset{n+r}{F}x$, es sey auch noch so weit von jenem nten entfernt, kleiner als jede gegebene Größe bleibt, wenn man erst n groß genug angenommen hat. Dieser Unterschied ist nähmlich der Zuwachs, den die ursprüngliche Reihe durch eine Fortsetzung über ihr ntes Glied hinaus erfährt; und dieser

Zu.

---

TRANSLATION

§6

*Corollary* 5. If the values of the sums of the first $n$, $n + 1$, $n + 2$, ..., $n + r$ terms of a series like those of §5 are denoted (§1) by $\overset{n}{F}x$, $\overset{n+1}{F}\,x$, $\overset{n+2}{F}\,x$, ..., $\overset{n+r}{F}\,x$, respectively, then the quantities

$$\overset{1}{F}x, \overset{2}{F}x, \overset{3}{F}x, \dots, \overset{n}{F}x, \dots, \overset{n+r}{F}x, \dots$$

represent a *new* series (called the *series of sums* of the previous one). By assumption this has the special property that the difference between its $n$th term $\overset{n}{F}x$ and every later

**36**

wenn es eine Größe, welche sich ändern darf, seyn soll; so wird man sie freylich jederzeit so annehmen

können, daß sie dem Gliede $\overset{n}{F}x$, welches man eben jetzt mit ihr vergleicht, recht nahe kommt, ja mit ihm völlig einerley ist. Daß aber die Voraussetzung auch einer unveränderlichen Größe, die diese Eigenschaft der Annäherung an die Glieder unsrer Reihe hat, keine Unmöglichkeit enthalte; folgt daraus, weil es bey dieser Voraussetzung möglich wird, diese Größe so genau, als man nur immer will, zu bestimmen. Denn gesetzt, man wollte X so genau bestimmen, daß der Unterschied zwischen dem angenommenen und dem wahren Werthe von X eine auch noch so kleine gegebene Größe d nicht überschreitet: so suche man nur in der gegebenen Reihe ein Glied $\overset{n}{F}x$ von der Beschaffenheit aus, daß jedes folgende $\overset{n+r}{F}x$ von ihm um weniger als $\pm$ d verschieden sey. Ein solches $\overset{n}{F}x$ muß es nach der Voraussetzung geben.

Ich sage nun, der Werth von $\overset{n}{F}x$ sey von dem wahren Werthe der Größe X höchstens um $\pm$ d verschieden. Denn wenn man bey einerley n, r nach Belieben vergrößert, so muß der Unterschied $X - \overset{n+r}{F}x = \pm\,\omega$ so klein werden können, als man nur immer will. Der Unterschied $\overset{n}{F}x - \overset{n+r}{F}x$ bleibt aber

**37**

aber jederzeit, so groß man auch r nehme, $< \pm$ d. Also muß auch der Unterschied

$$X - \overset{n}{F}x = (X - \overset{n+r}{F}x) - (\overset{n}{F}x - \overset{n+r}{F}x)$$

jederzeit $< \pm$ (d + $\omega$) verbleiben. Da aber derselbe bey einerley n eine beständige Größe ist, $\omega$ dagegen durch die Vergrößerung von r so klein gemacht werden kann, als man nur immer will: so muß $X - \overset{n}{F}x =$ oder $< \pm$ d seyn. Denn wäre es größer und z. B. $= \pm$ (d + e); so könnte unmöglich das Verhältniß d + e $< $ d + $\omega$, d. h. e $<$ $\omega$ bestehen, wenn man $\omega$ immer mehr verkleinert. Der wahre Werth von X ist also von dem Werthe, den das Glied $\overset{n}{F}x$ hat, höchstens um d verschieden; und läßt sich daher, da man d nach Belieben klein annehmen kann, so genau, als man nur immer will, bestimmen. Es gibt also eine reelle Größe, der sich die Glieder der von uns besprochenen Reihe so sehr, als man nur immer will, nähern, wenn man sie weit genug fortsetzt. Aber nur eine einzige dergleichen Größe gibt es. Denn nähmen wir an, daß es nebst X noch eine andre beständige Größe Y gäbe, der sich die Glieder der Reihe so sehr, als man nur immer will, nähern, wenn man sie weit genug fortsetzt: so müßten die Unterschiede $X - \overset{n+r}{F}x = \omega$, und $Y - \overset{n+r}{F}x = \omega'$ so klein werden können, als man nur immer will, wenn man r groß ge-

**38**

genug werden ließe. Dasselbe müßte also auch von ihrem eigenen Unterschiede, d. h. von $X - Y = \omega - \omega'$ gelten; welches wenn X und Y beständige Größen seyn sollen, unmöglich ist, falls man nicht X = Y voraussetzt.

term $\overset{n+r}{F}x$ (no matter how far from that $n$th term) stays smaller than any given quantity, provided $n$ has first been taken large enough. This difference is the increase produced in the *original* series by a continuation beyond its $n$th term, and [35] by the assumption, provided $n$ has been taken large enough, this increase should remain as small as we please.

$$\S7$$

*Theorem.* If a series of quantities

$$\overset{1}{F}x, \overset{2}{F}x, \overset{3}{F}x, \ldots, \overset{n}{F}x, \ldots, \overset{n+r}{F}x, \ldots$$

has the property that the difference between its $n$th term $\overset{n}{F}x$ and every later one $\overset{n+r}{F}x$, however far this latter term may be taken from the former, remains smaller than any given quantity if $n$ has been taken large enough, then there is always a certain *constant quantity*, and indeed only *one*, which the terms of this series approach and to which they can come as near as we please if the series is continued far enough.

*Proof.* It is clear from §6 that a series such as that described in the theorem is possible. But the hypothesis that there exists a quantity $X$ which the terms of this series approach as closely as we please when it is continued ever futher certainly contains nothing impossible, provided it is not assumed that this quantity be *unique* and *constant*. For [36] if it is to be a quantity which may vary then it can, of course, always be taken so that it is suitably near the term $\overset{n}{F}x$ with which it is just now being compared—even exactly the same as it. But also the assumption of a *constant* quantity with this property of proximity to the terms of our series contains nothing impossible because on this assumption it is possible to determine this quantity as accurately as we please. For suppose we want to determine $X$ so accurately that the difference between the assumed value and the true value of $X$ does not exceed a given quantity $d$, no matter how small. Then we simply look in the given series for a term $\overset{n}{F}x$ with the property that every succeeding term $\overset{n+r}{F}$ differs from it by less that $\pm d$. By the assumption there must be such an $\overset{n}{F}x$. Now I say that the value of $\overset{n}{F}$ differs from the true value of the quantity $X$ by at most $\pm d$. For if $r$ is increased arbitrarily, for the same $n$, the difference $X - \overset{n+r}{F}x = \pm\omega$ can become as small as we please. But the difference $\overset{n}{F}x - \overset{n+r}{F}x$ always remains [37] $< \pm d$, however large $r$ is taken. Therefore the difference

$$X - \overset{n}{F}x = (X - \overset{n+r}{F}x) - (\overset{n}{F}x - \overset{n+r}{F}x)$$

must also always remain $< \pm(d+\omega)$. But since for the same $n$ this is a *constant* quantity, while $\omega$ can be made as small as we please by increasing $r$, the $X - \overset{n}{F}x$ must be $=$ or $< \pm d$. For if it were *greater* and $= \pm(d + e)$, for example, it would be impossible for the relation $d + e < d + \omega$, i.e. $e < \omega$, to hold if $\omega$ is reduced further. The true value of $X$ therefore differs from the value of the term $\overset{n}{F}$ by at most $d$, and can therefore be determined as accurately as we please since $d$ can be taken arbitrarily small. There *is* therefore a *real quantity* to which the terms of the series under discussion approach as closely as we please if the series is continued far enough. But there is only *one* such quantity. For suppose that besides $X$ there was another *constant* quantity $Y$ which the terms of the series approach as much as we please it it is continued far enough, then the differences $X - \overset{n+r}{F}x = \omega$ and $Y - \overset{n+r}{F}x = \overset{1}{\omega}$ can be made as small as we please if $r$ [38] is allowed to be large enough. Therefore this must also hold for their own difference, i.e. for $X - Y = \omega - \overset{1}{\omega}$ which, if $X$ and $Y$ are to be *constant* quantities, is impossible unless one assumes $X = Y$.

### 16.1.2 Cauchy's treatment of sequences and series, 1821

The first comprehensive treatment of the convergence of infinite series was given by Cauchy in his *Cours d'analyse* of 1821. In the opening section of Chapter VI he introduced the sequences that are now named after him, with $n^{\text{th}}$ term $s_n$, say, and the property that as $n$ increases the difference $|s_{n+k} - s_n|$ for any value of $k$ must become arbitrarily small. Unlike Bolzano, Cauchy offered no proof that such sequences must converge but stated it as a self evident necessary and sufficient condition. As an example of a series that does *not* converge, Cauchy used the example $1 + \frac{1}{2} + \frac{1}{3} + \frac{1}{4} + \ldots$, where the individual terms decrease indefinitely, but which is not a 'Cauchy sequence' because $\frac{1}{n+1} + \frac{1}{n+2} + \cdots + \frac{1}{2n} > n \times \frac{1}{2n} = \frac{1}{2}$.

In §2 Cauchy gave convergence tests for series of positive terms, and in §3, a similar battery of tests for series with both positive and negative terms; these included the $n^{\text{th}}$ root test, the ratio test, and the alternating series test. In the last of these he already relied on the assumed convergence of Cauchy sequences. In §4 he moved on to power series, and defined what is now known as the radius of convergence. The extracts that follow are from §1, §3, and §4. Observe that there is as yet no $\varepsilon$, $\delta$ notation, and indeed very few proofs; persuasion is by means of examples rather than by formal argument.

Cauchy sequences
from Cauchy, *Cours d'analyse*, 1821, 123–126

# CHAPITRE VI.

*Des Séries convergentes et divergentes. Règles sur la convergence des Séries. Sommation de quelques Séries convergentes.*

—————

§. 1.$^{er}$ *Considérations générales sur les Séries.*

ON appelle *série* une suite indéfinie de quantités

$$u_0, \quad u_1, \quad u_2, \quad u_3, \quad \&c. \dots$$

qui dérivent les unes des autres suivant une loi déterminée. Ces quantités elles-mêmes sont les différens *termes* de la série que l'on considère. Soit

$$s_n = u_0 + u_1 + u_2 + \dots + u_{n-1}$$

la somme des $n$ premiers termes, $n$ désignant un nombre entier quelconque. Si, pour des valeurs de $n$ toujours croissantes, la somme $s_n$ s'approche indéfiniment d'une certaine limite $s$; la série sera dite *convergente,* et la limite en question s'appellera la *somme* de la série. Au contraire, si, tandis que $n$ croit indéfiniment, la somme $s_n$ ne s'approche d'aucune limite fixe; la série sera *divergente,* et n'aura plus de somme. Dans l'un et l'autre cas, le terme qui correspond à l'indice $n$, savoir $u_n$, sera ce qu'on nomme le *terme général.* Il suffit que l'on donne ce

124      COURS D'ANALYSE.

terme général en fonction de l'indice $n$, pour que la série soit complétement déterminée.

L'une des séries les plus simples est la progression géométrique

$$1, \quad x, \quad x^2, \quad x^3, \quad \&c. \ldots$$

qui a pour terme général $x^n$, c'est-à-dire, la puissance $n.^{me}$ de la quantité $x$. Si dans cette série on fait la somme des $n$ premiers termes, on trouvera

$$1 + x + x^2 + \ldots + x^{n-1} = \frac{1}{1-x} - \frac{x^n}{1-x};$$

et, comme pour des valeurs croissantes de $n$ la valeur numérique de la fraction $\frac{x^n}{1-x}$ converge vers la limite zéro, ou croît au-delà de toute limite, suivant qu'on suppose la valeur numérique de $x$ inférieure ou supérieure à l'unité, on doit conclure que dans la première hypothèse la progression

$$1, \quad x, \quad x^2, \quad x^3, \quad \&c. \ldots$$

est une série convergente qui a pour somme $\frac{1}{1-x}$, tandis que dans la seconde hypothèse la même progression est une série divergente qui n'a plus de somme.

D'après les principes ci-dessus établis, pour que la série

$$(1) \qquad u_0, \quad u_1, \quad u_2 \ldots u_n, \quad u_{n+1}, \quad \&c. \ldots$$

soit convergente, il est nécessaire et il suffit que des valeurs croissantes de $n$ fassent converger indéfiniment la somme

$$s_n = u_0 + u_1 + u_2 + \&c. \ldots + u_{n-1}$$

vers une limite fixe $s$ : en d'autres termes, il est né-cessaire et il suffit que, pour des valeurs infiniment grandes du nombre $n$, les sommes

$$s_n, \quad s_{n+1}, \quad s_{n+2}, \quad \&c. \ldots$$

diffèrent de la limite $s$, et par conséquent entre elles, de quantités infiniment petites. D'ailleurs, les diffé-rences successives entre la première somme $s_n$ et chacune des suivantes sont respectivement détermi-nées par les equations

$$s_{n+1} - s_n = u_n,$$
$$s_{n+2} - s_n = u_n + u_{n+1},$$
$$s_{n+3} - s_n = u_n + u_{n+1} + u_{n+2},$$
$$\&c. \ldots$$

Donc, pour que la série (1) soit convergente, il est d'abord nécessaire que le terme général $u_n$ décroisse indéfiniment, tandis que $n$ augmente ; mais cette condition ne suffit pas, et il faut encore que, pour des valeurs croissantes de $n$, les différentes sommes

$$u_n + u_{n+1},$$
$$u_n + u_{n+1} + u_{n+2},$$
$$\&c. \ldots$$

c'est-à-dire, les sommes des quantités

$$u_n, \quad u_{n+1}, \quad u_{n+2}, \quad \&c. \ldots$$

**126**          COURS D'ANALYSE.

prises, à partir de la première, en tel nombre que l'on voudra, finissent par obtenir constamment des valeurs numériques inférieures à toute limite assignable. Réciproquement, lorsque ces diverses conditions sont remplies, la convergence de la série est assurée.

TRANSLATION

## CHAPTER VI
*Convergent and divergent series. Rules on the convergence of series. Summation of some convergent series.*

§1. General considerations on series

A *series* [*série*] is an infinite sequence [*suite*] of quantities

$$u_0, u_1, u_2, u_3, \text{etc.} \dots$$

which are derived from one another according to a known law. These quantities themselves are the different *terms* of the series one is considering. Suppose

$$s_n = u_0 + u_1 + u_2 + \dots + u_{n-1}$$

is the sum of the first $n$ terms, where $n$ denotes any whole number. If, for values of $n$ always increasing, the sum $s_n$ approaches indefinitely to a certain limit $s$, the series will be said to be *convergent*, and the limit in question will be called the *sum* of the series. Conversely, if, while $n$ increases indefinitely, the sum $s_n$ does not approach any fixed limit, the series will be *divergent*, and will no longer have a sum. In either case, the term that corresponds to the index $n$, that is $u_n$, will be what one calls the *general term*. It suffices to give this [124] general term as a function of the index $n$ for the series to be completely determined.

One of the simplest series is the geometric progression

$$1, x, x^2, x^3, \text{etc.} \dots$$

which has for general term $x^n$, that is to say, the $n$th power of the quantity $x$. If in this series one takes the sum of the first $n$ terms, one will find

$$1 + x + x^2 + x^3 + \dots + x^{n-1} = \frac{1}{1-x} - \frac{x^n}{1-x};$$

and since, for increasing values of $n$, the absolute value of the fraction $\dfrac{x^n}{1-x}$ converges to the limit zero, or increases beyond every limit, according to whether one assumes the absolute value of $x$ to be less than or greater than one, we must conclude that under the first hypothesis the progression

$$1, \ x, \ x^2, \ x^3, \ \text{etc.} \ldots$$

is a convergent series which has for its sum $\dfrac{1}{1-x}$, while under the second hypothesis the same progression is a divergent series which no longer has a sum.

Following the principles established above, in order for the series

(1)                $$u_0, u_1, u_2 \ldots u_n, u_{n+1}, \text{etc.} \ldots$$

to be convergent, it is necessary and sufficient that the increasing values of $n$ make the sum [125]

$$s_n = u_0 + u_1 + u_2 + \text{etc.} \cdots + u_{n-1}$$

converge indefinitely towards a fixed limit $s$; in other words, it is necessary and sufficient that, for infinitely large values of the number $n$, the sums

$$s_n, s_{n+1}, s_{n+2} \ \text{etc.} \ldots$$

differ from the limit $s$, and consequently from each other, by infinitely small quantities. Besides, the successive differences between the first sum $s_n$ and each of the following sums are determined respectively by the equations

$$
\begin{aligned}
s_{n+1} - s_n &= u_n, \\
s_{n+2} - s_n &= u_n + u_{n+1}, \\
s_{n+3} - s_n &= u_n + u_{n+1} + u_{n+2}, \\
\text{etc.} \ldots &
\end{aligned}
$$

Therefore, for the series (1) to be convergent, it is first of all necessary that the general term $u_n$ should decrease indefinitely, while $n$ increases, but that condition is not sufficient, and it must also be that, for increasing values of $n$, the various sums

$$
\begin{aligned}
&u_n + u_{n+1}, \\
&u_n + u_{n+1} + u_{n+2}, \\
&\text{etc.} \ldots
\end{aligned}
$$

that is to say, the sums of the quantities

$$u_n, u_{n+1}, u_{n+2}, \text{etc.} \ldots$$

[126] starting with the first and taking however many one pleases, end up always taking absolute values less than any assignable limit. Conversely, when these various conditions are fulfilled, the convergence of the series is assured.

————————

## Convergence tests

from Cauchy, *Cours d'analyse*, 1821, 142–145

§. 3.$^e$ *Des Séries qui renferment des termes positifs*
*et des termes négatifs.*

Supposons que la série

$$(1) \qquad u_0, \ u_1, \ u_2 \dots u_n, \ \&\text{c.} \dots$$

se compose de termes, tantôt positifs, tantôt négatifs : et soient respectivement

$$(2) \qquad \rho_0, \ \rho_1, \ \rho_2 \dots \rho_n, \ \&\text{c.} \dots$$

les valeurs numériques de ces mêmes termes, en
sorte qu'on ait

$$u_0 = \pm \rho_0, \ u_1 = \pm \rho_1, \ u_2 = \pm \rho_2, \ \dots u_n = \pm \rho_n, \ \&\text{c.} \dots$$

La valeur numérique de la somme

$$u_0 + u_1 + u_2 + \dots + u_{n-1}$$

ne pouvant jamais surpasser

$$\rho_0 + \rho_1 + \rho_2 + \dots + \rho_{n-1},$$

il en résulte que la convergence de la série (2) en-
traînera toujours celle de la série (1). On doit ajouter
que la série (1) sera divergente, si quelques termes
de la série (2) finissent par croître au-delà de toute

limite assignable. Ce dernier cas se présente lorsque les plus grandes valeurs de $(\rho_n)^{\frac{1}{n}}$ convergent, pour des valeurs croissantes de $n$, vers une limite supérieure à l'unité. Au contraire, lorsque cette limite devient inférieure à l'unité, la série (2) est toujours convergente. On peut, en conséquence, énoncer le théorème suivant :

1.<sup>er</sup> Théorème. *Soit $\rho_n$ la valeur numérique du terme général $u_n$ de la série* (1); *et désignons par $k$ la limite vers laquelle convergent, tandis que $n$ croît indéfiniment, les plus grandes valeurs de l'expression* $(\rho_n)^{\frac{1}{n}}$. *La série* (1) *sera convergente, si l'on a $k < 1$, et divergente, si l'on a $k > 1$.*

Lorsque la fraction $\frac{\rho_{n+1}}{\rho_n}$, c'est-à-dire, la valeur numérique du rapport $\frac{u_{n+1}}{u_n}$, convergera vers une limite fixe, cette limite sera, en vertu du 4.<sup>e</sup> théorème [chap. II, §. 3.<sup>e</sup>], la valeur cherchée de $k$. Cette remarque conduit à la proposition que je vais écrire.

2.<sup>e</sup> Théorème. *Si, pour des valeurs croissantes de $n$, la valeur numérique du rapport*

$$\frac{u_{n+1}}{u_n}$$

*converge vers une limite fixe $k$, la série* (1) *sera convergente, toutes les fois que l'on aura $k < 1$, et divergente, toutes les fois que l'on aura $k > 1$.*

Par exemple, si l'on considère la série

144        COURS D'ANALYSE.

$$1, \ -\frac{1}{1}, \ +\frac{1}{1.2}, \ -\frac{1}{1.2.3}, \ +\&c\ldots,$$

on trouvera

$$\frac{u_{n+1}}{u_n} = -\frac{1}{n+1}, \quad k = \frac{1}{\infty} = 0\,;$$

d'où il résulte que la série sera convergente.

Le premier des deux théorèmes qu'on vient d'établir ne laisse d'incertitude sur la convergence ou la divergence d'une série que dans le cas particulier où la quantité représentée par $k$ devient égale à l'unité. Dans ce cas particulier, on peut quelquefois constater la convergence de la série proposée, soit en s'assurant que les valeurs numériques de ses différens termes forment une série convergente, soit en ayant égard au théorème suivant.

3.$^e$ THÉORÈME. *Si dans la série* (1) *la valeur numérique du terme général* $u_n$ *décroît constamment et indéfiniment, pour des valeurs croissantes de* $n$, *si de plus les différens termes sont alternativement positifs et négatifs, la série sera convergente.*

Considérons, par exemple, la série

$$(3) \quad 1, \ -\frac{1}{2}, \ +\frac{1}{3}, \ -\frac{1}{4}, \ +\&c..\pm\frac{1}{n}, \ \mp\frac{1}{n+1}, \&e.$$

La somme des termes dont le rang surpasse $n$, si on les suppose pris en nombre égal à $m$, sera

$$\pm\left(\frac{1}{n+1} - \frac{1}{n+2} + \frac{1}{n+3} - \frac{1}{n+4} + \&c\ldots \pm \frac{1}{n+m}\right).$$

Or la valeur numérique de cette somme, savoir,

$$\frac{1}{n+1} - \frac{1}{n+2} + \frac{1}{n+3} - \frac{1}{n+4} + \&c. \ldots \pm \frac{1}{n+m}$$

$$= \frac{1}{n+1} - \left(\frac{1}{n+2} - \frac{1}{n+3}\right) - \left(\frac{1}{n+4} - \frac{1}{n+5}\right) - \&c. \ldots$$

$$= \frac{1}{n+1} - \frac{1}{n+2} + \left(\frac{1}{n+3} - \frac{1}{n+4}\right) + \left(\frac{1}{n+5} - \frac{1}{n+6}\right) + \&c. \ldots,$$

étant évidemment comprise entre

$$\frac{1}{n+1} \quad \text{et} \quad \frac{1}{n+1} - \frac{1}{n+2},$$

décroîtra indéfiniment pour des valeurs croissantes de $n$, quel que soit $m$, ce qui suffit pour établir la convergence de la série proposée. Les mêmes raisonnemens peuvent évidemment s'appliquer à toutes les séries de ce genre.

TRANSLATION

§3. *Series which include positive terms and negative terms.*

Let us suppose that the series

(1)  $\quad\quad\quad u_0, u_1, u_2 \ldots u_n, \text{etc.} \ldots$

is composed of some positive, some negative terms; and let

(2)  $\quad\quad\quad \rho_0, \rho_1, \rho_2 \ldots \rho_n, \text{etc.} \ldots$

respectively be the absolute values of these same terms, so that one has

$$u_0 = \pm\rho_0, u_1 = \pm\rho_1, u_2 = \pm\rho_2, \ldots u_n = \pm\rho_n, \text{etc.} \ldots$$

The absolute value of the sum

$$u_0 + u_1 + u_2 + \cdots + u_{n-1}$$

may not exceed

$$\rho_0 + \rho_1 + \rho_2 + \cdots + \rho_{n-1},$$

and as a result the convergence of series (2) always entails the convergence of series (1). One must add that the series (1) will be divergent if some terms of series (2) eventually increase beyond any [143] assignable limit. This last case happens when the greatest values of $(\rho_n)^{\frac{1}{n}}$ converge, for increasing values of $n$, towards a limit greater than one.

Conversely, when this limit is less than one, series (2) is always convergent. One may consequently state the following theorem:

1ˢᵗ THEOREM. *Let $\rho_n$ be the absolute value of the general term $u_n$ of series (1); and let us denote by k the limit towards which the greatest values of the expression $(\rho_n)^{\frac{1}{n}}$ converge, while n increases indefinitely. The series (1) will be convergent if one has k < 1, and divergent if one has k > 1.*

When the fraction $\dfrac{\rho_{n+1}}{\rho_n}$, that is to say, the absolute value of the ratio $\dfrac{u_{n+1}}{u_n}$, converges towards a fixed limit, that limit will be, by virtue of Theorem 4 (Chapter II, §3), the sought value of $k$. This remark leads to the proposition that I am about to write.

2ⁿᵈ THEOREM. *If, for increasing values of n, the absolute value of the ratio*

$$\frac{u_{n+1}}{u_n}$$

*converges towards a fixed limit k, the series (1) will be convergent whenever one has k < 1, and divergent whenever one has k > 1.*

For example, if one considers the series [144]

$$1, -\frac{1}{1}, +\frac{1}{1.2}, -\frac{1}{1.2.3}, +\dots,$$

one will find

$$\frac{u_{n+1}}{u_n} = -\frac{1}{n+1}, \quad k = \frac{1}{\infty} = 0;$$

from which it follows that the series will be convergent.

The first of the two theorems we have just established leaves uncertainty over the convergence or divergence of a series in the particular case where the quantity represented by $k$ becomes equal to one. In this particular case, one may sometimes establish the convergence of the proposed series, either by assuring oneself that the absolute values of the various terms form a convergent series, or by having regard to the following theorem.

3ʳᵈ THEOREM. *If in series (1) the absolute value of the general term $u_n$ decreases steadily and indefinitely for increasing values of n, and if further the various terms are alternately positive and negative, the series will be convergent.*

Let us consider, for example, the series

(3)    $1, -\frac{1}{2}, +\frac{1}{3}, -\frac{1}{4}, + \text{etc.} \dots \pm \frac{1}{n}, \mp \frac{1}{n+1}, \text{etc.}$

The sum of the terms for which the rank exceeds $n$, if we assume that we take a number equal to $m$ of them, will be

$$\pm \left( \frac{1}{n+1} - \frac{1}{n+2} + \frac{1}{n+3} - \frac{1}{n+4} + \text{etc.} \dots \pm \frac{1}{n+m} \right).$$

Now the absolute value of this sum, that is, [145]

$$\frac{1}{n+1} - \frac{1}{n+2} + \frac{1}{n+3} - \frac{1}{n+4} + \text{etc.} \cdots \pm \frac{1}{n+m}$$

$$= \frac{1}{n+1} - \left(\frac{1}{n+2} - \frac{1}{n+3}\right) - \left(\frac{1}{n+4} - \frac{1}{n+5}\right) - \text{etc.} \ldots$$

$$= \frac{1}{n+1} - \frac{1}{n+2} + \left(\frac{1}{n+3} - \frac{1}{n+4}\right) + \left(\frac{1}{n+5} - \frac{1}{n+6}\right) + \text{etc.} \ldots,$$

being clearly contained between

$$\frac{1}{n+1} \quad \text{and} \quad \frac{1}{n+1} - \frac{1}{n+2},$$

will decrease indefinitely for increasing values of $n$, whatever $m$ may be, which suffices to establish the convergence of the proposed series. The same reasoning may clearly be applied to every series of this kind.

————————

## Power series and the radius of convergence
from Cauchy, *Cours d'analyse*, 1821, 150–152

§. 4.ᵉ *Des Séries ordonnées suivant les Puissances ascendantes et entières d'une variable.*

Soit

$$(1) \qquad a_0, \quad a_1 x, \quad a_2 x^2, \quad \ldots a_n x^n, \quad \&c \ldots$$

une série ordonnée suivant les puissances entières et ascendantes de la variable $x$,

(2)        $a_0, \ a_1, \ a_2, \ \ldots a_n$, &c. ...

désignant des coefficiens constans positifs ou négatifs. Soit de plus $A$ ce que devient pour la série (2) la quantité $k$ du paragraphe précédent [voy. le §. 3, 2.ᵉ théorème]. La même quantité, calculée pour la série (1), sera équivalente à la valeur numérique du produit

$$A \, x.$$

Par suite, la série (1) sera convergente, si cette valeur numérique est inférieure à l'unité, c'est-à-dire, en d'autres termes, si la valeur numérique de la variable $x$ est inférieure à $\frac{1}{A}$. Au contraire, la série (1) sera divergente, si la valeur numérique de $x$ surpasse $\frac{1}{A}$. On peut donc énoncer la proposition suivante.

1.ᵉʳ THÉORÈME. *Soit* $A$ *la limite vers laquelle converge, pour des valeurs croissantes de* $n$, *la racine* $n.^{me}$ *des plus grandes valeurs numériques de* $a_n$. *La série* (1) *sera convergente pour toutes les valeurs de* $x$ *comprises entre les limites*

$$x = -\frac{1}{A}, \quad x = +\frac{1}{A},$$

*et divergente pour toutes les valeurs de* $x$ *situées hors des mêmes limites.*

Lorsque la valeur numérique du rapport $\frac{a_{n+1}}{a_n}$

**152**    COURS D'ANALYSE.

converge vers une limite fixe, cette limite est [en vertu du 4.ᵉ théorème, chapitre II, §. 3] la valeur cherchée de $A$. Cette remarque conduit à une nouvelle proposition que je vais écrire.

2.ᵉ Théorème. *Si, pour des valeurs croissantes de n, la valeur numérique du rapport*

$$\frac{a_{n+1}}{a_n}$$

*converge vers la limite* $A$, *la série* (1) *sera convergente pour toutes les valeurs de* $x$ *comprises entre les limites*

$$-\frac{1}{A}, \quad +\frac{1}{A},$$

*et divergente pour toutes les valeurs de* $x$ *situées hors des mêmes limites.*

Corollaire 1.ᵉʳ Prenons pour exemple la série

$$(3) \qquad 1, \quad 2\,x, \quad 3\,x^2, \quad 4\,x^3, \quad \dots (n+1)\,x^n, \ \&c\dots$$

Comme on trouvera dans cette hypothèse

$$\frac{a_{n+1}}{a_n} = \frac{n+2}{n+1} = 1 + \frac{1}{n+1},$$

et par suite,

$$A = 1,$$

on en conclura que la série (3) est convergente pour toutes les valeurs de $x$ renfermées entre les limites

$$x = -1, \quad x = +1,$$

et divergente pour les valeurs de $x$ situées hors de ces limites.

TRANSLATION

### §4 *Series ordered according to increasing whole powers of a variable.*

Let

(1) $$a_0, a_1 x, a_2 x^2, \ldots a_n x^n, \text{etc.} \ldots$$

be a series ordered according to increasing whole powers of the variable $x$, where

(2) $$a_0, a_1, a_2, \ldots a_n, \text{etc.} \ldots$$

denote the constant positive or negative coefficients. Further, let $A$ be that which becomes for series (2) the quantity $k$ of the preceding paragraph (see §3, 2nd theorem). The same quantity, calculated for series (1), will be equivalent to the absolute value of the product

$$Ax.$$

It follows that series (1) will be convergent if that absolute value is less than one, that is to say, in other words, if the absolute value of the variable $x$ is less than $\frac{1}{A}$. Conversely, series (1) will be divergent if the numerical value of $x$ exceeds $\frac{1}{A}$. One may therefore state the following proposition.

1$^{\text{st}}$ THEOREM. *Let $A$ be the limit towards which, for increasing values of $n$, the $n^{th}$ roots of the greatest absolute values of $a_n$ converge. Series (1) will be convergent for all values of $x$ contained between the limits*

$$x = -\frac{1}{A}, \quad x = +\frac{1}{A},$$

*and divergent for all values of $x$ falling outside those same limits.*

When the absolute value of the ratio $\frac{a_{n+1}}{a_n}$ [152] converges towards a fixed limit, that limit is (by virtue of the 4th theorem, chapter II, §3) the sought value of $A$. This remark leads to a new proposition which I will state.

2$^{\text{nd}}$ THEOREM. *If, for increasing values of $n$, the absolute value of the ratio*

$$\frac{a_{n+1}}{a_n}$$

*converges towards the limit $A$, series (1) will be convergent for all values of $x$ contained between the limits*

$$-\frac{1}{A}, \quad +\frac{1}{A},$$

*and divergent for all values of $x$ situated outside these same limits.*

1$^{\text{st}}$ COROLLARY. Let us take for example the series

(3) $$1, 2x, 3x^2, 4x^3, \ldots (n+1)x^n, \text{etc.} \ldots,$$

Since one will find under this hypothesis that

$$\frac{a_{n+1}}{a_n} = \frac{n+2}{n+1} = 1 + \frac{1}{n+1},$$

and consequently

$$A = 1,$$

one may conclude that series (3) is convergent for all values of $x$ contained between the limits

$$x = -1, \quad x = +1,$$

and divergent for values of $x$ situated outside these limits.

------------

### 16.1.3 Abel's proof of the binomial theorem, 1826

Neither Cauchy nor Bolzano managed to prove that Cauchy sequences are convergent: Bolzano tried but failed; Cauchy merely stated it as obvious. Nevertheless, Cauchy sequences turned out to be an extraordinarily powerful tool. In 1826, only five years after the publication of the *Cours d'analyse*, Abel used them with great skill to give the first rigorous proof of the binomial theorem, namely, that if $|x| < 1$ then $(1 + x)^m = 1 + \frac{m}{1}x + \frac{m(m-1)}{1.2}x^2 + \frac{m(m-1)(m-2)}{1.2.3}x^3 + \ldots$ Mathematicians had been using this theorem freely and productively ever since Newton first presented it in the late seventeenth century (see, for example, 8.2, 9.2, and 14.1.1), but Newton's discovery had been based only on experiment and observation. As the eighteenth century progressed more than one mathematician had begun to raise questions about the validity of the infinite series on the right hand side: d'Alembert, for example, had investigated the values for which it converges (see 8.3.1), while Lagrange had made it his first test case for his calculation of the remainder term (see 8.3.2). Bolzano in 1816 wrote a lengthy paper on the binomial theorem, outlining the inadequacies of earlier treatments and attempting his own stricter proof, but still without complete success, and the first correct proof was given by Abel in 1826 in a paper entitled 'Recherches sur la série

$$1 + \frac{m}{1}x + \frac{m(m-1)}{1.2}x^2 + \frac{m(m-1)(m-2)}{1.2.3}x^3 + \ldots'.$$

Abel's proof may be broken down into four stages: first, several theorems about multiplication of series, proved from the assumed convergence of Cauchy sequences; second, a proof that the series $1 + \frac{m}{1}x + \frac{m(m-1)}{1.2}x^2 + \ldots$ converges for $|x| < 1$; third, if $\varphi(m) = 1 + \frac{m}{1}x + \frac{m(m-1)}{1.2}x^2 + \ldots$ then $\varphi(m)\varphi(n) = \varphi(m + n)$; fourth, from this last property, that $\varphi(m) = (1 + x)^m$.

Abel's proof was very long: he allowed both $x$ and $m$ to be complex, but always separated them into real and imaginary parts, which led to some fearsome algebraic manipulation; further, his notation was somewhat unreliable because he more than once gave new meanings to letters already in use. Nevertheless, the underlying concepts of his argument are as sophisticated as those in any modern proof. Here we give only the opening of Abel's paper to show his use of Cauchy sequences.

## Abel's proof of the binomial theorem

from Abel, 'Untersuchungen über die Reihe: $1 + \frac{m}{1}x + \frac{m(m-1)}{1.2}x^2 + \frac{m(m-1)(m-2)}{1.2.3}x^3 + \ldots$',
*Journal für die reine und angewandte Mathematik*, 1 (1826), 311–315

*Abel Untersuchungen über die Reihe* $1 + \frac{m}{1}x + \frac{m \cdot m - 1}{1 \cdot 2}x^2 \ldots\ldots$    **311**

## 29.

## Untersuchungen über die Reihe:

$$1 + \frac{m}{1}x + \frac{m \cdot (m-1)}{1 \cdot 2} \cdot x^2 + \frac{m \cdot (m-1) \cdot (m-2)}{1 \cdot 2 \cdot 3} \cdot x^3 + \ldots\ldots \text{u. s. w.}$$

(Von Herrn *N. H. Abel*.)

### 1.

Untersucht man das Raisonnement, dessen man sich gewöhnlich bedient, wo es sich um unendliche Reihen handelt, genauer, so wird man finden, daſs es im Ganzen wenig befriedigend, und daſs also die Zahl derjenigen Sätze von unendlichen Reihen, die als streng begründet angesehen werden können, nur sehr geringe ist. Man wendet gewöhnlich die Operationen der Analysis auf die unendlichen Reihen eben so an, als wären die Reihen endlich. Dieses scheint mir ohne besonderen Beweis nicht erlaubt. Sind z. B. zwei Reihen mit einander zu multipliciren, so setzt man

$$(u_0 + u_1 + u_2 + u_3 + \text{u. s. w.}) \, (v_0 + v_1 + v_2 + v_3 + \text{u. s. w.})$$
$$= u_0 v_0 + (u_0 v_1 + u_1 v_0) + (u_0 v_2 + u_1 v_1 + u_2 v_2) + \text{u. s. w.}$$
$$\ldots\ldots + (u_0 v_n + u_1 v_{n-1} + u_2 v_{n-2} + \ldots\ldots + u_n v_0) + \text{u. s. w.}$$

Diese Gleichung ist vollkommen richtig, wenn die beiden Reihen

$$u_0 + u_1 + \ldots\ldots \text{ und } v_0 + v_1 + \ldots\ldots$$

endlich sind. Sind sie aber unendlich, so müssen sie erstlich nothwendig c o n - v e r g i r e n, weil eine divergirende Reihe keine Summe hat, und dann muſs auch die Reihe im zweiten Gliede ebenfalls c o n v e r g i r e n. Nur mit dieser Einschränkung ist der obige Ausdruck richtig. Irre ich nicht, so ist diese Einschränkung bis jetzt nicht berücksichtigt worden. Es soll in gegenwärtigem Aufsatze geschehen. Eben so sind eine Menge ähnlicher Operationen zu rechtfertigen nöthig, z. B. das gewöhliche Verfahren, eine Gröſse durch eine unendliche Reihe zu dividiren, eine unendliche Reihe zu einer Potenz zu erheben, den Logarithmus, den Sinus, Cosinus davon zu nehmen, u. s. w.

Ein anderes Verfahren, welches man häufig in der Analysis antrifft, und welches nur zu oft auf Widersprüche führt, ist das: divergirende Reihen zur Berechnung numerischer Werthe von Reihen zu gebrauchen. Eine divergirende Reihe kann nie einer bestimmten Gröſse g l e i c h sein: sie ist blos ein Ausdruck, mit gewissen Eigenschaften, die sich auf die Operationen beziehen, denen die

Reihe unterworfen ist. Die divergirenden Reihen können zuweilen mit Nutzen als Symbole dienen, diese oder jene Sätze kürzer auszudrücken; aber man darf sie nie an die Stelle bestimmter Größen setzen. Thut man es, so kann man beweisen, was man will: Unmögliches sowohl als Mögliches.

Eine der merkwürdigsten Reihen der algebraischen Analysis ist folgende:

$$1 + \frac{m}{1}x + \frac{m(m-1)}{1 \cdot 2}x^2 + \frac{m \cdot (m-1)(m-2)}{1 \cdot 2 \cdot 3}x^3 + \ldots + \frac{m(m-1)\ldots m-(n-1)}{1 \cdot 2 \ldots \ldots \ldots n}x^n$$

u. s. w.

Ist $m$ eine ganze, positive Zahl, so läßt sich die Summe dieser Reihe, welche in diesem Falle endlich ist, bekanntlich durch $(1 + x)^m$ ausdrücken. Ist $m$ keine ganze Zahl, so geht die Reihe in's Unendliche fort, und sie wird convergiren oder divergiren, je nachdem die Größen $m$ und $x$ diese oder jene Werthe haben. In diesem Falle setzt man nun ebenfalls die Gleichung

$$(1 + x)^m = 1 + \frac{m}{1} \cdot x + \frac{m \cdot (m-1)}{1 \cdot 2} \cdot x^2 + \text{u. s. w.} \ldots\ldots;$$

aber dann drückt die Gleichheit weiter nichts aus, als daß die beiden Ausdrücke

$$(1 + x)^m, \quad 1 + \frac{m}{1} \cdot x + \frac{m \cdot (m-1)}{1 \cdot 2} \cdot x^2 + \ldots\ldots$$

gewisse Eigenschaften gemein haben, von welchen, für gewisse Werthe von $m$ und $x$, die numerische Gleichheit der Ausdrücke abhängt. Man nimmt an, daß die numerische Gleichheit immer Statt finden werde, wenn die Reihe convergent ist; dies ist aber bis jetzt noch nicht bewiesen worden. Es sind selbst nicht alle Fälle untersucht worden, wo die Reihe convergent ist. Selbst wenn man die Existenz der obigen Gleichung voraussetzte, müßte dennoch der Werth von $(1 + x)^m$ gesucht werden; denn der Ausdruck hat im Allgemeinen unendlich viele verschiedene Werthe, während die Reihe $1 + mx +$ u. s. w. nur einen einzigen hat.

Der Zweck dieser Abhandlung ist, die Ausfüllung einer Lücke zu versuchen, und zwar durch die vollständige Auflösung folgenden Problems:

„Die Summe der Reihe

$$1 + \frac{m}{1}x + \frac{m(m-1)}{1 \cdot 2}x^2 + \frac{m(m-1)(m-2)}{1 \cdot 2 \cdot 3}x^3 + \text{u. s. w.}$$

„für alle diejenigen reellen oder imaginairen Werthe von $x$ und $m$ zu finden, „für welche die Reihe convergirt."

### II.

Wir wollen zuerst einige nothwendige Sätze über die Reihen aufstellen.
Die

*Abel, Untersuchungen über die Reihe* $1 + \frac{m}{1}x + \frac{m\,\frac{1}{1}m-y}{1\,.\,2}x^2$ . ....   **313**

Die vortreffliche Schrift von *Cauchy „Cours d'analyse de l'école polytechnique"*, welche von jedem Analysten gelesen werden sollte, der die Strenge bei mathematischen Untersuchungen liebt, wird uns dabei zum Leitfaden dienen.

Erklärung. Eine beliebige Reihe

$$v_0 + v_1 + v_2 + \ldots\ldots + v_m \text{ u. s. w.}$$

soll convergent heifsen, wenn, für stets wachsende Werthe von $m$, die Summe $v_0 + v_1 + \ldots\ldots + v_m$ sich immerfort einer gewissen Gränze nähert. Diese Grenze soll Summe der Reihe heifsen. Im entgegengesetzten Falle soll die Reihe divergent heifsen, und hat alsdann keine Summe. Aus dieser Erklärung folgt, dafs, wenn eine Reihe convergiren soll, es nothwendig und hinreichend sein wird, dafs, für stets wachsende Werthe von $m$, die Summe $v_m + v_{m+1} + \ldots\ldots + v_{m+n}$ sich Null immerfort nähert, welchen Werth auch $n$ haben mag.

In irgend einer beliebigen Reihe wird also das allgemeine Glied $v_m$ sich Null stets nähern \*).

Lehrsatz I. Wenn man durch $\varrho_0, \varrho_1, \varrho_2 \ldots\ldots$ eine Reihe positiver Gröfsen bezeichnet, und der Quotient $\frac{\varrho_{m+1}}{\varrho_m}$ für stets wachsende Werthe von $m$, einer Grenze $a$ sich nähert, die gröfser ist als 1: so wird die Reihe

$$\varepsilon_0\varrho_0 + \varepsilon_1\varrho_1 + \varepsilon_2\varrho_2 + \ldots\ldots + \varepsilon_m\varrho_m + \ldots\ldots,$$

worin $\varepsilon_m$ eine Gröfse ist, die für stets wachsende Werthe von $m$, sich Null nicht nähert, nothwendig divergiren.

Lehrsatz II. Wenn in einer Reihe von positiven Gröfsen, wie $\varrho_0 + \varrho_1 + \varrho_2 \ldots\ldots + \varrho_m$, der Quotient $\frac{\varrho_{m+1}}{\varrho_m}$, für stets wachsende Werthe von $m$, sich einer Grenze $a$ nähert, welche kleiner ist als 1, so wird die Reihe

$$\varepsilon_0\varrho_0 + \varepsilon_1\varrho_1 + \varepsilon_2\varrho_2 + \ldots\ldots + \varepsilon_m\varrho_m,$$

worin $\varepsilon_0, \varepsilon_1, \varepsilon_2$ u. s. w. Gröfsen sind, die die Einheit nicht übersteigen, nothwendig convergiren.

In der That kann man, der Voraussetzung zufolge, $m$ immer grofs genug annehmen, dafs $\varrho_{m+1} < a\varrho_m, \varrho_{m+2} < a\varrho_{m+1}, \ldots\ldots \varrho_{m+n} < a\varrho_{m+n-1}$ ist. Hieraus folgt $\varrho_{m+k} < a^k \cdot \varrho_m$, und mithin

$$\varrho_m + \varrho_{m+1} + \ldots\ldots + \varrho_{m+n} < \varrho_m(1 + a + \ldots\ldots + a^n) < \frac{\varrho_m}{1-a},$$

---

\*) Anmerkung. Der Kürze wegen soll in dieser Abhandlung unter $\omega$ eine Gröfse verstanden werden, die kleiner sein kann, als jede gegebene, noch so kleine Gröfse.

I.                                                                 40

**314**    *Abel, Untersuchungen über die Reihe* $1 + \frac{m}{1} x + \frac{m \cdot (m-1)}{1 \cdot 2} x^2 \ldots\ldots$

und folglich um so mehr,

$$\varepsilon_m \varrho_m + \varepsilon_{m+1} \varrho_{m+1} + \ldots\ldots + \varepsilon_{m+n} \varrho_{m+n} < \frac{\varrho_m}{1-a}.$$

Da aber $\varrho_{m+k} < a^k \varrho_m$ und $a < 1$, so ist klar, dafs sich $\varrho_m$, und folglich auch die Summe

$$\varepsilon_m \varrho_m + \varepsilon_{m+1} \varrho_{m+1} + \ldots\ldots + \varepsilon_{m+n} \varrho_{m+n}$$

Null nähern wird.

Folglich ist die obige Reihe convergent.

**Lehrsatz III.** Bezeichnet man durch $t_0, t_1, t_2 \ldots\ldots t_m$ eine Reihe von beliebigen Gröfsen, und die Gröfse $p_m = t_0 + t_1 + t_2 + \ldots\ldots + t_m \ldots\ldots$ ist stets kleiner als eine bestimmte Gröfse $\delta$, so hat man

$$r = \varepsilon_0 t_0 + \varepsilon_1 t_1 + \varepsilon_2 t_2 + \ldots\ldots \varepsilon_m t_m < \delta . \varepsilon_0,$$

wo $\varepsilon_0, \varepsilon_1, \varepsilon_2$ positive, abnehmende Gröfsen bezeichnen.

In der That ist

$$t_0 = p_0, \ t_1 = p_1 - p_0, \ t_2 = p_2 - p_1, \text{ u. s. w.},$$

also

$$r = \varepsilon_0 p_0 + \varepsilon_1 (p_1 - p_0) + \varepsilon_2 (p_2 - p_1) + \ldots\ldots + \varepsilon_m (p_m - p_{m-1}),$$

oder auch

$$r = p_0 (\varepsilon_0 - \varepsilon_1) + p_1 (\varepsilon_1 - \varepsilon_2) + \ldots\ldots + p_{m-1} (\varepsilon_{m-1} - \varepsilon_m) + p_m \varepsilon_m.$$

Da aber $\varepsilon_0 - \varepsilon_1, \varepsilon_1 - \varepsilon_2, \ldots\ldots$ positiv sind, so ist die Gröfse $r$ offenbar kleiner als $\delta . \varepsilon_0$.

**Erklärung.** Eine Function $f(x)$ soll **stetige Function** von $x$, zwischen den Grenzen $x = o$, $x = b$ heifsen, wenn für einen beliebigen Werth von $x$, zwischen diesen Grenzen, die Gröfse $f(x - \beta)$ sich für stets abnehmende Werthe von $\beta$, der Grenze $f(x)$ nähert.

**Lehrsatz IV.** Wenn die Reihe

$$f(a) = v_0 + v_1 a + v_2 a^2 + \ldots\ldots + v_m a^m + \ldots\ldots$$

für einen gewissen Werth $\delta$ von $a$ convergirt, so wird sie auch für jeden kleineren Werth von $a$ convergiren, und von der Art seyn, dafs $f(a - \beta)$, für stets abnehmende Werthe von $\beta$, sich der Grenze $f(a)$ nähert, vorausgesezt, dafs $a$ gleich oder kleiner ist als $\delta$.

Es sey

$$v_0 + v_1 a + \ldots\ldots + v_{m-1} a^{m-1} = \varphi(a),$$
$$v_m a^m + v_{m+1} a^{m+1} + \text{u. s. w.} \ldots\ldots = \psi(a),$$

so ist

*Abel, Untersuchungen über die Reihe* $1 + \frac{m}{1}x + \frac{m\cdot(m-1)}{1\cdot2}x^2\ldots\ldots$    **315**

$$\psi(\alpha) = \left(\frac{\alpha}{\delta}\right)^m \cdot \varrho_m\delta^m + \left(\frac{\alpha}{\delta}\right)^{m+1} \cdot \varrho_{m+1}\delta^{m+1} + \text{u. s. w.,}$$

folglich, vermöge des Lehrsatzes (III.), $\psi(\alpha) < \left(\frac{\alpha}{\delta}\right)^m \cdot p$, wenn $p$ die gröfste der

Gröfsen $\varrho_m\delta^m$, $\varrho_m\delta^m + \varrho_{m+1}\delta^{m+1}$, $\varrho_m\delta^m + \varrho_{m+1}\delta^{m+1} + \varrho_{m+2}\delta^{m+2}$ u. s. w. bezeichnet.
Mithin kann man für jeden Werth von $\alpha$, der gleich oder kleiner ist, als $\delta$, $m$
grofs genug annehmen, dafs

$$\psi(\alpha) = \omega$$

ist. Nun ist $f(\alpha) = \varphi(\alpha) + \psi(\alpha)$; also $f(\alpha) - f(\alpha - \beta) = \varphi(\alpha) - \varphi(\alpha - \beta) + \omega$.
Da nun $\varphi(\alpha)$ eine ganze Function von $\alpha$ ist, so kann man $\beta$ klein genug an-
nehmen, dafs

$$\varphi(\alpha) - \varphi(\alpha - \beta) = \omega;$$

also ist auch auf gleiche Weise

$$f(\alpha) - f(\alpha - \beta) = \omega,$$

wodurch der Lehrsatz bewiesen wird.

---

## TRANSLATION

### 29.
#### Investigations on the series:

$$1 + \frac{m}{1}x + \frac{m(m-1)}{1.2}x^2 + \frac{m(m-1)(m-2)}{1.2.3}x^3 + \ldots \text{ etc.}$$

(From Herr *N. H. Abel*.)

#### 1.

If one subjects to a more precise examination the reasoning that one generally uses
when dealing with infinite series, one will find that, taken as a whole, it is not very
satisfactory, and that consequently the number of theorems concerning infinite series
that may be considered rigorously based is very limited. One normally applies the
operations of analysis to infinite series in the same way as if the series were finite. This
does not seem to me permissible without special proof. If for example one needs to
multiply two infinite series one by the other, one puts

$$(u_0 + u_1 + u_2 + u_3 + \text{etc.})(v_0 + v_1 + v_2 + v_3 + \text{etc.})$$

$$= u_0v_0 + (u_0v_1 + u_1v_0) + (u_0v_2 + u_1v_1 + u_2v_0) + \text{etc.}$$

$$\cdots + (u_0v_n + u_1v_{n-1} + u_2v_{n-2} + \text{etc.} + u_nv_0) + \text{etc.}$$

This equation is quite correct when the series

$$u_0 + u_1 + \ldots \quad \text{and} \quad v_0 + v_1 + \ldots$$

are finite. But if they are infinite, it is first necessary that they *converge*, for a divergent
series does not have a sum; then the series on the right hand side must likewise *converge*.

It is only with this restriction that the above expression is correct. But, if I am not mistaken, until now no one has taken notice of it. This is what it is proposed to do in this memoir. There are several other similar operations to justify, for example, the usual procedures for dividing a quantity by an infinite series, for raising an infinite series to a power, for determining its logarithm, its sine, its cosine, etc.

Another procedure that one frequently finds in analysis, and which quite often leads to contradictions, is that one makes use of divergent series for the calculation of numerical values of series. A divergent series can never be *equal* to a determined quantity; it is only an expression displaying certain properties which relate to the operations to which the [312] series is subject. Divergent series may sometime be used successfully as symbols to express such and such a proposition in an abbreviated manner; but one would never think to put them in place of determined quantities. If one does, one may prove anything one wants, the impossible as well as the possible.

One of the most remarkable series in algebraic analysis is the following:

$$1 + \frac{m}{1}x + \frac{m(m-1)}{1.2}x^2 + \frac{m(m-1)(m-2)}{1.2.3}x^3 + \ldots$$

$$+ \frac{m(m-1)(m-2)\ldots[m-(n-1)]}{1.2.3\ldots n}x^n \quad \text{etc.}$$

When $m$ is a positive whole number, one knows that the sum of this series, which in this case is finite, may be expressed as $(1+x)^m$. When $m$ is not a whole number, the series becomes infinite, and it will be convergent or divergent, according to the different values that one gives to $m$ and $x$. In this case one writes in the same way the equation

$$(1+x)^m = 1 + \frac{m}{1}x + \frac{m(m-1)}{1.2}x^2 + \text{etc.}\ldots ;$$

but now equality expresses only that the two expressions

$$(1+x)^m, \qquad 1 + \frac{m}{1}x + \frac{m(m-1)}{1.2}x^2 + \ldots$$

have certain common properties on which, for certain values of $m$ and $x$, the *numerical* equality of the expressions depends. One assumes that numerical equality will always hold when the series is convergent; but this is what until now has not yet been proved. No-one has even examined all the cases where the series is convergent. Even when one assumes the *existence* of the above equation, it still remains to find the *value* of $(1+x)^m$, for this expression has in general infinitely many different values, while the series $1 + mx + $ etc. has only one.

The aim of this memoir is to try to fill a gap with the complete solution of the following problem:

"Find the sum of the series

$$1 + \frac{m}{1}x + \frac{m(m-1)}{1.2}x^2 + \frac{m(m-1)(m-2)}{1.2.3}x^3 + \text{etc.}$$

for all real or imaginary values of $x$ and $m$ for which the series is convergent."

2.

We are first going to establish some necessary theorems on series. [313] The excellent work of Cauchy "*Cours d'analyse de l'école polytechnique*", which must be read by every analyst who loves rigour in mathematical research, will serve as our guide.

*Definition.* Any series

$$v_0 + v_1 + v_2 + \cdots + v_m \text{ etc.}$$

is said to be convergent, if for ever increasing values of $m$, the sum $v_0 + v_1 + \cdots + v_m$ approaches indefinitely to a certain limit. This limit will be called *the sum of the series.* In the contrary case the series is said to be divergent, and it does not have a sum. From this definition, for a series to be convergent, it is necessary and sufficient that for ever increasing values of $m$, the sum $v_m + v_{m+1} + \cdots + v_{m+n}$ approaches indefinitely to zero, whatever the value of $n$.

Therefore, in any convergent series whatever, the general term $v_m$ always approaches zero.*

*Theorem* I. If one denotes a series of positive quantities by $\rho_0$, $\rho_1$, $\rho_2$ ..., and the quotient $\dfrac{\rho_{m+1}}{\rho_m}$, for ever increasing values of $m$, approaches a limit $\alpha$ *greater than* 1, then the series

$$\varepsilon_0 \rho_0 + \varepsilon_1 \rho_1 + \varepsilon_2 \rho_2 + \cdots + \varepsilon_m \rho_m + \ldots,$$

where $\varepsilon_m$ is a quantity which, for ever increasing values of $m$, *does not approach zero*, will be necessarily *divergent*.

*Theorem* II. If in a series of positive quantities $\rho_0 + \rho_1 + \rho_2 + \cdots + \rho_m$ the quotient $\dfrac{\rho_{m+1}}{\rho_m}$, for ever increasing values of $m$, approaches a limit $\alpha$ *smaller than* 1, the series

$$\varepsilon_0 \rho_0 + \varepsilon_1 \rho_1 + \varepsilon_2 \rho_2 + \cdots + \varepsilon_m \rho_m,$$

where $\varepsilon_0$, $\varepsilon_1$, $\varepsilon_2$ etc. are quantities that are *never greater than* one, will be necessarily convergent.

Indeed, by assumption, one may always take $m$ large enough that $\rho_{m+1} < \alpha \rho_m$, $\rho_{m+2} < \alpha \rho_{m+1}$, $\ldots \rho_{m+n} < \alpha \rho_{m+n-1}$. It follows from there that $\rho_{m+k} < \alpha^k \rho_m$ and consequently

$$\rho_m + \rho_{m+1} + \cdots + \rho_{m+n} < \rho_m (1 + \alpha + \alpha^2 + \cdots + \alpha^n) < \frac{\rho_m}{1 - \alpha},$$

[314] therefore, for all the more reason,

$$\varepsilon_m \rho_m + \varepsilon_{m+1} \rho_{m+1} + \cdots + \varepsilon_{m+n} \rho_{m+n} < \frac{\rho_m}{1 - \alpha}.$$

---

* *Note.* For brevity, in this memoir we will understand by $\omega$ a quantity which may be smaller than any given quantity, however small.

Now, since $\rho_{m+k} < \alpha^k \rho_m$ and $\alpha < 1$, it is clear that $\rho_m$ and consequently the sum

$$\varepsilon_m \rho_m + \varepsilon_{m+1}\rho_{m+1} + \cdots + \varepsilon_{m+n}\rho_{m+n}$$

will approach zero.

The above series is therefore convergent.

*Theorem* III. On denoting by $t_0$, $t_1$, $t_2$ ...$t_m$ a series of any quantities whatever, if $p_m = t_0 + t_1 + t_2 + \ldots t_m \ldots$ is always less than a determined quantity $\delta$, one will have

$$r = \varepsilon_0 t_0 + \varepsilon_1 t_1 + \varepsilon_2 t_2 + \cdots + \varepsilon_m t_m < \delta \varepsilon_0,$$

where $\varepsilon_0, \varepsilon_1, \varepsilon_2$ ...denote positive decreasing quantities.

Indeed, one has

$$t_0 = p_0, \quad t_1 = p_1 - p_0, \quad t_2 = p_2 - p_1, \quad \text{etc.}$$

therefore

$$r = \varepsilon_0 p_0 + \varepsilon_1(p_1 - p_0) + \varepsilon_2(p_2 - p_1) + \cdots + \varepsilon_m(p_m - p_{m-1}),$$

or rather

$$r = p_0(\varepsilon_0 - \varepsilon_1) + p_1(\varepsilon_1 - \varepsilon_2) + \cdots + p_{m-1}(\varepsilon_{m-1} - \varepsilon_m) + p_m \varepsilon_m.$$

But $\varepsilon_0 - \varepsilon_1, \varepsilon_1 - \varepsilon_2,$ ...are positive, so the quantity $r$ will clearly be less than $\delta \varepsilon_0$.

*Definition.* A function $f(x)$ will be said to be a *continuous function* of $x$ between the limits $x = 0$ and $x = b$, if for any value of $x$ contained between these limits, the quantity $f(x - \beta)$, for ever decreasing values of $\beta$, approaches the limit $f(x)$.

*Theorem* IV. If the series

$$f(\alpha) = v_0 + v_1\alpha + v_2\alpha^2 + \cdots + v_m\alpha^m + \ldots$$

converges for a certain value $\delta$ of $\alpha$, it will also converge for every value *smaller than $\alpha$* and, for this kind of series, for ever decreasing values of $\beta$, the function $f(\alpha - \beta)$ will approach the limit $f(\alpha)$, assuming that $\alpha$ is equal to or less than $\delta$.

Suppose

$$v_0 + v_1\alpha + \cdots + v_{m-1}\alpha^{m-1} = \varphi(\alpha),$$

$$v_m\alpha^m + v_{m+1}\alpha^{m+1} + \text{etc.} \cdots = \psi(\alpha),$$

so [315]

$$\psi\alpha = \left(\frac{\alpha}{\delta}\right)^m v_m\delta^m + \left(\frac{\alpha}{\delta}\right)^{m+1} v_{m+1}\delta^{m+1} + \text{etc.},$$

therefore, from Theorem III, $\psi\alpha < \left(\frac{\alpha}{\delta}\right)^m p$, where $p$ denotes the greatest of the quantities $v_m\delta^m$, $v_m\delta^m + v_{m+1}\delta^{m+1}$, $v_m\delta^m + v_{m+1}\delta^{m+1} + v_{m+2}\delta^{m+2}$ etc. Therefore for every value of $\alpha$, equal to or less than $\delta$, one may take $m$ large enough that one will have

$$\psi(\alpha) = \omega.$$

Now $f(\alpha) = \varphi(\alpha) + \psi(\alpha)$, so $f(\alpha) - f(\alpha - \beta) = \varphi(\alpha) - \varphi(\alpha - \beta) + \omega$. Further, $\varphi(\alpha)$ is a polynomial in $\alpha$, so one may take $\beta$ small enough that

$$\varphi(\alpha) - \varphi(\alpha - \beta) = \omega;$$

so also one has in the same way

$$f(\alpha) - f(\alpha - \beta) = \omega,$$

which it was required to prove.

————————

## 16.2 UNIFORM CONVERGENCE

### 16.2.1 Cauchy's erroneous theorem, 1821

We have now seen many results from Cauchy's *Cours d'analyse* (1821) and *Resumé des leçons* (1823) that have since become standard features of the undergraduate curriculum. In Chapter VI of the *Cours d'analyse*, however, is a theorem that is certainly not taught nowadays because it turned out to be false: the theorem that an infinite sum of continuous functions is itself continuous. Although Cauchy did not say so, his claim was almost certainly a response to the emerging theory of Fourier series: Cauchy's argument, if correct, would imply that an infinite sum of sines and cosines must be continuous, whereas Fourier believed that even non-continuous functions could be expressed in this way.

————————————————————————————————————

### Cauchy's erroneous theorem
from Cauchy, *Cours d'analyse*, 1821, 130–132

————————————————————————————————————

La série

$$u_0, \quad u_1, \quad u_2, \quad u_3, \quad \&c. \ldots$$

étant supposée convergenté, si l'on désigne sa somme par $s$, et par $s_n$ la somme de ses $n$ premiers termes, on trouvera

$$s = u_0 + u_1 + u_2 + \ldots + u_{n-1} + u_n + u_{n+1} + \&c. \ldots$$

$$= s_n + u_n + u_{n+1} + \&c. \ldots ,$$

et par suite

$$s - s_n = u_n + u_{n+1} + \&c. \ldots .$$

De cette dernière équation il résulte que les quantités
tités

$$u_n, \quad u_{n+1}, \quad u_{n+2}, \quad \&c.\ldots$$

formeront une nouvelle série convergente dont la somme sera équivalente à $s - s_n$. Si l'on représente cette même somme par $r_n$, on aura

$$s = s_n + r_n;$$

et $r_n$ sera ce qu'on appelle le *reste* de la série (1) à partir du $n.^{me}$ terme.

Lorsque, les termes de la série (1) renfermant une même variable $x$, cette série est convergente, et ses différens termes fonctions continues de $x$, dans le voisinage d'une valeur particulière attribuée à cette variable ;

$$s_n, \quad r_n \quad \text{et} \quad s$$

sont encore trois fonctions de la variable $x$, dont la première est évidemment continue par rapport à $x$ dans le voisinage de la valeur particulière dont il s'agit. Cela posé, considérons les accroissemens que recoivent ces trois fonctions, lorsqu'on fait croitre $x$ d'une quantité infiniment petite $\alpha$. L'accroissement de $s_n$ sera, pour toutes les valeurs possibles de $n$, une quantité infiniment petite ; et celui de $r_n$ deviendra insensible en même temps que $r_n$, si l'on attribue à $n$ une valeur très-considérable. Par suite, l'accroissement de la fonction $s$ ne pourra être qu'une quantité infiniment petite. De cette remarque on déduit immédiatement la proposition suivante.

1.$^{er}$ Théorème. *Lorsque les différens termes de la série* (1) *sont des fonctions d'une même variable $x$,*

**132**          COURS D'ANALYSE.

*continues par rapport à cette variable dans le voi-*
*sinage d'une valeur particulière pour laquelle la*
*série est convergente, la somme s de la série est*
*aussi, dans le voisinage de cette valeur particu-*
*lière, fonction continue de x.*

TRANSLATION

The series

[(1)]                                  $u_0$, $u_1$, $u_2$, $u_3$, etc....

being assumed convergent, if one denotes its sum by $s$, and the sum of its first $n$ terms
by $s_n$, one will have

$$s = u_0 + u_1 + u_2 + \cdots + u_{n-1} + u_n + u_{n+1} + \text{etc.}...$$
$$= s_n + u_n + u_{n-1} + \text{etc.}...$$

and consequently

$$s - s_n = u_n + u_{n-1} + \text{etc.}.....$$

From this last equation, it follows that the quantities [131]

$$u_n, u_{n_1}, u_{n+2}, \text{etc.}...$$

will form a new convergent series whose sum will be equal to $s - s_n$. If one represents
this same sum by $r_n$, one will have

$$s = s_n + r_n;$$

and $r_n$ will be what one calls the *remainder* of series (1) from the $n^{\text{th}}$ term.

When, the terms of series (1) contain the same variable $x$, [and] this series is convergent, and the various terms are continuous functions of $x$ in the neighbourhood of
a particular value given to this variable, [then]

$$s_n, \quad r_n \quad \text{and} \quad s$$

are again three functions of the variable $x$, of which the first is clearly continuous with
respect to $x$ in the neighbourhood of the particular value we are concerned with. That
agreed, let us consider the increments that the three functions receive when one makes
$x$ increase by an infinitely small quantity $\alpha$. The increase in $s_n$ will be, for all possible
values of $n$, an infinitely small quantity; and that of $r_n$ will become indiscernible at
the same time as $r_n$, if one gives a very large value to $n$. It follows that the increase in
the function $s$ can only be an infinitely small quantity. From this remark one deduces
immediately the following proposition:

1$^{\text{st}}$ THEOREM. *When the various terms of series (1) are functions of the same variable x,*
[132] *continuous with respect to that variable in the neighbourhood of a particular value*
*for which the series is convergent, the sum s of the series is also, in the neighbourhood of*
*that particular value, a continuous function of x.*

### 16.2.2  Stokes and 'infinitely slow' convergence, 1847

An understanding that the convergence of a series of functions needs to be carefully handled developed only in the late 1840s, simultaneously but independently in the work of Phillip Seidel, a former pupil of Dirichlet, and George Gabriel Stokes in Cambridge. Both realized that for an infinite sum of continuous functions to be continuous, convergence must be of a particular kind, which Seidel (in 1848) described as not 'arbitrarily slow' and Stokes (in late 1847) as not 'infinitely slow'. Such ideas foreshadowed the later idea of uniform convergence, where a series of functions not only converges at every point, but does so at a uniform rate over a range of values.

Stokes' paper of 1847 was entitled 'On the critical values of the sums of periodic series'. His discussion of continuity in §1 shows that even by 1847 the Eulerian definition of a continuous function as one that can be expressed by a single formula had not entirely fallen out of use, but Stokes himself adopted the Bolzano–Cauchy definition: '$f(x)$ is called continuous when, for all values of $x$, the difference between $f(x)$ and $f(x \pm h)$ can be made smaller than any assignable quantity by sufficiently diminishing $h$'. In the same opening section, Stokes separated convergent series into two classes, either 'essentially' or 'accidentally' convergent; in modern terms absolutely or conditionally convergent. His definition of 'infinitely slow' convergence came only much later in the paper, in §38.

Stokes harked back to yet another old idea when he argued in §39 that $U$ is equal to the limit of $V$ because their difference can be made smaller than 'any assignable quantity', wording almost exactly the same as that used by Wallis two hundred years earlier (see 3.2.3 and 11.1.1).

The modern definition of uniform convergence was formulated a few years after the appearance of Stokes' paper, by Weierstrass in Berlin.

---

## Stokes and 'infinitely slow' convergence

from Stokes, 'On the critical values of the sums of periodic series', *Transactions of the Cambridge Philosophical Society*, 8 (1849), 561–562

---

### SECTION III.

*On the discontinuity of the sums of infinite series, and of the values of integrals taken between infinite limits.*

38.  LET        $u_1 + u_2 \ldots + u_n + \cdots$    ................................................... (66),

be a convergent infinite series having $U$ for its sum.  Let

$v_1 + v_2 \ldots + v_n + \cdots$    ................................................... (67),

be another infinite series of which the general term $v_n$ is a function of the positive variable $h$, and becomes equal to $u_n$ when $h$ vanishes.  Suppose that for a sufficiently small value of $h$ and all inferior values the series (67) is convergent, and has $V$ for its sum.  It might at first sight be supposed that the limit of $V$ for $h = 0$ was necessarily equal to $U$.  This however is not true.  For let the sum to $n$ terms of the series (67) be denoted by $f(n, h)$: then the limit of $V$ is the limit of $f(n, h)$ when $n$ first becomes infinite and then $h$ vanishes, whereas $U$ is the limit of $f(n, h)$ when $h$ first vanishes and then $n$ becomes infinite, and these limits may be different.  Whenever a discontinuous function is developed in a periodic series like (15) or (30) we have an instance of this; but it is easy to form two series, having nothing to do with periodic series, in which the same happens. For this purpose it is only requisite to take for $f(n, h) - U_n$, ($U_n$ being the sum of the first $n$ terms of (66),) a quantity which has different limiting values according to the order in which $n$ and $h$ are supposed to assume their limiting values, and which has for its finite difference a quantity which vanishes when $n$ becomes infinite, whether $h$ be a positive quantity sufficiently small or be actually zero.

For example, let

$$f(n,h) - U_n = \frac{2\,nh}{nh + 1}, \quad\quad\quad\quad\quad\quad\quad (68),$$

which vanishes when $n = 0$.   Then

$$\Delta \{f(n,h) - U_n\} = v_{n+1} - u_{n+1} = \frac{2\,h}{(nh + 1)\,(nh + h + 1)}.$$

Assume                          $U_n = 1 - \dfrac{1}{n + 1}$,   so that $u_n = \Delta U_{n-1} = \dfrac{1}{n\,(n + 1)}$,

and we get the series

$$\frac{1}{1 . 2} + \frac{1}{2 . 3} \cdots + \frac{1}{n\,(n + 1)} + \dots, \quad\quad\quad\quad\quad (69),$$

$$\frac{1 + 5\,h}{2\,(1 + h)} \cdots + \frac{h\,(h + 2)\,n^2 + h\,(4 - h)\,n + 1 - h}{n\,(n + 1)\,\{(n - 1)\,h + 1\}\,(nh + 1)} + \dots, \quad\quad (70).$$

which are both convergent, and of which the general terms become the same when $h$ vanishes. Yet the sum of the first is 1, whereas the sum of the second is 3.

If the numerator of the fraction on the right-hand side of (68) had been $pnh$ instead of $2nh$, the sum of the series (70) would have been $p + 1$, and therefore the limit to which the sum approaches when $h$ vanishes would have been $p + 1$. Hence we can form as many series as we please like (67) having different quantities for the limits of their sums when $h$ vanishes, and yet all having their $n^{\text{th}}$ terms becoming equal to $u_n$ when $h$ vanishes. This is equally true whether the series (66) be convergent or divergent, the series like (67) of course being always supposed to be convergent for all positive values of $h$ however small.

39. It is important for the purposes of the present paper to have a ready mode of ascertaining in what cases we may replace the limit of (67) by (66). Now it follows from the following theorem that this substitution may at once be made in an extensive class of cases.

THEOREM. The limit of $V$ can never differ from $U$ unless the convergency of the series (67) become infinitely slow when $h$ vanishes.

The convergency of the series is here said to become infinitely slow when, if $n$ be the number of terms which must be taken in order to render the sum of the neglected terms numerically less than a given quantity $e$ which may be as small as we please, $n$ increases beyond all limit as $h$ decreases beyond all limit.

DEMONSTRATION. If the convergency do not become infinitely slow, it will be possible to find a number $n_1$ so great that for the value of $h$ we begin with and for all inferior values greater than zero the sum of the neglected terms shall be numerically less than $e$. Now the limit of the sum of the first $n_1$ terms of (67) when $h$ vanishes is the sum of the first $n_1$ terms of (66). Hence if $e'$ be the numerical value of the sum of the terms after the $n_1^{\text{th}}$ of the series (66), $U$ and the limit of $V$ cannot differ by a quantity so great as $e + e'$. But $e$ and $e'$ may be made smaller than any assignable quantities, and therefore $U$ is equal to the limit of $V$.

## 16.3 COMPLETENESS OF THE REAL NUMBERS

Undergraduate mathematics courses today usually begin by defining real numbers, which become in turn the foundation of all subsequent work in analysis, underpinning the concepts of limit and continuity, and from these the calculus itself. Historically, however, as we have already seen, the story developed in the reverse direction: the rules of calculus were laid down by the end of the seventeenth century, and concerns about their validity did little to hinder anyone from using them. Not until the beginning of the nineteenth century were differentiation and integration properly understood as a process of taking limits. By then, Bolzano, Cauchy, and others were able to describe precisely what it meant to approach a limit, but no one yet questioned the *existence* of limits. That in turn was assured only much later in the nineteenth century, by work on the completeness of the real numbers, by Richard Dedekind, Georg Cantor, and many others. That final step in the rigorization of the calculus is the subject of this section, and is the last word in this book on real analysis, a story that has permeated so many of its previous chapters.

### 16.3.1 Bolzano and greatest lower bounds, 1817

Cauchy's 1821 proof of the intermediate value theorem (11.2.6) relied on the crucial assumption that a monotonic bounded sequence of real numbers converges to a limit. Bolzano in *Rein analytischer Beweis* four years earlier had used a different approach. First, he had tried to prove that every Cauchy sequence converges to a limit (see 16.1.2); assuming that this was the case, he could then prove that a set of real numbers that is bounded below has a greatest lower bound. This property is now known as the completeness axiom, but for Bolzano it was not an axiom but a theorem, derived from the convergence of Cauchy sequences. Bolzano went on to prove the intermediate value theorem as a direct consequence of the existence of a greatest lower bound.

By 1821, therefore, attempts to prove the intermediate value theorem had brought three important propositions into play:

1.  Cauchy sequences are convergent
    (an unsuccessful proof by Bolzano in 1817; accepted without proof by Cauchy in 1821).

2.  A set of numbers bounded below has a greatest lower bound
    (proved by Bolzano in 1817 on the basis of (1) ).

3.  A monotonic bounded sequence converges to a limit
    (taken for granted by Cauchy in 1821).

Each of propositions (1), (2), and (3) is equivalent to a statement of *completeness*, that is, that there are no gaps in the real numbers; any one of them can therefore be taken as an axiom from which the others can be derived. The existence of limits can be proved *only* by assuming one of these or an equivalent statement. This is why belief in the convergence of Cauchy sequences mattered so much to the mathematicians of the early nineteenth century, and why the completeness axiom is fundamental to modern analysis.

---

## Bolzano's greatest lower bound theorem

from Bolzano, *Rein analytischer Beweis*, 1817, §12, as translated by Steve Russ in Bolzano 2004, 269–271

---

§. 12.

Lehrſatz. Wenn eine Eigenſchaft M nicht allen Werthen einer veränderlichen Größe x, wohl aber allen, die kleiner ſind, als ein gewiſſer u, zukömmt: ſo gibt es allemahl eine Größe U, welche die größte derjenigen iſt, von denen behauptet werden kann, daß alle kleineren x die Eigenſchaft M beſitzen.

Be-

42

Beweis. 1. Weil die Eigenſchaft M von allen x, die kleiner ſind als u, und gleichwohl nicht von allen überhaupt gilt; ſo gibt es ſicher irgend eine Größe $V = u + D$ (wobey D etwas poſitives vorſtellt) von der ſich behaupten läßt, daß M nicht allen x, die $< V = u + D$ ſind, zukomme. Wenn ich daher die Frage aufwerfe, ob M wohl allen x, die $< u + \dfrac{D}{2^m}$ ſind, zukomme?

und den Exponenten m der Ordnung nach, erſt 0, dann 1, dann 2, dann 3, u. ſ. w. bedeuten laſſe: ſo bin ich gewiß, daß man die erſte meiner Fragen mir wird verneinen müſſen. Denn die Frage, ob M wohl allen x, die $< u + \dfrac{D}{2^0}$ ſind, zukomme, iſt einerley mit der, ob M allen x, die $< u + D$ ſind, zukomme; welches nach der Vorausſetzung zu verneinen iſt. Es kömmt nur darauf an, ob man mir auch alle folgenden Fragen, welche entſtehen, indem ich m nach und nach immer größer anſetze, verneinen wird. Sollte dieſes der Fall ſeyn; ſo iſt einleuchtend, daß u ſelbſt der größte der Werthe iſt, von welchen die Behauptung gilt, daß alle x, die kleiner als er ſind, die Eigenſchaft M beſitzen. Denn gäbe es noch einen größeren z. B. u + d; d. h. gälte die Behauptung, daß auch noch alle x, die $< u + d$ ſind, die Eigenſchaft M haben: ſo iſt doch offenbar, daß wenn ich m groß genug annehme,

u +

43

$u + \dfrac{D}{2^m}$ einmahl = oder $< u + d$ wird; und folglich müßte, wenn M allen x, die $< u + d$ ſind, zukömmt, daſſelbe auch allen, die $< u + \dfrac{D}{2^m}$ ſind, zukommen; alſo hätte mir dieſe Frage nicht verneint, ſondern bejahet werden müſſen. Es iſt daher erwieſen, daß es in dieſem Falle (wo man mir alle obigen Fragen verneint) eine gewiſſe Größe U (nähmlich u ſelbſt) gebe, welche die größte derjenigen iſt, von denen die Behauptung gilt, daß alle unter ihr ſtehende x die Eigenſchaft M beſitzen.

2. Wird mir dagegen die obige Frage einmahl bejahet, und iſt m der beſtimmte Werth des Exponenten, bey dem man ſie mir zuerſt bejahet (m kann auch 1 bedeuten; aber, wie wir geſehen, nicht 0): ſo weiß ich nun, daß die Eigenſchaft M allen x, die $< u + \dfrac{D}{2^m}$ ſind, aber ſchon nicht mehr allen, die $< u + \dfrac{D}{2^{m-1}}$ ſind, zukomme. Der Unterſchied zwiſchen $u + \dfrac{D}{2^{m-1}}$ und $u + \dfrac{D}{2^m}$ iſt aber $= \dfrac{D}{2^m}$. Wenn ich daher mit dieſem wieder, wie vorhin mit dem Unterſchiede D verfahre; d. h. wenn ich die Frage aufwerfe, ob M wohl allen x, die

$< u +$

$< u + \dfrac{D}{2^m} + \dfrac{D}{2^{m+n}}$ ſind, zukomme; und hier den Exponenten n erſt 0, dann 1, dann 2, u. ſ. w. be-deuten laſſe: ſo bin ich abermahl gewiß, daß man mir wenigſtens die erſte dieſer Fragen wird verneinen müſſen. Denn fragen, ob M allen x, die

$< u + \dfrac{D}{2^m} + \dfrac{D}{2^{m+0}}$ ſind, zukomme, heißt eben ſo viel, als fragen, ob M allen x, die $< u + \dfrac{D}{2^{n-1}}$ ſind, eigen ſey; was man ſchon vorhin verneinet hatte. Sollte man aber auch alle meine f o l g e n d e n Fragen verneinen, ſo groß ich auch n nach und nach mache: ſo würde, wie vorhin, erhellen, $u + \dfrac{D}{2^m}$ ſey jener größte Werth, oder das U, von welchem die Behauptung gilt, daß alle unter ihm ſtehenden x die Eigenſchaft M beſitzen.

3. Wird mir dagegen eine dieſer Fragen beja-het, und geſchieht dieß zuerſt bey dem beſtimmten Werthe n: ſo weiß ich nun, daß M allen x, die $< u + \dfrac{D}{2^m} + \dfrac{D}{2^{m+n}}$ ſind, zukomme, aber ſchon nicht mehr allen, die $< u + \dfrac{D}{2^m} + \dfrac{D}{2^{m+n-1}}$ ſind.

ſind. Der Unterſchied zwiſchen dieſen beyden Größen iſt $= \dfrac{D}{2^{m+n}}$; und ich verfahre mit ihm wieder, wie vorhin mit $\dfrac{D}{2^m}$. u. ſ. w.

4. Wenn ich auf dieſe Art ſo lange fortfahre, als man nur immer will; ſo ſieht man, daß das Re-ſultat, das ich zuletzt erhalte, eines von Beydem ſeyn muß.

a. Entweder ich finde einen Werth von der Form $u + \dfrac{D}{2^m} + \dfrac{D}{2^{m+n}} + \ldots + \dfrac{D}{2^{m+n..+r}}$, der ſich mir als der größte darſtellt, von welchem die Behauptung gilt, daß alle unter ihm ſtehende x die Eigenſchaft M beſitzen. Dieß geſchieht in dem Falle, wenn mir die Fragen, ob M allen x, die $< u + \dfrac{D}{2^m} + \dfrac{D}{2^{m+n}} + \ldots + \dfrac{D}{2^{m+n+..+r}}$ ſind, zukomme, für jeden Werth von s. verneinet werden.

b. Oder ich finde wenigſtens, daß M zwar allen x, die $< u + \dfrac{D}{2^m} + \dfrac{D}{2^{m+n}} + .. + \dfrac{D}{2^{m+n+..+r}}$ ſind, zukomme, aber ſchon nicht mehr allen, die $< u$

---

TRANSLATION

## §12

*Theorem.* If a property M does not apply to *all* values of a variable quantity x but does apply to *all* values *smaller* than a certain u, then there is always a quantity U which is the greatest of those of which it can be asserted that all smaller x possess the property M.

[42] *Proof.* I. Because the property M holds for all x *smaller* than u but nevertheless not for *all* x, there is certainly some quantity $V = u + D$ (where D represents someting positive) of which it can be asserted that M does not apply to all x which are $< V = u + D$. If I then raise the question of whether M *in fact applies to all x* which are $< u + \frac{D}{2^m}$ where the exponent m is in turn first 0, then 1, then 2, then 3, etc., I am sure the *first* of my questions will *have to be answered 'no'*. For the question of whether M applies to all x which are $< u + \frac{D}{2^0}$ is the same as that of whether M applies to all x which are $< u + D$, which is ruled out by assumption. What matters is whether all the *succeeding* questions, which arise as m gradually gets larger, will also be ruled out. Should this be the case, it is evident that u *itself* is the greatest value for which the assertion holds that all smaller x have property M. For if there were an even greater value, for example $u + d$, i.e. if the assertion held that also all x which are $< u + d$ have

**46**

$$< u + \frac{D}{2^m} + \frac{D}{2^{u}+n} + \ldots + \frac{D}{2^{m+n+\ldots+r-1}}$$

find. Hiebey steht es mir frey, die Anzahl der Glieder in diesen beyden Größen durch neue Fragen immer noch größer zu machen.

5. Ist nun der erste Fall vorhanden, so ist die Wahrheit des Lehrsatzes bereits erwiesen. Im zweyten Falle lasset uns bemerken, daß die Größe

$$u + \frac{D}{2^m} + \frac{D}{2^{m+n}} + \ldots + \frac{D}{2^{m+n+\ldots+r}}$$

eine Reihe vorstelle, deren Gliederzahl ich nach Belieben vermehren kann, und die zur Classe der §. 5 beschriebenen gehöret; weil sie, je nachdem m, n, ...r entweder alle = 1, oder zum Theile noch größer sind, entweder eben so, oder noch stärker abnimmt, als eine geometrische Progression, deren Exponent der echte Bruch ½ ist. Daraus ergibt sich, daß sie die Eigenschaft des §. 9 habe; d. h. daß es eine gewisse beständige Größe gebe, der sie so nahe kommen kann, als man nur immer will, wenn man die Menge ihrer Glieder hinlänglich vermehret. Sey diese Größe U; so behaupte ich, die Eigenschaft M gelte von allen x, die < U sind.

the property $M$, then it is obvious that if I take $m$ large enough, [43] $u + \frac{D}{2^m}$ will at some time be $=$ or $< u + d$. Consequently if $M$ applies to all $x$ which are $< u + d$, it also applies to all $x$ which are $< u + \frac{D}{2^m}$. We would therefore not have said 'no' to this question but would have had to say 'yes'. Thus it is proved that in this case (when we say 'no' to all the above questions) there is a certain quantity $U$ (namely $u$ itself) which is the greatest for which the assertion holds that all $x$ below it possess the property $M$.

2. However, if one of the above questions is *answered 'yes'* and $m$ is the particular value of the exponent for which this happens *first* ($m$ can be 1 but, as we have seen not 0), then I now know that the property $M$ applies to all $x$ which are $< u + \frac{D}{2^m}$ but not to all $x$ which are $< u + \frac{D}{2^{m-1}}$. But the difference between $u + \frac{D}{2^{m-1}}$ and $u + \frac{D}{2^m}$ is $= \frac{D}{2^m}$. If I therefore deal with this as I did before with the difference $D$, i.e. if I raise the question of whether $M$ applies to all $x$ which are [44]

$$< u + \frac{D}{2^m} + \frac{D}{2^{m+n}},$$

and here the exponent $n$ denotes first 0, then 1, then 2, etc., then I am sure once again that at least the *first* of these questions will have to be answered 'no'. For to ask whether $M$ applies to all $x$ which are

$$< u + \frac{D}{2^m} + \frac{D}{2^{m+0}}$$

is just the same as asking whether $M$ applies to all $x$ which are $< u + \frac{D}{2^{m-1}}$, which had previously been denied. But if all my *succeeding* questions are also to be answered negatively as I gradually make $n$ larger and larger, then it would appear, as before, that $u + \frac{D}{2^m}$ is that greatest value, or the $U$, for which the assertion holds that all $x$ below it possess the property $M$.

3. However, if one of these questions is answered positively and this happens first for the particular value $n$, then I now know $M$ applies to all $x$ which are

$$< u + \frac{D}{2^m} + \frac{D}{2^{m+n}}$$

but not to all $x$ which are

$$< u + \frac{D}{2^m} + \frac{D}{2^{m+n-1}}.$$

[45] The difference between these two quantities is $= \frac{D}{2^{m+n}}$ and I deal with this again as before with $\frac{D}{2^m}$, etc.

4. If I continue this way as long as I please it may be seen that the result that I finally obtain must be one of two things.

(a) Either I find a value of the form

$$u + \frac{D}{2^m} + \frac{D}{2^{m+n}} + \cdots + \frac{D}{2^{m+n+\cdots+r}}$$

which appears to be the greatest for which the assertion holds that all $x$ below it possess the property $M$. This happens in the case when the questions of whether $M$ applies to all $x$ which are

$$< u + \frac{D}{2^m} + \frac{D}{2^{m+n}} + \cdots + \frac{D}{2^{m+n+\cdots+r+s}}$$

are answered with 'no' for every value of $s$.

(b) Or I at least find that $M$ does indeed apply to all $x$ which are

$$< u + \frac{D}{2^m} + \frac{D}{2^{m+n}} + \cdots + \frac{D}{2^{m+n+\cdots+r}}$$

but not to all $x$ which are [46]

$$< u + \frac{D}{2^m} + \frac{D}{2^{m+n}} + \cdots + \frac{D}{2^{m+n+\cdots+r-1}}.$$

Here I am always free to make the number of terms in these two quantities even greater through new questions.

5. Now if the *first* case occurs the truth of the theorem is already proved. In the *second* case we may remark that the quantity

$$u + \frac{D}{2^m} + \frac{D}{2^{m+n}} + \cdots + \frac{D}{2^{m+n+\cdots+r}}$$

represents a series whose number of terms I can increase arbitrarily and which belongs to the class described in §5. This is because, depending on whether $m, n, \ldots, r$ are all $= 1$, or some of them are greater than 1, the series decreases at the same rate, or more rapidly than, a geometric progression whose ratio is the proper fraction $\frac{1}{2}$. From this it follows that it has the property of §9, i.e. there is a certain *constant quantity* to which it can come as close as we please if the number of its terms is increased sufficiently. Let this quantity be $U$; then I claim the property $M$ holds for all $x$ which are $< U$.

Bolzano completed the proof by supposing that the property does not hold for some $x = U - \delta$, and showing that this leads to a contradiction; and, similarly, that the supposition that $M$ holds for all $x < U + \varepsilon$ also leads to a contradiction.

### 16.3.2  Dedekind's definition of real numbers, 1858

Just as Cauchy, through teaching analysis to students at the École Polytechnique in the early 1820s, began to bring new rigour to definitions of limits, convergence, and continuity, so Richard Dedekind, teaching differential calculus at the Polytechnikum in Zürich some forty years later, was also forced to think afresh about the foundations of analysis, and to question the intuitive justifications that were still being given. Cauchy's assumption, for instance, that a monotonic bounded sequence must converge to a limit, was precisely one that Dedekind was troubled by. So great was his dissatisfaction with the usual geometrically based explanations that he resolved to find what he described as a purely arithmetic and rigorous foundation for analysis. This he succeeded in doing in November 1858, but did not publish his work until 1872, in *Stetigkeit und irrationale Zahlen* (*Continuity and irrational numbers*). The above account of how and why he came to the problem comes from his own Introduction to that treatise.

Dedekind saw that numbers (a concept from arithmetic) must have the same completeness or continuity as a straight line (a concept from geometry). His starting point was the observation that if units are marked off along an infinite straight line there are infinitely many points that do not correspond to any rational number, for example, the endpoint of the diagonal of a unit square (when the other end is placed at the origin). His aim was to define such non-rational, or irrational, numbers not just *geometrically*, but *arithmetically*, in terms of the rationals themselves.

Dedekind also pondered on the nature of continuity, and came up with an idea radically different from those presented earlier in the century by Bolzano and Cauchy (see 11.2). It is clear that every point on a straight line separates the line into two parts in such a way that every point of one part lies to the left of every point of the other. Conversely, claimed Dedekind, every such separation into two parts is produced by one and only one point.[3]

"If all points of a straight line fall into two classes in such a way that each point of the first class lies to the left of each point of the second class, then there exists one and only one point which brings about this separation of all points into two classes, this cutting of the line into two parts."

In this simple idea, argued Dedekind, lay the essence of continuity. It was a property he could not prove, but had to take as an assumption corresponding to our intuitive notion of continuity.[4]

---

3. "Zerfallen alle Punkte der Geraden in zwei Klassen von der Art, daß jeder Punkt der ersten Klasse links von jedem Punkte der zweiten Klasse liegt, so existiert ein und nur ein Punkt, welcher diese Einteilung aller Punkte in zwei Klassen, diese Zerschneidung der Graden in zwei Stücke hervorbringt." Dedekind 1930–32, 322.

4. 'Die Annahme dieser Eigenschaft der Linie ist nichts als ein Axiom, durch welches wir erst der Linie ihre Stetigkeit zuerkennen, durch welches wir die Stetigkeit in die Linie hineindenken.' Dedekind 1930–32, 323.

The assumption of this property for the line is nothing but an Axiom, through which alone we attribute continuity to the line, through which we understand continuity in the line.

A separation of the line into two parts on either side of a single point, Dedekind called a *cut* (*Schnitt*). Every rational number produces a cut, but there are also infinitely many cuts *not* produced by any rational number. These Dedekind called the irrationals. The rationals and irrationals taken together ensure the completeness, of the real numbers, to which Dedekind now gave the label $\mathfrak{R}$. It is not difficult to define an ordering of $\mathfrak{R}$, and it is also possible to define the operations of arithmetic in a way that corresponds to our natural understanding of them, which Dedekind went on to do in the remainder of his treatise.

---

## Dedekind cuts

from Dedekind, *Stetigkeit and irrationale Zahlen*, 1872, §4; from *Werke*, 1930–32, III, 323–325

---

### § 4.

### Schöpfung der irrationalen Zahlen.

Durch die letzten Worte ist schon hinreichend angedeutet, auf welche Art das unstetige Gebiet $R$ der rationalen Zahlen zu einem stetigen vervollständigt werden muß. In § 1 ist hervorgehoben (III), daß jede rationale Zahl $a$ eine Zerlegung des Systems $R$ in zwei Klassen $A_1$, $A_2$ von der Art hervorbringt, daß jede Zahl $a_1$ der ersten Klasse $A_1$ kleiner ist als jede Zahl $a_2$ der zweiten Klasse $A_2$; die Zahl $a$ ist entweder die größte Zahl der Klasse $A_1$, oder die kleinste Zahl der Klasse $A_2$. Ist nun irgendeine Einteilung des Systems $R$ in zwei Klassen $A_1$, $A_2$ gegeben, welche nur die charakteristische Eigenschaft besitzt, daß jede Zahl $a_1$ in $A_1$ kleiner ist als jede Zahl $a_2$ in $A_2$, so wollen wir der Kürze halber eine solche Einteilung einen Schnitt nennen und mit $(A_1, A_2)$ bezeichnen. Wir können dann sagen, daß jede rationale Zahl $a$ einen Schnitt oder eigentlich zwei Schnitte hervorbringt, welche wir aber nicht als wesentlich verschieden ansehen wollen; dieser Schnitt hat außerdem die Eigenschaft, daß entweder unter den Zahlen der ersten Klasse eine größte, oder unter den Zahlen der zweiten Klasse eine kleinste existiert. Und umgekehrt, besitzt ein Schnitt auch diese Eigenschaft, so wird er durch diese größte oder kleinste rationale Zahl hervorgebracht.

Aber man überzeugt sich leicht, daß auch unendlich viele Schnitte existieren, welche nicht durch rationale Zahlen hervorgebracht werden. Das nächstliegende Beispiel ist folgendes.

Es sei $D$ eine positive ganze Zahl, aber nicht das Quadrat einer ganzen Zahl, so gibt es eine positive ganze Zahl $\lambda$ von der Art, daß

$$\lambda^2 < D < (\lambda + 1)^2$$

wird.

Nimmt man in die zweite Klasse $A_2$ jede positive rationale Zahl $a_2$ auf, deren Quadrat $> D$ ist, in die erste Klasse $A_1$ aber alle anderen rationalen Zahlen $a_1$, so bildet diese Einteilung einen Schnitt $(A_1, A_2)$, d. h. jede Zahl $a_1$ ist kleiner als jede Zahl $a_2$. Ist nämlich $a_1 = 0$ oder negativ, so ist $a_1$ schon aus diesem Grunde kleiner als jede Zahl $a_2$, weil diese zufolge der Definition positiv ist; ist aber $a_1$ positiv, so ist ihr Quadrat $\leqq D$, und folglich ist $a_1$ kleiner als jede positive Zahl $a_2$, deren Quadrat $> D$ ist.

Dieser Schnitt wird aber durch keine rationale Zahl hervorgebracht. Um dies zu beweisen, muß vor allem gezeigt werden, daß es keine rationale Zahl gibt, deren Quadrat $= D$ ist. Obgleich dies aus den ersten Elementen der Zahlentheorie bekannt ist, so mag doch hier der folgende indirekte Beweis Platz finden. Gibt es eine rationale Zahl, deren Quadrat $= D$ ist, so gibt es auch zwei positive ganze Zahlen $t$, $u$, welche der Gleichung

$$t^2 - D u^2 = 0$$

genügen, und man darf annehmen, daß $u$ die kleinste positive ganze Zahl ist, welche die Eigenschaft besitzt, daß ihr Quadrat durch Multiplikation mit $D$ in das Quadrat einer ganzen Zahl $t$ verwandelt wird. Da nun offenbar

$$\lambda u < t < (\lambda + 1) u$$

ist, so wird die Zahl

$$u' = t - \lambda u$$

eine positive ganze Zahl, und zwar kleiner als $u$. Setzt man ferner

$$t' = D u - \lambda t,$$

so wird $t'$ ebenfalls eine positive ganze Zahl, und es ergibt sich

$$t'^2 - D\,u'^2 = (\lambda^2 - D)(t^2 - D\,u^2) = 0,$$

was mit der Annahme über $u$ im Widerspruch steht.

Mithin ist das Quadrat einer jeden rationalen Zahl $x$ entweder $< D$ oder $> D$. Hieraus folgt nun leicht, daß es weder in der Klasse $A_1$ eine größte, noch in der Klasse $A_2$ eine kleinste Zahl gibt. Setzt man nämlich

$$y = \frac{x\,(x^2 + 3\,D)}{3\,x^2 + D},$$

so ist

$$y - x = \frac{2\,x\,(D - x^2)}{3\,x^2 + D}$$

und

$$y^2 - D = \frac{(x^2 - D)^3}{(3\,x^2 + D)^2}.$$

Nimmt man hierin für $x$ eine positive Zahl aus der Klasse $A_1$, so ist $x^2 < D$, und folglich wird $y > x$, und $y^2 < D$, also gehört $y$ ebenfalls der Klasse $A_1$ an. Setzt man aber für $x$ eine Zahl aus der Klasse $A_2$, so ist $x^2 > D$, und folglich wird $y < x$, $y > 0$ und $y^2 > D$, also gehört $y$ ebenfalls der Klasse $A_2$ an. Dieser Schnitt wird daher durch keine rationale Zahl hervorgebracht.

In dieser Eigenschaft, daß nicht alle Schnitte durch rationale Zahlen hervorgebracht werden, besteht die Unvollständigkeit oder Unstetigkeit des Gebietes $R$ aller rationalen Zahlen.

Jedesmal nun, wenn ein Schnitt $(A_1, A_2)$ vorliegt, welcher durch keine rationale Zahl hervorgebracht wird, so erschaffen wir eine neue, eine irrationale Zahl $\alpha$, welche wir als durch diesen Schnitt $(A_1, A_2)$ vollständig definiert ansehen; wir werden sagen, daß die Zahl $\alpha$ diesem Schnitt entspricht, oder daß sie diesen Schnitt hervorbringt. Es entspricht also von jetzt ab jedem bestimmten Schnitt eine und nur eine bestimmte rationale oder irrationale Zahl und wir sehen zwei Zahlen stets und nur dann als verschieden oder ungleich an, wenn sie wesentlich verschiedenen Schnitten entsprechen.

## §4
### Creation of the irrational numbers

From what was said above it is already sufficiently clear in what way the discontinuous domain $R$ of rational numbers must be completed to become continuous. In §1, we emphasized (III), that each rational number $a$ produces a separation of the system $R$ into two classes $A_1$, $A_2$, in such a way that each number $a_1$ in the first class $A_1$ is smaller than each number $a_2$ in the second class $A_2$; the number $a$ is either the greatest number of class $A_1$ or the smallest number of class $A_2$. If now there is given an arbitrary separation of the system $R$ into two classes $A_1$, $A_2$, which possesses only the characteristic property that each number $a_1$ in $A_1$ is smaller than each number $a_2$ in $A_2$, then for short we shall call such a separation a *cut* and denote it by $(A_1, A_2)$. We can then say that each rational number $a$ produces a cut, or strictly two cuts but which we shall regard as not essentially different; this cut has the *further* property that there exists either amongst the numbers of the first class a greatest, or amongst the numbers of the second class a smallest. And conversely, [324] if a cut possesses this property, it is produced by this greatest or smallest rational number.

But one may easily persuade oneself, that there exist also infinitely many cuts which are not produced by rational numbers. The most convenient example is the following.

Let $D$ be a positive whole number, but not a square of a whole number. Then there exists a positive whole number $\lambda$ with the property that

$$\lambda^2 < D < (\lambda + 1)^2.$$

If we take into the second class $A_2$ each positive rational number $a_2$ of which the square is $> D$, but to the first class $A_1$ every other rational number $a_1$, this separation forms a cut $(A_1, A_2)$, that is, each number $a_1$ is smaller than each number $a_2$. For if $a_1 = 0$ or negative, then on these grounds $a_1$ is already smaller than each number $a_2$, since the latter by definition are positive; but if $a_1$ is positive, its square is $\leq D$, and it follows that $a_1$ is less than any positive number $a_2$ whose square is $> D$.

But this cut is produced by no rational number. To prove this it must first of all be shown that there is no rational number whose square $= D$. Although this is known from the first elements of number theory, the following indirect proof perhaps has a place here. If there is a rational number whose square $= D$, there are also two positive whole numbers $t$, $u$, which satisfy the equation

$$t^2 - Du^2 = 0,$$

and one may assume that $u$ is the *smallest* positive whole number which has this property, that its square under multiplication by $D$ is transformed into the square of a whole number $t$. Since clearly

$$\lambda u < t < (\lambda + 1)u$$

the number

$$u' = t - \lambda u$$

is a positive whole number, and certainly *smaller* than $u$. Further if one sets

$$t' = Du - \lambda t,$$

[325] then $t'$ will likewise be a positive whole number, and it comes out that

$$t'^2 - Du'^2 = (\lambda^2 - D)(t^2 - Du^2) = 0,$$

which contradicts what was assumed about $u$.

Hence the square of each rational number $x$ is either $< D$ or $> D$. From this it follows easily that there is neither a greatest number in the class $A_1$ nor a smallest number in the class $A_2$. For, if one sets

$$y = \frac{x(x^3 + 3D)}{3x^2 + D},$$

then

$$y - x = \frac{2x(D - x^2)}{3x^2 + D}$$

and

$$y^2 - D = \frac{(x^2 - D)^3}{(3x^2 + D)^2}.$$

If one here takes $x$ to be a positive number in the class $A_1$, then $x^2 < D$, and it follows that $y > x$ and $y^2 < D$, so $y$ likewise belongs to the class $A_1$. But if one takes $x$ to be a number in the class $A_2$, then $x^2 > D$, and it follows that $y < x, y > 0$ and $y^2 > D$, so $y$ likewise belongs to the class $A_2$. This cut is therefore produced by no rational number.

In this property, that not all cuts are produced by rational numbers, lies the incompleteness or discontinuity of the domain $R$ of all rational numbers.

Whenever then a cut $(A_1, A_2)$ lies before us, which is not produced by any rational number, we *create* a new, *irrational,* number $\alpha$, which we regard as fully defined by this cut $(A_1, A_2)$; we shall say that the number $\alpha$ corresponds to this cut, or that it produces this cut. Therefore, from now on there corresponds to each definite cut one and only one definite rational or irrational number and we regard two numbers as *different* or *unequal* if and only if they correspond to essentially different cuts.

────────────

In the final section of *Stetigkeit and irrationale Zahlen*, Dedekind returned to one of the statements that had concerned him at the beginning, and which Cauchy had taken for granted in 1821: that a bounded monotonic sequence must converge (see 11.2.6). Now he showed how this followed from, and was indeed equivalent to the continuity, or *completeness*, of $\mathfrak{R}$.

## Convergence of monotonic sequences

from Dedekind, *Stetigkeit and irrationale Zahlen*, 1872, §7, from *Werke*, 1930–32, III, 332

§ 7.

### Infinitesimal-Analysis.

Es soll hier nur noch zum Schluß der Zusammenhang beleuchtet werden, welcher zwischen unseren bisherigen Betrachtungen und gewissen Hauptsätzen der Infinitesimalanalysis besteht.

Man sagt, daß eine veränderliche Größe $x$, welche sukzessive bestimmte Zahlwerte durchläuft, sich einem festen Grenzwert $\alpha$ nähert, wenn $x$ im Laufe des Prozesses definitiv zwischen je zwei Zahlen zu liegen kommt, zwischen denen $\alpha$ selbst liegt, oder was dasselbe ist, wenn die Differenz $x - \alpha$ absolut genommen unter jeden gegebenen, von Null verschiedenen Wert definitiv herabsinkt.

Einer der wichtigsten Sätze lautet folgendermaßen: „Wächst eine Größe $x$ beständig, aber nicht über alle Grenzen, so nähert sie sich einem Grenzwert."

Ich beweise ihn auf folgende Art. Der Voraussetzung nach gibt es eine und folglich auch unendlich viele Zahlen $\alpha_2$ von der Art, daß stets $x < \alpha_2$ bleibt; ich bezeichne mit $\mathfrak{A}_2$ das System aller dieser Zahlen $\alpha_2$, mit $\mathfrak{A}_1$ das System aller anderen Zahlen $\alpha_1$; jede der letzteren hat die Eigenschaft, daß im Laufe des Prozesses definitiv $x \geqq \alpha_1$ wird, mithin ist jede Zahl $\alpha_1$ kleiner als jede Zahl $\alpha_2$, und folglich existiert eine Zahl $\alpha$, welche entweder die größte in $\mathfrak{A}_1$ oder die kleinste in $\mathfrak{A}_2$ ist (§ 5, IV). Das erstere kann nicht der Fall sein, weil $x$ nie aufhört, zu wachsen, also ist $\alpha$ die kleinste Zahl in $\mathfrak{A}_2$. Welche Zahl $\alpha_1$ man nun auch nehmen mag, so wird schließlich definitiv $\alpha_1 < x < \alpha$ sein, d. h. $x$ nähert sich dem Grenzwerte $\alpha$.

Dieser Satz ist äquivalent mit dem Prinzip der Stetigkeit, d. h. er verliert seine Gültigkeit, sobald man auch nur eine reelle Zahl in dem Gebiete $\mathfrak{R}$ als nicht vorhanden ansieht; oder anders ausgedrückt: ist dieser Satz richtig, so ist auch der Satz IV in § 5 richtig.

## §7
## *Infinitesimal analysis*

Finally it remains only to elucidate the connection which holds between our investigations up to now and certain principal theorems of infinitesimal analysis.

One says that a variable magnitude $x$, which runs through successive numerical values, approaches a fixed *limit* $\alpha$ when $x$ in the course of the process ultimately comes to lie between any two numbers between which $\alpha$ itself lies or, which is the same thing, when the absolute difference $x - \alpha$ ultimately sinks below any given value different from zero.

One of the most important theorems says the following: "If a magnitude $x$ grows steadily, but not beyond all limits; then it approaches a limit."

I prove this in the following way. According to the assumption there is one and consequently also infinitely many numbers $\alpha_2$, such that always $x < \alpha_2$; I denote by $\mathfrak{A}_2$ the system of all these numbers $\alpha_2$, and by $\mathfrak{A}_1$ the system of all other numbers $\alpha_1$; each of the latter has the property that, in the course of the process, ultimately $x \geq \alpha_1$, hence each number $\alpha_1$ is smaller than each number $\alpha_2$, and consequently there exists a number $\alpha$, which is either the greatest in $\mathfrak{A}_1$ or the least in $\mathfrak{A}_2$ (§5, IV). The former cannot be the case, since $x$ never stops growing, so $\alpha$ is the smallest number in $\mathfrak{A}_2$. Whatever number $\alpha_1$ one may now take, ultimately it will always be the case that $\alpha_1 < x < \alpha$, that is, $x$ approaches the limit $\alpha$.

This theorem is equivalent to the principle of continuity, that is, it loses its validity as soon as one regards even just one real number as not available in the domain $\mathfrak{R}$; or otherwise expressed: if this theorem is correct, then so also is Theorem IV in §5 correct.

### 16.3.3 Cantor's definition of real numbers, 1872

Georg Cantor corresponded with Dedekind during the 1870s on the nature and countability of real numbers, and in the same year that Dedekind published *Stetigkeit and irrationale Zahlen* Cantor too devised a definition of real numbers, but from a starting point quite different from Dedekind's. Since the underlying problem was to ensure the existence of a limit for a Cauchy sequence, the approach used by Cantor was to define numbers themselves in terms of Cauchy sequences. Thus, he supposed that a Cauchy sequence of rational numbers $a_1, a_2, ..., a_n, ...$ defines some number $b$. Cantor, somewhat confusingly, described this number as 'a definite limit' (*eine bestimmte Grenze*), but only in a loose sense which he would later clarify.

Cantor then showed that if some other Cauchy sequence has a similar limit $b'$, it is possible to decide whether $b = b'$ or $b < b'$ or $b > b'$, so that order is determined. He also showed how to define the usual operations of arithmetic on the quantities $b$. Thus these quantities have all the required properties of the real numbers.

---

### Cantor's sequences of rationals

from Cantor, 'Über die Ausdehnung eines Satzes aus der Theorie der Trigonometrischen Reihen', *Mathematische Annalen*, 1872, 123–125

---

### § 1.

Die rationalen Zahlen bilden die Grundlage für die Feststellung des weiteren Begriffes einer Zahlengrösse; ich will sie das Gebiet $A$ nennen (mit Einschluss der Null).

Wenn ich von einer Zahlengrösse im weiteren Sinne rede, so geschieht es zunächst in dem Falle, dass eine durch ein Gesetz gegebene unendliche Reihe von rationalen Zahlen:

(1)                    $a_1, \ a_2, \ ... \ a_n, \ .....$

vorliegt, welche die Beschaffenheit hat, dass die Differenz $a_{n+m} - a_n$

124                        G. Cantor.

mit wachsendem $n$ unendlich klein wird, was auch die positive ganze
Zahl $m$ sei, oder mit anderen Worten, dass bei beliebig angenom-
menem (positiven, rationalen) $\varepsilon$ eine ganze Zahl $n_1$ vorhanden ist, so
dass $(a_{n+m} - a_n) < \varepsilon$, wenn $n \gtreqless n_1$ und wenn $m$ eine beliebige positive ganze Zahl ist.

Diese Beschaffenheit der Reihe (1) drücke ich in den Worten aus:
„*Die Reihe* (1) *hat eine bestimmte Grenze b.*"

Es haben also diese Worte zunächst keinen anderen Sinn, als
den eines Ausdruckes für jene Beschaffenheit der Reihe, und aus dem
Umstande, dass wir mit der Reihe (1) ein besonderes Zeichen $b$ ver-
binden, folgt, dass bei verschiedenen derartigen Reihen auch verschiedene Zeichen $b$, $b'$, $b''$, ... zu bilden sind.

Ist eine zweite Reihe:

(1')                        $a_1'$, $a_2'$, ... $a_n'$, .....

gegeben, welche eine bestimmte Grenze $b'$ hat, so findet man, dass
die beiden Reihen (1) und (1') eine von den folgenden 3 Beziehungen
stets haben, die sich gegenseitig ausschliessen: Entweder 1. wird
$a_n - a_n'$ unendlich klein mit wachsendem $n$ oder 2. $a_n - a_n'$ bleibt
von einem gewissen $n$ an stets grösser, als eine positive (rationale)
Grösse $\varepsilon$ oder 3. $a_n - a_n'$ bleibt von einem gewissen $n$ an stets kleiner, als eine negative (rationale) Grösse $- \varepsilon$.

Wenn die erste Beziehung stattfindet, setze ich:

$$b = b',$$

bei der zweiten $b > b'$, bei der dritten $b < b'$.

Ebenso findet man, dass eine Reihe (1), welche eine Grenze $b$
hat, zu einer rationalen Zahl $a$ nur eine von den folgenden 3 Beziehungen hat.  Entweder:

1. wird $a_n - a$ unendlich klein mit wachsendem $n$, oder 2. $a_n - a$
bleibt von einem gewissen $n$ an immer grösser, als eine positive
(rationale) Grösse $\varepsilon$ oder 3. $a_n - a$ bleibt von einem gewissen $n$ an
immer kleiner, als eine negative (rationale) Grösse $- \varepsilon$.

Um das Bestehen dieser Beziehungen auszudrücken, setzen wir resp.:

$$b = a, \quad b > a, \quad b < a.$$

Aus diesen und den gleich folgenden Definitionen ergiebt sich als
*Folge*, dass, wenn $b$ die Grenze der Reihe (1) ist, alsdann $b - a_n$ mit
wachsendem $n$ unendlich klein wird, womit *nebenbei* die Bezeichnung
„Grenze der Reihe (1)" für $b$ eine gewisse Rechtfertigung findet.

Die Gesammtheit der Zahlengrössen $b$ möge durch $B$ bezeichnet
werden.

Mittelst obiger Festsetzungen lassen sich die Elementaroperatio-
nen, welche mit rationalen Zahlen vorgenommen werden, ausdehnen
auf die beiden Gebiete $A$ und $B$ zusammengenommen.

Sind nämlich $b$, $b'$, $b''$ drei Zahlengrössen aus $B$, so dienen die Formeln:

$$b \pm b' = b'', \quad b\,b' = b'', \quad \frac{b}{b'} = b''$$

als Ausdruck dafür, dass zwischen den den Zahlen $b$, $b'$, $b''$ entsprechenden Reihen:

$$a_1, \; a_2, \; \ldots \ldots$$
$$a_1', \; a_2', \; \ldots \ldots$$
$$a_1'', \; a_2'', \; \ldots \ldots$$

resp. die Beziehungen bestehen:

$$\lim (a_n \pm a_n' - a_n'') = 0, \quad \lim (a_n\, a_n' - a_n'') = 0,$$
$$\lim \left( \frac{a_n}{a_n'} - a_n'' \right) = 0,$$

wo ich auf die Bedeutung des Lim-Zeichens nach dem Vorhergehenden nicht näher einzugehen brauche. Aehnliche Definitionen werden für die Fälle aufgestellt, dass von den drei Zahlen eine oder zwei dem Gebiete $A$ angehören.

## TRANSLATION

### §1.

The rational numbers form the foundation for establishing an extended concept of numerical quantity; I will call them the domain $A$ (with zero included).

If I speak of a numerical quantity in the extended sense, then it happens first of all in this way, that we have an infnite sequence of rational numbers given by a law:

(1)                                  $a_1, a_2, \ldots a_n, \ldots$

which has the characteristic, that the difference $a_{n+m} - a_n$ [124] becomes infinitely small with increasing $n$, whatever the positive whole number $m$ may be or, in other words, that for an arbitrarily taken (positive, rational) $\varepsilon$ there exists a whole number $n_1$, such that $(a_{n+m} - a_n) < \varepsilon$, if $n \geq n_1$ and if $m$ is an arbitrary positive whole number.

I express this property of sequence (1) in words as: "*Sequence* (1) *has a definite limit b.*"

These words have thus in the first place no other meaning than as an expression of that property of the sequence, and from the circumstance that we connect with sequence (1) a particular symbol $b$, it follows that different sequences of this kind are represented by different symbols $b, b', b'', \ldots$.

If there is given a second sequence:

(1')                                  $a_1', a_2', \ldots a_n', \ldots$

which has a definite limit $b'$, one finds that the two sequences (1) and (1') always have one of the following 3 relationships, which are mutually exclusive: either 1. $a_n - a'_n$ becomes infinitely small with increasing $n$, or 2. $a_n - a'_n$ remains from a certain $n$ onwards always greater than a positive (rational) quantity $\varepsilon$, or 3. $a_n - a'_n$ remains from a certain $n$ onwards always smaller than a certain negative (rational) quantity $-\varepsilon$.

If the first relationship holds, I set:

$$b = b',$$

for the second $b > b'$, for the third $b < b'$.

Likewise one finds that a sequence (1) which has a limit $b$ has only one of the following three relationships to a rational number $a$. Either:

1. $a_n - a$ becomes infinitely small with increasing $n$, or 2. $a_n - a$ remains from a certain $n$ onwards always greater than a positive (rational) quantity $\varepsilon$, or 3. $a_n - a$ remains from a certain $n$ onwards always smaller than a negative (rational) quantity $-\varepsilon$.

In order to express that these relationships hold, we set respectively:

$$b = a, \quad b > a, \quad b < a.$$

From this, and the immediately following definitions, there results as a *consequence* that if $b$ is the limit of the sequence (1) then $b - a_n$ will become infinitely small with increasing $n$, which *at the same time* offers a certain justification for the description of $b$ as the "limit of sequence (1)".

The totality of numerical quantities $b$ may be denoted by $B$.

On the basis of the above definitions, the elementary operations that are effected with the rational numbers can be extended to the two domains $A$ and $B$ taken together. [125] Namely, if $b$, $b'$, $b''$ are three numerical quantities from $B$, then the formulas:

$$b \pm b' = b'' \quad bb' = b'' \quad \frac{b}{b'} = b''$$

express that, between the sequences:

$$a_1, a_2, \ldots$$
$$a'_1, a'_2, \ldots$$
$$a''_1, a''_2, \ldots$$

corresponding to the numbers $b$, $b'$, $b''$, respectively, there exist the relationships:

$$\lim(a_n \pm a'_n - a''_n) = 0, \qquad \lim(a_n a'_n - a''_n) = 0,$$

$$\lim\left(\frac{a_n}{a'_n} - a''_n\right) = 0,$$

where because of what has gone before I need not go into more detail on the meaning of the 'lim' symbol. Similar definitions are to be set up in the case that one or two of the three numbers belong to the domain $A$.

———————

# CHAPTER 17

# LINEAR ALGEBRA

L inear algebra is now an essential tool in many branches of mathematics, but tracing its history turns out to be surprisingly difficult. There are several reasons for this. One is that linear algebra is so basic that it arises in many different and apparently unrelated contexts. Another is that it includes a range of topics that do not at first appearance seem necessarily connected: linear equations, determinants, linear transformations, matrices, vector spaces, eigenvalues, and so on. Each of these subtopics has its own history, and only in the twentieth century were they finally united under the common umbrella of 'linear algebra'.

If we try to untangle the historical threads topic by topic, we again often find that there is at first no recognizable subject to work on. The theory of linear equations, for instance, as far as we have written records and with the exception of ancient China, has historically rarely attracted the same interest as the more challenging problems of solving quadratic or cubic equations, and there is no similar sense of continuity or progress. When systems of linear equations finally became important it was usually in the context of physical applications: solving differential equations or fitting data to hypotheses. These gave rise to special methods for special cases, from which a general theory emerged only later.

Sometimes in the history of linear algebra we find subjects without theories, at other times theories whose subjects have no name. Many important properties of determinants, for example, were understood before determinants themselves were identified and named, and the same was true for matrices and eigenvalues. In looking at precursors to the modern theory we must here more than ever avoid imposing our later concepts onto what earlier writers were thinking or doing, and allow them to speak in their own context.

A final and quite serious difficulty for the modern student is that much of the theory of what is now called linear algebra was developed in the context of investigating quadratic forms, expressions of the kind

$$ax^2 + 2bxy + cy^2.$$

Nineteenth-century mathematicians were thoroughly conversant with the theory of these forms, but modern students are not, and so the historical language of linear algebra can seem very unfamiliar. Once again we need to try to understand how the theory developed before the introduction of modern vocabulary and notation.

Linear algebra may be mathematically simple but its history is more complex than any other topic in this book. This chapter should therefore be viewed only as an attempt, but by no means the only possible one, to draw out some of the most significant threads of a very tangled tale.

## 17.1 LINEAR EQUATIONS AND DETERMINANTS

### 17.1.1 An early European example, 1559

The earliest surviving examples of problems involving simultaneous linear equations are to be found in the Chinese text known in English as *The nine chapters of the mathematical art*, compiled in the first century BC, though many of the problems in it would have been known considerably earlier. The eighth of the nine chapters is entitled (in translation) 'Rectangular arrays' and gives solutions for up to five equations in five unknowns by a method that is essentially a process of column reduction. Nothing of corresponding sophistication appeared in western texts until very much later.

Some of the first linear problems in western European texts appeared as puzzles of the following type:

A man in the east wanted to buy 100 assorted animals for 100 shillings. He ordered his servant to pay 5 shillings for a camel, one shilling for an ass and one shilling for 20 sheep. How many camels, asses, and sheep did he buy?

This particular problem was ascribed to Alcuin, head of the palace school in Aachen under Charlemagne from 781 to 796 AD, but the contents suggest that it originated much further east. Similar problems occur in many later texts with endless variations of what is to be bought and for how much, but the solutions are given without explanation and in general seem to have been found by intelligent guesswork.

One of the earliest European examples of simultaneous equations solved by a systematic method is to be found in the *Logistica* (*Arithmetic*) of 1559 by the French writer Jean Borrel (sometimes Latinized to Buteus), who was also one of the first European authors to work with notation for more than a single unknown quantity.

## A problem from Jean Borrel
from Borrel, *Logistica*, 1559, 190–191

Tres numeros inuenire, quorum primus cum triente reliquorum faciat 14. Se-
cundus cum aliorum quadrante 8. Tertius
item cum parte quinta reliquorum 8.

Pone primum esse 1 *A*, secundum 1 *B*, tertium
1 *C*. Erit igitur 1 *A*, $\frac{1}{3}$ *B*, $\frac{1}{3}$ *C* [ 14. Item
1 *B*, $\frac{1}{4}$ *A*, $\frac{1}{4}$ *C* [ 8. Et etiam 1 *C*, $\frac{1}{5}$ *A*, $\frac{1}{5}$
*B* [ 8. Ex his autem æquationem secundam fa-
ciendo, habebis pri-
mam, secundã, et ter-    3 *A*. 1 *B*. 1*C* [ 42 | 1$^a$
tiam, quales hic ap-    1 *A*. 4 *B*. 1*C* [ 32 | 2$^a$
posui. Ex tribus istis    1 *A*. 1 *B*. 5 *C* [ 40 | 3$^a$
æquatiõibus aliæ, vel
multiplicando, vel inuicem addendo sunt facien-
dæ, quousque per detractionem minorum ex maio-
ribus relinquatur sola quantitas vnius notæ, quod
fiet hoc modo. Multiplica æquationem secundam
in 3, fit 3 *A*, 12 *B*, 3*C* [ 96. Aufer primam, re-
stat

## *TERTIVS.*  191

*ftat* 11 $B$, 2 $C$ [ 54.

*Rurfum multiplica*
*æquationem tertiam*
*in* 3, *fit* 3 $A$, 3 $B$, 15
$C$ [ 120. *Detrahe*
*primam, reftat* 2 $B$,
14 $C$ [ 78. *Multi-*
*plica in* 11, *fit* 22 $B$,
154 $C$ [ 858. *Item*
*multiplica* 11 $B$, 2 $C$
[ 54, *in* 2; *fit* 22 $B$,
4 $C$ [ 108. *Aufer ex*
22 $B$, 154 $C$ [ 858,
*reftat* 150 $C$ [ 750].

$$3\ A,\ 12\ B,\ 3\ C\ [\ 96$$
$$3\ A,\ 1\ B,\ 1\ C\ [\ 42$$
$$\overline{\phantom{xxxxxx}}$$
$$11\ B.\ 2\ C\ [\ 54$$

$$3\ A.\ 3\ B.\ 15\ C\ [\ 120$$
$$3\ A.\ 1\ B.\ 1\ C\ [\ 42$$
$$\overline{\phantom{xxxxxx}}$$
$$2\ B.\ 14\ C\ [\ 78$$

$$22\ B.\ 154\ C\ [\ 858$$
$$22\ B.\ 4\ C\ [\ 108$$
$$\overline{\phantom{xxxxxx}}$$
$$150\ C\ [\ 750\ ]$$

*Partire in* 150, *prouenit* 5, *qui eft tertius numerus*
*C. Cum iam inueneris* 1 *C valere* 5, *ex æquatione,*
*quæ eft* 2 $B$, 14 $C$ [ 78, *aufer* 14 $C$, *hoc eft* 70, *fit*
*refiduum* 8, *quod valet* 2 $B$, *eft igitur* 4 *fecundus*
*numerus B. Vt autem habeas primum ab æquatio-*
*nis tertiæ numero* 40, *detrahe* 5 $C$, *et* 1 $B$, *hoc eft,*
29 *fit refiduum* 11, *qui primus eft numerus* $A$.
*funt itaque tres numeri* 11. 4. 5, *quos oportuit in-*
*uenire.*

*Notation*

Borrel used a comma to indicate addition, thus 3A, 12B, 3C, whereas a list of numbers was separated by stops, thus 11.4.5. He also used the symbol [ for equality.

### TRANSLATION

To find three numbers, of which the first with a third of the rest makes 14. The second with a quarter of the rest makes 8. Likewise the third with a fifth part of the rest makes 8.

*Put the first to be 1A, the second 1B, the third 1C. Therefore it will be that 1A, $\frac{1}{3}B$, $\frac{1}{3}C$ [14. Likewise 1B, $\frac{1}{4}A$, $\frac{1}{4}C$ [8. And also 1C, $\frac{1}{5}A$, $\frac{1}{5}B$ [8. Moreover, having made a second* *equation from these, you will have the first, second, and third, as I have put here.*

$$3A. \quad 1B. \quad 1C \quad [42 \quad |1^{st}$$
$$1A. \quad 4B. \quad 1C \quad [32 \quad |2^{nd}$$
$$1A. \quad 1B. \quad 5C \quad [40 \quad |3^{rd}$$

*From these three equations others are made, by multiplication, or by adding to each other, until by subtracting the smaller from the greater there remains a quantity of only one symbol, which is done in this way. Multiply the second equation by 3, it makes $3A, 12B, 3C$ [96. Take away the first, there remains $11B, 2C$ [54.*

$$\begin{array}{rrrl} 3A, & 12B, & 3C & [96 \\ 3A, & 1B, & 1C & [42 \\ \hline & 11B, & 2C & [54 \end{array}$$

$$\begin{array}{rrrl} 3A, & 3B, & 15C & [120 \\ 3A, & 1B, & 1C & [42 \\ \hline & 2B, & 14C & [78 \end{array}$$

$$\begin{array}{rrl} 22B, & 154C & [858 \\ 22B, & 4C & [108 \\ \hline & 150C & [750] \end{array}$$

[191] *Again multiply the third equation by 3, it makes $3A, 3B, 15C$ [120. Take away the first, there remains $2B, 14C$ [78. Multiply by 11, it makes $22B, 154C$ [858. Likewise multiply $11B, 2C$ [54 by 2, it makes $22B, 4C$ [108. Take that from $22B, 154C$ [858, there remains $150C$ [750]. Divide by 150, there comes 5, which is the number of all of C. Since now you will have $1C$ worth 5, from the equation which is $2B, 14C$ [78, take $14C$, that is 70, it leaves a remainder 8, which is worth $2B$, therefore 4 is the second number B. Moreover, so that you have the first from the equation where the number of the total is 40, subtract $5C$, and $1B$, that is, 29 and it leaves a remainder 11, which is the first number A. Therefore the three numbers are 11.4.5, which were to be found.*

### 17.1.2  Rules for solving three or four equations, 1748

By 1678 Leibniz had found (though did not publish) general solutions for systems of three or four linear equations, and used a double subscript to indicate the place of each coefficient in the array. In the eighteenth century, Maclaurin gave explicit rules for solving sets of two or three equations in his *Treatise of algebra*, written in 1729 but published only in 1748, two years after his death. His rules were based on the calculation of what are now called determinants, and Maclaurin saw how to extend the rules to equations in four unknowns, but lacking Leibniz's instinct for general notation would have had some difficulty in applying them.[1] A similar method was published by Gabriel Cramer in 1750 in his *Analyse des lignes courbes*, and was taught to school children as 'Cramer's rule' until the mid-twentieth century.

---

**Maclaurin's rules**

from Maclaurin, *A treatise of algebra*, 1748, 83–85

---

## THEOREM II.

§ 87. Suppofe now that there are three un-known Quantities and three Equations, then call the unknown Quantities *x*, *y*, and *z*.
   Thus,

$$\begin{cases} ax + by + cz = m \\ dx + ey + fz = n \\ gx + hy + kz = p \end{cases}$$

---

Then fhall $z = \dfrac{aep - ahn + dhm - dbp + gbn - gem}{aek - ahf + dhc - dbk + gbf - gec}$.

Where the Numerator confifts of all the dif-rent Products that can be made of three oppofite Coefficients taken from the Orders in which *z* is not found ; and the Denominator confifts of all the Products that can be made of the three op-

G 2                              pofite

---

1. Some kind of subscript notation is an essential prerequisite for handling general expressions in many areas of mathematics. Single subscript notation was invented by Brouncker and Wallis in the early 1650s in connection with recursion rules for continued fractions (see Wallis 1656, Proposition 190, 'Idem aliter'), and Leibniz in the course of his life devised more than fifty forms of index notation. The alternative, however, of gobbling up one letter of the alphabet after another, continued to be used not just by Maclaurin but by many later writers.

poſite Coefficients taken from the Orders that involve the three unknown Quantities. For, from the laſt, it appears, that

$$y = \frac{an - afz - dm + dcz}{ae - db},$$ and that

$$y = \frac{ap - akz - gm + gcz}{ab - gb};$$ therefore

$$\frac{an - afz - dm + dcz}{ae - db} = \frac{ap - akz - gm + gcz}{ab - gb},$$ and

$$\overline{an - afz - dm + dcz} \times ab - gb \times an - afz + gbdm -$$
$$- gbdcz = \overline{ap - gm - akz + gcz} \times ae - db \times ap - akz$$
$$+ gbdm - gbdcz.$$

Take $gbdm - gbdcz$ from both Sides, and divide by *a*, ſo ſhall

$$\overline{an - dm - afz + dcz} \times b - gbn + gbfz =$$
$$= ap - gm - akz + gcz \times e - dbp + dbkz.$$ Tranſpoſe and divide ſo ſhall you find,

$$x = \frac{aep - abn + dbm - dbp + gbn - gem}{aek - abf + dbc - dbk + gbf - gec}.$$ The Values of *x* and *y* are found after the ſame Manner, and have the ſame Denominator. Ex. gr.

$$y = \frac{afp - akn + dkm - dep + gcn - gfm}{aek - abf + dbc - dbk + gbf - gec}.$$

If any Term is wanting in any of the three given Equations, the Values of *z* and *y* will be found more ſimple. Suppoſe, for Example, that *f* and *k* are equal to nothing, then the Term *fz* will vaniſh in the ſecond Equation, and *kz* in the third, and $z = \frac{aep - anb + dbm - dbp + gbn - gem}{dbc - gec},$

$$y = \frac{gcn - dep}{dbc - gec}.$$

                                If

**Chap. 13.   A L G E B R A.      85**

If four Equations are  given, involvi g four unknown Quantities, their Values may be found much after the fame Manner, by·taking all the Products that can be made of four oppofite Co-efficients,  and always prefixing contrary Signs to thofe that involve the Products of two oppofite Coefficients.

### 17.1.3 Vandermonde's elimination theory, 1772

The *Mémoires* of the Paris Academy for 1772 contained two papers that dealt in different ways with the problem of solving simultaneous linear equations. The first was by Laplace, entitled 'Sur les solutions particulières des équations différentielles' ('On particular solutions of differential equations'), in which, among other things, he discussed systems of linear equations in several variables. The second was by Vandermonde, devoted specifically to the problem of elimination, and most of it was concerned with linear equations, with a short second part on equations of higher degree. The extract below is from the first part, where Vandermonde developed in all but name the theory of determinants.

## Vandermonde's elimination theory
from Vandermonde, 'Mémoire sur l'élimination', *Mémoires de l'Académie des Sciences*,
(1772), 516–520

516   MÉMOIRES DE L'ACADÉMIE ROYALE

# MÉMOIRE
## SUR L'ÉLIMINATION*.
### Par M. VANDERMONDE.

LE terme de toutes les Recherches générales sur l'Élimination des inconnues dans les équations algébriques, ou sur l'art de ramener les équations qui renferment plusieurs inconnues, à des équations qui n'en renferment qu'une, seroit d'obtenir une formule d'élimination générale & unique, sous la forme la plus concise & la plus commode, & où le nombre d'équations & leurs degrés fussent désignés par des lettres indéterminées. Nous sommes sans doute très-éloignés de ce terme, mais on peut entrevoir quelque possibilité de l'atteindre. C'est ce que je me propose de faire sentir dans ce Mémoire. Je donnerai pour un nombre $n$ d'équations du premier degré, une formule d'élimination qui est une espèce de fonction de $n$, & dont la forme est très-concise & très-commode ; & je ferai voir que les formules connues d'élimination entre deux équations de degrés élevés, paroissent propres à recevoir une forme systématique, & à devenir une espèce de fonction de leur degré commun. J'ai été bientôt arrêté dans cette recherche, & il sera facile d'en sentir la raison. Parmi les ressources qui nous manquent pour faire des progrès en ce genre, la plus indispensable seroit, sans doute, de réunir un nombre suffisant de coopérateurs.

---

* Ce Mémoire a été lû pour la première fois, à l'Académie le 12 Janvier 1771. Il contenoit différentes choses que j'ai supprimées ici, parce qu'elles ont été publiées depuis par d'autres Géomètres.

## ARTICLE I.er

### *Des Équations du premier degré.*

Je suppose que l'on représente par $\overset{1}{1}, \overset{2}{1}, \overset{3}{1}$, &c. $\overset{1}{2}, \overset{2}{2}, \overset{3}{2}$, &c. $\overset{1}{3}, \overset{2}{3}, \overset{3}{3}$, &c. &c. autant de différentes quantités générales, dont l'une quelconque soit $\overset{\alpha}{a}$, une autre quelconque soit $\overset{\beta}{b}$, &c. & que le produit des deux soit désigné à l'ordinaire par $\overset{\alpha}{a} \cdot \overset{\beta}{b}$.

Des deux nombres ordinaux $\alpha$ & a, le premier, par exemple, désignera de quelle équation est pris le coëfficient $\overset{\alpha}{a}$, & le second désignera le rang que tient ce coëfficient dans l'équation, comme on le verra ci-après.

Je suppose encore le système suivant d'abréviations, & que l'on fasse

$$\frac{\alpha \mid \beta}{a \mid b} = \frac{\alpha\ \beta}{a \cdot b} - \frac{\alpha\ \beta}{b \cdot a}$$

$$\frac{\alpha \mid \beta \mid \gamma}{a \mid b \mid c} = \frac{\alpha}{a} \cdot \frac{\beta \mid \gamma}{b \mid c} + \frac{\alpha}{b} \cdot \frac{\beta \mid \gamma}{c \mid a} + \frac{\alpha}{c} \cdot \frac{\beta \mid \gamma}{a \mid b}$$

$$\frac{\alpha \mid \beta \mid \gamma \mid \delta}{a \mid b \mid c \mid d} = \frac{\alpha}{a} \cdot \frac{\beta \mid \gamma \mid \delta}{b \mid c \mid d} - \frac{\alpha}{b} \cdot \frac{\beta \mid \gamma \mid \delta}{c \mid d \mid a} + \frac{\alpha}{c} \cdot \frac{\beta \mid \gamma \mid \delta}{d \mid a \mid b} - \frac{\alpha}{d} \cdot \frac{\beta \mid \gamma \mid \delta}{a \mid b \mid c}$$

$$\frac{\alpha \mid \beta \mid \gamma \mid \delta \mid \varepsilon}{a \mid b \mid c \mid d \mid e} = \frac{\alpha}{a} \cdot \frac{\beta \mid \gamma \mid \delta \mid \varepsilon}{b \mid c \mid d \mid e} + \frac{\alpha}{b} \cdot \frac{\beta \mid \gamma \mid \delta \mid \varepsilon}{c \mid d \mid e \mid a} + \frac{\alpha}{c} \cdot \frac{\beta \mid \gamma \mid \delta \mid \varepsilon}{d \mid e \mid a \mid b}$$

$$+ \frac{\alpha}{d} \cdot \frac{\beta \mid \gamma \mid \delta \mid \varepsilon}{e \mid a \mid b \mid c} + \frac{\alpha}{e} \cdot \frac{\beta \mid \gamma \mid \delta \mid \varepsilon}{a \mid b \mid c \mid d}$$

$$\frac{\alpha \mid \beta \mid \gamma \mid \delta \mid \varepsilon \mid \zeta}{a \mid b \mid c \mid d \mid e \mid f} = \frac{\alpha}{a} \cdot \frac{\beta \mid \gamma \mid \delta \mid \varepsilon \mid \zeta}{b \mid c \mid d \mid e \mid f} - \frac{\alpha}{b} \cdot \frac{\beta \mid \gamma \mid \delta \mid \varepsilon \mid \zeta}{c \mid d \mid e \mid f \mid a} + \&c.$$

318   MÉMOIRES DE L'ACADÉMIE ROYALE

Le fymbole —|—|— fert ici de caractériftique.

Les feules chofes à obferver font l'ordre des fignes, & la loi des permutations entre les lettres $a$, $b$, $c$, $d$, &c. qui me paroiffent fuffifamment indiqués ci-deffus.

Au lieu de tranfpofer les lettres $a$, $b$, $c$, $d$, &c. on pouvoit les laiffer dans l'ordre alphabétique, & tranfpofer au contraire les lettres $\alpha$, $\beta$, $\gamma$, $\delta$, &c. les réfultats auroient été parfaitement les mêmes; ce qui a lieu auffi par rapport aux conclufions fuivantes.

Premièrement, il eft clair que $\dfrac{\alpha\ \ |\ \ \beta}{a\ \ |\ \ b}$ repréfente deux termes différens, l'un pofitif, & l'autre négatif, réfultans d'autant de permutations poffibles de $a$ & $b$; que $\dfrac{\alpha\ |\ \beta\ |\ \gamma}{a\ |\ b\ |\ c}$ en repréfente fix, trois pofitifs & trois négatifs, réfultans d'autant de permutations poffibles de $a$, $b$ & $c$; que $\dfrac{\alpha\ |\ \beta\ |\ \gamma\ |\ \delta}{a\ |\ b\ |\ c\ |\ d}$ en repréfente vingt-quatre, douze pofitifs & douze négatifs, réfultans d'autant de permutations poffibles entre $a$, $b$, $c$ & $d$; & ainfi de fuite.

Mais de plus, la formation de ces quantités eft telle que l'unique changement qui puiffe réfulter d'une permutation, quelle qu'elle foit, faite entre les lettres du même alphabet, dans l'une de ces abréviations, fera un changement dans le figne de fa première valeur.

La démonftration de cette vérité & la recherche du figne réfultant d'une permutation déterminée, dépendent généralement de deux propofitions qui peuvent être énoncées ainfi qu'il fuit, en fe fervant de nombres pour indiquer le rang des lettres.

La première eft que

$$\frac{1\ |\ 2\ |\ 3\ |\ \cdots\ |\ m\ |\ m+1\ |\ \cdots\ |\ n}{1\ |\ 2\ |\ 3\ |\ \cdots\ |\ m\ |\ m+1\ |\ \cdots\ |\ n} = \frac{1\ |\ 2\ |\ 3\ |\ \cdots\ |\ n-m+1\ |\ n-m+2\ |\ n-m+3\ |\ \cdots\ |\ n}{m\ |\ m+1\ |\ m+2\ |\ \cdots\ |\ n\ |\ 1\ |\ 2\ |\ \cdots\ |\ m-1}$$

le figne —— n'ayant lieu que dans le cas où $n$ & $m$ font l'un & l'autre des nombres pairs.

La feconde eft que

$$\dfrac{1\,|\,2\,|\,3\,|\cdots|\,m\,|\,m+1\,|\cdots|\,n}{1\,|\,2\,|\,3\,|\cdots|\,m\,|\,m+1\,|\cdots|\,n} = -\,\dfrac{1\,|\,2\,|\,3\,|\cdots|\,m-1\,|\,m\,|\,m+1\,|\,m+2\,|\cdots|\,n}{1\,|\,2\,|\,3\,|\cdots|\,m-1\,|\,m+1\,|\,m\,|\,m+2\,|\cdots|\,n}.$$

Il fera facile de voir que, la première équation fuppofée, celle-ci n'a befoin d'être prouvée que pour un feul cas, comme, par exemple, celui de $m = n - 1$, c'eft-à-dire, celui où les deux lettres tranfpofées font les deux dernières.

Au lieu de démontrer généralement ces deux équations, ce qui exigeroit un calcul embarraffant plutôt que difficile, je me contenterai de développer les exemples les plus fimples; cela fuffira pour faifir l'efprit de la démonftration.

## Selon l'une & l'autre équation, on a

$$\dfrac{\alpha\,|\,\beta}{a\,|\,b} = -\,\dfrac{\alpha\,|\,\beta}{b\,|\,a}$$

mais felon l'ordre de formation prefcrit ci-deffus, $\dfrac{\alpha\,|\,\beta}{b\,|\,a}$

$$= \underset{b.a}{\alpha\ \beta} - \underset{a.b}{\alpha\ \beta}\quad \text{qui égale en effet} - \dfrac{\alpha\,|\,\beta}{a\,|\,b}.$$

Selon la première équation, on a

$$\dfrac{\alpha\,|\,\beta\,|\,\gamma}{a\,|\,b\,|\,c} = \dfrac{\alpha\,|\,\beta\,|\,\gamma}{b\,|\,c\,|\,a} = \dfrac{\alpha\,|\,\beta\,|\,\gamma}{c\,|\,a\,|\,b};$$

mais felon l'ordre de formation,

$$\dfrac{\alpha\,|\,\beta\,|\,\gamma}{b\,|\,c\,|\,a} = \underset{b.}{\alpha}\ \dfrac{\beta\,|\,\gamma}{c\,|\,a} + \underset{c.}{\alpha}\ \dfrac{\beta\,|\,\gamma}{a\,|\,b} + \underset{a.}{\alpha}\ \dfrac{\beta\,|\,\gamma}{b\,|\,c},$$

&

$$\dfrac{\alpha\,|\,\beta\,|\,\gamma}{c\,|\,a\,|\,b} = \underset{c.}{\alpha}\ \dfrac{\beta\,|\,\gamma}{a\,|\,b} + \underset{a.}{\alpha}\ \dfrac{\beta\,|\,\gamma}{b\,|\,c} + \underset{b.}{\alpha}\ \dfrac{\beta\,|\,\gamma}{c\,|\,a},$$

qui ne diffèrent du développement ci-deffus de $\dfrac{\alpha\,|\,\beta\,|\,\gamma}{a\,|\,b\,|\,c}$, que par une fimple tranfpofition entre les termes,

520   MÉMOIRES DE L'ACADÉMIE ROYALE

Selon la seconde, on a

$$\frac{\alpha\,|\,\beta\,|\,\gamma}{a\,|\,b\,|\,c} = -\;\frac{\alpha\,|\,\beta\,|\,\gamma}{b\,|\,a\,|\,c} = -\;\frac{\alpha\,|\,\beta\,|\,\gamma}{a\,|\,c\,|\,b};$$

mais on a déjà selon la première $\dfrac{\alpha\,|\,\beta\,|\,\gamma}{b\,|\,a\,|\,c} = \dfrac{\alpha\,|\,\beta\,|\,\gamma}{a\,|\,c\,|\,b};$

donc il suffit de prouver que selon l'ordre de formation

$$\frac{\alpha\,|\,\beta\,|\,\gamma}{a\,|\,b\,|\,c} = -\;\frac{\alpha\,|\,\beta\,|\,\gamma}{a\,|\,c\,|\,b}: \text{ or on a}$$

$$\frac{\alpha\,|\,\beta\,|\,\gamma}{a\,|\,c\,|\,b} = \frac{\alpha\;\;\beta\,|\,\gamma}{a.\;\;c\,|\,b} + \frac{\alpha\;\;\beta\,|\,\gamma}{c.\;\;b\,|\,a} + \frac{\alpha\;\;\beta\,|\,\gamma}{b.\;\;a\,|\,c}$$

( qui en suppofant $\dfrac{1\,|\,2}{1\,|\,2} = -\;\dfrac{1\,|\,2}{2\,|\,1}$, comme cela a

été prouvé ci-deffus ) eft,

$$= -\;\frac{\alpha\;\;\beta\,|\,\gamma}{a.\;\;b\,|\,c} - \frac{\alpha\;\;\beta\,|\,\gamma}{c.\;\;a\,|\,b} - \frac{\alpha\;\;\beta\,|\,\gamma}{b.\;\;c\,|\,a} = -\;\frac{\alpha\,|\,\beta\,|\,\gamma}{a\,|\,b\,|\,c}$$

Quant à $\dfrac{\alpha\,|\,\beta\,|\,\gamma}{c\,|\,b\,|\,a}$, il égale par conféquent $-\;\dfrac{\alpha\,|\,\beta\,|\,\gamma}{c\,|\,a\,|\,b}$,

ou $-\;\dfrac{\alpha\,|\,\beta\,|\,\gamma}{a\,|\,b\,|\,c}$.

TRANSLATION

## MEMOIR ON ELIMINATION
### by Monsieur Vandermonde

The ultimate aim of all general research on the elimination of unknowns in algebraic equations, or on the art of reducing equations which contain several unknowns to equations that contain only one, would be to obtain a general and unique elimination formula, in the most concise and useful form, in which the number of equations and their degrees would be denoted by general letters. We are without doubt very far from that end, but one may glimpse some possibility of attaining it. That is what I propose to show in this Memoir. I will give, for a number $n$ of equations of first degree, an elimination formula which is a kind of function of $n$, and whose form is very concise and very useful; and I will show that the known elimination formulas between two equations of higher degree, seem likely to take a systematic form, and to become a kind of function of their common degree. I was soon halted in this research, and it will be easy to give the reason for it. Among the resources we lack for making progress in this kind of work, the most indispensable would be, without doubt, to bring together a sufficient number of collaborators.

[517]

## 1$^{st}$ARTICLE

### Equations of first degree

I suppose that one represents by $\dfrac{1}{1}, \dfrac{2}{1}, \dfrac{3}{1}$ etc. $\dfrac{1}{2}, \dfrac{2}{2}, \dfrac{3}{2}$ etc. $\dfrac{1}{3}, \dfrac{2}{3}, \dfrac{3}{3}$

etc. etc. so many different general quantities, of which any one may be $\dfrac{\alpha}{a}$, another

may be $\dfrac{\beta}{b}$ etc., and that the product of the two is denoted in the ordinary way by

$\dfrac{\alpha}{a} \cdot \dfrac{\beta}{b}$.

Of the two ordinary numbers $\alpha$ and $a$, the first, for example, may denote the equation

from which the coefficient $\dfrac{a}{\alpha}$ is taken, and the second may denote the rank of that

coefficient in the equation, as one will see later.

I also assume the following system of abbreviations, and that one makes

$$\frac{\alpha \mid \beta}{a \mid b} = \frac{\alpha}{a}\frac{\beta}{b} - \frac{\alpha}{b} \cdot \frac{\beta}{a}.$$

$$\frac{\alpha \mid \beta \mid \gamma}{a \mid b \mid c} = \frac{\alpha}{a} \cdot \frac{\beta \mid \gamma}{b \mid c} + \frac{\alpha}{b} \cdot \frac{\beta \mid \gamma}{c \mid a} + \frac{\alpha}{c} \cdot \frac{\beta \mid \gamma}{a \mid b}.$$

$$\frac{\alpha \mid \beta \mid \gamma \mid \delta}{a \mid b \mid c \mid d} = \frac{\alpha}{a} \cdot \frac{\beta \mid \gamma \mid \delta}{b \mid c \mid d} - \frac{\alpha}{b} \cdot \frac{\beta \mid \gamma \mid \delta}{c \mid d \mid a} + \frac{\alpha}{c} \cdot \frac{\beta \mid \gamma \mid \delta}{d \mid a \mid b} - \frac{\alpha}{d} \cdot \frac{\beta \mid \gamma \mid \delta}{a \mid b \mid c}.$$

$$\frac{\alpha \mid \beta \mid \gamma \mid \delta \mid \varepsilon}{a \mid b \mid c \mid d \mid e} = \frac{\alpha}{a} \cdot \frac{\beta \mid \gamma \mid \delta \mid \varepsilon}{b \mid c \mid d \mid e} + \frac{\alpha}{b} \cdot \frac{\beta \mid \gamma \mid \delta \mid \varepsilon}{c \mid d \mid e \mid a} + \frac{\alpha}{c} \cdot \frac{\beta \mid \gamma \mid \delta \mid \varepsilon}{d \mid e \mid a \mid b}$$
$$+ \frac{\alpha}{d} \cdot \frac{\beta \mid \gamma \mid \delta \mid \varepsilon}{e \mid a \mid b \mid c} + \frac{\alpha}{e} \cdot \frac{\beta \mid \gamma \mid \delta \mid \varepsilon}{a \mid b \mid c \mid d}$$

$$\frac{\alpha \mid \beta \mid \gamma \mid \delta \mid \varepsilon \mid \zeta}{a \mid b \mid c \mid d \mid e \mid f} = \frac{\alpha}{a} \cdot \frac{\beta \mid \gamma \mid \delta \mid \varepsilon \mid \zeta}{b \mid c \mid d \mid e \mid f} - \frac{\alpha}{b} \cdot \frac{\beta \mid \gamma \mid \delta \mid \varepsilon \mid \zeta}{c \mid d \mid e \mid f \mid a} +$$
etc.

[518] The symbol $\left.\dfrac{}{}\right|\left|\right|$ serves here for a general sign.

The only things to observe are the order of signs, and the law of permutation between the letters $a$, $b$, $c$, $d$, etc. which seem to me sufficiently indicated above.

Instead of transposing the letters $a$, $b$, $c$, $d$, etc. one could have left them in alphabetic order, and alternatively transposed the letters $\alpha$, $\beta$, $\gamma$, $\delta$, etc. and the results would have been just the same; this holds also in regard to the following conclusions.

First, it is clear that $\dfrac{\alpha \mid \beta}{a \mid b}$ represents two different terms, one positive, and the other negative, resulting from the same number of possible permutations of $a$ and $b$;

that $\dfrac{\alpha \mid \beta \mid \gamma}{a \mid b \mid c}$ represents six, three positive and three negative, resulting from the

same number of possible permutations of $a$, $b$ and $c$; that $\dfrac{\alpha \mid \beta \mid \gamma \mid \delta}{a \mid b \mid c \mid d}$ represents twenty-four, twelve positive and twelve negative, resulting from the same number of possible permutations between *a*, *b*, *c* and *d*; and and so on.

But further, the formation of these quantities is such that the only change that can result from a permutation, whatever it may be, made between the letters of the same alphabet in one of these abbreviations, will be a change in the sign of the first value.

The demonstration that this is true and finding the resulting sign of a given permutation, depend generally on two propositions which may be stated as follows, making use of numbers to indicate the rank of the letters.

The first is that

$$
\frac{1 \mid 2 \mid 3 \mid \ldots \mid m \mid m+1 \mid \ldots \mid n}{1 \mid 2 \mid 3 \mid \ldots \mid m \mid m+1 \mid \ldots \mid n} =
$$

$$
\pm \frac{1 \mid 2 \mid 3 \mid \ldots \mid n-m+1 \mid n-m+2 \mid n-m+3 \mid \ldots \mid n}{m \mid m+1 \mid m+2 \mid \ldots \mid n \mid 1 \mid 2 \mid \ldots \mid m-1},
$$

[519] the sign − holding only in the case where *n* and *m* are both even numbers.

The second is that

$$
\frac{1 \mid 2 \mid 3 \mid \ldots \mid m \mid m+1 \mid \ldots \mid n}{1 \mid 2 \mid 3 \mid \ldots \mid m \mid m+1 \mid \ldots \mid n} =
$$

$$
- \frac{1 \mid 2 \mid 3 \mid \ldots \mid m-1 \mid m \mid m+1 \mid m+2 \mid \ldots \mid n}{1 \mid 2 \mid 3 \mid \ldots \mid m-1 \mid m+1 \mid m \mid m+2 \mid \ldots \mid n},
$$

It will be easy to see that, assuming the first equation, the latter need be proved only for a single case, as, for example, that of $m = n - 1$, that is to say, that where the two letters transposed are the two last.

Instead of proving these two equations generally, which requires a calculation that is cumbersome rather than difficult, I will content myself with expanding the simplest examples; this will suffice to show the spirit of the demonstration.

According to both equations, one has

$$
\frac{\alpha \mid \beta}{a \mid b} = - \frac{\alpha \mid \beta}{b \mid a}
$$

but according to the law of formation prescribed above, $\dfrac{\alpha \mid \beta}{a \mid b}$

$$
= \frac{\alpha}{b} \cdot \frac{\beta}{a} - \frac{\alpha}{a} \cdot \frac{\beta}{b} \quad \text{which indeed equals} \quad - \frac{\alpha \mid \beta}{a \mid b}.
$$

According to the first equation, one has

$$
\frac{\alpha \mid \beta \mid \gamma}{a \mid b \mid c} = \frac{\alpha \mid \beta \mid \gamma}{b \mid c \mid a} = \frac{\alpha \mid \beta \mid \gamma}{c \mid a \mid b};
$$

but according to the law of formation,

$$\begin{array}{|c|c|c|}\hline \alpha & \beta & \gamma \\\hline b & c & a \\\hline\end{array} = \begin{array}{|c|}\hline \alpha \\\hline b \\\hline\end{array} \cdot \begin{array}{|c|c|}\hline \beta & \gamma \\\hline c & a \\\hline\end{array} + \begin{array}{|c|}\hline \alpha \\\hline c \\\hline\end{array} \cdot \begin{array}{|c|c|}\hline \beta & \gamma \\\hline a & b \\\hline\end{array} + \begin{array}{|c|}\hline \alpha \\\hline a \\\hline\end{array} \cdot \begin{array}{|c|c|}\hline \beta & \gamma \\\hline b & c \\\hline\end{array},$$

and

$$\begin{array}{|c|c|c|}\hline \alpha & \beta & \gamma \\\hline c & a & b \\\hline\end{array} = \begin{array}{|c|}\hline \alpha \\\hline c \\\hline\end{array} \cdot \begin{array}{|c|c|}\hline \beta & \gamma \\\hline a & b \\\hline\end{array} + \begin{array}{|c|}\hline \alpha \\\hline a \\\hline\end{array} \cdot \begin{array}{|c|c|}\hline \beta & \gamma \\\hline b & c \\\hline\end{array} + \begin{array}{|c|}\hline \alpha \\\hline b \\\hline\end{array} \cdot \begin{array}{|c|c|}\hline \beta & \gamma \\\hline c & a \\\hline\end{array},$$

which does not differ from the above expansion of $\begin{array}{|c|c|c|}\hline \alpha & \beta & \gamma \\\hline a & b & c \\\hline\end{array}$, except by a simple transposition between the terms.

   [520] According to the second, one has

$$\begin{array}{|c|c|c|}\hline \alpha & \beta & \gamma \\\hline a & b & c \\\hline\end{array} = -\begin{array}{|c|c|c|}\hline \alpha & \beta & \gamma \\\hline b & a & c \\\hline\end{array} = -\begin{array}{|c|c|c|}\hline \alpha & \beta & \gamma \\\hline a & c & b \\\hline\end{array};$$

but one already has according to the first $\begin{array}{|c|c|c|}\hline \alpha & \beta & \gamma \\\hline b & a & c \\\hline\end{array} = \begin{array}{|c|c|c|}\hline \alpha & \beta & \gamma \\\hline a & c & b \\\hline\end{array}$; therefore it suffices to prove that according to the law of formation $\begin{array}{|c|c|c|}\hline \alpha & \beta & \gamma \\\hline a & b & c \\\hline\end{array} = -\begin{array}{|c|c|c|}\hline \alpha & \beta & \gamma \\\hline a & c & b \\\hline\end{array}$; now one has

$$\begin{array}{|c|c|c|}\hline \alpha & \beta & \gamma \\\hline a & c & b \\\hline\end{array} = \begin{array}{|c|}\hline \alpha \\\hline a \\\hline\end{array} \cdot \begin{array}{|c|c|}\hline \beta & \gamma \\\hline c & b \\\hline\end{array} + \begin{array}{|c|}\hline \alpha \\\hline c \\\hline\end{array} \cdot \begin{array}{|c|c|}\hline \beta & \gamma \\\hline b & a \\\hline\end{array} + \begin{array}{|c|}\hline \alpha \\\hline b \\\hline\end{array} \cdot \begin{array}{|c|c|}\hline \beta & \gamma \\\hline a & c \\\hline\end{array},$$

which (by supposing $\begin{array}{|c|c|}\hline 1 & 2 \\\hline 1 & 2 \\\hline\end{array} = -\begin{array}{|c|c|}\hline 1 & 2 \\\hline 2 & 1 \\\hline\end{array}$, since this has been proved above) is,

$$= -\begin{array}{|c|}\hline \alpha \\\hline a \\\hline\end{array} \cdot \begin{array}{|c|c|}\hline \beta & \gamma \\\hline b & c \\\hline\end{array} - \begin{array}{|c|}\hline \alpha \\\hline c \\\hline\end{array} \cdot \begin{array}{|c|c|}\hline \beta & \gamma \\\hline a & b \\\hline\end{array} - \begin{array}{|c|}\hline \alpha \\\hline b \\\hline\end{array} \cdot \begin{array}{|c|c|}\hline \beta & \gamma \\\hline c & a \\\hline\end{array} = -\begin{array}{|c|c|c|}\hline \alpha & \beta & \gamma \\\hline a & b & c \\\hline\end{array}.$$

As for $\begin{array}{|c|c|c|}\hline \alpha & \beta & \gamma \\\hline c & b & a \\\hline\end{array}$, it follows that it equals $-\begin{array}{|c|c|c|}\hline \alpha & \beta & \gamma \\\hline c & a & b \\\hline\end{array}$, or $-\begin{array}{|c|c|c|}\hline \alpha & \beta & \gamma \\\hline a & b & c \\\hline\end{array}$.

--------

### 17.1.4 Cauchy's definition of determinant, 1815

The quantities that we now call determinants arise naturally in the solution of linear equations, and it is clear that by 1772 much useful theory had already been worked out by Vandermonde and others. The word 'determinant', however, was first introduced in 1801 by Gauss in a quite different context. Gauss showed that certain properties of the quadratic form

$$ax^2 + 2bxy + cy^2$$

depend on the value of the quantity $b^2 - ac$, to which he gave the name determinant (in Latin, *determinans*). To see the relationship between Gauss's definition and the modern one we may write

$$ax^2 + 2bxy + cy^2 = \begin{pmatrix} x & y \end{pmatrix} \begin{pmatrix} a & b \\ b & c \end{pmatrix} \begin{pmatrix} x \\ y \end{pmatrix}.$$

in which it is apparent that $b^2 - ac$ is the determinant (in modern terms, apart from sign) of the central matrix.

The theory of determinants was consolidated by Cauchy in one of his earliest papers, presented to the Institut de France in 1812 and published in 1815. His subject was alternating functions, that is to say, functions whose value changes only in sign as the variables are permuted with each other. For Cauchy such investigations arose from Lagrange's 1771 paper on equations (see 12.3.1) but, as we have seen, Vandermonde had already treated a special class of such functions in 1772. In the first half of his paper Cauchy dealt with alternating functions in general, but in the second half he chose to concentrate on the kind that Vandermonde had treated. Recognizing at the same time the connection with Gauss's treatment of quadratic forms, Cauchy gave to these functions the name determinants (in French *déterminans*).

---

## Cauchy and determinants

from Cauchy, 'Mémoire sur les fonctions qui ne peuvent obtenir que deux valeurs égales et de signes contraires par suite des transpositions opérées entre les variables qu'elles renferment', *Journal de l'École Polytechnique*, 10 (1815), 51–54

---

Je vais maintenant examiner particulièrement une certaine espèce de fonctions symétriques alternées qui s'offrent d'elles-mêmes dans un grand nombre de recherches analytiques. C'est au moyen de ces fonctions qu'on exprime les valeurs générales des inconnues que renferment plusieurs équations du premier degré. Elles se représentent toutes les fois qu'on a des équations de condition à former, ainsi que dans la théorie générale de l'élimination. MM. *Laplace* et *Vandermonde* les ont considérées sous ce rapport dans les Mémoires de l'Académie des sciences (année 1772), et M. *Bezout* les a encore examinées depuis sous le même point de vue dans sa Théorie des équations. M. *Gauss* s'en est servi avec avantage dans ses Recherches analytiques, pour découvrir les propriétés générales des formes du second degré, c'est-à-dire, des polynomes du second degré à deux ou à plusieurs variables; et il a désigné ces mêmes fonctions sous le nom de *déterminans*. Je conserverai cette dénomination qui fournit un moyen facile d'énoncer les résultats; j'observerai seulement qu'on donne aussi quelquefois aux fonctions dont il s'agit le nom de *résultantes* à deux ou à plusieurs lettres. Ainsi les deux expressions suivantes, déterminant et résultante, devront être regardées comme synonymes.

---

## DEUXIÈME PARTIE.

*Des Fonctions symétriques alternées désignées sous le nom de Déterminans.*

### I.<sup>ère</sup> SECTION.

*Des Déterminans en général et des Systèmes symétriques.*

§. 1.<sup>er</sup> Soient $a_1$, $a_2$ ..... $a_n$ plusieurs quantités différentes en nombre égal à $n$. On a fait voir ci-dessus qu'en multipliant le produit

52                    A N A L Y S E.

de ces quantités, ou

$$a_1 a_2 a_3 \ldots \ldots a_n$$

par le produit de leurs différences respectives, ou par

$$(a_2-a_1)(a_3-a_1)\ldots(a_n-a_1)(a_3-a_2)\ldots(a_n-a_2)\ldots(a_n-a_{n-1})$$

on obtenait pour résultat la fonction symétrique alternée

$$S\left(\pm a_1 a_2^2 a_3^3 \ldots \ldots a_n^n\right),$$

qui par conséquent se trouve toujours égale au produit

$$a_1 a_2 a_3 \ldots a_n (a_2-a_1)(a_3-a_1)\ldots(a_n-a_1)(a_3-a_2)\ldots(a_n-a_2)\ldots(a_n-a_{n-1}).$$

Supposons maintenant que l'on développe ce dernier produit, et que dans chaque terme du développement on remplace l'exposant de chaque lettre par un second indice égal à l'exposant dont il s'agit, en écrivant par exemple $a_{r.s}$ au lieu de $a_r^s$, et $a_{s.r}$ au lieu de $a_s^r$, on obtiendra pour résultat une nouvelle fonction symétrique alternée, qui, au lieu d'être représentée par

$$S\left(\pm a_1{}^1 a_2{}^2 a_3{}^3 \ldots \ldots a_n{}^n\right),$$

sera représentée par

$$S\left(\pm a_{1.1} a_{2.2} a_{3.3} \ldots \ldots a_{n.n}\right),$$

le signe $S$ étant relatif aux premiers indices de chaque lettre. Telle est la forme la plus générale des fonctions que je désignerai dans la suite sous le nom de *déterminans*. Si l'on suppose successivement

$$n = 1, \quad n = 2, \quad \&c \ldots \ldots,$$

on trouvera

$$S\left(\pm a_{1.1} a_{2.2}\right) = a_{1.1} a_{2.2} - a_{2.1} a_{1.2};$$

$$S\left(\pm a_{1.1} a_{2.2} a_{3.3}\right) = a_{1.1} a_{2.2} a_{3.3} + a_{2.1} a_{3.2} a_{1.3} + a_{3.1} a_{1.2} a_{2.3},$$

$$- a_{1.1} a_{3.2} a_{2.3} - a_{3.1} a_{2.2} a_{1.3} - a_{2.1} a_{1.2} a_{3.3},$$

&c......

pour les déterminans du second, du troisième ordre, &c...... Les quantités affectées d'indices différens devant être généralement considérées comme inégales, on voit que le déterminant du second ordre renfermera quatre quantités différentes, savoir,

$$a_{1.1}, \quad a_{1.2},$$
$$a_{2.1}, \quad a_{2.2},$$

que le déterminant du troisième ordre en renfermera neuf, savoir,

$$a_{1.1}, \quad a_{1.2}, \quad a_{1.3},$$
$$a_{2.1}, \quad a_{2.2}, \quad a_{2.3},$$
$$a_{3.1}, \quad a_{3.2}, \quad a_{3.3},$$

&c......

En général, le déterminant du $n.^{ème}$ ordre, ou

$$S\left(\pm a_{1.1} a_{2.2} \ldots \ldots a_{n.n}\right),$$

renfermera un nombre égal à $n^2$ de quantités différentes, qui seront respectivement

$$(1) \begin{cases} a_{1.1}, \ a_{1.2}, \ a_{1.3} \ldots a_{1.n}, \\ a_{2.1}, \ a_{2.2}, \ a_{2.3} \ldots a_{2.n}, \\ a_{3.1}, \ a_{3.2}, \ a_{3.3} \ldots a_{3.n}, \\ \&c \ldots \ldots \\ a_{n.1}, \ a_{n.2}, \ a_{n.3} \ldots a_{n.n}, \end{cases}$$

Supposons ces mêmes quantités disposées en carré, comme on vient de le voir, sur un nombre égal à $n$ de lignes horizontales et sur autant de colonnes verticales, de manière que, des deux indices qui affectent chaque quantité, le premier varie seul dans chaque colonne verticale, et que le second varie seul dans chaque ligne horizontale, l'ensemble des quantités dont il s'agit formera un système que j'appellerai *système symétrique* de l'ordre $n$. Les quantités $a_{1.1}, a_{1.2} \ldots a_{2.1} \ldots a_{n.n}$

54    ANALYSE.

seront les différens termes du système, et la lettre $a$ dépouillée d'accens en sera la caractéristique. Enfin les quantités comprises dans une même ligne, soit horizontale, soit verticale, seront en nombre égal à $n$, et formeront une suite que j'appellerai dans le premier cas *suite hori-zontale*, et dans le second *suite verticale*. L'indice de chaque suite sera celui qui reste invariable dans tous les termes de la suite. Ainsi, par exemple, les indices des suites horizontales et ceux des suites verticales du système (1) sont respectivement égaux à

$$1, \quad 2, \quad 3 \ldots \ldots n.$$

J'appellerai termes *conjugués*, ceux que l'on peut déduire l'un de l'autre par une transposition opérée entre le premier et le second indice; ainsi $a_{2.3}$ et $a_{3.2}$ sont deux termes conjugués. Il existe des termes qui sont eux-mêmes leurs conjugués. Ce sont les termes dans lesquels les deux indices sont égaux entre eux, savoir,

$$a_{1.1}, \quad a_{2.2} \ldots \ldots a_{n.n};$$

je les appellerai termes *principaux* : ils sont tous situés dans le système (1) sur une diagonale du carré formé par le système.

Pour indiquer la relation qui existe entre le système (1) et le dé-terminant

$$S(\pm a_{1.1} a_{2.2} \ldots \ldots a_{n.n}),$$

je dirai que ce dernier appartient au système en question, ou, ce qui revient au même, que la fonction symétrique alternée

$$S(\pm a_{1.1} a_{2.2} \ldots \ldots a_{n.n})$$

est le déterminant de ce système.

Pour obtenir le déterminant du système (1), il suffit, comme on l'a dit ci-dessus, de remplacer les exposans des lettres par des indices dans le développement du produit

$$a_1 a_2 a_3 \ldots \ldots a_n (a_2 - a_1)(a_3 - a_1) \ldots \ldots (a_n - a_{n-1}).$$

*Notation*
Cauchy's $S(\pm a_1 a_2^2 \ldots a_n^n)$ is a general notation for a function of powers of $a_1, \ldots a_n$. It does *not* mean that each $a_k$ is raised to the $k$th power (as his later exposition makes clear).

TRANSLATION

I shall now examine in particular a certain kind of alternating symmetric functions which present themselves in a great number of analytic investigations. It is by means of these functions that one expresses the general values of unknowns contained in several equations of the first degree. They appear whenever one needs to form conditional equations, thus as in the general theory of elimination. Messieurs *Laplace* and *Vandermonde* have considered them in this respect in the Mémoires of the Academy of sciences (for the year 1772), and Monsieur *Bezout* has since examined them again from the same point of view in his *Theory of equations*. Monsieur *Gauss* has made use of them with advantage in his analytic investigations, to discover the the general properties of forms of second degree, that is to say, polynomials of second degree with two or several variables; and he has denoted these same functions by the name *determinants*. I will keep this name which supplies an easy way of stating the results; I will observe only that one sometimes also gives to the functions in question the name *resultants* in two or several letters. Thus the two following expressions, determinant and resultant, must be regarded as synonymous.

SECOND PART

*On alternating symmetric functions denoted by the name of determinants.*

1ST SECTION.

*On determinants in general and on symmetric systems.*

§1. LET $a_1, a_2 \ldots \ldots a_n$ be several different quantities, $n$ in number. We have shown above that by multiplying the product [52] of these quantities, or

$$a_1 a_2 a_3 \ldots \ldots a_n$$

by the product of their respective differences, or by

$$(a_2 - a_1)(a_3 - a_1) \ldots (a_n - a_1)(a_3 - a_2) \ldots (a_n - a_2) \ldots (a_n - a_{n-1}),$$

one obtained as a result the alternating symmetric function

$$S(\pm a_1 a_2{}^2 a_3{}^3 \ldots a_n{}^n),$$

which as a result is always equal to the product

$$a_1 a_2 a_3 \ldots a_n (a_2 - a_1)(a_3 - a_1) \ldots (a_n - a_1)(a_3 - a_2) \ldots (a_n - a_2) \ldots (a_n - a_{n-1}).$$

Suppose now that one expands this last product, and that in each term of the expansion one replaces the exponent of each letter by a second index equal to the exponent in question; by writing, for example, $a_{r.s}$ instead of $a_r^s$, and $a_{s.r}$ instead of $a_s^r$, one will obtain as a result a new alternating symmetric function, which, instead of being represented by

$$S(\pm a_1{}^1 a_2{}^2 a_3{}^3 \ldots a_n{}^n),$$

will be represented by

$$S(\pm a_{1.1} a_{2.2} a_{3.3} \ldots a_{n.n}),$$

where the symbol $S$ is relative to the first indices of each letter. Such is the most general form of the functions I shall denote in what follows by the name of *determinants*. If one supposes successively

$$n = 1, \ n = 2, \text{etc.} \ldots,$$

one will have

$$
\begin{aligned}
S(\pm a_{1.1} a_{2.2}) &= a_{1.1} a_{2.2} - a_{2.1} a_{1.2}, \\
S(\pm a_{1.1} a_{2.2} a_{3.3}) &= a_{1.1} a_{2.2} a_{3.3} + a_{2.1} a_{3.2} a_{1.3} + a_{3.1} a_{1.2} a_{2.3} \\
&\quad - a_{1.1} a_{3.2} a_{2.3} - a_{3.1} a_{2.2} a_{1.3} - a_{2.1} a_{1.2} a_{3.3},
\end{aligned}
$$

etc.…[53] for the determinants of second, and third order, etc. The quantities affected by different indices being considered in general as unequal, one sees that the determinant of second order contains four different quantities, namely,

$$
\begin{array}{cc}
a_{1.1}, & a_{1.2}, \\
a_{2.1}, & a_{2.2},
\end{array}
$$

and that the determinant of third order contains nine, that is,

$$
\begin{array}{ccc}
a_{1.1}, & a_{1.2}, & a_{1.3}, \\
a_{2.1}, & a_{2.2}, & a_{2.3}, \\
a_{3.1}, & a_{3.2}, & a_{3.3},
\end{array}
$$

etc. …

In general, the determinant of $n^{\text{th}}$ order, or

$$S(\pm a_{1.1} a_{2.2} \ldots a_{n.n}),$$

will contain a number $n^2$ of different quantities, which will be respectively (1)

$$
\left\{
\begin{array}{ccccc}
a_{1.1}, & a_{1.2}, & a_{1.3}, & \ldots & a_{1.n}, \\
a_{2.1}, & a_{2.2}, & a_{2.3}, & \ldots & a_{2.n}, \\
a_{3.1}, & a_{3.2}, & a_{3.3}, & \ldots & a_{3.n}, \\
\text{etc.} & & & & \\
a_{n.1}, & a_{n.2}, & a_{n.3}, & \ldots & a_{n.n}.
\end{array}
\right.
$$

Let us suppose these same quantities disposed in a square, as we have just seen, with a number $n$ of horizontal lines and with the same number of vertical columns, in such a way that, of the two indices that affect each quantity, the first changes only in each vertical column, and the second changes only in each horizontal line; together these quantities of which we speak will form a system which I will call a *symmetric system* of order $n$. The quantities $a_{1.1}, a_{1.2}, \ldots, a_{2.3}, \ldots, a_{n.n},$ [54] will be the different terms of the system, and the letter $a$ deprived of markings will be its general sign. Finally, the quantities contained in the same line, whether horizontal or vertical, will be $n$ in number, and will form a sequence which I will call in the first case the *horizontal sequence* and in the second the *vertical sequence*. The index of each sequence will be that which remains unchanged in all the terms of the sequence. Thus, for example, the indices of the horizontal sequences and those of the vertical sequences of system (1) are respectively equal to

$$1, 2, 3 \ldots n$$

I will call *conjugate* terms, those which one may derive from one another by a transposition carried out between the first and the second index; thus $a_{2,3}$ and $a_{3,2}$ are two conjugate terms. There exist terms which are their own conjugates. These are the terms in which the two indices are equal to each other, namely,

$$a_{1,1}, a_{2,2}.\ldots.a_{n,n};$$

I will call them *principal* terms; in system (1) they are all situated on a diagonal of the square formed by the system.

To indicate the relationship that exists between system (1) and the determinant

$$S(\pm a_{1,1} a_{2,2}.\ldots.a_{n,n}),$$

I will say that the last belongs to the system in question, or, which comes to the same thing, that the alternating symmetric function

$$S(\pm a_{1,1} a_{2,2}.\ldots.a_{n,n})$$

is the determinant of this system.

To obtain the determinant of system (1), it suffices, as we have said above, to replace the exponents of the letters by indices in the expansion of the product

$$a_1 a_2 a_3.\ldots.a_n(a_2 - a_1)(a_3 - a_1).\ldots.(a_n - a_{n-1}).$$

---

## 17.2 EIGENVALUE PROBLEMS

As with the theory of determinants, problems that gave rise to eigenvalues and eigenvectors existed long before any general theory was recognized or named. In the eighteenth century such problems arose in two areas: first, in the study of quadratic forms, and second, in the solution of sets of differential equations, and below we have an example of each.

### 17.2.1 Euler's quadratic surfaces, 1748

In Volume II of the *Introductio ad analysin infinitorum* of 1748, Euler included a study of surfaces that satisfy the general equation

$$\alpha z^2 + \beta yz + \gamma xz + \delta y^2 + \epsilon xy + \zeta x^2 + \eta z + \theta y + \iota x + \chi = 0.$$

These are quadratic surfaces, three-dimensional counterparts of conic sections, and including, for example, ellipsoids. One of the problems Euler investigated was the change of axes (from $x, y, z$ to $p, q, r$) required to give the equation its simplest possible form: $Ap^2 + Bq^2 + Cr^2 + K = 0$.

Such problems were not only of theoretical interest: Lagrange, for instance, made use of similar results in investigating the rotation of rigid bodies.[2]

---

2. See, for example, Lagrange 1773.

## Euler's change of axes

from Euler, *Introduction in analysin infinitorum*, 1748, II, §113–§115, here from the second edition, 1797

113. Quia , mutando pofitionem ternorum Axium , quibus Coordinatæ funt parallelæ , æquatio generalis ad formam fim-

## SECUNDI ORDINIS. 379

pliciorem reduci poteft , ifta reductione ita utamur , ut æqua- **CAP. V.** tionem generalem pro Superficiebus fecundi ordinis ad formam fimpliciffimam redigamus , quæ tamen omnes fpecies æque ac generalis in fe complectatur. Cum igitur æquatio generalis pro Superficiebus fecundi ordinis fit

$$\alpha zz + \beta yz + \gamma xz + \delta yy + \epsilon xy + \zeta xx + \eta z + \theta y + \iota x + \kappa = 0;$$

quæramus æquationem inter alias ternas Coordinatas $p$ , $q$ & $r$ , quæ quidem fe mutuo in eodem puncto , quo ternæ priores decuffent. Ad hoc ex §. 92. ftatuatur

$$x = p(\text{cof.}\,k.\text{cof.}\,m - \text{fin.}\,k.\text{fin.}\,m.\text{cof.}\,n) + q(\text{cof.}\,k.\text{fin.}\,m +$$
$$\text{fin.}\,k.\text{cof.}\,m.\text{cof.}\,n) - r.\text{fin.}\,k.\text{fin.}\,n$$

&

$$y = -p(\text{fin.}\,k.\text{cof.}\,m + \text{cof.}\,k.\text{fin.}\,m.\text{cof.}\,n) - q(\text{fin.}\,k.\text{fin.}\,m -$$
$$\text{cof.}\,k.\text{cof.}\,m.\text{cof.}\,n) - r.\text{cof.}\,k.\text{fin.}\,n$$

atque

$$z = -p.\text{fin.}\,m.\text{fin.}\,n + q.\text{cof.}\,m.\text{fin.}\,n + r.\text{cof.}\,n ,$$

unde refultet ifta æquatio

$$App + Bqq + Crr + Dpq + Epr + Fqr + Gp + Hq + Ir + K = 0.$$

114. Jam anguli illi arbitrarii $k$ , $m$ , & $n$ ita definiri potefunt , ut tres coëfficientes $D$ , $E$ , & $F$ evanefcant. Quanquam enim calculus nimis fit prolixus , quam ut angulorum illorum determinatio actu oftendi poffit ; tamen fi quis forte dubitet , an femper ifta eliminatio ad valores reales angulorum illorum perducat , is certe concedere debebit , duos faltem coëfficientes $D$ & $E$ nihilo æquales reddi poffe. Hoc autem fi fuerit effectum , pofitio tertii Axis , cui Ordinatæ $r$ funt parallelæ in plano ad Ordinatas $p$ normali , facile ita mutari poteft , ut etiam coëfficiens $F$ evanefcat. Statuatur enim $q = t.\text{fin.}\,i + u.\text{cof.}\,i$ & $r = t.\text{cof.}\,i - u.\text{fin.}\,i$ , ita ut , loco termini $qr$ , novus terminus $tu$ ingrediatur , cujus coëfficiens ope an-

APPEND. guli *i* nihilo æqualis fieri poterit. Hoc igitur modo æquatio generalis pro Superficiebus fecundi ordinis ad hanc formam perducetur

$$App + Bqq + Crr + Gp + Hq + Ir + K = 0.$$

· 115. Nunc præterea Coordinatæ *p , q , r* datis quantitatibus ita augeri diminuive poterunt , ut coëfficientes *G , H & I* evanefcant ; quod fiet mutato tantum puncto illo , unde omnes Coordinatæ initium habent. Atque hoc modo omnes Superficies fecundi ordinis in hac æquatione continebuntur

$$App + Bqq + Crr + K = 0,$$

ex qua intelligitur unumquodque trium planorum principalium per initium Coordinatarum ductorum Superficiem in duas partes fimiles & æquales bifecare. Omnis ergo Superficies fecundi ordinis non folum unum habet planum diametrale , fed adeo tria , quæ fe mutuo in eodem puncto normaliter interfecent ; quod punctum propterea Centrum Superficiei conftituet , etiamfi in nonnullis cafibus hoc Centrum in infinitum diftet. Simili fcilicet modo , quo omnes Sectiones conicæ Centro dicuntur præditæ , etiamfi in Parabola Centrum a Vertice infinite removeatur.

---

### TRANSLATION

113. Since, by changing the position of the three axes to which the co-ordinates are parallel, the general equation can be reduced to a simpler form, [379] we make use of that reduction, in order to reduce the general equation for surfaces of second degree to the simplest form, which nevertheless contains within it all the variables just as in the general form. Since therefore the general equation for surfaces of the second degree is

$$\alpha zz + \beta yz + \gamma xz + \delta yy + \epsilon xy + \zeta xx + \eta z + \theta y + \iota x + \chi = 0,$$

we seek an equation between three other co-ordinates *p*, *q* and *r*, which mutually describe the same point as the first three. For this we have from §92

$$x = p(\cos k.\cos m - \sin k.\sin m.\cos n) + q(\cos k.\sin m + \sin k.\cos m.\cos n) - r\sin k.\sin n$$

and

$$y = -p(\sin k.\cos m + \cos k.\sin m.\cos n) - q(\sin k.\sin m - \cos k.\cos m.\cos n) - r\cos k.\sin n$$

and

$$z = -p\sin m.\sin n + q\cos m.\sin n + r\cos n,$$

whence there results this equation

$$App + Bqq + Crr + Dpq + Epr + Fqr + Gp + Hq + Ir + K = 0.$$

114. Now the arbitrary angles $k$, $m$, and $n$ can be defined so that the three coefficients $D$, $E$, and $F$ vanish. For although the calculation is exceedingly long, by which the determination of those angles is actually shown, nevertheless if anyone truly doubts that this elimination always leads to real values for those angles, he must certainly concede this, that at least two coefficients $D$ and $E$ can be rendered equal to zero. Moreover, if this has been done, the position of the third axis, to which the ordinates $r$ are parallel in a plane perpendicular to the ordinates $p$, can easily be changed, so that the coefficient $F$ also vanishes. For we have $q = t.\sin i + u.\cos i$ and $r = t.\cos i - u.\sin i$, so that, in place of the term $qr$, there is included a new term $tu$, whose coefficient [380] can be made equal to zero by means of the angle $i$. Therefore in this way the general equation for surfaces of the second degree is brought to this form

$$App + Bqq + Crr + Gp + Hq + Ir + K = 0.$$

115. Now besides, the co-ordinates $p$, $q$, $r$ can be increased or decreased by given amounts, so that the coefficients $G$, $H$ and $I$ vanish; which may be done by changing the point from which all the co-ordinates originate. And in this way all surfaces of second degree are contained in this equation

$$App + Bqq + Crr + K = 0,$$

from which it is understood that each one of the three principal planes drawn through the origin of the co-ordinates bisects the surface in two similar and equal parts. Therefore every surface of second degree has not just one diametral plane, but three, which intersect each other perpendicularly in the same point; which point therefore constitutes the centre of the surface, although in some cases this centre is infinitely distant. In a similar way, obviously, to that in which all conic sections are said to have a centre, although in the parabola the centre is infinitely removed from the vertex.

––––––––––––

## 17.2.2 Laplace's symmetric system, 1787

In 1787 Laplace investigated the small perturbations that develop in the orbits of planets over long periods of time (*variations séculaires*). He considered a set of differential equations, which he labelled ($B$), of the form

$$\frac{dp^{(i)}}{dt} = q^{(i)}.\sum_{r=0}^{n}(i,r) - \sum_{r=0}^{n}q^{(r)}.[i,r]$$

$$\frac{dq^{(i)}}{dt} = -p^{(i)}.\sum_{r=0}^{n}(i,r) + \sum_{r=0}^{n}p^{(r)}.[i,r]$$

where $p^{(i)}$, $q^{(i)}$ are parameters representing the variation in orbit of the $i^{th}$ planet, and $(i, r)$ and $[i, r]$ are terms that depend in a specified way on the masses of the planets $m^{(i)}$, their mean distances from the sun $a^{(i)}$, and the mean speeds of the $i^{th}$ and $r^{th}$ planets. Laplace observed that the system is symmetric with respect to $i$ and $r$. By using the substitutions

$$p^{(i)} = M^{(i)}.\sin(ft + \beta)$$

$$q^{(i)} = M^{(i)}.\cos(ft + \beta)$$

he transformed his original equations to

$$fM^{(i)} = M^{(i)}.\sum_{r=0}^{n}(i, r) - \sum_{r=0}^{n} M^{(r)}.[i, r],$$

essentially eigenvalue equations with $n$ solutions $f_i$ for $f$.

Laplace observed that if the planetary perturbations are to remain small, all the values of $f_i$ must be real, and different from each other. Later it was to be understood that this follows from the symmetry of the equations, but Laplace's proof in this particular case was based on physical observation of the solar system.

---

### Laplace's planetary perturbations

from Laplace, 'Mémoire sur les variations séculaires des orbites des planètes', *Mémoires de l'Académie Royale de Paris*, (1787), 275–277 and 279

---

## I V.

REPRENONS maintenant les équations *(B)* de l'*art.* *11.* oï l'on y fuppofe fucceffivement $i = 0, i = 1, i = 2,$ ..... $i = n - 1$; on aura $2n$ équations différen- tielles linéaires du premier ordre, dont les intégrales doivent par conféquent renfermer $2n$ conftantes arbitraires. Sup- pofons

$$p^{(i)} = M^{(i)}.\text{fin.} (ft + \varepsilon) ; q^{(i)} = M^{(i)}.\text{cof.} (ft + \varepsilon) ;$$

en fubftituant ces valeurs dans les équations *(B)*, on aura

$$fM^{(i)} = M^{(i)}.\Sigma (i, r) - \Sigma. M^{(r)}.\boxed{i, r}.$$

Au moyen des $n$ équations que l'on formera par les fuppo- fitions de $i = 0, i = 1, ..... i = n - 1$, on pourra éliminer les conftantes $M^{(0)}, M^{(1)}$, &c. & l'on

Mm ij

aura une équation en $f$, du degré $n$; de plus, toutes les
conſtantes $M^{(o)}$, $M^{(1)}$, &c. ſeront données au moyen de
l'une d'elles, telle que $M^{(o)}$ qui reſtera arbitraire.

Soient $f$, $f'$, &c. les $n$ racines de l'équation en $f$; on
aura par la théorie connue des équations différentielles
linéaires,

$$p^{(i)} = M^{(i)} . \text{ſin.} (ft + \mathcal{C}) + N^{(i)} . \text{ſin.} (f't + \mathcal{C}') + \&c.$$
$$q^{(i)} = M^{(i)} . \text{coſ.} (ft + \mathcal{C}) + N^{(i)} . \text{coſ.} (f't + \mathcal{C}') + \&c.$$

Ces valeurs de $p^{(i)}$ & de $q^{(i)}$ ſeront complettes, puiſqu'elles
renfermeront les $2n$ arbitraires, $M^{(o)}$, $N^{(o)}$, &c. $\mathcal{C}$, $\mathcal{C}'$, &c

Maintenant ſi les racines $f$, $f'$, &c. ſont réelles & inégales; les valeurs de $p^{(i)}$ & de $q^{(i)}$ reſteront toujours fort
petites, & comme on a $\varepsilon^{(i)^2} = p^{(i)^2} + q^{(i)^2}$, les excentricités des orbites ſeront toujours peu conſidérables. Mais
il n'en eſt pas de même ſi quelques-unes de ces racines
ſont égales ou imaginaires; car alors les ſinus & les coſinus
ſe changent en arcs de cercle, ou en exponentielles. Les
excentricités des orbites ceſſeront donc, après un long
intervalle de temps, d'être fort petites; ce qui, en changeant
la conſtitution du ſyſtème ſolaire, détruiroit ſa ſtabilité
Par conſéquent, il importe de s'aſſurer que les valeurs de $f$, ne
peuvent être ni égales ni imaginaires. Cette recherche paroît
ſuppoſer la connoiſſance des maſſes des planètes, qui entrent
dans les coëfficiens de l'équation en $f$; mais il eſt très-
remarquable que quelles que ſoient ces maſſes, pourvu
qu'elles ſe meuvent toutes dans le même ſens, l'équation
en $f$ ne peut avoir que des racines réelles & inégales.

Pour le démontrer de la manière la plus générale, nous
obſerverons que dans le cas des racines imaginaires
valeur de $p^{(i)}$ contient des termes de la forme

$c$ étant le nombre dont le logarithme hyperbolique est l'unité, & $P^{(i)}$ étant une quantité réelle, puisque $p^{(i)}$ qui est égal à $e^{(i)} . \sin. \varpi^{(i)}$, est nécessairement réel. La valeur de $q^{(i)}$ renferme un terme correspondant de la forme $c^{g t} . Q^{(i)}$, $Q^{(i)}$ étant encore une quantité réelle ; la fonction $p^{(i)^2} + q^{(i)^2}$ renfermera donc le terme $c^{2 g t} . (P^{(i)^2} + Q^{(i)^2})$, & par conséquent le premier membre de l'équation

$$\Sigma' . m^{(i)} . \sqrt{(a^{(i)})} . (p^{(i)^2} + q^{(i)^2}) = \text{const.}$$

renfermera le terme

$$\Sigma' . m^{(i)} . \sqrt{(a^{(i)})} . (P^{(i)^2} + Q^{(i)^2}) . c^{2 g t}.$$

Si l'on suppose que l'exponentielle $c^{g t}$ soit la plus grande de toutes celles que renferment les valeurs de $p^{(i)}$ & de $q^{(i)}$ ; il est clair que le terme précédent ne peut être détruit par aucun autre, dans le premier membre de cette équation ; d'où il suit que ce membre ne peut se réduire à une constante, à moins que l'on ait

$$\Sigma' . m^{(i)} . \sqrt{(a^{(i)})} . (P^{(i)^2} + Q^{(i)^2}) = 0;$$

or cela est impossible lorsque les quantités $m^{(0)} . \sqrt{(a^{(0)})}$, $m^{(1)} \sqrt{(a^{(1)})}$, &c. sont toutes de même signe, ou, ce qui revient au même, lorsque toutes les planètes tournent dans le même sens ; les valeurs de $p^{(i)}$ & de $q^{(i)}$ ne peuvent donc point renfermer d'exponentielles, & l'équation en $f$ ne peut avoir que des racines réelles, dans le cas de la nature.

[...]

L'analyſe précédente ne peut s'appliquer qu'à un ſyſtème de planètes qui ſe meuvent toutes dans le même ſens, comme cela a lieu dans notre ſyſtème planétaire ; dans ce cas, on voit que le ſyſtème eſt ſtable, & ne s'éloigne jamais que très-peu, d'un état moyen autour duquel il oſcille avec une extrême lenteur. Mais cette propriété remarquable convient - elle également à un ſyſtème de planètes qui ſe meuvent en différens ſens ? c'eſt ce qu'il ſeroit très-difficile de déterminer. Comme cette recherche n'eſt d'aucune utilité dans l'aſtronomie, nous nous diſpen-ſerons de nous en occuper.

TRANSLATION

IV.

Let us now reconsider equations ($B$) of section II. If one there supposes successively $i = 0$, $i = 1$, $i = 2$, ... $i = n - 1$, one will have $2n$ linear differential equations of the first degree, of which the integrals must consequently contain $2n$ arbitrary constants. Let us suppose

$$p^{(i)} = M^{(i)}. \sin(ft + \beta); \quad q^{(i)} = M^{(i)}. \cos(ft + \beta);$$

by substituting these values into equations ($B$), one will have

$$fM^{(i)} = M^{(i)}. \sum (i, r) - \sum . M^{(r)}.[i, r].$$

By means of the $n$ equations one may form under the suppositions $i = 0$, $i = 1$, ... $i = n - 1$, one may eliminate the constants $M^{(0)}$, $M^{(1)}$, etc. and one [276] will have an equation in $f$, of degree $n$; further, all the constants $M^{(0)}$, $M^{(1)}$, etc. will be given in terms of one of them, such as $M^{(0)}$, which will remain arbitrary.

Let $f, f^1$, etc. be the $n$ roots of the equation in $f$; one will have by the known theory of linear differential equations,

$$p^{(i)} = M^{(i)}. \sin(ft + \beta) + N^{(i)}. \sin(f^1t + \beta^1) + \text{etc.}$$

$$q^{(i)} = M^{(i)}. \cos(ft + \beta) + N^{(i)}. \cos(f^1t + \beta^1) + \text{etc.}$$

These values of $p^{(i)}$ and $q^{(i)}$ will be complete, because they contain the $2n$ arbitrary constants, $M^{(0)}, N^{(0)}$, etc. $\beta, \beta^1$, etc.

Now if the roots $f, f^1$, etc. are real and unequal, the values of $p^{(i)}$ and $q^{(i)}$ will always remain very small, and since one has $e^{(i)2} = p^{(i)2} + q^{(i)2}$, the eccentricities of the orbits will remain barely significant. But it is not the same if some of these roots are equal or imaginary; for then the sines and cosines change into arcs of circles, or into exponentials. The eccentricities of the orbits will therefore cease, after a long period of time, to be very small; which would, by changing the constitution of the solar system, destroy its stability. Consequently, it matters to assure oneself that the values of $f$ can be neither equal nor imaginary. This question would seem to assume knowledge of the masses of the planets, which enter into the coefficients of the equation for $f$; but it is very remarkable that whatever their masses, provided they all move in the same direction, the equation in $f$ can only have real and unequal roots.

To demonstrate this in the most general manner, we may observe that in the case of imaginary roots, the value of $p^{(i)}$ contains terms of the form $c^{gt}.P^{(i)}$, [277] where $c$ is the number of which the hyperbolic logarithm is one, and $P^{(i)}$ is a real quantity, since $p^{(i)}$ which is equal to $e^{(i)} \sin \varpi^{(i)}$, is necessarily real. The value of $q^{(i)}$ contains a corresponding term of the form $c^{gt}.Q^{(i)}$, where $Q^{(i)}$ is again a real quantity; the function $p^{(i)^2} + q^{(i)^2}$ will therefore contain the term $c^{2gt}.(P^{(i)^2} + Q^{(i)^2})$, and consequently the first side of the equation

$$\sum^1 m^{(i)}.\sqrt{(a^{(i)})}.(p^{(i)^2} + q^{(i)^2}) = \text{constant}$$

will contain the term

$$\sum^1 m^{(i)}.\sqrt{(a^{(i)})}.(P^{(i)^2} + Q^{(i)^2}).c^{2gt}.$$

If one supposes that the exponential $c^{gt}$ is the largest of all those contained in the values of $p^{(i)}$ and $q^{(i)}$, it is clear that the above term cannot be destroyed by any other in the first side of this equation; from which it follows that this side cannot be reduced to a constant, unless one has

$$\sum^1 m^{(i)}.\sqrt{(a^{(i)})}.(P^{(i)^2} + Q^{(i)^2}) = 0.$$

Now that is impossible when the quantities $m^{(0)}.\sqrt{(a^{(0)})}$, $m^{(1)}.\sqrt{(a^{(1)})}$, etc. are all of the same sign, or, which comes to the same thing, when all the planets revolve in the same direction; the values of $p^{(i)}$ and $q^{(i)}$ cannot therefore contain exponentials, and the equation in $f$ can have only real roots, in the case of nature.

[...]

Laplace put forward a similar argument, again depending on the planets moving in the same direction, to show that the equation cannot have equal roots. In this case the $p^{(i)}$ would contain terms of the form $t^g.P^{(i)}$, and he argued, as above, that the square $t^{2g}$ of the highest power cannot be destroyed unless all coefficients $m^{(i)}$, $\sqrt{a^{(i)}}$, are zero. He ended his paper with the following remark.

[279] The above analysis can only be applied to a system of planets which all move in the same direction, as happens in our planetary system; in this case, one sees that the system is stable, and only ever moves away very little from a mean state around which it oscillates with extreme slowness. But does this remarkable property belong equally to a system of planets which move in different directions? This would be very difficult to determine. Since this research is of no use in astronomy, we will avoid engaging with it.

———————

### 17.2.3 Cauchy's theorems of 1829

In 1829 Cauchy produced a paper entitled 'Sur l'équation a l'aide de laquelle on détermine les inégalités séculaires des mouvements des planètes' ('On the equation by means of which one determines the secular inequalities of the movements of planets'), and therefore appeared to address the same problem that Laplace had treated in 1787 (see 17.2.2). His title, however, is somewhat misleading and appears to have been added only as an afterthought. The main subject of the paper was a different problem, previously treated by Euler and Lagrange (see 17.2.1), of transforming a general quadratic form

$$A_{xx}x^2 + A_{yy}y^2 + A_{zz}z^2 + \cdots + 2A_{xy}xy + 2A_{xz}xz + \ldots$$

into a simple sum of squares

$$s_1\xi^2 + s_2\eta^2 + s_3\zeta^2 + \ldots.$$

Cauchy stipulated, as had Lagrange, the condition

$$x^2 + y^2 + z^2 + \cdots = \xi^2 + \eta^2 + \zeta^2 + \cdots = 1$$

that is, that the transformation was of the kind we would now describe as orthogonal, but went further than Euler or Lagrange in working with any number of variables, rather than just the three required in physical applications.

Cauchy was able to show that $s_1, s_2, s_3, \ldots$ are the values of $s$ given by setting to zero the determinant of the array

$$
\begin{array}{llll}
A_{xx} - s, & A_{xy}, & A_{xz}, & \ldots \\
A_{xy}, & A_{yy} - s, & A_{yz}, & \ldots \\
A_{xz}, & A_{yz}, & A_{zz} - s, & \ldots \\
\ldots
\end{array}
$$

He went on to prove Theorem 1 of his paper, that the values of $s_1, s_2, \ldots s_n$, are real. His arguments were based on his own theory of determinants from almost twenty years earlier (see 17.1.4), and thus he performed a further important unification, between determinants, transformations of quadratic forms, and the emerging theory of eigenvalues.

At the end of the paper, Cauchy noted that the problem under discussion was relevant in geometry and mechanics, and that similar work was being done by Charles-François Sturm. The only mention of secular variation, other than in the title, is a passing reference which, like the title itself, appears to have been added later, probably after Cauchy became aware of the work of Sturm. Nevertheless, it is clear that at some point in writing the paper Cauchy recognized the underlying connection between the simplification of quadratic forms and the 'eigenvalue' problems of Laplace, and was able to shed light on both through his theory of determinants.

---

## Cauchy's theory of 'eigenvalues'

from Cauchy, 'Sur l'équation a l'aide de laquelle on détermine les inégalités séculaires des mouvements des planètes', *Exercices de mathématiques*, 1829, 140–142 and 159–160

---

# SUR L'ÉQUATION

## A L'AIDE DE LAQUELLE ON DÉTERMINE LES INÉGALITÉS SÉCULAIRES

# DES MOUVEMENTS DES PLANÈTES.

Soit

$$(1) \qquad s = f(x, y, z, \ldots)$$

une fonction réelle homogène et du second degré. Soient de plus

$$(2) \qquad \varphi(x, y, z, \ldots), \quad \chi(x, y, z, \ldots), \quad \psi(x, y, z, \ldots), \quad \text{etc.},$$

les dérivées partielles de $f(x, y, z, \ldots)$ prises par rapport aux variables $x$, $y$, $z$... Si l'on assujettit ces variables à l'équation de condition

$$(3) \qquad x^2 + y^2 + z^2 + \ldots = 1,$$

les *maxima* et *minima* de la fonction $s$ seront déterminés [voyez les Leçons sur le calcul infinitésimal, page 252] par la formule

$$(4) \qquad \frac{\varphi(x, y, z, \ldots)}{x} = \frac{\chi(x, y, z, \ldots)}{y} = \frac{\psi(x, y, z, \ldots)}{z} = \ldots,$$

D'ailleurs les diverses fractions que renferme la formule (4), étant égales entre elles, seront égales au rapport

$$\frac{x\varphi(x, y, z, \ldots) + y\chi(x, y, z, \ldots) + z\psi(x, y, z, \ldots) + \ldots}{x^2 + y^2 + z^2 + \ldots},$$

qui, en vertu de la condition (3) et du théorème des fonctions homogènes, se réduira simplement à

$$2f(x, y, z, \ldots) = 2s.$$

On aura donc encore

$$( 141 )$$

(5)
$$\frac{\varphi(x,y,z,\ldots)}{x} = \frac{\chi(x,y,z,\ldots)}{y} = \frac{\psi(x,y,z,\ldots)}{z} = \ldots = 2s\,,$$

ou, ce qui revient au même,

(6)
$$\frac{1}{2}\,\varphi(x,y,z,\ldots) = sx\,, \quad \frac{1}{2}\,\chi(x,y,z,\ldots) = sy\,, \quad \frac{1}{2}\,\psi(x,y,z,\ldots) = sz\,, \quad \text{etc.}$$

Soit maintenant

(7)
$$S = 0$$

l'équation que fournira l'élimination des variables $x$, $y$, $z$, $\ldots$ entre les formules (6). Les *maxima* et les *minima* de la fonction

$$s = f(x,y,z,\ldots)$$

ne pourront être que des racines de l'équation (7). D'ailleurs cette équation sera semblable à celle que l'on rencontre dans la théorie des inégalités séculaires des mouvements des planètes, et dont les racines, toutes réelles, jouissent de propriétés dignes de remarque. Quelques-unes de ces propriétés étaient déjà connues : nous allons les rappeler ici, et en indiquer de nouvelles.

Soit $n$ le nombre des variables $x$, $y$, $z$, $\ldots$. Désignons d'ailleurs, pour plus de commodité, par

$$A_{xx}\,, \quad A_{yy}\,, \quad A_{zz}\,, \quad \text{etc.}\ldots$$

les coefficients des carrés

$$x^2\,, \quad y^2\,, \quad z^2\,, \quad \text{etc.}\ldots$$

dans la fonction homogène $s = f(x,y,z,\ldots)$, et par

$$A_{xy} = A_{yx}\,, \quad A_{xz} = A_{zx}\,,\ldots A_{yz} = A_{zy}\,,\ldots$$

les coefficients des doubles produits

$$2xy\,, \quad 2xz\,, \ldots 2yz\,,\ldots\,,$$

ensorte qu'on ait

(8)
$$s = A_{xx}x^2 + A_{yy}y^2 + A_{zz}z^2 + \ldots$$
$$+ 2A_{xy}xy + 2A_{xz}xz + \ldots + 2A_{yz}yz + \ldots.$$

Les équations (6) deviendront

$$( 142 )$$

$$(9) \quad \left\{ \begin{array}{l} A_{xx}x + A_{xy}y + A_{xz}z + \ldots = sx\,, \\[4pt] A_{xy}x + A_{yy}y + A_{yz}z + \ldots = sy\,, \\[4pt] A_{xz}x + A_{yz}y + A_{zz}z + \ldots = sz\,, \\[4pt] \text{etc.}\ldots\,; \end{array} \right.$$

et pourront s'écrire comme il suit :

$$(10) \quad \left\{ \begin{array}{l} (A_{xx} - s)x + A_{xy}y + A_{xz}z + \ldots = 0\,, \\[4pt] A_{xy}x + (A_{yy} - s)y + A_{yz}z + \ldots = 0\,, \\[4pt] A_{xz}x + A_{yz}y + (A_{zz} - s)z + \ldots = 0\,, \\[4pt] \text{etc.}\ldots \end{array} \right.$$

Cela posé, il résulte des principes établis dans le troisième chapitre de l'*Analyse algébrique* [§ 2] que le premier membre de l'équation (8), ou $S$, sera une fonction alternée des quantités comprises dans le tableau

$$(11) \quad \left\{ \begin{array}{lll} A_{xx} - s\,, & A_{xy}\,, & A_{xz}\,, \ldots \\[4pt] A_{xy}\,, & A_{yy} - s\,, & A_{yz}\,, \ldots \\[4pt] A_{xz}\,, & A_{yz}\,, & A_{zz} - s\,, \ldots \\[4pt] \text{etc.}\ldots\,, \end{array} \right.$$

savoir, celle dont les différents termes sont représentés, aux signes près, par les produits qu'on obtient, lorsqu'on multiplie ces quantités, $n$ à $n$, de toutes les manières possibles, en ayant soin de faire entrer dans chaque produit un facteur pris dans chacune des lignes horizontales du tableau, et un facteur pris dans chacune des lignes verticales. En opérant ainsi, on trouvera, par exemple, pour $n = 2$,

$$(12) \quad S = (A_{xx} - s)(A_{yy} - s) - A^2_{xy}\,;$$

pour $n = 3$,

$$(13) \quad S =$$

$$(A_{xx} - s)(A_{yy} - s)(A_{zz} - s) - A^2_{yz}(A_{xx} - s) \cdot A^2_{xz}(A_{yy} - s) - A^2_{xy}(A_{zz} - s) + 2A_{xy}A_{xz}A_{yz}\,;$$

pour $n = 4$,

$$[\ldots]$$

Dans le cas particulier où les variables $x$, $y$, $z$ sont au nombre de trois seulement, l'équation (7) se réduit à celle qui se représente dans diverses questions de géométrie et de mécanique, par exemple, dans la théorie des moments d'inertie ; et le théorème 1.ᵉʳ fournit les règles que j'ai données dans le troisième volume des *Exercices* comme propres à déterminer les limites des racines de cette équation. Alors aussi les équations (22) sont semblables à celles qui existent entre les cosinus des angles que forment trois axes rectangulaires quelconques avec les axes coordonnés, supposés eux-mêmes rectangulaires, et le théorème 2 correspond à une proposition de géométrie, savoir, que par le centre d'une surface du second degré on peut mener trois plans perpendiculaires l'un à l'autre, et dont chacun la divise en deux parties symétriques.

( 160 )

J'observerai, en terminant cet article, qu'au moment où je n'en avais encore écrit qu'une partie, M. Sturm m'a dit être parvenu à démontrer fort simplement les théorèmes 1 et 2. Il se propose de publier incessamment le Mémoire qu'il a composé à ce sujet, et qui a été offert à l'Académie des sciences le même jour que le présent article.

TRANSLATION

## ON THE EQUATION
### BY THE AID OF WHICH ONE DETERMINES THE SECULAR INEQUALITIES
## OF THE MOVEMENTS OF THE PLANETS

Let

(1)
$$s = f(x, y, z, \dots)$$

be a real homogeneous function and of second degree. Further let

(2)
$$\varphi(x, y, z, \dots), \quad \chi(x, y, z, \dots), \quad \psi(x, y, z, \dots), \quad \text{etc.,}$$

be the partial derivatives of $f(x, y, z, \dots)$ taken with respect to the variables $x, y, z \dots$. If one subjects these variables to the conditional equation

(3)
$$x^2 + y^2 + z^2 + \dots = 1,$$

the *maxima* and *minima* of the function $s$ will be determined [see Leçons sur le calcul infinitésimal, page 252] by the formula

(4)
$$\frac{\varphi(x, y, z, \dots)}{x} = \frac{\chi(x, y, z, \dots)}{y} = \frac{\psi(x, y, z, \dots)}{z} = \dots.$$

Besides the various fractions contained in formula (4), being equal to each other, will be equal to the ratio

(5)
$$\frac{x\varphi(x, y, z, \dots) + y\chi(x, y, z, \dots) + z\psi(x, y, a, \dots) + \dots}{x^2 + y^2 + z^2 + \dots},$$

which, by virtue of condition (3) and the theory of homogeneous functions, will reduce simply to

$$2f(x, y, z, \ldots) = 2s.$$

One will therefore again have [141]

(5) $$\frac{\varphi(x, y, z, \ldots)}{x} = \frac{\chi(x, y, z, \ldots)}{y} = \frac{\psi(x, y, z, \ldots)}{z} = \cdots = 2s.$$

or, which comes to the same thing,

(6) $$\frac{1}{2}\varphi(x, y, z, \ldots) = sx, \quad \frac{1}{2}\chi(x, y, z, \ldots) = sy, \quad \frac{1}{2}\psi(x, y, z, \ldots) = sz,$$

etc. Now let

(7) $$S = 0$$

be the equation that eliminates the variables $x$, $y$, $z$, ...from the formulas in (6). The *maxima* and *minima* of the function

$$s = f(x, y, z, \ldots)$$

can be none other than the roots of equation (7). Besides, this equation will be similar to that which one meets in the theory of secular inequalities of the movements of planets, and whose roots, all real, display properties worthy of note. Some of these properties are already known: we will recall them here, and indicate new ones.

Let $n$ be the number of variables $x$, $y$, $z$, .... Let us besides, for greater convenience, denote by

$$A_{xx}, \quad A_{yy}, \quad A_{zz}, \quad \text{etc.} \ldots$$

the coefficients of the squares

$$x^2, \quad y^2, \quad z^2, \quad \text{etc.} \ldots$$

in the homogeneous function $s = f(x, y, z, \ldots)$, and by

$$A_{xy} = A_{yx}, \quad A_{xz} = A_{zx}, \ldots A_{yz} = A_{zy}, \ldots$$

the coefficients of the double products

$$2xy, \quad 2xz, \ldots 2yz, \ldots,$$

so that one has

(8) $$\begin{aligned} s = {} & A_{xx}x^2 + A_{yy}y^2 + A_{zz}z^2 + \ldots \\ & + 2A_{xy}xy + 2A_{xz}xz + \cdots + 2A_{yz}yz + \ldots \end{aligned}$$

Equations (6) will become [142]

(9)

$$\begin{aligned} A_{xx}x + A_{xy}y + A_{xz}z + \ldots &= sx, \\ A_{xy}x + A_{yy}y + A_{yz}z + \ldots &= sy, \\ A_{xz}x + A_{yz}y + A_{zz}z + \ldots &= sz. \\ \text{etc.} \ldots; \end{aligned}$$

and can be written as follows:

(10)

$$\begin{aligned}
(A_{xx} - s)x + A_{xy}y + A_{xz}z + \ldots &= 0, \\
A_{xy}x + (A_{yy} - s)y + A_{yz}z + \ldots &= 0, \\
A_{xz}x + A_{yz}y + (A_{zz} - s)z + \ldots &= 0, \\
\text{etc.} \ldots;
\end{aligned}$$

That said, it follows from the principles established in the third chapter of *Analyse algébrique* [= *Cours d'analyse*] (§2) that the first side of equation (8), or $S$, will be an alternating function of the quantities contained in the table

(11)

$$\begin{array}{cccc}
A_{xx} - s, & A_{xy}, & A_{xz}, & \ldots \\
A_{xy}, & A_{yy} - s, & A_{yz}, & \ldots \\
A_{xz}, & A_{yz}, & A_{zz} - s, & \ldots \\
\text{etc.} \ldots,
\end{array}$$

namely, whose different terms are represented, up to signs, by the products one obtains when one multiplies these quantities, $n$ by $n$, in all possible ways, taking care to enter in each product a factor taken from each of the horizontal lines of the table, and a factor taken from each of the vertical lines. Working thus, one will find, for example, for $n = 2$,

(12) $$S = (A_{xx} - s)(A_{yy} - s) - A_{xy}^2;$$

for $n = 3$,

(13) $$S = (A_{xx} - s)(A_{yy} - s)(A_{zz} - s) - A_{yz}^2(A_{xx} - s) - A_{zx}^2(A_{yy} - s) -$$

$$A_{xy}^2(A_{zz} - s) + 2A_{xy}A_{xz}A_{yz};$$

$$[\ldots]$$

[143] and generally one will obtain for $S$ a function of $s$ which will be a polynomial of degree $n$.

$$[\ldots]$$

Cauchy went on to state and prove Theorem 1: that the roots of equation (7) (equivalent to equation (11)) are real; and Theorem 2: that a general quadratic form can be transformed to a sum of squares, using a transformation that we would now describe as orthogonal. He ended his paper with the following observations.

$$[\ldots]$$

[159] In the particular case where the variables $x, y, z$ are only three in number, equation (7) reduces to that which appears in various questions in geometry and mechanics, for

example, in the theory of moments of inertia; and Theorem 1 supplies the rules that I have given in the third volume of the *Exercices* as appropriate for determining the limits of the roots of this equation. Then also equations (22) are similar to those that hold between the cosines of the angles formed by any three orthogonal axes with the co-ordinate axes, themselves assumed orthogonal, and Theorem 2 corresponds to a proposition in geometry, namely, that through the centre of a surface of second degree one may take three planes perpendicular to one another, each of which divides it into two symmetric parts.

[160] I will observe, on ending this article, that at a time when I had yet written only part of it, I was told that Monsieur Sturm had succeeded in demonstrating Theorems 1 and 2 very simply. He proposes to publish very soon the Memoir that he has composed on this subject, and which he has submitted to the Academy of Sciences on the same day as the present article.

――――――――

## 17.3 MATRICES

### 17.3.1 Gauss and linear transformations, 1801

As noted in 17.2.3 Gauss in 1801 defined the determinant of the quadratic form $ax^2 + 2bxy + cy^2$ to be $b^2 - ac$. He then went on to explore the problem of transforming quadratic forms using the linear substitutions

$$x = \alpha x' + \beta y'$$
$$y = \gamma x' + \delta y'.$$

He showed that the composition, or product, of this substitution with a second one,

$$x' = \alpha' x'' + \beta' y''$$
$$y' = \gamma' x'' + \delta' y'',$$

is a third substitution of the same type. Gauss's calculation demonstrates what is now the rule for multiplying $2 \times 2$ matrices. It also shows that, under his definition of a determinant, the determinant of the product is the product of the determinant.

# Gauss's linear transformations

from Gauss, *Disquisitiones arithmeticae*, 1801, *Werke*, I, 1863, 126–127

*Formae oppositae.*

159.

*Si forma F formam F' implicat, haec vero formam F'', forma F etiam formam F'' implicabit.*

Sint indeterminatae formarum *F, F', F''* respective $x, y$; $x', y'$; $x'', y''$ transeatque *F* in *F'* ponendo

$$x = \alpha x' + 6 y', \quad y = \gamma x' + \delta y'$$

*F'* in *F''* ponendo

$$x' = \alpha' x'' + 6' y'', \quad y' = \gamma' x'' + \delta' y''$$

patetque, *F* in *F''* transmutatum iri ponendo

$$x = \alpha(\alpha' x'' + 6' y'') + 6(\gamma' x'' + \delta' y''), \quad y = \gamma(\alpha' x'' + 6' y'') + \delta(\gamma' x'' + \delta' y'')$$

sive

$$x = (\alpha \alpha' + 6 \gamma') x'' + (\alpha 6' + 6 \delta') y'', \quad y = (\gamma \alpha' + \delta \gamma') x'' + (\gamma 6' + \delta \delta') y''$$

Quare *F* ipsam *F''* implicabit.

TRANSFORMATIO.    127

Quia

$$(\alpha \alpha' + 6 \gamma')(\gamma 6' + \delta \delta') - (\alpha 6' + 6 \delta')(\gamma \alpha' + \delta \gamma') = (\alpha \delta - 6 \gamma)(\alpha' \delta' - 6' \gamma')$$

adeoque positivus, si tum $\alpha \delta - 6 \gamma$ tum $\alpha' \delta' - 6' \gamma'$ positivus aut uterque negativus, negativus vero si alter horum numerorum positivus alter negativus: forma *F* formam *F'' proprie* implicabit, si *F* ipsam *F'* et *F'* ipsam *F''* eodem modo implicant, *improprie* si diverso.

TRANSLATION

## *Opposing forms*
159.

*If the form F transforms to the form F', and this in turn to form F'', then form F also transforms to form F''.*

Let $x, y$; $x', y'$; $x'', y''$ be the variables in the forms *F, F', F''*, respectively, and suppose *f* changes to *F'* by putting

$$x = \alpha x' + \beta y', \quad y = \gamma x' + \delta y'$$

and *F'* to *F''* by putting

$$x' = \alpha' x'' + \beta' y'', \quad y' = \gamma' x'' + \delta' y''$$

then it is clear that *F* goes to *F''* by putting

$$x = \alpha(\alpha' x'' + \beta' y'') + \beta(\gamma' x'' + \delta' y''),$$
$$y = \gamma(\alpha' x'' + \beta' y'') + \beta(\gamma' x'' + \delta' y'')$$

or

$$x = (\alpha\alpha' + \beta\gamma')x'' + (\alpha\beta' + \beta\delta')y'',$$
$$y = (\gamma\alpha' + \delta\gamma')x'' + (\gamma\beta' + \delta\delta')y''$$

Whence $F$ transforms to $F''$.

[127] And because

$$(\alpha\alpha' + \beta\gamma')(\gamma\beta' + \delta\delta') - (\alpha\beta' + \beta\delta')(\gamma\alpha' + \delta\gamma') = (\alpha\delta - \beta\gamma)(\alpha'\delta' - \beta'\gamma')$$

is positive if $\alpha\delta - \beta\gamma$ and $\alpha'\delta' - \beta'\gamma'$ are both positive or both negative, but negative if one of these numbers is positive and the other negative; the form $F$ transforms *properly* to $F''$, if $F$ transforms to $F'$ and $F'$ transforms to $F''$ in the same way, *improperly* if differently.

<hr/>

## 17.3.2  Cayley's theory of matrices, 1858

From what has been said already, it is clear that much of the theory that later came to be associated with matrices, for example, the rules of manipulation, a theory of determinants, and even a fledgling theory of eigenvalues, were already in existence by the early nineteenth century, long before matrices themselves were identified or named. An algebraic theory of matrices developed only after 1850 when James Joseph Sylvester, in correspondence with his friend and fellow lawyer Arthur Cayley, coined the term 'matrix' for an oblong array of terms. Cayley published 'A memoir on the theory of matrices' in the *Philosophical transactions of the Royal Society* in 1858, and in it laid the groundwork for matrix algebra. Thus Cayley did for matrices what Cauchy had done for substitutions in 1815 (see 13.1.1), establishing rules of notation and operation for these new objects in the mathematical canon.

Cayley's paper also contained the first formal statement of what is now known as the Cayley–Hamilton theorem, but Cayley proved it only for the very easy case of a $2 \times 2$ matrix. 'I have not thought it necessary', he remarked, 'to undertake the labour of a formal proof of the theorem in the general case of a matrix of any degree.' A proof by direct calculation in the general case in fact becomes impossibly complicated, but Cayley does not appear to have looked for alternative approaches. Just as in his earlier investigations into group theory (13.1.4), he succeeded in performing a few low level calculations but failed to see the larger picture, or to work with anything like the sophistication of his continental contemporaries.

Another problem raised by Cayley in 1858 was that of determining which matrices commute (or in his terminology 'are convertible') with a given matrix, but to this he was able to give only a partial answer.

# Cayley's definition of matrices

from Cayley, 'A memoir on the theory of matrices', *Philosophical transactions of the Royal Society*, 148 (1858), 17–19 and 23–24

[    17    ]

II. *A Memoir on the Theory of Matrices.*    By ARTHUR CAYLEY, *Esq., F.R.S.*

Received December 10, 1857,—Read January 14, 1858.

THE term matrix might be used in a more general sense, but in the present memoir I consider only square and rectangular matrices, and the term matrix used without quali- fication is to be understood as meaning a square matrix; in this restricted sense, a set of quantities arranged in the form of a square, *e. g.*

$$\left( \begin{array}{ccc} a, & b, & c \\ a', & b', & c' \\ a'', & b'', & c'' \end{array} \right)$$

is said to be a matrix. The notion of such a matrix arises naturally from an abbreviated notation for a set of linear equations, viz. the equations

$$X = ax + by + cz,$$
$$Y = a'x + b'y + c'z,$$
$$Z = a''x + b''y + c''z,$$

may be more simply represented by

$$(X, Y, Z) = \left( \begin{array}{ccc} a, & b, & c \\ a', & b', & c' \\ a'', & b'', & c'' \end{array} \right)(x, y, z),$$

and the consideration of such a system of equations leads to most of the fundamental notions in the theory of matrices. It will be seen that matrices (attending only to those of the same order) comport themselves as single quantities; they may be added, multiplied or compounded together, &c.: the law of the addition of matrices is pre- cisely similar to that for the addition of ordinary algebraical quantities; as regards their multiplication (or composition), there is the peculiarity that matrices are not in general convertible; it is nevertheless possible to form the powers (positive or negative, integral or fractional) of a matrix, and thence to arrive at the notion of a rational and integral function, or generally of any algebraical function, of a matrix. I obtain the remarkable theorem that any matrix whatever satisfies an algebraical equation of its own order, the coefficient of the highest power being unity, and those of the other powers functions of the terms of the matrix, the last coefficient being in fact the deter- minant; the rule for the formation of this equation may be stated in the following con- densed form, which will be intelligible after a perusal of the memoir, viz. the determi-

MDCCCLVIII.                    D

nant, formed out of the matrix diminished by the matrix considered as a single quantity involving the matrix unity, will be equal to zero. The theorem shows that every rational and integral function (or indeed every rational function) of a matrix may be considered as a rational and integral function, the degree of which is at most equal to that of the matrix, less unity; it even shows that in a sense, the same is true with respect to any algebraical function whatever of a matrix. One of the applications of the theorem is the finding of the general expression of the matrices which are convertible with a given matrix. The theory of rectangular matrices appears much less important than that of square matrices, and I have not entered into it further than by showing how some of the notions applicable to these may be extended to rectangular matrices.

1. For conciseness, the matrices written down at full length will in general be of the order 3, but it is to be understood that the definitions, reasonings, and conclusions apply to matrices of any degree whatever. And when two or more matrices are spoken of in connexion with each other, it is always implied (unless the contrary is expressed) that the matrices are of the same order.

2. The notation

$$\left(\begin{array}{ccc} a\,, & b\,, & c \\ a'\,, & b'\,, & c' \\ a''\,, & b''\,, & c'' \end{array}\;\middle|\;x, y, z\right)$$

represents the set of linear functions

$$\big((a, b, c\,\hbox{\char41} x, y, z),\ (a', b', c'\,\hbox{\char41} x, y, z),\ (a'', b'', c''\,\hbox{\char41} x, y, z)\big),$$

so that calling these $(X, Y, Z)$, we have

$$(X, Y, Z) = \left(\begin{array}{ccc} a\,, & b\,, & c \\ a'\,, & b'\,, & c' \\ a''\,, & b''\,, & c'' \end{array}\;\middle|\;x, y, z\right)$$

and, as remarked above, this formula leads to most of the fundamental notions in the theory.

3. The quantities $(X, Y, Z)$ will be identically zero, if all the terms of the matrix are zero, and we may say that

$$\left(\begin{array}{ccc} 0, & 0, & 0 \\ 0, & 0, & 0 \\ 0, & 0, & 0 \end{array}\right)$$

is the matrix zero.

Again, $(X, Y, Z)$ will be identically equal to $(x, y, z)$, if the matrix is

$$\left(\begin{array}{ccc} 1, & 0, & 0 \\ 0, & 1, & 0 \\ 0, & 0, & 1 \end{array}\right)$$

and this is said to be the matrix unity. We may of course, when for distinctness it is

required, say, the matrix zero, or (as the case may be) the matrix unity *of such an order*
The matrix zero may for the most part be represented simply by 0, and the matrix
unity by 1.

$$[\ldots]$$

21. The general theorem before referred to will be best understood by a complete
development of a particular case. Imagine a matrix

$$M = \left(\begin{array}{cc} a, & b \\ c, & d \end{array}\right),$$

and form the determinant

$$\left|\begin{array}{cc} a - M, & b \\ c, & d - M \end{array}\right|,$$

the developed expression of this determinant is

$$M^2 - (a+d)M^1 + (ad - bc)M^0;$$

the values of $M^2$, $M^1$, $M^0$ are

$$\left(\begin{array}{cc} a^2 + bc, & b(a+d) \\ c(a+d), & d^2 + bc \end{array}\right), \quad \left(\begin{array}{cc} a, & b \\ c, & d \end{array}\right), \quad \left(\begin{array}{cc} 1, & 0 \\ 0, & 1 \end{array}\right)$$

and substituting these values the determinant becomes equal to the matrix zero, viz. we
have

$$\left|\begin{array}{cc} a - M, & b \\ c, & d - M \end{array}\right| = \left(\begin{array}{cc} a^2 + bc, & b(a+d) \\ c(a+d), & d^2 + bc \end{array}\right) - (a+d)\left(\begin{array}{cc} a, & b \\ c, & d \end{array}\right) + (ad - bc)\left(\begin{array}{cc} 1, & 0 \\ 0, & 1 \end{array}\right)$$

$$= \left(\begin{array}{cc} (a^2 + bc) - (a+d)a + (ad - bc), & b(a+d) - (a+d)b \\ c(a+d) - (a+d)c, & d^2 + bc - (a+d)d + ad - bc \end{array}\right) = \left(\begin{array}{cc} 0, & 0 \\ 0, & 0 \end{array}\right),$$

that is,

$$\left|\begin{array}{cc} a - M, & b \\ c, & d - M \end{array}\right| = 0$$

where the matrix of the determinant is

$$\left(\begin{array}{cc} a, & b \\ c, & d \end{array}\right) - M\left(\begin{array}{cc} 1, & 0 \\ 0, & 1 \end{array}\right),$$

that is, it is the original matrix, diminished by the same matrix considered as a single quantity involving the matrix unity. And this is the general theorem, viz. the determinant, having for its matrix a given matrix less the same matrix considered as a single quantity involving the matrix unity, is equal to zero.

22. The following symbolical representation of the theorem is, I think, worth noticing: let the matrix M, considered as a single quantity, be represented by $\tilde{\text{M}}$, then writing 1 to denote the matrix unity, $\tilde{\text{M}}.1$ will represent the matrix M, considered as a single quantity involving the matrix unity. Upon the like principles of notation, $\tilde{1}.\text{M}$ will represent, or may be considered as representing, simply the matrix M, and the theorem is

$$\text{Det.} \; (\tilde{1}.\text{M} - \tilde{\text{M}}.1) = 0.$$

23. I have verified the theorem, in the next simplest case, of a matrix of the order 3, viz. if M be such a matrix, suppose

$$\text{M} = \left(\begin{array}{ccc} a, & b, & c \\ d, & e, & f \\ g, & h, & i \end{array}\right),$$

then the derived determinant vanishes, or we have

$$\left|\begin{array}{ccc} a-\text{M}, & b & , c \\ d & , & e-\text{M}, f \\ g & , & h & , i-\text{M} \end{array}\right| = 0,$$

or expanding,

$$\text{M}^3 - (a+e+i)\text{M}^2 + (ei+ia+ae-fh-cg-bd)\text{M} - (aei+bfg+cdh-afh-bdi-ceg) = 0;$$

but I have not thought it necessary to undertake the labour of a formal proof of the theorem in the general case of a matrix of any degree.

## 17.3.3   Frobenius and bilinear forms, 1878

Cayley's paper of 1858 opened up two important areas that Cayley himself only touched upon: the question of which matrices commute with a given matrix; and the Cayley–Hamilton theorem. The problem of commutativity was taken up by Jordan ten years later in the context of group theory and the commutativity of linear substitutions, and Jordan consequently discovered the canonical forms that are now named after him. Thus for Jordan, as earlier for Gauss, a result that arose in the first place from investigation of linear substitutions later became subsumed into matrix algebra

Cayley's second piece of unfinished business, a proof of the Cayley–Hamilton theorem, was completed in 1878 by Frobenius in a long and important paper entitled 'Über lineare Substitutionen und bilineare Formen' ('On linear substitutions and bilinear forms') and, as the title indicates, Frobenius too was working in the continental tradition of investigating linear substitutions. For Frobenius, a bilinear form $A$, in $2n$ variables $x_1, \ldots, x_n, y_1, \ldots, y_n$, was defined as

$$A = \sum_{i,j} a_{i,j} x_i y_j$$

where the $a_{i,j}$ are real or complex coefficients. In his 1878 paper he defined the product of two forms $A = \sum a_{i,j} x_i y_j$ and $B = \sum b_{i,j} x_i y_j$ as

$$AB = \sum_{\chi=1}^{n} \frac{\partial A}{\partial y_\chi} \frac{\partial B}{\partial x_\chi},$$

a definition that is exactly equivalent to multiplication of the matrix $A = (a_{i,j})$ by $B = (b_{i,j})$.

From this starting point, Frobenius extended the contemporary theory of linear transformations by defining, for example, *equivalent, similar,* and *congruent* forms, and *orthogonal* transformations. Thus, much of the later language and theory of matrices is to be found in his 1878 paper, but all of it expressed in terms of bilinear forms and transformations; there is no matrix, in the Cayleian sense of a rectangular array, anywhere in sight.

---

### Frobenuis and bilinear forms

from Frobenius, 'Über lineare Substitutionen und bilineare Formen', *Journal für die reine und angewandte Mathematik*, 84 (1878), 2–4

---

#### §. 1. Multiplication.

1.  Sind $A$ und $B$ zwei bilineare Formen der Variabeln $x_1, \ldots x_n$; $y_1, \ldots y_n$, so ist auch

$$P = \Sigma_1^n \frac{\partial A}{\partial y_\varkappa} \frac{\partial B}{\partial x_\varkappa}$$

eine bilineare Form derselben Variabeln. Dieselbe nenne ich aus den Formen $A$ und $B$ (in dieser Reihenfolge) *zusammengesetzt**). Es werden im Folgenden nur solche Operationen mit bilinearen Formen vorgenommen, bei welchen sie bilineare Formen bleiben****). Ich werde z. B. eine Form mit einer Constanten (von $x_1, y_1; \ldots x_n, y_n$ unabhängigen Grösse) multipliciren, zwei Formen addiren, eine Form, deren Coefficienten von einem Parameter abhängen, nach demselben differentiiren. Ich werde aber nicht zwei Formen mit einander multipliciren. Aus diesem Grunde kann kein Missverständniss entstehen, wenn ich die aus $A$ und $B$ zusammengesetzte Form $P$ mit

$$AB = \Sigma \frac{\partial A}{\partial y_\varkappa} \frac{\partial B}{\partial x_\varkappa}$$

bezeichne, und sie das *Product* der Formen $A$ und $B$, diese die *Factoren* von $P$ nenne. Für diese Bildung gilt

$\alpha$) das *distributive* Gesetz:

$$A(B+C) = AB + AC, \quad (A+B)C = AC + BC,$$
$$(A+B)(C+D) = AC + BC + AD + BD.$$

Sind $a$ und $b$ Constanten, so ist

$$(aA)B = A(aB) = a(AB),$$
$$(aA + bB)C = aAC + bBC.$$

$\beta$) das *associative* Gesetz:

$$(AB)C = A(BC),$$

daher diese Bildung kurz mit $ABC$ bezeichnet werden kann. Denn $AB$ entsteht, indem in $A$ die Variabeln $y_\varkappa$ durch $\dfrac{\partial B}{\partial x_\varkappa}$, lineare Functionen von $y_1, \ldots y_n$, ersetzt werden, oder indem in $B$ die Variabeln $x_\varkappa$ durch $\dfrac{\partial A}{\partial y_\varkappa}$, lineare Functionen von $x_1, \ldots x_n$, ersetzt werden. Die Form $(AB)C$ wird also gebildet, indem in $B$ erst die Variabeln $x_\varkappa$ durch die linearen Functionen $\dfrac{\partial A}{\partial y_\varkappa}$ von $x_1, \ldots x_n$ und dann die Variabeln $y_\varkappa$ durch die linearen Functionen $\dfrac{\partial C}{\partial x_\varkappa}$ von $y_1, \ldots y_n$ ersetzt werden. Die Reihenfolge dieser beiden Substitutionen ist aber offenbar gleichgültig.

$\gamma$) es gilt aber nicht allgemein das *commutative* Gesetz. Die Formen $AB$ und $BA$ sind im allgemeinen von einander verschieden. Ist $AB = BA$, so heissen die Formen $A$ und $B$ mit einander *vertauschbar*. Aus dem distributiven Gesetze folgt:

I. *Ist jede der Formen $A$, $B$, $C$, ... mit jeder der Formen $P$, $Q$, $R$, ... vertauschbar, so ist auch die Form $aA + bB + cC + \cdots$ mit der Form $pP + qQ + rR + \cdots$ vertauschbar.*

Sind ferner $B$ und $C$ beide mit $A$ vertauschbar, so folgt aus dem associativen Gesetze

$$A(BC) = (AB)C = (BA)C = B(AC) = B(CA) = (BC)A,$$

es ist also auch $BC$ mit $A$ vertauschbar. (Dies ist ein specieller Fall des *Jacobi-Poisson*schen Satzes aus der Theorie der partiellen Differentialgleichungen erster Ordnung.) Durch wiederholte Anwendung folgt daraus:

II. *Ist jede Form einer Reihe mit jeder Form einer anderen Reihe vertauschbar, so ist auch jede aus den Formen der ersten Reihe zusammengesetzte Form mit jeder aus denen der anderen Reihe zusammengesetzten vertauschbar.*

Eine Form, welche aus mehreren Formen durch die Operationen der Zusammensetzung, Multiplication mit constanten Coefficienten und Ad-

1*

4          *Frobenius, über lineare Substitutionen und bilineare Formen.*

dition (in endlicher Anzahl) gebildet ist, soll eine *ganze Function* jener
Formen genannt werden. Aus den obigen Sätzen folgt dann:

III. *Ist jede Form einer Reihe mit jeder Form einer anderen Reihe*
*vertauschbar, so ist auch jede ganze Function der Formen der ersten Reihe*
*mit jeder ganzen Function der Formen der anderen Reihe vertauschbar.*

2. Die Form, welche aus $A$ entsteht, indem die Variabeln $x_1, \ldots x_n$
mit $y_1, \ldots y_n$ vertauscht werden, heisst die *conjugirte Form* von $A$ (*Jacobi*,
dieses Journal Bd. 53, S. 265) und wird im Folgenden stets mit $A'$ bezeichnet werden. Die conjugirte Form von $aA$ ist $aA'$, die von $A + B$ ist
$A' + B'$. Die conjugirte Form von

ist

$$AB = \Sigma \frac{\partial A}{\partial y_\varkappa} \frac{\partial B}{\partial x_\varkappa}$$

$$\Sigma \frac{\partial A'}{\partial x_\varkappa} \frac{\partial B'}{\partial y_\varkappa} = B'A'.$$

IV. *Ist eine Form aus mehreren zusammengesetzt, so ist die conju-*
*girte Form aus den conjugirten in der umgekehrten Reihenfolge zusammen-*
*gesetzt.*

Ist $A$ mit $B$ vertauschbar, so ist daher auch $A'$ mit $B'$ vertauschbar.
Denn nimmt man in der Gleichung $AB = BA$ auf beiden Seiten die conjugirten Formen, so erhält man $B'A' = A'B'$.

Eine Form heisst *symmetrisch*, wenn sie ihrer conjugirten gleich ist,
*alternirend,* wenn sie ihr entgegengesetzt gleich ist. Jede Form kann, und
zwar nur in einer Weise, als Summe einer symmetrischen und einer alter-
nirenden Form dargestellt werden. Denn ist $A = S + T$, wo $S$ symmetrisch
und $T$ alternirend ist, so ist $A' = S - T$, und daher $S = \frac{1}{2}(A + A')$, $T = \frac{1}{2}(A - A')$.

Die Form $A'A$ ist nach Satz II. symmetrisch. Der Coefficient von
$x_\alpha y_\alpha$ in derselben ist $a_{1\alpha}^2 + a_{2\alpha}^2 + \cdots + a_{n\alpha}^2$. Sind daher die Coefficienten von
$A$ reell, so kann $A'A$ nur dann identisch verschwinden, wenn $A$ Null ist.
Sind allgemeiner die entsprechenden Coefficienten $a_{\alpha\beta}$ und $b_{\alpha\beta}$ der Formen
$A$ und $B$ conjugirte complexe Grössen, so kann $AB'$ nur verschwinden,
wenn $A$ Null ist. Denn der Coefficient von $x_\alpha y_\alpha$ ist in dieser Form
$a_{\alpha 1} b_{\alpha 1} + a_{\alpha 2} b_{\alpha 2} + \cdots + a_{\alpha n} b_{\alpha n}$.

3. Die Gleichung $P = AB$ ist eine symbolische Zusammenfassung
der $n^2$ Gleichungen

$$p_{\alpha\beta} = \underset{\varkappa}{\Sigma} a_{\alpha\varkappa} b_{\varkappa\beta} \quad (\alpha, \beta = 1, 2, \ldots n).$$

## §. 1. Multiplication.

1. If $A$ and $B$ are two bilinear forms in variables $x_1, x_2, \ldots x_n$; $y_1, y_2, \ldots y_n$, then

$$P = \sum_{1}^{n} \frac{\partial A}{\partial y_\chi} \frac{\partial B}{\partial x_\chi}$$

is also a bilinear form in the same variables. This I call the *composition* of the forms $A$ and $B$ (in this order). In what follows only such operations with bilinear forms will be considered, under which they remain bilinear forms. I will, for example, multiply a form by a constant (a quantity independent of $x_1, y_1; \ldots x_n, y_n$), add two forms, or differentiate a form whose coefficients depend on a parameter, with respect to that. But I will not multiply two forms with one another. For this reason there can arise no misunderstanding, if I denote the form $P$ composed from $A$ and $B$ as

$$AB = \sum_{1}^{n} \frac{\partial A}{\partial y_\chi} \frac{\partial B}{\partial x_\chi},$$

and call it the *product* of forms $A$ and $B$, and call them the *factors* of $P$. For this construct there hold

$\alpha$) the *distributive* law:

$$A(B + C) = AB + AC, \quad (A + B)C = AC + BC,$$

$$(A + B)(C + D) = AC + BC + AD + BD.$$

[3] If $a$ and $b$ are constants; then

$$(aA)B = A(aB) = a(AB),$$

$$(aA + bB)C = aAC + bBC.$$

$\beta$) the *associative* law:

$$(AB)C = A(BC),$$

so this construct can be described for short as $ABC$. Then $AB$ arises from $A$ by replacing the variables $y_\chi$ by $\dfrac{\partial B}{\partial x_\chi}$, linear functions in $y_1, y_2, \ldots y_n$, or from $B$ by replacing the variables $x_\chi$ by $\dfrac{\partial A}{\partial y_\chi}$, linear functions in $x_1, x_2, \ldots x_n$. Thus the form $(AB)C$ will be constructed by replacing in $B$ first the variables $x_\chi$ by $\dfrac{\partial A}{\partial y_\chi}$, linear functions in $x_1, x_2, \ldots x_n$, and then the variables $y_\chi$ by $\dfrac{\partial C}{\partial x_\chi}$, linear functions in $y_1, y_2, \ldots y_n$. The order of these two substitutions, however, is clearly immaterial.

$\gamma$) but there does not hold in general the *commutative* law. The forms $AB$ and $BA$ are in general different from each other. If $AB = BA$, the forms $A$ and $B$ are said to be *exchangeable* with each other. From the distributive law there follows:

I. *If each form $A$, $B$, $C$, ...is exchangeable with each of the forms $P$, $Q$, $R$, ..., then the form $aA + bB + cC + ...$ is also exchangeable with the form $pP + qQ + rR + ...$.*

Further if $B$ and $C$ are both exchangeable with $A$, then it follows from the associative law that

$$A(BC) = (AB)C = (BA)C = B(AC) = B(CA) = (BC)A,$$

so that $BC$ is also exchangeable with $A$. (This is a special case of the *Jacobi–Poisson* law from the theory of partial differential equations of the first order.) By repeated application there follows from this:

II. *If each form of a sequence is exchangeable with each form of another sequence, then each form composed of forms from the first sequence is also exchangeable with each composed of those from the second sequence.*

A form which is constructed from a number of forms by the operations (finite in number) of composition, multiplication with constant coefficients, and [4] addition, shall be called a *complete function* of these forms. From the above theorems there then follows:

III. *If each form of a sequence is exchangeable with each form of another sequence, then each complete function of forms from the first sequence is also exchangeable with each complete function of forms from the second sequence.*

2. The form, which arises from $A$, by exchanging the variables $x_1, \ldots x_n$ and $y_1, \ldots y_n$, is called the *conjugate form* of $A$ (*Jacobi*, this Journal, Vol. 53, p. 265) and in what follows will always be denoted by $A'$. The conjugate form of $aA$ is $aA'$, that of $A + B$ is $A' + B'$. The conjugate form of

$$AB = \sum \frac{\partial A}{\partial y_\chi} \frac{\partial B}{\partial x_\chi}$$

is

$$\sum \frac{\partial A'}{\partial x_\chi} \frac{\partial B'}{\partial y_\chi} = B'A'.$$

IV. *If a form is composed from several forms, then the conjugate form is composed from the conjugates in the reverse order.*

If $A$ is exchangeable with $B$, then $A'$ is also exchangeable with $B'$. For if one takes the conjugate form of both sides of the equation $AB = BA$, one has $B'A' = A'B'$.

A form is called *symmetric* if it is equal to its conjugate, *alternating* if it is equal to its opposite. Each form can be represented, and indeed in only one way, as the sum of a symmetric and an alternating form. For if $A = S + T$, where $S$ is symmetric and $T$ is alternating, then $A' = S - T$, and therefore $S = \frac{1}{2}(A + A')$, $T = \frac{1}{2}(A - A')$.

The form $A'A$ is symmetric by Theorem II. The coefficient of $x_\alpha y_\alpha$ in this is $a_{1\alpha}^2 + a_{2\alpha}^2 + \cdots + a_{n\alpha}^2$. If, therefore the coefficients of $A$ are real, then $A'A$ can vanish identically only if $A$ is null. More generally if the corresponding coefficients $a_{\alpha\beta}$ and $b_{\alpha\beta}$ of forms $A$ and $B$ are conjugate complex numbers, then $AB'$ can vanish only if $A$ is null. For the coefficient of $x_\alpha y_\alpha$ in this form is $a_{\alpha1}b_{\alpha1} + a_{\alpha2}b_{\alpha2} + \cdots + a_{\alpha n}b_{\alpha n}$.

3. The equation $P = AB$ is a symbolic summary of the $n^2$ equations

$$p_{\alpha\beta} = \sum_\chi a_{\alpha\chi} b_{\chi\beta} \quad (\alpha, \beta = 1, 2, \ldots n).$$

---

## 17.4 VECTORS AND VECTOR SPACES

### 17.4.1 Grassmann and vector spaces, 1862

The parallelogram law for the addition of forces first appeared in 1687 in Newton's *Principia*, as the first Corollary to the three laws of motion. By the early nineteenth century the mathematics of quantities that have both magnitude and direction was well understood, and complex numbers had joined physical entities like force or velocity as examples of such quantities (see, for example, Argand's treatment of complex numbers in 15.1.2). The more abstract concept of a vector space, whose elements need not be vectors in the traditional sense, emerged only gradually during the later part of the nineteenth century, and like so much else in linear algebra was not at first explicitly recognized. Dedekind's finite fields, for example, were finite dimensional vector spaces over $\mathbb{Q}$ complete with a specified basis (see 13.2.3).

The earliest examples of vector spaces are to be found in the work of Hermann Grassmann from the 1840s onwards. Grassmann was born in Stettin (now Szczecin in Poland) in 1809 and studied theology at the University of Berlin but was largely self-taught in mathematics and physics. In 1844 he wrote a treatise entitled *Ausdehnungslehre* (*Extension theory*) in which he put forward the idea of linear spaces generated by moving elements: an element (intuitively a point) generates an object of order 1 (a line), an object of order 1 generates an object of order 2 (a plane), and so on. Objects of the same order can be added to each other, or multiplied by real numbers. The *Ausdehnungslehre* contained the first seeds of the idea of a vector space, but the book made little or no immediate impression. In 1862 Grassmann produced a new and almost entirely reworked edition, and now he defined 'extensive quantities' $\alpha_1 e_1 + \alpha_2 e_2 + \ldots$ composed from 'units' $e_1$, $e_2$, $e_3$, …and real numbers $\alpha_1$, $\alpha_2$, …. The book also dealt with ideas of linear independence, subspaces, and dimension. It still had little impact, not least, perhaps, because of the obscurity of his writing, and it was not read seriously until after Grassmann himself had died.

In 1888 the *Ausdehnungslehre* was axiomatized by Giuseppe Peano, and at that stage the material was brought into a form very similar to that taught to students today, but it was not until the twentieth century that the importance of the concept of a vector space became more generally recognized.

## Grassman's extension theory
from Grassman, *Die Ausdehnungslehre*, 1862, 2–3, 4, 7–8

---

**3. Erklärung.** Einheit nenne ich jede Grösse, welche dazu dienen soll, um aus ihr eine Reihe von Grössen numerisch abzuleiten, und zwar nenne ich die Einheit eine ursprüngliche, wenn sie nicht aus einer anderen Einheit abgeleitet ist. Die Einheit der Zahlen, also die Eins, nenne ich die absolute Einheit, alle übrigen relative. Null soll nie als Einheit gelten.

**4. Erklärung.** Ein System von Einheiten nenne ich jeden Verein von Grössen, welche in keiner Zahlbeziehung zu einander stehen, und welche dazu dienen sollen, um aus ihnen durch beliebige Zahlen andere Grössen abzuleiten.

Anmerk. Hierher gehört auch der Fall, wo der Verein nur aus einer Einheit besteht (die jedoch nach Nr. 3 nicht null sein darf).

**5. Erklärung.** Extensive Grösse nenne ich jeden Ausdruck, welcher aus einem Systeme von Einheiten (welches sich jedoch nicht auf die absolute Einheit beschränkt) durch Zahlen abgeleitet ist, und zwar nenne ich diese Zahlen die zu den Einheiten gehörigen Ableitungszahlen jener Grösse; z. B. ist das Polynom

$$\alpha_1 e_1 + \alpha_2 e_2 + \cdots, \text{ oder} \sum \alpha e \text{ oder} \sum \alpha_r e_r$$

wenn $a_1$, $a_2$, $\cdots$ reelle Zahlen sind, und $e_1$, $e_2$, $\cdots$ ein System von Einheiten bilden, eine extensive Grösse, und zwar ist dieselbe aus den Einheiten $e_1$, $e_2$, $\cdots$ durch die zugehörigen Zahlen $\alpha_1$, $\alpha_2$, $\cdots$ abgeleitet. Nur wenn das System blos aus der absoluten Einheit (1) besteht, ist die abgeleitete Grösse keine extensive, sondern eine Zahlgrösse. Den Ausdruck Grösse überhaupt werde ich nur für diese beiden Gattungen derselben festhalten. Wenn die extensive Grösse aus den ursprünglichen Einheiten abgeleitet werden kann, so nenne ich jene Grösse eine extensive Grösse erster Stufe.

**8)**                                                                   **3**

Anmerk. Aus der Elementarmathematik setzen wir die Rechnungsgesetze für Zahlen, und auch für die sogenannten „benannten Zahlen", d. h. für die aus Einer Einheit abgeleiteten extensiven Grössen voraus; jedoch nur für den Fall, dass jene Einheit eine ursprüngliche ist.

**6.** Erklärung. Zwei extensive Grössen, die aus demselben System von Einheiten abgeleitet sind, addiren, heisst, ihre zu denselben Einheiten gehörigen Ableitungszahlen addiren, d. h.

$$\sum \overline{\alpha e} + \sum \overline{\beta e} = \sum \overline{(\alpha + \beta) \, e}$$

[...]

**10.** Erklärung. Eine extensive Grösse mit einer Zahl multipliciren heisst ihre sämmtlichen Ableitungszahlen mit dieser Zahl multipliciren, d. h.

$$\sum \overline{\alpha e} \cdot \beta = \beta \cdot \sum \overline{\alpha e} = \sum \overline{(\alpha \beta) \cdot e}$$

**11.** Erklärung.| Eine extensive Grösse durch eine Zahl, die nicht gleich null ist, dividiren, heisst ihre sämmtlichen Ableitungszahlen durch diese Zahl dividiren, d. h.

$$\sum \overline{\alpha e} : \beta = \sum \overline{\frac{\alpha}{\beta} \, e}$$

**12.** Für die Multiplikation und Division extensiver Grössen (a, b) durch Zahlen (β, γ) gelten die Fundamentalformeln:

1) $a\beta = \beta a$,

2) $a\beta\gamma = a(\beta\gamma)$,

3) $(a + b)\gamma = a\gamma + b\gamma$,

4) $a(\beta + \gamma) = a\beta + a\gamma$,

5) $a \cdot 1 = a$,

6) $a\beta = 0$ dann und nur dann, wenn entweder $a = 0$, oder $\beta = 0$,

7) $a : \beta = a \, \frac{1}{\beta}$, wenn $\beta \gtrless 0$ ist *).

Beweis. Es sei $a = \sum \overline{\alpha e}$, $b = \sum \overline{\beta e}$, wo die Summe sich auf das System der Einheiten $e_1 \ldots e_n$ bezieht, so ist

---

*) Das Zeichen $\gtrless$ zusammengesetzt aus $\gtr$ und $\lt$ soll ungleich bedeuten.

[...]

**16.** Erklärung. Zwischen n Grössen $a_1, \cdots a_n$ herrscht dann und nur dann eine Zahlbeziehung, wenn sich eine Gleichung

$$\alpha_1 \; a_1 + \cdots \alpha_n a_n = 0$$

aufstellen lässt, in welcher die Zahlen $\alpha_1, \ldots \alpha_n$ nicht alle zugleich null sind.

Beweis. Denn wenn in der Gleichung

$$\alpha_1 \; a_1 + \cdots \alpha_n a_n = 0$$

auch nur Eine der Zahlen $\alpha_1, \cdots \alpha_n$ von null verschieden ist, z. B. $\alpha_1$, so ist die mit dieser Zahl verbundene Grösse $a_1$ aus den übrigen numerisch ableitbar; denn dann ist

$$a_1 = - \frac{\alpha_2}{\alpha_1} a_2 - \frac{\alpha_3}{\alpha_1} a_3 - \cdots - \frac{\alpha_n}{a_1} a_n.$$

Umgekehrt, wenn irgend eine Zahlbeziehung zwischen den Grössen $a_1 \cdots a_n$ herrscht, z. B.

$$a_1 = \beta_2 a_2 + \beta_3 a_3 + \cdots \beta_n a_n$$

so wird

$$- a_1 + \beta_2 a_2 + \beta_3 a_3 + \cdots + \beta_n a_n = 0,$$

8                                                                (1 7

eine Gleichung, in welcher wenigstens der Koefficient von $a_1$ ungleich null ist.

3. *Explanation.* I call a *unit* any quantity that will serve for the purpose that from it there is derived a sequence of numerical [multiples of] quantities, and indeed I call the unit a *primitive unit* if it is not derived from another unit. The unit of numbers, that is, one, I call the *absolute* unit, all others *relative.* Zero must never serve as a unit.

4. *Explanation.* I call a *system of units* any collection of quantities, which stand in no numerical relation to one another, and which serve the purpose that from them other quantities are derived by means of arbitrary numbers.

Note. Here belongs also the case where the collection consists of only a single unit (which however according to No. 3 may not be zero).

5. *Explanation.* I call an *extensive quantity* any expression which is derived from a system of units (not restricted to the absolute unit) by means of numbers, and indeed I call the numbers that belong to the units the *derivation numbers* of that quantity; for example, the polynomial

$$\alpha_1 e_1 + \alpha_2 e_2 + \ldots, \quad \text{or} \quad \sum \alpha e \quad \text{or} \quad \sum \alpha_r e_r,$$

is an extensive quantity if $\alpha_1, \alpha_2, \ldots$are real numbers, and $e_1, e_2, \ldots$form a system of units, and indeed is the one derived from the units $e_1, e_2, \ldots$by means of the numbers $\alpha_1, \alpha_2, \ldots$belonging to them. Only if the system consists merely of the absolute unit (1), is the derived quantity not an *extensive* quantity, but a numerical quantity. In general I will keep to the expression quantity only for these two kinds. If the extensive quantity can be derived from the primitive units, then I call that quantity an extensive quantity of the *first level*.

[3] Note. From elementary mathematics we fix the rules of calculation for numbers, and also for the so-called 'named numbers', that is, for extensive quantities derived from a single unit; but only for the case that that unit is a primitive unit.

**6.** *Explanation.* To *add* two extensive quantities, derived from the same system of units, means to add the derivation numbers belonging to the same units, that is,

$$\sum \overline{\alpha e} + \sum \overline{\beta e} = \sum \overline{(\alpha + \beta)e}$$

[...]

There follows a similar definition of subtraction and proofs, from the definitions, of fundamental identities such as $a + b = b + a, a + b - b = a$, and so on.

[...]

[4] **10.** *Explanation.* To *multiply* an extensive quantity by a number means to multiply all its derivation numbers by that number, that is,

$$\sum \overline{\alpha e}.\beta = \beta. \sum \overline{\alpha e} = \sum \overline{(\alpha\beta).e}$$

**11.** *Explanation.* To *divide* an extensive quantity by a number that is not equal to zero, means to divide all its derivation numbers by this number, that is,

$$\sum \overline{\alpha e} : \beta = \sum \overline{\frac{\alpha}{\beta}e}$$

**12.** For the multiplication and division of extensive quantities $(a, b)$ by numbers $(\beta, \gamma)$ there hold the fundamental formulas:

1)    $\alpha\beta = \beta\alpha,$
2)    $\alpha\beta\gamma = \alpha(\beta\gamma),$
3)    $(a + b)\gamma = a\gamma + b\gamma,$
4)    $a(\beta + \gamma) = a\beta + a\gamma,$
5)    $a.1 = a$
6)    $a\beta = 0$    if and only if either $a = 0$, or $\beta = 0$,
7)    $\alpha : \beta = \alpha\frac{1}{\beta}$    if    $\beta > < 0.$ *)

*) The symbol $> <$ combined from $>$ and $<$ shall mean unequal.

[...]

[7] **16.** *Explanation.* Between $n$ quantities $a_1, \ldots a_n$ there holds a numerical relation if and only if an equation

$$\alpha_1 a_1 + \ldots \alpha_n a_n = 0$$

can be established in which the numbers $\alpha_1, \ldots \alpha_n$ are not all equal to zero at the same time.

*Proof.* For if in the equation

$$\alpha_1 a_1 + \ldots \alpha_n a_n = 0$$

even just one of the numbers $\alpha_1, \ldots \alpha_n$ is different from zero, for example, $\alpha_1$, then the quantity $a_1$ linked to this number is numerically derivable from the rest; for then

$$a_1 = -\frac{\alpha_2}{\alpha_1} a_2 - \frac{\alpha_3}{\alpha_1} a_3 - \cdots - \frac{\alpha_n}{[\alpha_1]} a_n.$$

Conversely, if any numerical relation holds between the quantities $a_1, \ldots a_n$, for example,

$$a_1 = \beta_2 a_2 + \beta_3 a_3 + \ldots \beta_n a_n,$$

then

$$-a_1 + \beta_2 a_2 + \beta_3 a_3 + \cdots + \beta_n a_n = 0,$$

[8] an equation in which at least the coefficient of $a_1$ is not equal to zero.

———————

# CHAPTER 18

# FOUNDATIONS

I t should give some pause for thought that a chapter entitled 'Foundations' comes so long after a chapter entitled 'Beginnings'. The first chapter of this book and the last, however, are in several ways closely related. Here at the end we will encounter once again the same topics that we met at the start: geometry, arithmetic, and the natural numbers, and again reduced to their most elementary forms. 'Elementary' is used here not in its colloquial sense of 'simple' or 'easy', but in a more literal sense (as in Euclid's *Elements*) of basic or fundamental, for in this present chapter we will see a renewed interest in the building blocks of mathematics: numbers, points, lines, and surfaces.

By the end of the nineteenth century it was clear that these objects can only be properly understood in terms of the relationships, assumed or derived, that hold between them. Hence we see also a revived concern with axioms and the mathematics that can be deduced from them, ancient ideas now appearing in a very new guise.

## 18.1 FOUNDATIONS OF GEOMETRY

Euclid's *Elements* is the earliest surviving attempt to deduce geometric truths from basic definitions, postulates, and axioms. *Definitions* described the basic concepts (points, lines, surfaces, numbers); *postulates* laid down what one was allowed to do (draw a line between two points, construct a circle with a given radius, etc.); while *axioms* were little more than self-evident truths (equal things added to equal things produce equal results; the whole is greater than its parts, etc.). From these Euclid was able to derive a series of increasingly sophisticated propositions, each using only those that had previously been proved.

This strict deductive method was by no means always followed by later writers, but it was always upheld as an ideal, not least because it guaranteed the indisputable truth of mathematics. Almost two thousand years after the compilation of the *Elements*, Newton's *Principia* was written in Euclidean style, but was one of the last examples of the genre in the early modern period because by then mathematics was rapidly running beyond classical constraints. During the eighteenth century every attempt to establish mathematics on rigorous logical foundations foundered on the treacherous rock of infinitely small quantities. At the time it hardly mattered: new and fertile ideas were emerging so fast that their authors did not trouble themselves too much about logical coherence. All the same, there were voices of caution, as we have seen in 10.2, from those who feared that mathematics was being constructed on the flimsiest of foundations.

Worse still, Euclid's *Elements*, which had for so long been one of the mainstays of European mathematics, itself came under increasing scrutiny. One postulate in particular had raised fundamental questions since the fifth century onwards. This was the fifth postulate of Book I, which states that two lines crossing a given line will meet on the side where the sum of the interior angles is less than two right angles. This can be rephrased in several equivalent forms, one of which is that the angle sum of a triangle is 180°. Another is that through any point there is one and only one line parallel to a given line (so that the postulate is commonly known as the 'parallel postulate').

As early as 450 AD Proclus had argued that the parallel postulate should be a theorem rather than a postulate, but repeated attempts over several centuries to prove it from the other axioms had all failed. Barrow in 1660 avoided the problem by upgrading the postulate to an axiom (see 1.2.1), thus treating it as a more or less self-evident truth. A hundred years later Johann Heinrich Lambert tried replacing it by an alternative axiom, namely that the angle sum of a triangle is *less* than 180°, hoping that this would lead to some inconsistency, but found none. This did not prevent several further attempts to prove the parallel postulate, but by the end of the eighteenth century it was under severe strain. During the nineteenth century it finally came to be recognized that the axioms of mathematics are not necessarily either fixed or obvious, but may be arbitrarily chosen, provided only that they do not lead to contradiction. So much for the indisputable truth of mathematics.

## 18.1.1 Hilbert's axiomatization of geometry, 1899

The discovery of geometries that are non-Euclidean was one of the motivations behind a new interest in the selection and statement of axioms, and by the end of the nineteenth century several branches of mathematics, not just geometry, had been placed on an axiomatic foundations. In 1882, for example, Heinrich Weber gave the following set of axioms for finite groups:[1]

*Definition.* A system $G$ of $h$ elements $\Theta_1, \Theta_2, \ldots, \Theta_h$ of whatever kind, is called a *group of degree h*, if it satisfies the following conditions:
I. By some rule, which we will call composition or multiplication, one may derive from two elements of the system a new element of the same systems. In symbols

$$\Theta_r \Theta_s = \Theta_t.$$

II. Always

$$(\Theta_r \Theta_s)\Theta_t = \Theta_r(\Theta_s \Theta_t) = \Theta_r \Theta_s \Theta_t.$$

III. From $\Theta\Theta_r = \Theta\Theta_s$ and from $\Theta_r\Theta = \Theta_s\Theta$ it follows that $\Theta_r = \Theta_s$.

Six years later, in 1888, Guiseppe Peano axiomatized what he called the 'geometric calculus' of Grassmann (see 17.4.1), and Dedekind's axioms for the natural numbers (see 18.2.2) also appeared that same year.

The prime example of a nineteenth-century axiomatic system, however, must be David Hilbert's re-axiomatization of Euclidean geometry itself, something that had by now come to be seen as essential to remove flaws and obscurities in the *Elements*. The first edition of Hilbert's *Grundlagen der Geometrie* (*Foundations of geometry*) was published in 1899, though the text went through many subsequent revisions and editions. Hilbert described certain objects $A$, $B$, $C$, …as points (*Punkte*); $a$, $b$, $c$, …as lines (*Geraden*); and $\alpha$, $\beta$, $\gamma$, …as planes (*Ebenen*); but unlike Euclid he did not attempt to define these things any further. Indeed, to rid the mind of any preconceptions Hilbert suggested that they could just as well be called 'chairs', 'tables', and 'beer mugs'. The only properties we may be certain of are those derived from the axioms themselves.

---

1. '*Definition.* Ein System $G$ von $h$ Elementen irgend welcher Art, $\Theta_1, \Theta_2, \ldots, \Theta_h$ heisst eine *Gruppe vom Grade h*, wenn es den folgenden Bedingungen genügt:
   I. Durch irgend eine Vorschrift, welche als Composition oder Multiplication bezeichnet wird, leite man aus zwei Elementen des Systems ein neues Element desselben Systems her. In zeichen

$$\Theta_r \Theta_s = \Theta_t.$$

   II. Es ist stets
$$(\Theta_r \Theta_s)\Theta_t = \Theta_r(\Theta_s \Theta_t) = \Theta_r \Theta_s \Theta_t.$$

   III. Aus $\Theta\Theta_r = \Theta\Theta_s$ und aus $\Theta_r\Theta = \Theta_s\Theta$ folgt $\Theta_r = \Theta_s$.'
Weber 1882, 301.

## Hilbert's geometric axioms

from Hilbert, *Grundlagen der Geometrie*, 1899, 4–7

### Kapitel I.

## Die fünf Axiomgruppen.

### § 1.

#### Die Elemente der Geometrie und die fünf Axiomgruppen.

Erklärung. Wir denken drei verschiedene Systeme von Dingen: die Dinge des ersten Systems nennen wir *Punkte* und bezeichnen sie mit *A, B, C, ...*; die Dinge des zweiten Systems nennen wir *Gerade* und bezeichnen sie mit *a, b, c, ...*; die Dinge des dritten Systems nennen wir *Ebenen* und bezeichnen sie mit *α, β, γ, ...*; die Punkte heissen auch die *Elemente der linearen Geometrie*, die Punkte und Geraden heissen die *Elemente der ebenen Geometrie* und die Punkte, Geraden und Ebenen heissen die *Elemente der räumlichen Geometrie* oder *des Raumes*.

Wir denken die Punkte, Geraden, Ebenen in gewissen gegenseitigen Beziehungen und bezeichnen diese Beziehungen durch Worte wie „liegen", „zwischen", „parallel", „congruent", „stetig"; die genaue und vollstandige Beschreibung dieser Beziehungen erfolgt durch die *Axiome der Geometrie*.

Die Axiome der Geometrie gliedern sich in fünf Gruppen; jede einzelne dieser Gruppen drückt gewisse zusammengehörige Grundthatsachen unserer Anschauung aus. Wir benennen diese Gruppen von Axiomen in folgender Weise:

I 1—7.    Axiome der *Verknüpfung*,
II 1—5.   Axiome der *Anordnung*,
III.      Axiom der *Parallelen* (*Euklidisches* Axiom),
IV 1—6.   Axiome der *Congruenz*,
V.        Axiom der *Stetigkeit* (*Archimedisches* Axiom).

Kap. I. Die fünf Axiomgruppen. § 2.                    5

## § 2.
### Die Axiomgruppe I: Axiome der Verknüpfung.

Die Axiome dieser Gruppe stellen zwischen den oben erklärten Begriffen Punkte, Geraden und Ebenen eine *Verknüpfung* her und lauten wie folgt:

I 1. *Zwei von einander verschiedene Punkte A, B bestimmen stets eine Gerade a; wir setzen AB = a oder BA = a.*

Statt „bestimmen" werden wir auch andere Wendungen brauchen, z. B. A „liegt auf" a, A „ist ein Punkt von" a, a „geht durch" A „und durch" B, a „verbindet" A „und" oder „mit" B u. s. w. Wenn A auf a und ausserdem auf einer anderen Geraden b liegt, so gebrauchen wir auch die Wendung: „die Geraden" a „und" b „haben den Punkt A gemein" u. s. w.

I 2. *Irgend zwei von einander verschiedene Punkte einer Geraden bestimmen diese Gerade; d. h. wenn AB = a und AC = a, und B $\neq$ C, so ist auch BC = a.*

I 3. *Drei nicht auf ein und derselben Geraden liegende Punkte A, B, C bestimmen stets eine Ebene α; wir setzen ABC = α.*

Wir gebrauchen auch die Wendungen: A, B, C „liegen in" α; A, B, C „sind Punkte von" α u. s. w.

I 4. *Irgend drei Punkte A, B, C einer Ebene α, die nicht auf ein und derselben Geraden liegen, bestimmen diese Ebene α.*

I 5. *Wenn zwei Punkte A, B einer Geraden a in einer Ebene α liegen, so liegt jeder Punkt von a in α.*

In diesem Falle sagen wir: die Gerade a liegt in der Ebene α u. s. w.

I 6. *Wenn zwei Ebenen α, β einen Punkt A gemein haben, so haben sie wenigstens noch einen weiteren Punkt B gemein.*

I 7. *Auf jeder Geraden giebt es wenigstens zwei Punkte, in jeder Ebene wenigstens drei nicht auf einer Geraden gelegene Punkte und im Raum giebt es wenigstens vier nicht in einer Ebene gelegene Punkte.*

Die Axiome I 1—2 enthalten nur Aussagen über die Punkte und Geraden, d. h. über die Elemente der ebenen Geometrie und mögen daher die *ebenen Axiome der Gruppe* I heissen, zum Unterschied von den Axiomen I 3—7, die ich kurz als die *räumlichen Axiome* bezeichne.

Von den Sätzen, die aus den Axiomen I 1—7 folgen, erwähne ich nur diese beiden:

S a t z  1.  Zwei Geraden einer Ebene haben einen oder keinen Punkt gemein; zwei Ebenen haben keinen Punkt oder eine Gerade gemein; eine Ebene und eine nicht in ihr liegende Gerade haben keinen oder einen Punkt gemein.

S a t z  2.  Durch eine Gerade und einen nicht auf ihr liegenden Punkt, so wie auch durch zwei verschiedene Geraden mit einem gemeinsamen Punkt giebt es stets eine und nur eine Ebene.

### § 3.

### Die Axiomgruppe II: Axiome der Anordnung [1]).

Die Axiome dieser Gruppe definiren den Begriff „zwischen" und ermöglichen auf Grund dieses Begriffes die *Anordnung* der Punkte auf einer Geraden, in einer Ebene und im Raume.

E r k l ä r u n g.  Die Punkte einer Geraden stehen in gewissen Beziehungen zu einander, zu deren Beschreibung uns insbesondere das Wort *„zwischen"* dient.

II 1.  *Wenn A, B, C Punkte einer Geraden sind, und B zwischen A und C liegt, so liegt B auch zwischen C und A.*

Fig. 1.

II 2.  *Wenn A und C zwei Punkte einer Geraden sind, so giebt es stets wenigstens einen Punkt B, der zwischen A und C liegt und wenigstens einen Punkt D, so dass C zwischen A und D liegt.*

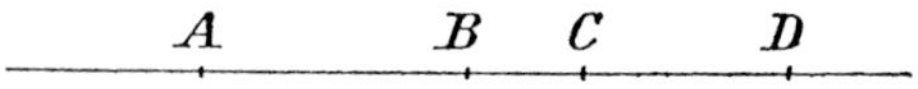

Fig. 2.

II 3.  *Unter irgend drei Punkten einer Geraden giebt es stets einen und nur einen, der zwischen den beiden andern liegt.*

II 4.  *Irgend vier Punkte A, B, C, D einer Geraden können stets so angeordnet werden, dass B zwischen A und C und auch zwischen A und D und ferner C zwischen A und D und auch zwischen B und D liegt.*

D e f i n i t i o n.  Das System zweier Punkte *A* und *B*, die auf einer Geraden *a* liegen, nennen wir eine *Strecke* und bezeichnen dieselbe mit *AB* oder *BA*. Die Punkte zwischen *A* und *B* heissen Punkte der Strecke *AB* oder auch *innerhalb* der Strecke *AB* ge-

---

1) Diese Axiome hat zuerst *M. Pasch* in seinen Vorlesungen über neuere Geometrie, Leipzig 1882, ausführlich untersucht. Insbesondere rührt das Axiom II 5 von *M. Pasch* her.

Kap. I. Die fünf Axiomgruppen. § 3, 4. 7

legen; alle übrigen Punkte der Geraden *a* heissen *ausserhalb* der Strecke *AB* gelegen. Die Punkte *A*, *B* heissen *Endpunkte* der Strecke *AB*.

II 5. *Es seien A, B, C drei nicht in gerader Linie gelegene Punkte und a eine Gerade in der Ebene ABC, die keinen der Punkte A, B, C trifft: wenn dann die Gerade a durch einen Punkt innerhalb der Strecke AB geht, so geht sie stets entweder durch einen Punkt der Strecke BC oder durch einen Punkt der Strecke AC.*

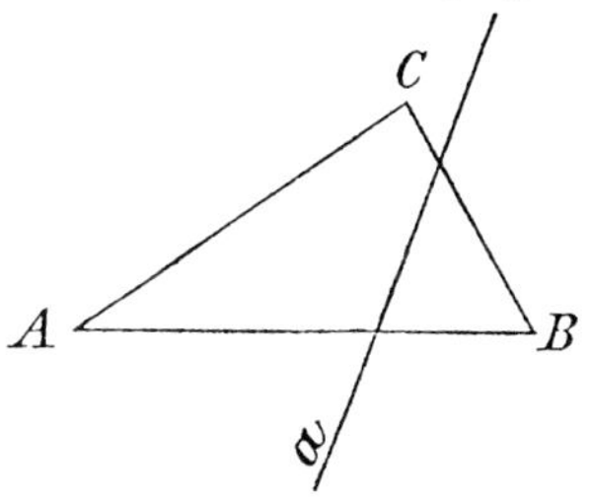

Fig. 3.

Die Axiome II 1—4 enthalten nur Aussagen über die Punkte auf einer Geraden und mögen daher die *linearen Axiome der Gruppe* II heissen; das Axiom II 5 enthält eine Aussage über die Elemente der ebenen Geometrie und heisse daher das *ebene Axiom der Gruppe* II.

TRANSLATION

## Chapter I.
## The five axiom groups.

§1.

### The elements of geometry and the five axiom groups.

*Explanation.* We imagine three different systems of things: the things of the *first* system we call *points* and denote them by $A, B, C, \ldots$; the things of the *second* system we call *lines* and denote them by $a, b, c, \ldots$; the things of the *third* system we call *planes* and denote them by $\alpha, \beta, \gamma, \ldots$; the points are also called the *elements of line geometry*, the points and lines are called the *elements of plane geometry*, and the points, lines and planes are called the *elements of spatial geometry* or of *space*.

We imagine the points, lines, planes in certain mutual relationships and describe these relationships by words like '*lie*', '*between*', '*parallel*', '*congruent*', '*continuous*'; the precise and complete description of these relationships follows from the *axioms of geometry*.

The axioms of geometry fall into five groups; each one of these groups describes certain basic facts of our observation, which belong together. We name these groups of axioms in the following way:

|     |         |                                                  |
|-----|---------|--------------------------------------------------|
| I   | 1 − 7.  | Axioms of *connection,*                          |
| II  | 1 − 5.  | Axioms of *order,*                               |
| III |         | Axiom of *parallels* (*Euclid's* axiom),         |
| IV  | 1 − 6.  | Axioms of *congruence,*                          |
| V   |         | Axiom of *continuity* (*Archimedes'* axiom).     |

[5]

## §2.
### Axiom group I: axioms of connection

The axioms of this group supply a *connection* between the concepts of points, lines and planes explained above and go as follows:

I 1. *Two points A, B different from each other always determine a line a; we put AB = a or BA = a.*

Instead of '*determine*' we will also use other turns of phrase, for example, A '*lies on*' a, A '*is a point of*' a, a '*goes through*' A '*and through*' B, a '*joins*' A '*and* ' or '*with*' B and so on. If A lies on a and at the same time on another line b, then we also use the phrase: '*the lines*' a '*and* 'b '*have the point A in common*' and so on.

I 2. *Any two points of a line, different from each other, determine that line; that is, if AB = a and AC = a, and B ≠ C, then also BC = a.*

I 3. *Three points A, B, C not lying on one and the same line always determine a plane α; we put ABC = α.*

We use also the phrases: A, B, C '*lie in*' α; A, B, C '*are points of*' α and so on.

I 4. *Any three points A, B, C of a plane α, not lying on one and the same line, determine this plane α.*

I 5. *If two points A, B of a line a lie in a plane α, then every point of a lies in α.*

In this case we say: *the line a lies in the plane α* and so on.

I 6. *If two planes α, β have a point A in common, then they have at least one further point B in common.*

I 7. *On every line there are at least two points, in every plane at least three points not lying on a line, and in space there are at least four points not lying in a plane.*

Axioms I 1–2 contain only statements about points and lines, that is, about the elements of plane geometry and can therefore be called the *plane axioms of group I,* to distinguish them from axioms I 3–7, which I call briefly the *spatial axioms.*

Of the theorems which follow from Axioms I 1–7, I mention only these two: [6] *Theorem 1.* Two lines of a plane have one or no points in common; two planes have no points or a line in common; a plane and a line not lying in it have one or no points in common.

*Theorem 2.* Through a line and a point not lying on it, as also through two different lines with a common point, there is always one and only one plane.

§3.

### Axiom group II: axioms of order.[1]

The axioms of this group define the concept 'between' and make possible on the basis of this concept the *ordering* of points on a line, in a plane and in space.

*Explanation.* The points of a line stand in a certain relationship to one another, which the word '*between*' in particular serves to describe to us.

II 1. *If A, B, C are points of a line, and B lies between A and C, then B also lies between C and A.*

II 2. *If A and C are two points of a line, then there is always at least one point B that lies between A and C, and at least one point D such that C lies between A and D.*

II 3. *Amongst any three points of a line there is always one and only one that lies between the other two.*

II 4. *Any four points A, B, C, D of a line can always be so labelled, that B lies between A and C and also between A and D, and further C between A and D and also between B and D.*

*Definition.* The system of two points A and B, that lie on a line a, we call a *segment* and denote it by AB or BA. The points between A and B are called points of the segment AB or also to lie *inside* the segment AB; [7] all remaining points of the line a are said to lie *outside* the segment AB. The points A, B are called the *endpoints* of the segment AB.

II 5. *Let A, B, C be three points not lying in a straight line and let a be a line in the plane ABC, which meets none of the points A, B, C; if then the line a goes through a point inside the segment AB, then it always goes either through a point of the segment BC or through a point of the segment AC.*

Axioms II 1–4 contain only statements about points on a line and may therefore be called the *line axioms of group* II; axiom II 5 contains a statement about the elements of plane geometry and is therefore called the *plane axiom of group* II.

---

[1] These axioms were first fully investigated by *M. Pasch* in his Vorlesungen über neuere Geometrie, Leipzig 1882. In particular axiom II 5 comes from M. Pasch.

———————

## 18.2 FOUNDATIONS OF ARITHMETIC

We have seen that even over the relatively short time span covered by this book the language of mathematics changed dramatically. The first important shift was away from the classical geometric descriptions of the seventeenth century to more formal and algebraic presentations in the eighteenth. In the nineteenth century, as analysis and algebra both became branches of mathematics in their own right, each acquired a language of its own. In analysis, concepts of limits and continuity, though geometric in origin, came to be written in terms of $\varepsilon, \delta$ inequalities; while in algebra, symbols began to stand for entirely new kinds of object: permutations, matrices, groups, and so on.

In the later part of the nineteenth century yet another kind of language emerged: the language of sets, which has now come to be used throughout all branches of mathematics. The idea of a set, or a collection of objects, is so basic and so general that it is difficult to pin down exactly when it emerged as a definite mathematical concept. One problem is the number of words with similar meaning that passed in and out of use. Galois, for instance, initially used the word *groupe* in its everyday informal sense for a collection of permutations, but later this took on a precise technical meaning. Similarly, Cauchy in a single paper in 1845, spoke of a *système de valeurs*, meaning simply a set or range of values, but also of a *système de substitutions conjuguées*, where *système* now had the more particular meaning of a set with some special structural properties (see 13.1.3). In French, Lebesgue's *ensemble*, from 1902, is perhaps the closest to the modern concept of a set (see 14.2.5).

German offered a similar variety of words. In Dedekind's writing, for example, we have *System* (used in Cauchy's sense for a set with some accompanying structure) and *Klasse* (see 16.3.2); while in Cantor's work we again find *System*, but also *Mannigfaltigkeit* (a multiplicity; Cantor 1891), and *Menge* (an amount, a crowd, lots of; Cantor 1895). By the latter, said Cantor, we are to understand 'a bringing together into a whole' ('Zusammenfassung zu einem Ganzen').

Sets are particularly helpful in handling properties of numbers, and both of the final extracts in this book make use of the concept, though the word itself does not appear; in the first the German word is *Inbegriff*, and in the second it is *System*; these are translated below as 'class' and 'system', respectively.

### 18.2.1 Cantor's countability proofs, 1874

As early as 1656, Wallis's attempts to square the circle had led him to suspect that the ratio of the perimeter of a circle to its diameter was neither a rational number nor a surd.[2] By 1685 he had developed his ideas further, and claimed that it was in fact impossible to pin down the required number by any finite or 'ordinary' equation.[3] In the early eighteenth century, Euler (following Leibniz) brought into standard use the terms 'algebraic' and 'transcendental'. Algebraic numbers are defined by an equation created from finitely many algebraic operations (for example, $\sqrt{2}$ satisfies $x^2 - 2 = 0$, and $\sqrt{-1}$ satisfies $x^2 + 1 = 0$); 'transcendental' numbers cannot be captured in such a way. Euler assumed that $\pi$, $e$, and logarithmic or trigonometric quantities in general were transcendental.

The first proof, as opposed to assumption, of the existence of transcendental numbers was given by Liouville in 1844, who demonstrated that $\xi = \sum_{n=1}^{\infty} 10^{-n!}$ is transcendental. He did so by proving that in a certain well-defined sense an algebraic number cannot be rapidly approximated by rationals, whereas $\xi$ can be. A proof that $e$ is transcendental was not found until thirty years later, by Charles Hermite in 1873, with a similar proof for $\pi$ by Carl Louis Lindemann in 1882.

---

2. Wallis 1656, *Scholium* to Proposition 190.    3. Wallis 1685, 315–317.

In 1874 Cantor proved that the algebraic numbers, though in one sense far more numerous than the rationals (they include surds and imaginary numbers, for example), are still countable, but that the real numbers are not, and putting these two results together he immediately inferred the existence of uncountably many transcendental numbers. Nowadays uncountability of the reals is usually demonstrated by a version of a diagonal argument devised by Cantor some twenty years later, in 1891. His first proof, however, was based on a quite different argument using nested intervals, and is the one reproduced here.

Cantor's word *Inbegriff* is not easy to translate. Strictly speaking it means 'an essential property', sometimes translated as 'concept' (see 14.2.4). Cantor was interested in the concept of being real and algebraic, and in all numbers that are of this kind. For this reason *Inbegriff* has sometimes been translated as 'set', but this is somewhat misleading because the looseness of the word 'set' fails to convey the sense of a common property that binds the numbers together. In the translation below I have chosen the word 'class' to convey the idea of a collection of numbers which share a special quality, that is, are of equal standing with one another.

### Cantor's countability proof

from Cantor, 'Über eine Eigenschaft des Inbegriffes aller reellen algebraischen Zahlen',
*Journal für die reine und angewandte Mathematik*, 1874, 258–261

# Ueber eine Eigenschaft des Inbegriffes aller reellen algebraischen Zahlen.

(Von Herrn *Cantor* in Halle a. S.)

Unter einer reellen algebraischen Zahl wird allgemein eine reelle Zahlgrösse $\omega$ verstanden, welche einer nicht identischen Gleichung von der Form genügt:

$$(1.) \quad a_0\, \omega^n + a_1\, \omega^{n-1} + \cdots + a_n = 0,$$

wo $n$, $a_0, a_1, \cdots a_n$ ganze Zahlen sind; wir können uns hierbei die Zahlen $n$ und $a_0$ positiv, die Coefficienten $a_0, a_1, \cdots a_n$ ohne gemeinschaftlichen Theiler und die Gleichung (1.) irreductibel denken; mit diesen Festsetzungen wird erreicht, dass nach den bekannten Grundsätzen der Arithmetik und Algebra die Gleichung (1.), welcher eine reelle algebraische Zahl genügt, eine völlig bestimmte ist; umgekehrt gehören bekanntlich zu einer Gleichung von der Form (1.) höchstens soviel reelle algebraische Zahlen $\omega$, welche ihr genügen, als ihr Grad $n$ angiebt. Die reellen algebraischen Zahlen bilden in ihrer Gesammtheit einen Inbegriff von Zahlgrössen, welcher mit $(\omega)$ bezeichnet werde; es hat derselbe, wie aus einfachen Betrachtungen hervorgeht, eine solche Beschaffenheit, dass in jeder Nähe irgend einer gedachten Zahl $\alpha$ unendlich viele Zahlen aus $(\omega)$ liegen; um so auffallender dürfte daher für den ersten Anblick die Bemerkung sein, dass man den Inbegriff $(\omega)$ dem Inbegriffe aller ganzen positiven Zahlen $\nu$, welcher durch das Zeichen $(\nu)$ angedeutet werde, eindeutig zuordnen kann, so dass zu jeder algebraischen Zahl $\omega$ eine bestimmte ganze positive Zahl $\nu$ und umgekehrt zu jeder positiven ganzen Zahl $\nu$ eine völlig bestimmte reelle algebraische Zahl $\omega$ gehört, dass also, um mit anderen Worten dasselbe zu bezeichnen, der Inbegriff $(\omega)$ in der Form einer unendlichen gesetzmässigen Reihe:

$$(2.) \quad \omega_1, \omega_2, \cdots \omega_\nu, \cdots$$

gedacht werden kann, in welcher sämmtliche Individuen von ($\omega$) vorkommen und ein jedes von ihnen sich an einer bestimmten Stelle in (2.), welche durch den zugehörigen Index gegeben ist, befindet. Sobald man ein Gesetz gefunden hat, nach welchem eine solche Zuordnung gedacht werden kann, lässt sich dasselbe nach Willkür modificiren; es wird daher genügen, wenn ich in §. 1 denjenigen Anordnungsmodus mittheile, welcher wie mir scheint, die wenigsten Umstände in Anspruch nimmt.

Um von dieser Eigenschaft des Inbegriffes aller reellen algebraischen Zahlen eine Anwendung zu geben, füge ich zu dem §. 1 den §. 2 hinzu, in welchem ich zeige, dass, wenn eine beliebige Reihe reeller Zahlgrössen von der Form (2.) vorliegt, man in jedem vorgegebenen Intervalle ($\alpha \cdots \beta$) Zahlen $\eta$ bestimmen kann, welche nicht in (2.) enthalten sind; combinirt man die Inhalte dieser beiden Paragraphen, so ist damit ein neuer Beweis des zuerst von *Liouville* bewiesenen Satzes gegeben, dass es in jedem vorgegebenen Intervalle ($\alpha \cdots \beta$) unendlich viele transcendente, d. h. nicht algebraische reelle Zahlen giebt. Ferner stellt sich der Satz in §. 2 als der Grund dar, warum Inbegriffe reeller Zahlgrössen, die ein sogenanntes Continuum bilden (etwa die sämmtlichen reellen Zahlen, welche $\geqq 0$ und $\leqq 1$ sind) sich nicht eindeutig auf den Inbegriff ($\nu$) beziehen lassen; so fand ich den deutlichen Unterschied zwischen einem sogenannten Continuum und einem Inbegriffe von der Art der Gesammtheit aller reellen algebraischen Zahlen.

## §. 1

Gehen wir auf die Gleichung (1.), welcher eine algebraische Zahl $\omega$ genügt und welche nach den gedachten Festsetzungen eine völlig bestimmte ist, zurück, so möge die Summe der absoluten Beträge ihrer Coefficienten, vermehrt um die Zahl $n-1$, wo $n$ den Grad von $\omega$ angiebt, die *Höhe* der Zahl $\omega$ genannt und mit $N$ bezeichnet werden; es ist also, unter Anwendung einer üblich gewordenen Bezeichnungsweise:

(3.)    $N = n-1 + [a_0] + [a_1] + \cdots + [a_n].$

Die Höhe $N$ ist darnach für jede reelle algebraische Zahl $\omega$ eine bestimmte positive ganze Zahl; umgekehrt giebt es zu jedem positiven ganzzahligen Werthe von $N$ nur eine endliche Anzahl algebraischer reeller Zahlen mit der Höhe $N$; die Anzahl derselben sei $\varphi(N)$; es ist beispielsweise $\varphi(1) = 1$; $\varphi(2) = 2$; $\varphi(3) = 4$. Es lassen sich alsdann die Zahlen des Inbegriffes $(\omega)$, d. h. sämmtliche algebraischen reellen Zahlen folgendermassen anordnen; man nehme als erste Zahl $\omega_1$ die eine Zahl mit der Höhe $N = 1$; lasse auf sie, der Grösse nach steigend, die $\varphi(2) = 2$ algebraischen reellen Zahlen mit der Höhe $N = 2$ folgen, bezeichne sie mit $\omega_2$, $\omega_3$; an diese mögen sich die $\varphi(3) = 4$ Zahlen mit der Höhe $N = 3$, ihrer Grösse nach aufsteigend, anschliessen; allgemein mögen, nachdem in dieser Weise sämmtliche Zahlen aus $(\omega)$ bis zu einer gewissen Höhe $N = N_1$ abgezählt und an einen bestimmten Platz gewiesen sind, die reellen algebraischen Zahlen mit der Höhe $N = N_1 + 1$ auf sie folgen und zwar der Grösse nach aufsteigend; so erhält man den Inbegriff $(\omega)$ aller reellen algebraischen Zahlen in der Form:

$$\omega_1, \ \omega_2, \ \cdots \ \omega_\nu, \ \cdots \cdots$$

und kann mit Rücksicht auf diese Anordnung von der $\nu$ten reellen algebraischen Zahl reden, wobei keine einzige aus dem Inbegriffe $(\omega)$ vergessen ist. —

### §. 2.

Wenn eine nach irgend einem Gesetze gegebene unendliche Reihe von einander verschiedener reeller Zahlgrössen:

$$(4.) \quad \omega_1, \ \omega_2, \ \cdots \ \omega_\nu, \ \cdots \cdots$$

vorliegt, so lässt sich in jedem vorgegebenen Intervalle $(\alpha \cdots \beta)$ eine Zahl $\eta$ (und folglich unendlich viele solcher Zahlen) bestimmen, welche in der Reihe (4.) nicht vorkommt; dies soll nun bewiesen werden.

Wir gehen zu dem Ende von dem Intervalle $(\alpha \cdots \beta)$ aus, welches uns beliebig vorgegeben sei, und es sei $\alpha < \beta$; die ersten beiden Zahlen unserer Reihe (4.), welche im Innern dieses Intervalles (mit Ausschluss der Grenzen liegen, mögen mit $\alpha'$, $\beta'$ bezeichnet werden, und es sei $\alpha' < \beta'$; ebenso bezeichne man in unserer Reihe die ersten beiden Zahlen, welche im Innern von $(\alpha' \cdots \beta')$ liegen, mit $\alpha''$, $\beta''$, und es sei $\alpha'' < \beta''$, und nach demselben Gesetze bilde man ein folgendes Intervall $(\alpha''' \cdots \beta''')$ u. s. w. Hier sind also $\alpha'$, $\alpha'' \cdots$ der Definition nach bestimmte Zahlen unserer Reihe (4.), deren Indices im fortwährenden Steigen sich befinden, und das Gleiche gilt von den Zahlen $\beta'$, $\beta'' \cdots$; ferner nehmen die Zahlen $\alpha'$, $\alpha'', \cdots$

ihrer Grösse nach fortwährend zu, die Zahlen $\beta'$, $\beta''$, $\cdots$ nehmen ihrer Grösse nach fortwährend ab; von den Intervallen $(\alpha \cdots \beta)$, $(\alpha' \cdots \beta')$, $(\alpha'' \cdots \beta'')$, $\cdots$ schliesst ein jedes alle auf dasselbe folgenden ein. — Hierbei sind nun zwei Fälle denkbar.

*Entweder* die Anzahl der so gebildeten Intervalle ist endlich; das letzte von ihnen sei $(\alpha^{(\nu)} \cdots \beta^{(\nu)})$; da im Innern desselben höchstens eine Zahl der Reihe (4.) liegen kann, so kann eine Zahl $\eta$ in diesem Intervalle angenommen werden, welche nicht in (4.) enthalten ist, und es ist somit der Satz für diesen Fall bewiesen. —

*Oder* die Anzahl der gebildeten Intervalle ist unendlich gross; dann haben die Grössen $\alpha$, $\alpha'$, $\alpha''$, $\cdots$, weil sie fortwährend ihrer Grösse nach zunehmen, ohne ins Unendliche zu wachsen, einen bestimmten Grenzwerth $\alpha^\infty$; ein gleiches gilt für die Grössen $\beta$, $\beta'$, $\beta''$, $\cdots$, weil sie fortwährend ihrer Grösse nach abnehmen, ihr Grenzwerth sei $\beta^\infty$; ist $\alpha^\infty = \beta^\infty$ (ein Fall, der bei dem Inbegriffe $(\omega)$ aller reellen algebraischen Zahlen stets eintritt), so überzeugt man sich leicht, wenn man nur auf die Definition der Intervalle zurückblickt, dass die Zahl $\eta = \alpha^\infty = \beta^\infty$ nicht in unserer Reihe enthalten sein kann[*]; ist aber $\alpha^\infty < \beta^\infty$, so genügt jede Zahl $\eta$ im Innern des Intervalles $(\alpha^\infty \cdots \beta^\infty)$ oder auch an den Grenzen desselben der gestellten Forderung, nicht in der Reihe (4.) enthalten zu sein. —

Die in diesem Aufsatze bewiesenen Sätze lassen Erweiterungen nach verschiedenen Richtungen zu, von welchen hier nur eine erwähnt sei:

„Ist $\omega_1$, $\omega_2$, $\cdots \omega_n$, $\cdots$ eine endliche oder unendliche Reihe von einander linear unabhängiger Zahlen (so dass keine Gleichung von der Form $a_1 \omega_1 + a_2 \omega_2 + \cdots + a_n \omega_n = 0$ mit ganzzahligen Coefficienten, die nicht sämmtlich verschwinden, möglich ist) und denkt man sich den Inbegriff $(\Omega)$ aller derjenigen Zahlen $\Omega$, welche sich als rationale Functionen mit ganzzahligen Coefficienten aus den gegebenen Zahlen $\omega$ darstellen lassen, so giebt es in jedem Intervalle $(\alpha \cdots \beta)$ unendlich viele Zahlen, die nicht in $(\Omega)$ enthalten sind.“

In der That überzeugt man sich durch eine ähnliche Schlussweise,

---

[*] Wäre die Zahl $\eta$ in unserer Reihe enthalten, so hätte man $\eta = \omega_p$, wo $p$ ein bestimmter Index ist; dies ist aber nicht möglich, denn $\omega_p$ liegt n i c h t im Innern des Intervalles $(\alpha^{(p)} \cdots \beta^{(p)})$, während die Zahl $\eta$ ihrer Definition nach im Innern dieses Intervalles liegt.

TRANSLATION

## On a property of the class of all real algebraic numbers.

$\left(\text{from Herr } Cantor \text{ in Halle an der Saale}\right)$

Generally by a real algebraic number will be understood a real numerical quantity $\omega$, which satisfies a non-identical equation of the form:

(1.)     $$a_0\omega^n + a_1\omega^{n-1} + \cdots + a_n = 0,$$

where $n, a_0, a_1, \ldots a_n$ are whole numbers; we can here take the numbers $n$ and $a_0$ as positive, the coefficients $a_0, a_1, \ldots a_n$ as without common divisors, and equation (1.) as irreducible; with these specifications it comes about that, by the known principles of arithmetic and algebra, equation (1.), which is satisfied by a real algebraic number, is completely determined; conversely, as is known, there belong to an equation of form (1.) at most so many real algebraic numbers $\omega$ that satisfy it as are given by its degree $n$. The real algebraic numbers taken together form a class of numbers which will be denoted by $(\omega)$; it has the property, as emerges from simple examination, that in any neighbourhood of a given number $\alpha$ there lie infinitely many numbers from $(\omega)$; so at first sight it is all the more striking that one can uniquely assign the class $(\omega)$ to the class of all positive whole numbers, $\nu$, which will be denoted by the symbol $(\nu)$, so that to each algebraic number $\omega$ there belongs a definite positive whole number $\nu$, and conversely to each positive whole number $\nu$ a fully determined real algebraic number $\omega$, that is, to describe the same thing in other words, the class $(\omega)$ can be thought of in the form of an infinite regulated sequence

(2.)     $$\omega_1, \omega_2 \ldots \omega_\nu, \ldots$$

[259] in which all individuals of $(\omega)$ appear and each one of them is found at a definite place in (2.), which is given by the index belonging to it. As soon as one has found a law by which such a correspondence can be conceived, it can be modified at will; it will therefore suffice if, in §1, I communicate that method of ordering which, as it seems to me, takes the least trouble to state.

In order to give an application of this property of the class of all real algebraic numbers, after §1 I adjoin §2, in which I show that, if there is presented an arbitrary sequence of real numerical quantities of the form (2.), one can in every preassigned interval $(\alpha \ldots \beta)$ determine numbers $\eta$, which are not contained in (2.); if one combines the contents of these two paragraphs, then this gives a new proof of the theorem first proved by *Liouville*, that in every preassigned interval $(\alpha \ldots \beta)$ there exist infinitely many numbers that are transcendental, that is, not algebraic. Further, the theorem in §2 presents itself as the reason that classes of real numbers that form a so-called continuum (for example, all real numbers which are $\geq 0$ and $\leq 1$) cannot be related uniquely to the class $(\nu)$; thus I have found a clear difference between a so-called continuum and a class of the kind of the totality of real algebraic numbers.

§1.

Let us return to equation (1.), which an algebraic number $\omega$ satisfies and which under the aforementioned conditions is fully determined; the sum of the absolute values of its coefficients, increased by the number $n - 1$, where $n$ gives the degree of $\omega$, may be called the *height* of the number $\omega$ and will be denoted by $N$; that is, making use of a commonly known notation:

(3.) $$N = n - 1 + [a_0] + [a_1] + \cdots + [a_n].$$

Accordingly, the height $N$ for each real algebraic number $\omega$ is a determined positive whole number; conversely, for each positive whole number value of $N$ there are only a finite number of algebraic real numbers with height $N$; let $\phi(N)$ be the number of them; then, [260] for instance, $\phi(1) = 1$; $\phi(2) = 2$; $\phi(3) = 4$. Then the numbers of the class $(\omega)$, that is, all algebraic real numbers, can be ordered in the following way: one takes as first number $\omega_1$ the one number with height $N = 1$; let there follow, in order of increasing size, the $\phi(2) = 2$ algebraic real numbers with height $N = 2$, and denote them by $\omega_2, \omega_3$; to these may be appended the $\phi(3) = 4$ numbers with height $N = 3$, in order of increasing size; in general, after all the numbers of $(\omega)$ up to a certain height $N = N_1$ have been enumerated and put in a definite place in this way, the real algebraic numbers with the height $N = N_1 + 1$ may follow them and indeed in order of increasing size; so one obtains the class $(\omega)$ of all real algebraic numbers in the form:

$$\omega_1, \omega_2, \ldots \omega_\nu, \ldots$$

and with respect to this ordering, by which not a single member of the class is forgotten, one can speak of the $\nu^{th}$ real algebraic number.

§2.

If there is prsented an infinite sequence (4.) of real numbers distinct from each other, given by any law at all:

(4.) $$\omega_1, \omega_2, \ldots \omega_\nu, \ldots$$

then there can be determined in every preassigned interval $(\alpha \ldots \beta)$ a number $\eta$ (and consequently infinitely many such numbers), which does not occur in sequence (4.); this will now be proved.

We start from the end of the interval $(\alpha \ldots \beta)$, which is arbitrarily presented to us, and suppose $\alpha < \beta$; the first two numbers of our sequence (4.) that lie in the interior of this interval (excluding the boundaries) may be denoted by $\alpha'$, $\beta'$, and suppose $\alpha' < \beta'$; likewise, one denotes the first two numbers in our sequence that lie in the interior of $(\alpha' \ldots \beta')$ by $\alpha''$, $\beta''$, and suppose $\alpha'' < \beta''$, and by the same rule one forms a next interval $(\alpha''' \ldots \beta''')$, and so on. Thus there are found $\alpha', \alpha'' \ldots$, by definition certain numbers of our sequence (4.), whose indices are strictly increasing, and the same holds for the numbers $\beta', \beta'', \ldots$; further, the numbers $\alpha', \alpha'', \ldots$ [261] strictly increase in size, the numbers $\beta', \beta'', \ldots$ strictly decrease in size; each one of the intervals $(\alpha \ldots \beta), (\alpha' \ldots \beta'), (\alpha'' \ldots \beta''), \ldots$ encloses all those that follow it. — Now there are only two conceivable cases.

*Either* the number of intervals so formed is finite; let the last of them be $(\alpha^{(\nu)} \ldots \beta^{(\nu)})$; since there can lie at most one number of the sequence (4.) in the interior of this, it follows that a number $\eta$ can be taken in this interval, which is not contained in (4.), and the assertion is proved for this case. —

*Or* the number of intervals so formed is infinitely large; then the quantities $\alpha$, $\alpha'$, $\alpha''$, ..., because they are strictly increasing in size without growing infinite, have a definite limit $\alpha^\infty$; the same holds for the quantities $\beta$, $\beta'$, $\beta''$, ..., because they are strictly decreasing in size; let their limit be $\beta^\infty$. If $\alpha^\infty = \beta^\infty$ (a case that always occurs for the class $(\omega)$ of all real algebraic numbers), then one easily convinces oneself, if one merely looks back to the definition of the intervals, that the number $\eta = \alpha^\infty = \beta^\infty$ cannot be contained in our sequence; but if $\alpha^\infty < \beta^\infty$, then every number $\eta$ in the interior of the interval $(\alpha^\infty \ldots \beta^\infty)$ or even at the boundaries of it satisfies the stated requirement, that it be not contained in the sequence (4.). —

* If the number $\eta$ were contained in our sequence, then one would have $\eta = \omega_p$, where $p$ is a certain index; this is not possible, however, for $\omega_p$ does *not* lie in the interior of the interval $(\alpha^{(p)} \ldots \beta^{(p)})$, whereas the number $\eta$ by its definition does lie in the interior of the interval.

---

### 18.2.2  Dedekind's definition of natural numbers, 1888

By the late nineteenth century there existed several viable definitions of the real numbers. In 16.3, for example, we saw those produced by Dedekind and Cantor. Any definition of real numbers, however, must ultimately be based on the more elementary starting point of the natural numbers, and defining the natural numbers is not at all easy. Euclid's attempt in the third century BC was hardly improved upon for two thousand years.

In 1888 Dedekind, after many years of work, published a seminal essay entitled *Was sind und was sollen die Zahlen* (*What are and what should numbers be*), in which he provided an axiomatic definition of the natural numbers using the language of sets and mappings. First he had to establish a good deal of groundwork and vocabulary. What he described as a 'similar image' (*ähnliche Abbildung*) is what we would now call a one-one mapping, with the property that $\phi(a) = \phi(b)$ only if $a = b$, but to keep more closely to Dedekind's terminology it has been translated here as 'similar mapping'. The 'chain' (*Kette*) of an element $n$ is the set $\{n, \phi(n), \phi(\phi(n)), \phi(\phi(\phi(n))), \ldots\}$ and was denoted by Dedekind as $n_0$. He also used the notation $a'$ for $\phi(a)$ and $A'$ for $\phi(A)$ (see 9.3.1).

From his definitions Dedekind was able to show that the sequence $N$ of natural numbers is the *only* number chain containing the base element 1. Thus, just as in Euclid's definition, the unit element 1 is the crucial component of the entire system. The essential difference between Euclid's system and Dedekind's, however, is that in the former numbers are simply collections of units, whereas in the latter there is an inbuilt ordering. From this Dedekind was able to prove the principle of mathematical induction: that a theorem holds for all numbers of a chain $m_0$ if it holds for some $n = m$ (in $m_0$), and if validity for any $n$ implies validity for its successor $\phi(n)$. In the final sections of the treatise he also defined the usual operations of addition, multiplication, and raising to powers, thus showing that his natural numbers have all the properties required for arithmetic.

# Dedekind's definition of the natural numbers

from Dedekind, *Was sind und was sollen die Zahlen*, 1888, §6; from *Werke*, 1930–32, III, 359–360

§ 6.

Einfach unendliche Systeme. Reihe der natürlichen Zahlen.

71. Erklärung. Ein System $N$ heißt einfach unendlich, wenn es eine solche ähnliche Abbildung $\varphi$ von $N$ in sich selbst gibt, daß $N$ als Kette (44) eines Elementes erscheint, welches nicht in $\varphi(N)$ enthalten ist. Wir nennen dies Element, das wir im folgenden durch das Symbol 1 bezeichnen wollen, das Grundelement von $N$ und sagen zugleich, das einfach unendliche System $N$ sei durch diese Abbildung $\varphi$ geordnet. Behalten wir die früheren bequemen Bezeichnungen für die Bilder und Ketten bei (§ 4), so besteht mithin das Wesen eines einfach unendlichen Systems $N$ in der Existenz einer Abbildung $\varphi$ von $N$ und eines Elementes 1, die den folgenden Bedingungen $\alpha, \beta, \gamma, \delta$ genügen:

$\alpha$. $N' \, 3 \, N$.

$\beta$. $N = 1_0$.

$\gamma$. Das Element 1 ist nicht in $N'$ enthalten.

$\delta$. Die Abbildung $\varphi$ ist ähnlich.

Offenbar folgt aus $\alpha, \gamma, \delta$, daß jedes einfach unendliche System $N$ wirklich ein unendliches System ist (64), weil es einem echten Teile $N'$ seiner selbst ähnlich ist.

72. Satz. In jedem unendlichen System $S$ ist ein einfach unendliches System $N$ als Teil enthalten.

Beweis. Es gibt nach 64 eine solche ähnliche Abbildung $\varphi$ von $S$, daß $\varphi(S)$ oder $S'$ ein echter Teil von $S$ wird; es gibt also ein Element 1 in $S$, welches nicht in $S'$ enthalten ist. Die Kette

— 360 —

$N = 1_0$, welche dieser Abbildung $\varphi$ des Systems $S$ in sich selbst entspricht (44), ist ein einfach unendliches, durch $\varphi$ geordnetes System; denn die charakteristischen Bedingungen $\alpha$, $\beta$, $\gamma$, $\delta$ in 71 sind offenbar sämtlich erfüllt.

73. Erklärung. Wenn man bei der Betrachtung eines einfach unendlichen, durch eine Abbildung $\varphi$ geordneten Systems $N$ von der besonderen Beschaffenheit der Elemente gänzlich absieht, lediglich ihre Unterscheidbarkeit festhält und nur die Beziehungen auffaßt, in die sie durch die ordnende Abbildung $\varphi$ zueinander gesetzt sind, so heißen diese Elemente natürliche Zahlen oder Ordinalzahlen oder auch schlechthin Zahlen, und das Grundelement 1 heißt die Grundzahl der Zahlenreihe $N$. In Rücksicht auf diese Befreiung der Elemente von jedem anderen Inhalt (Abstraktion) kann man die Zahlen mit Recht eine freie Schöpfung des menschlichen Geistes nennen. Die Beziehungen oder Gesetze, welche ganz allein aus den Bedingungen $\alpha$, $\beta$, $\gamma$, $\delta$ in 71 abgeleitet werden und deshalb in allen geordneten einfach unendlichen Systemen immer dieselben sind, wie auch die den einzelnen Elementen zufällig gegebenen Namen lauten mögen (vgl. 134), bilden den nächsten Gegenstand der Wissenschaft von den Zahlen oder der Arithmetik.

*Notation*
Dedekind used a symbol similar to 3 to indicate inclusion, that is, $A \ 3 \ B$ for what we would now write as $A \subset B$, but since it is difficult to reproduce exactly, and to avoid confusion, it is replaced below by the modern symbol $\subset$.

## TRANSLATION

### §6. *Simply infinite systems. Sequences of natural numbers.*

71. *Explanation.* A system $N$ is called *simply infinite* if there exists a similar mapping $\phi$ of $N$ into itself, such that $N$ appears as chain (44) of one element which is not contained in $\phi(N)$. We call this element, which we will denote in the following by the symbol 1, the *base element* of $N$ and at the same time say that the simply infinite system $N$ is *ordered* by means of this mapping $\phi$. If we keep the earlier convenient symbols for images and chains from (§4), then the essential nature of a simply infinite system $N$ lies in the existence of a mapping $\phi$ of $N$ and an element 1, satisfying the following conditions $\alpha$, $\beta$, $\gamma$, $\delta$:

$\alpha$.   $N' \subset N$.

$\beta$.   $N = 1_0$.

$\gamma$.   The element 1 is not contained in $N'$.

$\delta$.   The mapping $\phi$ is similar.

Clearly it follows from $\alpha, \gamma, \delta$, that every simply infinite system $N$ really is an infinite system (64), because it is similar to a proper part $N'$ of itself.

72. *Theorem.* In every infinite system $S$ there is a simply infinite system $N$ contained in it as a part.

*Proof.* By (64) there is a similar mapping $\phi$ of $S$ such that $\phi(S)$ or $S'$ becomes a proper part of $S$; thus there exists an element 1 in $S$, which is not contained in $S'$. The chain [360] $N = 1_0$, which corresponds to this mapping $\phi$ of the system $S$ into itself (44), is a simply infinite system, ordered by $\phi$; for the characteristic conditions $\alpha, \beta, \gamma, \delta$ in (71) are clearly all satisfied.

73. *Explanation.* If in considering a simply infinite system $N$ ordered by a mapping $\phi$ one entirely neglects the special character of the elements, simply keeping their distinguishability and concentrating only on the relationships in which they are placed to one another by the ordering mapping $\phi$, then these elements are called *natural numbers* or *ordinal numbers* or also in a word *numbers*, and the base element 1 is called the *base number* of the *number sequence N*. With regard to this freeing of the elements from all other content (abstraction) one can rightly call numbers a free creation of the human mind. The relationships or laws, which are derived from conditions $\alpha, \beta, \gamma, \delta$ in (71) only, and are therefore always the same in all ordered simply infinite systems, whatever names the individual elements may happen to have been assigned (see 134), constitute the principle object of the *science of numbers* or *arithmetic.*

# PEOPLE, INSTITUTIONS, AND JOURNALS

This is a summary of the main mathematicians, institutions, and journals mentioned in the text. One of its purposes is to provide a quick reference guide to dates and places. The other is to emphasize that personal communications and friendships were often significant in the development and spread of mathematical ideas, hence the brief notes on *Institutional affiliations* and *Friends, colleagues, and correspondents* where appropriate.

## PEOPLE

**Abel, Niels Henrik** (near Stavanger, Norway, 1802–Oslo, 1829)
    *Institutional affiliations*: none; was offered a teaching post in Berlin a few days before he died.
    *Friends, colleagues, correspondents*: befriended by August Leopold Crelle who published much of his work.

**d'Alembert, Jean le Rond** (Paris, 1717–Paris, 1783)
    *Institutional affiliations*: member of the Paris Academy; mathematical editor of the *Encylopédie*.
    *Friends, colleagues, correspondents*: corresponded with Daniel Bernoulli, Euler, and many others.

**Ampère, André-Marie** (Lyon, 1775–Paris, 1836)
    *Institutional affiliations*: taught at the École Polytechnique from 1803.
    *Friends, colleagues, correspondents*: worked with Lagrange, Cauchy, Poisson, and others at the École Polytechnique.

**Apollonius of Perga** (fl. *c.* 185 AD)
    Almost nothing known of his life except that he spent some time in Alexandria.

**Archimedes** (died Syracuse, 212 BC)
    Almost nothing known of his life except that he probably visited Alexandria.
    *Friends, colleagues, correspondents*: corresponded with Conon, Dositheus, Eratosthenes in Alexandria.

**Argand, Jean Robert** (Paris, 1768–Paris, 1822)
    Thought to have been a Parisian bookkeeper.

**Bayes, Thomas** (London, 1702–Tunbridge Wells, Kent, 1761)
    *Institutional affiliations*: Fellow of the Royal Society from 1742.

**Bernoulli, Jacob** (Basel, 1654–Basel, 1705)
    *Institutional affiliations*: Professor of mathematics at Basel from 1687.
    *Friends, colleagues, correspondents*: corresponded with Leibniz, his own brother Johann Bernoulli, and others.

**Bernoulli, Johann** (Basel, 1667–Basel, 1748)
    *Institutional affiliations*: Professor of mathematics at Groningen from 1695; Professor of mathematics at Basel from 1705; member of the Academies of Paris, Berlin, St Petersburg, and Fellow of the Royal Society.

*Friends, colleagues, correspondents*: corresponded with Leibniz, Euler, and many others; taught calculus to l'Hôpital.

**Boethius, Anicius Manlius Severinus** (Rome, *c.* 480–near Pavia, 524)
Born into an eminent Roman family; imprisoned for political resistance 524; executed 524.

**Bolzano, Bernard** (Prague, 1781–Prague, 1848)
*Institutional affiliations*: Professor of philosophy of religion at Prague 1805–1819 and 1825–1831.

**Bombelli, Rafael** (Bologna, 1526–1572)
Lived mostly in Bologna where he worked on a land reclamation project.

**Briggs, Henry** (Halifax, England, 1561–Oxford, 1630)
*Institutional affiliations*: Gresham Professor of Geometry 1596; Savilian Professor of Geometry, Oxford, 1620.
*Friends, colleagues, correspondents*: worked closely with Napier on logarithms 1615–17.

**Brouncker, William** (*c.* 1620–1684)
*Institutional affiliations*: first President of the Royal Society 1663–67; President of Gresham College 1664–67.
*Friends, colleagues, correspondents*: worked with Wallis and corresponded with Fermat during the 1650s.

**Cantor, Georg** (St Petersburg, 1845–Halle, Germany, 1918)
*Institutional affiliations*: studied at Zürich and Berlin, where he was taught by Weierstrass, Kummer, and Kronecker; taught at the University of Halle from 1869.
*Friends, colleagues, correspondents*: corresponded with Dedekind; later came under bitter attack from Kronecker.

**Cardano, Girolamo** (Pavia, 1501–Rome, 1576)
*Institutional affiliations*: practised medicine in Padua from 1526 and Milan from 1534; later held chairs of medicine at Pavia and Bologna.
*Friends, colleagues, correspondents*: worked with Ludovico Ferrari.

**Cauchy, Augustin-Louis** (Arcueil, near Paris, 1789–Paris, 1857)
*Institutional affiliations*: taught at the École Polytechnique 1815–30; Turin 1830–33; Paris 1834–57; member of the Paris Academy.
*Friends, colleagues, correspondents*: protégé of Lagrange and Laplace, contemporary of Ampère, Poisson, Fourier, and others at the École Polytechnique.

**Cavalieri, Bonaventura** (Milan, ?1598–Bologna, 1647)
*Institutional affiliations*: entered the Augustinian Gesuati order as a child; lecturer at the University of Bologna from 1629.
*Friends, colleagues, correspondents*: met Castelli and Galileo in Pisa before 1620 and later corresponded at length with Galileo.

**Cayley, Arthur** (Richmond, Surrey, 1821–Cambridge, 1895)
*Institutional affiliations*: graduated as Senior Wrangler and Smith's prizewinner from Trinity College, Cambridge, 1842; worked as a lawyer in London from 1845; Sadlerian Professor of Mathematics at Cambridge from 1863.
*Friends, colleagues, correspondents*: close friend and colleague of James Jospeh Sylvester.

**Collins, John** (Wood Eaton, near Oxford, 1625–London, 1683)
*Institutional affiliations*: spent his early life at sea, later as an accountant in various government offices; Fellow of the Royal Society from 1667.
*Friends, colleagues, correspondents*: knew and corresponded with most of the mathematicians of his day; his letters are a source of major importance for our understanding of seventeenth-century English mathematics.

**Dedekind, Richard** (Braunschweig, 1831–Braunschweig, 1916)

*Institutional affiliations*: studied at Göttingen under Gauss; taught at the Polytechnikum in Zürich from 1858 and at the Polytechnikum in Braunschweig from 1862.

*Friends, colleagues, correspondents*: studied under Gauss at Göttingen; became close friends with Riemann and later Dirichlet; corresponded with Cantor.

**Descartes, René** (La Haye, France, 1596–Stockholm, 1650)

*Institutional affiliations*: none; based in Paris 1620–28 and in the Netherlands 1628–49

*Friends, colleagues, correspondents*: corresponded with other mathematicians through Mersenne.

**Euclid** (*c.* 250 BC)

Nothing known.

**Euler, Leonhard** (Basel, 1707–St Petersburg, 1783)

*Institutional affiliations*: St Petersburg Academy 1727–41; Berlin Academy 1741–66; St Petersburg Academy from 1766.

*Friends, colleagues, correspondents*: was taught by Johann Bernoulli in Basel, and remained close to various members of the Bernoulli clan; prolific correspondent with the Bernoullis, d'Alembert, Lagrange, and many others.

**Fermat, Pierre de** (Beaumont-de-Lomagne, near Toulouse, 1601–Castres, 1665)

*Institutional affiliations*: none; spent his life as an official of the *parlement* of Toulouse.

*Friends, colleagues, correspondents*: corresponded with Mersenne, Descartes, Pascal, Torricelli, Wallis, Brouncker.

**Ferrari, Ludovico** (Bologna, 1522–Bologna, 1565)

*Institutional affiliations*: taught mathematics in Milan and later Bologna.

*Friends, colleagues, correspondents*: spent some years from 1536 in the household of Cardano.

**Fibonacci**, see Leonardo Pisano

**Fourier, Jean Baptiste Joseph** (Auxerre, France, 1768–Paris, 1830)

*Institutional affiliations*: lecturer at the École Polytechnique 1795–98; joined Napoleon's Egyptian campaign, then became an administrator in Grenoble 1801; returned to Paris only in 1815; member of the Paris Academy from 1816.

*Friends, colleagues, correspondents*: contemporary of Cauchy, Lacroix, Poisson, and others at the Paris Academy.

**Frobenius, Ferdinand Georg** (Berlin, 1849–Berlin, 1917)

*Institutional affiliations*: studied at Göttingen and Berlin; Assistant Professor at Berlin 1874 and at the Polytechnikum in Zürich from 1875; Professor at Berlin from 1892.

*Friends, colleagues, correspondents*: contemporary of Kummer and Weierstrass in Berlin in the early 1870s.

**Galois, Évariste** (Bourg-la-Reine, near Paris, 1811–Paris, 1832)

*Institutional affiliations*: none; twice failed the entrance examination to the École Polytechnique.

*Friends, colleagues, correspondents*: left his work in the care of his friend Auguste Chevalier.

**Gauss, Karl Friedrich** (Braunschweig, 1777–Göttingen, 1855)

*Institutional affiliations*: studied at Göttingen and Braunschweig; Director of the Göttingen Observatory from 1807; amongst his last students were Dedekind and Riemann.

**Grassmann, Hermann Günther** (Stettin (now Sczcecin, Poland), 1809–Stettin, 1877)

*Institutional affiliations*: none; taught himself mathematics and physics and became a school teacher in Stettin; from 1848 onwards worked on comparative linguistics, particularly Sanskrit.

**Gregory, James** (near Aberdeen, Scotland, 1683–Edinburgh, 1675)

*Institutional affiliations*: Professor of Mathematics at St Andrews from 1668; Professor of Mathematics at Edinburgh from 1674.

*Friends, colleagues, correspondents*: studied in Padua under Stefano degli Angeli, a former pupil of Torricelli.

**Harriot, Thomas** ([Oxford], *c.*1560–London, 1621)

*Institutional affiliations*: none; worked under the patronage of the ninth Earl of Northumberland.

*Friends, colleagues, correspondents*: a close friend of Nathaniel Torporley, who worked for a time with Viète; later corresponded briefly with Kepler; otherwise communicated his findings only to a small circle of personal acquaintants.

**Hilbert, David** (Königsberg (now Kaliningrad), 1862–Göttingen, 1943)

*Institutional affiliations*: Privatdozent at University of Königsberg from 1886; Professor at Königsberg from 1892; Professor of Mathematics at Göttingen from 1895.

*Friends, colleagues, correspondents*: deeply influenced by Kronecker, but nevertheless upheld the work of Cantor.

**Hoüel, Guillaume-Jules** (Thaon, Normandy, 1823–Bordeaux, 1886)

*Institutional affiliations*: Professor of Pure Mathematics at Bordeaux.

**Hudde, Jan** (Amsterdam, 1628–Amsterdam, 1704)

*Institutional affiliations*: none; spent most of his life in Amsterdam as a civic official.

*Friends, colleagues, correspondents*: learned mathematics from Frans van Schooten (the younger) who published some of his papers.

**Huygens, Christiaan** (The Hague, Netherlands, 1629–The Hague, 1695 )

*Institutional affiliations*: Fellow of the Royal Society from its foundation in 1663, and of the Paris Academy from its foundation in 1666.

*Friends, colleagues, correspondents*: studied mathematics with Frans van Schooten; taught Leibniz in the 1670s; knew and corresponded with most of the French and English mathematicians of his day.

**al-Khwārizmī, abū ja'far Muhammad ibn Mūsā** (*fl.* 800–847)

Little is known about his life; under Caliph al-Ma'mūn (813–833) he was based in some capacity at the Dār al-Hikma in Baghdad.

**Kummer, Ernst Eduard** (Sorau (Zary, now Poland), 1810–Berlin, 1893)

*Institutional affiliations*: Professor at the University of Breslau (now Wroclaw, Poland); succeeded Dirichlet as Professor at Berlin in 1855.

*Friends, colleagues, correspondents*: friend of Jacobi and Dirichlet; joined in Berlin by Kronecker and Weierstrass.

**Lacroix, Sylvestre François** (Paris, 1765–Paris, 1843)

*Institutional affiliations*: succeeded Lagrange at the École Polytechnique in 1799; later held chairs at the Sorbonne and Collège de France.

*Friends, colleagues, correspondents*: contemporary of Laplace, Cauchy, Poisson, and others at the École Polytechnique.

**Lagrange, Joseph Louis** (Turin, 1736–Paris, 1813)

*Institutional affiliations*: foreign member of the Berlin Academy from 1756; replaced Lagrange at the Berlin Academy in 1766; taught at the École Polytechniqe in Paris from 1787.

*Friends, colleagues, correspondents*: corresponded with Euler from 1754; mentor to the young Cauchy; contemporary of Laplace, Poisson, and others at the École Polytechnique.

**Landen, John** (1719–1790)

A surveyor who spent most of his life in the countryside around Peterborough, East Anglia.

**Laplace, Pierre Simon de** (Beaumont-en-Auge, Normandy–Paris, 1827)

*Institutional affiliations*: member of the Paris Academy 1773; played important roles in the Écoles Polytechnique and Normale; the most influential mathematician of his day in France.

*Friends, colleagues, correspondents*: contemporary of Lagrange, Cauchy, Poisson, Fourier, and others in Paris.

**Lebesgue, Henri Léon** (Beauvais, 1875–Paris, 1941)

*Institutional affiliations*: studied at the Sorbonne; member of the Paris Academy from 1922.

**Leibniz, Gottfried Wilhelm** (Leipzig, 1646–Hannover, 1716)

*Institutional affiliations*: Fellow of the Royal Society from 1673; helped to found the Berlin Academy in 1700.

*Friends, colleagues, correspondents*: studied in Paris under Huygens; knew and corresponded with mathematicians throughout Europe.

**Maclaurin, Colin** (Kilmodan, Scotland, 1698–Edinburgh, 1746)

*Institutional affiliations*: Professor of Mathematics at Aberdeen from 1717; Fellow of the Royal Society from 1719; succeeded James Gregory as Professor of Mathematics at Edinburgh.

*Friends, colleagues, correspondents*: staunch supporter of Newton, who recommended him for his position in Aberdeen.

**Mercator, Nicolaus** (Schleswig-Holstein [now Germany], *c.* 1619–Paris, 1687)

*Institutional affiliations*: came to England in 1653 and made a living as a tutor of mathematics; Fellow of the Royal Society from 1666.

**Mersenne, Marin** (Oizé, France, 1588–Paris, 1648)

*Institutional affiliations*: entered the Minim convent in Paris in 1619.

*Friends, colleagues, correspondents*: corresponded with, and sometimes met, most of the leading scientists and mathematicians of the day, acting as a trusted intermediary and promoting an exchange of ideas across Europe.

**de Moivre, Abraham** (Vitry-le-François, France, 1667–London, 1745)

*Institutional affiliations*: forced to emigrate to England after the revocation of the edict of Nantes; Fellow of the Royal Society from 1697; later a member of the Academies of Berlin and Paris.

**Napier, John** (Edinburgh, 1550–Edinburgh, 1617)

*Institutional affiliations*: none; landowner at Gartes, Scotland.

*Friends, colleagues, correspondents*: after publishing his work on logarithms collaborated with Briggs.

**Newton, Isaac** (Woolsthorpe, Lincolnshire, 1642–London, 1727)

*Institutional affiliations*: entered Trinity College, Cambridge, 1661; Lucasian Professor of Mathematics at Cambridge from 1669; President of the Royal Society from 1703.

*Friends, colleagues, correspondents*: communicated his early work to Barrow and Collins; in 1676 corresponded with Leibniz through Collins; later known to all the mathematicians of his day but rarely developed close friendships.

**Nichomachus of Gerasa** (*fl. c.* 100 AD)

Appears to have come from Gerasa in Palestine; his date is inferred only from the fact that his *Introduction to arithmetic* was reasonably well known by the mid second century AD.

**Pascal, Blaise** (Clermont-Ferrand, 1623–Paris, 1662)

*Institutional affiliations*: none; spent most of his life in Paris.

*Friends, colleagues, correspondents*: corresponded with Mersenne, Fermat.

**Pisano, Leonardo** (Fibonacci) (Pisa, *c.*1170–probably Pisa, after *c.*1240)

Spent most of his early years in north Africa and the countries bordering the Mediterranean; nothing else is known about his life, except that he was awarded a yearly salary by the city of Pisa in 1240.

**Poisson, Siméon-Denis** (Pithiviers, 1781–Paris, 1840)

*Institutional affiliations*: taught at the École Polytechnique from 1800 onwards.

*Friends, colleagues, correspondents*: studied under Lagrange and Laplace who were later his colleagues at the École Polytechnique.

**Riemann, Georg Friedrich Bernhard** (Breselenz, northern Germany, 1826–Lake Maggiore, Italy, 1866)

*Institutional affiliations*: taught at Göttingen from 1854; succeeded Dirichlet as Professor at Göttingen in 1859.

*Friends, colleagues, correspondents*: influenced by Jacobi and Dirichlet in Berlin in 1847; studied under Gauss in Göttingen.

**Sacrobosco, Johannes** (died Paris, 1244 or 1256)

Almost nothing known of his life, but he appears to have belonged to the monastery of Holywood (in Latin *sacer boscus*) in Nithsdale, Scotland; lived in Paris from about 1220.

**Stevin, Simon** (Bruges, 1540–The Hague, 1620)

*Institutional affiliations*: none; engineer, and later quartermaster-general of the army of the Netherlands; tutor to Maurice, prince of Orange.

**Stokes, George Gabriel** (Skreen, County Sligo, Ireland, 1819–Cambridge, 1903)

*Institutional affiliations*: graduated as Senior Wrangler and Smith's prizewinner from Pembroke College, Cambridge, 1841; Lucasian Professor of Mathematics at Cambridge from 1849; President of the Royal Society from 1885.

**Taylor, Brook** (Edmonton, Middlesex, 1685–London, 1731)

*Institutional affiliations*: graduated in law from St John's College, Cambridge from 1709; Fellow of the Royal Society from 1711.

**Torricelli, Evangelista** (Faenze, Italy, 1608–Florence, 1647)

*Institutional affiliations*: succeeded Galileo as mathematician and philosopher to Duke Ferdinand II.

*Friends, colleagues, correspondents*: studied in Rome under Castelli, a former pupil of Galileo; corresponded with a number of Italian and French mathematicians.

**Tschirnhaus, Ehrenfried Walter von** (near Görlitz, Germany, 1651–Dresden, 1708)

*Institutional affiliations*: none.

*Friends, colleagues, correspondents*: met members of the Royal Society in London, Huygens and Leibniz in Paris, and many other leading scientists and mathematicians throughout Europe.

**Vandermonde, Alexandre-Théophile** (Paris, 1735–Paris, 1796)

*Institutional affiliations*: trained for a career in music and wrote only four mathematical papers; member of the Paris Academy from 1771.

**Viète, François** (Fontenay-le-Comte, western France, 1540–Paris, 1603)

*Institutional affiliations*: trained as a lawyer and spent most of his life in high government office.

**Wallis, John** (Ashford, Kent, 1616–Oxford, 1703)

*Institutional affiliations*: Savilian Professor of Geometry at Oxford from 1649.

*Friends, colleagues, correspondents*: worked with Brouncker in the 1650s; corresponded with mathematicians throughout Europe.

**Weierstrass, Karl Theodor Wilhelm** (Ostenfelde, Germany, 1815–Berlin, 1897)

*Institutional affiliations*: trained as a teacher and taught elementary mathematics and other subjects until 1856; Associate Professor at Berlin from 1856; full Professor from 1864.

## INSTITUTIONS

**University of Bologna**,  founded 1088.

**University of Oxford**,  founded in the late eleventh century; Savilian Chairs of Geometry and Astronomy established by Henry Savile in 1619.

**University of Cambridge**,  founded in the early thirteenth century; Lucasian Chair of Mathematics established in 1663.

**University of Pavia**,  founded 1361.

**University of St Andrews**,  founded 1413.

**University of Basel**,  founded 1459.

**Gresham College, London**,  established by Thomas Gresham in 1575 to provide free public lectures in geometry, astronomy, and other subjects in the City of London.

**Royal Society**,  established in 1660; early meetings were held at Gresham College.

**Paris Academy of Sciences**,  established 1666.

**Berlin Academy of Sciences**,  founded in 1700 as the Berlin-Brandenburg Society of Scientists.

**St Petersburg Academy**,  founded by Leibniz in 1725.

**University of Göttingen**,  established 1734.

**École Polytechnique**,  established 1794.

**University of Berlin**,  established 1810.

**London Mathematical Society**,  established 1865.


## JOURNALS

*Philosophical transactions of the Royal Society*,  established 1665.

*Acta eruditorum*,  published from 1682 to 1731 when it was succeeded by the *Nova acta eruditorum*.

*Mémoires de l'Académie Royale des Sciences de Paris*,  published from 1699 to 1790.

*Mémoires de l'Académie des Sciences et des Belles-Lettres de Berlin*,  published from 1745 to 1769.

*Nouveaux mémoires de l'Académie des Sciences et Belles-Lettres*,  published from 1770 to 1786.

*Journal de l'École Polytechnique*,  published from 1795. The first two volumes are a collection of lecture notes, which had been printed in individual *Cahiers* between 1795 and 1800, and were thus effectively textbooks for the courses at the École; after that the *Journal* became a repository of new research.

*Bulletin des sciences mathématiques, physiques et chemiques*,  known as Bulletin de Férussac,  established 1824.

*Journal für die reine und angewandte Mathematik*,  known as Crelle's journal,  established in 1826 by August Leopold Crelle.

*Comptes rendus* (of the Paris Academy),  established 1835.

*Journal de mathématiques pures et appliquées*,  known as Liouville's journal, established in 1836 by Joseph Liouville.

*Mathematische Annalen*,  established 1868.

# BIBLIOGRAPHY

## PRIMARY SOURCES

Collected works, where they exist, are given as the first entry for each author. All other entries are in chronological order of publication.

Abel, Niels Henrik, *Oeuvres complètes de Niels Henrik Abel* (second edition), edited by Ludvig Sylow and Sophus Lie, 2 vols, Christiana, 1881 (= *Oeuvres*).

Abel, Niels Henrik, 'Mémoire sur les équations algébriques, où l'on démontre l'impossibilité de la résolution de l'équation générale du cinquième degré', first printed in Christiana (now Oslo) in 1824; and in *Oeuvres*, I, 28–33.

Abel, Niels Henrik, 'Beweis der Unmöglichkeit algebraische Gleichungen von höheren Graden als dem vierten allgemein aufzulösen', *Journal für die reine und angewandte Mathematik* (= Crelle's journal), 1 (1826), 65–84; and as 'Démonstration de l'impossibilité de la résolution algébrique des équations générales qui passent le quatrième degré' in *Oeuvres*, I, 66–87.

Abel, Niels Henrik, 'Untersuchungen über die Reihe: $1 + \frac{m}{1}x + \frac{m(m-1)}{1.2}x^2 + \frac{m(m-1)(m-2)}{1.2.3}x^3 + \dots$', *Journal für die reine und angewandte Mathematik* (= Crelle's journal), 1 (1826), 311–339.

d'Alembert, Jean le Rond, *Opuscules mathématiques, ou mémoires sur différens sujets de géométrie, de méchanique, d'optique, d'astronomie etc.*, 8 vols, Paris, 1761–80 (= *Opuscules*).

d'Alembert, Jean le Rond, 'Récherches sur la courbe que forme une corde tenduë mise en vibration', *Mémoires de l'Académie Royale des Sciences à Berlin*, 3 (1747), 214–219.

d'Alembert, Jean le Rond, *Encyclopédie, ou, Dictionnaire raisonné des sciences, des arts et des métiers. …Mis en ordre et publié par M. Diderot, de l'Académie Royale des Sciences et des Belles-Lettres de Prusse; et quant à la partie mathématique, par M. d'Alembert, de l'Académie Royale des Sciences de Paris….*, 16 vols, Paris, 1751–65.

d'Alembert, 'Réflexions sur les suites et sur les racines imaginaires'; in *Opuscules*, V, 171–215.

Ampère, André-Marie, 'Recherches sur quelques points de la théorie des fonctions dérivées qui conduisent à une nouvelle démonstration de la série de Taylor, et à l'expression finie des termes qu'on néglige lorsqu'on arrête cette série à un terme quelconque', *Journal de l'École Polytechnique*, Cahier 13, 6 (1806), 148–181.

Anonymous, *The nine chapters on the mathematical art: companion and commentary*, edited and translated by Kangshen Shen, John N Crossley, and Anthony W-C Lunn, Oxford University Press, 1999.

Apollonius, *Apollonii Pergaei conicorum libri quattuor*, edited and translated by Federico Commandino, Bologna, 1566.

Apollonius, *Apollonii Pergaei conicorum libri octo*, edited and translated by Edmund Halley, Oxford, 1710.

Arbuthnot, John, *Of the laws of chance, or, a method of calculation of the hazards of game*, London, 1692.

Archimedes, *Archimedis opera non nulla*, edited and translated by Federico Commandino, Venice, 1558.

Argand, [Jean Robert], *Essai sur une manière de représenter les quantités imaginaires dans les constructions géométriques*; reprinted by Jules Hoüel, Paris, 1874.

Bayes, Thomas, 'An essay towards solving a problem in the doctrine of chances', *Philosophical transactions of the Royal Society*, 53 (1763), 370–418.

Berkeley, George, *The analyst; or, a discourse addressed to an infidel mathematician*, London, 1734.

Bernoulli Jacob, *Jacobi Bernoulli basileensis opera*, edited by Gabriel Cramer, 2 vols, Geneva, 1744 (= *Opera*).

Bernoulli, Jacob, 'Analysis problematis antehac propositi, de inventione lineae descensus a corpore gravi percurrendae uniformiter, sic ut temporibus aequalibus aequales altitudines emetiatur: et alterius cujusdam problematis propositio', *Acta eruditorum*, (1690), 217–219; and in *Opera*, I, 421–423.

Bernoulli, Jacob, 'Solutio problematum fraternorum, peculiari programmate […] una cum propositione reciproca aliorum', *Acta eruditorum*, (1697) 211–217; and in *Opera*, II, 768–778.

Bernoulli, Jacob, *Ars conjectandi*, Basel, 1713.

Bernoulli, Johann, *Johannis Bernoulli […] Opera omnia*, 4 vols, Lausanne and Geneva, 1742 (= *Opera*).

Bernoulli, Johann, 'Lettre de Mr. Bernoulli […] du 15 Octobre 1697', *Journal des Savans*, (1697), 458; partially reprinted as 'Solutio problematum quae Jacobus Bernoullius […] frater fratri proposuit', *Acta eruditorum*, (1698), 52–56.

Bernoulli, Johann, 'Solution d'un problème concernant le calcul intégral, avec quelques abregés par raport à ce calcul', *Mémoires de l'Académie Royale des Sciences*, (1702), 296–305; reprinted as 'Problema exhibitum a Jo. Bernoullo', *Acta eruditorum*, (1703), 26–31; and in *Opera*, I, 393–399.

Bernoulli, Johann, 'Solution du probleme proposé par M. Jacques Bernoulli […] trouvé en deux manières par M. Jean Bernoulli son frère', *Mémoires de l'Académie Royale des Sciences*, (1706), 235–245; and in *Opera*, I, 424–435.

Bernoulli, Johann, 'Remarques sur ce qu'on a donné jusqu'ici de solutions des problèmes sur les isoperimetres', *Mémoires de l'Académie Royale des Sciences*, (1718), 100–135; reprinted as 'De solutionibus quae extant problematum isoperimetricorum', *Acta eruditorum*, (1718), 16–31 and 74–88; and in *Opera*, II, 235–269.

Boethius, Anicius Manlius Severinus, *De institutione arithmeticae*, translated by Michael Masi in *Boethian number theory: a translation of the De institutione arithmetica*, Studies in Classical Antiquity vol 6, Amsterdam: Rodopi, 1983.

Bolzano, Bernard, *The mathematical works of Bernard Bolzano*, edited and translated by Steve Russ, Oxford University Press 2004 (= *Works*).

Bolzano, Bernard, *Der binomische Lehrsatz, und als Folgerung aus ihm der polynomische, und die Reihen die zur Berechnung des Logarithmen und Exponentialgrössen dienen, genauer als bisher erwiesen*, Prague, 1816; and in *Works*, 153–248.

Bolzano, Bernard, *Rein analytischer Beweis des Lehrsatzes, daß zwischen je zwei Werten, die ein entgegengesetztes Resultat gewähren, wenigstens eine reelle Wurzel der Gleichung liege*, Prague: Gottlieb Haase, 1817; reprinted in *Abhandlungen der königlichen böhmischen Gesellschaft der Wissenschaften*, 5 (1818); and in *Works*, 249–277.

Borrell, Jean (= Johann Buteo), *Logistica, quae et arithmetica vulgo dicitur*, Lyons, 1559.

Briggs, Henry, *Arithmetica logarithmica, sive logarithmorum chiliades triginta*, London, 1624.

Brouncker, William, 'The squaring of the hyperbola by an infinite series of rational numbers', *Philosophical transactions of the Royal Society*, 3 (1668), 645–649.

Calinger, Ronald, (ed), *Classics of mathematics*, Moore Publishing Co., 1982; reprinted New Jersey: Prentice Hall, 1995.

Cantor, Georg, *Gesammelte Abhandlungen mathematischen und philosophischen Inhalts*, edited by Ernst Zermelo, Berlin: Springer, 1932; reprinted in facsimile Hildesheim: Olms, 1962 (= *Abhandlungen*).

Cantor, Georg, 'Über die Ausdehnung eines Satzes aus der Theorie der trigonometrischen Reihen', *Mathematische Annalen*, 5 (1872), 123–132; and in *Abhandlungen*, 92–102.

Cantor, Georg, 'Über eine Eigenschaft des Inbegriffes aller reellen algebraischen Zahlen', *Journal für die reine und angewandte Mathematik* (= Crelle's journal), 77 (1874), 258–262; and in *Abhandlungen*, 115–118.

Cantor, Georg, 'Über eine elementare Frage der Mannigfaltigkeitslehre', *Jahresbericht der Deutschen Mathematiker-Vereinigung*, 1 (1891), 75–78; and in *Abhandlungen*, 278–281.

Cantor, Georg, 'Beiträge zur Begründung der transfiniten Mengenlehre', *Mathematische Annalen*, 46 (1895), 481–512 and 49 (1897), 207–246; and in *Abhandlungen*, 282–356; translated by Philip Edward Bertrand Jourdain as *Contributions to the founding of the transfinite numbers*, Chicago: Open Court, 1915; reprinted New York: Dover, 1955.

Cardano, Girolamo, *Artis magnae, sive, de regulis algebraicis, liber unus* (= *Ars magna*), Nuremberg, 1545; translated by T Richard Witmer as *Ars magna, or, the rules of algebra*, Cambridge, MA: MIT Press, 1968; reprinted New York: Dover, 1993.

Cardano, Girolamo, 'Liber de ludo aleae', translated by Sydney Henry Gould in *Cardano the gambling scholar*, Princeton: Princeton University Press, 1953; reprinted New York: Dover, 1965.

Cauchy, Augustin-Louis, *Oeuvres complètes d'Augustin Cauchy*, series (1) 12 vols, series (2) 15 vols, Paris, 1882–1974 (= *Oeuvres*).

Cauchy, Augustin-Louis, 'Sur le nombre des valeurs qu'un fonction peut acquérir, lorsqu'on y permute de toutes les manières possibles les quantités qu'elle renferme', *Journal de l'École Polytechnique*, Cahier 17, 10 (1815), 1–28; and in *Oeuvres* (2), I, 64–90.

Cauchy, Augustin-Louis, 'Sur les fonctions qui ne peuvent obtenir que deux valeurs égales et de signes contraires par suite des transpositions opérées entre les variables qu'elles renferment', *Journal de l'École Polytechnique*, Cahier 17, 10 (1815), 29–112; and in *Oeuvres* (2), I, 91–169.

Cauchy, Augustin-Louis, *Cours d'analyse de l'École Royale Polytechnique*, I$^{re}$ partie, *Analyse algébrique*, Paris, 1821; and in *Oeuvres* (2) III, 17–471.

Cauchy, Augustin-Louis, *Resumé des leçons données à l'École Royale Polytechnique, sur le calcul infinitésimal*, Paris, 1823; and in *Oeuvres* (2) IV, 13–609.

Cauchy, Augustin-Louis, 'Sur un nouveau genre de calcul analogue au calcul infinitésimal', *Exercices de Mathématiques*, 1 (1826), 11–24; and in *Oeuvres* (2), VI, 23–37.

Cauchy, Augustin-Louis, 'Mémoire sur les intégrales définies', *Mémoires présentés par divers savans à l'Académie Royale des Sciences de l'Institut de France* (1), 1 (1827), 601–799; and in *Oeuvres* (1), I, 329–475.

Cauchy, Augustin-Louis, 'Sur l'équation a l'aide de laquelle on détermine les inégalités séculaires des mouvements des planètes', *Exercices de mathématiques*, 4 (1829), 140–160; and in *Oeuvres*, (2), IX, 174–195.

Cauchy, Augustin-Louis, 'Formules pour le développement des fonctions en séries' in 'Résumé d'un mémoire sur la mécanique céleste et sur un nouveau calcul appelé calcul des limites', Lithograph, Turin, 1833; and in *Oeuvres* (2) XII, 48–112.

Cauchy, Augustin-Louis, 'Sur le nombre des valeurs égales ou inégales que peut acquérir une fonction de $n$ variables indépendantes, quand on y permute ces variables entre elles d'une manière quelconque', *Comptes rendus de l'Académie des Sciences*, 21 (1845), 593–607; and in *Oeuvres* (1), IX, 277–293.

Cavalieri, Bonaventura, *Geometria indivisibilibus continuorum nove quadam ratione promota*, Bologna, 1635.

Cayley, Arthur, *The collected mathematical papers of Arthur Cayley*, edited by Cayley (vols 1–7) and A R Forsyth (vols 8–13), Cambridge: The University Press, 1889–97 (= *Papers*).

Cayley, Arthur, 'On a property of the caustic by refraction of the circle', *Philosophical magazine* (4), 6 (1853), 427–431; and in *Papers*, II, 118–122.

Cayley, Arthur, 'On the theory of groups, as depending on the symbolic equation $\theta^n = 1$', *Philosophical magazine* (4), 7 (1854), 41–47 and 408–409; and in *Papers*, II, 123–130 and 131–132.

Cayley, Arthur, 'A memoir on the theory of matrices', *Philosophical transactions of the Royal Society*, 148 (1858), 17–37; and in *Papers*, II, 475–496.

Cayley, Arthur, 'On the theory of groups, as depending on the symbolic equation $\theta^n = 1$', *Philosophical magazine*, 18 (1859), 34–37; and in *Papers*, IV, 88–91.

Cayley, Arthur, 'A theorem on groups', *Mathematische Annalen*, 13 (1878), 561–565; and in *Papers*, X, 149–152.

Cayley, Arthur, 'On the theory of groups', *Proceedings of the London Mathematical Society*, 9 (1878), 126–133; and in *Papers*, X, 324–330.

Cayley, Arthur, 'Desiderata and suggestions', *American journal of mathematics*, 1 (1878), 50–52 and 174–176; and in *Papers*, X, 401–405.

Dedekind, Richard, *Gesammelte mathematische Werke*, edited by Robert Fricke, Emmy Noether, and Öystein Ore, 3 vols, Braunschweig, 1930–32; reprinted in 2 vols, with the first 220 pages of the original vol 3 omitted, New York: Chelsea, 1969 (= *Werke*).

Dedekind, Richard, *Stetigkeit und irrationale Zahlen*, Braunschweig, 1872; and in *Werke*, III, 315–334; translated by Wooster Woodruff Beman in *Essays on the theory of numbers*, Chicago: Open Court, 1901; reprinted New York: Dover, 1963.

Dedekind, Richard, 'Sur la théorie des nombres entiers algébriques', *Bulletin des sciences mathématiques et astronomiques*, in five parts: series (1), 11 (1876), 278–288; series (2), 1 (1877), §1–§4, 17–41; §5–§12, 69–92; §13–§18, 144–164; §19–§30, 207–248; Introduction and §1–§11 in *Werke*, III, 262–296; and in the eleventh supplement to Dirichlet's *Vorlesungen*, third edition, 1879; translated by John Stillwell as *Theory of algebraic integers*, Cambridge University Press, 1996.

Dedekind, Richard, *Was sind und was sollen die Zahlen?*, Braunschweig, 1888; and in *Werke*, III, 335–391; translated by Wooster Woodruff Beman in *Essays on the theory of numbers*, Chicago: Open Court, 1901; reprinted New York: Dover, 1963.

Descartes, René, *La géométrie*, appended to *Discours de la méthode*, Leiden, 1637; translated by David Eugene Smith and Marcia L Latham as *The geometry of René Descartes*, Chicago: Open Court, 1925; reprinted New York: Dover, 1954.

Diophantus of Alexandria, *Diophanti Alexandrini arithmeticorum libri sex*, edited by Claude Gaspar Bachet, Paris, 1621.

Diophantus of Alexandria, *Diophanti Alexandrini arithmeticorum libri sex …cum obseruationibus P. de Fermat*, edited by Samuel Fermat, Toulouse, 1670.

Diophantus of Alexandria, *Books IV to VII of Diophantus' Arithmetica: in the Arabic translation attributed to Qusta ibn Luqa*, edited by Jacques Sesiano, New York: Springer, 1982.

Dirichlet, Peter Gustav Lejeune-, *Vorlesungen über Zahlentheorie*, edited by Richard Dedekind, Braunschweig, 1863; second edition 1871; third edition 1879; fourth edition 1894.

Euclid, *Elements*, translated by Henry Billingsley as *The elements of geometrie*, London, 1570.

Euclid, *Elements*, translated by Isaac Barrow as *Euclide's Elements; the whole fifteen books compendiously demonstrated*, London, 1660.

Euler, Leonhard, *Opera omnia*, series (1) 30 vols, series (2) 32 vols to date, series (3) 12 vols to date, Euler Committee of the Swiss Academy of Sciences, Leipzig, 1911– (= *Opera*).

Euler, Leonhard, *Introductio in analysin infinitorum*, Lausanne, 1748; second edition Lyons, 1797; and in *Opera*, (1), XIII and IX.

Euler, Leonhard, 'De vibratione chordarum exercitatio', *Nova acta eruditorum*, (1749), 512–527; also published in French as 'Sur la vibration des cordes', *Mémoires de l'Académie des Sciences à Berlin*, 4 (1748), 69–85; both versions in *Opera*, (2), X, 50–77.

Euler, Leonhard, 'Remarques sur les mémoires précedens de M. Bernoulli', *Mémoires de l'Académie des Sciences à Berlin*, 9 (1753), 196–222; and in *Opera*, (2), X, 233–254.

Euler, Leonhard, *Institutiones calculi differentialis, cum eius usu in analysi finitorum ac doctrina serierum*, Berlin, 1755; and in *Opera*, (1), X.

Euler, Leonhard, *Institutiones calculi integralis*, 3 vols, St Petersburg, 1768–70; republished with a new 4th volume, St Petersburg, 1792–94; and in *Opera*, (1), XI–XIII.

Ewald, William, *From Kant to Hilbert: a source book in the foundations of mathematics*, 2 vols, Oxford: Clarendon Press, 1996; reprinted in paperback 1999.

Fauvel, John and Gray, Jeremy, (eds) *The history of mathematics: a reader*, Basingstoke: Macmillan, 1987.

Fermat, Pierre de, *Varia opera mathematica*, Toulouse, 1679 (= *Varia opera*).

Fermat, Pierre de, *Oeuvres de Fermat*, edited by Paul Tannery and Charles Henry, 4 vols, Paris, 1891–1912 (= *Oeuvres*).

Fermat, Pierre de, statement of 'Fermat's last theorem' for cubes, in Wallis, *Commercium epistolicum*, 1658, 158–161; and in Wallis, *Opera*, II, 844–845, and Fermat, *Oeuvres*, II, 374–378.

Fermat, Pierre de, 'Methodus ad disquirendam maximam et minimam et de tangentibus linearum curvarum', [1629], in *Varia opera*, 63–64; and in *Oeuvres*, I, 133–136.

Fermat, Pierre de, 'Ad locos planos et solidos isagoge', [1630s], in *Varia opera*, 1–8; and in *Oeuvres*, I, 91–103.

Fermat, Pierre de, letters outlining Fermat's 'little theorem', [1640], in *Varia opera*, 176–178 and 162–164; and in *Oeuvres*, II, 193–199 and 206–212.

Fermat, Pierre de, letters on games of chance, [1654], in *Varia opera*, 179–188; and in *Oeuvres*, II, 288–314.

Fermat, Pierre de, 'De aequationum localium transmutatione et emendatione ad multimodam curvilineorum inter se vel cum rectilineis comparationem, cui annectitur proportionis geometricae in quadrandis infinitis parabolis et hyperbolis usus', [1657–58], in *Varia opera*, 44–57; and in *Oeuvres*, I, 255–285.

Fourier, Jean Baptiste Joseph, *Oeuvres de Fourier*, edited by Gaston Darboux, 2 vols, Paris, 1888–1890 (= *Oeuvres*).

Fourier, Jean Baptiste Joseph, *Théorie analytique de la chaleur*, Paris, 1822; and in *Oeuvres*, I, xv–541; translated by Alexander Freeman as *The analytical theory of heat*, Cambridge, 1878; reprinted New York: Dover, *c.* 1955.

Frobenius, Ferdinand Georg, *Gesammelte Abhandlungen*, edited by Jean-Pierre Serre, 3 vols, Berlin: Springer, 1968 (= *Abhandlungen*).

Frobenius, Ferdinand Georg, 'Über lineare Substitutionen und bilineare Formen', *Journal für die reine und angewandte Mathematik* (= Crelle's journal), 84 (1878), 1–63; and in *Abhandlungen*, I, 343–405.

Galois, Évariste, 'Oeuvres mathématiques d'Évariste Galois', edited by Joseph Liouville, *Journal de mathématiques pures et appliquées* (= Liouville's journal), 11 (1846), 381–444 (= *Oeuvres*).

Galois, Évariste, *Écrits et mémoires mathématiques*, edited by Robert Bourgne and Jean-Paul Azra, Paris: Gauthier-Villars, 1962 (= *Écrits*).

Galois, Évariste, 'Sur la théorie des nombres', *Bulletin des sciences mathématiques, physiques et chimiques* (= *Bulletin de Férussac*), 13 (1830), 428–435; and in *Écrits*, 112–127.

Galois, Évariste, 'Mémoire sur les conditions de résolubilité des équations par radicaux' (= 'Premier mémoire'), [1831], in *Oeuvres*, 417–433; and in *Écrits*, 37–71; translated by Harold M Edwards as 'Memoir on the conditions for solvability of equations by radicals' in *Galois theory*, New York: Springer, 1984, 101–113.

Galois, Évariste, letter to Auguste Chevalier, [1832], in *Oeuvres*, 408–415; and in *Écrits*, 172–185.

Gauss, Carl Friedrich, *Carl Friedrich Gauss Werke*, edited by E J Schering, 9 vols, Göttingen, 1863–1903.

Gauss, Carl Friedrich, *Disquisitiones arithmeticae*, Leipzig, 1801; and in *Werke*, I, 9–463.

Grassmann, Hermann, *Die Ausdehnungslehre*, Berlin: Enslin, 1862; translated by Lloyd C Kannenburg as *Extension theory*, Providence RI: American Mathematical Society and London Mathematical Society, 2000.

Gregory, James, *James Gregory: Tercentenary memorial volume*, edited by H W Turnbull, London: for the Royal Society of Edinburgh, 1939.

Halliwell-Phillipps, James Orchard, (ed), *Rara mathematica: or, a collection of treatises on the mathematics and subjects connected with them, from ancient inedited manuscripts*, London, 1839.

Harriot, Thomas, *Artis analyticae praxis, ad aequationes algebraicas nova expedita, et generali methodo, resolvendas: tractatus*, London, 1631.

Harriot, Thomas, manuscript writings on equations, translated by Jacqueline Stedall in *The greate invention of algebra: Thomas Harriot's treatise on equations*, Oxford University Press, 2003.

Heine, Eduard, 'Die Elemente der Functionenlehre', *Journal für die reine und angewandte Mathematik* (= Crelle's journal), 74 (1872), 172–188.

Hilbert, David, *Grundlagen der Geometrie*, in *Festschrift zur Feier der Enthüllung des Gauss-Weber-Denkmals in Göttingen*, Leipzig, 1899; translated by E J Townsend as *The foundations of geometry*, London: Kegan Paul, Trench, Trübner, 1902.

Hobbes, Thomas, *Elements of philosophy, the first section, concerning body. Written in Latine …and now translated into English. To which are added six lessons to the professors of mathematicks of the institution of Sr Henry Savile, in the University of Oxford*, London, 1656.

Hoüel, Guillaume Jules, *Théorie élémentaire des quantités complexes*, 3 vols in 1, Paris, 1867–74.

Hudde, Jan, *De reductione aequationum*, 1657, in van Schooten 1659, I, 407–506.

Huygens, Christiaan, *De ratiociniis in ludo aleae*, in van Schooten 1657; translated by John Arbuthnot, *Of the laws of chance, or, a method of calculation of the hazards of game*, London, 1692.

al-Khwārizmī, *Al-jabr wa'l-muqābala*; translated by Louis Charles Karpinski in *Robert of Chester's Latin translation of the algebra of al-Khwarizmi*, New York, 1915.

Kummer, Ernst Eduard, 'De numeris complexis, qui radicibus unitatis et numeris integris realibus constant', *Journal de mathématiques pures et appliquées* (= Liouville's journal), 12 (1847), 185–212.

Kummer, Ernst Eduard, 'Zur Theorie der complexen Zahlen', *Journal für die reine und angewandte Mathematik* (= Crelle's journal), 35 (1847), 319–326.

Kummer, Ernst, 'Über die Zerlegung der aus Wurzeln der Einheit gebildeten complexen Zahlen in ihre Primfactoren', *Journal für die reine und angewandte Mathematik* (= Crelle's journal), 35 (1847), 327–367.

Lacroix, Sylvestre François, *Traité du calcul différentiel et du calcul intégral*, 3 vols, Paris, 1797–1800; second edition, revised and augmented, 3 vols, Paris, 1810–19.

Lacroix, Sylvestre François, *Traité élémentaire du calcul différentiel et du calcul intégral*, Paris, 1802; translated by Charles Babbage, George Peacock, and John Herschel, as *An elementary treatise on the differential and integral calculus*, Cambridge, 1816.

Lagrange, Joseph Louis, *Oeuvres de Lagrange*, edited by Joseph Alfred Serret, 14 vols, Paris, 1867–92 (= *Oeuvres*).

Lagrange, Joseph Louis, 'Réflexions sur la résolution algébrique des équations', *Nouveaux mémoires de l'Académie Royale des Sciences à Berlin*, 1 (1770), 134–215, and 2 (1771), 138–253; and in *Oeuvres*, III, 203–421.

Lagrange, Joseph Louis, 'Nouvelle solution du problème du mouvement de rotation d'un corps de figure quelconque qui n'est animé par aucune force accélératrice', *Nouveaux mémoires de l'Académie Royale des Sciences à Berlin*, 4 (1773), 85–105; and in *Oeuvres*, III, 577–616.

Lagrange, Joseph Louis, *Théorie des fonctions analytiques: contenant les principes du calcul différentiel, dégagés de toute considération d'infiniment petits, d'évanouissans, de limites et de fluxions, et réduits à l'analyse algébrique des quantités finies*, first edition, Paris, 1797; second, augmented, edition, Paris, 1813; the first edition was reprinted in *Journal de l'École Polytechnique*, Cahier 9, 3 (1801), 1–277, but in some bound copies it has been replaced by the second edition of 1813, with pagination 1–383; and in *Oeuvres*, IX, 15–413.

Landen, John, *A discourse concerning the residual analysis: a new branch of the algebraic art*, London, 1758.

Laplace, Pierre Simon de, *Oeuvres complètes*, Académie de Sciences, 14 vols, Paris, 1878–1912 (= *Oeuvres*).

Laplace, Pierre Simon de, 'Mémoire sur les variations séculaires des orbites des planètes', *Mémoires de l'Académie Royale des Sciences*, (1787), 267–279; and in *Oeuvres*, XL, 295–306.

Laplace, Pierre Simon de, 'Mémoire sur les approximations des formules qui sont fonctions de très grands nombres', *Mémoires de l'Académie Royale des Sciences*, 10 (1809–10), 353–415; and in Laplace, 1812, 88–175, and in *Oeuvres*, XII, 310–353.

Laplace, Pierre Simon de, *Théorie analytique des probabilités*, Paris, 1812.

Lebesgue, Henri, 'Sur une généralisation de l'intégrale définie', *Comptes rendus*, 132 (1901), 1025–1028.

Leibniz, Gottfried Wilhelm, 'De vera proportione circuli ad quadratum circumscriptum in numeris rationalibus', *Acta eruditorum*, (1682), 41–46.

Leibniz, Gottfried Wilhelm, 'Nova methodus pro maximis et minimis, itemque tangentibus, …', *Acta eruditorum*, (1684), 467–473.

Leonardo of Pisa (= Fibonacci), *Liber abaci*, translated by L E Sigler as *Fibonacci's Liber abaci: Leonardo Pisano's book of calculation*, New York: Springer 2002; reprinted 2003.

Maclaurin, Colin, *A treatise of fluxions*, 2 vols, Edinburgh, 1742.

Maclaurin, Colin, *A treatise of algebra*, London, 1748.

Mercator, Nicolaus, *Logarithmotechnia, sive, methodus construendi logarithmos*, London, 1668.

Mersenne, Marin, *Cogitata physico-mathematica*, Paris, 1644.

de Moivre, Abraham, 'Aequationum quarundam potestatis tertia, quintae, septimae, nonae, et superiorum, ad infinitum usque pergendo, in terminis finitis, ad instar regularum pro cubicis quae vocantur Cardani, resolutio analytica', *Philosophical transactions of the Royal Society*, (1707), 2368–2371.

de Moivre, Abraham, *Miscellaneis analyticis supplementum*, appended with its own pagination to *Miscellanea analytica de seriebus et quadraturis*, London, 1730.

de Moivre, Abraham, *The doctrine of chances: or a method of calculating the probability of events in play*, London, 1718; for second and third editions, corrected and enlarged, see de Moivre, 1738.

de Moivre, Abraham, *The doctrine of chance: or, a method of calculating the probabilities of events in play*, London, 1738 and 1756.

Napier, John, *Mirifici logarithmorum canonis descriptio*, Edinburgh, 1614; translated by Edward Wright as *A description of the admirable table of logarithms*, London, 1616.

Napier, John, *Mirifici logarithmorum canonis constructio*, edited by Henry Briggs, Edinburgh, 1619.

Newton, Isaac, *The correspondence of Isaac Newton*, edited by H W Turnbull, 7 vols, Cambridge University Press, for the Royal Society, 1959–77 (= *Correspondence*).

Newton, Isaac, *The mathematical papers of Isaac Newton*, edited by D T Whiteside, 8 vols, Cambridge University Press, 1967–81 (= *Papers*).

Newton, Isaac, discovery of the general binomial theorem, [1664–65], in *Papers*, I, 122–134 (and frontispiece).

Newton, Isaac, 'De analysi per aequationes numero terminorum infinitas', [1669], published by William Jones as *Analysis per quantitatum series, fluxiones, ac differentias*, London, 1711; and in *Papers*, II, 206–247.

Newton, Isaac, treatise on fluxions and infinite series, [1671], translated by John Colson as *The method of fluxions, and infinite series*, London, 1736; and in *Papers*, III, 28–353.

Newton, Isaac, *Epistola prior*, 13 June 1676, partly published in Wallis, *A treatise of algebra*, London, 1685, 341–346; and in full in *Correspondence*, II, 20–47.

Newton, Isaac *Philosophiae naturalis principia mathematica*, London, 1687; second edition, amended and enlarged, Cambridge, 1713; third edition, London, 1726; translated by Andrew Motte as *The mathematical principles of natural philosophy*, London, 1729, reprinted London: Dawson, 1968; and by Isaac Bernard Cohen and Anne Miller Whitman in *The principia: mathematical principles of natural philosophy*, Berkeley: University of California Press, 1999.

Newton, Isaac, *Two treatises of the species and magnitude of curvilinear figures* appended to Newton, *Opticks: or, a treatise on the reflexions, refractions, inflexions and colours of light*, London, 1704.

Nicomachus of Gerasa, *Arithmetica*, translated by Martin Kuther d'Ooge as *Introduction to arithmetic*, New York: Macmillan, 1926.

Nissen, H J, Damerow P, and Englund K, *Archaic bookkeeping: early writing and techniques of economic administration in the ancient Near East*, Chicago University Press, 1993.

Oughtred, William, *Arithmeticae in numeris et speciebus institutio: quae tum logisticae, tum analyticae, atque adeo totius mathematicus quasi clavis est* (= *Clavis mathematicae*), London, 1631; augmented and reordered for the second edition 1647 (English) and 1648 (Latin).

Pascal, Blaise, letters to Fermat on games of chance, July–October 1654, see Fermat [1654].

Poisson, Siméon-Denis, 'Mémoire sur les intégrales définies', *Journal de l'École Polytechnique*, Cahier 16, 9 (1813), 215–246.

Riemann, Bernhard, *Gesammelte mathematische Werke und wissenschaftlicher Nachlass*, edited by Richard Dedekind and Heinrich Weber, Leipzig, 1876 (= *Werke*).

Riemann, *Über die Darstellbarkeit einer Function durch eine trigonometrische Reihe* (Habilitationsschrift), *Abhandlungen der Königlichen Gesellschaft der Wissenschaften zu Göttingen*, 13 (1854); and in *Werke*, 213–253.

Riemann, *Grundlagen für eine allgemeine Theorie der Functionen einer veränderlichen complexen Grösse* (Inauguraldissertation), Göttingen, 1851, printed as a 32-page pamphlet, Göttingen, 1867; and in *Werke*, 3–47.

Rigaud, Stephen Peter, (ed), *Correspondence of scientific men of the seventeenth century*, 2 vols, Oxford, 1841.

Roberval, Gilles Personne de, 'Traité des indivisibles' in *Divers ouvrages de mathématique et de physique, par Messieurs de l'Académie Royale des Sciences*, Paris, 1693; and in *Mémoires de l'Académie Royale des Sciences depuis 1666 jusqu'à 1699*, 6 (1730).

de Saint Vincent, Grégoire, *Opus geometricum quadraturae circuli et sectionum coni decem libris comprehensum*, Antwerp, 1647.

Schooten, Frans van, (ed), *Exercitationum mathematicarum libri quinque*, Leiden, 1657.

Schooten, Frans van, (ed), *Geometria*, 2 vols, Amsterdam, 1659–61.

Smith, David Eugene, *A source book in mathematics*, New York: McGraw-Hill, 1929; reprinted New York: Dover, 1959.

Stevin, Simon, *De thiende*, Leiden, 1585.

Stevin, Simon, *La disme*, in *L'arithmetique …aussi l'algebre …Encore un livre particulier de la pratique d'arithmetique*, Leiden, 1585.

Stokes, George Gabriel, *Mathematical and physical papers*, edited by Joseph Larmor, 5 vols, Cambridge, 1880–1905 (= *Papers*).

Stokes, George Gabriel, 'On the critical values of the sums of periodic series', *Transactions of the Cambridge Philosophical Society*, 8 (1849), 533–583; and in *Papers*, I, 236–313.

Struik, Dirk Jan, (ed) *A source book in mathematics 1200–1800*, Cambridge, MA: Harvard University Press, 1969; reprinted Princeton: University Press, 1986.

Tartaglia, Niccolo, *Quesiti et inventioni diverse*, Venice, 1546.

Taylor, Brook, *Methodus incrementorum directa et inversa*, London, 1715.

Torricelli, Evangelista, *De sphaera et solidis sphaeralibus libri duo. …De dimensione parabolae, solidique hyperbolici problemata duo*, also known as *Opera geometrica E. Torricelli*, Florence, 1644.

Tschirnhaus, Ehrenfried Walter von, 'Nova methodus auferendi omnes terminos intermedios ex data aequatione', *Acta eruditorum*, (1683), 204–207.

Vandermonde, Alexandre-Théophile, 'Mémoire sur la résolution des équations', *Mémoires de l'Académie Royale des Sciences*, (1771), 47–55 and 365–416.

Vandermonde, Alexandre-Théophile, 'Mémoire sur l'élimination', *Mémoires de l'Académie Royale des Sciences*, (1772), 516–532.

Viète, François, *F. Vietae opera mathematica*, edited by Frans van Schooten, Leiden, 1646 (= *Opera*); partly translated by T Richard Witmer as *The analytic art*, Kent State University Press, 1983.

Viète, François, *In artem analyticem isagoge, seorsim excussa ab opere restitutae mathematicae analyseos, seu algebra nova*, Tours, 1591.

Viète, François, *Zeteticorum libri quinque*, Tours, 1593.

Viète, François, *Effectionum geometricarum canonica recensio*, Tours, 1593.

Viète, François, *De numerosa potestatum ad exegesin resolutione*, Paris, 1600.

Wallis, John, *Operum mathematicorum pars prima, pars altera*, 2 vols, Oxford, 1656–57 (= *Operum*).

Wallis, John, *Opera mathematica*, 3 vols, 1693–99; reprinted in facsimile, Hildesheim: Olms, 1972 (= *Opera*).

Wallis, John, *The correspondence of John Wallis*, edited by Philip Beeley and Christoph Scriba, 2 vols to date, Oxford University Press, 2003– (= *Correspondence*).

Wallis, John, *De sectionibus conicis tractatus*, [1656], in *Operum*, II, 49–108; and in *Opera*, I, 291–354.

Wallis, John, *Arithmetica infinitorum*, [1656], in *Operum*, II, 1–199 (new pagination); and in *Opera*, I, 355–478; translated by Jacqueline Stedall as *The arithmetic of infinitesimals: John Wallis 1656*, New York: Springer, 2004.

Wallis, John, (ed), *Commercium epistolicum, de quaestionibus quibusdam mathematicis nuper habitum*, Oxford, 1658; and in *Opera*, II, 757–860; also in *Correspondence*, I, 274–502 passim.

Wallis, John, *Tractatus duo. Prior, de cycloide …Posterior, epistolaris …de cissoide …et de curvarum, …*, Oxford, 1659; and in *Opera*, I, 489–569.

Wallis, John, *A treatise of algebra both historical and practical*, London, 1685; and in Latin, augmented, in *Opera*, II, 1–482.

Weber, Heinrich, 'Beweis des Satzes, dass jede eigentlich primitive quadratische Form unendlich viele Primzahlen darzustellen fähig ist', *Mathematische Annalen*, 20 (1882), 301–329.

## SECONDARY SOURCES AND FURTHER READING

Andersen, Kirsti, 'Cavalieri's method of indivisibles', *Archive for history of exact sciences*, 31 (1985), 291–367.

Auger, Léon, *Un savant méconnu, Gilles Personne de Roberval, 1602–1675: son activité intellectuelle dans les domaines mathématique, physique, mécanique et philosophique*, Paris: A Blanchard, 1962.

Baron, Margaret E, *The origins of the infinitesimal calculus*, Oxford: Pergamon Press, 1969.

Belhoste, Bruno, *Augustin-Louis Cauchy: a biography*, translated from French by Frank Ragland, New York: Springer, 1991.

Bos, Henk J M, *Redefining geometrical exactness: Descartes' transformation of the Early Modern concept of construction*, New York: Springer, 2001.

Bottazzini, Umberto, *The higher calculus: a history of real and complex analysis from Euler to Weierstrass*, translated from Italian by Warren Van Egmond, New York: Springer, 1986.

Burn, Bob, 'Gregory of St Vincent and the rectangular hyperbola', *Mathematical gazette*, 84 (2000), 480–485.

Burn, Robert P, 'Alphonse Antonio de Sarasa and logarithms', *Historia mathematica*, 28 (2001), 1–17.

Burn, Bob, 'Fermat's little theorem – proofs that Fermat might have used', *Mathematical gazette*, 86 (2002), 415–422.

Burn, Robert P, 'The vice: some historically inspired and proof-generated steps to limits of sequences', *Educational studies in mathematics*, 60 (2005), 269–295.

Burnett, Charles, *The introduction of Arabic learning into England*, London: British Library, 1997.

Cajori, Florian, *A history of mathematical notations*, 2 vols, Chicago: Open Court, 1928–29; reprinted New York: Dover, 1993.

Child, James Mark, *The early mathematical manuscripts of Leibniz*, Chicago: Open Court, 1920.

Crowe, Michael J, *A history of vector analysis: the evolution of the idea of a vectorial system*, University of Notre Dame Press, 1967.

Cuomo, Serafina, *Ancient mathematics*, London: Routledge, 2001.

Dickson, Leonard Eugene, *History of the theory of numbers*, 3 vols, Washington: Carnegie Institute, 1919–23; reprinted New York: Chelsea Publishing Company, 1971 and Providence, RI: American Mathematical Society, 1999.

Dugac, Pierre, 'Eléments d'analyse de Karl Weierstrass', *Archive for history of exact sciences*, 10 (1973), 41–176.

Dunham, William, *The calculus gallery: masterpieces from Newton to Lebesgue*, Princeton University Press, 2005.

Edwards, Charles Henry, *The historical development of the calculus*, New York: Springer, 1979.

Edwards, Harold M, *Fermat's last theorem: a genetic introduction to algebraic number theory*, New York: Springer, 1977.

Freudenthal, H, 'Did Cauchy plagiarise Bolzano?', *Archive for the history of exact sciences*, 7 (1971), 375–392.

Grabiner, Judith V, *The origins of Cauchy's rigorous calculus*, Cambridge, MA: MIT Press, 1981; reprinted New York: Dover, 2005.

Grattan-Guinness, Ivor, *The development of the foundations of mathematical analysis from Euler to Riemann*, Cambridge, MA: MIT Press, 1970.

Grattan-Guinness, Ivor, (ed), *From the calculus to set theory, 1630–1910: an introductory history*, London: Duckworth, 1980.

Grattan-Guinness, Ivor (ed), *Landmark writings in western mathematics 1640–1940*, Amsterdam: Elsevier, 2005.

Gutras, Dimitri, *Greek thought, Arabic culture: the Graeco-Arabic translation movement in Baghdad and early 'Abbāsid society (2nd–4th/8th–10th centuries)*, London: Routledge, 1998.

Hawkins, Thomas, 'The theory of matrices in the 19th century', *Proceedings of the International Congress of Mathematicians*, Vancouver, 1974, II, 561–570.

Hawkins, Thomas, *Lebesgue's theory of integration: its origins and development*, Madison: University of Wisconsin Press, 1970; second edition, New York: Chelsea, 1975.

Hawkins, Thomas, 'Another look at Cayley and the theory of matrices', *Archives internationales d'histoire des sciences*, 27 (1977), 82–112.

Hawkins, Thomas, 'Weierstrass and the theory of matrices', *Archive for history of exact sciences*, 17 (1977), 119–163.

Heath, Thomas Little, *A history of Greek mathematics*, 2 vols, Oxford: Clarendon Press, 1921; reprinted New York: Dover, 1981.

Hoare G T Q, and Lord, N J, '"Intégrale, longueur, aire" the centenary of the Lebesgue integral', *Mathematical gazette*, 86 (2002), 3–27.

Hofmann, Joseph E, *Leibniz in Paris 1672–1676*, Cambridge University Press, 1974.

Jahnke, Hans Niels, (ed), *A history of analysis*, Providence, RI: American Mathematical Society and London Mathematical Society, 2003.

Jesseph, Douglas M, *Squaring the circle: the war between Hobbes and Wallis*, University of Chicago Press, 1999.

Katz, Victor J, (ed), *The mathematics of Egypt, Mesopotamia, China, India, and Islam: a sourcebook*, Princeton University Press, 2007.

Knobloch, Eberhard, 'Déterminants et élimination chez Leibniz', *Revue d'histoire des sciences*, 54 (2002), 143–164.

Kunitzsch, Paul, 'The transmission of Hindu-Arabic numerals reconsidered', in *The enterprise of science in Islam*, Jan P Hogendijk and Abdelhamid I Sabra (eds), Cambridge, MA: MIT Press, 2003.

Maanen, Jan van, 'Hendrick van Heuraet (1634–1660?): his life and mathematical work', *Centaurus*, 27 (1984), 235–284.

Mahoney, Sean, *The mathematical career of Pierre de Fermat 1601–1665*, Princeton University Press, 1973; revised second edition, 1994.

Neugebauer, O and Sacks, A J, *Mathematical cuneiform texts*, American Oriental Society Series, vol. 29, New Haven, CT: American Oriental Society and the American Schools of Oriental Research, 1945.

Neumann, Peter M, '*Galois theory*. By Harold M. Edwards', in *American mathematical monthly*, 5 (1986), 407–411.

Neumann, Peter M, 'On the date of Cauchy's contributions to the founding of the theory of groups', *Bulletin of the Australian Mathematical Society*, 40 (1989), 293–302.

Neumann, Peter M, 'What groups were: a study of the development of the axiomatics of group theory', *Bulletin of the Australian Mathematical Society*, 60 (1999), 285–301.

Ore, Oystein, *Number theory and its history*, New York: McGraw-Hill, 1948; reprinted New York: Dover, 1988.

Parshall, Karen Hunger, 'The art of algebra from al-Khwārizmī to Viète: a study in the natural selection of ideas', *History of science*, 26 (1988), 129–164.

Pedersen, Olaf, 'In quest of Sacrobosco', *Journal for the history of astronomy*, 16 (1985), 175–221.

Robson, Eleanor, 'Words and pictures: new light on Plimpton 322', *American mathematical monthly*, 109 (2002), 105–120.

Robson, Eleanor, *Mathematics in ancient Iraq: a social history*, Princeton University Press, 2008.

Ronan, Mark, *Symmetry and the Monster*, Oxford: Oxford University Press, 2006.

Rose, Paul Lawrence, *The Italian renaissance of mathematics*, Geneva: Librairie Droz, 1975.

du Sautoy, Marcus, *The music of the primes: why an unsolved problem in mathematics matters*, London: Fourth Estate, 2003.

Schubring, Gert, 'Argand and the early work on graphical representation: new sources and interpretations', in *Around Caspar Wessel and the geometric representation of complex numbers*, Proceedings of the Wessel Symposium at the Royal Danish Academy of Sciences and Letters, Copenhagen, 1998, 125–146.

Sesiano, Jacques, *Books IV to VII of Diophantus' Arithmetica: in the Arabic translation attributed to Qusta Ibn Luqa*, New York: Springer, 1982.

Singh, Simon, *Fermat's last theorem*, London: Fourth Estate, 2002.

Smithies, Frank, *Cauchy and the creation of complex function theory*, Cambridge University Press, 1997.

Stedall, Jacqueline Anne, *A discourse concerning algebra: English algebra to 1685*, Oxford University Press, 2002.

Todhunter, Isaac, *A history of the mathematical theory of probability from the time of Pascal to that of Laplace*, Cambridge: Macmillan, 1865.

Toti Rigatelli, Laura, 'The theory of equations from Cardano to Galois, 1540–1830' in Grattan-Guinness, (ed), *Companion encyclopedia of the history and philosophy of the mathematical sciences*, 2 vols, London: Routledge, 1994 and 2003, I, 713–721.

Toti Rigatelli, Laura, *Évariste Galois 1811–1832*, translated from Italian by John Denton, Basel: Birkhaüser, 1996.

Turnbull, H W, (ed), *James Gregory: Tercentenary memorial volume*, London: for the Royal Society of Edinburgh, 1939.

Walker, Evelyn, *A study of the traité des indivisibles of Gilles Personne de Roberval*, New York: Columbia University, 1932.

Weil, André, *Number theory: an approach through history from Hammurapi to Legendre*, Boston: Birkhäuser, 1984.

Westfall, Richard S, *Never at rest: a biography of Isaac Newton*, Cambridge University Press, 1980.

Whiteside, D T, 'Henry Briggs: the binomial theorem anticipated', *Mathematical gazette*, 45 (1961), 9–12.

Whiteside, D T, 'Newton's discovery of the general binomial theorem', *Mathematical gazette*, 45 (1961), 175–180.

Whiteside, D T, (ed), *The mathematical papers of Isaac Newton*, 8 vols, Cambridge University Press, 1967–81.

Youschkevitch, A P , 'The concept of function up to the middle of the 19th century', *Archive for history of exact sciences*, 16 (1976), 37–85.

## DIGITAL ARCHIVES

Many resources are now available electronically. Some of the sites listed below are accessible only through libraries, but others are openly available.

### Books and journals

*English*

Early English Books Online (EEBO)
  http://eebo.chadwyck.com
  (Catalogue of all books published in Britain or in English up to 1700, with digitized page images)

Eighteenth Century Collections Online (ECCO)
  http://galenet.galegroup.com/servlet/ECCO
  (A similar resource to EEBO, but for the eighteenth century)

JSTOR http://www.jstor.org
  (Archive of journals in English)

*French*

Portail documentaire mathématique
  http://portail.mathdoc.fr/Fondsnum/
  (Central resource for books and journals in French)

Oeuvres complètes
  http://portail.mathdoc.fr/OEUVRES/
  (Collected works of some leading French and German mathematicians)

Paris Academy of Sciences
  http://www.academie-sciences.fr/archives/histoire_memoire.htm
  (Archives of the Paris Academy)

*German*

Göttinger Digitalisierungs-Zentrum
  http://gdz.sub.uni-goettingen.de/en/index.html
  (Central resource for books and journals in German)

Digizeitschriften
  http://docsrv2.digizeitschriften.de/
  (Archive of leading journals in German)

Akademiebibliothek
  http://bibliothek.bbaw.de/bibliothek/digital/index.html
  (Journals and other material published by the Berlin Academy up to 1900)

*Dutch*

Science in the Netherlands
http://www.historyofscience.nl
(Some important Dutch mathematical and scientific texts)

**Special interest sites**

Archimedes project
  http://echo.mpiwg-berlin.mpg.de/content/historymechanics/archimdesecho
  (Research library in the history of mechanics)

Euclid's *Elements*
  http://aleph0.clarku.edu/~djoyce/java/elements
  (Interactive version of Euclid's *Elements*, prepared by David Joyce)

Euler archive
  http://www.math.dartmouth.edu/~euler/

# INDEX

*See also* the list of contents on pages vii–xi